DMU 0574018 01 3
WITHDRA[WN]
DE MONTFORT UNI[VERSITY]
LIBRARY
AF744552

GOOD FAITH IN THE JURISPRUDENCE OF THE WTO

What does the concept of good faith express? This book is the first to discuss what good faith means in international trade law. As a reference guide for scholars and practitioners it analyses the case law of WTO dispute settlement practice.

The book describes how, why and when the concept of good faith links the WTO Agreements with other public international norms. The concept of good faith appears frequently in treaties and customary rules, but is most often considered a general principle of law. WTO law uses the corrolaries of *pacta sunt servanda*, the prohibition of *abus de droit* and the protection of legitimate expectation alongside the principle of good faith.

An analysis of GATT 1947 and WTO case law reveals that the function of good faith varies. The Panel reports and the Appellate Body decisions make different use of it. The Appellate Body is prepared to apply the principle to WTO provisions only, while Panels use it more freely and substantively; that is, they apply good faith to fill lacunae in any of the WTO covered agreements.

Also, adjudicators use the principle differently, depending on whether it relates to the agreements covered by the WTO or the procedural law of WTO dispute settlement. As it applies to the former, good faith is used to strike a balance between, on the one hand, the obligation to liberalise trade, and on the other hand, the right to invoke an exception to trade liberalisation for the protection of the environment, culture, public morals, human life or health. In this way, good faith safeguards the gains of multilateral trade liberalisation against unlawful interests such as disguised protectionism.

The book also introduces the novel field of WTO procedural law governing trade dispute litigation. In the Dispute Settlement Understanding (DSU), good faith appears in the standard of review, rules of evidence and fact-finding, standing, duty of prior consultation, right of establishment of a panel, *ex officio* investigations, withdrawal of notices of appeal, and the raising of objections. In all these areas it ensures that the rules of dispute resolution are not abused. The Appellate Body has even gone so far as to derive a new standard from the principle of good faith that demands that disputes are settled fairly, promptly and effectively.

Insights into good faith in WTO law are not only important for trade law professionals. Current applications and future operations of the principle are likely to be of strategic value for answering the increasingly pressing question of how WTO law and other international agreements ought to be reconciled.

VOLUME 4 in the series Studies in International Trade Law

Studies in International Trade Law
Titles in this series:

Volume 1 *Basic Legal Instruments for the Liberalisation of Trade*
by Federico Ortino

Volume 2 *The Power to Protect: Trade, Health, and Uncertainty in the WTO*
by Catherine Button

Volume 3 *The WTO, the Internet and Trade in Digital Products*
by Sacha Wunsch-Vincent

Good Faith in the Jurisprudence of the WTO

The Protection of Legitimate Expectations, Good Faith Interpretation and Fair Dispute Settlement

Marion Panizzon

Inauguraldissertation zur Erlangung der Würde eines Doctor iuris der Rechtswissenschaftlichen Fakultät der Universität Bern. Die Fakultät hat diese Arbeit am 26. August 2004 auf Antrag der beiden Gutachter, Prof Dr Thomas Cottier und Prof Dr Gabrielle Marceau, als Dissertation angenommen, ohne damit zu den darin ausgesprochenen Auffassungen Stellung nehmen zu wollen.

•HART•
PUBLISHING

OXFORD AND PORTLAND, OREGON
2006

Schulthess §

Published in North America (US and Canada) by
Hart Publishing
c/o International Specialized Book Services
920 NE 58th Avenue, Suite 300
Portland, OR 97213-3786
USA
Tel: +1-503-287-3093 or toll-free: +1-800-944-6190
Fax: +1-503-280-8832
Email: orders@isbs.com
Website: www.isbs.com

© Marion Panizzon 2006

Marion Panizzon has asserted her right under the Copyright, Designs and Patents Act 1988 to be identified as the author of this work.

All rights reserved. No part of this publication may be reproduced, stored in a retrieval system, or transmitted, in any form or by any mean, without the prior permission of Hart Publishing, or as expressly permitted by law or under the terms agreed with the appropriate reprographic rights organisation. Enquiries concerning reproduction which may not be covered by the above should be addressed to Hart Publishing at the address below.

Hart Publishing, 16C Worcester Place, Oxford, OX1 2JW
Telephone: +44 (0)1865 517530 Fax: +44 (0)1865 510710
Email: mail@hartpub.co.uk
Website: www.hartpub.co.uk

British Library Cataloguing in Publication Data
Data Available
ISBN-13: 978–1–84113–620–2 (hardback)
ISBN-10: 1–84113–620–4 (hardback)

ISBN (Switzerland): 3–7255–5195–2

Typeset by Hope Services, Abingdon
Printed and bound in Great Britain by
TJ International, Padstow, Cornwall

DE MONTFORT UNIVERSITY LIBRARY:
B/code
Fund: 08 Date: 12/6/07
Sequence:
Class: 341.754
Suffix: PAN

Acknowledgements

This book could not have been possible without the thoughtful guidance of Thomas Cottier, so it is with a grateful thanks to him that the discussion of the rule, role and reach of good faith in WTO jurisprudence shall be introduced. The second reviewer, Gabrielle Marceau, has greatly improved what was originally a doctoral thesis by viewing it from a practitioner's perspective and for this input, I thank her too.

During my time as editorial assistant for the Journal of International Economic Law at Georgetown University Law Center, John H Jackson was influential in the formulation of the initial hypothesis that WTO law may be interpreted with general principles and customary rules of public international law.

Much inspiration in the initial stages of this work has also come from Michael Byers and Jerome Reichman at Duke University School of Law and I thank both for shaping my understanding of the WTO.

I am grateful for the excellent research environment of the Swiss Institute of Comparative Law in Lausanne which facilitated the writing of this book. I thank Bertil Cottier and the Institute's board for awarding me a *van Calker* stipend.

While at the University of Zurich, Christine Breining-Kaufmann and Rolf H Weber allowed me the time to complete this book and I thank them for this opportunity. I thank Helen Keller at the University of Zurich for encouragement and support and Thomas Wälde of the University of Dundee for his practical input.

I further thank all my colleagues and staff at the World Trade Institute of the University of Berne for their moral support and, specifically, for reading and commenting on the manuscript, Krista Nadakavukaren-Schefer, Maya Hertig Randall, Mats Oesch, Daniel Wüger, Nikolas Stürchler and Susan Kaplan.

For their friendship and support that predates and extends beyond the writing of this my first book, I thank my friends Julia v Buttlar-v Keussler, Krista Nadakavukaren-Schefer, Monika Szwarc-Kuczer, Charles Newcomb, Petra Kühn, Christoph Konrad, Carlotta Anderau, Jérôme Neri, Henri Culot, Christine Christ v Wedel, Cécile Mayor and Anne-Catherine Hahn. My most heartfelt thanks are for Benedict F Christ who has accompanied me with patience and kindness.

This book is dedicated to my beloved parents, Nicole and Renato Panizzon-Guisan, as well as to my sister and brother. They offered me numerous opportunities to grow and to expand my horizons.

Zurich, April 2006.

Summary of Contents

Contents

Abbreviations

AB	Appellate Body
ACP	African, Carribean and Pacific Group of States
AD	Anti-Dumping
ADA	Anti-Dumping Agreement/ Agreement on Implementation of Article VI of the General Agreement on Tariffs and Trade 1994
ADP	Automatic Data-Processing Machines
A.J.I.L.	American Journal of International Law
ASCM	Agreement on Subsidies and Countervailing Measures
ASG	Agreement on Safeguards
ASPS	Agreement on the Application of Sanitary and Phytosanitary Measures
ATBT	Agreement on Technical Barriers to Trade
ATC	Agreement on Textiles and Clothing
BGE	Bundesgerichtsentscheid (Switzerland)
CBD	Convention on Biological Diversity
CDSOA	Continued Dumping and Subsidy Offset Act (US)
CIT	Court of International Trade (US)
CITES	Convention on International Trade in Endangered Species of Wild Flora and Fauna
CFI	European Court of First Instance
CML Rev	Common Market Law Review
CSI	California Steel Industries Inc. (US)
CVA	Canadian Value-Added Tax
CVD	Countervailing Duty
DSB	Dispute Settlement Body
DSU	Dispute Settlement Understanding/ Understanding on Rules and Procedures Governing the Settlement of Disputes
EC	European Communities
EEA	European Economic Area
EEC	European Economic Community
ECJ	European Court of Justice
EJIL	European Journal of International Law
EU	European Union
FSC	Foreign Sales Corporation (US)

GATT	General Agreement on Tariffs and Trade (GATT 47) and (GATT 94)
GATS	General Agreement on Trade in Services
GPA	Government Procurement Agreement
Harv Int'l LJ	Harvard International Law Journal
HFCS	High Fructose Corn Syrup
HS	Harmonized System
ICAO	International Civil Aviation Organization
ICC	International Criminal Court
ICJ	International Court of Justice
ICSID	International Centre for Settlement of Investment Disputes
ICTY	International Criminal Tribunal for the Former Yugoslavia
ILC	International Law Commission
ILOAT	International Labour Organization Administrative Tribunal
IMF	International Monetary Fund
IPRs	Intellectual Property Rights
ITLOS	International Tribunal for the Law of the Sea
JIEL	Journal of International Economic Law
KSC	Kawasaki Steel Corporation (Japan)
LAN	Local Area Network
MEAs	Multilateral Environmental Agreements
MFN	Most-Favored Nation
NAFTA	North American Free Trade Association
NVNI	Non-Violation Nullification and Impairment
NT	National Treatment
NTO	National Treatment Obligation
OFAC	Office of Foreign Assets Control (US)
OMC	Organisation Mondiale du Commerce
PCIJ	Permanent Court of International Justice
PLE	Protection of Legitimate Expectations
SPS	Sanitary and Phytosanitary Measures
TIM	Trade Integration Mechanism (World Bank and IMF)
TPRM	Trade Policy Review Mechanism
TRIPS	Agreement on Trade-Related Aspects of Intellectual Property Rights
UK	United Kingdom
UN	United Nations
UNAT	UN Secretary General, members of his or her staff
UNCLOS	United Nations Convention on the Law of the Sea
UNTS	United Nations Treaty Series

US	United States
USDOC	US Department of Commerce
VCLT	Vienna Convention on the Law of Treaties
VER	Voluntary Export Restraints
WB	World Bank
WCO	World Customs Organization
WTO	World Trade Organization
YBILC	Yearbook of the International Law Commission

Table of Cases

WTO PANEL AND APPELLATE BODY REPORTS

The full citation of GATT 47 and WTO Panel and Appellate Body Reports follows the format used by the *WTO Analytical Index: Guide to WTO Law and Practice* (2003), pp. 9 – 27. All decisions can be accessed at <http://www.world tradelaw.net.>. The italicized title renders the title as used in the footnotes.

GATT 47 PANEL REPORTS

DECISIONS AND ARBITRAL AWARDS OF THE INTERNATIONAL COURT OF JUSTICE, AND THE PERMANENT COURT

DECISION OF THE INTERNATIONAL CRIMINAL TRIBUNAL FOR THE FORMER YUGOSLAVIA

DECISION OF THE INTERNATIONAL TRIBUNAL FOR THE LAW OF THE SEA

DECISIONS OF THE EUROPEAN COURT OF JUSTICE AND EUROPEAN COURT OF FIRST INSTANCE

DECISIONS OF NATIONAL COURTS (SWITZERLAND AND US)

Table of Treaties, Statutes and Documents

WTO DECISIONS, DECLARATIONS AND OTHER DOCUMENTS

GATT 1947 UNDERSTANDING AND AGREEMENT

ILC DOCUMENTS

MISCELLANEOUS UN CHARTERS AND RESOLUTIONS

1

Introduction

> Good faith, observes Cicero, requires that a man should consider as well as what he intends, as what he says. . . . It is a right, which natural reason dictates, that every one who receives a promise, should have the power to compel the promiser to do what a fair interpretation of his words suggests. . . . Isocrates, treating of agreements, . . . maintains that the laws enacted on this subject are the common laws of all mankind, not only Greeks, but barbarians also.
>
> Hugo Grotius, *The Rights of War and Peace*[1]

IN MANY INSTANCES the Member States of the World Trade Organization (WTO), acting as parties to a dispute before the WTO Dispute Settlement Body (DSB), have asked the Panel to interpret provisions of the WTO Agreements with the principle of good faith.[2] Parties to WTO disputes have included discussions on the interpretation of good faith as a term of reference in their submissions to the WTO Dispute Settlement Body. A fortiori, parties have claimed either the violation of the principle of good faith, or, have claimed through non-violation nullification and impairment of benefits the frustration of their legitimate expectations. Good faith also sets the threshold for the Appellate Body's (AB) review of the factual determinations by the Panels. The good faith corollaries of protection of legitimate expectations calls upon the WTO judiciaries to follow previously adopted dispute settlement reports. Codified within Articles 3.10 and 4.3 of the Dispute Settlement Understanding (DSU),[3] good faith holds the WTO Member States to the standard of fair,

[1] Book II, ch XVI, Paris, 1625, Latin in the original.

[2] *Cf* Marrakesh Agreement Establishing the WTO at Marrakesh on 15 April 1994 [hereinafter 'WTO (Marrakesh) Agreement'] is the constituent treaty of the WTO. Art II contains a description of the term 'WTO Agreements', which are, pursuant to Art II:2 WTO (Marrakesh) Agreement, '[t]he agreements and associated legal instruments included in Annexes 1, 2 and 3 (hereinafter referred to as "Multilateral Trade Agreements")' and what Art II:3 calls '[t]he agreements and associated legal instruments included in Annex 4 (hereinafter referred to as "Plurilateral Trade Agreements")'. In contrast to the Multilateral Trade Agreements, the 'Plurilateral Trade Agreements do not create either obligations or rights for members that have not accepted them'.

[3] See Understanding on Rules and Procedures Governing the Settlement of Disputes, Annex 2 of the Marrakesh Agreement Establishing the World Trade Organization of 15 April 1994, in 'The Results of the Uruguay Round of "Multilateral Trade Negotiations": The Legal Texts', GATT Secretariat, June 1994, WTO, Geneva [hereinafter 'DSU'].

prompt and effective dispute settlement procedures. Appellate Body decisions have derived this procedural good faith standard from Articles 3.10 and 4.3 DSU. Thereby, the AB has construed detailed procedural rules for settling disputes pursuant to the WTO's compulsory dispute settlement regime.[4] Good faith's contribution to the emergence of an effective and fully equipped body of WTO procedural law may spill over to the less developed ones of 'international procedural law', whether these apply to adjudication before the International Court of Justice or any other international law.[5]

By settling trade disputes the Panels and the AB have developed a body of jurisprudence around the WTO covered agreements.[6] The Panels and the AB have referred—beyond the positive limits of the WTO Agreements—to the 'law of treaties', meaning the body of rules governing the law of international treaties, foremost codified in the Vienna Convention on the Law of Treaties (VCLT).[8]

In addition to drawing from the 'law of treaties', the WTO Members' terms of reference call upon the other sources of 'general public international law'.[9] The *US–Gasoline* AB Report is the baseline decision for introducing into the 'GATT/WTO *acquis*' sources of international law outside the WTO Agreements.[10] As the AB in *US–Gasoline* says, the General Agreement on Tariffs and Trade (GATT)[11] is 'not to be read in clinical isolation from public international law'.[12]

Multiple such references to 'non-WTO' international law exist.[13] The WTO judiciary has been inspired particularly by 'related treaties', which are those international agreements, 'whose origins lie[s] outside the WTO legal system

[4] See, eg Cameron and Campbell, 1998; Waincymer, 2002; Iwasawa, 2002, pp 287ff on compulsory dispute settlement in the WTO.

[5] Thirlway, 1996, p 389, for discussion of the term, content, structure and development of the law governing international judicial procedure.

[6] Art 1:1 DSU defines the 'covered agreements' as 'the provisions of the agreements listed in Appendix 1 to this Understanding', which are the WTO (Marrakesh) Agreement, the Multilateral Trade Agreements (pursuant to Art II:2 WTO (Marrakesh) Agreement) and the Plurilateral Trade Agreements (see Art II:3 WTO (Marrakesh) Agreement).

[7] See, eg Vierdag, 1996, p 145, on the identity, substance, function and scope of what is meant by the term 'law of treaties', which is the law governing the negotiation, adoption, authentication, ratification, reservations, entry into force, and furthermore, the application and interpretation, the implementation, change and termination of international treaties and conventions.

[8] See VCLT (1969) 8 International Legal Materials 679, done at Vienna on 23 May 1969, entered into force on 27 January 1980, 1155 UNTS 331 (1980), available at http://www.un.org/law/ilc/texts/treaties.htm.

[9] See, eg Joyner, 2005, p 4, who defines 'public international law' as 'consist[ing] of rules that are generally recognised as binding the members of the international community in their relations with one another' and Jeremy Bentham (1789), the first scholar to coin the term 'public international law', as 'the body of rules and norms that governs the interaction between states as well as between other international persons'.

[10] Cottier et al, 2005, p 113.

[11] See GATT, Annex 1A, Marrakesh Agreement Establishing the WTO, in 'The Results of the Uruguay Round of Multilateral Trade Negotiations, The Legal Texts', GATT Secretariat, June 1994, WTO, Geneva [hereinafter 'GATT 94'].

[12] *US–Gasoline*, AB Report, p 17.

[13] Pauwelyn, 2003b, pp 449–51.

and which are not formally part of the GATT/WTO *acquis*.'[14] For example the Agreement on Trade-related Intellectual Property Rights (TRIPS) directly refers to applicable substantive provisions of the major intellectual property conventions (eg Paris Convention);[15] GATT Article XV:2 exempts WTO Member States from certain liberalization obligations when balance-of-payments and other financial obligations are required by the International Monetary Fund (IMF). Apart from such legislative references to related treaties, there exist purely judicial references to international agreements listed nowhere in any WTO Agreement. It is contested whether such treaties related to the WTO form part, of the WTO 'applicable law'.[16] Such contested linkages between the WTO and other trade-related international agreements, include the Multilateral Environmental Agreements (MEAs), namely the Convention on Biological Diversity (CBD) and the Convention on International Trade in Endangered Species of Wild Flora and Fauna (CITES), and, furthermore the United Nations Convention on the Law of the Sea (UNCLOS), regional integration treaties, such as the North American Free Trade Association (NAFTA), the Treaty of the European Union and last, but not least, the various bilateral investment treaties (BITs).

Furthermore, the WTO judiciary has referred to rules of custom, namely to *pacta sunt servanda*, non-retroactivity and estoppel. Two of these rules, the principles of *pacta sunt servanda* and non-retroactivity of treaties, are codified in Articles 26 and 28 VCLT, respectively.[17] All three of these rules of custom guide 'the application of WTO law'.[18]

In addition to treaties and custom, the GATT 1947, the WTO Panels and the AB have considered the general principle of law of good faith and its corrollaries of *abus de droit* and estoppel, as well as the good faith rule of treaty interpretation of Article 31 VCLT.[19]

[14] Cottier et al, 2005, p 113.

[15] See TRIPS, Annex 1C of the Marrakesh Agreement Establishing the WTO of 15 April 1994, in 'The Results of the Uruguay Round of Multilateral Trade Negotiations', The Legal Texts, GATT Secretariat, June 1994, WTO, Geneva.

[16] Pauwelyn, 2001, pp 560, who introduced the term 'applicable law' for the WTO, in order to emphasise that WTO jurisdiction is limited to the WTO Agreements, but WTO applicable law extends to general international law and, specifically, non-WTO treaties; see Pauwelyn, 2003a, p 460; see also Bartels, 2001, pp 449–519, who deems 'international law from all sources . . . potentially applicable as WTO law'.

[17] See *EC–Sardines*, AB Report, para 278; *US–Line Pipe Safeguards*, AB Report, fn 117 to para 110; *US–Offset Act ('Byrd Amendment')*, AB Report, para 296, on *pacta sunt servanda*, see *Brazil–Coconut*, AB Report, p 15; *EC–Bananas*, AB Report, para 236; *Canada–Patent Term*, AB Report, para 73; *EC–Sardines*, AB Report, para 200 on non-retroactivity of treaties.

[18] Zeitler, 2005, p 729.

[19] See, eg *EC–LAN*, paras 83, 86; *India–Patents*, AB Report, paras 43, 45–6, 55; *EC–Poultry*, AB Report, para 147; *Argentina–Textiles*, AB Report, paras 42, 47; *US–Section 211 ('Havana Club')*, paras 328, 340; *US–Cotton Subsidies*, AB Report, paras 613, 623 on treaty interpretation; of a total of 73 issued AB Reports as of 11 December 2005, a little more than 0.25% (23 AB Reports) expressly relate to Art 31 VCLT when interpreting one of the WTO Agreements.

The AB has not referred to equity and is less likely to recognise emergent principles of international law or soft law as WTO sources of law.[20]

The Panels have always gone step further than the AB in applying non-WTO sources of international law, but at first they approached such jurisprudence tentatively. In 2001, Pauwelyn could still say that the '[P]anel limited its reference to customary international law, but it should have referred to the broader class of general international law, including both general customary international law and general principles of law'.[21] The AB has been even more radical in turning down the use of sources of law other than the WTO Agreements. It has, for example said that Article 3.2 DSU prohibits the 'imputation into a treaty of words that are not there or the importation into a treaty of concepts that were not intended'.[22] Yet, the AB has also issued statements that seem to embrace such other sources of international law, namely the principles of *pacta sunt servanda*[23] and prohibition of abuse of rights.[24]

How can such conflicting statements be explained? The answer lies in the distinction between the jurisdiction of the WTO and WTO 'applicable law'.[25] The jurisdiction of the WTO is, pursuant to Article 1:1 DSU, limited to claims brought under, first, the agreements 'listed in Appendix 1' of the DSU (the so-called 'covered agreements'), secondly, those brought under the WTO (Marrakesh) Agreement and, thirdly, those about the rights and obligations of the DSU 'taken in isolation or in combination with any covered agreement'.[26] According to Pauwelyn, the limited jurisdiction of the WTO neither 'mean[s] that the applicable law available to a WTO Panel is necessarily limited to WTO covered agreements',[27] nor that there is a 'need for the WTO treaty to explicitly incorporate such non-WTO justifications'.[28] While Pauwelyn counts sources of international law, such as custom or general principles of law, as applicable law to the WTO, he seems to deny such sources the quality of sources of WTO law.[29]

Focusing on one such source of international law, the general principles of good faith and its corollary in custom, *pacta sunt servanda*, this study aims to

20 *EC–Hormones*, AB Report, para 123 and fn 92; against Cottier et al, 2005, p 113.
21 Pauwelyn, 2001, p 543 and fn 61.
22 *India–Patents*, AB Report, para 45.
23 See *EC–Sardines*, AB Report, para 278:

> [W]e must assume that Members of the WTO will abide by their treaty obligations in good faith, as required by the principle of *pacta sunt servanda* articulated in Art 26 of the Vienna Convention. And, always in dispute settlement, every Member of the WTO must assume the good faith of every other Member (footnotes omitted).

24 See *US–Shrimp*, AB Report, para 158; *US–Cotton Yarn*, AB Report, fn 53 to para 83.
25 See Pauwelyn, 2003a, pp 460–3.
26 Art 1:1 DSU.
27 Pauwelyn, 2003a, p 460.
28 *Ibid*, p 459.
29 *Ibid*, pp 40–52.

assess whether, beyond WTO applicable law, these principles are also WTO legal sources. This study will shed light on the application in WTO law of one particular general principle of law and customary rule, namely good faith and its corollaries of *pacta sunt servanda*, protection of legitimate expectations (PLE), prohibition of *abus de droit* and estoppel.

After first acknowledging the existence of general principles of law in WTO jurisdiction, this book will secondly examine if the WTO judiciary offers protection to good faith and legitimate expectations and prohibits an abuse of rights. Thirdly, the book will investigate why the GATT 1947 and the WTO Panels consider applying the principle of good faith for resolving WTO disputes.

The hypothesis is that the AB has only acknowledged claims of good faith when the claims have strengthened the trade liberalization obligations of the WTO Agreements. By way of being adopted with the reservation that it will not be applied by the WTO judiciary unless it supports the goals and objectives of the WTO Agreements, namely progressive and multilateral trade liberalization, good faith has only a one-dimensional content in WTO law. The way the AB has used good faith, the principle emanates from the customary rule of *pacta sunt servanda*, which says that treaties must be performed and implemented in good faith. As such, good faith stands for consent and ensures the application of the positive treaty provisions of the WTO Agreement.

The WTO judiciary either identifies good faith as implicitly contained in a specific provision or applies good faith as a source of WTO law, but one outside such positive treaty obligations. However, any interpretation of a WTO obligation is conditioned by the pro-trade content of good faith. Good faith limits the use of the exceptions from trade liberalization. For example, in Article XX GATT, it ensures that free trade values remain unencumbered by environmental, labour, health and cultural standards. If this hypothesis is correct, the AB would acknowledge the existence of a legal principle of good faith, only under the condition that it expresses a pro-trade concept protecting a WTO Member's expectations as to free trade in general, and multilaterally agreed conditions of competition in particular, including reduction of tariffs, concessions in services, implementation of intellectual property protection, rules-based use of trade remedies, fair use of the dispute settlement system.

Some scholars argue that when the Panels or the AB seek the guidance of a general principle of law, such an application of a source of law outside the WTO Agreements amounts to judicial activism prohibited by Article 3.2 DSU. To such scholars, general principles of law, in contrast to the positive rights and obligations of the WTO Agreements would 'add to or diminish' the WTO Members' rights and obligations.[30]

[30] *Cf* Bloche, 2002, p 826 and fn 4 with further references, who seems to adopt the view that general principles only serve interpretive purposes in the WTO; similarly, Lennard, 2001, p 41, who refers to the sources of international law used by the Panels and the AB as sources 'bearing upon interpretation' of the WTO Agreements; similarly cautious Bronckers, 2001, p 56, '[T]he case law

Others have responded that while '[g]eneral principles of law are rarely referred to in GATT, they are per se part of the legal order of GATT although they derive their existence from sources outside the GATT legal order . . .'.[31] The general principle of good faith is one such non-WTO source of law applied by the Panels and the AB.

A first concept of good faith WTO practice has referred to is the general rule of interpretation in Article 31(1) of the VCLT, which maintains that only an interpretation in good faith is a valid analysis of an international treaty provision. However, the Panels and the AB of the WTO disagree as to the precise role of good faith in interpretation.

Divergence between the Panels and the AB also extends to the notion and function of good faith. Views also diverge on the notion and function of the corollaries of good faith, namely, *pacta sunt servanda* and prohibition of *abus de droit*. Many Panel reports referring to a general principle of good faith or to one of its corollaries have been overturned by the AB.

Thus, the issue of good faith fuels the debate about enlarging for some and diminishing for others the WTO's jurisdictional scope. While resolving a dispute over a tariff classification, a trade remedy or the depth of patent protection, there is often included in the Panel report an obiter dictum relating to good faith which serves to define the borders of WTO jurisdiction within the limits of public international law.

A further purpose of this study is to examine the jurisprudence's process of delimiting the borders of WTO law. It will also be to identify a precursor role of the WTO judiciaries for other international tribunals, and to understand the pivotal role of good faith and its corollaries therein. While the emphasis will be put on good faith, a secondary focus will be on understanding the substantive trade law issues behind the disputes examined. The process of substitution, as the replacement of good faith for the underlying trade issue shall be termed, will shed more light on the seemingly complex, technical nature of disputes over tariffs, quotas and trade remedies.

The study is embedded in the context of what Petersmann in 1999 identified as one of the challenges ahead for the legal rules of the WTO trading system as follows:

> The small, but growing WTO jurisprudence on dispute settlement procedures illustrates the 'evolutionary approach to interpretation' in WTO legal practice, as well as the growing influence of general international law principles and dispute settlement

of the Appellate Body, which pays considerable attention to interpretative rules and developments of public international law, the WTO has become more open-minded than its predecessors'; against Cottier and Schefer, 2000, pp 60–2, openly support the view that good faith and legitimate expectations apply as substantive law in the WTO, albeit only in cases of Non-Violation Nullification and Impairment (NVNI) complaints; generally, Bartels, 2001, p 499 deems 'international law from all sources . . . potentially applicable as WTO law'; see Pauwelyn, 2003a, pp 25–34, for more authors and views on what type of (international) law the WTO Agreements represent and which sources of international law apply to the WTO.

[31] Benedek, 1990, pp 417, 131.

practices of other international courts on WTO legal practice, especially on the progressive refinement of WTO dispute settlement procedures.[32]

Only through the analysis of the jurisprudence of the WTO Panels and the AB, which is the principal source of good faith expressions in the WTO, can the sources, role and function of good faith in the WTO be examined and particularities of a WTO good faith principle be identified. By organizing the case law of the WTO judicial bodies, the study will discuss whether the Panels or the AB, directly apply, in WTO treaty law, good faith as the source of law and interpretation in its function as a general principle of law in public international law, or whether the WTO judiciary has created its own good faith principle.

Chapters one to six of this study discuss the various substantive expressions of good faith throughout the WTO Agreements as applied in WTO adjudication. Substantive good faith neither means interpreting an existing legal provision pursuant to the premise of good faith, nor does it refer to the procedural principle of good faith as it applies to the settlement of trade disputes under the DSU.[33] Substantive good faith as discussed in chapters one to six, fills in gaps of WTO law, where the solution of a trade dispute may not be found in the positive law of the WTO Agreements or where a positive rule is being abused. Substantive good faith includes a study into the concept and corollaries of good faith as it appears in the Panel and AB Reports applying the rules and provisions of the WTO Agreements, namely, the PLE, the customary rule of *pacta sunt servanda* and the prohibition of *abus de droit*. Firstly, the WTO's substantive uses of good faith separate into:

— specific WTO provisions implying 'expressions of good faith', eg the Chapeau of Article XX GATT, Article 6 of the Anti-Dumping Agreement/Agreement on Implementation of Article VI of the GATT 1994 (ADA), Articles 7 and 8 TRIPS;
— direct applications of the general principle of law as an 'autonomous source of rights and obligations';[34]
— 'well-established' judge-made principles, eg the PLE;
— grey areas, where Panel and AB practice and fail to clarify whether they apply general public international law concepts of good faith directly and, thus, consider a general principle of law applicable law within the jurisdiction of the WTO, or whether in the Panels' or the AB's estimation, the normative value good faith finds its limits in the individual rules of one of the WTO Agreements, such as the introductory clause of Article XX GATT 94, the so-called Chapeau of Article XX GATT 94, which 'is . . . but one expression of the principle of good faith'.[35]

[32] Petersmann, 1999, p 216.
[33] See Art 3.2 DSU.
[34] Kolb, 1998, p 662.
[35] *US–Shrimp*, AB Report, para 158; see also *US–Japan Hot-rolled Steel*, AB Report, para 10: 'We see this provision [para 2 Annex II, ADA] as another detailed expression of the principle of good faith'.

Chapters seven to ten explore the interpretive uses the WTO judiciary makes of good faith. The reception in WTO law of the VCLT, namely the 'general rule of treaty interpretation' contained in Article 31(1) of the VCLT, is examined. While good faith is applied substantively when there is a gap in the law, good faith interpretation describes the process of extracting an implied meaning of good faith (an 'expression of good faith') from within the wording of the language of a right or obligation in the WTO Agreements. The text of the provision may clearly refer to some expression of good faith or be ambigious, vague or otherwise unclear. The WTO judiciary will in all cases embark upon interpretation, which depicts the analytical legal reasoning of the language of a provision, in lieu of a direct application of the provision as a rule of law to the facts in the case. Such legal analysis, for international treaties, follows specific rules, which are laid down in the VCLT. However, both the sources and methods of these rules of interpretation, as well as the chronological order in which these are to be used, is contested. According to the VCLT, the provision at hand must be interpreted in the light of its text, context, object and purpose and in good faith.

First, one will analyse whether the WTO Panels and the AB adhere to the approach furthered by the International Law Commission (ILC), whereby next to sources of text, context and object and purpose, the VCLT rules on interpretation of Article 31 require a 'good faith interpretation' of a treaty. Secondly, and if it is demonstrated that the VCLT becomes applicable WTO law under Article 3.2 of the WTO DSU,[36] the question is whether it has been applied in the practice of interpreting the WTO Agreements.[37] Thirdly, one will investigate whether or not the WTO judiciary has created a good faith rule of interpretation of its own.

Chapters ten to twelve look first into another category where concepts of good faith are applied in WTO practice—the substantive good faith rules of WTO procedural law, which this book calls in shortened form, 'procedural good faith obligations'. They are codified in Articles 3.10 and 4.3 of the DSU. Secondly, in WTO dispute settlement, good faith standards created by AB jurisprudence, which demand the 'fair, prompt and effective' settlement of WTO disputes are identified and discussed. The standard of good faith underlying dispute resolution together with the good faith obligations under Articles 3.10 and 4.3 DSU, balance the due process rights of the WTO Members parties to a dispute with their obligations towards a functioning WTO dispute settle-

[36] See DSU Art 3.2; see *US–Gasoline*, AB Report, p 17; see also *US–Shrimp*, AB Report, para 157 and fn 152, with reference to Art 31 VCLT; *US–Japan Hot-rolled Steel*, AB Report, para 101; *US–Section 211 ('Havana Club')*, Panel Report, para 8.57; *India–Patents*, Panel Report, para 7.18; *EC–LAN*, Panel Report, para 8.25; *US–Section 301*, Panel Report, para 7.67, for references to 'good faith interpretation'.

[37] *India–Patents*, Panel Report, para 7.18; *EC–LAN*, Panel Report, para 8.25; see also *US–Section 301, Panel Report*, para 7.67; see also Cottier and Schefer, 2000, pp 61–2; against *India–Patents* AB Report, paras 43–8; *EC–LAN* AB Report, para 83.

ment system.[38] Commonly, procedural rules are divided into those aimed at the settlement of disputes and as such ensuring the correct implementation of WTO law by domestic authorities. The latter procedural obligations apply mostly to trade remedies, such as anti-dumping and countervailing duties, as well as to safeguard measures. This study will consider to what extent good faith shapes WTO procedural law, and will discuss how good faith might define the limits of due process rights thereby restraining an abusive exercise of due process rights. It will be discussed whether balancing due process rights with a view to achieving a reasonable resolution of the substantive dispute prevents the escalation of abusive litigation techniques in trade disputes and how good faith controls WTO procedure during its various stages, such as which obligations it imposes upon litigating members and why it imposes duties on the Panels.[39]

In the concluding chapter (chapter thirteen), the limits of good faith protection in the WTO are tested. A WTO adjudicator may not expand the rights and the obligations of the WTO members. Indications in WTO appellate practice suggest that the WTO Panels may have overstepped this limit of Article 3.2 DSU by importing into WTO adjudication expressions of good faith. This study will seek to corroborate such evidence in the light of AB decisions overturning the Panels with the argument that the import of the general principle of law of good faith, with the exception of the well-accepted customary rule of *pacta sunt servanda*, is a prohibited 'aggrandiz[ation]' of the 'rights and obligations of members'.[40]

[38] *US–FSC*, AB Report, para 166.
[39] Ehlermann, 2002, p 606.
[40] Art 3.2 last sentence of the DSU.

2

Concepts and Contents of Good Faith in International Law

> To claim for good faith that it is the basis of international law would be to ascribe to the ethical element behind, and in, international law a place which appears to minimise more than is warranted the equally, if not more, important functions fulfilled by the working principles behind international law.[1]

> The principle of good faith is 'the fundamental principle of every legal system'.[2]

GOOD FAITH IS a general principle of international law.[3] General principles of law function to 'make the law of nations a viable system for application in a judicial process. . .'.[4] The obligation to protect good faith, together with standards of good faith implied in treaty provisions, the underlying or ensuing customary rule of *pacta sunt servanda* as well as the customary rule of estoppel, and the good faith-related concepts of equity and fairness are sources known to public international law.[5] Doctrine and jurisprudence confirm that good faith is an 'essential principle of international law'[6] but deny good faith a standing as a 'fundamental principle of international law'.[7]

Even if the principle of good faith fails to qualify as a 'fundamental' or 'overriding' principle of international law,[8] because it is not part of *ius cogens*, as, for example, the prohibition of the use of force, it nevertheless forms a 'fundamental principle of any legal system'.[9]

There is a debate in the doctrine whether the principle of good faith is a moral principle devoid of normative content or whether it expresses normative values, such as a right, an obligation or standards and, thus, constitutes a source of law. For the ILC, on the one hand, 'the expression "in good faith" should also

[1] Schwarzenberger, 1955, p 324.

[2] Cheng, 1987, p 105.

[3] See Schwarzenberger, 1955, pp 325–6; O'Connor, 1991, p 119; *US–Shrimp*, AB Report, para 158.

[4] Brownlie, 1998b, pp 15–19.

[5] See *ibid*, 1998a, p 18.

[6] Cheng, 1987, p 105.

[7] Degan, 1997, p 83; see also Brownlie, 1998a, p 19; against Zoller, 1977, p 12.

[8] Brownlie, 1998a, p 515, good faith is not part of the 'overriding principles of international law . . . forming a body of *ius cogens*'.

[9] See Degan, 1997, p 141; against Hilf, 2001, p 128.

certainly be retained, for those words were the very essence of the rule stated. The obligation was not only moral, but also a legal one'.[10] For Zoller, on the other hand, good faith belongs to the realm of morality and policy.[11]

GOOD FAITH AND ITS SOURCES IN PUBLIC INTERNATIONAL LAW

The sources of international law have been listed in what has been called the 'deplorable' Article 38(1) ICJ Statute.[12] While Article 38(1) depicts the sources of international law, it refrains from laying down with authority how such sources stand in legal relation to each other.[13] Article 38(1) cites the sources, but neither puts them on a theoretical foundation nor catalogues the sources systematically, by hierarchical order, or other rule, by which the judge could be informed on the normative value of each source in relationship to another. As with any other general principle of law, it remains unclear whether the general principle of law of good faith primes custom, and *in concreto*, the customary rule of *pacta sunt servanda*. Does the customary rule of *pacta sunt servanda* stand at a hierarchically higher level higher than the principle of PLE, which, in some instances, may reach further than the limits of consensus put down by *pacta sunt servanda*?

The Deficiencies of Article 38(1) of the Statute of the ICJ

Article 38(1) ICJ on the sources of international law leaves it up to the international lawyer and tribunal to find the rules of international law applicable in a case. As Article 38(1) ICJ Statute lists these, they are nothing but a 'disorderly' and often 'intellectually incoherent' mixture of rules of logic and past practice of organization of the sources of international law.[14] On the one hand, the deficiencies of Article 38(1) ICJ Statute have serious consequences, namely the one of treating consent and custom as interchangeable legal sources. On the other hand, it must be borne in mind that the object and purpose of the ICJ Statute is to assist the judiciary, the ICJ, or any other international court or tribunal abiding by its rules, in the settlement of disputes, even if the Statute had originally been designed for the ICJ only. It cannot be expected of Article 38(1) ICJ Statute to establish a sourcebook for every international court and tribunal. The purpose of Article 38(1) ICJ Statute has not been to design a theory of

[10] See Yearbook of the International Law Commission (YBILC) 1964, vol I, p 29.

[11] See Zoller, 1977, pp 348–50, 351–2, 354, at p 351, 'la bonne foi . . . n'est qu'un principe de base . . . qui ne peut avoir une effectivité juridique que dans la mesure où on lui donne une forme juridique suffisante'.

[12] Allot, 1996, p 34.

[13] See *ibid*.

[14] *Ibid*.

sources of international law, involving the task of codifying all sources of international law as well as the one of defining their relationships to each other. While the sources of law codified in Article 38(1) ICJ Statute are helpful to analyse what the sources of good faith expressions in the WTO jurisprudence may be, both Article 38(1) and corresponding ICJ jurisprudence must be taken *cum grano salis*.

If the Statute governing the ICJ's adjudicatory tasks has neither clarified the relationship of the sources of international law nor set up a coherent theory of the legal foundations of international law, the ICJ's case law has done even less to remedy the deficiencies of Article 38(1) ICJ Statute. The ICJ neglects to 'identify the source it is applying, whether by reference to particular subparagraphs of article 38(1) or otherwise'. The same holds true of the WTO adjudicators.[15]

Treaty Law and Practice

The duty to respect good faith in international treaty relations is found codified in many international agreements. The most wide-ranging such good faith duty is Article 2.2 of the UN Charter, which obliges UN Member States 'to ensure to all of them the rights and benefits resulting from membership, shall fulfill in good faith the obligations assumed by them in accordance with the present Charter'.[16] This universal duty to fulfill the treaty obligations under the UN Charter in good faith,[17] not only binds the UN Member States but also the UN organs.

Müller distinguishes two purposes behind the debated inclusion of this provision in the Charter. First, the express enunciation of good faith in treaty law serves the purpose of countering the positivistic and legalistic treaty law as well as to offer an alternative in case there is no treaty law lest there be a legal vacuum.[18]

Secondly, Article 2.2 of the UN Charter was installed to give a chance to balance legally the different political interests, influences and weights of the UN Member States.[19] In this sense Müller cites that while states are entitled to enjoy fully the rights that flow out of the equal sovereignty of states as contained in the text of Article 2.1 UN Charter, the good faith clause ensures that States 'comply faithfully with their international duties and obligations'.[20] However, public

[15] Mendelson, 1996, p 64.

[16] Art 2.2 Charter of the United Nations of 24 October 1945, entry into force 24 October 1945, available at http://www.un.org/aboutun/charter/ [hereinafter 'UN Charter']; see also Zoller, 1977, p 6.

[17] See Art 2.2 UN Charter; see Müller, 1995a, pp 89–97 for a discussion of Art 2.2 UN Charter; see also Rosenne, 1989, p 159.

[18] See Müller, 1971, p 228.

[19] See *ibid*, p 233.

[20] *Ibid* and fn 17. However, the author also mentions opinions—most prominently Hans Kelsen's—that the clause of Art 2, para 2, UN Charter has no legal value whatsoever.

international tribunals are very cautious to acknowledge the bad faith of a Member State.[21]

The UN Charter of Economic Rights and Duties of States, and the UN General Assembly Resolution 1803(XVII) on Permanent Sovereignty over Natural Resources, contain codified expressions of *pacta sunt servanda*.[22]

Codifications of the Duty to Settle Disputes in Good Faith and Prohibitions of Abuse of Procedure

In *Case Concerning the Aerial Incident of 10 August 1999 (Pakistan v India)*, the ICJ derived from the general duty of UN Members to respect good faith in Article 2.2. UN Charter the more specific duty to settle disputes in good faith.[23] This duty to respect good faith in dispute settlement procedure has become the most important good faith obligation in international treaty law, including the law of the WTO Agreements as the following examples will show. In 1982 the UN adopt the Manila Declaration on the Peaceful Settlement of International Disputes annexed to the General Assembly Resolution 37/10 of 15 November 1982, where paragraph 5 to chapter I holds UN Members to settle disputes in good faith.[24]

Manila Declaration on the Peaceful Settlement of International Disputes, Paragraphs 5 and 11:

> 5. States shall seek in good faith and in a spirit of cooperation an early and equitable settlement of their international disputes by any of the following means: negotiation, inquiry, mediation, conciliation, arbitration, judicial settlement, resort to regional arrangements or agencies or other peaceful means of their own choice, including good offices. In seeking such a settlement, the parties shall agree on such peaceful means as may be appropriate to the circumstances and the nature of their dispute.
>
> 11. States shall in accordance with international law implement in good faith all the provisions of agreements concluded by them for the settlement of their disputes.[25]

[21] See Zoller, 1977, p 141.

[22] See UN Charter of Economic Rights and Duties of States, ch I; see also UN General Assembly Resolution 1803(XVII) of 14 December 1962, para 8, available at http://www.unhchr.ch/french/html/menu3/b/c_natres_fr.htm; see also White, 1996, p 232 and fns 9 and 10.

[23] See *Case Concerning the Aerial Incident of 10 August 1999 (Pakistan v India)*, Jurisdiction of the Court, para 53.

[24] See para 5, Charter I, Annex to the General Assembly, Resolution 37/10, Peaceful Settlement of Disputes between States, 15 November 1982, UN Document A/RES/37/10, available at http://www.un.org/documents/ga/res/37/a37r010.htm; see Rosenne, 1989, pp 161–2 for a summary discussion of the good faith duties in the Manila Declaration; see also Peters, 2002, pp 131–2.

[25] See para 11, Charter I, Annex to the General Assembly, Resolution 37/10, Peaceful Settlement of Disputes between States, 15 November 1982, UN Document A/RES/37/10, available at http://www.un.org/documents/ga/res/37/a37r010.htm.

As of 2000, there are nine judgments of the ICJ that establish the duty to settle disputes in good faith.[26] In addition to Art 2.2 UN Charter and the UN Manila Declaration, the following other codifications in international treaties of the duty to settle disputes in good faith exist.

The principle of good faith in the judicial settlement of disputes is said to be implicitly at the basis of the International Criminal Court Statute (ICC Statute) Article 86, which requires States to 'fully [reference to good faith] cooperate with the Court in the investigation and prosecution of crimes within the jurisdiction of the Court'.[27] In international criminal judgments, the duty to provide information as a specific emanation of the good faith obligation in disputes, was concretised in the 1997 *Blaskic* Supoena Judgment, where the Appeals Chamber of the International Criminal Tribunal for the Former Yugoslavia (CTFY) held that 'The degree of bona fide cooperation and assistance' is an element the Tribunal will take into account 'throughout the whole process of scrutinizing the documents . . .'.[28]

Article 23 of the International Centre for Settlement of Investment Disputes (ICSID) conciliation rules establishes an express duty to resolve disputes in good faith.[29] Article 11 of the 1996 Permanent Court of Arbitration Optional Conciliation Rules holds states engaging in arbitration proceedings to cooperate in good faith and to produce documents to the conciliator.[30] The principle against the abuse of procedure has been codified frequently in human rights treaties, and protects both the individual in the procedures installed for its benefit against the State, and the State against the abuse of procedure by individuals before international organs.[31] Another explicit duty to settle disputes in good faith is contained in Article 294 UNCLOS.

As for the case law, specialised UN Courts, namely the International Criminal Tribunal for the Former Yugoslavia (ICTY) and the International Tribunal for

[26] See, eg *Case Concerning the Aerial Incident 10 August 1999 (Pakistan v India)*, where in para 30, Pakistan alleged that the reservation valid for Commonwealth States amounts as a disguised discrimination among others to a breach of good faith, an argument that the Court denied; Ambatielos *(Greece v United Kingdom)* (1951–1953), p 23; Military and Paramilitary Activities in and against Nicaragua (1984–1991), para 21; Application of the Convention on the Prevention and Punishment of the Crime of Genocide (1993–), p 336 and 349; see Kolb, 2000, pp 640–6, for a summary and discussion of all cases as of relating to abuse of judicial process.

[27] Art 86 Rome Statute of the ICC; see also Peters, 2002, pp 131–3, for a cross-comparison of the principle of good faith as a source of states' duty to cooperate specifically in dispute settlement procedures in different various treaties.

[28] Case no IT-95-14-T, *Prosecutor v Tihomir Blaskic*, Judgment of 29 October 1997, para 68, cited in Peters, 2002, p 132.

[29] See UNCLOS of 10 December 1982, Montego Bay Convention on the Law of the Sea; Art 23 ICSID Rules of Procedure for Conciliation Proceedings (Conciliation Rules), January 1985, available at http://www.worldbank.org/icsid/basicdoc/basicdoc.htm.

[30] See the text of Art 11: Cooperation of Parties with Conciliator, Art 11, 'The parties will in good faith cooperate with the conciliator and, in particular, will endeavour to comply with requests by the conciliator to submit written materials, provide evidence and attend meetings', available at http://pca-cpa.org/ENGLISH/BD/conciliationenglish.htm; see also Peters, 2002, pp 131–2.

[31] See Kolb, 2000, p 638.

the Law of the Sea (ITLOS), have further consolidated procedural rules by using good faith to compel states to cooperate in dispute settlement, as seen in Article 294 of UNCLOS (1982), Article 23 ICSID Conciliation Rules (1985) and in case law of the CTFY, *Prosecutor v Tihomir Blaskic* (1997).[32] But a tribunal will not always hold states responsible to procedural good faith, as *The 'Camouco' Case (Panama v France) Prompt Release* (ITLOS, 2000), shows, where France introduced the argument of abuse of process, but ITLOS left the claim unsubstantiated.[33]

The Duty to Settle Disputes in Good Faith Contained in the DSU

For the WTO Agreements, the duty to settle disputes is expressly codified in Articles 3.10 and 4.3 of the DSU, described in chapters eleven to twelve below. The UNCLOS and the DSU codifications of the general principle of good faith, are very much alike. Both are codified expressions of the general principle of law not to abuse procedural rights, and both share a similar concern with balancing the power of different Member States.

However Article 294 of the UNCLOS Convention goes one step further than Article 3.10 DSU, since it provides for a preliminary proceeding in which the tribunal may reject a case for the reason that a claim constitutes an abuse of legal process. The WTO DSU by contrast does not allow such a legal consequence (preliminary proceeding) for its members' failure to engage in dispute settlement in good faith.

The prohibition on abusing procedural rights is codified in Article 294 of the UNCLOS.[34] It stems from the concern to find a measure of equilibrium between the interests of coastal states and land-locked states, which in particular want to see their rights safeguarded under the Convention.[35]

A similar concern could have guided the WTO legislator's idea behind Articles 3.7, 3.10 and 4.3 DSU, when they established the DSU, the one of finding an equilibrium between the powerful economic actors and the less powerful ones, that do not possess the market power to instigate a dispute, far less to defend themselves against the abuse of due process rights by litigation techniques.

As opposed to the WTO judiciary, which has derived far-reaching procedural guarantees under Article 3.10 DSU, especially as of the recent trade remedy cases (year 2000 onwards), there are no comparable, explicit corrective mechanisms installed to counter an abuse of substantive WTO law (rights not contained in

[32] UNCLOS Art 294 (1982); case No IT-95-14-T, *Prosecutor v Tihomir Blaskic*, Judgment of 29 October 1997, para 68, cited in Peters, 2002, p 132.

[33] *Camouco* (*Panama v France*) (Application for prompt release), Verbatim Record of the Public Sitting of 27 January 2000, ITLOS/PV.00/2/Rev. 1, available at http://www.itlos.org.

[34] See UNCLOS.

[35] See Kolb, 2000, p 639.

the DSU). The WTO judiciary compares well to international jurisprudence on this point, as there are some parallels in the use of 'procedural good faith'. For ITLOS, ICJ, ICTY and the WTO's AB, the specific expression derived of the duty to settle disputes in good faith, namely to provide the judiciary with evidence, is a new instrument to secure members' compliance and one which has been used only since the late nineties. It is a sign for the increasing juridification of international organizations' dispute resolution mechanisms and the acceptance thereof by many nations.[36]

As states will increasingly accept requirements of fairness in international forums, such international organizations will become more rule-oriented and less exposed to the power plays often displayed by excessive use of litigation techniques.[37] At the WTO, the AB is in line with international jurisprudence's recent trend towards juridification. However, there is no good faith obligation at the WTO, codified or implicit, that is comparable to Article 2.2 UN Charter.[38]

The WTO does not have a comprehensive duty to respect good faith. Rather, the codified enunciations of good faith (in the DSU) are all concentrated on aspects of legal process in Articles 3.10 and 4.3 of the DSU, where the duty to settle disputes in good faith is explicitly mentioned. Thus, it is understandable that WTO case law is full of citations of the general principle of law of good faith, since the WTO bridges this gap by referring to the general principle of good faith. Thus, it is up to the adjudicator to draw from general principles if it needs to fill a gap in the WTO agreements or if there is the need to balance interests at stake.

General Principles of Law

The concept of good faith has been associated with the international legal source of 'general principles of law'. General principles of law are a source of international law under Article 38(1)(c) ICJ Statute.[39] The Permanent Court of International Justice (PCIJ) in the *Chorzow Factory Case* left undecided whether the term 'general' refers to 'principles of international law' or to 'a general conception of law'.[40] Equally undecided is doctrine, since the language of Article 38(1)(c) of the ICJ Statute is unclear as to which general principles are relevant. Do they include some or all of the following?

[36] *Cf* Cottier and Oesch, 2001, p 28, who noted the term 'juridification of dispute settlement'; *cf* Kuyper, 1995, p 90, who introduced the term 'judicialization' of the WTO.

[37] *Cf* Jackson, 1999, pp 110–11, who marks the term 'rule-orientation'.

[38] See Art 2.2 UN Charter; see also Müller, 1995, pp 89–97, for a discussion of Art 2.2 UN Charter.

[39] See Art 38(1)(c) ICJ Statute.

[40] *Chorzow Factory Case*, PCIJ, Ser A, No 17, p 29, cited in Kosekenniemi, 1985, p 123.

— general principles of municipal law;
— general principles of international law, generated by state practice ('principles of international law proper'), such as freedom of the seas or diplomatic immunity;
— general principles of legal systems generally ('basic or fundamental' principles of international law, such as the *ius cogens* principles[41]); or
— general principles of legal systems specifically as to rules of judicial and arbitral procedure (due process, fair trial, etc).[42]

In addition to their classification as to their content, 'principles of international law' may further be divided into the international legal principles the ICJ has recognised (eg, freedom of maritime communication in the *Corfu Channel Case*, good faith in the *Nuclear Tests Case*, estoppel in the *Temple of Preah Vihear Case*, effective nationality in the *Nottebohm Case*, etc[43]) and those the ICJ may not (yet) have acknowledged) but which are contained in the UN's Friendly Relations Declaration.[44]

One could go one step further to distinguish, among the principles the ICJ has recognised, those, which the WTO AB has recognised (such as *pacta sunt servanda* and non-retroactivity) from 'principles of international law' the ICJ has recognised, but which the WTO AB has not (yet) recognised—good faith, equity, estoppel, PLE, precautionary principle.

Institutional Principle in International Organizations

What Amerasinghe calls institutional principles and what Schermers before him calls 'general rules for international organs', is the notion for describing 'institutional issues [. . .] common to all or to most international organs'.[45]

The question is whether the WTO, as a public international organization pursuant to Articles I, II and VIII of its constituent treaty, the so-called WTO (Marrakech) Agreement,[46] draws from good faith for operational, procedural

[41] Koskenniemi, 1985, pp 124–5.

[42] Mendelson, 1996, p 79–80.

[43] See Koskenniemi, 1985, p 123, for a more complete enumeration of general principles of international law recognised by the ICJ.

[44] See *The Declaration on the Principles of International Law concerning Friendly Relations and Cooperation among States in Accordance with the Charter of the UN*, 24 October 1970, which lists the principles of non-use of force, peaceful settlement of disputes, non-interference in the internal affairs of other States, cooperation in accordance with the UN Charter, equal rights and self-determination of Peoples, sovereign equality of States, good faith in the fulfillment of the obligations of the UN Charter.

[45] See Schermers, 1980, p 112.

[46] Art I, *Establishment of the Organization*, 'The World Trade Organization' (hereinafter referred to as 'the WTO') is hereby established; Art II, *Scope of the WTO*, para 2, 'The WTO shall provide the common institutional framework for the conduct of trade relations among its members in matters related to the agreements and associated legal instruments included in the Annexes to this Agreement'; Art VIII, *Status of the WTO*, para 1, 'The WTO shall have legal personality, and shall be accorded by each of its members such legal capacity as may be necessary for the exercise of its functions'.

and internal guidance.[47] In order to answer whether good faith structures and organises the WTO as an institutional principle, one would have to examine jurisprudence for expressions of good faith controlling the behaviour of certain organs of the WTO, namely the duties of the Panels, the AB, the Secretariat or the Director-General. One is most likely to find, through jurisprudential analysis, an institutional good faith duty in the relationship between the Panels and the AB as described below in chapter twelve.

The hypothesis is that good faith may very well be an institutional principle of the WTO in the realm of dispute settlement, where AB jurisprudence short of establishing a rule of binding precedent maintains that Panels are bound by good faith to respect similarly situated AB decisions. Whether a quasi-rule of precedent may qualify as an institutional principle simply because it binds the lower to the higher judicial organ is one argument of this study.

Two examples for good faith-related institutional principles at the WTO are first, equitable geographical representation of interests and, secondly, equitable representation of specific interests. The concept of an institutional principle of equitable representation goes back to Schermers and Blokker, who introduced the notion for international organizations in general in 1980.[48]

In comparison to the WTO, EC case law distinguishes institutional from non-institutional principles depending upon their impact on the European Unions (EU) supranationality. The *Opel Austria* case illustrates this difference between institutional and non-institutional principles by stating that institutional principles are those that are binding between states, and non-institutional ones are those of an international organization vis-à-vis an individual. The European Court of First Instance (CFI) held in *Opel Austria* (1997) that the Council had frustrated Austria's legitimate expectations protected by the EC–Austria bilateral agreement still in force for the couple of days left before Austria's entry into the EEA. The EC Council had violated the international law obligation of good faith under the EEA, when it adopted, just a few days before Austria's entry into the EEA, a tariff regulation that had the effect of prospectively offsetting the benefits Austrian economic operators were just about to enjoy under the new legal regime of the EEA.

In *Opel Austria*, the CFI explicitly used general public international law to support its conclusion that the individual economic operator, Opel Austria was entitled to protection of its legitimate expectations and that Austria was entitled to oppose according to the principle of good faith, the creation of a regulation that would become illegal within the few days of Austria's entry into the EEA.[49]

[47] See Amerasinghe, 1996, pp 15–20.

[48] See Schermers, 1980, pp 145–54.

[49] See Case T-115/94, *Opel Austria GmbH v Council* [1997] ECR-II-39, paras 89–95; see de Witte, 2000, p 156, who discusses the case.

In the *Opel Austria* case, for instance, the CFI considers the EC at fault under the general principle of law of good faith, but finds that the principle of legitimate expectations, as a 'non-institutional principle', only protects individuals (and not Member States).[50] Thus, it was only the individual economic operator, Opel Austria, which could rely on the protection of its legitimate expectations to oppose the tariff increase imposed by the regulation. Austria (which at this time was not yet member of the EEA) itself could only rely on the general principle of law of good faith.[51]

GOOD FAITH PROTECTION AND CORROLARIES

> We cannot do without power, except of course in the lovely utopias of the anarchists. But it can be held in check and counterbalanced so that it does not become excessive. It is possible to take away its unauthorised functions that quell the individual, that being [. . .] is the touchstone of society and whose rights we must respect and guarantee. Violating these rights inevitably unleashes a series of escalating *abuses*, which like concentric waves sweep away the very idea of [. . .] justice (emphasis added).
>
> Mario Vargas Llosa, 'Confessions of a Liberal', Irving Kristol Award 2005 Recipient's Speech before the American Enterprise Institute, 3 March 2005

Good Faith

The principle of good faith is a legal concept about the substance and the process of communication between individuals and among states. It requires states to enter into relationships 'honestly and fairly' and be guided by truthful motives and purposes.[52] Within treaty law, good faith most prominently figures in two places:

(1) It is a source and method of treaty interpretation pursuant to Article 31(1) VCLT. The content of the interpretative principle of good faith is to ensure that the interpretation of the treaty terms remains a balanced and fair one. It limits the extent of literal interpretation if there is the risk that such an interpretation may result in one party 'gaining an unfair or unjust advantage over another party'.[53]

(2) It imposes certain duties to the signatories to a treaty prior ratification, namely to make every good faith effort 'to obtain the consent of the sovereign'.[54]

[50] de Witte, 2000, p 156; similarly, Canal-Forgues, 2001, p 9.
[51] See de Witte, 2000, p 156.
[52] D'Amato, 1992, p 599.
[53] *Ibid.*
[54] *Ibid.*

Given that good faith expresses 'complex', 'polar' values,[55] good faith is associated with concepts of equity, such as aquiescence and estoppel. In addition, good faith has close ties to the customary rule of *pacta sunt servanda*, the general principles of law of the PLE and the prohibition of *abus de droit*. Kolb has organised good faith around an extrinsic and intrinsic concept, which this study will apply. With extrinsic and intrinsic concepts Kolb distinguishes the principle of good faith from related concepts, ie corrolaries of the principle of good faith, such as equity, estoppel, *pacta sunt servanda* and prohibition of abus de droit (see below, chapter three).

Corrolaires of equity, namely acquiescence, estoppel and detrimental reliance will not be analyzed in detail for WTO law, given that the case law of the WTO has not (yet) adopted or related to these principles in any major way.

Equity

As a general principle of law removed from 'any particular system of jurisprudence or the municipal law of any state',[56] equity is perhaps the only principle to 'provide constraint on state consent by bringing objective notions of fairness and distributive justice into international law'.[57] While there are international treaties expressly codify 'recourse to equity', such as Articles 59, 69, 70(4), 83 UNCLOS, no such reference to equity is found in any of the WTO Agreements.[58] The ICJ has had more and more frequent recourse to equity or equitable principles.[59] But, there has not been any WTO Panel or AB decision so far, substantiating an argument on the basis of equity. In contrast to the lack of equity in WTO jurisprudence, the ICJ not only has referred to equity in quantitative terms but has proposed a doctrine of equity for public international law in order to establish the function and content of the concept for public international law.[60]

Any discussion of equity and equitable principles applicable to the rights and obligations of the WTO Agreements forming part of the adjudication thereof or filling in a gap in the law of the WTO must take into account the jurisprudential dicta of the ICJ on this issue, as it is mostly the ICJ judges, who have developed and applied the concept of equity in international norms.[61]

[55] Cheng, 1987, p 105; see also Zoller, 1977, p 12, 'En dépit de ses difficultés d'approche et de son contenu singulièrement complexe, la bonne foi est reconnue par l'ensemble de la doctrine comme l'un des principes fondamentaux du droit international'; similarly Kennedy, 1992, p 345.

[56] Lowe, 1992, p 54.

[57] Charlesworth and Chinkin, 2000, p 79.

[58] *Ibid* and fn 112.

[59] See, eg *ibid*.

[60] See Weil, 1996, p 121, 'la Cour internationale a eu recours de plus en plus fréquemment à ce concept, dont elle a entrepris en même temps de préciser la fonction et le contenu'.

[61] See Weil, 1996, pp 123–4.

The ICJ, in the *Continental Shelf Case (Libyan Arab Jamahiriya/Malta)* of 1985, found that equity is, next to law, an emanation of justice.[62] Equity is thus on par with law. This opinion found that a judgment must be equitable, ie the interpretation in equity of a rule of international law shall be given priority over other interpretative means, but only to the extent that the result remains consistent with the (positive) law.[63] Secondly, and as an immediate result from the first equation, the ICJ separates equity from judgments *ex aequo ac bono*, and thus drives a split between objective values of justice (equity) and subjective case-by-case justice (*ex aequo ac bono*).[64]

In relation to a rule of positive law, scholarship defines three functions for equity. It can firstly be implied in treaty provisions, where it will function as a means of judicial interpretation (equity *infra legem*).[65] Treaty rights and obligations either directly mandate the judge to make, within the limits of judicial discretion, a consideration of equity, or such rights and obligations may implicitly contains a notion of equity, the latter which is the case in the WTO Agreements, where no provision either contains an explicit reference to judicial discretion or to equitable principles. In this *infra legem* function of 'work[ing] within the limits of the law more or less as a mechanism of judicial interpretation',[66] equity shares, what Weil calls an integrative relationship ('rapport d'intégration') to the positive law of a treaty provision.[67]

Secondly, equity can be juxtaposed to a rule and realise the function of a corrective to the law (*contra legem* equity).[68] In its *contra legem* function, equity is criticised by positivists, who fear an undue limitation on state sovereignty and an overbroad increase of discretionary power of the judiciary.[69] Thirdly, equity may substitute for a missing or ambiguous rule (equity *praeter legem*).[70] Where equity juxtaposes a legal norm (equity *contra legem*) it is difficult to distinguish what exactly separates it from a judgment *ex aequo ac bono*.[71]

Equity is a source of international law and finds concretization in what the ICJ calls equitable principles, *pacta sunt servanda*, good faith protection, prohibition of *abus de droit*, obligation to repair damage, etc.[72] The assertation that equity is in par with the law produces two consequences:

— As mentioned above, equity is separated from the subjective concept of judging a case *ex aequo ac bono*.

[62] *Cf ibid*, pp 122–3.
[63] See *ibid*, 124–6; see also Cottier and Schefer, 2000, pp 54–5.
[64] *Ibid*, pp 126ff.
[65] See *ibid*, pp 134–44; see also Janis, 1995, p 109.
[66] See Janis, 1995, p 109.
[67] Weil, 1996, p 134.
[68] See *ibid*, pp 130–1; see also Janis, 1995, p 109.
[69] See Janis, 1995, p 109.
[70] Weil, 1996, pp 131–4.
[71] See *ibid*, pp 126–9.
[72] *Ibid*, pp 124–6.

— The assertion begs the question whether equity, just as positive treaty law, acquires the status of a formal source of law.

The ICJ and some authors deny such an assumption with the argument that Article 38(1) ICJ does not list equity as being among the formal sources of public international law.[73] If equity is not a source of international law of its own, the next question is whether equity must be subsumed under a rule of custom or whether it qualifies as a general principle of law. The debate over the source quality of equity remains open-ended to this day.[74] However, even if related to or constituting a rule of custom, equity nevertheless assumes the functions of a typical general principle of international law, ie filling in a gap in the law or concretizing the open-endedness of a norm. It does so for the judge to avoid a *non-liquet* ruling, because a *nou-liquet* would dangerously compromise the completeness of the public international order (see section below, 'Function of Normativity in Public International Law').

Equity has been most frequently used by the ICJ in maritime and territorial transboundary cases. Equity is often the only way to solve these heavily technical and facts-based cases in order to demarcate boundaries.[75] From its function of assisting the judge in technical, facts-intensive cases to find a fair outcome for both parties, equity is similar to estoppel, the latter which Sinclair characterises as being used in international law in 'territorial disputes with deep historical roots'.[76]

'A less traditional but equally important current use of equity in international law concerns the new international economic order', where equity speaks to the concerns of developing countries relating to the unfair distribution of resources on the one hand, and the protectionist use of labour, environmental, sanitary and phytosanitary measures (SPS) by industrialised nations to block the importation of agricultural and non-agricultural goods originating in developing countries, into their markets.[77] This is where equity acquires a specific meaning for the WTO (in addition to other organizations or international agreements concerned with development issues, namely the Charter of Economic Rights and Duties of States)'.[78] However, such references in the WTO Agreements as well as in other organizations' foundational charters, resolutions and other internal documents, such as memoranda, guidelines, including for dispute settlement, amount to another, perhaps more substantive function of equity in the sense of distributional justice, 'economic and political

[73] *Ibid*, p 127.
[74] *Cf Ibid*.
[75] See Janis, 1995, p 113; see also Weil, 1996, p 122.
[76] Sinclair, 1996, p 104.
[77] Janis, 1995, p 111.
[78] See UN Res 3281 (XXIX), Charter of Economic Rights and Duties of States of 12 December 1974.

fairness' and equitable sharing of benefits than the one described originally in ICJ case law as identifying the role and delimiting the discretion of a judge.[79]

Equity is a contested concept of international law. It is said to protect the rights of the already privileged.[80] Within the field of international economic law, equity has been applied to resource allocation, but not to international trade law in the sense of the WTO Agreements. Since equity is burdened with the criticism of favouring the entities (states, individuals) already protected in the law, it may be a good thing that the WTO judiciary is not introducing the concept in a WTO already divided over issues of distributive justice.

Estoppel and Aquiescence

Estoppel is a concept based in Anglo-American common law of contracts. It made its entry into public international law with the advent of international arbitration through the settlement of boundary disputes between the US and Great Britain under the Jay Treaties. The concept of estoppel was introduced in an inter-state context in the British Guiana and Alaska arbitration controversy, where it functioned to resolve 'procedural technicalities'.[81]

Considered by some as a general principle of international law, by others as a rule of custom, and by Brownlie as a principle creating special relations, estoppel is founded upon the principle of good faith.[82] Similarly to the principle of good faith, estoppel protects adverse reliance on the consistency of conduct by one or both parties to a dispute. In contrast to the principle of acquiescence described below, estoppel does not require an 'element of detriment or prejudice caused by the state's attitude'.[83] Nevertheless, the criteria for the principle of estoppel to vest are strict and more narrowly described with the requirements of 'clear and consistent acceptance',[84] than the ones of the principle of good faith.[85] However, estoppel is not vested with the 'coherence' of good faith or any other principle of international law, due to its fragmented and incidental forms of applications.[86]

Its key function is to protect the applicant state against being misled by the respondent state acting as if it had agreed to a statement made by the applicant state, when in fact the respondent state does not agree. Estoppel sanctions the behaviour of a respondent state giving the wrong impression about the

[79] Janis, 1995, pp 111–12.
[80] See, eg Koskenniemi, 1990, p 4; Lowe, 1992, p 78; Charlesworth and Chinkin, 2000, p 80.
[81] See Lauterpracht, 1933, p 149.
[82] See Sinclair, 1996, p 106; against Kolb, 2000, p 357.
[83] Brownlie, 1998b, p 27.
[84] *Ibid.*
[85] Sinclair, 1996, pp 107–8.
[86] *Ibid*, p 104, with reference to Brownlie.

applicant state's offer or action, if such behaviour leads to a detrimental change for the applicant state or to a benefit for the respondent state. The legal effect of estoppel is to preclude the respondent state from denying the conclusion its conduct suggested.[87] Its fundament is based upon the idea of preclusion, which is one corrolary of the notion of good faith.[88] Estoppel realises a measure of protection for the legitimate expectations of a party in the consistency of a conduct, if the party suffers by having relied on the conduct. Thus, in order to vest, the party must have relied on the assurances or other conduct of another party 'in such a way that it would be prejudiced were the other party later to change its position'.[89]

By being based upon the concept of 'detrimental reliance' (Vertrauensschaden),[90] the principle of estoppel is a *lex specialis* of the principle of PLE, which itself is a 'concretization of the principle of good faith'.[91] If the conduct extends for a long period of time, the principle of estoppel, according to Kolb, acquires a customary basis.[92] In that sense the principle of estoppel is the mirror image of the one of acquiescence.

Acquiescence is a claim whereby a state did accept or agree to a matter but makes it appear to the other as if it had not.[93] For Müller and Cottier, acquiescence is a sort of 'qualified inaction', or 'toleration', which is insofar qualified as it generates a legally binding effect.[94] The criteria for silence to bind a party pursuant to the principle of acquiescence, because an action, such as a protest, would have been required by the law of acquiescence are firstly, either a 'notoriety of claims challenging a legal situation', or the 'assertion of alleged rights', or 'attribution to a state acting in good faith of having had knowledge of such claims'.[95] A second prerequisite is the 'prolonged abstentation from reaction, especially by states particularly interested, concerned and affected by these claims/rights'.[96] Without there being the necessity of a showing of a detriment, as is prerequisite for a claim of estoppel to vest, legal protection (of reliance on legititmate expectations and/or confidence) through acquiescence is based alone on the 'time factor', ie the long duration of inaction by the party holding the *right de jure*, and the 'gradual accumulation of indications symbolizing the seriousness of the claim'.[97]

[87] See *ibid*, pp 105, 108.
[88] See *ibid*, p 106.
[89] Kolb, p 359.
[90] *Ibid*, p 365
[91] *Ibid*, p 378
[92] See *ibid*, p 360.
[93] Estoppel in international law is not to be confused with the concept of promissory estoppel in Anglo-American law of contracts, nor of collateral estoppel or doctrine of interference under US patent law.
[94] Müller and Cottier, 1992, p 14.
[95] *Ibid*.
[96] *Ibid*, p 15.
[97] Müller and Cottier, 1992, p 15.

The jurisprudence of the WTO AB resorts explicitly once to estoppel in *EC–Sugar Subsidies*, where it impliedly uncovered evidence of inconsistency in the conduct of the US appellant. Furthermore, in *US–Foreign Sales Corporation (FSC)*, the US, the appellant, had alleged that the EU was precluded from bringing an appeal conditioned upon the Panel's treatment or not, of the administrative pricing issue, and then, for the EU to engage as the appellee (respondent) in an appeal brought by the US against the EU. It is the AB who brought in an implied notion of estoppel, arguing that the US had first accepted the establishment of the Panel, and that based on the US' subsequent conduct in the interpretation of the Agreement on Subsidies and Countervailing Measures (ASCM), the US could not change its position by arguing that the EU's claims should have been dismissed and that the Panel's findings should have been reversed.[98]

Even more briefly, AB jurisprudence relates to the principle of acquiescence in *US–Gambling*.[99] To analyse the meaning of estoppel for WTO law in-depth one would have to compare with WTO ICJ jurisprudence. For the ICJ estoppel predominantly functions to uncover the inconsistency of state conduct in maritime and land boundary cases, such as in *North Sea Continental Shelf, Gulf of Maine, Temple of Preah Vihear, Anglo–Norwegian Fisheries, Passage through Great Belt, Military an Paramilitary Activities in and against Nicaragua, Barcelona Traction (second phase) and Land, Island and Maritime Frontier Dispute (El Salvador/Honduras)*.[100]

Since estoppel and acquiescence are yet nascent principles in the case law of the WTO, this study will not deal in depth with these. It suffices to say that estoppel constituted an implicit, but nevertheless important procedural ground of complaint in the *US–FSC* case. However, the AB refused to consider the argument by the Panel that the US had failed to file an objection on time and that the US was therefore precluded from raising the same objection later, under the label of an 'expression of estoppel'. However, in substance, the AB did agree with the Panel. In the subsequent *EC–Sugar Subsidies* case, the AB referred explicitly to the 'estoppel principle'[101] but again refused to acknowledge the principle's presence as constituting WTO law: 'it is far from clear that the estoppel principle applies in the context of WTO dispute settlement'.[102] Most probably, the AB refuses to decide upon a case by referring to the estoppel principle because it does not want to be perceived as unlawfully aggrandizing the scope of WTO jurisdiction by introducing concepts of international law that are not positively inscribed in the WTO Agreements. Another reason for why the AB in the *EC–Sugar Subsidies* decision firstly refuses to substantiate the EC's claim

[98] See *US–FSC*, AB Report, paras 162–6.

[99] Other WTO AB Reports where WTO Members brought a claim of acquiescence are *Guatemala–Cement and Argentina–Textiles.*

[100] See Sinclair, 1996, pp 106–20.

[101] *EC–Sugar Subsidies*, AB Report, para 309.

[102] *Ibid.*

that Australia, Brazil and Thailand should be estopped from 'alleging that the European Communities' exports of C sugar are in excess of its export subsidy reduction commitments',[103] and secondly, does not take a clear stand as to whether the principle of estoppel applies or not to WTO law,[104] is that estoppel is a principle, as Brownlie says, creating a special relation between states',[105] and thus founded on reciprocity and bilateralism rather than on the multilateralism as applied by the WTO.

Pacta Sunt Servanda

Another corrolary of good faith is the customary rule of *pacta sunt servanda*. The concept of *pacta sunt servanda* is today considered a customary rule of law, and thus vested with more authority than a general principle of international law. *Pacta sunt servanda* is 'a rule existing independently of the will of the parties' and 'commands' simultaneously the application and interpretation, and even the negotiation of treaties. Because of this characteristic as 'metanorm', it is, at the same time, treaty law, customary law and a general principle of law.[106] Its function is to protect the ordering principles of law, including the one of good faith, and thus to solidify and guarantee the foundations of the legal system.

Even if the term was coined by the Romans (it is attributed to Cicero's *Officiis*), Roman *ius civile* did not recognise the principle, given that the *ius civile* derived the binding force of contracts from strict typology and formal structures. It is only in the *ius gentium*, the law among the nations, which Romans applied to other peoples, where contracts were based on good faith alone (as opposed to form and typology) that the principle of *pacta sunt servanda* served the purpose of maintaining the legal order.[107]

Its contemporary basis lies in the *Age of Reason* where it is considered one among the many attempts at structuring society and creating a legal, political economic order hailed as progress for humankind. *Pacta sunt servanda* thus emanates from the spirit of respect for the legal order.[108]

In international law, a first school of thought considers *pacta sunt servanda* to reflect the 'specific character of the international community'.[109] For a second school of thought, the basic principle of *pacta sunt servanda* is common to all

[103] *Ibid*, para 346(h).
[104] See *EC–Sugar Subsidies*, AB Report, para 346(h).
[105] Brownlie, 1998b, pp 24, 27.
[106] Scobbie 1997, p 271, citing Sir Hersch Lauterpracht, Kelsen's *Pure Science of Law*, 1933, CP, vol 2, pp 419–20; see also Koskenniemi, 1997, p 224; see also YBILC, 1966, vol II, p 60.
[107] See Kolb, 2000, pp 86–92.
[108] See *ibid*, p 86.
[109] Schachter, 1991, p 53.

legal systems of whatever kind.[110] In contrast to the first school of thought, this second school of thought considers *pacta sunt servanda* to being deeply rooted in the practice of States.[111]

There is a close connection between the principle of good faith and the customary rule of *pacta sunt servanda*. For most scholars, good faith underlies *pacta sunt servanda*, and *pacta sunt servanda* is the tool forcing states to perform and implement a treaty in good faith. As Kolb says, sometimes good faith dominates the principle of *pacta sunt servanda*, of which it [*pacta* . . .] is the executory expression.[112] Viewed as the foundational principle, good faith comes closer to the original Roman *ius gentium* function of *pacta sunt servanda*. While good faith was the principle holding a foreigner and a Roman citizen to their agreement *(pactum nudum)*, which was neither upheld by a particular formal expression nor could be identified as belonging to a certain contract type of *ius civile*, *pacta sunt servanda* would enforce the reliance in good faith of the party.

Another discussion relates to the normative value of *pacta sunt servanda*. If *pacta sunt servanda* declares that a treaty deploys the effect of obligatorily binding the parties, then some say it must be *ius cogens*. However, Judge Bedjaoui counters with the argument that if *ius cogens* conflicts with a treaty, *ius cogens* will prime treaty rights and obligations and limit the parties' obligations to perform the treaty.[113] Degan declares that among general principles of law, even the fundamental principle' of *pacta sunt servanda* is no peremptory norm of general international law (*ius cogens*).[114] Kennedy, describing positivists 'defending the authoritativeness of treaties', says that these have 'raised the soft norm *pacta sunt servanda* to a new status'.[115] Zoller goes even less far and declares that *pacta sunt servanda* has interpretive value only, as it ensures that a treaty is not restrained by a mere literal, formalist interpretation.[116] The only limits for *pacta sunt servanda* according to Judge Bedjaoui are principles of *ius cogens*.[117]

Since an evolutionary treaty interpretation liberates the treaty interpretation from the constraints of the will of the parties agreed upon originally, such an interpretation is inconsistent with *pacta sunt servanda*, but not necessarily with *ius cogens*. *Pacta sunt servanda* delimits the extent of evolutionary

[110] *Ibid*.

[111] Degan, 1997, p 74.

[112] See Kolb, 2000, p 93, 'Parfois la bonne foi domine le principe *pacta sunt servanda* qui en est l'expression exécutoire'.

[113] *Case Concerning the Gabcikovo-Nagymaros Project–(Hungary/Slovakia)*, 25 September 1997, Individual Opinion of Judge Bedjaoui, para 5(a).

[114] Degan, 1997, p 141 and 395.

[115] Kennedy, 1992, 1992, p 25.

[116] Zoller, 1977, p 95.

[117] See *Case Concerning the Gabcikovo-Nagymaros Project (Hungary/Slovakia)* 25 September 1997, Individual Opinion of Judge Bedjaoui, para 5(a).

treaty interpretation or, according to Bedjaoui, prohibits it, because the rules of the VCLT protect the intentions of the parties at the time of the conclusion of the treaty (principle of contemporaneity) and not evolving concepts.[118]

Article 2.2 of the UN Charter codifies an obligation of *pacta sunt servanda* that 'All Members, in order to ensure to all of them the rights and benefits resulting from membership, shall fulfill in good faith the obligations assumed by them in accordance with the present Charter'.[119]

Pacta sunt servanda is moreover codified in Article 26 VCLT. Article 26 of the VCLT, entitled '[p]acta sunt servanda', states: 'Every treaty in force is binding upon the parties to it and must be performed by them in good faith'. The VCLT drafters considered good faith and *pacta sunt servanda* to be equals, and in earlier drafts wanted to link the two explicitly by an additional secondary aspect to the rule that is now Article 26.[120]

Petersmann, in 1999, argued that 'the classical international law principle of *pacta sunt servanda*' no longer fits the scope of the contemporary content of the itnernational rule of law.[121] Under today's international rule of law, states are no longer bound only by the international agreements they entered into willingly and consensually; in addition, states are held to human rights standards and the duty to maintain democratic peace irrespective of their political system's concrete attitude to those values. For Petersmann, therefore, the principle of *pacta sunt servanda*—which to some degree stands for the bygone principle of sovereignty of states and the requirement of consensus of the 'classical' international legal order—must be replaced by an international level of constitutional 'checks and balances', to be achieved by democratic participation, compulsory jurisdiction for judicial review and transparent decision-making of international organizations.[122]

Goldsmith and Posener note that most international lawyers today would subscribe to a statement that states may even be bound by silence, as in the failure to object to an emerging customary norm, because consent no longer is a real

[118] *Ibid*, paras 6(b), 7(i) and (ii).

[119] Art 2.2 UN Charter; see also Zoller, 1977, p 6. *Pacta sunt servanda* was applied in general public international case law in the *Case Concerning Gabcikovo-Nagymaros Project (Hungary/Slovakia)* 25 September 1997, where Czechoslovakia found that if Hungary were allowed to give the 1977 treaty between both parties an evolutionary meaning it would amount to unilaterally terminating the treaty, which is prohibited by *pacta sunt servanda*. The Court found that evolutionary interpretation does not preclude a treaty from good faith compliance and the 1977 to still be binding on both parties. 'The Court would set a precedent with disturbing implications for treaty relations and the integrity of the rule *pacta sunt servanda* if it were to conclude that a treaty in force between States, which the parties have implemented in considerable measure . . . over a period of years, might be unilaterally set aside on grounds of reciprocal non-compliance'.

[120] YBILC, 1966, vol II, p 61, referring to YBILC, 1964, vol II, p 7.

[121] Petersmann, 1998, p 244, '[T]he world-wide recognition of human rights entails that the classical international law principle of *pacta sunt servanda* may no longer be a sufficient basis for the "rule of international law" if the international rules do not protect human rights and democratic peace'.

[122] *Ibid*, see also p 209.

requirement. Ascribing even less legal authority to *pacta sunt servanda* than Petersmann, Goldsmith and Posener, argue that the theory of consent, reflected in *pacta sunt servanda* for treaty compliance, is 'neither a necessary nor a sufficient basis for creating an international legal obligation'.[123]

Prohibition of *Abus de Droit*

A first distinction must be made between the notion of *abus de droit* to describe a specific legal situation and the prohibition of such an *abus de droit*.[124] While the first is well accepted in international law, the legal instrument of prohibiting such an abuse of rights is more common to international institutional law, where it applies to the abuse of power by Member States of an international organization or by the organs in charge of running such an organization.[125] An abuse of rights may only arise where a state or an individual or an organ has either a right (property rights), or a competence (decisions of administrative organs) which it is entitled to exercise. Contrarily, when a state, an organ or an individual violates an existing specific obligation, no such situation of an abuse of rights arises, because in those cases the state, organ or individual, which acted, had no right at all.[126]

The Legal Context of Abus de Droit

Given that *abus de droit* is a general principle of law, it is an abstract concept that may be turned into operational rules only when filled with specific content, which is achieved by is subdividing the general principle of law into specific legal situations.[127] *Abus de droit* doctrine seperates into three situations according to general international legal theory and practice. The first ensures a fair interdependence of rights and obligations. It describes situations whereby a state exercises its rights in such a way as to hinder another state in the enjoyment of its own rights, leading to an injury. A prohibition of *abus de droit* in this first function equilibrates treaty rights with treaty obligations (balancing of interests).[128] This first situation of *abus de droit*, whereupon a judge is called upon to readjust a disproportionate manifestation of interest linked to an expression of sovereignty by a state to a more balanced form of interest, compatible with

[123] Goldsmith and Posener, 2005, p 189.
[124] See Kiss, 1992, pp 4–5.
[125] *Ibid*, pp 5–7.
[126] *Ibid*, p 5.
[127] See Kolb, 2000, p 463.
[128] See Cheng, 1987, pp 123–32; see also Kolb, 2000, p 466.

the community of states, is most common in the international law of natural resources and the law of the sea.[129]

When a WTO Member State makes excessive use of an exception to the multilateral trading system, such as when the US, for environmental purposes, imposed obligations on Malaysia and others that went beyond the exercise of such rights under Article XX GATT, the *US–Shrimp* AB Report found it to be an abuse of the environmental exception in the GATT Agreement. Another *abus de droit* situation arises where a WTO Member State exercises its procedural rights in a way that either hinders the Panel in seeking evidence or hinders another party in exercising its due process rights (see below chapters eight to twelve).

Where a right is exercised intentionally for an end which is different from that for which the right had been created and, as a result, injury is caused (the *abus de droit* doctrine will step in to prohibit such a malicious or fictitious exercise of a right). Such a ficticious exercise of a right is prohibited, meaning that evading a treaty obligation is considered a violation of law.[130] Bad faith or an intention to cause harm is required for this second situation. A classic example for a fictitious exercise of rights is the *Free Zones of Upper Savoy and District of Gex Case*, where the court said: 'A reservation must be made as regards the case of abuses of right, since it is certain that France must not evade the obligation to maintain the zones by erecting a customs barrier under the guise of a control cordon'.[131]

The third situation developing out of *abus de droit* relates to the prohibition of an abuse of discretion, without the intention to harm (*détournement de pouvoir*). It usually arises in administrative practice within states or by the organs of an international organization.[132] The constitutive element for this situation is an expression of arbitrariness in the action of the state. Prohibition of arbitrariness is closely related to the prohibition of discrimination and the concepts are used 'interchangeably', with the result that both concepts function as standards more than express prohibitions of international law.[133]

Prohibition of Abuse of Rights

The principle prohibiting *abus de droit* delimits the exercise of legal power by states. Whether or not the *abus de droit* prohibition attains the status of a general principle of law, it is a judicial concept. As such, the judge is required to

[129] See Kolb, 2000, pp 466–7; see also Kiss, 1992, p 5, referring for the law of the sea to UNCLOS Art 300, which expressly prohibits an abuse of rights in the exercise of the rights under the Convention.

[130] See Cheng, 1987, pp 121–32; see also Kiss, 1992, p 5.

[131] *Free Zones of Upper Savoy and District of Gex case*, PCIJ Series A/B, No 46, p 167; see also Cheng, 1987, p 123; Degan, 1997, p 57, for the case's implications for *abus de droit*.

[132] See Kiss, 1992, p 5.

[133] See Kolb, 2000, pp 468–9, with further references.

balance rights and obligations in order to find a reasonable result. Nonetheless, the prohibition of *abus de droit* does not go so far as to oblige the judge to find an equitable result. True to its terms, it limits itself to prohibiting an unreasonable result.

Abus de droit is a concept developed for civil law and made its entry into international law when the private law model, namely that of contracts, was drawn up for a better understanding of the character of treaties in international law.[134] Pursuant to the private law analogy for international law, the addressee of the prohibition of *abus de droit* is the 'state, which obviously abuses its rights of internal sovereignty, in disregard of the obligations to foreign states and fundamental duties of humanity'.[135]

However, there are scholars who find that the prohibition of *abus de droit* has a foundation of its own right in public international law and does not need to rely on the analogy of contracts:

> In many cases the use of a right degenerates into a socially reprehensible abuse of right, not because of the sinister intention of the person exercising the right, but owning to the fact that, as result of social changes unaccompanied by corresponding developments in the law, an assertion of a right grounded in the existing law becomes mischevious and intolerable.[136]

Lauterpracht argues that because international law, in contrast to domestic law, does not dispose of a legislator entitled to adjust legal norms to societal change, the concept of *abus de droit* adjusts the behaviour of states to corresponding developments in the law among states. The concept of *abus de droit* entitles the judiciary to create a new tort, thus 'destroy[ing] the hitherto recognised freedom of action and creat[ing] a new right to legal protection from injurious interference'.[137]

Scholarship of international law considers the prohibition of *abus de droit* as a general principle of law, which forms, in Anglo-American law, the foundation for the law of torts, and, in the national legal systems of codifications, emanates more from administrative or public law, where the *abus de droit* prohibition delimits the power of the state government vis-à-vis citizens.[138]

In international legal theory there are thus two schools of thought about the underlying concepts of the doctrine of abuse of rights. The first comes from private law of contracts and torts and bases the doctrine upon equal and fair expectations among the partners engaging in a contractual relationship. The starting point is that each party to the contract has a right to assume that it will not be frustrated by another. The only difference to the private law of contracts is that

[134] Vaughan, 2000, p 218.
[135] Lauterpracht, 1933, p 287 with further references.
[136] *Ibid*, pp 286–7.
[137] *Ibid*, p 287.
[138] *Ibid*, pp 292–7.

the parties in international law are not individuals but states. This concept of *abus de droit* doctrine relates closely to the one of PLE and the one of good faith.

The other school of thought argues from a more institutional design perspective by stating that it is the lack of a legislator in international law that has propagated the prohibition of *abus de droit* as a tool of change.[139] Adhering to the institutional function of the *abus de droit* doctrine one can say that it goes somewhat against the legitimate expectations concept, as it may run counter to such expectations, intentionally, to create a new solution, just as it might run in parallel to such expectations. As a promoter of change, the prohibition of *abus de droit* does stand opposed to the quasi-precedential function of legitimate expectations, the latter, which create a duty to follow similarly situated past Panel and AB reports.

However, the 'principle of change inherent in the prohibition of abuse of rights', 'is a principle which enables courts to take cognizance, without recourse to legislation, of changes in conditions and social developments'.[140] The *abus de droit* prohibition thus becomes related to *clausula rebus sic stantibus*, and at the WTO it may be a promoter of changes in the law when, perhaps, negotiations fail to address a new development.

The institutional foundation of *abus de droit* doctrine in the law of the WTO Agreements conflicts with the express duty of caution, which Articles 3.2 and 19.2 DSU impose upon a WTO judiciary tempted to adopt the role of a legislator, which at least the institutional rationale of the *abus de droit* doctrine requires.[141] Thus, the *abus de droit* doctrine might have, in the law of the WTO Agreements, a more limited scope of application than in public international law, where no treaty imposes such an express limitation upon the judicial power of either the ICJ, or, as regards specialised tribunals, the ITLOS.

However, a third strand of doctrine finds another foundation for the prohibition of *abus de droit*, one that is consistent with Article 3.2 DSU as it is not based on the expansive role of international judges. According to Cottier and Schefer, '[r]ooted' in good faith, *abus de droit* doctrine requires every right to prohibition be exercised honestly and loyally.[142] It follows that the scope of *abus de droit* is narrower than the duty to act in good faith. Cheng and Zoller, before Cottier and Schefer, confirmed for public international law that the duties of good faith are more encompassing than the prohibition of *abus de droit*.[143]

Which of the two doctrines does the WTO AB tend to espouse?

[139] *Ibid*, pp 286–7.
[140] *Ibid*, p 299.
[141] Van den Bossche, 2005, p 185.
[142] Cottier and Schefer, 1997, p 178; see Cheng, 1987, p 132.
[143] See Cheng, 1987, p 132; see also Zoller, 1977, p 353.

Good Faith Limits of the Abus de Droit *Prohibition*

Beyond *abus de droit*, only good faith can sanction a morally or socially inappropriate behaviour.[144] Thus, beyond the 'limit of the law', which is *abus de droit*, a member's behaviour can only be sanctioned under the principle of good faith.[145]

The *abus de droit* doctrine has its limits where its 'elasticity' risks give too much power into the hands of international tribunals. Given the shortage of legislated solutions, international tribunals under the prohibition of *abus de droit* may be called upon to balance the 'conflicting factors in individual cases' that could not be resolved through treaty interpretation for lack of existing legal rules on the specific issue *in casu*.[146] In international law there are no checks and balances to guarantee that international tribunals will dispose of this power responsibly and in accordance with the requirements of international peace and justice and in the light of the 'growing integration of the international community', as opposed to giving in to unilateral pressure by militaries or economically superior world powers.[147]

The more 'rudimentary' the international community's law-creating machinery, the higher the risk of 'unscrupulous' appeals and the higher the responsibility of the court to render these inoperative. At the WTO with its compulsory jurisdiction, the judicial machinery is better equipped to address the dangers of an overbroad use by querulant parties of the principle of prohibition of abuse of rights. In addition, the DSU, in Articles 3.10 and 4.3, has expressly codified a prohibition to abuse the principle of *abus de droit* in dispute settlement procedures. Through Articles 3.10 and 4.3 DSU, as will be discussed in chapters eleven and twelve below, the WTO judiciary may not only address, but has a positive legal basis to enforce what Lauterpracht calls 'petty', 'short-sighted and petulant' cases and appeals that are based upon abuse of rights claim in disregard of the purpose of trade law and the interest of multilateral trade liberalization.[148]

[144] See Zoller, 1977, p 353.
[145] Cheng, 1987, p 132.
[146] Lauterpracht, 1933, p 306.
[147] *Ibid.*
[148] *Ibid.*

NORMATIVITY OF GOOD FAITH CONSIDERATIONS

Good Faith as a General Principle of Law

The principle of good faith may acquire the following degrees of normality:

— It may form either a duty or an obligation in an international agreement or convention pursuant to Article 38(1)(a) ICJ Statute;
— It may be a general principle of law pursuant to Article 38(1)(c) ICJ Statute;
— A corrolary of good faith, the concept of *pacta sunt servanda* enters international jurisdiction as a rule of custom under Article 38(1)(b) ICJ Statute. Good faith may be a rule of custom of its own, with no relation to *pacta sunt servanda,* if the two conditions of customary international law, 'result of practical application' and *opinio iuris* (Article 38(1)(b))[149];
— Good faith may enter a judicial decision, or a teaching of publicists under Article 38(1)(d) ICJ Statute;
— Good faith is an implicit source of international law, not mentioned in Article 38(1)(a–d) ICJ Statute. As such implicit evidence of international law, good faith either represents a unilateral act, or acts through a resolution of an international organization;[150]
— It can be a 'general principle of law' according to Article 38(1)(c) ICJ Statute, in addition, or, simultaneously to, functioning as the primary means of interpretation of Article 31(1) VCLT;
— Good faith is sometimes a source of soft law, such as private codes of conduct, gentlemens' agreements etc. As soft law, good faith may have the prospects of gaining normativity as an emergent principle of international law. However, emergent principles of international law are not yet a source listed nor otherwise recognised under Article 38(1) ICJ Statute. Nevertheless, soft law forms an inherent part of international legal sources today.

The concept of good faith is a legal one, because it forms a source of international law under Article 38(1) ICJ Statute. Another reason for why the principle of good faith is foremost a legal and not only a moral principle or a principle of public policy is that the single most important treaty on the law of treaties, the VCLT, addresses good faith in Article 26 as a part of *pacta sunt servanda*, and in Article 31 as an indispensable element of treaty interpretation.[151] General principles of interpretation outside 31(1) VCLT do not originate from

[149] Hilf, 2001, p 123.
[150] *cf* Mendelson, 1996, p 85.
[151] See VCLT, Preamble, para 3, Arts 26, 31(1) and 32(b).

'good faith' in the first paragraph of Article 31 VCLT.[152] Rather, they are either 'relevant rules . . . applicable between the parties' under Article 31(3)(c) or express a 'special meaning' the parties to a treaty may have had in mind under Article 31(4).

Finally, other elements of good faith interpretation may count towards supplementary means of interpretation under Article 32 VCLT. Of course, next to the VCLT 'classical sources of interpretation', other non-WTO treaties, customary law and general principles can all be relevant for the interpretation of the WTO Agreements under Article 31(3)(c).[153] If one focuses on maxims or general principles for the interpretation of treaties, it is often 'difficult' to distinguish their source-quality.[154]

As a legal principle, good faith protection on the one hand is a principle of national law, a building block for many, but not all of the worlds' legal systems. Good faith protection is a legal concept of Anglo-American contract law in the context of injurious reliance based upon frustrated expectations (see below). EC case law recognises the principle of good faith as 'the corrolary in public international law of the principle of PLE', the latter which is a legal concept of the 'Community's legal order' founded upon the legal traditions of the EC Member States.[155] It is to be asked whether it exists as a legal concept of Chinese or Islamic legal culture.

To the WTO AB in *US–Shrimp*, the legal concept of good faith protection has as a two-fold function and content: The principle of good faith stands on the one hand for a source of law accepted by major national legal systems, and on the other hand it acts as a general principle of public international law under Article 38(1)(c.) ICJ Statute: 'This principle, at once a general principle of law and a general principle of international law, controls the exercise of rights by states'.[156] The WTO AB does not question the authority of good faith as an international legal concept even if not all the national legal systems of WTO Member States today protect good faith. However, one must say that the WTO AB integrated the general principle of good faith into its jurisprudence in 1998, at a time when neither China nor the Islamic republics were members of the WTO.

[152] Against Lennard, 2002, p 55, 'WTO Panels and the AB have relied on several interpretative "maxims". . . . These are not explicitly referred to in the Vienna Convention, but they have been treated in WTO for a as emerging naturally from the expressed principles in the Vienna Convention. In particular, they are often seen as deriving from the requirement to interpret treaties in good faith . . .'

[153] Hilf, 2001, pp 122–3.

[154] *Ibid*, p 123.

[155] T-115/94 *Opel Austria v Council* [1997] ECR II-39, paras 93–4; see also Petersmann, 1998b, p 190.

[156] See *US–Shrimp*, AB Report, para 158.

Differences of Degree between Principles and Rules

Legal theorists have written about a possible difference between 'principles' and 'rules' and whether or not a hierarchical relation exists between the two.[157] Dworkin (1978) has identified differences between rules and principles in strict 'logical' terms.[158] Rules have 'all-or-nothing' consequences, and principles express a measure of 'weight or importance'.[159] For Soetman (1991), in contrast, rules and principles do not have a different logical structure that allows for a distinction between the two.[160]

Most recently, Verheij et al (1998) find with Dworkin that rules and principles have a logical structure, but they depart from Dworkin in believing that since the logical structure of a rule is no different than the one of a principle, they must be distinguished by the different types of relationships they engage in with either other rules or principles ('integrated view on rules and principles').[161] In their view, rules lead directly to their conclusion, while principles lead to conclusions in a two-step process, by which principles inform about the reasons first, before the reasons are weighed in order to draw a conclusion. Secondly, when rules conflict, the conclusion will be a contradiction because, as mentioned in the first hypothesis, rules lead directly to a conclusion. When principles conflict, however, the conflicting principles only result in reasons 'plead[ing] for incompatible solutions', but no contradiction results from the conflict.[162] The final conclusion is reached by weighing the pros and cons of the different, conflicting reasons. Thirdly, acording to Verheij et al 'rules are independent from other rules and principles and lead to their conclusions in isolation, while principles interact with other principles'.[163]

This third distinction by Verheij et al is probably the most relevant one for the principle of good faith and the rule of *pacta sunt servanda* in the WTO. The AB, as the 'keeper of the agreements' watching over the slightest *pacta sunt servanda* attempt at judicial enlargement of its jurisdiction, takes good care to insist on *pacta sunt servanda* being a rule that may not 'interact' with other rules or principles. Keeping *pacta sunt servanda* in the category of rules prevent it from interacting with good faith and other legal principles, which may then expand the WTO jurisdiction under the WTO Agreements, contrary to the clear meaning of Article 3.2 DSU.

Of course, the usage of the terms 'rules' and 'principles' is contested as well. For Soeteman, *pacta sunt servanda* is a 'principle-like rule', and not a typical rule.[164]

[157] See Mendelson, 1996, p 80.

[158] Dworkin, 1978, p 24, 'The difference between legal principles and legal rules is a logical distinction'.

[159] *Ibid*, pp 22 and 71ff.

[160] See Soetman, 1991, p 34 (translated from the original in Dutch by Verheij et al, 1998, p 5).

[161] Verheij et al, 1998, p 3.

[162] *Ibid*, pp 45.

[163] *Ibid*, p 5.

[164] Soeteman, 1991, p 33.

The ICJ, however, has refused to establish a distinction between 'principles' and 'rules' of international law.[165]

The distinction between rules and principles touches upon the role of principles in international law and bears systemic consequences. If principles are considered sources of international law, including WTO law, the completeness but not the comprehensiveness of the international legal system, including the WTO treaty system, is affirmed and vice-versa (see sections, 'Completeness' and 'A Complete WTO Legal System') below.[166]

Normative and Descriptive Theories of Principles

Under a theory proclaiming principles to prime rules, the principle of good faith would prime in general international and WTO law, a treaty rule, ie a provision of the WTO Agreements. The theory described above, which distinguishes a principle from a rule adopts a formal (descriptive) definition for a principle. 'The principle underlies and preempts the rule. Under such a descriptive theory of principles, a principle is the "representation" by which the norm can be found and applied', the principle precedes the norm/rule. Virally observes that the role of principles in public international law may be one of extending the scope of jurisdiction to catch up with the history behind the law. It seems that Virally is adopting a formal, as opposed to a normative, theory of general principles for international law, which understands principles as tools in the hands of positive law but not as legal sources of their own:

> Le recours à des principes d'une grande abstraction lui permet d'allonger considérablement son enjambée et, peut-être, de rattraper l'histoire. Un tel recours s'avère particulièrement nécessaire dans l'ordre juridique international pour compenser la densité trop faible du réseau des règles qui le constituent. Il peut l'aider aussi, aujourd'hui, de façon efficace, à compenser la lenteur et l'insuffisance des ses modes de formation et c'est, sans aucun doute, une des raisons de la place prise par les "principes" dans la pratique contemporaine.[167]

Normative theory, however, understands the sources of international law as directly applicable substantive law. Under normative theory of principles, a 'principle' such as good faith, is equal to, and interchangeable with, a 'rule' of good faith. The normative theory concludes that the principle (of good faith), as well as the rule (of good faith) are, under the normative aspect, ie from the viewpoint of their legal value, identical sources of law, since both are legally binding norms.

Only standards, under such a normative theory of principles, stand apart from both principles and rules. The 'good faith standard of interpretation', for

[165] See Weil, 1996, p 80 and fn 67.
[166] *Cf* Lowe, 2000, pp 208–11.
[167] Virally, 1990, p 204.

example, under normative theory of sources, has a different normative effect than the principle/rule of good faith. Standards limit the 'conditions of all legal process', but do not create norms (rights and obligations) of their own.[168]

Despite the normative distinction between standards and principles/rules, Koskenniemi says that as a standard of interpretation, a principle also 'applies' (to interpretation) and thus carries binding force and, consequently, also some normative effect.

The Function of Normativity in Public International Law

Under a formal as opposed to normative theory of principles, a principle describes and represents the norm but does not directly apply as a source of law to a situation of fact. Under the formal theory of principles, one must distinguish whether good faith acts as a source of international law under Article 38(1) ICJ Statute or as a standard of interpretation under the VCLT.[169] From a formal viewpoint of the sources of international law, the standard of interpretation of good faith is not to be confused with the principle of good faith, the latter which is a source of law under Article 38(1)(c) ICJ Statute.

Under the normative theory of sources, the principle of good faith may function in international law either as a general principle of law, thereby applying as a substantive rule composing either rights or obligations, or as a standard. As a standard, good faith constitutes therefore a 'general principle of interpretation' and as a rule/principle, it functions as a 'general principle of law'. The principles of equity, estoppel and prohibition of abuse of rights, related to the principle of good faith, are considered such interpretative standards.

Does the WTO judiciary makes a hierarchical distinction between a rule and a principle? And if so, how do the Panels and the AB define the legal concept of good faith, as a principle or as a rule?

Completeness of the International Legal System It has been argued that if the international legal system considers principles to be sources of its norms and standards of interpretation, such an international legal system has reached the stage of completeness. The completeness of international law is preconditioned upon its fundamental principles and legal institutions being in place.[170] Evidence for the international legal system's completeness is that system's ability to 'modify itself to cope with the need for change and development'.[171] According to Lowe, the fundamental principles and legal institutions are the

[168] See Koskenniemi, 1985, pp 127–8.
[169] *Ibid*, p 127.
[170] See Lowe, 2000, pp 207–8.
[171] *Ibid*, p 208.

tools and the sources of renewal and development. It is only through principles and legal institutions that international law becomes effective as a 'system'.[172]

General principles of law, such as good faith, are especially important in the process of systemizing law, as they are, first, general enough to reach beyond the limits of the problems that have incited their creation. Secondly, general principles of law are vague enough to actively self-generate norms, and thus renew a legal system continuously, beyond simply developing the system as a 'copy-book of precedents'.[173] General principles of law are, thirdly, flexible enough to enable the judiciary to develop solutions to kinds of questions that have not previously arisen. General principles of law are thus evidence that an international legal system is confident enough to abandon *non-liquet* rulings.[174] Public international law theory[175] and practice (*Free Zones, Chorzow Factory, Eastern Greenland, Arbitral Award of the King of Spain, Temple of Preah Vihear, Corfu Chanel* and *Right of Passage over Indian Territory* etc)[176] maintain that, within the limits of the social reality the law ought to reflect, one of the functions of general principles of law is to fill in gaps.

The principle of good faith may be a substitute for a gap in the law of international relations. As most general principles of international law, good faith functions to avoid a *non-liquet*. The general principle of law of good faith will thus assist an international court or tribunal in finding the material to fill in the absence or insufficiency of a rule of law. The role of general principles of law in the international legal system is to hold back an international tribunal from refusing to give a decision after it has assumed jurisdiction (*non-liquet*).[177] However, in international law, there exists non-norm governed conduct (rechtsfreier Raum) where 'a conduct is neither prohibited, not required, nor permitted by norms'. Such non-norm governed conduct is not to be confused with norm-permitted conduct.[178] According to Sir Hersch Lauterpracht's approach to Article 38(1)(c) ICJ Statute, the role of general principles of law (and of customary international law) is to prohibit *non-liquet* rulings of international

[172] See Lowe, 2000, p 209.

[173] *Ibid*, p 210.

[174] See *ibid*, p 211; see also Lauterpracht, 1933, pp 63ff; 127ff.

[175] See, eg Cheng, 1987, p 390, '[T]hey [general principles of law] apply directly to the facts of the case wherever there is no formulated rule governing the matter'; Schachter, 1991, p 57; Degan, 1997, p 16; Brownlie, 1998a, pp 17–18; against Virally, 1990, p 212, 'A cause de leur extrême abstraction, les principes ne représentent que des règles de droit incomplètes, autorisants trop d'interprétations divergentes pour remplir de façon satisfaisante la fonction essentielle du droit, qui est de servir de guide aux acteurs de la vie sociale . . .'; compare, Koskenniemi, 1989, pp 24–5, 'Although such rules are sometimes treates as if they provided a fully determined solution, it is clearly more common to consider them as pragmatic directives which on the whole would seem to give the most satisfactory solution'.

[176] See Brownlie, 1998a, pp 17–18, for an overview.

[177] See Dekker and Werner, p 229, with reference to Sir Hersch Lauterpracht, 1958, 'Some Observations on the Prohibition of "Non-Liquet" and the Completeness of the Law', in *Symbolae Verzijl*, Nijhoff, The Hague, pp 196–221.

[178] See *ibid*, p 236.

courts and tribunals under the jurisdiction of international law.[179] By ruling out the legality of *non-liquet*, general principles of law thus realise three functions of international law. First, general principles of law preserve the peace, secondly, they realise the peaceful settlement of disputes and thirdly they concretise the law.[180] Given that the role of general principles of law is to prohibit *non-liquet* rulings, their function is one of assuring the completeness of international law. If the WTO legal system accepts general principles of law as one of its sources, it rules out the legality of *non-liquet* rulings, ie the WTO legal system affirms that it does not accept its judiciary to issue *non-liquet* rulings, that it requires its judiciary to fill in the gaps of WTO law and that it presumes the WTO legal system to be a complete one.

The principle of good faith in the WTO legal system may thus function to identify gaps in the law and to distinguish these from non-norm governed conduct, ie conduct in international trade, which falls under the jurisdiction of the WTO legal system but is neither permitted nor prohibited and not required by the law of the WTO Agreements.

But what is the contribution of the principle of good faith specifically? Does it contribute to the completeness of the international legal system on its own? Does the principle of good faith contribute, in addition to the self-generating function of a general principle of law, just by the normative value good faith expresses? How does the systemic value of the general principle of law of good faith contribute to the completeness of the international legal system in general and the WTO treaty system in particular? Has the WTO legal system, from the viewpoint of the international legal system, reached completeness yet? Although it cannot be isolated from international law in general, it is the WTO legal system that specifically addresses issues of international trade. The question then becomes whether the WTO legal system is complete for the realm of international trade law. If the answer to this question is yes, we must then ask: does the use of the principle of good faith in WTO law and practice contribute to the completeness of the WTO legal system?

Comprehensiveness of the WTO *Agreements* While completeness raises the question of how far norms may reach beyond the scope of the problems that they were created to address, the comprehensiveness of a legal system distinguishes the aspects of international life regulated by international law from the areas international law does not cover. Among those uncovered areas, there may be some like natural resources, for example, which are considered unregulated, so that they may be freely exploited without regulatory constraint. Such areas are unregulated but still fall under a legal regime (in the case described, the national sovereignty of the state over natural resources). Substituting

[179] *Ibid*, p 230 with reference to Lauterpracht, 1933, pp 66–7.
[180] *Ibid*, pp 230–2.

non-regulation for liberalization and freedom of action therefore does not diminish the completeness of a legal system. It is only where an area regulated by law or identified by a rule is judged inappropriate by a court to rule upon.[181]

The question of whether the WTO legal system is to be considered comprehensive or not, may be examined by identifying areas of international trade that are covered by the law of the WTO Agreements, but for which the Panels and/or the AB issue a judgment of non-justiciability. The question of comprehensiveness of the WTO legal system must not be confused with the one of completeness. While the first relates to acknowledging incompetence by the WTO judiciary, the second is one of declaring a 'posture of abstention' and is proportional to the confidence in a legal system and its judiciary.[182] For the WTO, this will be discussed below in chapter 6, 'The Notion of Extended Protection of Legitimate Expectations'.

The Standard of Good Faith Interpretation

According to H Lauterpracht, good faith interpretation means to privilege all interpretation, which preserves the validity of the treaty (*favorem validitatis*).[183] In his Separate Opinion to the *Admissibility of Hearings of Petitioners by the Committee on South-West Africa* (ICJ Advisory Opinion, 1956), H Lauterpracht says:

> The third possibility, which appears to me . . . in accordance with good faith and common sense, is to interpret the instrument as continuing in validity and as fully applicable . . . to maintain the effectiveness, though not more than that, of the . . . instrument . . . The essence of that Opinion was that the Court declined to apply literally the legal régime which it was called upon to interpret . . . Actually, the Opinion did no more than give effect to the . . . legal instrument before it. That is the true function of interpretation.[184]

However, Lauterpracht did not discuss whether the essence of a treaty was better arrived at through subjective treaty interpretation, which would take into account the will at the time of the treaty negotiatiors (volontarist), or through an objective standard of reasonable interpretation.

[181] See Vaughan, 2000, p 210.

[182] *Ibid*, pp 210–11.

[183] See Kolb, 2000, p 277.

[184] See *Admissibility of Hearings of Petitioners by the Committee on South-West Africa*, ICJ, Advisory Opinion of June 1, 1956, Separate Opinion of Judge Sir Hersch Lauterpracht, in H Lauterpracht (ed), *International Law Reports*, Year 1956, London, 1960, p 60.

From Subjective to Objective Standards

As early as 1676, scholars found that 'rules depend for their efficacy upon mutual good faith'.[185] But it took until the 1960s for the objective 'standard of reasonable expectation' to definitely replace the voluntarist-subjective interpretation of treaties.[186] Scholars in the 20th century have linked the interpretation in good faith of contracts between private parties (*bonae fidei negotia*), to the interpretation of international agreements in good faith.

In the 1960s, general public international law doctrine, national courts,[187] and the ICJ[188] began to agree that the 'standard of reasonable expectation'[189] had superseded volontarist treaty interpretation. Müller explains this shift from a volontarist view of international law to a constitutional approach with the following argument: 'Also for public international law the opinion is shared that the standard of reasonable expectation has superseded expressions of will, or, at least, it is supplementing the interpretative methods of treaties.'[190] Bernhardt, similarly, finds that a minimum consensus of treaty interpretation exists and that good faith plays a part in it:

> In the light of the many and principled controversies among scholars relating to the interpretation of public international law, it is especially appreciated that there is unanimity in the fundamental interpretative approach: Interpretation and application of international treaties are, to an important degree subject to the objective principle of objective good faith and equity/fairness.[191]

For the Swiss Supreme Court any interpretation of international treaties must abide by the standard of reasonable expectations, because treaties are *bona fidei*

[185] O'Connor, 1991, p 66, with further references.

[186] Müller, 1971, p 145.

[187] See Bundesgerichtsentscheid (Switzerland) (BGE) 94 (1986) I, Urteil vom 22. November 1968 i.S. Frigerio gegen das Eidg. Verkehrs-und Energiewirtschaftsdepartement, p 673, confirmed in BGE 97 359 (1971) I, p 673, Erw. 5, Urteil vom 17. Februar 1971 i.S. Bundesrepublik Deutschland gegen Kanton Schaffhausen, p 366, Erw. 5 (for the examples of the Swiss Supreme Court); see also *Maximov v United States*, 299 F.2d 565 (1962); aff'd US 49 (1963), for the US, cited in McDougal et al, 1994, p 86.

[188] The *Island of Timor Case* (1914), *Case Concerning the Factory at Chorzow* (Jurisdiction) PCIJ Ser. A No 9 (1927), South West Africa Cases, (1962) ICJ Rep 319.

[189] Müller, 1971, p 145; O'Connor, 1991, p 109, who uses the term 'standard of behaviour', for describing the function of good faith in Art 31(1) VCLT.

[190] *Ibid*, 'Auch für das Völkerrecht wird heute die Meinung vertreten, dass das Vertrauensprinzip das Willensprinzip überwunden habe oder doch ergänzend die Auslegung völkerrechtlicher Verträge bestimme . . .'.

[191] Bernhardt, 1963, p 23, 'Angesichts der zahlreichen und grundsätzlichen Kontroversen in der völkerrechtlichen Auslegungslehre ist es besonders zu begrüssen, dass in der Grundfrage Einigkeit besteht; Interpretation und Anwendung internationaler Verträge stehen in besonderem Masse unter dem Gebot von Treu und Glauben und Billigkeit'.

negotia.[192] Müller nevertheless finds that the principle of good faith has only rarely materialised in a concrete result for the interpretation of a treaty.[193]

The Standard of Reasonableness

Since good faith interpretation enhances the rule of law it must be an objective standard, 'consensual engagements must be interpreted . . . as *bonae fidei negotia*. It as a rule of law, that good faith becomes fully integrated in the modern codified law of treaties'.[194] For Kolb and others, good faith interpretation on the one hand depicts the essence of the interpretation of international agreements, such as that good faith must guide each and every interpretative process involving an international treaty provision.[195] On the other hand, good faith interpretation stands, according to Kolb, for a particular, if not peculiar set of methods of treaty interpretation.

As the cardinal rule of treaty interpretation, a good faith analysis of the meaning of the text of a treaty means to:

> not excessively adhere to the letter of the text, it involves condemning a malicious attachement to the text, painstaken architectural constructs with language or its fraudulent use, or any unreasonable allegation, all of which serve to twist the true sense of the treaty in disrespect for its spirit.

Good faith interpretation, in this general sense may be 'equated to the standard of reasonablness, to non-abusive interpretation and even to a finding of an equitable result.[196]

The particular methods of treaty interpretation related to good faith are, eg a behavioural analysis of the actions of the parties to a dispute and the interpretation in *favorem validitatis* purported by H Lauterpracht as described

[192] BGE 94 (1986) I, Urteil vom 22. November 1968 i.S. Frigerio gegen das Eidg. Verkehrs-und Energiewirtschaftsdepartement, p 673, 'Die Staatsverträge sind ihrer Natur nach, "bona fidei negotia"; für die Auslegung gilt allgemein die Vertrauenstheorie'. confirmed in BGE 97 359 (1971) I, p 673, Erw. 5, Urteil vom 17. Februar 1971 i.S. Bundesrepublik Deutschland gegen Kanton Schaffhausen, p 366, Erw. 5.

[193] Müller, 1971, pp 145–6, 'Obwohl die Auslegung der Verträge nach den Grundsätzen von Treu und Glauben als unbestrittenes Prinzip gilt, sind daraus doch selten konkrete Folgerungen im Sinne des Vertrauensschutzes gezogen worden'.

[194] Rosenne, 1989, p 179.

[195] See Kolb, 2000, pp 264–5 with reference in particular to Virally, who is attributed the statement that good faith informs, in the interpretative process, of how far the contractual engagement to execute a treaty shall reach (translated by author).

[196] *Ibid*, p 264 (translated by the author), original French reads:

> Interpréter et executer une obligation juridique de bonne foi, c'est de recherc̀her l'exécution selon son esprit sans l'attachement malicieux au texte, les architectures dolosives ou frauduleuses, les allegations déraisonnables, qui, loin de chercher à servir l'esprit de l'accord, n'ont pour but que d'en tourner le veritable sens. C'est de manière équivalente que l'on dit qu'il faut interpréter un traité raisonnablement et de manière non abusive, et parfois même que l'on préconise une interprétation équitable.

above.[197] More details on the the meaning, uses and limits of good faith interpretation will be described below in chapters seven to ten.

As an introduction to the standard of good faith interpretation in the WTO, one can point out that the references to good faith as an element of the interpretative process began in GATT/WTO case law with the decision to apply the VCLT rules of treaty interpretation first to the GATT and later to the WTO.[198] It took the IJC 11 years from the VCLT's inception to recognise in 1991 (*Arbitral Award of 31 July 1989*) Articles 31 and 32 of the VCLT.[199] Only three years after the ICJ issued in 1991 (*Arbitral Award of 31 July 1989*) its first 'textually oriented recognition' of the VCLT of 1969,[200] two GATT 1947 Panels openly recognised the relevancy of VCLT for GATT interpretation. Thus, while the 'wider body of international law', at least until the environmental disputes, did not find itself impregnated by GATT/WTO law, GATT/WTO jurisprudence in contrast made serious efforts to be in synchronization with interpretive rules of general public international law.[201]

In contrast to the ICJ, the WTO AB since its very first case (*US–Gasoline* in 1996) has declared that it will abide by the VCLT rules for the interpretation of its agreements.[202] The ICJ's 'lateness and hesitation' in recognizing the VCLT stemmed from the 'doctrinal division among the various schools of interpretation of treaties'.[203]

What, in comparison to ICJ practice, seems to be the WTO AB's quick and open recognition of customary rules of interpretation was hailed a primer in the history of international adjudicative organs.[204] Apparently, the WTO AB was not very much concerned about scholarly debates on treaty interpretation. It simply considered the VCLT system a solid enough basis for its work. WTO jurisprudence in 1996 moved to declare the VCLT a codification of customary rules of interpretation of public international law. The AB did so in order also

[197] See Kolb, 2000, pp 272–8.

[198] In addition to GATT 1947 Panel decisions declaring the interpretive rules of the VCLT applicable, there were also GATT Panel and later WTO decisions declaring the VCLT rules governing the application of treaties applicable to the GATT 1947, such as the rule on retroactivity (Art 28) of the VCLT in the *US–Non-Rubber Footwear*, Panel Report, paras 4.5 and 4.10; *Brazil–Coconut*, Panel Report, p 15; *EC–Bananas*, AB Report, paras 235–7; *EC–Hormones*, AB Report, paras 126–8; see also Cameron and Gray, 2001, pp 271–2, on the issue of Art 28 VCLT and WTO law and Art 27 VCLT in *Canada–Gold Coins*, para 53.

[199] *Arbitral Award of 31 July 1989, (Guinea-Bissau v Senegal)*, ICJ Judgment of 12 November 1991, pp 69–70, 'These principles [natural and ordinary meaning etc.] are reflected in Arts 31 and 32 of the VCLT, which may in many respects, be considered as a codification of existing customary international law on the point'.

[200] Bernardez, 1998 p 733.

[201] Cottier and Oesch, 2001, p 36, however, as the authors maintain, GATT 1947 jurisprudence rarely referred to substantive and procedural general public international law. See also Lennard, 2002, p 86.

[202] Ehlermann, 2002, p 615.

[203] Bernardez, 1998 pp 732–3.

[204] See Ehlermann, 2002, pp 616, 618.

to bind those WTO Members that had not ratified the VCLT, most prominently the US.[205] Only two years before the AB, did the ICJ in the 1994 *Territorial Dispute (Libyan Arab Jamahiriya/Chad)* case, declare VCLT Article 31 applicable to non-parties as customary international law.[206]

Public Policy and the Moral Standard of Good Faith

In addition to functioning as a standard of interpretation for the law of treaties and as a general principle of law, good faith sets thresholds of moral and political conduct. Since this study is about the legal dimensions of the juridical concepts of good faith, the moral, as well as the political standard, are described for reasons of comprehensiveness only.

Zoller defines the concept of good faith by negation. For Zoller, good faith has neither a juridical value nor a legal function. No legal rules emanate from the concept of good faith, because it neither forms a source of rights and obligations,[207] nor states the law as a legal standard:[208]

> It results that good faith, as a normative principle, that is, considered as the obligation to hold one's engagement, has no legal consistency whatsoever . . . This is way the principle of good faith is a moral principle and nothing more than that.[209]

Political Context

An 'extra-juridical' concept involving politics and morale exists for Kolb as well, but, alongside a juridical concept of good faith.[210] The 'extra-juridical' concept of political good faith, first, equates concepts of loyalty and sincerity, in view of justifying and/or dissimulating the underlying political interests or power. Secondly, a policy of good faith void of any normative value exists for Kolb. It applies to situations where juridical good faith is set in an entirely political con-

[205] See Restatement (Third) of the Foreign Relations Law of the United States 112(2) (1987), 325 cnt, which suggests that the US ascribes to the interpretive provisions of the VCLT as these, 'represent [] generally accepted principles and the United States has also appeared willing to accept them despite differences of nuance and emphasis', cited in van Alstine, 1998, fn 71 to p 706.

[206] See *Territorial Dispute (Libyan Arab Jamahiriya/Chad)*, Judgment, ICJ Reports 1994, p 21, para 41; the ICJ reiterated that Art 31 VCLT reflects customary international law in *Maritime Delimitation and Territorial Questions between Qatar and Bahrain (Qatar v Bahrain)*, Jurisdiction and Admissibility, Judgment, ICJ Reports 1995, p 18, para 33; *Oil Platforms (Islamic Republic of Iran v United States of America)*, Preliminary Objections, Judgment, ICJ Reports 1996 (II), p 812, para 23; *Kasikili/Sedudu Island (Botswana/Namibia)*, Judgment, ICJ Reports 1999 (II), p 1059, para 18; most recently *Case Concerning Sovereignty over Pulau Ligitan and Pulau Sipadan, (Indonesia/Malaysia)*, ICJ Judgment 17 December 2002, para 37.

[207] See Zoller, 1977, pp 339, 345.

[208] Kolb, 1998, p 662.

[209] Zoller, 1977, p 345, 'Il en résulte que la bonne foi, en tant que principe normatif, compris comme l'obligation de tenir ses engagements, n'a pas de consistance proprement juridique . . . C'est pourquoi le principe de bonne foi est un principe moral et rien de plus'.

[210] See Kolb, 2000, p 82.

text, such as in gentlemen's agreements, and other forms of international understandings that lack binding character, but nevertheless are, guided by the general principle of law of good faith. In such non-binding understandings, the principle of good faith, remains juridical in a political context. In contrast the juridical concept of good faith forms one among the many other cornerstones of an international legal order, governed by treaties with binding norms and compulsory jurisdiction.[211]

International Ethos

A moral concept of good faith was debated at the time of the League of Nations, when H Lauterpracht and others found that an international ethos of humanity, justice, mutual supportiveness and the fundamental principles of good faith and loyalty preconditioned the international legal order. Just as with the political principle of good faith, the boundaries between the moral and juridical principles are blurry.

Should the moral concept of good faith form the substantive content of a positive treaty provision, the moral principle of good faith becomes a legal and, thus, enforceable concept. Thus, to Zoller, the concept of good faith acquires a legally binding effect when equipped with the legal format of positive rule.[213]

The distinction between the legal, the moral and the political concept has fostered, but, has more often been confounded with, the international legal separation between good faith in an objective sense ('Treu und Glauben') and subjective good faith ('Vertrauensschutz'). While good faith in a subjective sense has often been mistaken with the PLE, it emanates from and relates to an equitable function of good faith. Müller has identified the relationship between the moral principle of good faith and subjective good faith: 'The duty of good faith does not so much aim at realizing a subjective morality, as much as it requires a behaviour of mutual respectfulness guided by objective guideposts'.[214]

Finally, compared to its corrolaries of *pacta sunt servanda* and prohibition of abus de droit, good faith is the only concept which, beyond the positive law of a treaty obligation or of a general principle of law, may have an impact on a non-legal situation, such as sanctioning a morally or socially inappropriate behaviour.[215]

[211] *Ibid*, pp 82–4.
[212] *Ibid*, pp 82–5.
[213] See Zoller, 1977, pp 339, 345.
[214] Müller, 1971, p 128, 'Das Gebot von Treu und Glauben zielt nicht so sehr auf die subjektive Moralität, sondern es fordert ein an objektiven Massstäben gegenseitiger Rücksichtnahme orientiertes Verhalten'.
[215] See Zoller, 1977, p 353.

3

Good Faith and its Corrolaries in the Law of the WTO Agreements

> The Appellate Body was prudent enough not to surprise WTO Members with the introduction of too many legal concepts from the various sources of public international law.[1]

THIS CHAPTER DISCUSSES how the content of good faith varies depending upon the normative value attributed to it. Functions of good faith principles in public international law are compared to how good faith applies in WTO legal practice. Compelled either by the parties' terms of reference or by their own judgment, the WTO Panels have applied the principle of good faith, interpreted certain obligations of the WTO Agreements in good faith or created standards of (procedural) good faith.

The goal of chapter three is to analyse WTO Panel and AB decisions to assess to what extent the WTO judiciary refers to expressions of good faith, including the protection of legitimate expectations, *pacta sunt servanda*, the prohibition of *abus de droit*, equity, acquiescence and estoppel.

How good faith manifests itself in WTO case law must be separated from the normative value of good faith, as in how much legal, moral and political value good faith carries in WTO law, practice and policy. The normativity of good faith in the substantive law (as opposed to the procedural law of the WTO Agreements) will be the object of the following chapter four. Three other chapters, ten to twelve below, will introduce the role and normative function of procedural good faith, which stands for good faith as it applies to WTO dispute settlement.

CLASSIFICATIONS OF GOOD FAITH AND COROLLARIES IN WTO LAW

In order to organise the different legal principles protecting expressions of good faith in the WTO, this study refers to the method Kolb has used for classifying

[1] Hilf and Puth, 2002, p 216.

good faith concepts and corollaries in international law. Kolb distinguishes the intrinsic principle of good faith, *la bonne foi en tant que principe juridique* [good faith as a legal principle] from the extrinsic *notions juridiques voisines* [related legal concepts],[2] including equity, estoppel, *pacta sunt servanda* and prohibition of *abus de droit*. This distinction will also be applied to this study of the expressions of good faith codified in the WTO Agreements as rights and obligations, or found in the decisions by the panels or the AB.

Kolb's classification of good faith applies to general international law as well to the WTO, as the subset of specific rules of international law regulating trade and trade-related matters. The WTO Agreements, being treaties, constitute sources of international law alongside other treaties (which may be 'related treaties' if these regulate trade issues) and general principles of law and custom.

What scholars have convincingly laid out and the AB has confirmed in its very first report on *US–Gasoline*, is, that the WTO legal system forms part of the general international legal order. In the words of the *US–Gasoline* judgment, the WTO legal system created by the WTO Agreements and jurisprudence is 'not to be read in clinical isolation from public international law'.[3] What *US–Gasoline* does is to allow the AB to seek interpretative advice in sources of public international law. However, the AB limits such references to the customary rules of interpretation, which are the only sources of international law outside the WTO covered agreements that the WTO adjudicator may seek guidance from. There is no such thing as a freepass for applying all international law or all sources of international law becoming part of WTO law.

Nevertheless, even if the WTO Agreements are considered a source of international law, it is unclear whether or not other sources of international law, namely related treaties, general principles of law, and custom could fall within the scope of WTO jurisdiction and, as a consequence, shall be applied by the Panels and the AB of the WTO.

WTO case law either reflects a reference to, or contains a measure of:

— the general principle of law of good faith
— the customary rule of *pacta sunt servanda*
— the doctrine of negotiating in good faith
— the doctrine of implementing WTO obligations in good faith
— the prohibition of *abus de droit*
— the general principle of estoppel

[2] Kolb, 1998, p 662, 'La délimitation de la bonne foi par rapport à des notions juridiques voisines'.

[3] See *US–Gasoline*, AB Report, p 17.

The protection of legitimate expectations is GATT-specific and forms the seventh type of an expression of good faith in WTO law. Since it is GATT/WTO-specific, it is discussed separately in chapter 6.

GOOD FAITH AS GENERAL PRINCIPLE OF LAW

What does it mean when jurisprudence refers to the general principle of law of good faith as 'recognized' or 'implied' in a provision of substantive WTO law or when good faith is 'expressed' in a WTO provision? This question firstly says something about the content of good faith in the context of a particular WTO covered agreement. Secondly, such statements of the judiciary may inform about the legal source: either good faith emanates from a treaty provision of one of the WTO Agreements 'expressing' such a general principle of law, or the legal source of WTO good faith is the general principle of law of good faith with corrolaries (prohibition of abus de droit, estoppel) applied directly, or the customary rule of *pacta sunt servanda.* This second question also informs about the normative value of good faith for the WTO legal system and will thus be discussed below.

US–Shrimp Appellate Body Report (1998): General Exceptions of Article XX GATT 94 Chapeau

The AB unveiled that the Chapeau of Article XX is 'but one expression of the principle of good faith' and that '[t]his principle, is at once a general principle of law and a general principle of international law'.[4] The Chapeau provides for a safety valve against protectionism, when WTO Members invoke one of the specific exceptions to Most Favoured Nations (MFN) or NT enumerated in the list of Article XX(a–j) GATT 94.

The AB overturned the Panel and the Panel's sequencing of Article XX GATT 94, when it introduced the Chapeau as the ultimate test for justifying the provisionally GATT-consistent domestic measure.[5] Panel practice on Article XX GATT before *US–Shrimp* had been to first determine whether the policy goal of a measure is justified under the Chapeau of Article XX, followed by examining whether the domestic measure would fall under one of the policy goals listed under Article XX(a–j) GATT.[6] In the affirmative, such a finding would lead to an examination of the measure under a specific exemption of Article XX.

[4] *Ibid*, para 157.
[5] *Ibid*, paras 122–3.
[6] See *US–Gasoline*, AB Report, para 7.29; *US–Shrimp* AB Report, paras 113–16.

Because the *US–Shrimp* Panel found a violation of the Chapeau, the *US–Shrimp* Panel did not engage in the second test of examining whether or not the scope of *US–Section 609* would fall under a policy exceptions of Article XX(a–j) GATT.[7] The AB in *US–Shrimp* overturned the Panel on this point with the argument that the Panel had followed an incorrect sequencing of Article XX GATT examinations. To the AB, the GATT-consistency of the domestic measure's policy goal no longer counted for the Chapeau of Article XX; rather, the measure and its application would have to be subjected to the additional test under the Chapeau after its policy goal, and thus the measure itself would be determined provisionally justified under Article XX(a–j).[8] Only this 'two-tier' approach could ensure that the measure was not an arbitrary, discriminatory and disguised restriction to trade because it would examine the relationship between the measure and its propagated goal.[9]

Hence, the AB decided to match the Chapeau with the general principle of international law of good faith in order to solidly ground its reversal of Panel practice. In order to prove that the Chapeau limits the exercise of the specific exemptions, the AB first referred to the Chapeau's language and its negotiating history and ended by resorting to the general principle of law.

Not only does the Chapeau express a notion of good faith, another 'application of this general principle' [of good faith] is the *abus de droit* doctrine.[10] The AB finds that already *US–Gasoline* had based its reading of the Chapeau on the prohibition of *abus de droit*.[11]

The Panel and the AB reports agree on the result of sanctioning the US for its arbitrary and discriminating shrimp embargo.[12] The only difference between the Panel and AB reports lies in their method of sequencing.[13] The AB examines and finds that *US–Section 609* is provisionally justified under the specific exception of Article XX(g) but that ultimately, *US–Section 609* violates the Chapeau of Article XX. The Panel, in contrast, had directly arrived at the conclusion that *US Section 609* was arbitrary and discriminatory vis–à–vis other WTO Members.

The AB imparts upon the prohibition of *abus de droit* in the context of Article XX, a WTO-specific function, ie the prohibition of discrimination. *US–Shrimp* is therefore further discussed under the heading of *abus de droit* doctrine. The AB, in any case, has directly applied the prohibition of *abus de droit*, in addition to declaring Chapeau of Article XX but an 'expression' of good faith.

[7] *Ibid*, para 7.62; *US–Shrimp* AB Report, para 112.
[8] *US–Shrimp* AB Report, para 149.
[9] *Ibid*, paras 147, 149–50.
[10] *Ibid*, para 158.
[11] *Ibid*, para 151 referring to *US–Gasoline*, AB Report, p 22.
[12] *US–Shrimp* Panel Report, para 7.62; *US–Shrimp* AB Report, paras 186, 187(c).
[13] *US–Shrimp* AB Report, paras 117–19.

EC–Hormones Appellate Body Report (1998): Good Faith in Risk Assessment of Article 5.2 of the Agreement on the Application of Sanitary and Phytosanitary Measures (ASPS)

The AB is prepared to recognise the imposition of a trade restriction for sanitary and phytosanitary reasons, if it is 'based on a risk assessment'[14] pursuant to the ASPS.[15] Specifically, there needs to be a rational relationship between the measure and the risk assessed.[16] The scientific conclusion about the risk, which constitutes the risk assessment, can by the standards of AB jurisprudence even be scientific evidence reflecting 'divergent' as opposed to 'mainstream' opinion.[17] However, because the AB lacks the standard of review for such issues of facts, it counterbalances this gap by holding members responsible under good faith, when these choose the diverging opinion to provide the evidence:[18]

> In most cases, responsible and representative governments tend to base their legislative and administrative measures on 'mainstream' scientific opinion. In other cases, equally responsible and representative governments may act in good faith on the basis of what, at a given time, may be a divergent opinion coming from qualified and respected sources.[19]

The good faith standard imposed on WTO Member States for choosing the most reasoned and responsible evidence, relates to the broader 'reasonable relationship' required between the risk assessment and the sanitary and/or phytosanitary measure.[20] In analogy to the reasonable relationship between assessment and measure, member governments will be under a stricter good faith duty regarding evidence chosen, where the risk involved is 'life threatening' and 'constitutes a clear and imminent threat to public health and safety'.[21] However, it is uncertain whether the good faith duty extends also to the quality of the *sources* of evidence.[22] The AB only refers to 'governments act[ing] in good faith', thus omitting to clarify whether a government that bases itself on divergent scientific opinion must be guided by good faith considerations, or

[14] See Arts 5.1 and 5.2 ASPS; *EC–Hormones*, AB Report para 148.

[15] ASPS, Annex 1A of the Marrakesh Agreement Establishing the WTO of 15 April 1994, in The *Results of the Uruguay Round of Multilateral Trade Negotiations, The Legal Texts*, GATT Secretariat, June 1994, WTO, Geneva.

[16] See *EC–Hormones*, AB Report, para 193.

[17] *Ibid*, para 194; see Pauwelyn, 2003c, pp 179–82 on minority scientific opinion in the context of Art 5 ASPS.

[18] See Oesch, 2003b, pp 15, 84–95, who finds that *EC–Hormones* established a standard of review somewhere between *de novo* and 'total deference'.

[19] *EC–Hormones*, AB Report, para 194; see also *Japan–Agricultural Products*, AB Report, para 77, where the AB referred to this statement.

[20] See *EC–Hormones*, AB Report, para 194.

[21] *Ibid*.

[22] See Pauwelyn, 2003c, p 180.

whether the risk assessment, which a government conducts on the basis of divergent evidence must be performed in good faith. While the first interpretation would enhance the effectiveness of Article 5.2 ASPS, the second, narrower one, would pay more respect to considerations of state sovereignty. By defining the level of safety of scientific evidence and balancing that level with the degree of market openness, good faith provides for a balanced interpretation of the ASPS. In doing so, it takes on the identical function of *infra legem* good faith it had already embraced for the interpretation of the Chapeau of Article XX.

US–Cotton Yarn Appellate Body Report (2001): the Good Faith Obligation to Withdraw a Safeguard Measure

Practice in *US–Cotton Yarn* (2001) introduces a good faith obligation that all WTO Member States must observe, if their safeguard measures have been declared lawful by the Panel or the AB. Later on, post-determination evidence relied upon for demonstrating that pre-determination facts would never have justified the safeguard under WTO standards in the first place. Therefore, the AB in *US–Cotton Yarn* argued, WTO Member States are under the good faith duty to withdraw pre-determination safeguard measures.

There is a gap in Article 6.2 of the Agreement on Textiles and Clothing (ATC),[23] in combination with Article 6 of the Agreement on Safeguards (ASG),[24] by which a member can circumvent the discovery of a factual error after it finds that the conditions for a safeguard measure were fulfilled, and, thereupon, continue to impose the safeguard. The AB cannot overturn a Panel decision finding for the US, when *ex post facto* the safeguard measure was found unjustified, because it had no *de novo* standard of review relating to issues of fact, and neither does the Panel have the power to substitute its own judgment for that of a member.[25] Nevertheless, the AB suggests that the US would have abused its right to impose provisional safeguard measures under Article 6.2 ATC, if it had neglected to withdraw the safeguard after the US census data for 1998 showed that the safeguard revealed itself to be unfounded.[26]

The AB plays with the idea to sanction with good faith a WTO Member State for not withdrawing a safeguard when post-determination evidence relating to pre-determination facts reveals that the safeguard was unfounded. However,

[23] ATC, Annex 1A of the Marrakesh Agreement Establishing the WTO of 15 April 1994, in 'The Results of the Uruguay Round of Multilateral Trade Negotiations', The Legal Texts, GATT Secretariat, June 1994, WTO, Geneva.

[24] ASG, Annex 1A of the Marrakesh Agreement Establishing the WTO of 15 April 1994, in 'The Results of the Uruguay Round of Multilateral Trade Negotiations', The Legal Texts, GATT Secretariat, June 1994, WTO, Geneva.

[25] *US–Cotton Yarn*, AB Report, para 78.

[26] *Ibid*, paras 62–3, 81.

the AB neglects to concretise the duty and fails to hold the US liable for violating the duty to respect good faith. Had the AB held the US liable under the good faith argument, the US would have had to remove the later discovered, unfounded safeguard measure:

> There is no need for the purpose of this appeal to express a view on the question whether an importing member would be under an *obligation*, flowing from the 'pervasive' general principle of *good faith* that underlies all treaties, to *withdraw* a safeguard measure if post–determination evidence relating to pre-determination facts were to emerge revealing that a determination was based on such a critical factual error that one of the conditions required by Article 6 turns out never to have been met (emphasis in the original, footnotes omitted).[27]

The AB acknowledges that Article 6 ATC specifies neither the procedure nor the organ of the determination. Thus, it suggests that there might be a gap.[28] The AB fills in this gap by drawing an analogy to Article 6 of the Agreement on Safeguards under which WTO Members intending to impose a safeguard ought to make a 'preliminary determination' into the 'clear evidence' that increased imports would cause or threaten serious injury. Such a duty, the AB finds, is one of 'due diligence'.[29] However, the AB finds that even if a member could not have known at the time of determination that there was data contradicting its safeguard, the member would be obliged under good faith, but not Article 6.2 ATC, to remove its safeguard. However, the AB left this last finding unsubstantiated.[30]

Although the AB left this finding unsubstantiated, it nevertheless imposes a good faith duty upon the WTO Member States.[31] If a Panel reviews evidence a Member could not have known at the time that Member had made its determination in due diligence, it would be infringing upon the Member's due process right, namely, Article 11 DSU.[32] Therefore, the AB says, the duty of good faith to withdraw the safeguard measure even before that safeguard is found justified binds the WTO Member State imposing the safeguard, if that Member had evidence that the safeguard was unfounded (pre-determination evidence of post-determination fact).[33]

However, in this case, the AB did not find it necessary to examine whether the US should be held responsible under good faith, to withdraw the safeguard, because the AB found the Panel to have exceeded its discretion under Article 11 DSU by considering the 1998 US Census data, which the Panel could not have known at the point in time when the US made its determination of facts before the DSB. Nevertheless, the AB did pronounce the US safeguard unjustified.[34]

[27] *Ibid*, para 81 and fn 52 and 53.
[28] *Ibid*, para 76.
[29] *Ibid*, paras 76–9.
[30] *Ibid*, para 81.
[31] See *ibid*, para 81.
[32] See *ibid*, paras 74–80.
[33] *Ibid*, para 81.
[34] *US–Cotton Yarn*, AB Report, paras 78, 80, 128.

US–Japan Hot-rolled Steel Panel and Appellate Body Reports (2001) and *Egypt–Steel Rebar AD* Panel Report (2002): Good Faith in Anti-Dumping Investigations

The development of the good faith principle in WTO rules of procedure and related practice, specifically, good faith in anti-dumping investigations and dispute settlements is prejudiced upon 'trade remedy' cases that involve the US steel industry, namely, as of December 2005, *US–Japan Hot-rolled Steel, US–Steel Safeguard, US–Line Pipe Safeguards, US–Corrosion-resistant Steel Sunset Review, US–German Steel, US–Lead and Bismuth Carbon Steel* and *US–OCTG Sunset Review*.

The *US–Japan Hot-rolled Steel* case introduces two issues of good faith obligations, both relating to the procedure prescribed in the ADA for imposing anti-dumping duties upon another WTO Member State.

First there is the obligation of the importing WTO Member State to respect a standard of reasonableness when conducting anti-dumping investigations pursuant to paragraphs 2 and 5 of Annex II of the ADA. This expression of good faith *infra legem* contained in Annex II paragraphs 2 and 5 ADA was taken up in the later *Egypt–Steel Rebar AD* Panel report of 8 August 2002 and confirmed in *US–Steel Safeguard* of 10 November 2003, *US–Corrosion-resistant Steel Sunset Review* of 15 December 2003, *US–OCTG Sunset Review* of 2 November 2005.

The second expression of good faith, the *US–Japan Hot-rolled Steel* Panel and AB Reports of 2001 find, relates to the duty of the investigating authorities of the importing WTO Member State to conduct an objective examination under Annex II and Article 3.1 ADA.

US–Japan Hot-rolled Steel *Panel Report (2001): the Reasonableness of Anti-dumping Investigations*

When the US Department of Commerce (USDOC) imposed anti-dumping duties on imports of hot-rolled steel and other related products from Japan on 29 June 1999, Japan's response was to bring the dispute before the WTO by requesting the establishment of a Panel. While preparing the US response to Japan's complaint, the USDOC requested information from the Japanese steel producer Kawasaki Steel Corporation (KSC) and its US affiliate, the California Steel Industries Inc (CSI). Annex II ADA provides that Member States have to compel their industries to comply with the requests of another party to a litigation. Subsequently, KSC submitted the requested information to the USDOC in paper form. The US considered this submission insufficient and requested computer taped questionnaires instead of hand-written ones.

Subsequently, the US argued before the Panel that Japan did not comply with the US submission request. In the US' view, Japan had acted against the object and purpose of Annex II ADA and thus violated its duty to comply with such provisions in good faith. The Panel instead ruled in Japan's favour that the Japanese submission of evidence was sufficient. The Panel also found that the US anti-dumping laws, regulations, and administrative procedures were inconsistent with numerous provisions of the ADA and its Annex II.

US–Japan Hot-rolled Steel *Appellate Body Report (2001): Good Faith in 'Using the Facts Available'*

On 25 April 2001, the US filed a notice of appeal claiming that:

> the Panel . . . erred in finding that an unbiased and objective investigating authority evaluating the evidence before USDOC could not reasonably have concluded that KSC had not failed, under the duty of Article 6.8 ADA to 'cooperate' in providing requested information.[35]

Japan responded that the evidence the USDOC required from KSC and CSI was an unreasonable demand that violated the standard of good faith. To Japan, the USDOC had requested, under the Annex II of the ADA (to which Article 6.8 ADA refers), more than it should have reasonably required from the industry allegedly engaged in dumping.[36]

The AB 'notes that paragraph 2 of Annex II [ADA] authorises investigating authorities to request responses to questionnaires in a particular medium', as, for example, computer tape.[37] The principle of good faith implied in paragraph 2 Annex II ADA, however, limits the investigating importing party's scope of requests to reasonable requests: 'but, at the same time, states that such a request should not be "maintained" ', if it were to impose 'an "*unreasonable extra burden*" on the interested party', that is, would '*entail unreasonable additional cost and trouble*' (emphasis added by the AB).[38] Good faith *infra legem* paragraph 2 Annex II ADA functions to 'strike a balance between the effort that they can expect interested parties to make in responding to questionnaires, and the practical ability of those interested parties to comply fully with all demands made of them by the investigating authorities':[39]

> We see this provision as another detailed expression of the principle of good faith, which is, at once, a general principle of law and a principle of general international law, that informs the provisions of the Anti-Dumping Agreement, as well as the other covered agreements. This organic principle of good faith, in this particular context, restrains investigating authorities from imposing on exporters burdens which, in the circumstances, are not reasonable.[40]

35 *US–Japan Hot-rolled Steel*, AB Report, para 11.
36 *Ibid*, para 19.
37 *Ibid*, para 101.
38 *Ibid*.
39 *Ibid*.
40 *Ibid*.

Paragraph 5 of Annex II ADA implies another good faith standard. In paragraph 5 Annex II ADA, good faith prohibits the investigating authorities of the importing WTO Member State to discard information that is 'not ideal in all respects', unless the exporting WTO Member State had not acted 'to the best of its ability', when supplying the information to the importing WTO Member States antidumping investigations authorities.[41]

Paragraphs 2 and 5 Annex II ADA together with Articles 6.8 and 6.13 ADA are, examples of good faith *infra legem*, or, in the WTO terminology 'implied'. Even if the AB does not use the terminology of *infra legem*, good faith is found implied in paragraphs 2 and 5 Annex II ADA to which Articles 6.8 and 6.13 ADA refer to. The function of good faith *infra legem* in Articles 6.8 and 6.13 in combination with paragraphs 2 and 5 Annex II ADA, is a balancing one:

> We, therefore, see paragraphs 2 and 5 of Annex II of the ADA as reflecting a careful balance between the interests of investigating authorities and exporters.[42]

Infra legem good faith requires:

> the investigating authorities to engage in a balancing of interests: the primary function of investigating authorities are not entitled to insist upon *absolute* standards or impose *unreasonable* burdens upon those exporters. We also observe that Article 6.13 of the ADA provides: The authorities shall take *due account of any difficulties experienced by interested parties*, in particular small companies, in supplying information requested, *and shall provide any assistance practicable* (emphasis added by the AB).[43]

The importing WTO Member State (which in the dispute, is the party bringing a claim against the dumping) has the right to require that the interested (eg exporting parties) make the best effort to provide information about the alleged dumping. This positive right contained in paragraphs 2 and 5 Annex II ADA, is set off by the implied good faith standard, against the practical ability of these interested parties to comply fully with all demands made of them by the investigating authorities. The AB found that the Japanese steel industry had cooperated in good faith with the USDOC. In the AB's view it was the US who had infringed upon this duty of balancing, which the good faith standard of paragraphs 2 and 5 Annex II ADA impliedly required, by requesting information from Japanese government authorities in a way that was unreasonable as to cost and trouble.[44]

[41] *Ibid*, para 100.
[42] *Ibid*, para 102.
[43] *Ibid*.
[44] *Ibid*, para 240(a–b).

US–Japan Hot-rolled Steel *Panel and Appellate Body Reports (2001): Duty of Objective Examination by Investigating Authorities*

Pursuant to *US–Japan Hot-rolled Steel,* the importing WTO Member State, before lawfully imposing anti-dumping duties, is to respect the ' "fundamental, substantive obligation" with respect to the injury determination' under Article 3.1 ADA.[45] Specifically, the domestic investigating authorities of the importing WTO Member State must conduct an 'objective examination', based upon 'positive evidence'. The AB identified this obligation to conduct an 'objective examination' as a procedural expression of good faith and created the obligation that the *process* of examination must 'conform to the dictates of the basic principles of good faith and fundamental fairness'.[46]

Good faith in *US–Japan Hot-rolled Steel* functions formatively, *infra legem.* It fills in the meaning of the term 'objective examination' by imposing the duty of a fair and unbiased investigative process upon the importing member.[47] The word 'objective', which qualifies the word 'examination', indicates essentially that the 'examination' process must conform to the dictates of the basic principles of good faith and fundamental fairness. In short, an 'objective examination' requires that the domestic industry, and the effects of dumped imports, be investigated in an unbiased manner, without favouring the interests of any interested party, or group of interested parties, in the investigation. The duty of the investigating authorities to conduct an 'objective examination' recognises that the determination will be influenced by the objectivity, or any lack thereof, of the investigative process.[48]

Article 3.1 ADA is, in addition to paragraphs 2 and 5 Annex II ADA, another source for the AB decision to reflect good faith in the ADA. The AB implied that the 'general principle of good faith' in Article 3.1 ADA was 'yet another expression of the general principle of good faith in the ADA'.[49]

The measure of good faith implied in Article 3.1 ADA also contains a procedural component. In substance, Article 3.1 ADA functions to ensure that the anti-dumping investigation procedure prescribed by the ADA is conducted fairly, orderly and in a timely fashion. As such, Article 3.1 ADA compares with the due process requirements imposed under the Chapeau of Article XX GATT 94, and also with the similar due process obligation relating to the procedure for settling disputes in good faith under Article 3.10 DSU, as discussed below in chapter ten.[50]

[45] *Ibid*, para 192.

[46] *Ibid*, para 193.

[47] *Cf* Schwarzenberger, 1955, p 325, who defines the *formative* function of good faith as the 'creation of rules of an essentially relative and elastic character'.

[48] *US–Japan Hot-rolled Steel*, AB Report, para 193.

[49] *Ibid*, fn 141 to para 193.

[50] See *US–Shrimp*, AB Report, paras 181–2.

Egypt–Steel Rebar AD *Panel Report (2002): 'Level of Good Faith Cooperation' in Relation to Value of Information*

In the later *Egypt–Steel Rebar AD* Panel decision of 8 August 2002, the Panel followed the *US–Japan Hot-rolled Steel* AB's interpretation of good faith *infra legem* implied in Annex II ADA. Thus, in *Egypt–Steel Rebar AD*, the Panel reiterates that Annex II ADA implies that good faith must ensure that the level of cooperation between investigating and investigated party remains a balanced one:

> As we have noted, paragraphs 3 and 5, in addition to some of the other provisions of Annex II, have to do with assessing whether the information submitted by interested parties must be used. Thus, paragraph 5 is a complement to paragraph 3 and the two must be read together in considering the IA's obligations in respect of submitted information. In particular, we believe that under the pertinent phrases in these two paragraphs taken together, information that is of a very high quality, although not perfect, must not be considered unverifiable solely because of its minor flaws, so long as the submitter has acted to the best of its ability. That is, so long as the level of good faith cooperation by the interested party is high, slightly imperfect information should not be dismissed as unverifiable.[51]

The Panel in *Egypt–Steel Rebar AD*, which was never appealed, adds on to the meaning of good faith implied in paragraphs 2 and 5 Annex II ADA.

***US–Section 211 ('Havana Club')* Panel (2001) and Appellate Body Report (2002): Good Faith Implementation of the TRIPS Agreement**

In *US–Japan Hot-rolled Steel* AB Report (2001), the principle of good faith had protected the exporting party from unreasonable procederual requests by the importing party's anti-dunping investigating authorities. In *US–Section 211 ('Havanna Club')*, the Panel found that Article 7 TRIPS imposes a duty on WTO Member States to implement the TRIPS Agreement in good faith:

> Moreover, Article 7 of the TRIPS Agreement states that one of the objectives is that [t]he protection and enforcement of intellectual property rights should contribute . . . to a balance of rights and obligations. We consider this expression to be a form of the good faith principle. The AB in *United States–Shrimps* stated that this principle 'controls the exercise of rights by states'. One application of this principle, the application widely known as the doctrine of *abus de droit*, prohibits the abusive exercise of a state's rights and enjoins that whenever the assertion of a right 'impinges on the field covered by [a] treaty obligation, it must be exercised bona fide, that is to say reasonably. An abusive exercise by a member of its own treaty right thus results in a breach of the treaty rights of the other members and, as well, a violation of the treaty obliga-

[51] *Egypt–Steel Rebar*, Panel Report, para 7.161.

> tion of the member so acting'. Members must therefore implement the provisions of the TRIPS Agreement in a manner consistent with the good faith principle enshrined in Article 7 of the TRIPS Agreement.[52]

Article 7 TRIPS constitutes the first recognition of a good faith obligation in the TRIPS Agreement.

> The members must therefore implement the provisions of the TRIPS Agreement in a manner consistent with the good faith principle enshrined in Article 7 of the TRIPS Agreement.[53]

While the Panel in *US–Section 211 ('Havana Club')* identified Article 7 TRIPS as an expression of good faith *infra legem*, and formulated the first good faith obligation of the TRIPS Agreement, *a fortiori*, the AB in *US–Section 211 ('Havana Club')* generalised this duty of good faith implementation to all of the treaties regrouped under the WTO (Marrakech) Agreement, ie the GATT and the 'covered agreements',[54] the General Agreement on Trade in Services (GATS), the TRIPS and the DSU:

> '[I]t cannot be assumed that the WTO Member will fail to implement its obligations under the WTO Agreement in good faith'.[55]

The function good faith assumes in Article 7 TRIPS according to *US–Section 211 ('Havana Club')* derives from *pacta sunt servanda*. Therefore, the good faith duty of assuring the correct implementation of the TRIPS in good faith under Article 7 TRIPS will be discussed in more detail in the next section focusing specifically on *pacta sunt servanda*.

PACTA SUNT SERVANDA

A second emanation of good faith that the Panels and the AB apply as part of WTO law is *pacta sunt servanda,* the duty to perform treaty obligations in good faith. *Pacta sunt servanda* also encompasses two corollaries:

— the duty to negotiate in good faith and
— the duty to implement treaty obligations in good faith.

[52] *US–Section 211 ('Havana Club')*, Panel Report, para 8.57.
[53] *Ibid.*
[54] See 'Agreements Covered by the Understanding', Appendix 1 to the DSU; these include the WTO Marrakech Agreement Establishing the WTO and its annexed legal instruments, except for Annex 3 [hereinafter 'covered agreements'].
[55] *US–Section 211 ('Havana Club')*, AB Report, para 259.

Performing WTO Obligations in Good Faith

Pacta sunt servanda is a customary legal principle forming part of the body of rules binding upon all state parties to international treaties, including the WTO Agreements. The VCLT, as the main codification on the international law of treaties, enshrines the duty to 'fulfill, perform and execute [. . .] treaty obligations in accordance with the "pervasive" principle of good faith' in Article 26.[56] Even if WTO DSU Article 3.2 calls upon the WTO judiciary to apply, from the body of rules governing the international law of treaties, the rules on treaty interpretation only, the AB in its *US–Offset Act ('Byrd Amendment')* decision has integrated the rule of *pacta sunt servanda* of Article 26 VCLT into the WTO *acquis* in 2003:

> Article 26 of the Vienna Convention, entitled *Pacta Sunt Servanda*, provides that '[e]very treaty in force is binding upon the parties to it and must be performed by them in good faith'. The US itself affirmed 'that WTO Members must uphold their obligations under the covered agreements in good faith'.[57]

The 2003 *US–Offset Act ('Byrd Amendment')* ruling is the result of a development in case law, that began with the *Belgian Family Allowances* GATT 1947 Panel Report of 1952[58] and, in a slightly different form, with the *US–Malt Beverages GATT 1947* Panel Report of 1992,[59] to which the WTO Panel Report on the *Korea–Government Procurement Panel* decision seems to have referred in 2000.

In *Korea–Government Procurement*, the Panel established *pacta sunt servanda* for the first time in WTO law. The Panel had derived *pacta sunt servanda* from the 'well-established GATT principle' of legitimate expectations. It had not directly imported *pacta sunt servanda*, from customary international law.[60] The 2003 *US–Offset Act ('Byrd Amendment')* AB report confirmed the

[56] *US–Offset Act ('Byrd Amendment')*, AB Report, para 105.

[57] *Ibid*, para 296.

[58] See *Belgian Family Allowances*, GATT 1947 Panel Report adopted 7 November 1952, BISD 1S/59.

[59] *US–Malt Beverages*, GATT 1947 Panel Report adopted 19 June 1992 November 1952, BISD 1S/59, para 5.79, where the question was whether or not the central government was responsible for GATT-inconsistent acts of its subfederal entities, when, according to that GATT Member State's internal division of powers between central government and subfederal entities mean that the central government in the particular area governed by GATT law, never had jurisdiction, or had delegated that jurisdiction to the subfederal entities. The Panel referred to Art 27 VCLT which says that the duty to perform international treaty obligations in good faith may not be circumvented by invoking national legislative divison of powers; 'Art XXIV:12 that this provision was designed to apply only to those measures by regional or local governments or authorities which the central government cannot control because they fall outside its jurisdiction under the constitutional distribution of powers'. The Panel agreed with this interpretation in view of the general principle of international treaty law that a party to a treaty may not invoke the provisions of its internal law as justification for its failure to perform a treaty obligation.

[60] Compare *India–Patents*, Panel Report, para 7.20 with *Korea–Government Procurement*, Panel Report, para 7.93ff.

Korea–Government Procurement Panel's finding and affirmed that *pacta sunt servanda* forms an integral part of WTO jurisdiction, constituting a binding obligation upon the WTO Member States.

WTO Case Law

US–Offset Act ('Byrd Amendment') *Panel Report (2003)*

The Panel had found that the US's Continued Dumping and Subsidy Offset Act (CDSOA) Article undermined the value of Article 5.4 ADA and Article 11.4 ASCM for the trading partners of the US. The CDSOA provides for financial incentives if industry supports the US government dumping investigations. WTO law, particularly Articles 5.4 ADA and 11.4 ASCM, maintains that quantitative assessment of imports should trigger an investigation into an alleged dumping accusation. The CDSOA, to the Panel distorted the object and purpose of Articles 5.4 ADA and 11.4 ASCM because:

— under the CDSOA there were more petitions in support of anti-dumping duties from domestic industry than would have been the case without the CDSOA
— the CDSOA denied the US' trading partners, who were subject to the US' anti-dumping investigation a 'meaningful test of whether the petition has the required support of industry'

Therefore, the US did not in good faith in promoting this outcome.

Specifically the Panel found evidence that:

> given the low costs of supporting a petition, and the strong likelihood that all producers will feel obliged to keep open their eligibility for offset payments for reasons of competitive parity, we could conclude that the majority of petitions will achieve the levels of support required under ADA Article 5.4 and ASCM Article 11.4.[61]

Article 5.4 ADA does not require an investigation into the motives or intent of a domestic producer choosing to support a petition, but only requires statistical thresholds be met. With the CDSOA a greater number of producers support a petition to investigate than would exist without the CDSOA. Notwithstanding the 'wrong motives', with the CDSOA there are producers, which, unaffected by the dumping, simply rally for support of dumping investigations to benefit from the distribution of offset payments:

> [T]he CDSOA may be regarded as having undermined the value of AD Article 5.4/ASCM Article 11.4 to the countries with whom the United States trades, and the United States may be regarded as not having acted in good faith in promoting this outcome.[62]

[61] *US–Offset Act ('Byrd Amendment')*, Panel Report, para 7.63.
[62] *Ibid.*

Further, the Panel said:

> The importance of the principle of good faith as a general rule of conduct in international relations is well established. Good faith requires a party to a treaty to refrain from acting in a manner, which would defeat the object and purpose of the treaty as a whole or the treaty provision in question.[63]

The Panel found that the CDSOA 'implies a return to the situation which existed before the introduction of ADA Article 5.4 and ASCM Article 11.4'.[64] Instead of examining whether the support actually existed, it was simply assumed to exist and there was not in all cases 'evidence of the industry-wide concern of injury being caused by dumped or subsidised imports'.[65] Thus, the Panel suggested US conduct was contrary to good faith because the US CDSOA reflects a mistrust of the multilateral objectives of the WTO to reduce or eliminate unfair barriers to trade, such as anti-dumping duties, in order to realize trade liberalization.

The US acted contrary to good faith because the US legislation, the CDSOA, has the effect of undermining the objectives of Articles 5.4 ADA and 11.4 ASCM. The CDSOA renders these WTO provisions 'completely meaningless'.[66] Not only did the Panel accuse the US of creating, via the CDSOA, a legal situation incompatible with good faith as a general rule of conduct in international relations, but *a fortiori* the Panel held the US responsible for violating the customary rule of *pacta sunt servanda,* which demands that a party to a treaty 'refrain from acting in manner which could defeat the object and purpose of the treaty as a whole or the treaty provision in question'.[67] While the Panel may not, under the international legal presumption of good faith, presume the US to have acted in bad faith, the Panel nevertheless considers the CDSOA as a violation of the duty to perform the ASCM and ADA in good faith (*pacta sunt servanda*).

US–Offset Act ('Byrd Amendment') *Appellate Body Report (2003)*

The US appealed against the Panel's decision claiming that the Panel had misapplied the 'constituent elements test' as defined by the AB in the *US–1916 Act* decision.[68]

The US criticises the Panel for finding it had failed to act in good faith. According to the US, there is no basis in the WTO Agreement for a Panel to conclude that a member has not acted in good faith 'or to enforce a principle of

[63] *US–Offset Act ('Byrd Amendment')*, Panel Report, para 7.64 (footnotes omitted).
[64] *Ibid*, para 7.65.
[65] *Ibid*.
[66] *Ibid*, AB Report, para 279.
[67] *Ibid*, Panel Report, para 7.64
[68] *Ibid*, AB Report, para 16.

"good faith" as a substantive obligation agreed to by WTO Members'. The US based its argumentation against the existence of a substantive good faith principle in WTO law on the fact that

> dispute settlement Panels are subject to clear and unequivocal limits on their mandate: they may clarify 'existing provisions' of WTO agreements and may examine the measures at issue in the light of the relevant provisions of the covered agreements.[69]

Brazil countered that the US 'may be regarded as not having acted in good faith in promoting this outcome'.[70] According to Brazil, the incentive to file or support anti-dumping and countervailing duty petitions created by CDSOA payments further raises the potential for a minority of domestic producers to be able to 'control and initiate anti-dumping and/or countervailing duty proceedings'.[71]

The other appellees, namely the EC, India, Indonesia and Thailand, joined Brazil, in submitting that the obligation to perform a treaty obligation in good faith means that such obligations 'must not be evaded by a merely literal interpretation'. For the appellees, *pacta sunt servanda* and good faith mean that the parties 'must abstain from acts that are calculated to frustrate the object and purpose of the treaty'.[72]

The AB 'expresses . . . concern' with the Panel's approach in interpreting Article 5.4 ADA and Article 11.4 ASCM.[73] The AB says that it

> fail[s] to see how the Panel's interpretation of those provisions may be said to be based on the ordinary meaning of the words found in those provisions and, hence, we do not believe the Panel properly applied the principles of interpretation codified in the Vienna Convention.[74]

The AB then conducted a textual analysis following the VCLT rules. The AB's analysis concluded that the texts of Articles 5.4 ADA and 11.4 ASCM Agreement do not support the Panel, which had argued that applying for an investigation shall include an examination into the motives of the domestic producers.[75] Thus, the AB embarked upon an investigation into the object and purpose of the Offset Act,[76] and finally upon an examination into the Panel's argument that the US had violated a substantive good faith obligation.[77]

The AB very clearly distinguishes the principle of 'good faith interpretation' from the material principle of good faith, expressed in this case as *pacta sunt servanda*. Even though the AB was quick to point out that it had used the

[69] *Ibid*, para 28 and fn 36, referring to Arts 3.2 and 7.1 DSU.
[70] *Ibid*, para 56; see also para 278, where the AB takes up Brazil's formulation.
[71] *Ibid*.
[72] *Ibid*, para 88.
[73] *Ibid*, para 281.
[74] *Ibid* and fn 226 referring to Art 17.6(ii) ADA, which is similar to 3.2 DSU.
[75] *Ibid*, para 285.
[76] *Ibid*, paras 287–94.
[77] *Ibid*, paras 295–9.

substantive principle of good faith in previous cases (the *US–Shrimp* and the *US–Hot-rolled Steel* cases), it nevertheless felt that the AB had peeled out the principle of substantive good faith from layers of somewhat nebulous WTO jurisprudence on the issue of good faith:

> The principle of good faith may therefore be said to inform a *treaty interpreter's* task. Moreover, *performance* of treaties is also governed by good faith. Hence, Article 26 of the Vienna Convention, entitled *Pacta sunt servanda*, to which several appellees referred in their submissions, provides that '[e]very treaty in force is binding upon the parties to it and must be performed by them in good faith' (emphasis added).[78]

The AB decision has been received with criticism American. doctrine in particular views it as irreconcilable with the prohibition of Article 3.2 DSU to import via adjudication a substantive general principle of law into the WTO *acquis*:

> Although the AB rejected a finding of lack of good faith in the evidence in that case, it affirmed that a finding can be made that a WTO Members has failed to act in good faith seemingly independently from any violation of a substantive obligation under one of the Agreements.[79]

The AB's discussion of good faith involves two aspects. The first is 'good faith interpretation', which we will describe in chapters 7 to 9 and which relates possibly to the value Articles 5.4 ADA and 11.4 ASCM had for the US trading partners and which the CDSOA undermined as a result of increasing support for petitions to investigate dumping based on financial incentives rather than on the showing of a true industry concern. The second manifestation of good faith relates to the Panels' finding that the US defeated the object and purpose of Articles 5.4 ADA and 11.4 ASCM. The Panel, who searched for the most accurate source for the substantive principle of good faith applicable to the CDSOA, based itself on *pacta sunt servanda* and its derivative, the principle that a VCLT signatory must abstain from acts calculated to frustrate the object and purpose of the treaty.

The AB overturned the Panel because it found the evidence insufficient to conclude that the US had violated an obligation of good faith.[80] The AB's first argument is that because it found the US CDSOA not to violate the WTO Anti-Dumping Agreement, good faith 'does not have the relevance it had for the Panel' (who had found the US CDSOA to violate the ADA).[81] Secondly, and more importantly, the AB seems to hint at the fact that even if it had found the US in violation, such a finding would not have sufficed to condemn the US of disrespecting *pacta sunt servanda*. The AB argued that the Panel would have had 'to prove more than a mere treaty violation'.[82] The AB thus suggests that

[78] *US–Offset Act ('Byrd Amendment')*, AB Report, para 298; *US–Offset Act ('Byrd Amendment')* Panel Report, para 7.64 and fn 314.

[79] *Ibid*; *US–Offset Act ('Byrd Amendment')*, Panel Report, para 7.64 and fn 314 (footnotes omitted).

[80] See *ibid*, para 299.

[81] *Ibid*, para 295.

[82] *Ibid*, para 298.

the Panel would have had to prove an intention to act contrary to good faith, ie to show that the US had 'calculated to frustrate the object and purpose of the treaty'.[83] Thus, the AB seems to adhere to the ILC' s approach to *pacta sunt servanda*, as well as to share the appellees (EC and others) view, requiring in addition to an objective violation of a treaty provision, the fulfillment of a subjective element, such as the intentional, ie calculated, frustration of the object and purpose of an agreement.[84]

Scholarly Discussion of the Decisions

To the *US–Offset Act ('Byrd Amendment')* Panel it is possible to act contrary to good faith and to violate a treaty provision. To the AB firstly, a claim of good faith may be substantiated only in the absence of a treaty violation:

> . . . [G]iven our conclusion that the CDSOA does not constitute a violation of Article 5.4 of the Anti-Dumping Agreement and Article 11.4 of the ASCM Agreement, the issue of whether the US 'may be regarded as not having acted in good faith' in enacting the CDSOA does not have the relevance it had for the Panel.[85]

Secondly, contradicting its first statement, a treaty violation is an insufficient basis for a claim of good faith violation:

> Nothing, however, in the covered agreements supports the conclusion that simply because a WTO Member is found to have violated a substantive treaty provision, it has therefore not acted in good faith. In our view, it would be necessary to prove more than mere violation to support such a conclusion.[86]

Consequently, the AB's view on good faith performance of treaties is that it can be only sanctioned if a conduct is more seriously damaging than a mere treaty violation, or if the conduct in question is less serious than a treaty violation. The confusing statement of the AB may be understood if one identifies US conduct with the terms of *praeter legem* and *contra legem* good faith. It may be that the AB wanted to say that a violation of good faith would only vest in two narrowly defined situations. Without using the term of good faith *praeter legem*, the AB may have thought of applying good faith to the WTO, first, if the principle of good faith acts *praeter legem* to fill in a gap in the WTO Agreements. Secondly, good faith may be applied by the WTO judiciary *contra legem*: if the importing party, *in concreto*, the US, acts in a way that obstructs the object and purpose of a WTO provision and, in result, renders that provision meaningless, the duty to perform the WTO Agreements in good faith would vest and sanction such an abuse of rights.

83 *Ibid*, para 88.
84 *Ibid*, para 7.64 and fn 314; *US–Offset Act ('Byrd Amendment')*, AB Report, para 88.
85 AB Report, para 295.
86 AB Report, para 298.

Abus de Droit

The Panel held that the US by encouraging dumping investigations based on financial incentives instead of actual industry concerns had decreased the value of Articles 5.4 ADA and 11.4 ASCM Agreement in the eyes of its trading partners and the WTO, because instead of reflecting real industry concerns,

— the dumping investigation would be initiated for non-injury related reasons; and
— the number of dumping investigations would be artificially kept high, ie would occur more often than if only the truly affected producers would support the petitions.

The Panel found that the CDSOA created a situation of *abus de droit* insofar as the US 'defeat[ed] the object and purpose of the treaty as a whole or the treaty provision in question'.[87] As a foundation for its concept, the Panel refered to D'Amato and to the ILC Commission's Yearbook of 1966, vol II, page 211.[88] The ILC says, 'a party must abstain from acts *calculated* to frustrate the object and purpose of the treaty' (emphasis added).[89] The EC and the other appellees take up this element of intent ('acts . . . calculated to frustrate') in their appeal.[90]

Pacta Sunt Servanda *Prohibiting the Abuse of WTO Rights*

In addition to identifying an *abus de droit*, the Panel issued a prohibition to abuse rights. The Panel sanctioned the US for creating a situation of *abus de droit* by using the customary rule of *pacta sunt servanda* (encompassing the duty to perform treaties in good faith) as opposed to applying the prohibition of *abus de droit*. To the Panel, *pacta sunt servanda* is the applicable principle for firstly, prohibiting that the ADA provisions on how to conduct a fair investigation into dumping allegations are abused. Secondly, *pacta sunt servanda* also serves to sanction the US for issuing a new law. Thus, the Panel finds that by creating a situation of *abus de droit*, the US had simultaneously violated the duty to perform the ADA in good faith.

The AB disagrees with the Panel's analysis that the US had violated its duty of *pacta sunt servanda* by creating artificial incentives for industry to vote in favour of imposing anti-dumping duties on imported goods. Therefore, the AB overturn the finding of the Panel and held that since the CDSOA does not violate Articles 5.4 ADA and 11.4 ASCM Agreement, the US cannot be found to have acted contrary to good faith.[91]

[87] *US–Offset Act ('Byrd Amendment')*, Panel Report, para 7.64.
[88] See *US–Offset Act ('Byrd Amendment')*, Panel Report, fn 314 to para 7.64.
[89] *Ibid*, fn 314 to para 7.64, citing YBILC, 1966, vol II, p 211; see also Charme, 1992, pp 71ff.
[90] *US–Offset Act ('Byrd Amendment')*, AB Report, para 88.
[91] See *US–Offset Act ('Byrd Amendment')*, AB Report, para 295.

The AB in the *US–Offset Act ('Byrd Amendment')* adopted a textual view of *pacta sunt servanda,* which it had abandoned in *US–Line Pipe Safeguards* for a more teleological one.[92] In *US–Offset Act ('Byrd Amendment'),* the AB used *pacta sunt servanda* to confirm its textual interpretation of Articles 5.4 ADA and 11 ASCM Agreement that a showing of how a member arrived at gathering enough support for an anti-dumping investigation does not interest the WTO.[93]

Until the *US–Offset Act ('Byrd Amendment')* case, neither a Panel nor the AB had attempted to concretise the concept that treaties must be performed in good faith. Only in 2003 did the AB in the *US–Offset Act ('Byrd Amendment')* case identify *pacta sunt servanda* as a potentially new (substantive) function of the principle of good faith. Previous Panels and AB decisions had founded concepts of good faith either on legitimate expectations as to conditions of competition based upon the GATT *acquis* or 'good faith interpretation' in Article 31 VCLT, and good faith guarding against an abuse of right under Article 31(3)(c) VCLT.

Limited by the clear language of Article 3.2 DSU, which recognises only the customary international rules of *interpretation* as opposed to the entire set of rules on the international law of treaties, the AB in *US–Offset Act ('Byrd Amendment')* declared for the first time in its 10 years of jurisprudence that it would take *pacta sunt servanda* into account even if it is strictly speaking not (yet) WTO law.

The AB derived its legitimacy towards a broad interpretation of Article 3.2 DSU, because, as it points out, several appellees had expressly referred to *pacta sunt servanda* in their terms of reference (Article 7 DSU):

> Hence, Article 26 of the VCLT, entitled pacta sunt servanda, to which several appellees referred to in their submissions, provides that '(e)very treaty in force is binding upon the parties to it and must be performed by them in good faith'.[94]

Since even the appellant, the US, had affirmed 'that WTO Members must uphold their obligations under the covered agreements in good faith',[95] the AB must have felt empowered to define the confines of WTO jurisdiction with the customary rule of *pacta sunt servanda.*

The WTO-specific Rule of *Pacta Sunt Servanda*

This section will enumerate the three constitutive elements WTO jurisprudence has developed for *pacta sunt servanda* to become binding on a WTO Member State, namely the absence of discrimination, the limitation of sovereignty and the restraint on textual interpretation.

[92] See *US–Line Pipe Safeguards*, AB Report, paras 106, 108.
[93] See *US–Offset Act ('Byrd Amendment')*, AB Report, paras 283–4, 291.
[94] *Ibid*, para 296.
[95] *Ibid.*

Reinforcing the Non-discrimination Obligation

It is said that human rights jurisprudence suggests that *pacta sunt servanda* enforces the principle that treaties must be applied as to ensure the absence of discrimination, both in fact and in law.[96] In analogy, a *pacta sunt servanda* obligation requiring the absence of discrimination for WTO law would entail two elements: the elimination of discrimination between foreign and domestic economic operators, whether these be producers (GATT), service providers (GATS),[97] rightholders (TRIPS), investors under the Agreement on Trade-related Investment Measures (TRIMs)[98] or government and sub-federal public authorities under the Government Procurement Agreement (GPA);[99] and the elimination of discrimination among foreign competitors on a domestic market.

Other Limitations on National Sovereignty

Pacta sunt servanda reinforces 'an obligatory relation',[100] whereby the states' rights to exercise their sovereign rights become, in the area of markets and trade, more limited by WTO law. *Pacta sunt servanda* is the guardian of the WTO Member States' mutual consent and level of concessions. *Pacta sunt servanda* limits the abuse of sovereignty, including unilateral application, and stands for the interpretation and termination of international treaties. By holding the WTO Member States that are bound to the VCLT rule of performing treaties in good faith (Article 26 VCLT), it ensures legal security and predictability of the WTO Agreements within the legal system of international treaties. WTO jurisprudence finds an analogy in the Individual Opinion of Judge Bedjaoui in the *Case concerning the Gabcikovo–Nagymaros Project—(Hungary/Slovakia)*, 25 September 1997. In his individual opinion, Judge Bedjaoui illustrated what legal implications for the community of sovereign states, the prnciple of *pacta sunt servanda* has:

> La survivance du traité . . . montre . . . qu'il n'est pas question de légaliser les atteintes portées au principe *pacta sunt servanda*. . . . il paraît encore plus essentiel, surtout pour un organe judiciaire mondial soucieux de faire respecter le droit international, de montrer urbi et orbi que les traités ne sont pas 'chiffons de papier' et que leur vio-

[96] YBILC, 1964, vol II, p 8, referring to *Rights of United States Nationals in Morocco*, ICJ Reports, 1952, p 212; see also *Treatment of Polish Nationals in Danzig*, PCIJ 1932, Series A/B No 44, p 28; *Minority Schools in Albania*, PCIJ 1935, Series A/B, No 64, pp 19–20.

[97] See GATS, Annex 1B, Marrakesh Agreement Establishing the WTO, in 'The Results of the Uruguay Round of Multilateral Trade Negotiations', GATT Secretariat, June 1994, WTO, Geneva.

[98] Agreement on Trade-related Investment Measures (TRIMS), Annex 1A of the Marrakesh Agreement Establishing the WTO of 15 April 1994, in 'The Results of the Uruguay Round of Multilateral Trade Negotiations', The Legal Texts, GATT Secretariat, June 1994, WTO, Geneva.

[99] GPA, Annex 4 of the Marrakesh Agreement Establishing the WTO of 15 April 1994, in 'The Results of the Uruguay Round of Multilateral Trade Negotiations', The Legal Texts, GATT Secretariat, June 1994, WTO, Geneva.

[100] *Cf* YBILC, 1964, vol II, p 8.

lation ne peut les anéantir. Hors de leur consentement mutuel, les Etats ne peuvent et ne doivent pas se défaire aussi aisément de leurs obligations contractuelles. Il est impératif de renforcer la sécurité juridique des engagements internationaux.[101]

Treaty Interpretation and Rule Stability

Pacta sunt servanda prevents the divergent interpretations of a rule leading to the non-application of a treaty. *Pacta sunt servanda* in Article 26 VCLT closely connects with Article 31 VCLT, the general rule of treaty interpretation.[102] As an example, *pacta sunt servanda* of Article 26 VCLT in combination with 'good faith interpretation' of Article 31 VCLT may limit the impact of textual interpretation and can thus be used *contra legem.*

The VCLT drafters found that *pacta sunt servanda* not only has the 'negative' function of *contra legem*, in the sense that it does 'not only [require] the parties to refrain from certain acts', but that it may also entail the obligation 'that they [the parties] give effect to the spirit of the treaty'.[103] *Pacta sunt servanda,* according to the VCLT drafters, has two contradicting contents. First, it means giving full effect to a treaty, which may involve creative jurisprudence. Secondly, *pacta sunt servanda* secures the stability of a rule, by limiting an overbroad, teleological interpretation to a strictly textual rule analysis.

In international legal scholarship, Kennedy confirms the VCLT drafters, by defining the function of *pacta sunt servanda* as a dialectic one. *Pacta sunt servanda* is on the one hand a 'dualist' principle, which may either be used to emphasize 'binding'[ness], to ensure the security and predictability of treaty relations. As such, *pacta sunt servanda* confines the international adjudicator to a textual interpretation.[104] On the other hand, *pacta sunt servanda* may mean interpretation in 'good faith', which is an interpretative method stressing the peace and confidence enhancing effects of treaties.[105] As a rule of good faith, *pacta sunt servanda* empowers the adjudicator to bolder interpretation, leading to an equity enhancing, *contra* or *praeter legem* function.[106]

However, the downside of this polyvalent principle of *pacta sunt servanda* is, according to Kennedy, its 'polarity', which renders *pacta sunt servanda* susceptible to 'rhetorical' manipulations by the adjudicator depending on the doctrine he/she wishes to emphasize in a given case.[107] Müller calls *pacta sunt servanda* the 'good-faith clause', and adds that the 'drive to protect confidence creates legal ties'. Thus, Müller seems to prioritise or at least to emphasize the *pacta sunt servanda* creative function over the more static one of preserving a treaty's legal

[101] *Case Concerning the Gabcikovo–Nagymaros Project (Hungary/Slovakia*, 25 September 1997, Individual Opinion of Judge Bedjaoui, para 63.

[102] *cf* YBILC, 1964, vol II, p 8; *cf* YBILC, 1966, p 219.

[103] *cf* YBILC, 1964, vol I, p 30.

[104] Kennedy, 1992, p 43.

[105] See *ibid*, pp 43–4.

[106] *Cf* Zoller, 1977, p 95.

[107] Kennedy, 1992, p 44, who uses the term 'rhetorical management'.

security.[108] Judge Bedjaoui in the *Case concerning the Gabcikovo–Nagymaros Project,* in contrast to Müller, emphasized that *pacta sunt servanda* has the one and only function of guaranteeing legal security and the stability of treaty relations.[109] In WTO law, the *India–Patents* and *EC–LAN* AB reports have, without expressly mentioning Article 26 VCLT, concurred with the security enhancing function of *pacta sunt servanda.*[110] In *US–Offset Act ('Byrd Amendment'),* the AB however seems to have reversed its strict textualist interpretation of the function of *pacta sunt servanda* and expressly referred to Article 26 VCLT.

The divide between these two perspectives of *pacta sunt servanda* materialises on the issue of treaty violation. While the textualists (ICJ) maintain that acting contrary to good faith is equivalent to a rule-violation, the good faith school (Müller, Kennedy, Zoller) believes that a treaty violation does not in all cases amount to a violation of *pacta sunt servanda.* A party may act contrary to good faith despite a rule-consistent behaviour:

> Un manquement à la bonne foi dans l'exécution du traité n'est pas l'équivalent d'une violation de l'engagement international lui-même. Un Etat peut parfaitement remplir ses obligations découlant d'un traité, mais violer le principe de bonne foi.[111]

This division has led the WTO Panels to clash with the textualist AB over the availability of NVNI complaints. Cottier and Schefer concur that a violation of *pacta sunt servanda* may lay the grounds for both a claim of violation and a NVNI complaint. The only difference between a violation and non-violation type complaint for breach of *pacta sunt servanda* would be that in the case of a violation, Article 22 DSU would require that the inconsistent measure be removed, while in a non-violation type complaint, the breaching party would have to compensate the other party adequately. Under GATT XXIII, however, adequate compensation could be demanded under both violation and NVNI complaints.

This shift in concept leads Cottier and Schefer to observe that as grounds for complaint, *pacta sunt servanda* has moved towards the 'European more absolute, perception of *pacta sunt servanda*'. But given the remedies for NVNI complaints contained in Article 26 of the DSU, *pacta sunt servanda* may also 'continue to follow Anglo-American traditions'.[112]

DUTY TO NEGOTIATE IN GOOD FAITH

The duty to negotiate in good faith is a corollary of the customary rule of international law of *pacta sunt servanda*, and this section will examine it as to its

108 *Cf* Müller, 1971, 1995, p 95.

109 See *Case Concerning the Gabcikovo–Nagymaros Project (Hungary/Slovakia)*, 25 September 1997, Individual Opinion of Judge Bedjaoui, para 63.

110 See *India–Patents*, AB Report, para 47; *EC–LAN*, AB Report, para 82.

111 Zoller, 1977, p 81.

112 Cottier and Schefer, 1997, p 172.

direct application and thus immediate impact upon the WTO rights and obligations. It is part of the pre-contractual good faith obligations. As it applies in WTO law, the duty to negotiate in good faith should not be confused with pre-contractual good faith obligations. The duty to negotiate in good faith appears in WTO jurisprudence in the context of the Chapeau of Article XX GATT, but there is no duty for WTO Members to negotiate new or to amend in good faith existing rights and obligations, as well as to offer new concessions in the framework of a WTO Ministerial Conference.

Foundation in International Law

In public international law, the duty to negotiate in good faith forms part of customary law and is considered binding upon all nations, regardless of their expressions of will and consent:

> Article 18 Vienna Convention on the Law of Treaties
>
> General public international under Article 18 VCLT codifies the obligation of a State not to frustrate the object of a treaty prior to its entry into force. Although it does not actually mention good faith, Article 18 VCLT nevertheless 'specifically requires the maintenance of a certain standard of good faith between negotiating States even before the conclusion and entry into force of the treaty'.[113]

Most international law doctrine and jurisprudence deal with the particular aspect of good faith negotiations between the signing and the entry into force of a treaty.[114] Most prominently, cases brought under the US–British Jay Treaty of 1794 and the later Treaty of Ghent of 1814, between the same parties, as well as arbitrage and a few PCIJ cases, extract the elements of a presumption that states in negotiating treaties among each other should be obliged to respect:[115]

> [P]roposed nothing which is illusory or merely nominal.[116]
>
> [H]ave intended anything which would under the circumstances, have been unreasonable, absurd or contradictory, or which leads to impossible consequences.[117]
>
> [I]n case of doubt, words are to be interpreted against the party which has proposed them, and according to the meaning that the other party would reasonably and naturally have understood.[118]

[113] YBILC, 1966 vol II, p 60.

[114] *Cf* Zoller, 1977, pp 68–78; Kolb, 2000, pp 204–5, 213–17, 220–30.

[115] See Cheng, 1987, pp 106–11; see also The Avalon Project at Yale Law School, British–American Diplomacy 1782–1863, available at http://www.yale.edu/lawweb/avalon/diplomacy/britian/brtreaty.htm.

[116] Cheng, 1987, p 106, with references to the Jay Treaty cases ('illusory') and the Treaty of Ghent cases ('nominal').

[117] *Ibid*, with further references.

[118] *Ibid*, p 108, with further references.

In general public international law, the duty to negotiate in good faith goes beyond the prohibition of negotiating in bad faith.[119] The constitutive elements are the absence of fraud and the reasonable attitude of the parties in the light of the object and purpose of a treaty ('Pflicht, das Vertragsziel nicht zu vereiteln').[120] Fraud in negotiation is to lead the other party into erroneous belief, to have the intention of harming the other party to cheat on the other party, as well as corrupting a government representative.[121] The negative criteria are all subjective criteria that have not (yet) been well received in public international law.[122]

Corrolary of Pacta Sunt Servanda *and Other Applications*

In public international law, the principle to negotiate in good faith was introduced in the *North Sea Continental Shelf* (1969) case.[123] The contentious issue was, whether the principle to negotiate in good faith was an extra-legal criteria emerging from the general principle of good faith in international law, or whether it existed within a positive legal rule (*infra legem*) and was held mandatory by that legal rule. Judge Morelli in his dissenting opinion held that it was an 'extra-legal' criteria, emerging from the general principle of law of good faith, which the 'legal rule makes it obligatory to apply, but which remain outside the legal rule'.[124] The ICJ Advisory Opinion *Legality of the Threat or Use of Nuclear Weapons* (1996) further concretised the duty to negotiate in good faith under Article VI of the Non-Proliferation Treaty. The ICJ held found that the obligation to negotiate in good faith contains the dual requirement of conduct and result:

> The legal import of that obligation goes beyond that of a mere obligation of conduct; the obligation involved here is an obligation to achieve a precise result that appears to impose a stricter duty than the AB's statement in *US–Shrimp (Article 21.5)*, nuclear disarmament in all its aspects by adopting a particular course of conduct, namely, the pursuit of negotiations on the matter in good faith.

This twofold obligation to pursue and to conclude negotiations formally concerns the 182 state parties to the Treaty on the Non-proliferation of Nuclear Weapons, or, in other words, the vast majority of the international community. The WTO AB, at least in a statement from *US–Shrimp (Article 21.5)*, has adopted a less strict good faith in negotiations requirement, which it finds applies only to the conduct, but does not require a specific result.

There are also limits to the duty to negotiate in good faith. On this point, general international legal doctrine and AB jurisprudence agree that the duty to

[119] See Müller, 1971, pp 156–64; see also Zoller, 1977, p 49; *cf* Cheng, 1987, pp 106–9.
[120] See Müller, pp 156–64.
[121] See Zoller, 1977, pp 50–1.
[122] *Ibid*, p 51.
[123] See North Sea Continental Shelf, Judgment, ICJ Rep 1969, p 47.
[124] *Ibid*, Dissenting Opinion of Judge Morelli, p 213.

negotiate in good faith is not a duty to *conclude* the treaty.[125] Compare Zoller's statement in 1977 that '[l]a simple obligation de négocier n'emporte jamais l'obligation de conclure l'accord et, d'une manière générale, "l'engagement de négocier n'implique pas celui de s'entendre"[126] with the almost identical statement by the AB in 2001: '[r]equiring that a multilateral agreement be *concluded* . . . would not be reasonable' (emphasis added by the author).[127]

As Müller says and Kolb confirms, there are dangers to over regulating the duty to negotiation in good faith, as it could turn out to be a disincentive for concluding treaties, and treaties are, in the final analysis, indispensable for the maintenance of peace.[128]

WTO Case Law

Should the WTO judiciary consider WTO jurisdiction as part of the international legal system, the WTO Member States would be bound by the VCLT rules on the law of treaties. In that sense, the rule of *pacta sunt servanda* may not be qualified as an aggrandizment of WTO Member rights and obligations pursuant to the limitation on the scope of WTO jurisdiction under Article 3.2 of the DSU. For GATT 94, the duty to negotiate in good faith is another expression, or, at minimum, a corollary of the WTO principle of non-discrimination.[129]

As illustrated by the WTO dispute settlement reports below, the WTO Panels and the AB derive the duty to negotiate in good faith not only from the customary rule of *pacta sunt servanda* but, in addition, from the GATT -specific non-discrimination obligation. The content of this GATT-specific non-discrimination obligation prohibits a WTO Member State from negotiating only with some and not with other WTO Members. It has been applied to WTO law in order to assess whether the extraterritorial effect of domestic measure, which had been provisionally justified under an Article XX GATT exception, was justified under that WTO Member's trading partners expectations in a non-discriminatory and non-trade restrictive application of that measure under the Chapeau of Article XX GATT.[130] The AB held, as described in more detail below, that good faith in negotiations functions as a standard under the Chapeau of Article XX GATT for measuring whether the domestic legislation was discriminatory or trade restrictive by WTO/GATT standards. It functions as a presumption that a WTO Member State, before resorting to the extraterritorial, unilateral application of its domestic laws, first has made a good faith effort to

125 Compare *North Sea Continental Shelf Case*, Separate Opinion of Judge Ammoun, p 136 with *North Sea Continental Shelf Case*, Dissenting Opinion of Judge Morelli, p 213.
126 Zoller, 1977, pp 64–5.
127 *US–Shrimp (Art 21.5)*, AB Report, para 123.
128 See Müller, 1971, p 161; see also Kolb, 2000, p 201.
129 See *US–Shrimp*, AB Report, para 172; *US–Shrimp (Art 21.5)*, AB Report, paras 119, 122.
130 *Ibid*; see also Marceau, 1999, p 104.

resolve the non-trade policy issue by means of negotiating a multilateral treaty among the WTO Member States. Furthermore, this good faith effort presumes a WTO Member State's domestic regulation to be WTO-consistent under the terms of non-discrimination and least trade restrictive of the Chapeau of Article XX GATT.

US–Shrimp *Panel Report (1998)*

In *US–Shrimp* (1998), the Panel held[131] and the AB confirmed[132] that the US has the right to uphold protective legislation even if it had extraterritorial effect, as long as it undertakes a *serious good faith effort to negotiate* a multilateral convention to achieve its intended regulatory purpose, *in casu*, the protection of sea turtles, prior to the entry into force of its legislative act.[133] The Panel held that failure to undertake the good faith effort of negotiating multilaterally before unilaterally enacting the domestic regulation amounted to a protectionist abuse of the environmental exception of Article XX(g) GATT 94.

Good faith in negotiations is yet another expression of good faith attributed to the Chapeau of Article XX.[134] It is somewhat more self-standing than the *abus de droit* prohibition expressed by the Chapeau because, in contrast to that, it is more removed from the constitutive elements of the Chapeau.

US–Shrimp (Article 21.5) *Appellate Body Report (2001)*

In *US–Shrimp (Article 21.5)* (the compliance case succeeding the *US–Shrimp* AB decision), the US had (as it had been required to by the *US–Shrimp* AB decision) altered its approach and undertaken to negotiate an international convention on the protection of sea turtles.

In *US–Shrimp (Article 21.5)*, the AB examined whether the *US–Shrimp (Article 21.5)* Panel Report had correctly found that the new US measure complied with Article XX GATT 94:

> no longer constitutes a means of 'arbitrary or unjustifiable discrimination between countries where the same conditions prevail' and is, therefore, within the scope of measures permitted under Article XX of the GATT 94.[135]

Malaysia claimed that serious good faith efforts to *negotiate* an agreement would be insufficient to satisfy the requirements of the Chapeau of Article XX.

[131] See *US–Shrimp*, Panel Report, para 7.56.

[132] *Ibid*, AB Report, para166.

[133] See *US–Shrimp (Art 21.5)*, Panel Report, para 6.1; *US–Shrimp (Art 21.5)* AB Report, para 112ff. The AB Report, paras 167, 171, 172 speaks about serious efforts, but does not relate these to the notion of good faith; *US–Shrimp*, Panel Report, para 7.56 speaks about 'good faith negotiations'.

[134] The other good faith functions expressed in the Chapeau of Art XX GATT 94 are the prohibition against *abus de droit* and the general principle of law of good faith used substantively and interpretatively; see *US–Shrimp*, AB Report, paras 158, 163, 181.

[135] *US–Shrimp (Art 21.5)*, AB Report, paras 111–12.

The *US–Shrimp* AB Report had instead required that an international agreement be *concluded*, because a mere obligation to *negotiate* would result in:

> The absurd situation where any WTO Member would be able to offer to negotiate in good faith on an agreement incorporating its unilaterally defined standards before claiming that its measure is justified under Article XX of the GATT 94 and in the event of failure to conclude an agreement, claim that the measure applying the unilateral standards could not constitute unjustifiable discrimination.[136]

The AB disagreed with Malaysia's reading of the *US–Shrimp* AB Report and Malaysia's finding of error in the *US–Shrimp (Article 21.5)* Panel Report. Because the US had negotiated with some but not all exporting countries affected by its measure before the imposition of the measure, the *US–Shrimp (Article 21.5)* AB Report maintained:

> . . . [T]he United States could conceivably respect this obligation [Chapeau of Article XX GATT 94], and the conclusion of an international agreement might nevertheless not be possible despite the serious, good faith efforts of the United States. Requiring that a multilateral agreement be *concluded* by the United States in order to avoid 'arbitrary or unjustifiable discrimination'. . . would mean that any country party to the negotiations with the United States, whether a WTO Member or not, would have, in effect, a veto over whether the United States could fulfill its WTO obligations. Such a requirement would not be reasonable.[137]

Nonetheless, in result, but for a different reason, the AB agreed with the result of the *US–Shrimp (Article 21.5)* Panel Report and found the US in violation of the obligation to avoid arbitrary or unjustifiable discrimination in its regulatory measures.

The AB cited its *US–Shrimp* AB Report where it had found the US in violation of the obligation to avoid arbitrary or unjustifiable discrimination.

In its submission before the AB, Malaysia had disagreed with the Panel's decision to use the conclusion by the US of the Inter-American Convention as a benchmark for measuring whether the US negotiating efforts amounted to serious good faith efforts. For Malaysia the Inter-American Convention could not be used as a legal standard, but merely served as an example.

The AB upheld:

> the Panel's finding that, in view of the serious, good faith efforts made by the United States to negotiate an international agreement, 'Section 609 is now applied in a manner that no longer constitutes a means of unjustifiable or arbitrary discrimination, as identified by the Appellate Body in its Report',[138] . . . as long as . . . the ongoing serious good faith efforts to reach a multilateral agreement, remain satisfied.[139]

[136] *Ibid*, paras 113, 115.
[137] *Ibid*, para 122.
[138] *Ibid*, para 134.
[139] *Ibid*, para 153(b).

In *US–Shrimp (Article 21.5)* the AB defended the use of the Inter-American Convention as a guide for assessing the serious good faith efforts of the US:

> In our view, in assessing the serious, good faith efforts made by the United States, the Panel did not err in using the Inter-American Convention as an *example*. In our view, also, the Panel was correct in proceeding then to an analysis broadly in line with this principle and, ultimately, was correct as well in concluding that the efforts made by the United States in the Indian Ocean and South-East Asia region constitute serious, good faith efforts comparable to those that led to the conclusion of the Inter-American Convention. We find no fault with this analysis.[140]

In *US–Shrimp (Article 21.5)*, the AB did not propose any new and additional criteria to measure the serious good faith effort to negotiate a bilateral or multilateral agreement before imposing on exporting members a unilateral and non-consensual import prohibition.

Canada criticized the lack of interpretive guidance by the AB as 'difficult for Panels in future disputes to determine' and 'difficult for WTO Members themselves to determine when they have met the criteria'.[141]

However, in one footnote, the AB reversed the Panel's finding on the particular point of *how much* effort is considered serious *depending on which* WTO *Member is imposing the import ban* under Article XX GATT 94:

> We do wish to note, though, that there is one observation by the Panel with which we do not agree. In assessing the good faith efforts made by the United States, the Panel stated that: The United States is a *demandeur* in this field and given its scientific, diplomatic and financial means, it is reasonable to expect rather more than less from that member in terms of serious good faith efforts. Indeed, the capacity of persuasion of the United States is illustrated by the successful negotiation of the Inter-American Convention. (Panel Report, paragraph 5.76) this line of reasoning does not persuade us. As we stated in our previous Report, the Chapeau of Article XX is 'but one expression of the principle of good faith'. (Appellate Body Report, *United States–Shrimp, supra*, footnote 24, paragraph 158) This *good faith* notion applies to *all* WTO *Members equally* (emphasis added).[142]

Korea–Government Procurement *Panel Report (2000)*

The *Korea–Government Procurement* decision will be described *in extenso* below in chapter six, in connection with the PLE. Here we will treat the case only where it is pertinent to the duty to negotiate in good faith.

The Panel related to the duty to negotiate in good faith on the one hand with the PLE as to the competitive bidding opportunities the US was entitled to, as

[140] *US–Shrimp (Art 21.5)*, AB Report, para 133.

[141] Dispute Settlement Update: '*Shrimp–Turtle* & *US–Canada Lumber*' in 5 Bridges, 8 November 2001.

[142] *US–Shrimp* AB Report, fn 97 to para 134.

regards its construction service providers on a Korean airport project, on the other hand.[143] Specifically, the Panel applied the 'general rules of customary international law on good faith and error in treaty negotiations'. Since Korea had not committed yet to actual concessions, the Panel could not base the US non-violation claim upon the GATT principle of frustration of legitimate expectations.[144] With respect to altering the plurilaterally agreed bidding deadlines and procedure, the US had claimed a frustration of its legitimate expectations, when Korea had, to the detriment of the US, introduced inadequate bidding deadlines and other restrictive measures, with the result that the the value of the assurances given under the negotiations and upon which the US had based its expectations had decreased.[145]

However, since the plurilateral negotiations on the GPA were still ongoing, no actual commitments existed yet, and there was no equal level playing field upon which the US could build an NVNI case.

Nevertheless, based upon the measures Korea had introduced, which basically offset the value of the assurances of concessions Korea had given the US when negotiating the accession to the GPA, the Panel found a 'gap' in substantive law which needed to be filled—with 'principles of international [substantive] law'.[146] 'In this case, it was the negotiations which allegedly gave rise to the reasonable expectations rather than any concessions'.[147]

To fill the gap in WTO law, the Panel found 'the duty to negotiate in good faith to be applicable WTO law'.[148] It consequently applied the customary rule of *pacta sunt servanda*, which, in a 'further development', it considerd to include the notion of NVNI, which, in turn, 'is an extension of the good faith requirement'.[149] In so doing, the Panel declared that 'we are of the view that the customary rules of international law apply to the WTO treaties and to the process of treaty formation under the WTO'.[150] Specifically, the Panel sees 'no conflict or inconsistency' with the WTO Agreements, if it were to 'review the claim of nullification or impairment raised by the United States within the framework of principles of international law which are generally applicable not only to performance of treaties but also to treaty negotiation'.[151]

After affirming that the customary rule of *pacta sunt servanda* was applicable to the WTO and explaining how it related to PLE,[152] the Panel then had to apply the duty to negotiate in good faith to the facts of the case. It found that Korea had violated a 'general rule of customary international law'[153] by not 'negotiating on

143 See *Korea–Government Procurement*, Panel Report, para 7.117.
144 *Ibid*, para 7.101.
145 *Ibid*, paras 7.87 and 7.118.
146 *Ibid*, para 7.101.
147 *Ibid*, para 7.120.
148 *Ibid*, para 7.95.
149 *Ibid*, paras 7.93 and 7.95.
150 *Ibid*, para 7.95
151 *Ibid*, paras 7.96, 7.101.
152 *Ibid*, para 7.101.
153 *Ibid*.

a full and forthcoming basis',[154] specifically by not providing 'full, timely and complete',[155] and 'frank' and 'forthright answers' and the negotiations having been deficient in 'transparence and openness':

> It was objectively clear what the US question was about. And Korea, knowing that, then had an obligation to make a full and frank response. The integrity of the negotiating system requires no less'.[156] The Panel then went on to say that the WTO Member States have 'a right to expect full and forthright answers to their questions submitted during negotiations, particularly with respect to schedules of affirmative commitments such as those appended to the GPA.[157]

The Panel did lay open which sources and materials it had used for its declaration that the rule of *pacta sunt servanda* includes a duty to negotiate in good faith. But it may have been influenced by the US submission, which most likely had referred to elements of the duty to negotiate in good faith in the cases under the US–British Jay and Ghent Treaties of 1794 and 1814.

The Panel also clarified that in case of doubt the situation had to be interpreted against the offeror, ie against Korea:

> [T]he duty to demonstrate good faith and transparency in GPA negotiations is particularly strong for the 'offering' party, this does not relieve the other negotiating partners from their duty of diligence to verify these offers as best as they can.[158]

Nevertheless, in result the US was found responsible for not keeping sufficiently informed, and for not having objected to Korea's introduction of measures. The US should have realised when Korea introduced the measures that these would have an impact on US bidding opportunities or even offset US competitive bidding opportunities. Thus, the case was not decided over the issue of good faith. Good faith in negotiations therefore remained *obiter dictum*, and no appeal has yet referred to, or overturned, the Panel's reasoning in *Korea–Government Procurement*.

Scholarly Discussion of the Decisions

The WTO's future trading rules will not be drafted in an equitable, fair and balanced manner unless the good faith obligation to negotiate in 'transparency and openness' is expanded beyond the plurilateral GPA.[159] By bringing together conflicting interests at the drafting stage, the duty to negotiate in good faith will increase, in analogy to Brown Weiss, the 'legitimacy' of the WTO's Ministerial trade negotiating rounds in the eyes of 'global civil society' and the

[154] See *Korea–Government Procurement*, Panel Report, para 7.100.
[155] *Ibid*, para 7.110.
[156] *Ibid*.
[157] See *ibid*, para 7.119; see also paras 7.120–7.122.
[158] *Ibid*, para 7.125; see also para 7.113.
[159] *Ibid*, para 7.121.

'disenchanted' of trade liberalization, as it will preempt the second, more costly, judicial balancing that characterizes the process of dispute resolution.[160]

In the same year the *Korea–Government Panel* was issued, Cottier and Schefer mentioned that not only should 'good faith permeate the Organization's legal operations' but also it should enter its '*diplomatic*' ones.[161] Among the other good faith obligations that they suggest the WTO should respect, there is the duty to negotiate in good faith, which they understand even more broadly than the Panel in the *Korea–Government Procurement* decision:

> [G]ood faith must characterise the drafting of the accession protocol; good faith must determine the behaviour of members in meetings of the Ministerial Conference and the General Council meetings; good faith must characterise the multilateral and plurilateral negotiations for new obligations.[162]

WTO-specific Doctrine of the Duty to Negotiate in Good Faith

The WTO principle of good faith in negotiations may be a GATT-specific obligation in its own right. The duty to negotiate in good faith relates to the requirement that the exercise of Article XX exceptions shall be non-discriminatory. The GATT-specific obligation to negotiate in good faith means that if a serious negotiation of multilateral solution can be shown to precede the imposition of unilateral and extraterritorial trade restrictions, the measure is likely non-discriminatory under the Chapeau of Article XX GATT 94 standards.

The obligation to conduct good faith negotiations is one element of the GATT 94 non-discrimination principle. It is argued that non-discrimination determines the modalities of how a negotiation must be lead, in order for the negotiation to respect good faith and legitimate expectations. More specifically, the AB considers the duty to negotiate in good faith to be one element of the non-discrimination principle, and inherently expressed within the meaning of the Chapeau of Article XX, as the *US–Shrimp* AB Report details in the following paragraph:[163]

> The Panel first recalls that the Appellate Body considered "the *failure of the United States to engage the appellees*", as well as other members exporting shrimp to the United States, in serious across-the-board negotiations . . . bears heavily in any appraisal of justifiable or unjustifiable discrimination within the meaning of the Chapeau of Article XX (emphasis in the original).[164]

[160] Brown Weiss, 2000, p 370.
[161] Cottier and Schefer, 2000, p 57.
[162] *Ibid.*
[163] See *US–Shrimp*, AB Report, para 172; *US–Shrimp (Art 21.5)*, AB Report, paras 119, 122.
[164] *US–Shrimp (Art 21.5)*, Panel Report, para 5.63.

According to the AB, the conduct good faith prohibits under the non-discrimination principle of the Chapeau of Article XX of GATT 94, is to 'negotiate seriously with some but not with others'.[165]

> In *United States–Shrimp*, we stated that the measure . . . there resulted in 'unjustifiable discrimination', in part because, as applied, the United States treated WTO Members differently.[166]

Under the Chapeau of Article XX GATT 94, the respondent must prove four elements in order to refute the allegation that it has engaged in unjustified discrimination. The good faith efforts to reach international agreements must be firstly, '*comparable from one forum of negotiation to the other*', in the sense that [secondly,] *comparable efforts* are made, [thirdly,] *comparable resources* are invested and [fourthly,] *comparable energies* are devoted to securing an international agreement. 'The negotiations need not be identical'.[167]

However, even if all four elements are fulfilled, there is no guarantee that the effort to negotiate before adopting a measure is non-discriminatory:

> So long as such comparable efforts are made, *it is more likely* that 'arbitrary or unjustifiable discrimination' will be avoided between countries where an importing member concludes an agreement with one group of countries, but fails to do so with another group of countries (emphasis added).[168]

The duty to negotiate in good faith could provide all WTO Members excluded from 'green rooms' (essentially 'closed-door' deliberations on new treaty text) with the tool to enforce their own right of participation.[169] Minimally, the duty to negotiate in good faith will empower politically and economically less powerful WTO Members with the pressure to step up the demand for increased transparency in the WTO's decision-making process.[170] The duty to negotiate in good faith will foster the 'acceptance of the WTO' and 'trust in, the international trading system'.[171]

WTO practice limits national sovereignty through the PLE in favour of free trade, as can be seen in the *Korea–Government Procurement* Panel decision, which was never appealed. The duty to negotiate in good faith protects legitimate expectations as to the negotiation of concessions, which are invocable in a NVNI complaint: '[F]ull and forthright answers to their questions submitted during negotiations, particularly with respect to Schedules of affirmative commitments such as those appended to the GPA'.[172] '[A]n obligation to make

[165] *Ibid*, AB Report, para 172; see also Marceau, 1999, p 104.
[166] *Ibid (Art 21.5)*, AB Report, para 119.
[167] *Ibid*, para 122.
[168] *Ibid*.
[169] *cf* Esty, 2002, pp 12–14.
[170] *Ibid*.
[171] Cottier and Schefer, 2000, p 57.
[172] *Korea–Government Procurement*, Panel Report, para 7.119.

a full and frank response'.[173] '[A] particular duty of transparency and openness on the "offering" party in negotiations on concessions under the GPA'.[174]

A very concrete result of the good faith duty to negotiate fairly pursuant to the *Korea–Government Procurement* Panel report was that Ministers included paragraph 26 on transparency in government procurement to the Doha Ministerial Declaration and agreed at Doha to establish the 'Working Group on Transparency in Government Procurement', which issues yearly reports to the General Council.[175]

Paragraph 26 does not mention any good faith duties for governments offering bidding opportunities, or for WTO Members as regards the negotiation of new multilateral agreements on transparence in government procurement; and, *a fortiori,* it does not concretise the elements of good faith duties that the *Korea–Government Procurement* Panel had started doing. Furthermore, the binding nature of such Ministerial Decisions remains unclear. Paragraph 26 of the Doha Declaration nevertheless may be seen as the concrete effect of a Panel decision:

> Recognizing the case for a multilateral agreement on transparency in government procurement and the need for enhanced technical assistance and capacity building in this area, we agree that negotiations will take place after the Fifth Session of the Ministerial Conference on the basis of a decision to be taken, by explicit consensus, at that Session on modalities of negotiations. These negotiations will build on the progress made in the Working Group on Transparency in Government Procurement by that time and take into account participants' development priorities, especially those of least-developed country participants. Negotiations shall be limited to the transparency aspects and therefore will not restrict the scope for countries to give preferences to domestic supplies and suppliers. We commit ourselves to ensuring adequate technical assistance and support for capacity building both during the negotiations and after their conclusion.[176]

For Marceau, the failure to conduct multilateral negotiations did not amount to a violation of the WTO Agreement per se, but the 'refusal to exhaust the MEA's mechanisms—hence to consult fully and properly with the most appropriate and expert forum' could be an element used by a Panel or the AB when assessing the good faith of a party to the WTO dispute settlement process.[177]

For Howse, the AB ruling in *US–Shrimp* did not lead to a *sui generis* duty to negotiate, only to a duty not to discriminate in one's negotiating behaviour. What the AB said was that it held that one reason that the US scheme was being

[173] *Ibid*, para 7.110.

[174] *Ibid*, para 7.121.

[175] See, eg Report (2003) of the Working Group on Transparency in Government Procurement to the General Council, 15 July 2003, WTO Document WT/WGTGP/7.

[176] See Doha Ministerial Declaration of 14 November 2001, 20 November 2001, WTO Document WT/MIN(01)/DEC/1.

[177] Marceau, 2001, pp 1125–6.

applied with unjustified discrimination was that the US had engaged in serious negotiations with one group of countries and not others, ie not the complainants.[178]

In *US–Shrimp*, the statutory American shrimp processing method was not per se illegal, but rather could have the effect of impairing the object and purpose of Article XX(g) GATT if the shrimp ban was upheld. Thus, the good faith obligation to negotiate was derived from law (Article XX(g) GATT).

In contrast, the *US–Line Pipe from Korea* decision derived the duty to negotiate in good faith directly from *pacta sunt servanda* codified in Article 26 VCLT.[179] In this case, the good faith negotiations constituted the obligation between the exporting and importing members to reach an adequate understanding on the level of compensation countering the adverse effects of the safeguard measure pertaining to their trade.

IMPLEMENTING WTO OBLIGATIONS IN GOOD FAITH

Another corollary of the customary rule of *pacta sunt servanda* is the duty to implement international treaty obligations in good faith. In addition to recognizing *pacta sunt servanda* and its corollary to negotiate in good faith (see above), the AB in 2002 recognised that the obligations of Members under the WTO Agreements have to be implemented in good faith.

As the *US–Section 211 ('Havana Club')* AB Report shows, the duty to implement WTO obligations in good faith is, as of today, standard appellate practice. The Panel found it to be implicitly 'enshrined' in Article 7 TRIPS.[180] Two years before the AB's express recognition of this self-standing obligation, Cottier and Schefer had formulated the postulate that 'good faith must accompany the implementation and adherence to the obligations of the WTO in a member's domestic legal system'. According to the authors, a duty to implement the WTO obligations in good faith guarantees the 'viability of . . . the international trading system', but must be accompanied by the recognition of other 'important' applications of good faith, notably in the negotiations and pre-accession phases.[181]

US–Section 211 ('Havana Club') Appellate Body Report (2002)

In the first case to address the national treatment (NT) obligation as it relates to the TRIPS Agreement, the EC argued that US legislation (Section 211(a)(2) and (b)) and administrative practice by the Office of Foreign Assets Control (OFAC)

[178] See email exchange with Professor Howse, 12 February 2003.
[179] See *US–Line Pipe Safeguards*, AB Report, para 110.
[180] *US–Section 211 ('Havanna Club')*, Panel Report, para 8.57
[181] Cottier and Schefer, 2000, p 57.

had violated both NT obligations, the one under the TRIPS Agreement, Article 3(1) and the other under the Paris Convention of 1967, Article 2(1).[182]

The EC claimed that US Section 211(a)(2) applied and thus imposed restrictions on only Cuban and other foreign successors-in-interest to the original owners.[183] The Panel argued that the less favourable treatment of non-US nationals under Section 211(a)(2), who, if successor-in-interest to a 'designated national', could not have their rights protected by US courts, was offset by OFAC's practice under Section 515.201 of the Cuban Assets Control Regulation. The OFAC's practice under the Cuban Assets Control Regulation was not to issue specific licenses to United States nationals to become successors-in-interest to 'designated nationals'.[184] However, the EC argued on appeal that the administrative practice of the OFAC did not cure the less favourable treatment accorded to *foreign* successors in interest under Section 211(a)(2).[185]

The Panel relied on previous Panel reports to argue that where discretionary authority is vested in the executive branch of a WTO Member, it cannot be assumed that the member will use this authority in violation of its international obligations.[186]

For non-US nationals there was an extra hurdle: US nationals face only *one* proceeding, while non-US nationals face *two*. Consequently, the EC claimed on appeal that Section 211(a)(2), as it relates to successors-in-interest, violates the NT obligation in the TRIPS Agreement and the Paris Convention (1967).[189] Thus, the AB considered first the Panel's reasoning with respect to the plain reading of Section 211(a)(2), which the Panel found rightly to afford less favourable treatment to non-US nationals.[190] Also, the AB on the basis of the good faith principle in implementing WTO obligations, agreed with the Panel's finding that the OFAC's administrative practice should not be assumed to be an exercise of executive authority inconsistent with WTO obligations. The AB says:

> [W]here discretionary authority is vested in the executive branch of a WTO Member, it cannot be assumed that the WTO Member will fail to implement its obligations under the *WTO Agreement* in good faith.[191]

However, the AB found that assuming that the OFAC had not acted inconsistently with the WTO is not enough to relieve the US of a conclusion that

182 See *US–Section 211 ('Havana Club')*, AB Report, para 233.
183 *Ibid*, para 244.
184 *Ibid*, paras 248 and 249.
185 *Ibid*, para 250.
186 *Ibid*, paras 250–51.
187 *Ibid*, para 251.
188 *Ibid*, para 254.
189 *Ibid*, paras 255–6.
190 *Ibid*, para 258.
191 *Ibid*, para 259.

Section 211(a)(2) does not accord less favourable treatment to non-US nationals who are successors-in-interest to a 'designated national'.[192]

The AB found it necessary to examine the argument made by the EC about the 'extra-hurdle' for non US-nationals.[193] It found that Section 211(a)(2) would only then apply non-discriminatorily to US and non-US license applications, if 'in every individual situation where a non-United States successor-in-interest seeks to assert its rights', US courts would be required 'not to recognise, enforce or otherwise validate any assertion of rights'.[194] For the AB, even the *possibility* that non-US successors-in-interest face two hurdles is *inherently less favourable* than the undisputed fact that US successors-in-interest face only one.[195]

Thus, the AB held Section 211(a)(2) inconsistent (despite its finding that an executive authority with discretionary powers is assumed to implement WTO obligations in good faith) with Articles 2(1) of the Paris Convention of 1967 and Article 3(1) of the TRIPS Agreement[196] and reversed the Panel's finding.[197]

The WTO adopts the general public international approach to good faith in implementing obligations because it 'presumes' that were an executive authority acts on behalf of a State, it does so consistently with that State's international obligations. Similarly to *abus de droit* in the Chapeau of Article XX, the AB links the principle of good faith in implementation to two non-discrimination provisions, Article 3(1) TRIPS and 2(1) of the Paris Convention of 1967.[198] However, in the final analysis the AB did not find the US in violation of the non-discrimination provisions for failure of US *administrative* organs to remove the extra-hurdle in the procedure for non-US nationals (good faith). Instead, the AB bases the violation of good faith upon the *hypothetical* discriminatory treatment of non US-nationals before US *courts*.[199]

In the final analysis, it is to be observed that the *US–Section 211 ('Havana Club')* case involved a much less self-standing duty to implement TRIPS in good faith than the reference in the AB Report. While the Panel had twice linked good faith in implementation to Article 7 TRIPS, the AB did not even mention Article 7 TRIPS but nevertheless held the US responsible under a good faith obligation: 'We consider this expression [Article 7 of the TRIPS Agreement] to be a form of the good faith principle'. 'Members must therefore implement the provisions of the TRIPS Agreement in a manner consistent with the good faith principle enshrined in Article 7 of the TRIPS Agreement'.[200] '[I]t cannot be assumed that

[192] See *US–Section 211 ('Havana Club')* AB Report, paras 260–9.
[193] *Ibid*, para 260.
[194] *Ibid*, para 264; see also para 267.
[195] See *ibid*, para 265.
[196] *Ibid*, para 268.
[197] *Ibid*, para 269.
[198] *Ibid*, para 259.
[199] *Ibid*, paras 264, 267, 269.
[200] *Ibid*, para 8.57.

the WTO Member will fail to implement its obligations under the *WTO Agreement* in good faith (emphasis in the original)'.[201]

Not only does the AB detach the duty to implement in good faith from Article 7 TRIPS specifically, it even goes so far as to declare (and emphasize) that the requirement applies to the WTO Agreement generally. In sum, the AB has introduced a self-standing obligation to implement all WTO Agreements in good faith, based upon a Panel decision that had applied such a duty to the TRIPS Agreement only.

Overview of International Legal Theory and Practice

In general public international law, there is no *explicit* codification of the principle that good faith may require a Party to conform its internal laws to its international treaty obligations. The Swiss delegate to the ILC Convention had initiated the move to abort an express codification of this principle in the VCLT.[202] Similar to good faith in treaty *negotiations*, good faith in treaty *implementation* is derived from the duty to *perform* treaties in good faith under Article 26 VCLT.[203] Good faith in treaty implementation is an emanation of *pacta*, rather than of good faith, because it does not have to do with justice; rather it holds the parties to the rules they have agreed to be bound by.[204] The ICJ has to date not recognised an obligation for parties to modify their internal laws in order to comply with their external obligations.[205]

Doctrine says that states may be responsible for 'remov[ing] all obstacles in their internal law in order that a treaty can be carried out and respected by all these organs in good faith'.[206] This obligation not only requires necessary legislative modifications, but also 'putting to disposal, if necessary, sufficient financial funds'.[207] The mirror-image rule to this principle is Article 27 VCLT in combination with Article 46, which says that only a fundamentally important and manifest, ie 'objectively evident' (by any other State acting normally and in good faith) violation of internal law by the international obligation may remove the state from its obligation to implement a treaty in good faith.[208]

201 *Ibid*, para 259.
202 See Zoller, 1977, p 94, referring to the Swiss delegate Bindschedler.
203 See Degan, 1997, p 407; *cf* Zoller, 1977, p 94.
204 See Zoller, 1977, p 94.
205 *Ibid*.
206 Degan, 1997, p 407.
207 *Ibid*.
208 *Ibid*, p 406; see also Müller, 1971, pp 200, 204.

Conclusions

As long as certain WTO Member States and doctrine do not recognise the substantive legal quality of a self-standing general principle of law of good faith, the AB will refuse to apply it beyond interpreting already existing WTO provisions, or beyond WTO Members consensus, *pacta sunt servanda*.[209] Consequently, most references to good faith, as opposed to *pacta sunt servanda*, have stopped short of positively applying the actual general principle or customary rule. Other times, the principle or rule has simply figured as *obiter dicta*, or, finally, denied a substantive effect for lack of evidence. Therefore, the exceptions, where a self-standing, general principle of law of good faith was actually applied as substantive WTO law, are all the more noteworthy: in *US–Cotton Yarn*, the AB raised the question about whether 'an importing member is under the *obligation*, flowing from the pervasive general principle of good faith that underlies all treaties'.[210] In *US–Offset Act ('Byrd Amendment')*, the AB found that WTO Members must respect *pacta sunt servanda*, thereby confirming the *Korea–Government Procurement* Panel decision, which had declared this customary international rule applicable WTO law.[211] Such exceptional recognitions of substantive good faith are of limited practical and precedential value for the following two reasons:

— The incorporation of the general principle of law of good faith has had the status of an *obiter dictum* only.
— The principle of good faith was rejected as unfounded for lack of evidence.[212]

ABUS DE DROIT DOCTRINE

Next to *pacta sunt servanda*, the *abus de droit* doctrine is another corrolary of the good faith principle used by both the Panels and the AB in the adjudication of WTO cases. Pursuant to the distinction which has to be made between the recognition by a legal system of a situation of *abus de droit* and the prohibition of such an abuse of rights, described above, the status of *abus de droit* theory in WTO law and practice shall be analyzed through this lens. The goal is to determine whether the Panels and/or the AB go beyond finding, in the context of WTO adjudication, a legal situation of *abus de droit* and outrightly formulate a prohibition of *abus de droit*.

[209] *Cf US–Offset Act ('Byrd Amendment')*, AB Report, paras 296, 297; see McRae, 2003, p 713.

[210] *US–Cotton Yarn*, AB Report, para 81, emphasis in the original.

[211] See *US–Offset Act ('Byrd Amendment')*, AB Report, paras 296, 297; see *Korea–Government Procurement*, Panel Report, paras 7.93ff.

[212] See *US–Cotton Yarn*, AB Report, para 81 (obiter dictum); *US–Byrd Amendment*, AB Report, para 299 (lack of evidence); *Korea–Government Procurement*, Panel Report, para 7.119 (lack of evidence).

Specific Situations of *Abus de Droit* in WTO Practice

WTO practice has sometimes made use of the notion of *abus de droit* as 'an application of [the] general principle [of law of good faith]'.[213]

The first instance of an *abus de droit* adjudication in WTO practice is the *Australia–Subsidy* decision under GATT 47.[214] Yet, the doctrine of *abus de droit* was only explicitly recognised in the *US–Shrimp* case. While in the *Australia–Subsidy* decision, *abus de droit* was related to the PLE of members as to conditions of competition in the context of a NVNI complaint,[215] *US–Shrimp* linked the concept to a violation of substantive WTO law, ie the Chapeau of Article XX GATT 94.[216]

In *Australia–Subsidy* it was the GATT-consistent lifting of a subsidy, which upset the competitive relationship between Chile and Australia, that triggered *abus de droit*. In 2001, Cameron and Gray, identified this GATT 47 case as the first case implicitly recognizing a doctrine of *abus de droit*.[217] However, some WTO scholars, namely Hilf and Canal-Forgues in 2001 and Lennard in 2002, have not followed the AB's characterisation of the US's import embargo on turtle-unfriendly shrimp as an *abus* of Article XX(g). Hilf (while agreeing that the Chapeau of Article XX expresses a balancing function of good faith) maintains that the Chapeau of Article XX enforces the principle of 'multilateralism' and 'cooperation' over and above unilateral trade sanctions; in other words, the Chapeau is not an expression of *abus de droit*.[218]

In *US–Shrimp,* US turtle protection laws, which were provisionally justified under Article XX(g), were applied in a discriminatory and arbitrary manner. Cottier and Schefer have confirmed that the AB in its 'landmark' *US–Shrimp* decision gave the 'first explicit recognition of abuse of rights in WTO law'.[219] The authors however demand more of the AB insofar as they would like it to specify whether the *abus de droit* doctrine truly 'expound[s] the essence and specific function of this elusive provision'.[220]

For Cheng and Schwarzenberger, *abus de droit* has a balancing function in general public international law.[221] Cheng described the delimiting function of *abus de droit* with words that were later reflected in the AB's definition of *abus de droit*: 'The exact line dividing the right from the obligation, or, in other words,

213 *US–Shrimp*, AB Report, para 158; similarly, *US–Cotton Yarn*, AB Report, para 81 and fn 53; see *US–Section 211 ('Havana Club')*, Panel Report, para 8.57.

214 See Cottier and Schefer, 1997, p 178; see also Cameron and Gray, 2001, pp 294–5.

215 See *Australia–Subsidy*, para 12.

216 See *US–Shrimp*, AB Report, para 158.

217 See Cameron and Gray, 2001, pp 294–5, with references to *US–Shrimp*. The authors maintain—contrary to Cottier and Schefer, who 'directly apply' *abus de droit*—that it 'underlies' Art XX GATT.

218 Hilf, 2001, pp 119, 128ff.

219 Cottier and Schefer, 2000, p 65.

220 *Ibid*.

221 See Cheng, 1987, p 132; Schwarzenberger, 1955, p 324.

the line delimiting the rights of both parties is traced at a point where there is a reasonable balance between the conflicting interests involved'.[222]

The AB together with WTO scholars, namely Hilf, Cameron and Gray, treat *abus de droit* as a means to balance the rights of members to invoke an exception to trade liberalization on the one hand with their WTO duties to keep markets open and non-discriminating on the other hand.[223] Canal-Forgues views the AB's application of the Chapeau of Article XX to the US shrimp embargo as giving *effet utile* to Article XX(g). He does not mention *abus de droit*.[224] Lennard finds that to compare Article XX Chapeau to *abus de droit* doctrine leads us down an 'uncertain path', 'full of highly subjective concepts', which could 'lead to a greatly expanded role for the Panels and the AB (perhaps in effect developing a general "equitable" jurisdiction . . .)'.[225]

Among the scholars opposed to *abus de droit* doctrine making its entrance into the WTO via Article XX, Lennard finds that since *abus de droit* compares with equity law jurisdiction, equity is part of *abus de droit*. The study here finds that equity may be inherent in the prohibition of *abus de droit*, but not necessarily vice versa.[226]

The *Abus de Droit* Prohibition as a Good Faith Obligation of the WTO

The AB has gone further than to recognize the existence of an *abus de droit* doctrine. It has prohibited under WTO law, the legal situation of *abus de droit*.[227] The AB considers *abus de droit* as an obligation, and similarly to Cheng's and Zoller's perspective, good faith obligations and prohibitions of abuse of rights as the two sides of the same coin. When a conduct is unreasonable, for the AB, it is synonymous with a violation of good faith obligations.[228] Pursuant to this WTO jurisprudence, with its specific emphasis on market access and non-discrimination, the prohibition of *abus de droit qua* loyalty and honesty means the absence of protectionism and discrimination.

With the assumption of an obligation, the scope of a right becomes precisely delimited, and the line between lawfulness and abuse is flexible to future adjustments.[229] This is exactly the function of the Chapeau of Article XX: the exercise of a specific exemption is restricted if it conflicts with one of the three obligations

[222] See Cheng, 1987, p 132; Schwarzenberger, 1955, p 324.
[223] See Hilf, 2001, pp 128ff; see Cameron and Gray, 2001, p 295.
[224] *Cf* Canal-Forgues, 2001, p 22.
[225] Lennard, 2002, pp 67–8.
[226] *Cf* Cottier and Schefer, 2001, p 64, who consider *abus de droit* as an 'equitable doctrine' along with the principles of estoppel and acquiescence; similarly, Lennard, 2002, p 70.
[227] *Cf* Kiss, 1992, p 5.
[228] See Cheng, 1987, p 132; see also Zoller, 1977, p 353; against Schwarzenberger, 1955, p 318.
[229] Cheng, 1987, pp 123–4.

a member has assumed under the Chapeau of Article XX (non-discrimination, no disguised and no arbitrary restriction on trade).

The prohibition of an *abus de droit* extends even to the conduct of WTO negotiations:

> Whether in dispute settlement or in negotiations, good faith needs to be set out as a principle to which all members must adhere: Members' abuses of their rights must be prevented and the protection of members' legitimate expectations must be afforded if the WTO system is to maintain its authority as an institution of justice as well as an acceptable source for the promulgation of binding rules.[230]

In the WTO, *abus de droit* can be the object of both a violation and a NVNI claim.[231]

The Abus de Droit Prohibition as a Corrolary of Good Faith Obligations

The prohibition of *abus de droit* imposes *substantive* limits upon the domestic measures provisionally justified under a specific exemption. The measure and its application must be *flexible* as to aims. For example, an environmental objective must be flexible as to the manner in which trade is restricted, in order to allow affected WTO Members to adopt *comparable* as opposed to identical solutions.[232] The law qualifying for an Article XX exception must '*not be rigid, unbending*' and may not offer only a '*single*' solution for attaining the environmental (or other) policy objective.[233]

Moreover, the prohibition against *abus de droit* imposes not only substantive criteria on the measure qualifying for an exception but also prescribes how it should be applied, that is prohibits a measure 'otherwise fair and just on its face, is actually applied in an arbitrary or unjustifiable manner'.[234]

The AB found that the prohibition of *abus de droit* imposes on the US certification process for shrimp exporting licenses the conditions of '*basic fairness and due process*'.[235] Because the US treated members whose applications for certification were rejected in a '*singularly casual and informal manner*', the AB found the US in violation of procedural good faith.[236] By imposing such due process requirements, good faith regulates the relationship between members' domestic law and WTO treaty obligations. Good faith in the Chapeau of Article XX ensures that 'broader public deliberation' debates the problem before a trade restriction is imposed.[237]

230 Cottier and Schefer, 1997, p 67.
231 *Ibid*, 2000, pp 51–3.
232 See *US–Shrimp*, AB Report, paras 163, 177.
233 *Ibid*, para 177; Marceau, 1999, pp 103–5.
234 *US–Shrimp*, AB Report, para 160; Marceau, 1999, p 105.
235 *US–Shrimp*, AB Report, para 181.
236 *Ibid*.
237 Howse, 2000, pp 42–51.

The AB relates the prohibition against *abus de droit* to the obligation of a reasonable exercise of a right described by scholars and the ICJ case law as sanctionable under 'breach of contract'.[238]

'Balancing Test'

In addition to finding that the Chapeau of Article XX functions as a prohibition of *abus de droit* the AB has tried to accomplish its 'task' of 'locat[ing] and marki[ing] out a line of equilibrium' between the right of a member to invoke the exception and the rights of other members through the application of various substantive provisions.[239] But is the balancing test is a function of *abus de droit* or rather one of good faith? This relates to the more general question of the relationship between *abus de droit* and equity. Specifically, it is to be asked whether *abus de droit* contains an element of equity, which has been related to the balancing test.[240]

The balancing test, or the regulative function of good faith, is designed to counterbalance the effects of *abus de droit*. It is interesting that the AB on the one hand imposes the intrusive standard of *abus de droit*, which clearly prioritises free trade values, upon members invoking an exception, and then on the other hand engages in balancing tests.[241] However, it is possible that the AB has wanted to soften the harshness and unilateral emphasis on free trade with *abus de droit* in the context of an exception from trade liberalization rules, by equity law jurisdiction. With the balancing test, the AB corrected the Panel's jurisprudence of *abus de droit*, which had 'tilted towards one particular value among the competing values at stake, namely that of free trade'.[242] Thus, the balancing test and *abus de droit* are two functions of good faith, which must be kept separate. It is not because a judge uses *abus de droit*, that the legislator has meant to empower the judiciary to decide in equity.[243] It appears from *US–Shrimp* jurisprudence however, that the WTO AB has the right to infuse its judgments with notions of equity.

Cottier and Schefer argue that equity is Anglo-American (common) law's response to the Continental concept of *abus de droit*. Thus, in their view, these are not two mutually supportive concepts but one and the same principle.[244]

Marceau argues that it is from the balancing test, rather than from the prohibition against *abus de droit*, that the substantive and procedural requirements of flexibility, due process, etc are derived. To the contrary, it is the prohibition against *abus de droit* creates these substantive rules, and the balancing test is a corollary of the wider function of good faith, which in turn encompasses both

238 *US–Shrimp*, AB Report, fn 156 to para 158.
239 See *ibid*, para 159.
240 See Schwarzenberger, 1955, p 321.
241 Compare *US–Shrimp*, AB Report, para 158, with *US–Shrimp*, AB Report, para 159.
242 Howse, 2000, pp 52–3.
243 *Cf* Schwarzenberger, 1955, p 321.
244 See Cottier and Schefer, 2000, pp 54–5.

the prohibition of *abus de droit* and equity law jurisdiction.[245] Cameron and Gray even opine that *abus de droit* doctrine 'is rooted in the principles of good faith *and equity*' (emphasis added).[246] Thus, in their view, the balancing function is a direct corollary of *abus de droit*.

Cheng agrees that the prohibition against *abus de droit* encompasses a notion of fairness, and the AB in *US–Shrimp* even cites Cheng's argumentation.[247] However, Cheng refers to the fairness and equity that a party must observe when exercising its rights, and does not specify as to whether the notion of *abus de droit* contains the additional authorisation of the adjudicator to infuse equity into his/her decisions in the context of *abus de droit*.

Schwarzenberger contrarily says that in order to avoid *abus de droit* becoming 'itself an abuse and intolerable nuisance', it must be purged of 'exuberances' and restricted to situations of 'manifest injustice and iniquity'.[248] Thus, a balancing function understood as an equity law jurisdiction is not contained in the notion of *abus de droit*.[249]

Abus de droit is not invoked as a self-standing general principle of law, but rather is integrated into the Chapeau by a truly teleological interpretation of the AB, derived from the principles of interpretation of good faith and its corollary of effectiveness.[250] *Abus de droit* since *US–Shrimp* has only been used in *US–Cotton Yarn,* in which the AB related to the *US–Shrimp acquis*.[251]

The AB thus considers *abus de droit* doctrine a branch of good faith, committed to 'marking out' the 'delicate' 'line of equilibrium' that separates a 'fair and just' exercise of a right (both procedural and substantive), which reason demands, from 'arbitrary', 'unjustifiable' and 'distortive' exercise of a right, which is an 'abuse or misuse' of a right.[252]

WTO Case Law: Sanctioning the Abuse of Public Policy Exceptions and Trade Defenses

Abus de droit has either prevented the abuse of the Article XX(g) GATT 94 exception *(US–Shrimp)* or was mentioned but not acted upon, to prevent the misuse of a transitory textiles safeguard measure *(US–Cotton Yarn)*.

245 *Cf* Schwarzenberger, 1955, p 324; see also Cameron and Gray, 2001, p 294.

246 Cameron and Gray, 2001, p 294.

247 See *US–Shrimp*, AB Report, fn 156 to para 158, referring to Cheng, 1987, p 125.

248 Schwarzenberger, 1955, p 307, 321, who on the other hand seems to admit that a judge may, if the parties agree to the balancing functions, exercise equity law jurisdiction.

249 *Cf* Cheng, 1987, p 132.

250 See *US–Shrimp*, AB Report, fn 157 to para 158, interpretation with good faith under Art 31(3)(c); see Canal-Forgues, 2001, p 22, who sustains the thesis that *US–Shrimp* implicitly refers to the principle of effectiveness in treaty interpretation, which is a corollary to rule 31(1) VCLT, refers to *US–Shrimp*, AB Report, para 121.

251 See *US–Cotton Yarn*, AB Report, para 81; see, eg McRae, 2003, pp 714–15, for a voice against integrating general public integration law into the WTO legal order; see, eg McNelis, 2003, p 651, 'militating in favour of broader obligations' and specifically for the integration of good faith into the WTO; *cf* de Witte, 2000, p 159, for the situation in EC law.

252 *US–Shrimp*, AB Report, paras 158–60.

The Prohibition against Abusing the Article XX GATT Exception: US–Shrimp *Appellate Report (1998)*

The AB resorts to *abus de droit* under GATT 94 to prevent, through the Chapeau, the abuse of Article XX specific exceptions. So far, there has been no complaint that a WTO Member has abused an Article XXIV GATT exception (regional trade agreements), and no such situation has been portrayed in the light of *abus de droit* (*Turkey–Textiles* AB Report).[253] The other Article XX GATT exceptions cases (*EC–Asbestos, Thailand–Cigarettes, US–Gasoline*), except for *US–Shrimp*, have addressed neither good faith nor *abus de droit.*

The misuse of the trade remedies, such as safeguards, countervailing and anti-dumping duties, forms the other 'block' of cases determined by good faith. In trade remedy cases, *abus de droit* has been used to ensure the fair use of trade remedies, especially the fair use of investigation procedures leading to their imposition. So far, the only case to use *abus de droit* specifically was *US–Cotton Yarn.* In the other trade remedy cases (*US–FSC, Thailand–Steel, US–Lamb, Mexico–HFCS (Article 21.5), Chile–Agricultural Products*) good faith was used to ensure fair dispute settlement procedures, and, for that purpose, the codified expression of good faith Articles 3.10 and 4.3 DSU.

In *US–Shrimp*, the AB was called upon to define both

— the scope of the exemption of Article XX(g) GATT—specifically whether it covered the legislated environmental protection of living natural resources;[254] and
— the scope of the Chapeau of Article XX—namely if and within what limits it was still GATT-consistent to apply domestic environmental laws extraterritorially.[255]

The AB made use of good faith simultaneously as an interpretive (good faith as relevant international law applicable in the relations between the parties under Article 31(3)(c) VCLT) and as a substantive tool *(abus de droit)* to solve the issue.[256]

Upon examining the negotiating history of the Chapeau, the AB found that the UK Government had already proposed in 1946: '[I]n order to prevent abuse of the exceptions of Article 32 [which a subsequently became Article XX]', the Chapeau of this provision should be qualified.[257] Moreover, it found that the Panel in *US–Gasoline* had stated that 'the purpose and object of the introductory clauses of Article XX is generally the prevention of "*abuse of the exceptions of* [*Article XX*]" '.[258]

[253] See *Turkey–Textiles*, AB Report, paras 42–64, specifically, fn 13 to para 45.

[254] See *US–Shrimp*, AB Report, paras 127–45.

[255] *Ibid*, paras 146–86.

[256] *Cf* Cottier and Schefer, 2000, p 65; see *US–Shrimp*, AB Report, para 159, 'The task of interpreting and applying the Chapeau . . .'.

[257] *US–Shrimp*, AB Report, para 157.

[258] *Ibid*, para 119.

The AB was more favourable to the conflicting values of non-discriminatory and non-protectionist international trade engaged in a formative use of the general principle of good faith and developed the Chapeau as a rule for limiting the rights of members under the specific exemptions of Article XX.[259] *Abus de droit qua* Article XX Chapeau limits the use of exceptions in favour of the clearly prioritised obligations of the substantive provisions of the GATT:

> One application of this general principle [of good faith], the application widely known as the doctrine of *abus de droit*, prohibits the abusive exercise of a state's rights and enjoins that whenever the assertion of a right 'impinges on the field covered by [a] treaty obligation, it must be exercised bona fide, that is to say, reasonably'. An abusive exercise by a member of its own treaty right thus results in a breach of the treaty rights of the other Members and, as well, a violation of the treaty obligation of the Member so acting' (footnote omitted).[260]

The Prohibition against Abusing a Trade Remedy: US–Cotton Yarn *Appellate Body Report (2001)*

The *US–Shrimp* approach to *abus de droit* doctrine was briefly referred to as a footnote when the AB suggestively implied that members are under a good faith obligation to withdraw a safeguard measure on their own initiative if post-determination evidence of pre-determination facts reveal such a factual error that the safeguard measure should not have been imposed in the first place.[261] By upholding the US's safeguard on cotton imports from Pakistan despite the factual error discovered in the aftermath of the safeguard investigation, the AB not only implies 'that there is no need . . . to express a view' on whether or not there exists a good faith obligaion for members to withdraw an unfounded safeguard. The AB also refuses to expressly condemn the US for committing an abuse of rights.[262] In *US–Shrimp*, the *abus de droit* doctrine affected the legality of the US measure using the exception of Article XX(g) GATT.

However, the AB did caution the US that it could have condemned the US of abusing its due process rights for the following reason: The US would have abused the Panel's obligation, emanating from the US' due process rights, to pay due respect to the US investigation authorities, if the US had had the intention of covering up the insuffciency of the investigating authorities. However, the AB lacked the evidence to accuse the US of an intentional cover-up of the volume imports of Pakistani cotton and damage to the US cotton industry. The US managed to portray the Panel's investigation into the US census Data, as a violation of its due process rights, which had been violated by the Panel's failure to respect

[259] cf Schwarzenberger, 1955, pp 324ff on the formative use and creative functions of the general principle of law of good faith.

[260] *US–Shrimp*, AB Report, para 158.

[261] See *US–Cotton Yarn*, AB Report, fn 53 to para 81; see Lester and Leitner, 2003b, p 9, for a discussion of the case.

[262] *Ibid*, para 81.

the policy space of the US' investigating authorities.[263] The US investigating authorities had found no data at the time of investigating the injury or threat of injury to domestic cotton producers that could have defied imposing the safeguard. The Panel had considered the US Census data of 1998, which had not been available to the US investigating authorities, with the result that the AB had no choice but to condemn it for exceeding its standard of review.[264] The *abus de droit* doctrine did not condemn the US for basing its safeguard on *ex post facto* unjustified evidence since the US authorities had exercised due diligence). Though the claim was left unsubstantiated by the AB it held the US responsible for knowingly choosing to investigate a trade remedy at a time when the US census data was not yet available. The US had done this so it could not be accused of failing to comply with due diligence required under Article 6 of the ATC and Article 6 ASG. Thus, the US abused the protective shield afforded by the Panel's limited standard of review, which does not allow it to investigate instead of the domestic authorities, since, without its limited standard of review, the Panel would have been empowered to ask the US to withdraw the safeguard.[265]

Conclusions

The doctrine of *abus de droit* stands somewhat in the middle between a direct 'application of the general principle of law of good faith' in WTO practice and a mere expression of good faith in a WTO treaty provision.[266] Moreover, it is debated whether *abus de droit* is part of good faith, or whether it is broader or narrower than good faith, as one can either act unreasonably but still be in good faith, or not act in good faith but act consistently and reasonably with strict law. In the second scenario, the state will be (if there is no obligation to respect good faith) left unsanctioned by positive legal WTO obligations and the *abus de droit* doctrine controlling lawful uses.

PROTECTION OF LEGITIMATE EXPECTATIONS

Since the concept of PLE will be discussed in detail in chapter six, this section will only outline its main features as a concept of international law in relation to the principle of good faith.

[263] *Ibid*, paras 62, 64, 74, 78, 80.
[264] *Ibid*, para 80.
[265] See *US–Cotton Yarn*, AB Report, paras 74–81 and fn 53 to para 81.
[266] *Japan–Alcoholic Beverages*, AB Report, para 158; see *US–Cotton Yarn*, AB Report, para 81 and fn 53.

Foundations

The PLE guarantees the 'equal conditions of competition' (*Italy–Agricultural Machinery*)[267] or, to put it another way, the 'equal competitive relationship between imported and domestic products' (*Japan–Alcoholic Beverages*).[268] The protection of legitimate expectations:

— safeguards the negotiated level of tariffs or other concessions (*Germany–Sardines, Japan–Film, Korea–Government Procurement*);[269]
— has a gap-filling function, insofar as it ensures that the conditions of competition are not offset by fact-patterns not yet regulated by WTO law (*Japan–Film*);[270]
— protects current trade and the predictability of future trade (*India–Patents*); [271]
— protects trading partners from a detrimental change in their competitive opportunities, which manifests itself when the value of tariff concessions is 'offset' (*EEC–Oilseeds I, Japan–Film*)[272] by measures not yet prohibited by WTO law;
ensures that the conditions of competition, usually a certain level of tariff concessions, are not rendered meaningless by measures otherwise consistent with strict GATT/WTO rule (*Australia–Subsidy* and *EEC–Oilseeds II*);[273]
— ensures that the 'effective equality of competitive opportunities between imported products from different countries and between imported and domestic products' are maintained (*Japan–Film*);[274] and lastly,
— protects concessions other than tariffs, such as the assurances given under a waiver according to Article XXV:5 (*US–Sugar Waiver*),[275] the specific commitments under GATS (Articles VI:5, XXIII:3),[276] or even negotiations of commitments for access to projects under the GPA (*Korea–Government Procurement*).[277]

[267] *Italy–Agricultural Machinery*, Panel Report, para 13; see also *India–Patents*, Panel Report, para 7.20.

[268] *US–Gasoline*, AB Report, p 16.

[269] See, eg *Germany–Sardines*, para 16; *Japan–Film*, Panel Report, paras 10.63–10.329; *Korea–Government Procurement*, Panel Report, para 7.93ff.

[270] See *Japan–Film*, Panel Report, paras 10.72–10.77; see *Korea–Government Procurement*, Panel Report, para 7.101.

[271] See *India–Patents*, Panel Report, para 7.30, referring to *US–Taxes on Petroleum (Superfund)*, see also paras 7.34–7.41.

[272] *EEC–Oilseeds I*, Panel Report, para 148; see, eg *Japan–Film*, Panel Report, paras 10.38, 10.77, for a later WTO case.

[273] See *Australia–Subsidy*, Panel Report, paras 10, 12; *EEC–Oilseeds II*, para 81.

[274] *Japan–Film*, Panel Report, para 10.86.

[275] See *US–Sugar Waiver*, Panel Report, paras 5.14–5.16, 5.20–6.3

[276] See Cottier and Schefer, 1997, pp 155–6; see Roessler, 1997, pp 134–5; see Cho, 1999, pp 324–5.

[277] See *Korea–Government Procurement*, Panel Report, paras 7.109–7.111.

GATT 47 Practice on the Protection of Legitimate Expectations

The Panels of GATT 1947 have created the GATT-specific principle of protecting the legitimate expectations as to the conditions of competition to prevent negotiated concessions from being offset by measures consistent on their face but actually contrary to the underlying principles of GATT 47. In the words of *Japan–Film,* PLE protects the 'relative conditions of competition which existed between domestic and foreign products as a consequence of the relevant tariff concessions have been upset'.[278] Since the 1950s, the GATT 1947 Panels have protected the legitimate expectations of Members as to the competitive opportunities the negotiated tariff concessions realise for products on foreign markets.[279]

GATT 94 Panel Practice on the Protection of Legitimate Expectations

WTO Panels have continued to apply this judge-made law, expanding the concept of legitimate expectations as to the conditions of competition accruing under both the GPA and the TRIPS.[280]

However, under GATT 94, only a single Panel has substantiated PLE, in relation to a violation of Article II GATT 94 (*EC–LAN* Panel Report).[281] One Panel, *India–Patents,* has substantiated PLE relating to a more general benefit than the the level of negotiated tariff concessions.[282] For lack of evidence, the Panel in *EC–Asbestos* refused to substantiate a claim of PLE on grounds of a violation complaint.[283] Similarly, the *Korea–Government Procurement* Panel—for lack of a causal link between the Korean measures and damage to the competitive opportunities for the US service providers on Korean government procurement bids[284]—refused to substantiate the claim that the GPA should protect expectations 'accru[ing] pursuant to the negotiation rather than pursuant to a concession', ie in addition to reasonable expectations arising out of already negotiated concessions.[285] Similarly, no complaint has yet been brought alleging that 'the attainment of any objective of that [GATT 94] Agreement is being impeded' as an alternative NVNI cause of action foreseen by Article 26 DSU.

[278] *Japan–Film*, Panel Report, para 10.86.

[279] See *Australia–Subsidy*, pp 4–5.

[280] See, eg *US–Underwear*, Panel Report, para 7.20; *India–Patents*, Panel Report, para 7.18; *EC–LAN*, Panel Report, paras 8.23–8.26, 8.28.

[281] See *EC–LAN*, Panel Report, para 8.24.

[282] See *India–Patents*, Panel Report, para 8.25, where PLE related to the security and predictability members under the TRIPS transitory regime should nevertheless be providing to others under Art 70 TRIPS.

[283] See *EC–Asbestos*, Panel Report, para 8.303.

[284] See *Korea–Government Procurement*, Panel Report, paras 7.118–7.119.

[285] *Ibid*, para 7.120; see also WTO Analytical Index, 2003, p 381.

Evasive Appellate Body Reports

The AB had confirmed Panel practice that legitimate expectations are a 'well-established GATT principle'.[286] However, the AB limits a self-standing PLE, under either non-violation or violation complaints, to the 'GATT *acquis*', and refuses to recognise PLE for enforcing other-than-tariff-based-conditions of competition, for example, the worsening of the predictability of future trade in the context of a failure to implement a transitory patent filing system, as in *India–Patents*.[287]

The WTO AB has been criticised for its handling of the well-established GATT instrument of protecting of legitimate expectations, as well as for its incorrect understanding of Article 31 VCLT, which protects legitimate expectations in the context of 'good faith interpretation'. More specifically, scholars have been disappointed that the AB refuses to expand 'legitimate expectations as to conditions of competition' to protect a Member's justified hopes that the WTO Members under the TRIPS transitory regime will realise the TRIPS mailbox system for patent application in order to concretise the legal security and the predictability necessary 'to plan future trade'.[288] The only slight expansions of the concept of PLE by the AB was, firstly, in the *India–Patents* AB Report, where the AB conceded that legitimate expectations arising out of an unforeseeable change in competitive opportunities can be subsumed under a broad interpretation of the non-discrimination obligations in Article III GATT, Article XVII:3 GATS, thus potentially forming a violation complaint (GATT Article XXVIII:1(a), GATS Article XXIII:1 and 2.)[289] Secondly, in *EC–Asbestos* AB the AB was prepared to allow a NVNI if brought together with a violation complaint.[290]

Comparisons with Protection of Legitimate Expectations in EU Case Law

The use of PLE in the CFI *Opel–Austria* decision lends itself to comparison with the WTO, with the difference that the WTO, being an intergovernmental as opposed to supranational organization, does not know the situation where a WTO Member could hold a WTO organ responsible under the concept of legitimate expectations. While the 'well-established GATT principle' of PLE usually

[286] *India–Patents*, Panel Report, para 7.20.

[287] *Ibid*, AB Report, para 43.

[288] Cottier and Schefer, 2000, p 68, 'While the Appellate Body is to be applauded for its apparent recognition of the need to prevent the abuse of WTO-granted rights by Members, it still reveals a lack of understanding of the principle of the protection of legitimate expectations and the consequences of breaches of good faith'. See *India–Patents*, Panel Report, para 7.30, 'As the Superfund Panel pointed out, such rules and disciplines "are not only to protect current trade but also to create the predictability needed to plan future trade"' (footnote omitted).

[289] *Cf India–Patents*, AB Report, para 40; against *EC–LAN*, AB Report, para 80.

[290] *EC–Asbestos*, AB Report, para 187; see also Ohlhoff, 2003, p 738.

protects WTO Member States legitimate expectations as to conditions of competition accruing through negotiated tariff or other concessions, the EC principle protects individuals (economic operators) from unexpected actions of the EC's administrative bodies (and not from other EC Member States).[291]

The second difference is that when the Panel linked up legitimate expectations to international law it chose the customary international rule of *pacta sunt servanda*, while the CFI has preferred the general principle of good faith. The reason is once more the institutional difference between a supranational legal order (EC) that necessarily leaves its judiciary more leeway, and an intergovernmental international organization (WTO), where the adjudicators are strictly limited by the consensus of members.

Thus, while WTO adjudicators trace back the origins of PLE in the customary international rule of *pacta sunt servanda* as the fundamental principle of consensus-based treaty law,[292] the EC's judiciaries (the CFI and the European Court of Justice (ECJ)) are more flexible and may find the foundations of their PLE principle in the general principle of good faith.

The possibility for even WTO law to extend the scope of protection of PLE from states to private market participants was addressed in the *India–Patents* Panel decision, but was overturned by the AB.[293] The Panel was perhaps influenced by EC notions of legitimate expectations, which protect economic operators against breach of promises by EC institutions.[294] In *India–Patents* the US claimed that India's legally uncertain administrative/judicial practices, especially in the light of its legislators' lack of implementation of WTO obligation, had infringed the rights of its patent-holding economic operators to plan future trade.[295] The AB denied the US the protection of its legitimate expectations and addressed explicitly the situation of its private rights holders, which of course were also denied protection of their expectations.[296]

Canal-Forgues lauds the *India–Patents* Panels' decision for elevating the usually subjective concept of legitimate expectations (akin to EC and European national laws) to an objectivities concept expressing WTO Members' reasonable expectations.[297]

Since the WTO is intergovernmental and does not protect individual actors, claims by exporters alleging the violation of legitimate expectations are situated

[291] *Cf* Lang, 2000, p 170.

[292] *Cf* Degan, 1997, pp 75–83, 394–7.

[293] Compare Schermers and Walbroeck, pp 79–83, 64ff; Canal-Forgues, 2001, p 9, with Cottier and Schefer, 1997, pp 163–4; against Lang, 2000, p 174, who argues that the principle of legitimate expectations in EC law, stands for 'flexibility' and conflicts with the principle of legal certainty, the latter which primes the principle of legitimate expectations.

[294] See Canal-Forgues, 2001, pp 9–10; *cf* Lang, 2000, p 170, for the protection of economic operators' expectations in EC case law; see also specifically on EC case-law de Witte, 2000, p 156.

[295] See *India–Patents* (US), Panel Report, para 7.35; see also *India–Patents* (EC), Panel Report, para 7.56.

[296] See *India–Patents*, AB Report, para 48.

[297] See Canal-Forgues, 2001, pp 9–10.

in a legal vacuum. Thus, in the WTO, such claims may be brought by WTO Member States only as so-called true non-violation complaints.[298]

Constitutive Elements

The disputed measure must be non-foreseeable, which renders the expectation 'legitimate'.[299] The *Japan–Film* Panel on the one hand creates the presumption that if a measure has been introduced after the negotiations of concessions, 'the complaining party should not be held to have anticipated these measures'.[300] The *EC–Asbestos* Panel on the other hand restricted the definition of non-foreseeability by stating that where the respondent and international attitude generally 'create[s] a climate' that should lead the complaining Member 'to anticipate a change in the attitude of the importing countries', such a 'climate' renders any expectation no longer legitimate by the WTO.[301]

If the elements are proven, the harmful measure does not have to be withdrawn as under a violation type complaint. Article 26:1(b) DSU simply asks the wrongful member in a NVNI case to provide for 'mutually satisfactory adjustment'.[302]

WTO Specificities

The GATT/WTO foundations for opening the multilateral trading system to considerations of good faith, fairness and (limitedly) equity, lie in early GATT 1947 Panel practice of protecting legitimate expectations.

For a long time, GATT/WTO jurisprudence separated the expression of legitimate expectations contained in Articles I, II and III GATT from the protection of legitimate expectations under the non-violation remedy, which compensated for the gaps in treaty law. Such gaps had enabled the circumvention of tariff concessions.

Beginning with *India–Patents* and continued under *Korea–Government Procurement,* Panel practice finally recognised the PLE as a self-standing, 'doctrine', an 'extended *pacta sunt servanda*'.[303]

As of today, there are only three adopted reports in which NVNI as the basis of complaint was recognised (*Australia–Subsidy* (1950), *Germany–Sardines* (1952), *EEC–Oilseeds II* (1990)).[304] All three cases were decided under GATT 47. In all of these, legitimate expectations relating to tariff concessions were

[298] See Cottier and Schefer, 1997, p 182.

[299] See *Australia–Subsidy*, p 6, cited in Cottier and Schefer, 1997, p 162.

[300] *Japan–Film*, Panel Report, para 10.80; see also WTO Analytical Index, 2003, pp 375–6.

[301] *EC–Asbestos*, Panel Report, paras 8.295–8.297; see also WTO Analytical Index, 2003, pp 377–8.

[302] Art 26:1(b) DSU; see, eg Cottier and Schefer, 1997, pp 154–5, 180; Matsushita et al, 2003, pp 34–5; Ohlhoff, 2003, p 740.

[303] *India–Patents*, AB Report, para 41; *Korea–Government Procurement*, Panel Report, para 7.102.

[304] See Jackson et al 1995, pp 362–3.

claimed to be frustrated under the concept of NVNI complaints pursuant to Article XXIII:1(b) GATT 47.[305] The *India–Patents* Panel Report in 1997 adds the *German Import Duties on Starch* (1955) decision to the GATT 47 decisions; here a Panel or working party had successfully substantiated a NVNI ground of complaint.[306] However, the abovementioned *German Import Duties on Starch* report remained unadopted.

The *EC–Asbestos* AB Report (2001) lists three additional cases in which the Panel/working party successfully substantiated a claim on the grounds of a NVNI complaint, but where the report remained unadopted: *EC–Citrus Products* (1985), *EEC–Canned Fruit* (1985), and *EEC–Oilseeds I* (1989).[307] According to the *EC–Asbestos* AB Report, a NVNI ground of complaint was moreover alleged in seven additional cases but remained unsubstantiated by the Panel/working party:

— *Uruguayan Recourse to Article XXIII* (1962)
— *Spain–Soybean Oil* (1981)
— *United States Trade Measures Affecting Nicaragua* (1986)
— *Japan–Trade in Semi-Conductors* (1988)
— *USA–Restrictions on the Importation of Sugar and Sugar-Containing Products Applied under the 1955 Waiver* (1990)
— *Japan–Film* (1998)
— *Korea–Government Procurement* (2000).

Petersmann has identified three additional cases in which a Panel/working party considered NVNI grounds of complaint without substantiating the claim:

— *Cuban Import Restrictions on Textiles* (1948)
— *French Import Restrictions, Article XXIV:6* (1962)
— *Renegotiations between Canada and the EEC and Japan–Nullification or Impairment of the Benefits Accruing to the EEC under the General Agreement and Impediment to the Attainment of GATT objectives* (1974).

In addition to *Japan–Film* and *Korea–Government Procurement*, there are four additional WTO Panel reports that do not substantiate NVNI claims:

— *EC–LAN*[308]
— *India–Patents*[309]
— *EC–Asbestos*[310]
— *US–Offset Act (Byrd Amendment)*.[311]

[305] See Cottier and Schefer, 1997, fn 56 to p 158; see also Ohlhoff, 2003, p 738.
[306] See *India–Patents*, AB Report, fn 25 to para 39.
[307] See *EC–Asbestos*, AB Report, fn 188 to para 186; see also Ohlhoff, 2003, fn 418 to p 738.
[308] See *EC–LAN*, Panel Report, para 8.60.
[309] See *India–Patents*, Panel Report, para 7.63
[310] See *EC–Asbestos*, AB Report, paras 186–91.
[311] See *US–Offset Act ('Byrd Amendment')*, Panel Report, paras 7.120–7.132.

No AB Report has protected the concept of PLE or substantiated a NVNI ground of complaint to this day.

Future Developments

Protection of Concessions under Negotiation

The *Korea–Government Procurement* (2000) Panel found a ground of complaint to sanction Korea for nullifying and impairing the US legitimate expectations as to 'competitive bidding opportunities'. These had been assured with the exchange of concessions when Korea negotiated its terms of accession to the GPA. In the case, Korea was offsetting the value of these concesions vis-à-vis its trading partners by setting up inadequate bid deadlines and insufficient challenge procedures.[312]

Protection of Future Trade Opportunities

The kernel of the *India–Patents* case was to introduce the element of good faith into the concept of PLE.[313] The competitive opportunities of foreign patent applicants were being detrimentally modified and resulted in 'legal insecurity' as regards patent applications in India. Instead of assuring a positive IP protection regime, India had merely offered a defensive protection, in the sense that certain TRIPS-inconsistent legislation would not be enforced. The Panel found such legal insecurity to impair 'the predictability needed to plan future trade', for which the WTO legal system stands for (*India– Patents*).[314]

With such an application of the Vienna rules on good faith treaty interpretation, the *India–Patents* Panel protects what are legitimate expectations as to the predictability of future trade, which the transitory patent registration procedures under Article 70 TRIPS would guarantee.

EQUITY

WTO law and practice contain no express reference to the concept of equity. The concept of equity has been used, if at all, as a policy guideline for reforming the WTO trading system in view of rebalancing the existing trade rules,[315] namely in the areas of intellectual property,[316] market access,[317] agriculture,

[312] *Korea–Government Procurement*, Panel Report, para 7.95.

[313] See *India–Patents*, Panel Report, paras 7.30–7.38.

[314] *Ibid.*

[315] *Cf* Dollar, 2001, pp 217–21.

[316] See, eg Cottier and Panizzon, 2004, pp 371ff; Panizzon and Cottier, 2005, pp 227ff on proposals to integrate an Intellectual Property Rights (IPR) protection of traditional knowledge as a measure of equity for re-equilibrating the WTO TRIPS IPR regime with the concerns of developing countries; see, eg Abbott, 2002, pp 469ff for access to medicines for public health in developing countries into the WTO TRIPS Agreement as another IPR-related measure of equity.

[317] See, eg Deardorff, 2001, pp 159ff on market access for developing countries as an instrument for achieving equity in the WTO.

labour mobility,[318] transfer of technology,[319] and South-South (regional) technical, sanitary and phytosanitary product standards[320] for achieving better acceptance of the WTO in developing countries. Specifically calibrated legal instruments for developing countries may express another measure of equity in the WTO Agreements, for example, Special and Differential Treatment, Enabling Clause exceptions to multilateral trading rules, preferential tariffs of the General System of Preferences, transitory intellectual property regime.

Franck credits the WTO for realizing a measure of equity in what he calls 'process legitimacy', meaning the substitution of the 'aggressive unilateralism' of economically powerful states against smaller and weaker nations, with the WTO's dispute settlement system's multilateral rules and remedies. In this studys' view, the WTO's instruments for achieving an equitable trading of the world' resources goes beyond the DSU and includes political guidelines as well as legal instruments, mainly in the realm of exceptions from multilateral rules, transfer of technology and preferential tariffs.[321]

An example for the political rather than legal quality of references in the WTO to equity, may be the statement of a former WTO Director-General in what aspires to be the WTO Secretariat's directive of the WTO's future. Thus, Supachai Panitchpakdi introduced the very first World Trade Report (WTR) in 2003 with the following words: 'There is a powerful case to be made that enhanced market access for poor countries' products, and greater equity in WTO rules, can bolster development efforts'.[322]

Earlier, in 1996, the concept of equity was used similarly as an argument to render the WTO more responsive to developing countries' concerns. Thus, equity in the WTO:

— is a concept that developing countries at the WTO have appropriated in relation to their concerns with the WTO's multilateral trading system, namely in relation to higher environmental, labour, health and intellectual property standards in industrialised countries impacting negatively on developing countries' comparative advantage in cheaper production;[323]
— is a concept used to promote the negotiations of future WTO rules, or to reform existing WTO ones; and

[318] See, eg Sapir, 2001, pp 191–200 on labour mobility for achieving equity in the WTO.
[319] See Dollar, 2001, pp 212–14.
[320] See Cottier and Panizzon, forthcoming 2006 on how international standards, namely in the TBT and the SPS, could be recalibrated for South–South trade in analogy to the model of Art 12:4 Agreement on Technical Barriers to Trade (ATBT), whereby developing countries may use among themselves standards that are lower than the international ones.
[321] Franck, 1995, p 433–4.
[322] WTO Press Release 348 of 14 August 2003, 'World Trade Report 2003, new WTO report focuses on questions of development', http://www.wto.org/english/news_e/pres03_e/pr348_e.htm December 2005).
[323] See, eg Raghavan, 2001, 'Developing nations reject labour issues in WTO', in South North Development Monitor No 4564 of 2 December 2001, available at Third World Network, http://www.twnside.org.sg/title/deb9-cn.htm (29 December 2005); see also Cottier and Panizzon, 2004, pp 371ff.

— is addressed as a 'complementary' issue outside the scope of WTO law[324] but within the realm of inter-institutional cooperation, such as the World Bank (WB) and IMF initative of 2003 to provide for trade-related adjustment assistance to developing WTO Member States in the framework of the Doha Development Round[325] or the already existing IMF 'Trade Integration Mechanism' (TIM).[326] These instruments provide financial relief to those WTO Member States where economic operators have become temporary victims of a new round of trade liberalization.

The equitable instruments of the WB and the IMF aim only indirectly at distributive justice in multilateral trade. The instruments of these institutions are economic ones, such as multilateral lending and compensatory financing, which may allow developing countries to build the line of credit and the public infrastructure necessary for engaging in global trade.[327] The Bretton Woods Institutions' instruments do not directly intervene in the trade flows as the WTO's legal measures do. However, since 2004, the WTO has engaged in a sort of Bretton Woods-type macro-economic stabilization programme. An initiative that is within the WTO but outside compulsory jurisdiction of the WTO DSU, is 'trade facilitation'.[328] Trade facilitation is laid down for WTO Members in Annex D 'Modalities for Negotiations on Trade Facilitation' of the Doha Development Round's 'July 2004 Package'.[329] According to Dollar, such 'complementary institutions and policies' may 'foster equity' as to participation of the poor in the global economy, within the WTO or other international institutions.[330]

In contrast to the principle of good faith and its corrolaries discussed in this book, the concept of equity in the WTO is neither recognised as a juridical concept nor used as a jurisprudential principle. As of today, equity is far from being adopted by the WTO Panels and the AB in their adjudication of WTO disputes, but it may play a role in rebalancing and reforming the WTO Agreements' texts

[324] Dollar, 2001, p 217, speaking of the '[i]mportance of complementary institutions and policies' to compensate for losses incurred where 'international institutions have oversold the benefits of liberalization'.

[325] IMF Press Release No 03/140 of 21 August 2003, 'IMF and World Bank Announce Plans to Support Developing Countries with Trade-Related Adjustment Needs in WTO Round, Reaffirm the Importance of a Successful Trade Round to Developing Countries', http://www.imf.org/external/np/sec/pr/2003/pr03140.htm (29 December 2005).

[326] IMF Factsheet of September 2005, 'The IMFs TIM', http://www.imf.org/external/x10/changecss/changestyle.aspx (29 December 2005), the TIM assists 'member countries to meet balance of payments shortfalls that might result from multilateral trade liberalization. The TIM is not a special lending facility, but rather a policy designed to make resources more predictably available under existing IMF facilities'.

[327] *Cf* Franck, 1995, pp 418–22.

[328] See generally McLinden, 2005, pp 179–89.

[329] Decision adopted by the General Council on 1 August 2004, WTO Document WT/L/579 of 2 August 2004, http://www.wto.org/english/tratop_e/dda_e/draft_text_gc_dg_31july04_e.htm#annexd (29 December 2005) [hereinafter 'July 2004 Package'], Annex D Modalities for Negotiations on Trade Facilitation.

[330] Dollar, 2001, p 220.

in WTO Ministerial Conferences and new trade rounds, such as the Doha Development Round. If equity has played a role in WTO policy at all, it is expressed in terms of 'flexibility', which the Doha Ministerial Declaration on the TRIPs and Public Health used to describe the concessions that industrialised countries are bound to make, for example, compulsory licensing in emergency situations, in order to ensure that developing countries are equipped with the necessary medicines to fight off pandemics.[331]

ESTOPPEL

The WTO judiciary has had only a few cases mentioning equity or discussing the status of the concept for WTO law, and most of these were GATT 1947 cases. In *EEC–Bananas I* the EEC argued that the Panel should prevent the complaining parties from invoking their rights under Part II of the General Agreement by applying the principle of 'estoppel'. The complaining parties had not only 'slept upon their rights' but they had allowed Member States of the European Economic Community (EEC) to continue with the application of the banana import restrictions while deriving negotiating benefits in other areas of international trade from EEC Member States.[332] In this case, the concept of estoppel was based on the notions of equity and good faith performance of rights, and prevented a party from asserting a right under international law without abrogating it materially. The Panel stated:

> This rule of law was firmly established in customary international law, often applied by international tribunals, and was partly codified in Article 45 of the Vienna Convention on the Law of Treaties (1969).[333]

In the WTO context so far, estoppel has been referred to in connection with good faith and this only once by the AB in *EC–Sugar Subsidies*.[334] Except for quoting the Panel,[335] the AB chooses neither to address nor to apply the good faith corollary of estoppel, although the Panel had used it against the EC. On appeal, the EC had claimed that the Panel 'misconstrued and misapplied' the principle of estoppel. Relying on the notion that the principle of estoppel relates to questions of fact instead of law, which of course are outside the AB's scope

[331] Declaration on the TRIPS Agreement and Public Health of 14 November 2001, WTO Document WT/MIN(01)/DEC/2 of 20 November 2001 http://www.wto.org/english/thewto_e/minist_e/min01_e/mindecl_trips_e.htm (29 December 2005), paras 4 and 5.

[332] See *EEC–Bananas I*, para 1.40.

[333] *Ibid*, paras 1.40–1.41; see, eg the arguments of estoppel brought by Mexico in *US–Tuna I (Tuna–Dolphin I)*, para 3.48; Turkey in *Turkey–Consultations*, para 22; the US in *US–Section 337*, para 3.66; the EEC in *EEC–Oilseeds I*, para 117, *EEC–Wheat Flour*, para 2.16, *EEC–Pasta*, para 3.5, by the US in *US–Auto Taxes*, para 3.192, in *US–Sugar Waiver*, and by Japan in *Japan–Alcohol*, para 4.15.

[334] *EC–Sugar Subsidies*, AB Report, paras 38ff.

[335] See *ibid*, para 77.

of review, the AB managed to circumvent the issue.[336] Since the AB refuses to enter the debate about the status and content of the principle for the WTO, there is no AB jurisprudence on estoppel yet.

CONCLUSIONS

The general principles of good faith and its corrolaries, namely the PLE, colour the interpretation and arguably form part of the 'applicable law' of the WTO.[337] Whether or not good faith unfolds legal protection of rights and obligations under the treaty law of the WTO agreements, or merely acts as a standard for interpreting the WTO treaty rules, will be examined in chapters seven to ten below.

This section has firstly found that WTO Members are held by the 'well-established GATT principle' of PLE not to offset the conditions of competition guaranteed by the WTO Agreements. Secondly, WTO Members have the right under the PLE to demand that WTO adjudicators respect earlier adopted decisions. Thirdly, WTO practice has linked the GATT principle of PLE to the customary rule of *pacta sunt servanda,* in order to broaden the scope of NVNI-complaints. To fill the gap legitimacy of expanding the concept of PLE to include the protection of the 'predictability needed to plan future trade' as applied *in concreto* to the TRIPS, and, to ensure that reasonable reliance on concessions is given during accession negotiations to WTO Members joining the plurilateral GPA, the Panel referred to *pacta sunt servanda.*

Abus de droit jurisprudence began to be implemented by WTO adjudicators in 1998 with *US–Shrimp,* and continued in 2001 with *US–Cotton Yarn. Pacta sunt servanda* entered the WTO only later, namely in the cases adjudicated between 2000–2003, such as *Korea–Government Procurement* in 2000; *US–Section 211 ('Havana-Club')* in 2002, and *US–Offset Act ('Byrd Amendment')* in 2003.

PLE, *pacta sunt servanda* and *abus de droit* are recognised principles of WTO legal practice, requiring WTO Members to negotiate, perform and implement the obligations of the WTO Agreements in good faith. Whether or not *pacta sunt servanda* and *abus de droit* doctrine will become part of the WTO *acquis* just as PLE is considered part of the 'GATT *acquis*' will depend on how closely future Panels and the AB follow WTO previous practice on these principles.[338] Whether or not they will some day be consulted as subsidiary means of WTO treaty interpretation, hinges upon the formulation and installation of a WTO

[336] See *ibid*, paras 38ff.

[337] Pauwelyn, 2001, pp 560; and id, 2003a, p 460, who introduced the term 'applicable law' for the WTO (see above ch 1); see also Bartels, 2001, pp 449–519.

[338] *Japan–Alcohol*, AB Report, p 14; see also *US–Line Pipe Safeguards*, AB Report, para 174, for a value of previous adopted WTO reports as a subsidiary means of treaty interpretation under the VCLT.

law on *stare decisis*. Under current WTO practice, these principles create the legitimate expectation, if they are contained in an adopted report, that they will be followed by later Panels and the AB.[339] In other words, the answer as to whether the customary rule of international law of *pacta sunt servanda,* its emanations of good faith in negotiation and in implementation, and the general principle of law of a prohibition of *abus de droit*, will become 'well-established' WTO principles, will depend upon, as Cottier and Oesch have said, the emergence of a WTO doctrine of precedent.[340]

[339] See *Japan–Alcohol*, AB Report, p 14; *India–Patents*, AB Report, para 34; *US–Line Pipe Safeguards*, AB Report, para 174.

[340] See Cottier and Oesch, 2001, pp 40–1.

4

The Normativity of Good Faith in the WTO Legal System

ALL WTO LEGAL concepts of good faith emanate from the WTO Panels and AB jurisprudence, with two exceptions. Two WTO treaty provisions, both in the DSU, expressly mention good faith. These are Article 3.10 DSU regarding the duty to resolve disputes in good faith and Article 4.3 DSU regarding the duty to conduct consultations in good faith.

Usually, the concept of good faith is introduced into an ongoing trade dispute by the WTO Member State parties in their terms of reference. Either the Panels or both the Panels and the AB then take up these references and decide what weight and value the concept should be given in the context of the specific case, but in view of the rights and obligations under the WTO Agreements.

Good faith in WTO law may apply as a general principle of law to resolve a gap of jurisdiction in the WTO Agreement. It may also underlie a rule of a specific WTO Agreement and thus *imply* the application of the general principle. When implied in the meaning of a WTO rule, the judiciary ought to interpret the rule in good faith, usually by uncovering the underlying conflict of interests, thereafter balancing these according to the case-by-case context.

The issue of what standing and a which value legal principle is to be attributed in a particular legal system touches upon the normative value of such a principle. The normative value itself, differs depending upon the functions given to general principles of law: *praeter legem*, *infra legem* and *contra legem*.[1] For good faith specifically, Schwarzenberger introduced an additional category for a principle's normative function, which may or may not coincide with the classical division mentioned above, namely, a balancing or regulative (*infra legem* or *contra legem*) or a formative (*praeter legem*) function of good faith.[2]

[1] See, eg Weil, 1996, pp 129–44.

[2] Schwarzenberger, 1955, p 325, who defines the *formative* function of good faith as the 'creation of rules of an essentially relative and elastic character', and introduces the one of *regulative* (balancing) good faith.

NORMATIVE FUNCTIONS: *PRAETER*, *INFRA* AND *CONTRA LEGEM* GOOD FAITH

At the WTO, just like in any other international legal order, good faith has (regulative) *infra legem*,[3] corrective (jurisdictional) *contra legem*,[4] and gap-filling (constitutive) *praeter legem* functions.[5]

Good Faith *Praeter Legem*

The customary rule of *pacta sunt servanda* evokes good faith's formative, *praeter legem* function of gap-closing (constitutive good faith), or, put differently, the prohibition of a *nonliquet*. *Pacta sunt servanda* implies that an international legal system based upon a treaty is a complete one, especially when, as with the WTO Agreements, the Member States are bound by a compulsory jurisdiction.[6] Within such a complete legal system, good faith and *pacta sunt servanda* ensure that all gaps will be closed. Another good faith corrolary with a *praeter legem* function for situations where the WTO Agreements do not provide for an explicit rule is the principle of PLE as described below in chapter six.[7]

Good Faith *Infra Legem*

The balancing function of good faith in the WTO on the one hand materialises when the general principle of good faith is applied to a situation of fact. On the other hand, a balancing function of good faith (*infra legem*) may be implied in a treaty provision, and be used interpretatively to balance the right of a WTO Member State to invoke an exception (human, animal, plant life or health, public order, environment, labour standards, cultural diversity or internal security) pursuant to Article XX(a–j) GATT with the obligation to apply the exception both in a non-discriminatory fashion and in the least trade restrictive way.

[3] *Cf US–Shrimp*, AB Report, paras 156–9.

[4] *Cf US–Japan Hot-rolled Steel*, AB Report, para 101.

[5] *Cf Korea–Government Procurement*, Panel Report, para 7.101; see also *Japan–Film*, Panel Report, paras 10.72–10.77.

[6] *Cf* Schachter, 1991, p 53, for whom *pacta sunt servanda* is a typical example of a principle specific to international law and unrelated to the municipal traditions of States; against Degan, 1997, p 74, for whom 'the basic principle of *pacta sunt servanda* is common to all legal systems of whatever kind. It is rooted in the practice of States and is accepted by them as a customary rule of international law'; but see Brownlie, 1998a, p 19, for whom '"general principles of law" overlap that of the present section [general principles of international law]'. General principles of international law contain for Brownlie, 'the principles of consent, reciprocity, equality of states, good faith, domestic jurisdiction and the freedom of seas'; similarly, Virally, 1990, p 195, who adopts a more functionalist perspective of what constitutes a general principle of international law.

[7] See Cottier and Schefer, 1997, p 147, for the concept of legitimate expectations as a 'gap closing device' in GATT/ WTO law.

Good Faith *Contra Legem*

The prohibition of *abus de droit* embodies the corrective function of good faith.[8] The way the principle of good faith materialises in the introductory paragraph of Article XX GATT, the so-called 'Chapeau', it may also be used as a corrective (good faith *contra legem*) and stand for the prohibition against abusing the list of exceptions in Article XX(a–j) GATT for protectionist reasons.

While not yet tested in case law in the way that Article XX GATT has been interpreted in *US–Shrimp*, other provisions throughout the WTO Agreements may imply the balancing function of good faith *infra legem*. Good faith may balance the values of trade liberalization and technological development with the public interest concerns, namely socio-economic values and public health, food safety and nutrition, transfer of technology, environmental protection, preservation of cultural heritage in addition to Article XX (a–j) GATT, as listed under Article XI GATT, Article XIV (a–e) and Article XIVbis GATS, as well as Articles 7 and 8 TRIPS.

VARYING DEGREES OF NORMATIVITY

Codifications in the Dispute Settlement Understanding

Articles 3.10 and 4.3 of the DSU are the only provisions in the treaty system of the WTO to explicitly impose good faith obligations upon WTO Members.[9] Articles 3.10 and 4.3 DSU require those WTO Member States engaging in dispute settlement procedures to act in good faith, namely by engaging in consultations (Article 4.3 DSU), or to resolve disputes in good faith (Article 3.10 DSU). As the analysis of cases in chapters eleven and twelve will show, WTO judicial practice has derived many detailed good faith obligations for both WTO Members and the Panels from the codifications in Article 3.10 and 4.3 DSU. As such, WTO adjudication on good faith issues dealing with the procedural intricacies of the dispute settlement process has not only contributed to the development of a body of WTO-specific procedural law of dispute settlement, but has also shaped an emerging body of rules, which Thirlway summarizes under the term of 'international judicial procedure'.[10]

[8] See generally Schwarzenberger, 1955, who introduces the notions of *formative* (law-creating) and *regulative* (balancing) good faith, see, eg Zoller, 1977, pp 109–11, who cites authors tracing *abus de droit* to traditions of civil law.

[9] Arts 3.10 and 4.3 DSU.

[10] Thirlway, 1996, p 389.

Standards of Good Faith in Dispute Resolution

Not only does the legal concepts of good faith in the WTO colour the rights and obligations of the WTO Members codified in the various provisions of the different WTO Agreements, but good faith may also function as a standard, as a treshhold by which to measure certain behaviour. Panel and appellate jurisprudence have implied a standard of good faith under the obligation to engage in dispute settlement proceedings only if these could provide for a 'fruitful' resolution of the dispute. Good faith thus implied in Article 3.7 DSU, where it is part of the meaning of 'fruitful[ness]', expresses a standard. As a standard, good faith has a lesser degree of normativity than the one it has as an outright obligation of Articles 3.10 and 4.3 DSU. The standard implied under Article 3.7 DSU stands for a prohibition against abusing dispute settlement rules and procedures. In dispute settlement, there may be other good faith standards, associated with Article 3.10 DSU, as the case law below will show.

In Continental European legal tradition of informal, cooperative relationships, whereby the underlying tradition and a need to upkeep 'trust' is key to dispute resolution,[11] good faith plays an important role in litigation. Good faith may guide the litigation process among the parties to a dispute and between these and the judiciary. Furthermore, good faith may form the basis for the legitimate expectations of the parties vis-à-vis the judicial branch including the reliance on precedents.[12]

In contrast, the American tradition of litigation through the adverserial process does not rely on good faith, but rather on the socratic method of answer and response through rhetorical debate, intervention, disclosure and transparency.[13]

Among scholars and practioners, it is debated whether good faith may serve as a guiding principle or standard in WTO litigation outside the precedential value of reports.[14] In the last decade, the WTO legal system, specifically its dispute resolution regime, has become, some claim, the 'backbone of the peace-time world order'.[15] Increasingly, the WTO trading regime is undergoing a 'legalization'[16] process, moving away from a power-oriented form of trade diplomacy towards a rule-oriented constitutionalised international trade law system.[17] One

[11] Levi-Faur, 2005, p 453.

[12] *Cf* Jackson, 1998, p 74.

[13] Levi-Faur, 2005, p 453.

[14] See, eg Pauwelyn, 2003b, p 124, describing the 'Americanization' of the WTO DSU, which is a process Pauwelyn portrays as 'bringing in the lawyers'.

[15] Ohlhoff and Schloemann, 1998, p 302.

[16] *Ibid*, p 303; see generally Pauwelyn, 2003b, p 124ff, for the notion of 'legalization' of the WTO.

[17] See Jackson and Croley, 1996, p 195; Jackson, 1999; Cameron and Campbell, 1998, p 21; Ohlhoff and Schloemann, 1998, p 303; Cottier, 2000, p 221; Petersmann, 2000, pp 111ff; Oesch, 2003b, p 242; Cottier and Hertig, 2004, pp 261–328, the term 'constitutionalization' of the WTO, term was probably first introduced by Jackson and Croley in 1996, Jackson in 1999 depicted the WTO Agreements as a 'trade constitution, the discussion on the constitutionalization of the WTO' was thereupon taken up by Petersmann, Cameron and Campbell, Cottier, Ohlhoff and Schloemann, amongst others.

aspect of such a law-oriented WTO is the so-called move away from the alternative methods of dispute resolution that the DSU provides for under Article 5. The trend lies in adverserial dispute resolution, eg, the litigation of trade disputes in the Panel process and its subsequent possibility for appeal. This is a development towards a 'juridification',[18] 'jurisdictionalization',[19] and 'Americanization' of WTO dispute settlement.[20] If the analysis is correct, then it will not be long before references to a good faith standard guiding dispute resolution will vanish from WTO jurisprudence to be replaced by detailed, formal and prescriptive rules of procedure.[21]

Good Faith 'Implied' in, 'Inherent' to, and 'Underlying' WTO Treaty Provisions

Often, the WTO judiciary considers the general principle of law of good faith to be implied in certain WTO provisisons. Thus, the AB has copied over from general public international law concepts of good faith into certain individual rules of the WTO Agreements, for example by considering 'the Chapeau of Article XX, [as] . . . but one expression of the principle of good faith'.[22] A second example of implied good faith relates to risk assessment based on divergent scientific opinion, which complies with Article 5.2 SPS Agreement as long as 'governments . . . act in good faith'.[23] A third example for a WTO Panel reading the principle of good faith into a WTO treaty provision concerns the implicit application of good faith in the TRIPS Agreement, where a Article 7 TRIPS 'enshrine[s]' good faith.[24]

When general principles of law are reflected in positive law rather than applied by court practice, 'they constitute the *source* of various rules of law, which are merely the expression of these principles' [italics added].[25] When inherently contained in a WTO treaty provision, good faith often takes on an equilibriating function, such as the balancing of interests (regulative good faith).[26] However, the customary international rule of *pacta sunt servanda,* when found to be implied in a WTO treaty provison, evokes good faith's formative function of gap-closing (constitutive, *praeter legem* good faith),[27] while

[18] Oesch, 2003b, p 234.

[19] Stern, 2000, p 266.

[20] Pauwelyn, 2003b, p 124.

[21] *Cf* Levi-Faur, 2005, p 452.

[22] *US–Shrimp*, AB Report, para 158; see also *US–Japan Hot-rolled Steel*, AB Report, para 10, '[w]e see this provision [para 2 Annex II, Anti-Dumping Agreement (ADA)] as another detailed expression of the principle of good faith'.

[23] *EC–Hormones*, AB Report, para 194 interpreting Art 5.2 ASPS.

[24] *US–Section 211 ('Havana Club')*, Panel Report, para 8.57.

[25] Cheng, 1987, p 390.

[26] *Cf US–Shrimp*, AB Report, paras 156–9.

[27] *Cf* Schachter, 1991, p 53, for whom *pacta sunt servanda* is a typical example of a principle specific to international law and unrelated to the municipal traditions of States; against Degan, 1997, p 74, for whom 'the basic principle of *pacta sunt servanda* is common to all legal systems of whatever kind. It is rooted in the practice of States and is accepted by them as a customary rule of

an implied reference to the general principle of law of prohibiting *abus de droit* embodies the corrective function.[28]

Implied good faith signals to the WTO Panel or AB to interpret by the rule of good faith under Article 31(1) VCLT in addition to using the pure textual approaches (plain meaning of a rule), the contextual or the teleological methods.

Implied good faith is often confounded with good faith interpretation under Article 31(1) VCLT. However, it is not quite clear whether implied good faith *(infra legem)* is identical to good faith interpretation (see below). In any case both good faith interpretation and implied good faith are inherent in a WTO treaty provision (good faith *infra legem*).

The difference between interpretation of a WTO provision in good faith pursuant to Article 31(1) VCLT and implied good faith may be the one of different functions within *infra legem* good faith. While only a notion of good faith implied in a treaty provision will call upon the adjudicator to engage in a balancing of values, a good faith interpretation may apply to any WTO treaty rule, independantly of whether or not that rule embodies a measure of good faith. In addition, such a good faith interpretation may not imply a balancing of interests in every single case.

The balancing of interests usually requires to weigh the right of a WTO Member to invoke an exception of human health, of environmental protection or of internal security under the exhaustive list of Article XX GATT against that member's obligation (in the Chapeau of Article XX) to apply the exception in a non-discriminatory way and not to abuse it for protectionist reasons.[29]

Balancing requires the interests of global trade liberalization to be reconciled with the concern to protect domestic, regional and international public interest, such as 'public health' and 'nutrition', 'transfer of technology', environmental protection and preservation of cultural heritage, expressed in the substantive law of the other WTO 'covered agreements'.

What WTO adjudicators have called 'expressions' of good faith are,[30] similarly to the term 'implied' good faith, instances where the WTO adjudicator has not yet had the courage or did not find the necessity to detach the good faith protection from a WTO provision. Expressions of good faith in the different WTO treaty rules could thus be described as self-standing good faith obligations 'in-waiting'.

international law'; but see Brownlie, 1998a, p 19, for whom ' "general principles of law" overlap that of the present section [general principles of international law]'. General principles of international law contain for Brownlie, 'the principles of consent, reciprocity, equality of states, good faith, domestic jurisdiction and the freedom of seas'; similarly, Virally, 1990, pp 195, who adopts a more functionalist perspective of what constitutes a general principle of international law.

[28] See generally Schwarzenberger, 1955, who introduces the notions of *formative* (law-creating) and *regulative* (balancing) good faith, see, eg Zoller, 1977, pp 109–11, who cites authors tracing *abus de droit* to traditions of civil law.

[29] *Cf US–Shrimp*, AB Report, para 159; see also Cameron and Campbell, 1998, p 25 on 'balance'.

[30] *US–Shrimp*, AB Report, para 158; similarly *US–Japan Hot-rolled Steel*, AB Report, para 101.

The most prominent example is the prohibition of *abus de droit*, which the *US–Shrimp* AB Report reads into the Chapeau of Article XX GATT 94. Nonetheless, expressions of good faith protection identified in the various provisions of the WTO Agreements offer a stronger protection than 'good faith interpretation'.

The Panels and the AB monitor, through the principle of good faith, whether an expansive or even creative interpretation of the exceptions is warranted under the wording, context and object and purpose of the Chapeau of Article XX GATT. By reading good faith obligations into the scope of the general exceptions to WTO agreements, such as Article XX GATT or Article XIV GATS, the Panels and, most often, the AB have succeeded in controlling or pushing back expansive and creationist readings of exceptions to the liberalization obligations of GATT Article XX. The judiciary of the WTO uses the principle of good faith and the rule of 'good faith interpretation' under Article 31 VCLT to separate the 'wheat' of real trade disputes from the 'chaff' of non-trade disputes, the latter emerging through extensive and creative interpretation of the WTO Agreements' exception clauses.[31]

'Good Faith Interpretation' of WTO Law

In scholarship, Bloche and Lennard argue that the express relationship the WTO Panels and, sometimes, the AB construe between a WTO treaty provision and the general principle of law of good faith, serves interpretive purposes only.[32] Bronckers, characterizing WTO appellate practice specifically, also subscribes to the idea that the AB applies only those rules of general public international law that provide for interpretative guidance, but would not seek to apply (yet) general principles of law to WTO rights and obligations.[33] On the other side of the spectrum, Cottier and Schefer argue that good faith and legitimate expectations apply as substantive law in the WTO, with the only limitation that such substantive application of the general principle of good faith is reserved for cases of NVNI complaints only.[34] Bartels, even more generously, deems 'international law from all sources . . . potentially applicable as WTO law'.[35]

The controversy in international treaty law as to the scope of the sources and methods of treaty interpretation contained in Articles 31 and 32 VCLT, also

[31] Cameron and Campbell, 1998, p 21.

[32] See Bloche, 2002, p 826 and fn 4 with further references; similarly, Lennard, 2001, p 41 who refers to the sources of international law used by the Panels and the AB as sources 'bearing upon interpretation' of the WTO Agreements.

[33] See Bronckers, 2001, p 56, '[T]he case law of the Appellate Body, which pays considerable attention to interpretative rules and developments of public international law, the WTO has become more open-minded than its predecessors'.

[34] See Cottier and Schefer, 2000, pp 60–2.

[35] Bartels, 2001, p 499.

extends to the WTO. The controversy is about whether or not Articles 31 and 32 VCLT require what scholars call 'good faith interpretation', meaning interpreting the words of a provision not only under the aspect of language, context, object and purpose but also under the aspect of good faith.

A second controversy splits WTO trade lawyers. Does Article 3.2 DSU confine treaty interpretation of the WTO Agreements to Articles 31 and 32 VCLT?[36] Or may WTO treaty interpretation draw from interpretative maxims outside the VCLT?[37] Such extra-VCLT sources of interpretation might include corrolaries of the rule of 'good faith interpretation', eg the good faith-based customary rule of *pacta sunt servanda*,[38] the principle of estoppel[39] and the prohibition of *abus de droit*.[40] The legal notions of *pacta sunt servanda* and equity are 'neighbouring', kindred, or related to the principle of good faith. In addition to their interpretative function outside of the VCLT, such good faith corolaries have a substantive content as normative principles *infra, contra* or even *praeter* legem.[41] The majority believes that the interpretation of a WTO norm may only go so far as it is still 'in accordance with "the customary rules of interpretation of public international law" '.[42]

Direct Application by the Panels and the AB of the General Principle of Good Faith

The direct application of general principles of law amounts to a *praeter legem* function of good faith. The normative implications of good faith *praeter legem* have been described by Cheng as follows:

> Thirdly, they apply directly to the facts of the case wherever there is no formulated rule governing the matter. In a system like international law, where precisely formu-

[36] See, eg *EC–Poultry*, AB Report, para 83, where the EC–Brazil Oilseeds Agreement was determined a supplementary means of WTO interpretation (Art 32 VCLT), the HS and World Customs Organization (WCO) either Art 31(3)(c) or Art 32 VCLT; *EC–LAN*, AB Report, para 89, CITES is 31(3)(c); *US–Shrimp* AB Report, fn 120 to para 133; *US–Shrimp Art 21.5*, Panel Report, para 5.57.

[37] See generally Palmeter and Mavroidis, 1998, pp 398–413; McRae, 1998, pp 98–110; Ohlhoff and Schloemann, 1998, pp 302–29; Trachtmann, 1999, pp 333–77; Garcia–Rubio, 2001, pp 67–82, Pauwelyn, 2001, pp 535–87; Pauwelyn, 2003a, 2003, pp 25–88, for the notion, scope and limits of WTO jurisdiction.

[38] See, eg *Belgian Family Allowances*, GATT 1947 Panel Report adopted 7 November 1952, BISD 1S/59; *Korea–Government Procurement*, Panel Report, para 7.93–7.103, for *pacta sunt servanda* in GATT 1947 and WTO Panel reports; *EC–Sardines*, AB Report, para 278; *US–Offset Act (Byrd Amendment)*, AB Report, para 296, for the only two WTO AB Reports on *pacta sunt servanda*.

[39] See *EC–Sugar Subsidies*, AB Report, paras 38ff with reference to *EC–Sugar Subsidies*, Panel Report, para 77, for the only reference in WTO dispute practice to the principle of estoppel today.

[40] See *US–Shrimp*, AB Report, para 158; see *US–Section 211 ('Havana Club')*, AB Report, para 259; *US–Cotton Yarn*, AB Report, para 81 and fn 53 to para 81, for the prohibition of *abus de droit* in WTO appellate practice.

[41] See Kolb, 1998, p 662.

[42] Art 3.2 DSU, second sentence.

> lated rules are few, the third function of general principles of law acquires special significance and has contributed greatly towards defining the legal relations between States.[43]

In numerous cases, good faith finds practical solutions when the WTO Agreements do not provide for an explicit rule.[44] This is the gap-filling (constitutive) *praeter legem* function of good faith.[45] Even though the WTO Agreements provide for a comprehensive set of rules, situations may arise in which WTO members feel that there is an unforeseen or unintentional gap in the agreements. Because the WTO obligations are often watered down in the course of their negotiation among the more than 120 nations which today form the Member States of the WTO, many provisions of the WTO are quite 'vague'.[46] Whether such 'vague' and indeterminate provisions are gaps, and may be filled with content, is a key question. If the answer is yes, then we must ask whether the principle of good faith may construe an appropriate substitute rule.

A second group of *lacunae* involves matters that have not been regulated in the WTO Agreements because a topic was dropped during the negotiation process when a consensus could not be reached. Certain scholars claim that even under such circumstances the principle of good faith may be used to create a makeshift rule for temporarily solving a particular legal problem (until a new rule is multilaterally negotiated and consented to).[47]

Compared to the Panels, who have at least in one case recognised substantive international law to be part of the WTO legal order,[48] the AB has lagged behind and has declared only its own treaty law, that is, WTO provisions, to be 'but an expression of the general principle of law of good faith'.[49] In declaring a WTO treaty provision a manifestation of good faith, the WTO judicial bodies, specifically the AB, step directly applying the general principle of law away from, in other words any 'source' of law other than treaty law; but they nonetheless go a step further than merely interpreting with a general principle of law (see below).

The AB's cautious stance on general principles of law is no surprise, since a similar view persists in general public international law, where some jurists deny general principles of law not only *substantive* law quality but any legal effect, including *interpretive* value. In the deliberations of the ILC relating to the VCLT, one finds some voices retrograding general principles of law to principles of '[. . .] logic and good sense valuable as guides only to assist in

[43] Cheng, 1987, p 390.

[44] See Cottier and Schefer, 1997, p 147, for the concept of legitimate expectations as a 'gap closing device' in GATT/ WTO law.

[45] *Cf Korea–Government Procurement*, Panel Report, para 7.101; see also *Japan–Film*, Panel Report, paras 10.72–10.77.

[46] Goldsmith and Posner, 2005, p 161.

[47] *Cf* Pauwelyn, 2004, pp 136–7.

[48] See *Korea–Government Procurement*, Panel Report, paras 7.93–7.96; see Pauwelyn 2001, p 543, lauding the overture of the Panel to substantive law.

[49] *US–Shrimp*, AB Report, para 158.

appreciating the meaning which the parties may have intended to attach to the expressions that they employed in a document'.[50]

The 'well-established GATT principle' of legitimate expectations applies directly to compensate, in the context of NVNI complaints, for negated values of negotiated concessions (*Australia–Subsidy, EEC–Oilseeds I, Korea–Government Procurement*).[51]

PLE moreover applies in the context of violation complaints to assure the 'predictability needed to plan future trade, ie by requiring that India comply in good faith with the minimal requirements of the TRIPS transitory regime for developing countries, by installing a mailbox system for patent applications (*India–Patents*)'.[52]

Equally, the prohibition of *abus de droit*, which the AB tentatively adopted as a self-standing rule in the *US–Shrimp* case, is directly applied in the later *US–Cotton Yarn* case as an independent 'obligation' to ensure the timing of evidence submissions in safeguard actions giving the opposing party a fair chance to respond.[53]

General principles of law fill in gaps when there are no rules to assist the judge in finding a solution. Müller finds that there is a tendency for good faith to concretise in positive rules.[54] If manifested in such a concrete rule, good faith comes closest to unfolding obligatory force. Substantive good faith protection *praeter legem* is rooted in the GATT 1947 Panels' and working parties' decision to protect the legitimate expectations as to conditions of competition of a trading partner where no GATT positive law had been violated.

Substantive good faith later became a cause of action for non-violation nullification and impairment complaints (NVNI), a corollary to *pacta sunt servanda*, and guaranteed the precedential value of adopted Panel and appellate reports for later decisions.

Judge-made and WTO-specific Good Faith Principle

The WTO Panels and the AB have not only referred to the general public international principle of good faith, but also engaged in judicially creating a corrolary of good faith. Known as a 'well-established GATT principle',[55] the PLE on the one hand distinguishes itself from references to the general principle of good faith by being WTO-specific as opposed to referring to a more general source of law; it is also a judicial creation as opposed to general principle of law.

[50] YBILC, 1966, vol II, p 218.
[51] See, eg *Australia–Subsidy*, Panel Report, para 12; *EEC–Oilseeds I*, Panel Report, para 148; *Korea–Government Procurement*, Panel Report paras 7.87, 7.100ff.
[52] *India–Patents*, Panel Report, para 7.30; see also *EC–LAN*, Panel Report, para 8.25.
[53] Compare *US–Shrimp*, AB Report, para 158 with *US–Cotton Yarn*, AB Report, para 81.
[54] See Müller, 1971, p 256.
[55] *India–Patents*, AB Report, para 45.

In creating a principle specifically for WTO law and by applying certain principles derived from the muncipal laws of the WTO members,[56] the WTO adjudicators have conformed to Brownlie's analysis: 'An international tribunal chooses, edits, and adapts elements from better-developed systems: the result is a new element of international law (. . .)'.[57]

Influenced by Cottier and Schefer, both Petersmann and Ohlhoff find that the PLE has evolved beyond its status as a WTO-specific expression of good faith, to become 'specific applications of the equity-based international law principle of good faith'.[58]

[56] See Hilf, 2001, pp 111–30; see also Hilf and Puth, 2002, pp 199–218.

[57] See Brownlie, 1998b, pp 15–19.

[58] Cottier and Schefer, 1997, p 148; Petersmann, 1991, p 225, respectively; see also Ohlhoff, 2003, pp 740–1.

5

Schloraly Views and Judicial Arguments about the Functions of WTO Good Faith

SCHOLARLY VIEWS ON THE ROLE OF GOOD FAITH IN WTO JURISPRUDENCE

IN ADDITION TO the two explicit good faith obligations codified in Articles 3.10 and 4.3 of the DSU and the implicit good faith expressions derived from the GATT-principle of the PLE, scholarship on good faith in the WTO has relied on dispute settlement cases. The following section will examine the two main schools of thought on good faith, namely the volontarists and the integrationists. These two schools differ chiefly in the varying importance they attribute to the principle of good faith in WTO jurisprudence. For the volontarists, good faith is only part of the interpretation process of the WTO rights and obligations pursuant to the good faith rule of interpretation under Article 31(1) VCLT. For the integrationists, the limits of WTO jurisdiction are wider, because in addition to its interpretive function, the general principle of good faith may be directly applied in WTO practice, most often when a solution is necessary to fill in the gap in the positive law of a WTO Agreement.

The 'Volontarist' School of Good Faith Interpretation

One school of thought argues that if any non-WTO law were to constitute applicable law in a WTO dispute, it would be limited to a single treaty, ie the VCLT.[1] Under this school of thought, member State consent to DSU 3.2 extends only to 'customary rules of interpretation' codified in the VCLT. This volontarist view of WTO jurisdiction is opposed to the application of 'customary international law'[2] other than the interpretive rules of the VCLT.[3] For the

[1] See Jackson, 1999, pp 120–1; see also Bloche, 2002, p 826 and fn 4.

[2] Against *Korea–Government Procurement*, Panel Report, para 7.96.

[3] McRae, 2003, pp 712–13; see Degan, 1997, p 74, 'for volontarists it is a crucial problem because, . . ., they simply do not recognise general principles of law which have not been consented to by States'.

volontarists, deference to national investigating authorities in anti-dumping, ountervailing duty and safeguard actions, prime fairness to the trading partner.[4] Emanating from this view, the general principles of law generally, and the principle of good faith specifically, merely *interpret* WTO norms. As McRae says:

> Principles of public international law do not leapfrog into treaty regimes and add to substantive obligations under those regimes. They exist alongside of and are relevant to the interpretation and application of the substantive treaty rules.[5]

The 'Integrationist' School of Good Faith Application

What this study terms the 'integrationist' school of thought consists of propononents in favour of directly applying into WTO jurisdiction, the general principle of law of good faith, together with its corollaries of PLE, *pacta sunt servanda* and the prohibition of *abus de droit*. The integrationist school of thought believes that the general principles of law exist as source of law in their own right, and that they have found expression in the Panels' but also the AB's jurisprudence.

Pauwelyn is a proponent of the integrationist school. In the following excerpt he sides with the progressive *Korea–Measures Affecting Government Procurement* Panel:

> The Panel correctly rejected the argument *a contrario* that the reference in DSU Article 3.2 only to rules of treaty interpretation of customary international law mean that all other international law is excluded.[6]

Pauwelyn's later work directly counters Trachtman's stand against an application of general international law to the WTO as well as Steger's legitimacy concern with the argument that general principles of law, specifically the ones of good faith, apply when there is a gap in the positive law of the WTO treaties: 'WTO Panel can apply general international law as a fallback when it is faced with certain questions not regulated in the WTO treaty itself'.[7]

Marceau, another proponent of the view that general principles of law have a fixed place in the law and practice of the WTO, conclusively suggests that the correct *interpretation* of Article 31 VCLT 'in certain cases requires Panels and the Appellate Body to use or to take into account various other treaties, custom and general principles of law'.[8]

[4] *Cf* Jackson, 1999, p 347, who asks, '. . . will such deference result in increasing abdication of judicial responsibilities to maintain fairness and completeness of decisions, . . .'.

[5] McRae, 2003, p 715; see McRae, 2003, p 713.

[6] Pauwelyn, 2001, p 543; against McRae, 2003, pp 712–13; more cautiously, Hilf, 2001, p 122.

[7] Pauwelyn, 2004, p 136.

[8] Marceau, 2001, p 1103.

According to Mengozzi, GATT 47 Panels were already applying 'customary law principles' when referring to custom in order to concretise 'extremely vague obligations'.[9] Consequently, 'a series of customary law principles which are often applied to international conventions containing general rules easily found their way into GATT 47 jurisprudence: the useful effects principle, . . . the principle according to which the contracting parties of an international agreement will apply it in good faith.'[10]

The integrationist view concludes from the application of the precautionary principle as substantive law by the AB in *EC–Hormones*, that the WTO Panels and the AB are 'open' not only to 'customary or general principles of law', but also to 'non-trade international law'.[11]

Hilf is more cautious and does not directly address the question whether the reference in WTO practice to a 'principle' amounts to a reference to law or whether the principles only have a standing as a question of fact.[12] McNelis more strongly advocates in favour of WTO jurisdiction being broadened by extraneous sources.

McNelis finds that the AB in the *US–Offset Act ('Byrd Amendment')* case introduced for the first time a substantive good faith obligation.[13] Ohlhoff also maintains that both the AB and the Panels use general principles of law. However, if the principle is used substantively, it is only for support of an argument already found in WTO law.[14]

For Mavroidis and Palmeter general principles of law apply directly to WTO law, because Article 38(1) of the ICJ Statute applies via Article 7 DSU *mutatis mutandis* to the WTO.[15]

This thesis propagates what Pauwelyn defines as the 'broader view on what Panels can do as treaty interpretation',[16] and favours the integration of good faith into WTO law including by deriving expressions of good faith from general public international sources of law and interpretation. The WTO Agreements permit references to good faith interpretation, even though the basis in Article 3.2. DSU could benefit from a clarifying authoritative interpretation pursuant to Article IX:2 WTO Agreement.[17]

It is thereby proposed to adopt such a clarifying interpretive understanding, declaring the customary rule of *pacta sunt servanda*—the underlying basis of

[9] Mengozzi, 1995, pp 119–20.

[10] *Ibid.*

[11] Trebilcock and Howse, 1999, p 74.

[12] Hilf, 2001, pp 116, 122.

[13] See McNelis, 2003, pp 657–8; see also *US–Offset Act ('Byrd Amendment')*, AB Report, paras 283–4.

[14] See Ohlhoff, 2003, p 699.

[15] See Palmeter and Mavroidis, 1998, p399; see also Lennard, 2002, pp 40–1, citing the *Guatemala–Cement*, Panel Report, paras 6.382–6.383, in which the Panel did not consider Guatemala's reference to Art 38(1) ICJ Statute.

[16] Pauwelyn, 2004, p 137.

[17] See Art IX:2 WTO (Marrakech) Agreement; see generally Ehlermann and Ehring, 2005, pp 803–24, on authoritative interpretation.

international treaty law—to be applicable WTO law, and the general principle of law of prohibiting *abus de droit,* a directly applicable WTO principle.

JUDICIAL VIEWS ON THE LIMITS OF GOOD FAITH IN WTO JURISDICTION

The WTO's judicial bodies increasingly refer to various expressions of good faith and corollaries, appearing to exceed in many instances what Article 3.2 DSU describes as the limited scope of WTO jurisdiction.[18] The Panels and the AB of the WTO thus have taken on a pioneering role among international tribunals, namely the International Tribunal on the Law of the Sea (ITLOS), the ICJ, and the ad hoc tribunals of the International Center for the Settlement of Investment Disputes (ICSID), by referencing the VCLT law of treaties. It was only in 2003 that, possibly inspired by the WTO AB, the ICJ in the *Oil Platforms* case started expressly referencing the VCLT.

Congruence

Panel and appellate practice, as well as doctrine, agree that the general principle of law of good faith, may 'inform a treaty interpreter's task'.[19] Thus, WTO jurisprudence and doctrine have unanimously accepted that the VCLT's rule of 'good faith interpretation' forms part of WTO jurisdiction.[20] Moreover, the WTO Panels and the AB agree that good faith 'is, at once, a general principle of law and a principle of general international law'.[21] The WTO judiciary thereby apparently confirms the views already taken by Cicero, Isocrates and Grotius, that good faith is inherent of any legal system as it governs the relationship both among states and among individuals, as well as between a state and an individual by either protecting one's legitimate expectations, by preventing abuses of a right or filling an obligation with content. Despite good faith's manifest presence in WTO law, many issues remain open and division exists on many elements of good faith in the WTO.

[18] See *US–Section 301*, Panel Report, para 7.21; see also *US–Gasoline*, AB Report, p 17; *Japan–Alcohol*, AB Report, p 11; *EC–LAN*, AB Report, para 84; *US–Shrimp*, AB Report, para 114.

[19] *US–Offset Act ('Byrd Amendment')*, AB Report, para 296; see also *US–Shrimp*, AB Report, para 158; *cf* McRae, 2003, pp 710–16; Ehlermann, 2002, pp 616–18, who is one of the few members of the AB to have published 'off the bench'.

[20] See *US–Gasoline*, AB Report, p 17.

[21] *US–Japan Hot-rolled Steel*, AB Report, para 101; see also *US–Shrimp*, AB Report, para 158; *US–Cotton Yarn*, AB Report, fn 53 to para 81; *US–Byrd Amendment*, AB Report, para 297; *US–FSC*, AB Report, para 166, for additional references to good faith as a 'general principle of law and a general principle of international law'.

Divergence

Since the inception of the WTO in 1994, and increasingly in the case law of the last half decade, the Panels have referred to the general principle of law of good faith. The AB, on the other hand, has been more cautious in embracing the principle of good faith.

The Panels and the AB, as well as scholars, are divided over the meaning attributed to 'good faith interpretation', namely the impact of the good faith element in the interpretive process.

Usually, WTO practice refers to the 'fundamental rule of treaty interpretation' in Article 31(1) VCLT, which it prefers over the general principle of law of good faith used interpretively.[22] As long as the WTO interpreter expressly refers to customary rules of interpretation of VCLT, interpreting the WTO Agreements in good faith is consistent with Article 3.2 DSU, since 'Articles 31 and 32 have attained the status of rules of customary international law'.

However, the Panels and the AB are divided over the meaning, in the interpretive process, of 'good faith' under Article 31(1) VCLT.[23] A restrictive adoption of good faith as a tool of interpretation is nothing new to international judiciaries. The ILC, the ICJ, and academic doctrine also cannot agree on the rationale for good faith in this customary rule of interpretation.[24] Opinions are divided between those advocating for good faith to commit the interpreter to a standard of reasonableness, and those arguing that good faith has no proper interpretive value when compared to the functions of meaning, context and the object and purpose of a norm.[25]

Article 3.2 DSU defines the 'rights and obligations' of WTO Members, as the WTO Marrakech Agreement provides for in referring to the Annexes 1–4, the latter which are the agreements best known under the term of 'covered agreements'. Considering that Article 3.2 of the DSU restricts the jurisdiction of the WTO to the WTO 'covered agreements', the AB has not found a proper legal basis in the WTO Agreements for applying the principle of good faith, except for Article 3.10 DSU imposing upon WTO Members the obligation to bring a trade dispute only in good faith.[26]

While the Panels have been reprimanded by the AB for allegedly unlawfully expanding the scope of jurisdiction of the WTO as defined and bound by Article 3.2 DSU, the AB's jurisprudence in this regard has been comparatively quite

[22] *US–Line Pipe Safeguards*, AB Report, para 244.

[23] Compare *India–Patents*, Panel Report, para 7.24, with *India–Patents*, AB Report, paras 45–7; similarly compare *EC–LAN*, Panel Report, paras 8.25–8.26, with *EC–LAN*, AB Report, paras 83–6.

[24] See Müller, 1971, p 121–4; Lennard, 2003, p 22.

[25] See eg, YBILC, 1966, vol II, pp 219–21; Müller, 1971, pp 123–53; Korhonen, 1996, p 7–8; O'Connor, 1991, p 109; Lennard, 2002, pp 20–2; against McRae, 2003, p 711, 'implicit in the text/context/object and purpose trilogy of Art 31'.

[26] *Cf* Ohlhoff and Schloemann, 1998, pp 326–7.

progressive. Without falling into the pitfall of judicial creativity, the AB has also managed to take in non-WTO sources of law, without locking them in as applicable law but only as a means of interpreting existing WTO provisions.

6

Protection of Legitimate Expectations as GATT-specific Good Faith

> The non-violation nullification and impairment doctrine goes further than just respect for the object and purpose of the treaty as expressed in its terminology. One must respect actual provisions (ie, concessions) as far as their material effect on competitive opportunities is concerned. It is an extension of the good faith requirement in this sense.[1]

AMONG ALL THE other emanations of good faith in WTO law and practice, the PLE is the only GATT/WTO-specific 'doctrine of good faith'.[2] The PLE is a self-standing good faith principle which the WTO Panels, and even earlier, the GATT 47 adjudicators directly applied as a 'well-established GATT principle'.[3] Because PLE is considered an expression of good faith, under Article 31 VCLT, PLE also 'informs a treaty interpreter's task' and guides the interpretation of the WTO Agreements.[4]

This chapter discusses the development and foundations of the PLE in the GATT 47 and the WTO with an introduction followed by a short illustration of its historical development from GATT 47 to WTO law. First, the 'traditional' concept of the PLE 'as to conditions of competition' is discussed. Second, the development of what this study calls the 'extended' PLE will be examined. Next, this study will seek to understand the alternative and more recent developments of the traditional concept of PLE 'as to conditions of competition'. It will discuss how the basis for the PLE cause of action today is broader than the narrower concept of 'conditions of competition'.

PLE may be based upon frustrated MFN treatment, relate to 'the predictability to plan future trade' mentioned in the GATT and WTO preambles, and may even contain claims that refer to the customary rule of international law of *pacta sunt servanda*. In addition to an expanded base of a complaint, the type of complaint under which PLE may be brought has broadened. While supposedly

[1] *Korea–Government Procurement*, Panel Report, para 7.95.

[2] See Cottier and Schefer, 1997, p 182.

[3] *India–Patents*, Panel Report, para 7.20.

[4] *Cf US–Offset Act ('Byrd Amendment')*, AB Report, para 298; *US–Offset Act ('Byrd Amendment')*; *US–Shrimp*, AB Report, para 158.

strictly reserved for NNVI-type complaints, PLE has also been brought under violation-type complaints, or under what is called 'broad' NVNI-type complaints. However, PLE may not be brought under overbroad NVNI-type complaints, which are defined as 'wrong' NVNI complaints.

This chapter will also discuss the limits of extending the GATT/WTO-specific principle of PLE to violation-type complaints. We will examine the resistance that the AB has put up regarding any extension of the principle, whether it be substantive, such as when the PLE cause of action is brought under the TRIPS, or procedural, such as when PLE is based upon a violation-type complaint.

Lastly,we will look briefly at legitimate expectations as to the precedential value of adopted Panel and AB Reports, although this will be discussed in more detail as part of the procedural functions of WTO good faith in chapter twelve below.

ECONOMIC RATIONALE AND LEGAL FOUNDATIONS

Consolidation of the Negotiated Level of Liberalization Commitments

The preamble to the WTO (Marrakech) Agreement calls for 'entering into reciprocal and mutually advantageous arrangements directed to the substantial reduction of tariffs and other barriers to trade', and for 'eliminate[ing] . . . discriminatory treatment in trade relations'.[5] Thus, the mandate of the WTO is to protect the *acquis* of trade liberalization, beyond the obligations of the positive rules of the agreements. The principle of protecting legitimate expectations ensures that the level of negotiated reductions of trade barriers is not offset by actions consistent with positive rights and obligations, but inconsistent with the overall level of multilaterally negotiated liberalization commitments. Thereby PLE contributes 'to eliminate discriminatory treatment in international commerce'.[6]

Pescatore criticises the WTO for having, 'in the guise of principles conveniently termed to be "principles of GATT law"' resolved disputes by having 'imported [principles] into GATT from the outside'.[7] However, the opposite is probably true. The GATT/WTO established PLE because there was no such concept in public international law at the time.[8]

The GATT 47 Panels introduced the concept of PLE as to conditions of competition by deriving it from Article III GATT 94. As such it is considered the GATT/WTO's earliest and only WTO-specific expression of good faith. PLE is explicitly mentioned in Article XVII:3 GATS. However, jurisprudence and

[5] WTO (Marrakech) Agreement, Preamble, para 3.
[6] *Canada–Wheat*, AB Report, para 95.
[7] Pescatore, 1993, p 12.
[8] See Cottier and Schefer, 1997, pp 167–8, 180–1; see also Cottier and Schefer, 2000, pp 58–9.

scholarship have found it implicitly contained in Articles II and III GATT. Moreover, it is an inherent element of the cause of action of non-violation complaints, the latter regulated by Articles XXIII(b) and (c) GATT 94 and Article 26 DSU.[9]

Under GATT 94, legitimate expectations protect the negotiated tariff concessions from being '*de facto* withdrawn' by a member, who instead of 'withdrawing a concession *de jure* in exchange of compensation or equivalent withdrawals of concessions by affected contracting parties', circumvents by an action or omission Article XXVIII GATT 94 on the 'Modification of Schedules'.[10]

The Judge-made Principle

PLE typically is a judicial concept.[11] The 'well-established' principle specific to GATT/WTO law was created by the GATT 47 Panels and in the course of time was further developed by the Panels of the WTO.[12] However, its enforceability has not yet been fully accepted by the AB, who nevertheless concedes that the PLE is derived from Article III GATT 94 and 'in part from Article XXIII, the basic dispute settlement provision of the GATT (and the WTO)'.[13]

Because of its origins in GATT jurisprudence, PLE, when used *substantively*, is a GATT/WTO Panel creation.[14] When used *interpretively*, however, PLE stems from the rule of interpretation in good faith under Article 31 VCLT. In 2000, substantive uses also related the precept first developed under the GATT of 1947, to the customary international rule of *pacta sunt servanda*.

Today, the 'precept'[15] reaches beyond the traditional meaning of conditions *of* competition under Article III GATT/Article XVII:3 GATS to more elusive protection of legal security and predictability to plan as the preconditions *for* competition such as trade, non-foreseeable changes both as to a member's tariff schedule or as to competitive bidding opportunities assured in the negotiations to the plurilateral GPA but subsequently changed as of the actual schedule of concession.

Not only may the PLE be invoked in cases of WTO-consistent measures, but the claims of nullification and impairment of a benefit through the frustration of a legitimate expectation may also be brought regarding WTO-inconsistent

[9] *Cf* Cheng, 1987, p 390, on the three functions attributed to general principles of law.
[10] Petersmann, 1991, p 226.
[11] *India–Patents*, Panel Report, para 7.22.
[12] *Ibid.*
[13] *Ibid*; see *India–Patents*, AB Report, para 34, which cites the Panel.
[14] *Cf* Cottier and Schefer, 2000, p 59, who say that the concept of NVNI complaints, related to the one of PLE will be reduced as the WTO undertakes to use more of general principles of law; see also *India–Patents*, Panel Report, para 7.20 and fns 81–4, for a list of cases using the PLE substantively as a GATT-specific principle.
[15] *India–Patents*, Panel Report, para 7.30.

measures, and thus in combination with a violation type complaint.[16] The *EC–Asbestos* AB Report of 1996 was pioneering on this question and found that if the violation of a provision triggers the frustration of a legitimate expectation concurrently, the claim can be brought as a separate NVNI-type complaint in a non-violation cause of action.[17] If the distinction between a non-violation and a violation complaint is not yet made, the basis of the claim is nullification or impairment of benefits.

FUNCTION AND CONTENT OF PROTECTION OF LEGITIMATE EXPECTATIONS

Conditions of Competition

The PLE 'as to conditions of competition' is the origin of good faith protection, which was to emerge in the jurisprudence relating to the WTO Agreements in 1996. The PLE as to conditions of competition constitutes the basis only for substantive good faith principles; it does not form the basis for the procedural obligations to respect good faith in the DSU. This section will describe the most traditional among the existing types of protection of legitimate expectation known to the GATT/WTO legal system.

The initial basis upon which the GATT/WTO adjudicators founded the PLE are 'the conditions competition' which a foreign market operator may rely on in an internal market liberalised by the multilaterally negotiated tariff concessions.[18] PLE is not only the earliest reference ever to good faith in the GATT/WTO legal system, but also a genuine GATT/WTO-specific expression of good faith. Among the multifaceted references to good faith in WTO practice, it is the best integrated principle. As the *India–Patents* Panel declared, it is a 'well-established GATT principle'.[19]

The PLE 'as to conditions of competition' is a principle designed to prevent negotiated tariff concessions from being 'adversely modif[ied]'[20] by an otherwise 'internationally legal act'.[21] It stands for the basic GATT-specific value of market access. Legitimate expectations 'as to conditions of competition' assure that the advantages negotiated between the contracting parties, such as better market access, but also non-discriminatory conditions on the domestic market, are reflected in the reality that the assurances of freer trade are not offset by

[16] See *EC–Asbestos*, AB Report, para 187.
[17] *Ibid.*
[18] *Italy–Agricultural Machinery*, Panel Report, para 12.
[19] *India–Patents*, Panel Report, para 7.22.
[20] *Italy–Agricultural Machinery*, Panel Report, para 12; see, eg *Canada–Autos*, Panel Report, para 10.80 for a later WTO case.
[21] Matsushita et al, 2003, p 86.

other measures. Legitimate expectations protect the 'value' of exchanged trade concessions:[22]

> [T]he main value of a tariff concession is that it provides an assurance of better market access through improved price competition. Contracting parties negotiate tariff concessions primarily to obtain that advantage. They must therefore be assumed to base their tariff negotiations on the expectation that the price effect of the tariff concessions will not be systematically offset. If no right of redress were given to them in such a case they would be reluctant to make tariff concessions and the General Agreement would no longer be useful as a legal framework for incorporating the results of trade negotiations.[23]

With the exception of Articles VI:5(a)(ii) and XVII:3 GATS, the PLE is not an expressly codified right. As a principle of GATT/WTO law, the advantage of PLE is that it applies equally to each of the WTO Agreements. Some provisions may contain an implicit recognition of PLE, such as Articles II and III GATT.

The PLE is related to other basic principles of the GATT/WTO legal system. Foremost, PLE 'as to conditions of competition' ensures 'compliance' with the non-discrimination obligation. PLE ensures the 'effective equality of competitive opportunities between imported products from different countries and between imported and domestic products':[24]

> [I]n an Article XXIII:1(b) case the issue is not whether equality of competitive conditions exists but whether the relative conditions of competition which existed between domestic and foreign products as a consequence of the relevant tariff concessions have been upset.[25]

Legitimate expectations 'as to conditions of competition', economically, do not protect the 'trade flows' (also called 'trade volumes'[26]) but rather the 'price effect' of concessions (*EEC–Oilseeds I*).[27] Viewed from the perspective of the negotiated value of concessions, legitimate expectations as to the 'conditions of competition' protect the 'value' or 'balance' of negotiated tariffs or other concessions.[28] As such, PLE as to conditions of competition underlying Article III GATT have been described as offering only 'relative' protection.[29]

22 *EC–LAN*, Panel Report, paras 8.69, 8.71; Petersmann, 1991, pp 224–5.
23 *EEC–Oilseeds I*, Panel Report, para 148.
24 *Japan–Film*, Panel Report, para 10.86.
25 *Ibid.*
26 *EEC–Oilseeds I*, Panel Report, para 151; see also *India–Patents*, AB Report, para 40, for a list of cases on the issue.
27 *EEC–Oilseeds I*, Panel Report, paras 147–8.
28 *EEC–Oilseeds I*, Panel Report, paras 114, 148.
29 *Japan–Film*, Panel Report, para 10.86.

The Substantive Element of GATT Article III

Italy–Agricultural Machinery *GATT 47 Panel Report (1958): 'Provide Equal Conditions of Competition'*

At a time when the UK was not yet part of the EC common market, it brought a case under the GATT alleging that an Italian law providing Italian purchasers of agricultural machinery with a rebate when buying Italian tractors amounted to a distortion of the conditions of competition between foreign and domestic tractors, prohibited by the non-discrimination provision of Article III. Since the credit facilities offered for each purchase of Italian machinery were not made available to purchases of imported tractors, the UK declared that 'these products did not enjoy the equality of treatment which should be accorded to them'.[30] The UK found this unequal treatment particularly unfair, because the tariff rates on tractors were bound pursuant to Article II GATT.

The Panel found Italian law—even if it did not directly affect the sale or purchase of products—unlawful, because it had the effect of subsidising Italian tractors. Under Article III GATT such discriminatory effects were prohibited insofar as they would 'adversely modify the conditions of competition between the domestic and imported products on the internal market'.[31] The Panel found Italy to have violated the non-discrimination obligation under GATT Article III—because the UK tractor industry deprived by Italy's bound tariff for agricultural products meant that the UK tractor industry could not offset the price difference of the subsidy by rolling back the price effect onto Italian consumers through a higher export tariff; the UK tractor industry was therefore unable to counter the adverse effect of the Italian subsidy on its competitive opportunities on the Italian market.

Neither the Panel nor the UK alleged a nullification or impairment of a reasonably expected benefit for the reason that the value of Italy's tariff concession had been impaired. Nevertheless, the *Italy–Agricultural Machinery* definitions of discrimination that might lay 'adversely modify the conditions of competition'[33] and 'equal conditions of competition'[34] lay the groundwork for defining the concept of legitimate expectations as to conditions of competition and their frustration through the impairment of the negotiated level of tariff concessions, whether or not the adverse measure circumvents or violates GATT law. As the Panel put it: '[T]he drafters of the Article intended to cover in paragraph 4 not only the laws and regulations which directly governed the conditions of sale or purchase, but also any laws or regulations which might adversely modify the conditions of competition between the domestic and imported products on the internal market'.[35]

[30] *Italy–Agricultural Machinery*, para 5.
[31] *Ibid*, para 12.
[32] See *ibid*, para 12.
[33] *Ibid*.
[34] *Ibid*, para 13.
[35] *Ibid*, para 12.

[I]f the scope of Article III were limited in the way the Italian delegation suggested to a specific type of laws and regulations, the *value* of the *bindings* under Article II of the Agreement *and* of the general rules of *non-discrimination* as between imported and domestic products could be easily evaded.[36]

The Panel agreed with the UK that the Article III:4 GATT requirement to guarantee 'equal conditions of competition' reflected the 'drafters' intent'.[37] In result, the Panel suggested the Contracting Parties ask Italy to eliminate the adverse effects of its law on foreign tractor importers by 'extends[ing] the availability of the credit facility to permit a fair choice between purchases of tractors of domestic and foreign origin'.[38]

Italy–Agricultural Machinery in 1958 had already set the precedent for expanding the scope of Article III GATT to include the prohibition of any domestic measures with a discriminatory effect in terms of the competitiveness between foreign and domestic products on the internal market:

The selection of the word 'affecting' would imply, in the opinion of the Panel, that the drafters of the Article intended to cover in paragraph 4 not only the laws and regulations which directly governed the conditions of sale or purchase but also any laws or regulations which might adversely modify the conditions of competition between the domestic and imported products on the internal market.[39]

For *Italy–Agricultural Machinery,* the object and purpose of Article III GATT is 'to provide equal conditions of competition, once goods had been cleared through customs'.[40] Future NVNI cases, namely *India–Patents* of 1998, expanded the meaning of 'conditions of competition' to encompass not only modifications of negotiated concessions impairing competitive opportunities but also (beyond negotiated concessions) other terms of trade with an impact on the access to and competition in domestic market for foreign products.[41]

Japan–Alcohol (1996): *'Expectations of the Equal Competitive Relationship'*

Japan's shochu was more favourably taxed than vodka and the imported distilled liquors were not similarly taxed to 'directly competitive or substitutable products' from Japan, thus affording 'protection to domestic products in violation of Article III:2, second sentence, of [GATT]'.[42]

The *Japan–Alcohol* Panel found and the AB confirmed that Japan's Liquor Tax Law had the effect of affording shochu GATT-prohibited protection in

36 *Ibid*, para 15.
37 *Ibid*, para 13.
38 *Ibid*, para 24.
39 *Ibid*, Panel Report, para 12.
40 *Ibid*, para 13.
41 See *India–Patents*, Panel Report, para 7.20.
42 *Japan–Alcohol*, AB Report, p 32; see also *Japan–Alcohol*, Panel Report, paras 7.1 and 7.2.

relation to 'other distilled liquors'[43] (often foreign), as well as to vodka under Article III GATT first sentence.[44]

Japan's Liquor Tax Law was found to unfairly change the conditions of competition, which members could expect under Article III, by preferably modifying the competitive opportunities in favour of shochu.[45]

Japan–Alcohol does not protect the EC's expectations as to the competitive opportunities for its liquors; rather the AB decision is directly based upon the prohibition of discriminatory treatment of EC liquor and vodka under Article III GATT 94. *Japan–Alcohol* does not deal with the concept of the nullification or impairment of a benefit, for which the EC should be compensated under Article 26.1(b) DSU.

Implicitly, although not substantiating a NVNI-type complaint, the AB recognised that claims of frustration of legitimate expectations as to conditions of competition can be brought as violation complaints pursuant to Article III GATT in combination with Article XXIII:1(a) GATT.

Japan–Alcohol stands in contrast to the *EC–LAN* AB Report. In *EC–LAN*, the AB had stated that legitimate expectations could only be protected through NVNI claims: 'The concept of "*reasonable expectations*", which the Panel refers to as "legitimate expectations", is a concept that was developed in the context of *NVNI* complaints' (emphasis added).[46]

Japan–Alcohol constitutes the first decision under the WTO and the first report at an appellate level to expressly recognise that GATT Article III may also protect *expectations* as to the 'equality of competitive conditions of competition for imported in relation to domestic products'.[47] 'The broad and fundamental purpose of Article III is to avoid protectionism in the application of internal tax and regulatory measures'. More specifically, the purpose of Article III:

> is to ensure that internal measures 'not be applied to imported or domestic products so as to afford protection to domestic production'. Toward this end, Article III obliges members of the WTO to provide equality of competitive conditions for imported products in relation to domestic products. . . . Article III protects expectations not of any particular trade volume but rather of the equal competitive relationship between imported and domestic products (emphasis added).[48]

Secondly, the AB broadened the scope of violation complaints to include not only discriminatory treatment of foreign products with respect to tariffs but also 'internal taxes and other internal regulatory measures'.[49]

As the precedent to *India–Patents*, *Japan–Alcohol* acknowledged previous practice which recognised that legitimate expectations can form the object of

[43] *Japan–Alcohol*, AB Report, pp 25–31.
[44] See *ibid*, pp 21, 32.
[45] *Ibid*, p 16.
[46] *EC–LAN*, AB Report, para 80.
[47] *Japan–Alcohol*, AB Report, p 16.
[48] See *ibid*.
[49] *Ibid*, p 17.

violation complaints, as long as the expectation can be situated in the context of a broad interpretation of the non-discrimination obligation in GATT Article III:

> In the context of violation complaints made under Article XXIII:1(a), it is true that Panels examining claims under Articles III and XI of the GATT have frequently stated that the purpose of these articles is to protect the expectations of members concerning the competitive relationship between imported and domestic products, as opposed to expectations concerning trade volumes (emphasis added).[50]

India–Patents reiterates the somewhat ambiguous statement of *Japan–Alcohol,* which leaves the issue open as to whether or not a claim of legitimate expectations—absent of a proof of actual, *de jure* violation of the non-discrimination provision of Article III GATT—can stand or not. Nevertheless, the *India–Patents* AB report clarified *Japan–Alcohol* insofar as it recognised that the 'purpose' of Article III is to protect the legitimate expectations as to the competitive relationships between imported and domestic products.[51]

The Substantive Element of GATS Article XVII Paragraph 3

The GATS negotiators codified the well-established GATT principle of maintaining the conditions of competition. Not only does the NT obligation under GATS Article XVII:3 NT prohibit explicit discriminatory treatment between foreign and domestic service suppliers, it also considers the modification of conditions of competition a violation of the non-discrimination obligation:

> Formally identical or formally different treatment shall be considered to be less favourable if it modifies the conditions of competition in favour of services or service suppliers of the Member compared to like services or service suppliers of any other Member.[52]

EC–Bananas (US) *Panel Report (1997): 'Creates Less Favourable Conditions of Competition for like Service Supplier'*

The *EC–Bananas* Panel found the EC's operator category rules to discriminate against 'non-EC owned or controlled service suppliers . . . provid[ing] wholesale trade services in bananas in and to the EC' (Chiquita, Dole Del Monte and Noboa), violating the GATS Article XVII:3 guaranteed conditions of competition.[53]

> In the Uruguay Round, the drafters of the GATS were aware that the term *affecting* had been interpreted in prior GATT Panel reports to cover not only laws and regulations which directly govern the conditions of sale or purchase but also any laws or

[50] *India–Patents*, AB Report, para 40.
[51] *Ibid.*
[52] GATS Art XVII, para 3.
[53] *EC–Bananas (US)*, Panel Report, paras 7.327, 7.330, 7.341.

> regulations which might adversely modify conditions of competition between like domestic and imported products.[54]
>
> [W]e conclude that service suppliers of Complainants' origin are subject to less favourable conditions of competition in their ability to compete in the wholesale services market for bananas than service suppliers of EC (or ACP) origin.[55]
>
> . . . [A]lthough operator category rules arguably apply on a formally identical basis regardless of the origin of the service or the service supplier concerned, service suppliers of Complainants' origin are subject to less favourable conditions of competition in the meaning of Article XVII:2–3 than service suppliers of EC origin, as a result of the allocation to Category B operators of 30 per cent of the licences required for in-quota imports of third-country and non-traditional ACP bananas.[56]

A Note from the European Commission confirms the EC's discriminatory intent when establishing the licensing system for third-country and non-traditional ACP banana suppliers:

> [It] is intended to 'cross subsidise' the latter category of operators with tariff quota rents in order to offset the higher costs of production, to strengthen their competitive position and to encourage them to continue marketing bananas of EC and traditional ACP origin.[57]
>
> Consequently, we find that the allocation to Category B operators of 30 per cent of the licences allowing the importation of third-country and non-traditional ACP bananas at in-quota tariff rates creates less favourable conditions of competition for like service suppliers of Complainants' origin and is therefore inconsistent with the requirements of Article XVII of GATS.[58]

Moreover, the Panel extended the no less favourable treatment requirement to the MFN clause, so that among the foreign suppliers, identical competitive opportunities would be guaranteed. In other words, the conditions of competition requirement was applied to ensure non-discrimination not only between foreign and domestic suppliers pursuant to NT, but also *among the different foreign* bananas suppliers, which amounts to equal treatment pursuant to the MFN obligation, of non-traditional operators and ACP third-country operators.[59]

Canada–Autos *Panel Report (2000): 'Less Favourable as Formally Different or Formally Identical Treatment which Modifies the Conditions of Competition'*

In *Canada–Autos,* the issue was the Canadian value-added tax (CVA). The EC and Japan alleged that the CVA resulted in 'upsetting the balance of conditions of competition for sales of like imported motor vehicles'.[60]

[54] *EC–Bananas (US)*, Panel Report, para 7.281, footnotes omitted.
[55] *Ibid*, para 7.336.
[56] See *ibid*, para 7.338.
[57] *Ibid*, para 7.339.
[58] *Ibid*, para 7.182.
[59] See *ibid*, para 7.304.

The CVA was part of Canada's import duty scheme, which allowed motor vehicle manufacturers to qualify for an import duty exemption. In order to qualify for such a rebate, a manufacturer had to reach a certain limit of manufacturing costs. While Canada maintained that this treshhold could easily be reached by totaling the labour costs alone, the respondants—the EC and Japan—countered that the CVA required to qualify for a rebate 'include[d] the costs of domestic parts, materials and non-permanent equipment'. The foreign motor vehicle manufacturers importing into Canada therefore maintained that by excluding from the definition of CVA the costs of like imported products, the CVA requirements affected the 'internal sale, . . . or use' of products because they modify the conditions of competition between domestic and imported products.[61]

The Canadian government defended its definition of CVA by stating that it did not require the use of domestic over imported products for the import duty exemption, and that the use of domestic products was a local content requirement unrelated to the tax calculation scheme.[62]

Not only did the complainants base their claim on the less favourable treatment of imported motor vehicle parts, which would lead to offsetting the fair competition among foreign and domestic products, they also alleged that the exclusion from the definition of CVA of the costs of imported products would affect the trade in services, because 'it modifies the conditions of competition between the beneficiaries of the duty-free treatment and other wholesale trade service suppliers of imported motor vehicles which do not benefit from the same treatment'.[63] In particular, the cost of foreign services offered in Canada would be higher than the domestically offered services, because the costs of the products the service provider would have to purchase would be higher for the foreign service providers. In our view, the CVA requirements does indeed affect the conditions of competition between services supplied in Canada and services supplied from outside Canada through modes 1 and 2, even where a manufacturer meets its CVA requirements on the basis of labour costs alone.[64]

The Panel likewise concluded that due to the CVA requirements, the auto manufactures benfitting from the import duty exemption would end up preferring to use Canadian services rather than 'like' services supplied from another member, and that the CVA did 'modify [. . .] the conditions of competition in favour of services supplied within Canada'.[65]

Another issue in *Canada–Autos,* relating to the PLE as to no less favourable competitive conditions for foreign service suppliers, arose in connection with the scope of footnote 10 to Article XVII:1. The footnote exempts from the

[60] *Canada–Autos*, Panel Report, para 4.3.
[61] *Ibid*, para 10.76.
[62] See *ibid*, para 10.77.
[63] See *ibid*, para 10.237.
[64] *Ibid*, para 10.304.
[65] *Ibid*, para 10.307.

GATS non-discrimination obligation, foreign service or service suppliers whose foreignness constitutes an 'inherent competitive disadvantage'. The Panel argued that a member may not introduce measures modifying the competitive opportunities for such services and suppliers that are already disadvantaged because of their foreign—ie non-national—origin.[66]

In contrast, the GATS concept of reasonable expectations is more limited in scope, insofar as it only vests if the measure at issue does *not* conflict with the GATS' rules (Article XIII:3 GATS).[67] Just as with GATT, GATS requires a nullification or impairment of benefits to be shown in order for a frustration of reasonable expectations to be substantiated. As Cottier and Schefer argue, the significant difference to GATT, which applies the nullification and impairment condition to both violation and NVNI complaints, is that GATS relates the concept of nullification and impairment to the reasonable expectations specifically, and thus reserves the concept only for cases concerning the frustration of legitimate expectations. [68] Consequently, the GATS has eliminated the difference between violation and NVNI based upon whether nullification and impairment are *presumed* (violation cases) or must be *proven* (NVNI).[69]

Differences between Protection of Legitimate Expectations under GATT and GATS

In contrast to both GATT Article XXIII:1(b) and Article 26 DSU, which provide for NVNI remedies—whether or not the offending measure conflicts with the agreements—GATS Article XXIII:3 expressly limits the coverage of reasonable expectations to GATS-consistent measures:

> If any Member considers that any benefit it could have reasonably have expected to accrue to it under a specific commitment of another Member under Part III of this Agreement is being nullified or impaired as a result of the application of any measure which does not conflict with the provisions of this Agreement, it may have recourse to the DSU.[70]

Another difference between these the GATT 94 and the GATS, is that GATS Article XXIII:3 replaces, by 'explicitly stating', the requirement of reasonable expectations 'the concept of nullification and impairment of benefits', used in GATT Article XXIII:1(b). GATS is seen to have 'broken new ground' and contributed to containing 'potentially far reaching and arbitrary use' of nullification and impairment concept for legal measures, by no longer using the concept of nullification and impairment to distinguish a violations from an NVNI claim.[71]

[66] See *Canada–Autos*, Panel Report, paras 10.300–10.308.
[67] Roessler, 1997, p 135.
[68] See Cottier and Schefer, 1997, p 157.
[69] *Ibid*, pp 157–8; see also Matsushita et al, 2003, pp 85–6.
[70] Compare WTO Analytical Index, 2003, pp 368–9 and Art 26 DSU with Art XXIII:3 GATS.
[71] Cottier and Schefer, 1997, pp 157–8.

Article VI:5(a)(ii) GATS constitutes GATS' second 'legal obligation' to respect reasonable expectations:

> In sectors in which a Member has undertaken specific commitments, pending the entry into force of disciplines developed in these sectors pursuant to paragraph 4, the Member shall not apply licensing and qualification requirements and technical standards that nullify or impair such specific commitments in a manner which:
>
> (ii) could not reasonably have been expected of that Member at the time the specific commitments in those sectors were made.[72]

Under GATS a member has a legitimate expectation that foreign services and service suppliers will not be treated less favourably than domestic ones. Specifically, a member may not apply licensing, qualification and technical standards and requirements to the 'committed' service sectors unless they could have reasonably been anticipated at the time the commitments were made. Until today, no case law has elucidated the meaning, function and scope of GATS Article VI:5(a)(ii).[73]

The question then is what the purpose of the GATS NVNI provision in Article XXIII:3 is. Both the protection of the legitimate expectations as to no less favourable treatment for foreign service suppliers in Article XVII, paragraph 3 and as to no unreasonable changes in licensing/technical requirements for specific commitments, Article VI:5(a)(ii), will be brought under a violation type complaint.

GATS Article XVII:3 is in fact founded upon the body of jurisprudence which formed around GATT Article III, more than anything else, as the *EC–Bananas* (US) Panel illuminates:

> Thus, the formulation of both Articles II and XVII of GATS derives from the 'treatment no less favourable' standard of the GATT national treatment provisions in Article III of GATT, which has been consistently interpreted by past Panel reports to be concerned with conditions of competition between like domestic and imported products on internal markets.[74]

The *US–Copyright* Panel in 2000, confirmed the *EC–Banana's* dictum that PLE under GATS Article XVII, paragraph 3 incorporated by analogy the *acquis* of GATT Article III. The only difference between PLE under GATT Article III and GATS Article XVII, paragraph 3, is that the GATS charges the member modifying the competitive opportunities for third-country services and service suppliers with 'violating' the non-discriminatory treatment obligation:

> [W]e also recall that, eg, in the dispute *EC–Bananas III*, the Panel and the Appellate Body introduced concepts, as developed in dispute settlement practice under Article III of GATT, into the national treatment clause of Article XVII of GATS whose

[72] See Roessler, 1997, p 135.
[73] *cf* WTO Analytical Index, 2003, p 1108.
[74] *EC–Bananas (US)*, Panel Report, para 468 (footnote omitted).

wording is based on the GATT national treatment clause and interpretations developed in GATT dispute settlement practice.[75]

Finally, the 2001 *US–FSC (Article 21.5)* Panel Report pronounced on the similar issue of PLE between GATT Article III jurisprudence and Article XVII:3 GATS: 'Clearly, provisions relating to national treatment under the *GATS* were modeled after Article III of the GATT and reflect jurisprudence developed thereunder'.[76]

Given the 'huge differences in the nature of goods and services', Cho is skeptical that GATS can 'rely entirely on the GATT for guidance'.[77] Cottier and Schefer also pointed out that because Article XVII:3 GATS does not require or even 'mention . . . the term "nullification" and "impairment"' of a benefit, GATS in comparison to GATT has abolished the antiquated and ambiguous concept of NVNI complaints.[78] As Cottier and Schefer say, under GATS, there is either the violation of an obligation or a specific commitment, or the prohibition to frustrate legitimate expectations of benefits relating to a modification of conditions of competition under Article XVII:3.[79] As Cottier and Schefer emphasize, 'both are legal concepts', and thus, both are violation grounds for complaint.[80] Even if the GATS framework is an incomplete legal order,[81] PLE still does gap-filling in the form of NVNI complaints, just as PLE under GATT Article XXIII:1(b) does.[82] Additionally, because under GATS the specific commitments emanate from the members' unilateral initiative, and responsibility and are not multilaterally negotiated concessions, a measure a member introduces to 'offset' its own commitment cannot be sanctionable.[83]

The GATS negotiators somewhat reduced the legal avenues for complaints 'contained' the option of expanding the GATS jurisdiction judicially to new areas via NVNI complaints. While under GATT, for infringements of reasonable expectations, there were two legal avenues (if related to conditions of competition, violation complaints under the non-discrimination obligation of Article III, if induced by an area of law not yet covered by the WTO, such as competition policies, NVNI nullification and impairment under Article

[75] *US–Copyright*, Panel Report, para 6.185.

[76] *US–FSC (Art 21.5)*,Panel Report, para 8.143; see also *Korea–Beef*, Panel Report para 624, for the analogy between Art III: 4 GATT and GATS Art XVII:3

[77] Cho, 1998, pp 324–5.

[78] Cottier and Schefer, 1997, p 157.

[79] See *ibid*.

[80] *Ibid*.

[81] See GATS Art VI:4 ('develop any necessary disciplines') and GATS Art XV ('developing the necessary multilateral disciplines').

[82] *Cf* Roessler, 1997, p 135, however, Roessler, in contrast to my opinion also finds GATT to be an incomplete legal order, 'And, like the GATT, the GATS framework of obligations does not cover the full range of policies affecting trade in services, and consequently does not effectively protect all the economic benefits that WTO Members expect from the specific commitments they obtained by making counter-commitments'.

[83] See Cho, 1998, p 325.

XXIII:1(b)), under GATS there is only one for both frustration of legitimate expectations and outright violations of obligations.

Under GATS, the specific commitments are unilateral concessions, not mutually interdependent, ie 'bound' like the tariffs under GATT. Thus, the specific commitments being simple, unilateral statements, provide for no legal basis in a complaint.[84] Overall, the GATS containment of NVNI complaints should not be understood to be an intentional decision to curb NVNIs by design, developed out from the lessons learned by overbroad NVNI complaints.[85]

Instead it is GATS' distinctive design, which less intently than the one of the GATT, promotes legalisation, but more emphatically embraces development through further negotiations, essentially summarised with the instrument of 'progressive liberalization'. While the GATT seems to consider itself a 'completed' legal system, where the few gaps can be quickly managed by a NVNI complaint, the GATS, inversely, assesses itself as a legal system in development, which will further construct its laws by negotiations only.

The Procedural Element of Successful Non-violation Nullification and Impairment

A complainant has to show four elements for an unforeseeable measure to legitimately impair the attainment of a benefit. The impairment usually is the frustration of a legitimate expectation. The constitutive elements for a NVNI-type complaint have been described at length elsewhere, so that they are only briefly listed here.[86]

'True' Non-violation Nullification and Impairment and Constitutive Elements

Benefit, Impairment, Non-forseeable Measures, Causality A nullification and impairment can be a 'disadvantage to the complaining party' but can also result in a 'benefit to the responding party'.[87] Moreover, Article 26 DSU sanctions a measure and/or its application which 'impede the attainment of an objective'.[88]

Since a NVNI ground of complaint is based on the lack of a positive legal obligation, GATT practice early on sought to make up for this legal insecurity by requiring a 'detailed justification' from the complaining party pursuant to Article 26(a) DSU.[89]

In 1962, the *Uruguayan Recourse to Article XXIII* Panel decision introduced the requirement of a 'detailed submission incumbent on the country invoking

[84] *Ibid.*
[85] Against Cottier and Schefer, 1997, pp 157–8.
[86] See, eg *ibid*, pp 158–63; Petersmann, 1991, pp 210–26; Cho, 1998, pp 316–18.
[87] *Ibid*, p 161, the benefit to the responding member situation has never arisen in practice.
[88] Art 26 DSU.
[89] *Cf* Cho, 1998, pp 316–18; Ohlhoff, pp 739–40.

Article XXIII', in cases 'where there is no infringement of the GATT provisions'.[90] The *EC–Asbestos* Panel in 2000 found the fact that Article XXIII(b) GATT 47 cases are 'exceptional courses of action' justifies 'requiring the complaining party, as opposed to the respondent, to carry the burden of presenting a detailed justification in support of its complaint'.[91]

Rendering Concessions 'Meaningless' A NVNI complaint pursuant to Article 26 DSU vests when a benefit that could legitimately have been expected to accrue is impaired. The 'benefit impaired' relates to the negotiated concessions, which are rendered 'meaningless'[92] 'as a result of the application by a Member of any measure'[93] taken in 'the absence of substantive [WTO] legal rules',[94] or by 'measures consistent with th[e] Agreement[s]' (*EEC–Oilseeds I*).[95]

Because the legitimate expectations of the US did not relate to conditions of competition created by tariff or other *concessions*, but instead to an 'entitlement to a benefit that had accrued pursuant to the *negotiation*', the Panel 'noted' that the 'basis' for the *Korea–Government Procurement* NVNI claim was 'different' from the one for a 'traditional NVNI case'.[96]

In consequence, *Korea–Government Procurement* qualifies as what Hudec has called a 'wrong' NVNI case. Cho writes that 'wrong cases' have 'over-extend [. . .] the jurisdiction of the WTO dispute settlement system' and 'pose the risk of over-adjudication'. In sum, these could become associated with 'judicial overreach', a development in the WTO which 'has brought the WTO judicial branch into the disreputation among developing and developed country Members alike'.[97]

[90] *Uruguayan Recourse to Art XXIII*, Panel Report, para 15.

[91] *EC–Asbestos*, Panel Report, para 8.276. The dispute was based on a French Decree defining a temporary exception for 'certain existing materials, products or devices containing chrysotile fibre when . . . no substitute for that fibre is available' and, based on current scientific knowledge, 'poses a lesser occupational health risk than chrysotile fibre'. Canada, as the complainant, did not contest the toxicity of asbestos, but maintained that chrysotile asbestos, the only form of the substance still allowed to be used in France, was safe in circumstances of properly controlled use and should not be banned outright. Canada claimed that the Decree infringed the provisions relating to technical regulations and standards, ie Art 2 ATBT, violated the principle of non-discrimination, and was contrary to the GATT prohibition on quantitative import restrictions. Canada also claimed that the French ban nullified or impaired comparative advantages accruing to Canada within the meaning of article XXIII:1(b) of the GATT. The *EC–Asbestos* Panel at first instance found that the 'prohibition' provision of the Decree was not covered by the TBT Agreement, whereas the 'exceptions' in Art 2 were covered. The Panel found that the measure was justified on the grounds of human health in accordance with article XX(b) of the GATT and fulfilled the conditions set out in the Chapeau of that same article. The Panel also determined that Canada had failed to establish that the Decree had subsequently nullified or impaired benefits that accrued to Canada in accordance with Art XXIII:1(b) of the GATT. See Footer and Zia-Zarifi, 2002, pp 120–42, for a summary of the case.

[92] See *EEC–Oilseeds I*, para 81.

[93] Art 26 DSU.

[94] *India–Patents*, AB Report, para 41.

[95] *EEC–Oilseeds I*, Panel Report, para 144.

[96] See *Korea–Government Procurement*, Panel Report, paras 7.84, 7.87.

[97] Cho, 1998, pp 329–30, with references to Hudec, who introduced the term of 'wrong NVNI complaints'; see Barfield, 2001, pp 45ff for 'judicial overreach' at the WTO and its critics.

The existence of NVNI complaints at the WTO as well as the notion of legitimate expectations as to conditions of competition have been brought into relation with good faith and completeness of the WTO as a legal system.

Panel case law in *India–Patents* and *EC–LAN* has associated the PLE with 'good faith interpretation' under Article 31 VCLT. In *Korea–Government Procurement*, the Panel further expanded the relationship of legitimate expectations. In *Korea-Government Procurement*, PLE played the role of the 'good faith [element of] interpretation' under the 'general rule of interpretation' of Article 31(1) VCLT.[98] A fortiori the Panel found PLE expressed in the substantive legal rule of *pacta sunt servanda*.

Scholarship by Cottier and Schefer maintains that NVNI is 'an implicit incorporation of the principle of the PLE in the trading system' and that '[t]he protection of good faith clearly is at the core of NVNI complaints'.[99] Most recently, authors such as Ohlhoff and Bagchi have confirmed the connection between good faith and legitimate expectations by statements such as: 'Indeed, Panels and the Appellate Body of the WTO have thus far interpreted a relatively robust notion of good faith, sufficient to encompass the controversial notion of a NVNI nullification or impairment'.[100]

In past Panel practice, there have also been 'wrong' NVNI complaints where the adjudicator prohibits domestic measures in an area not yet covered by WTO law, when such measures circumvent existing WTO law. In such 'wrong' cases the WTO adjudicator takes on a legislator's task. Such cases today have so far concentrated exclusively on a single new area, that of anticompetitive practices. The issue for the GATT 47 Panel of whether or not to enter into such 'wrong' NVNI-type complaints, was whether or not GATT law should allow the 'toleration of restrictive business practices by private companies' like in the *Japan–Semiconductors* case, were legitimate expectations in competitive conditions of one contracting party were frustrated by the other contracting party's deficient competition policy.[101]

Such overbroad cases seek out judicial resolutions instead of negotiated solutions. Cottier and Schefer maintain that it would enhance legal security at the WTO and solidify the predictability of its decisions, if the WTO judiciary would replace the NVNI-type remedy through a violation-type remedy on the basis of a violation of the general principle of law of good faith, which has in the meantime also been recognised by general public international law.[102]

[98] *India–Patents*, Panel Report, para 7.18; *EC–LAN*, Panel Report, para 8.25; see also *US–Section 301*, Panel Report, para 7.67.

[99] Cottier and Schefer, 1997, p 148; see also Cottier and Schefer, 2000, p 58; see also Cottier and Oesch, 2001, p 36.

[100] Bagchi, 2003, p 1540.

[101] See *Japan–Film*, Panel Report, paras 10.49–10.50.

'Requiring a Mutually Satisfactory Adjustment' There is no WTO case law to clarify the meaning of the 'mutually satisfactory adjustment' remedy. However, scholarship has advanced the following proposals and concerns for giving content to the remedy of 'mutually satisfactory adjustment'.

Matsushita, Schoenbaum and Mavroidis as well as Petersmann have warned that the adjustment should not create a MFN-*in*consistent solution to the dispute, and that any adjustment compensating for the loss of competitive opportunity should thus be offered on an MFN-basis, ie *erga omnes*.[103]

Cottier and Schefer argue for amending the remedy, in order for it to congrue with 'removing the harming measures' of violation complaints. While the removal of the measure should be the 'prime obligation', the 'parties suffering from such fundamental changes' would 'retain the right to renegotiate market access conditions with principle suppliers'.[104]

Petersmann finds that such 'mutually satisfactory adjustment' can either consist of offering 'compensatory trade liberalization' or of 'compensatory withdrawals' of 'substantially equivalent concessions initially negotiated with the applicant contracting party' under Article XXVIII GATT 94.[105]

'True' Non-violation Nullification and Impairment Cases

The action for traditional forms of protecting legitimate expectations under the GATT 47, the GATT 94, the GATS and the TRIPS are NVNI-complaints. This section will start by listing case law followed by an analysis of the 'true' NVNI action.

Australia–Subsidy *GATT 47 Panel Report (1950)* The concept of PLE was created to protect the value of a tariff concession granted by one member from being impaired by otherwise GATT-consistent, but unforeseeable behaviour of that same member towards its trading partners.

In *Australia–Subsidy*, the working party found that Chile could not have been expected to foresee at the time that it negotiated for duty-free binding on sodium nitrate, that Australia would lift its war-time fertilizer subsidy on sodium nitrate, from which Chilean imports into Australia had been benefiting:[106]

> . . . [T]he action of the Australian Government which resulted in upsetting the competitive relationship between sodium nitrate and ammonium sulphate could not reasonably have been anticipated by the Chilean Government, . . .[107]

102 See Cottier and Schefer, 1997, p 148; Cottier and Schefer, 2000, pp 58–9.
103 See Matsushita et al 2003, pp 86; see also Petersmann, 1991, p 226.
104 Cottier and Schefer, 1997, p 181.
105 Petersmann, 1991, p 226.
106 *Australia–Subsidy*, para 12.
107 *Ibid.*

The working party considered whether Chile had suffered an injury, expressed by an impairment of a benefit accruing to Chile under the GATT Article XXIII:1(b).

While the lifting of a subsidy regularly is a GATT-consistent and an encouraged action, in *Australia–Subsidy* it amounted to an abuse of rights, because it impaired the value of the concession granted to Chile. The Panel found that Chile could neither have reasonably been asked to have expected the price for ammonium sulphate compared to the one for sodium nitrate to rise, nor, for Australia to remove the subsidy from which Chile had also benefitted, before lifting it on another fertilizer (ammonium sulphate), because in the past Australia had treated both fertilizers equally.[108] In reaching this conclusion the Working Party considered that the removal of a subsidy, in itself, would not normally result in nullification or impairment. In the case under consideration, the inequality created and the treatment that Chile could reasonably have expected at the time of the negotiation—after taking into consideration all pertinent circumstances—were important elements in the working party's conclusions.[109]

The finding of the working party revolved around the issue of foreseeability. The question was whether Chile had reason to assume that the subsidy would remain applicable to both fertilizers as long as there remained a local nitrogenous fertilizer shortage or whether it should have foreseen the end of the war-time fertilizer subsidy.[110]

Even if the Australian government had not acted 'unreasonabl[y]', the working party nevertheless stated that Chile could at the time of the 1947 negotiations not have expected Australia to treat the fertilizers dissimilarly.[111] As the working party report reads:

> The Australian Government, in granting a subsidy on account of the war-time fertilizer shortage and continuing it in the post-war period had grouped the two fertilizers together and treated them uniformly.[112]

While finding that Australia had not violated GATT law, the working party still concluded that there was a prima facie impairment of a concession granted to Chile as a result of a measure which did not conflict with the provisions of the General Agreement.[113] Chile did not ask that it be released from its obligations to import sodium nitrate duty-free; thus, the working party hoped that a satisfactory adjustment between the two members according to Article XXIII: 1 could be found.[114]

While the working party conceded that the value of concessions granted to Chile had been impaired, it found no infringement of the Agreement by Australia.[115]

108 See Cottier and Schefer, 1997, p 178.
109 *Australia–Subsidy*, para 12.
110 See *ibid*.
111 *Ibid*.
112 *Ibid*.
113 See *ibid*, para 13.
114 See *ibid*, paras 13–14; see Cottier and Schefer, 1997, pp 159–63; Petersmann, 1991, pp 200–4, for a discussion of the case.
115 *Australia–Subsidy*, para 13.

But beginning with the later *US–Taxes on Petroleum (Superfund)* case, a violation of a treaty provision was to become a prima facie case of nullification and impairment. The Panels (and later the AB) would find it no longer necessary to check whether or not a GATT violation also constituted nullification or impairment.[116] In NVNI cases there would be no such presumption, and nullification and impairment would have to be established by the complainant(s).[117] Article 26:1(a) DSU codifies this burden of proof for the complaining party.

In the *India–Patents* case the AB said that in order to establish nullification or impairment, it was no longer necessary to determine whether legitimate expectations had been impaired, once a prima facie case of violation had been established.[118] Nevertheless, the case figures as a milestone for the recognition that Article III GATT integrates a protection for legitimate expectations as to the conditions of competition.

Japan–Alcohol clarifies two issues: Firstly, the decision confirmed the *Superfund* Panel of 1987, which had said: 'Article III:2, first sentence, obliges contracting parties to establish certain competitive conditions for imported products in relation to domestic products'.[119] *Japan–Alcohol* extends *Superfund's* jurisprudence by specifying that 'Article III protects *expectations* not of any particular trade volume but rather of the equal competitive relationship between imported and domestic products' (emphasis added).[120]

In sum, the jurisprudence that the Panels and later the AB established with the above mentioned cases shows that in a violation case, the PLE was already contained in the prima facie case of nullification and impairment, while in NVNI cases the Panel would have to prove that the legitimate expectations of a Party had been nullified or impaired. Thus, it is only partially true that legitimate expectations are only protected in the framework of a NVNI complaint. In a violation complaint, they are not an issue to be established by the Panel, but they are nevertheless contained in the claim of violation.[121]

A broad reading of 'nullification and impairment' to include a 'change of the competitive relationship of the parties'[122] is sometimes also advanced as the origin of PLE.[123] Such an expanded notion of interpretation of nullification and impairment, which emphasizes 'an element of flexibility to take into account elements other than strict adherence to or violation of treaty provisions',[124] constituted the cause of action for the *Germany–Sardines (1953)* NVNI-complaint, where Norway invoked the frustration of a 'traditional' concept of the PLE.

[116] See *US–Taxes on Petroleum (Superfund)*, para 5.1.3; see Jackson et al, 2002, p 273, for a discussion of the case.

[117] See *EEC–Oilseeds I*, para 151.

[118] See *India–Patents*, AB Report, para 40.

[119] *US–Taxes on Petroleum (Superfund)*, Panel Report, para 5.1.9.

[120] *Japan–Alcohol*, AB Report, p 16.

[121] See *India–Patents*, AB Report, para 41.

[122] Cottier and Schefer, 1997, p 160.

[123] See *ibid*, 2000, pp 57–8.

[124] *Ibid*, p 58.

Germany–Sardines *GATT 47 Panel Report (1953)* In *Germany–Sardines*, Norway accused Germany of changing its treatment of preparations of sardines to less favourable than the equal treatment negotiated at the Torquay Round of Multilateral GATT trade negotiations. The Panel found that since Norway could not have foreseen Germany's unilateral action at Torquay, and because Germany's action 'substantially reduced the value of the concessions obtained by Norway that Norway had actually suffered a nullification and impairment of a benefit accruing to it under the General Agreement'.[125] Even though in this case there was no violation of a GATT provision, the Panel found:

> The measures taken by the German Government have nullified the validity of the assumptions which governed the attitude of the Norwegian delegation and substantially reduced the value of the concessions obtained by Norway, . . . the Norwegian Government is justified in claiming that it had suffered an impairment of a benefit accruing to it under the General Agreement.[126]

The Panel recommended that Germany restore the competitive relationship which existed at the time the Norwegian Government negotiated at Torquay, and which Norway could reasonably have expected to continue.[127]

In this case, there was no GATT-consistent action which turned out to be an abuse of a right because it reduced the value of tariff concessions; rather it was the less favourable treatment given despite the assurance of an equal treatment that upset the competitive relationship between the preparations of two groups of sardines.

Two years later, in the 1955 decision of *Germany–Starch and Potato Flour*, the Netherlands, Belgium and Luxemburg contended that the value of their tariff concessions vis-à-vis Germany had decreased because Germany had failed to bring down to Benelux rates its duties on certain starch products as had been promised by the Head of the German delegation. The Panel found that already the 'firm promise' of granting the tariff binding sufficed to create legitimate expectations.[128] The promise was neither made part of the formal schedule of tariff concessions nor deposited formally with the Secretariat, but simply contained in a letter by the chief of the German delegation.[129] This case was never settled[130] but simply 'noted'.[131]

EEC–Oilseeds I GATT 47 Panel Report (1989) In direct contrast to *Australia–Subsidy*, where withdrawing a subsidy had impaired the value of tariff concessions accorded to Chile and violated its legitimate expectations, the

125 *Germany–Sardines*, para 17.

126 *Ibid*.

127 See *ibid*, para 18; see also Cottier and Schefer, 1997, pp 159–63; Petersmann, 1991, pp 204–5, for a discussion of the case.

128 See *Germany–Starch and Potato Flour*, pp 77, 79; see von Bogdandy, 1992, p 98 and Cottier and Schefer, 1997, pp 159–63, for a discussion of the case.

129 See Petersman, 1991, 206.

130 See Jackson et al, 1995, p 363.

131 Petersmann, 1991, 206.

scenario of *EEC–Oilseeds I* is directly opposite: the contested issue of the case was not the lifting of a subsidy from which *foreign* fertilisers had benefitted, but the *introduction* of a subsidy to *domestic* producers at the expense of foreign ones. The EEC's subsidy on EEC oilseed was alleged to directly circumvent the duty free bindings on oilseed, agreed during the Dillon Round, and thus impaired the EEC's trading partners' expectation that all oilseed be exposed to global price competition:[132]

> The idea underlying them is that the improved competitive opportunities that can legitimately be expected from a tariff concession can be frustrated not only by measures proscribed by the General Agreement but also by measures consistent with that Agreement.[133]

The EC argued that no nullification or impairment could arise in the absence of any violation of specific obligations of the General Agreement.[134] The US in contrast argued that nullification and impairment could occur if a trading partner introduces a domestic measure subsequent to the adoption of the tariff concession and if that measure

— could not have reasonably been anticipated by the party bringing the complaint at the time of the negotiation of the concession; and
— upset the competitive position of the imported products (ie altered the pre-existing market relationship in the host country).[135]

The EC countered that it is not legitimate to expect the absence of production subsidies, even after the grant of a tariff concession, because Articles III:8(b) and XVI: 1 explicitly recognise the right of contracting parties to grant production subsidies. This right would be effectively eliminated if its exercise were assumed to impair tariff concessions:[136]

> The recognition of the legitimacy of an expectation relating to the use of production subsidies therefore in no way prevents a contracting party from using production subsidies consistently with the General Agreement; it merely delineates the scope of the protection of a negotiated balance of concessions. For these reasons the Panel found that the US may be assumed not to have anticipated the introduction of subsidies which protect Community producers of oilseeds completely from the movement of prices for imports and thereby prevent tariff concessions from having any impact on the competitive relationship between domestic and imported oilseeds.[137]

Declaring that legitimate expectations balance the scope of the protective albeit GATT-consistent measures, with the volume of trade liberalization

[132] See *EEC–Oilseeds I*, paras 131, 143; see Jackson et al, 1995, pp 357–64; Cottier and Schefer, 1997, pp 159, 162; Petersmann, 1991, pp 217–18; von Bogdandy, 1992, pp 102–3, for a discussion of the case.

[133] *Ibid*, para 144.

[134] See *ibid*, Panel Report, para 55.

[135] *Ibid*, para 58.

[136] *Ibid*, para 147.

[137] *Ibid*, para 148.

achieved through negotiated tariff concessions, the GATT Panel can be said to have refered to a well-described function of good faith in public international law, which is—according to Schwarzenberger, Zoller and others—that good faith functions to delimit the scope of rights and obligations:[138]

> For these reasons the Panel found that benefits accruing to the United States under Article II of the General Agreement in respect of the zero tariff bindings for oilseeds in the Community Schedule of Concessions were impaired as a result of subsidy schemes which operate to protect Community producers of oilseeds completely from the movement of prices of imports and thereby prevent the oilseeds tariff concessions from having any impact on the competitive relationship between domestic and imported oilseeds.[139]

US–Offset Act ('Byrd Amendment') *Appellate Body Report (2003)* When it appealed the *US–Offset Act ('Byrd Amendment')* Panel Report, the US asked the AB whether or not the Panel had erred in finding firstly that the US had not violated its obligations under Article 5.4 ADA and Article 11.4 of the ASCM.[140] However, the AB found that the US must be regarded as not having acted in good faith.[141]

While the issue of violation/NVNI complaints under Articles 26 DSU and XXIII: 1(b) GATT 94 did not arise directly, the AB issued two ambiguous if not contradictory statements on the correlation between a violation of WTO law and an action that is contrary to good faith. In the opening statement on good faith, the AB says: 'Given our conclusion that the CDSOA does not constitute a violation of Article 5.4 of the Anti-Dumping Agreement and Article 11.4 of the ASCM Agreement, the issue of whether the United States "may be regarded as not having acted in good faith" in enacting the CDSOA does not have the relevance it had for the Panel'.[142]

> Nothing, however, in the covered agreements supports the conclusion that simply because a WTO Member is found to have violated a substantive treaty provision, it has therefore not acted in good faith. In our view, it would be necessary to prove more than mere violation to support such a conclusion.[143]

The AB seemed to suggest that NVNI complaints no longer are the remedy of choice to protect good faith, because 'more than a mere violation must be shown'. With this statement, the AB directly overturned its findings of the earlier paragraph, where it implied that good faith could be protected only in the absence of a violation. Demanding that *more* than a *mere violation* must be

[138] See Schwarzenberger, 1955, pp 324ff; Zoller, 1977, pp 45, 343–6.

[139] *EEC–Oilseeds I*, Panel Report, para 152; see similarly, *EEC–Oilseeds II*, Panel Report, paras 85 and 90.

[140] ASCM, Annex 1A of the Marrakesh Agreement Establishing the WTO of 15 April 1994, *in* The Results of the Uruguay Round of Multilateral Trade Negotiations, The Legal Texts, GATT Secretariat, June 1994, WTO, Geneva.

[141] See *US–Offset Act ('Byrd Amendment')*, Panel Report, paras 7.63–7.64.

[142] *Ibid*, AB Report, para 295.

[143] *Ibid*, para 298.

proven, suggests that violation complaints are the only possible carriers of good faith claims, because this would entail that an additional, possibly subjective element would have to be proven in order to distinguish the good faith violation from any ordinary rule-violation. However, the AB statement that more than a mere violation must be proven for a good faith cause of action to stand, leaves many questions open, for instance:

— Must a subjective element of the intent to act inconsistently with WTO law be shown in order for the general principle of good faith to become enforceable in addition to a rule violation?
— Is acting contrary to good faith a cause of action for a NVNI-type complaint, or may a good faith violation be cause of action supplementary to the violation basis of a claim?

Conclusions 'True' NVNI cases compensate for the benefit impaired, which is the competitive trading opportunity a tariff or other concession has granted a WTO Member. In what Cottier and Schefer call 'true' and 'real' NVNI complaints,[144] Cho 'supplementary-mode' NVNI cases,[145] and the Panels 'traditional NVNI claim',[146] a direct causal link connects the measure offsetting the benefit with the negotiated concessions or the concessions under negotiations.

It remains debatable whether or not a cause of action demanding legal protection of one's legitimate expectations must always be brought under a NVNI-type complaint or whether a claim of frustration of legitimate expectations may also be brought under a violation complaint.[147] There are at least three reasons for this dilemma:

— Under the GATS most cases involving the PLE will be dealt with under violation complaints.[148] The reason for this is that Article XVII:3 GATS explicitly codifies the obligation to protect the reasonable expectations as to conditions of competition, so that the violation of PLE will amount to violating the text of a rule, as opposed to violating some sort of implicit principle. The fact that the GATS, in a further development from the GATT 94, has abolished the requirement of showing a violation of reasonable expectations, has led to the expanded PLE in recent jurisprudence, where an NVNI-type complaint is no longer necessary for bringing a PLE cause of action
— TRIPS does not cover NVNI complaints at all.
— The GATT 94 concept of NVNI also includes measures that violate GATT.[149] Under the GATS, a violation of PLE could be brought under Article XVII:3 as mentioned above, but it would be limited to allegations

[144] See Cottier and Schefer, 1997, p 182, who use the term 'real' or 'true' NVNI complaints.
[145] Cho, 1998, p 318.
[146] *Korea–Government Procurement*, Panel Report, para 7.84.
[147] Cottier and Schefer, 1997, p 181.
[148] See *ibid*.
[149] Art XXIII:3 GATS.

of a frustration of legitimate expectations pertaining to conditions of competition.

In a 'true' NVNI case, the impairment of a benefit relates to a concrete, identifiable improvement of multilateral trade. The improvement a member can legitimately expect may:

— accrue under the negotiated level of tariff or other concessions;
— be based upon the negotiation concessions; or
— relate to goal of the WTO, which is protected by the customary rule of *pacta sunt servanda*.

Traditionally, the benefit impaired has been the legitimate expectation as to the competitive opportunity guaranteed by a tariff or other concession.[150] The 'true' NVNI complaint precisely defines the competitive opportunity offset either as a tariff or another concession. Moreover, the

> products in question in NVNI cases seem to have a relatively close relationship; they are 'identical' or 'directly competitive' products', . . . which implies that to some extent supplementary mode NVNI cases, . . . play a pragmatic role of filling in the gap let by the general obligations in the GATT, including the Article III (national treatment) obligations.[151]

Since *Korea–Government Procurement*, the benefit can extend to a legitimate expectation as to a competitive opportunity generated by the negotiation of a concession.[152] The Panel found that what it termed 'traditional' NVNI complaints to be 'extended *pacta sunt servanda*'.[153] Thus, in *Korea–Government Procurement*, the Panel laid open the nexus between GATT/WTO NVNI complaints and the general principle of law of good faith, which is a correlation that Cottier and Schefer had identified in 1997.[154]

In order to avoid confusion between 'true' NVNI complaints, and ones that might be *considered* 'true' NVNI complaints but where there is no tariff or other concession offset, it is proposed to use the term 'broad' NVNI complaint for *Korea–Government Procurement*-type cases. This notion would regroup all those situations brought under a NVNI-type complaint, where the legitimate expectation relates to a more abstract benefit than a tariff or other negotiated concession, yet is narrow enough to be protected by a general principle of law, such as *pacta sunt servanda*, or perhaps, state responsibility.

The *US–Copyright* and *Canada–Pharmaceutical* cases, described below under the section entitled 'Extended Protection of Legitimate Expectations', do not fall under the 'broad' NVNI-type complaints, even though the legitimate expectation claim at their basis is more 'extended' than the nullification and impairment

[150] See Cho, 1998, pp 316–18.
[151] *Ibid*, p 318.
[152] See *Korea–Government Procurement*, Panel Report, para 7.93.
[153] *Ibid*, para 7.103.
[154] See Cottier and Schefer, 1997, p 148.

of a tariff concession. The reason is that for *US–Copyright* and *Canada–Pharmaceutical* the PLE brought a cause of action under a violation-type complaint and not a NVNI-type, probably because large parts of both cases related to the TRIPS, which still keeps the NVNI-type complaint suspended from applying to its substantive provisions.

In all the other cases where a legitimate expectation as to a competitive opportunity cannot be subsumed either under negotiated concessions or under the more extended notion of PLE referring to a general principle of law or a customary international rule, the situation is for the legislator to regulate and thus not a 'case' for the adjudicator; hence, they are (using Hudec's words) 'wrong' cases.[155]

In the *Japan–Film* Panel ruling, the Panel denied the US a NVNI ground of complaint because it failed to show how measures of promotion, distribution or restriction upon large stores selling film, 'nullifie[s] or impair[s] benefits accruing to the United States in respect of competitive market-access expectations for imported film or paper'.[156]

In *Japan–Film* the US's cause of action was general anti-competitive behaviour by Japan, whether it was private actions tolerated by Japan or anticompetitive government regulation. The discriminatory treatment against the US film producers was without any relation to a GATT-specific benefit such as tariffs, and resembled more a politically motivated attempt to broaden the WTO's scope of jurisdiction by competition law. *Japan–Film* thus qualifies as an 'independent-mode' or 'wrong' NVNI case.[157]

'Wrong', 'Overbroad' and 'Broad' Non-violation Nullification and Impairment Cases

'Wrong cases' involve the impairment of legally unreasonable but politically important expectations. The question is firstly, whether or not case law of the Panels has legitimately offered protection to such constellations. Secondly, the question is whether the Panels have gone too far in extending the relief for the frustration of legitimate expectations ('wrong' cases) where they have mistakenly understood the protection of legitimate expectations to provide for an 'overbroad' sense. The issue of resolving 'wrong' NVNI complaints has gained importance with ongoing negotiations as to whether or not to establish the NVNI remedy within TRIPS.

How can one recognise what Hudec terms 'wrong' NVNI complaints? In a 'wrong' NVNI complaint, a member claims the frustration of a legitimate expectations as to equal competitive opportunities for its products, services or

[155] Cho, 1998, pp 329–30, with references to Hudec, who introduced the term of 'wrong NVNI complaints'. See Barfield, 2001, pp 45ff for 'judicial overreach' at the WTO and its critics.

[156] See *Japan–Film*, Panel Report, para 10.366.

[157] Cho, 1998, p 319.

nationals, on the internal market, based on a 'broad[er]' benefit than tariffs or another type of concession.[158]

Cottier and Schefer define 'wrong' NVNI complaints as 'constellations in which legally unreasonable, but politically very important, expectations are impaired by the action of others', which are not at all specific to the trade area, but exist 'in any other domain of human conduct'.[159]

Roessler articulates the concern that expanding 'the application of Article XXIII:1(b) . . . to benefits generated by the general policy obligations set out in the WTO Agreements that go beyond their good faith performance', would be 'inconsistent with the intent of Article 3.2 DSU'.[160] Similarly to the later *Korea–Government Procurement* Panel, Roessler sets out the general principle of performing treaties in good faith, ie *pacta sunt servanda,* as the threshold for distinguishing a 'true' from an 'overbroad' NVNI complaint.[161] In this context, Cho says:

> [T]hese cases include issues where current Members have not yet established relevant substantive norms on which Panel decisions can be based or cases in which sovereign questions arise as to whether a Panel should second-guess the policy determination of a Member country.[162]

Most agree that such politically motivated NVNI complaints, which often function to fill in the gaps in the law of the WTO Agreements, should be contained. Proposals are, firstly, to negotiate a new set of WTO rules for filling in gaps in yet unregulated areas of cross-border trade. Secondly, one would have to encourage the WTO judiciary to increase its references to principles of general public international law.

However, there are voices advocating for maintaining a broad existence of NVNI complaints, in order to keep up the flexibility associated with 'maintain[ing] the balance of interests even in cases where the substantial law does not cover the issues at hand'.[163] Some even fear that under the WTO, compared to the old GATT, where a member could veto the adoption of such a 'wrong' Panel report, 'wrong' NVNI complaints will proliferate, because the WTO no longer is equipped with such a 'screening mechanism . . . to expel irrelevant cases'.[164]

Already successfully tested in the *Korea–Government Procurement* case, a method for dismissing 'wrong', that is, 'overbroad' NVNI complaints, is to charge the complaining member with knowledge of the change in circumstances or of the gap in the law, to the effect that its NVNI complaint will remain unsubstantiated for lack of non-foreseeability.[165]

[158] *Cf ibid*, pp 330–1 referring to Hudec.
[159] Cottier and Schefer, 1997, p 182.
[160] Roessler, 1997, p 142.
[161] See *Korea–Government Procurement*, Panel Report, paras 7.93–7.102.
[162] Cho, 1998, p 330.
[163] Von Bogdandy, 1992, p 110.
[164] Cho, 1998, p 330.
[165] See *Korea–Government Procurement*, Panel Report, para 7.119.

So far, only in the *Korea–Government Procurement* did the Panel successfully broaden the scope of an NVNI cause of action without violating the separation of judicial and adjudicative powers in the WTO. The Panel in *Korea–Government Procurement* substituted the missing basis for claiming PLE with the customary rule of *pacta sunt servanda*. By proxy of *pacta sunt servanda*, the Panel avoided engaging in 'overbroad' interpretation of the facts and law in the case and thereby escaped the accusation of creating a category of 'wrong' PLE.

The *Korea–Government Procurement* case shows that as long as PLE is based upon NVNI action, PLE is validly extended, and the 'broadened' PLE is the legitimate cause of action of a 'broad' but not 'overbroad' NVNI complaint.

The specific constellation of the *Korea–Government Procurement* case leads this study to identify a third category of NVNI-type complaints, in addition to 'true', 'wrong' and 'overbroad' complaints, a category which this study calls 'broad' NVNI complaints. 'Broad' NVNI may be defined as those complaints, where the WTO legal basis for claiming the frustration of legitimate expectations is missing, but where a general principle of law or customary international law steps in to fill that gap of substantive law.

'Broad' NVNI complaints qualify as a 'procedural extension of the concept of PLE' and are further described below in the section on the extensions of the concept of PLE, particularly under the heading of 'procedural extensions'.

Compared with an extended definition of PLE, a 'broad' NVNI describes the broadening of the scope of the NVNI cause of action, while 'extending' relates to the scope underlying the basis of a 'broad' claim, which is the 'extended' PLE. In sum, an 'extended' PLE and a 'broad' NVNI complaint may go hand-in-hand.

Japan–Semi-Conductors *GATT 47 Panel Report (1988): a 'Wrong Case'* The EEC had asked the Panel to examine whether or not an export barrier (such as voluntary export restraints, export cartels and export taxes) as opposed to the standard import barriers, could form the basis of a NVNI complaint.[166] The Panel did not consider the argument raised because the EC was unable to demonstrate evidence of a competitive disadvantage vis-à-vis exports from the US, which were allegedly bound in an agreement between the US and Japan aiming at access of US products on the Japanese market and preventing Japanese dumping on the US market. The EEC had alleged that the voluntary export restraints (VERs) that existed between the US and Japan, though not covered by GATT law, were nevertheless inconsistent with the GATT objectives.[167] The case was adopted but for the NVNI ground of complaint, for which the EEC had brought insufficient evidence.

[166] See *Japan–Semi-Conductors*, para 33; see Cottier and Schefer, 1997, pp 159, 162; Petersmann, 1991, pp 213–14; von Bogdandy, 1992, pp 100–1, for a discussion of the case.

[167] *Japan–Semi-Conductors*, para 131; see Petersmann, 1991, p 217; for a discussion of the case.

The case is important for demonstrating that non-standard trade barriers, even outside direct government control, can negatively influence negotiated tariff concessions.[168] It is to be kept in mind that through linkage of WTO law with related treaties (CBD, World Health Organization, Food and Agriculture Organization), the rules of which contain trade-specific obligations, there might be more such non-standard, 'wrong' NVNI complaints in the future, when WTO Members allege that a specific trade obligation or prohibition of such a related treaty, infringes upon the negotiated tariff or other concessions of the WTO. Authorising NVNI complaints for non-standard trade measures would much expand the scope of NVNI complaints. To some authors as well as to the AB, such PLE based on 'wrong' type of complaints would destabilise the predictability and security of the multilateral trading system. Others to the contrary stress the benefits for trade if such 'overbroad' complains were legitimate.

In *Japan–Film*, the US claimed that the benefits from trade liberalization for the Kodak Film company had been impaired by actions that neither solely targeted foreign importers nor were taken by the government. Since Japan's measures were not found in violation of GATT law, the US had been deprived of the grounds for a violation-type complaint. However, the US had claimed and the Panel confirmed that the US could bring a non-violation-type complaint on the basis that its legitimate expectations as to fair conditions of competetion had been frustrated. The US had claimed that the benefits from GATT liberalization had been impaired because Japan's laws were tolerating monopolies.[169] However, the Panel found that since Japans regulation functioned effectively as an incentive for Japans film producers to monopolise production and conclude price agreements to the detriment of foreign companies, the US claim that its reasonable expectations as to benefits arising from the negotiated tariff reductions brought under a NVNI cause of action, were justified:

> We reach this conclusion in considering the purpose of Article XXIII:1(b), which is to protect the balance of concessions under GATT by providing a means to redress government actions not otherwise regulated by GATT rules that nonetheless nullify or impair a Member's legitimate expectations of benefits from tariff negotiations. To achieve this purpose, in our view, it is important that the kinds of government actions considered being measures covered by Article XXIII:1(b) should not be defined *in an unduly restrictive manner* (footnotes omitted, emphasis added).[170]

Korea–Government Procurement *Panel Report (2001): a 'Broad Case'* The *Korea–Government Procurement* case of 2001 'extended *pacta sunt servanda*' and 'broadened' the NVNI-complaint (see below for a more complete description of the case). Therefore the *Korea–Government Procurement* case will be discussed twice, once from the perspective of a 'broad'—but not necessarily

[168] See von Bogdandy, 1992, pp 100–1.
[169] See *Japan–Film*, Panel Report, paras 10.49–10.50.
[170] *Ibid*, para 10.50.

'wrong'—NVNI-complaint and, further below, from the viewpoint of an 'extended' PLE, which—for *Korea–Government Procurement*—manifests itself by deriving the PLE cause of action on the duty to negotiate in good faith, which itself is based in the customary rule of *pacta sunt servanda*.

Two years after *Japan–Film*, the Panel in the *Korea–Government Procurement* decision used the general principle of international law to expand the notion of a 'true' NVNI complaint.

If Korea offset the US service providers' competitive bidding opportunities by inadequate submission procedures and bidding deadlines it unlawfully modified such terms of negotiation agreed upon between Korea and the US and thus, the Panel found Korea to have violated the duty to negotiate in good faith. The Panel thus found that the impaired competitive opportunity constituted the grounds of a NVNI despite the fact that no 'actual Schedule commitment[s]' formed the grounds of complaint.[171] Thus, the Panel admitted a NVNI complaint in the absence of actual concessions, but on the grounds that Korea had violated its duty to negotiate in good faith.[172]

Capsizing the general principle of law of good faith in order to create a more law-based, 'true' NVNI ground of complaint, to replace the fact that there were 'no concessions given by Korea', was an important development for the 'well-established GATT principle' of legitimate expectations.

The decisive role the Panel attributed to general public international law in this case has gained only little and negative attention in recent scholarship.[173] On the one hand McRae has criticised the decision as an example of an unlawful importation of additional obligations under the disguise of public international law. McRae, in contrast to the Panel and mainstream doctrine, maintains the scope of Article 3.2 DSU authorises only interpretive references to public international law, but prohibits incorporating supplementary international law obligations into the WTO.[174]

> The . . . concern . . . is whether the treaty obligations of WTO Members are to be supplemented by additional obligations derived from customary international law. On the face of it, Article 3.2 DSU says that they cannot . . . This distinction was ignored by the Panel in *Korea–Government Procurement* which took the view that unless expressly or implicitly excluded by the WTO Agreements, public international law can be invoked by a Panel as the basis for a substantive finding against a Member.[175]

When the Panel employed to good faith to fill in the gap of Korea's missing scheduled concessions, it proved that the WTO's legalisation can go hand in hand with its integration into general public international law. As the custom-

[171] *Korea–Government Procurement*, Panel Report, para 7.118.

[172] See *ibid*, paras 7.93–7.119.

[173] *Ibid* para 7.117; see, eg Hilf, 2001, p 122; Pauwelyn, 2001, p 543; Lennard, 2002, p 43; Canal-Forgues, 2003, p 119, for four authors who have identified the value of the *Korea–Government Procurement* Panel Report for the WTO's relationship to general public international law.

[174] See McRae, 2003, pp 711, 713.

[175] *Ibid*, p 713.

ary rule of *pacta sunt servanda* prevents judicial law-making (Article 3.2 DSU) it simultaneously completes the WTO's gaps. The *Korea–Government Procurement* Panel promotes the WTO system's openness towards international law.

THE NOTION OF 'EXTENDED' PROTECTION OF LEGITIMATE EXPECTATIONS IN THE *KOREA–GOVERNMENT PROCUREMENT* PANEL REPORT

The theme of this next section is what the *Korea–Government Procurement* Panel called 'extended' PLE. The diverging decisions by the Panels and the AB on PLE mirrors the two camps in scholarship, namely:

— Those who represent the WTO as a rule-oriented legal system guided by the mission of containing equity law jurisdiction and 'limiting the use of flexibilities' to a minimum; and in sharp contrast,
— to want to use PLE as a 'catalyst for integrat[ing]' the WTO legal system into the broader one of international law more generally.

In *Korea-Government Procurement* the Panel was undecided whether a PLE cause of action could be extended beyond the protection of conditions of competition on a foreign market, to the duty to negotiate in good faith.

To extend the PLE cause of action according to the Panels, would mean to enable PLE to vindicate the duty to negotiate in good faith, to protect the predictability of trade opportunities in the future and to protect expectations as to equal treatment in relation to the MFN (instead of under the NT clause). The NVNI choice of action has usually been the incorrect type of complaint for claiming the frustration of a legitimate expectation, in an 'extended' sense, so that the *Korea–Government Procurement* Panel found 'extended' PLE claims to have to be brought in a violation-type complaint instead.

Extending Protection of Legitimate Expectations and its Limits in a Rule-oriented WTO

The conditions of competition, which amount to the 'benefit' protected by legitimate expectations, relate either to tariff concessions (GATT) or to the specific commitments (GATS). However, under an extended concept of PLE, PLE may protect even the 'reasonable expectation of enjoying competitive bidding opportunities' under the plurilateral GPA.[176] Moreover, the concept of extended PLE could also encompass benefits impaired or reasonable expectations frustrated by violations of explicit treaty goals, such as the security and predictability of a

[176] *Korea–Government Procurement*, Panel Report, para 7.103.

transitory patent system under TRIPS Article 70.[177] This is in contrast to claims of violation of positive rights and obligations incumbent on WTO Member States. A claim of frustration of expectations legitimately derived from treaty goals amounts to holding a WTO Member State responsible for the expectations it creates, as opposed to holding that Member State responsible for fulfilling its rights and obligations under the WTO Agreements:

> There is no denying that economic operators—in this case potential patent applicants—are influenced by the legal insecurity created by the continued existence of mandatory legislation that requires the rejection of product patent applications in respect of pharmaceutical and agricultural chemical products.[178]

Conditions of competition are not a reserved domain of trade in goods under GATT Article III GATT, but are a 'precept . . . governing the [entire] multilateral trading system' (*India–Patents, Panel Report*).[179] Consequently, Panel jurisprudence has established legitimate expectations as to competitive opportunities as a principle applicable to all the WTO Agreements (*India–Patents,* Panel Report). To this day, appellate practice has not accepted the comprehensive PLE throughout all the WTO Agreements. The AB equates the PLE cause of action to non-violation nullification and impairment (NVNI), whereas the Panels recognise that PLE may be the cause of action of a violation complaint (*India–Patents,* Panel Report, 1998).

GATT 47 and GATT 94 practice 'extended' the GATT/WTO-specific principle of PLE.[180] The earliest expansion of the scope of PLE occurred with the *Australia–Subsidy* decision of 1950. Doctrine subsequently depicted PLE in *Australia–Subsidy* to function as a prohibition of *abus de droit*.[181] The *India–Patents* (1997) and *EC–LAN* (1998) Panel Reports found PLE to express an element of 'good faith interpretation',[182] which the 'customary rule of interpretation of public international law' had codified under Article 31 VCLT (see above).[183] Additionally, the *EC–LAN* Panel Report established that legitimate expectations would protect tariff treatment, and it sufficed that the tariff treatment had only been 'contemplated' by a schedule pursuant to Article II:5 GATT (*EC–LAN*).[184] Again, the *EC LAN* Panel, based on the earlier *India–Patents* Panel decision, propagated the possibility of protecting legitimate expectations under a violation-type complaint, as codified under Article XXIII:1(a) GATT 94

[177] See *India–Patents*, Panel Report, paras 7.21, 7.34–7.35, 7.41–7.43, 7.62.

[178] *Ibid*, para 7.35.

[179] *Ibid*, para 7.30.

[180] *Cf Korea–Government Procurement*, Panel Report, paras 7.102ff, which describes PLE as an 'extended *pacta sunt servanda*'.

[181] See Cottier and Schefer, 1997, p 178.

[182] *India–Patents*, Panel Report, para 7.18; *EC–LAN*, Panel Report, para 8.25; see also *US–Section 301*, *Panel Report*, para 7.67, of 2000, which takes up the expression.

[183] See *India–Patents*, Panel Report, paras 7.18; *EC–LAN*, Panel Report, para 8.19.

[184] See *EC–LAN*, Panel Report, paras 8.23ff.

and Article 23 DSU. The *EC–Asbestos* AB Report confirmed that legitimate expectations may be protected under a claim of violation of Articles I, II:5, III GATT and, conceivably, Article XVII:3 GATS, except that such a claim of violation will have to be brought additionally, instead of alternatively, to a claim of rule-violation.[185]

Most recently, the *Korea–Government Procurement* Panel of 2000 found that PLE could be derived from the 'principle of international law' of *pacta sunt servanda*, which includes among others the duty to negotiate in good faith.[186]

Procedural Extensions: 'Broad' Non-violation Complaints and Violation Complaints

This section describes how the procedural extension of the NVNI-type complaint or the violation-type complaint relates to the substantive extension of the PLE cause of action. As the *Korea–Government Procurement* Panel decision (described above) has shown, a broad scope of protection through a NVNI claim is legitimate WTO practice today, as long as the underlying PLE cause of action has been legitimately expanded by a general principle of law stepping into the gap of WTO law.

The issue of whether or not it is possible to claim protection of one's legitimate expectations through a violation complaint is controversial. A claim of frustration of a legitimate expectation will not in and of itself constitute the grounds for a violation complaint; rather the inconsistent measure in violation of a WTO provision simultaneously nullifies and impairs an additional benefit addressed by the legitimate expectation.

Protection of Legitimate Expectations under 'Broad' Non-violation Nullification and Impairment Complaints

The following section refers to the section on 'broad' NVNI-complaints above, where the Panel had introduced with *Korea–Government Procurement* a decision that procedurally extended the scope of PLE by construing a 'broad' but legitimate NVNI-type complaint, based upon a notion of PLE extended by the customary rule of *pacta sunt servanda*.

[185] See *India–Patents*, Panel Report, para 7.40; *EC–LAN*, Panel Report, para 8.23; *EC–Asbestos*, Panel Report, para 8.263; *EC–Asbestos*, AB Report, para 187; against *India–Patents*, AB Report, para 42; *EC–LAN*, AB Report, para 80.

[186] *Korea–Government Procurement*, Panel Report, paras 7.93, 7.120.

Protection of Legitimate Expectations under Violation Complaints

India–Patents *and* EC–LAN *Panel Reports (1998)* Alleging the frustration of legitimate expectations in a violation complaint are the *India-Patents* case (January 1998), where the violation of the 'well-established GATT principle' of 'conditions of competition' was at stake, and the *EC–LAN* (June 1998) case, where the violation of Article II:5 relating to tariff classification under GATT was at the basis of a request for PLE.[187]

The Panels in both *India-Patents* and *EC–LAN* maintained that Articles I, II:5 and III GATT encompass a protection for legitimate expectations so that a frustration of such can be brought in a violation complaint:[188]

> The fact that the Oilseeds Panel report concerns a NVNI complaint does not affect the validity of this reasoning in cases where an actual violation of tariff commitments is alleged. If anything, such a direct violation would involve a situation where expectations concerning tariff concessions were even more firmly grounded.[189]

The Panel in *EC–LAN* appeared to find that those provisions in the WTO Agreements which implicitly refer to some sort of legitimate expectation, will be violated when such expectations are frustrated. Such provisions are not only Article II GATT as in the present case, but also include Articles III GATT and XVII:3(b) GATS:

> We now turn to the examination of whether the actual tariff treatment of LAN equipment entitles the United States to legitimate expectations in this regard sufficient to establish its claim of a violation of Article II of GATT 94 by the European Communities (emphasis added).[190]

The US claimed that legitimate expectations may be alleged in the context of a violation complaint under Articles II or III GATT:

> The United States believes that the Panel properly relied on the concept of 'legitimate expectations' and that the decision in India-Patents does not require the rejection of the Panel's use of 'legitimate expectations' as a factor in its analysis of whether the European Communities is in violation of its obligations under Article II of the GATT 94.[191]

In result, the Panel sided with the US with one reservation. The Panel did not agree completely with the US that PLE should be separated from claims under Article II or III GATT. Neither this Panel nor its predecessor, the *India–Patents* Panel, found that there existed any good reason for separating legitimate expectations and Articles II and III GATT. To the contrary, the *India–Patents* and

[187] *India–Patents*, Panel Report, para 7.20; see *EC–LAN*, Panel Report, paras 8.23–8.28, 8.31.

[188] See *India–Patents*, Panel Report, para 7.20; *EC–LAN*, Panel Report, paras 40–1(US), para 8.23 (Panel).

[189] *EC–LAN*, Panel Report, para 8.23.

[190] *Ibid*, para 8.45.

[191] See *ibid*, para 40.

EC–LAN Panels found that in order to protect the respective parties' legitimate expectations it was necessary to build upon those provisions:

> In the view of the United States, it is both possible and necessary to distinguish between the concepts employed in enforcing obligations under Articles III or XI of the GATT, the concepts involved in a 'NVNI nullification or impairment complaint' and the concept of 'legitimate expectations' employed by the Panel in the present dispute. According to the United States, all three concepts are intellectually and historically distinct and independent.[192]

The EC appealed to the AB to overturn the Panel's finding because it had as in *India–Patents* before:

> meld[ed] the legally-distinct bases for 'violation' and 'NVNI' complaints under Article XXIII of the GATT 94 into a uniform cause of action which is not consistent with Article XXIII.[193]

The EC made this statement because it believed that the *EC–LAN* case

> was not concerned with the affectation of competitive relationship between imported and domestic products, but rather with the tariff treatment of certain products compared to the concessions scheduled by the EC in the WTO.[194]
>
> [E]ven more erroneously, . . . the context that the present Panel considered to be relevant for the interpretation of Schedule LXXX in a violation complaint has been deduced from the interpretation of Article II in a NVNI complaint.[195]

India–Patents *and* EC–LAN *Appellate Body Reports (1998)* Conservative AB practice in *India–Patents* and *EC–LAN* overturned the progressive Panel decisions on the issue of PLE, and reinstated the status quo, holding that PLE may be protected only via a NVNI-type complaint. Both the *India–Patents* and *EC–LAN* AB Reports argued that PLE as to conditions of competition under Articles III GATT, and as to tariff classification under Article II:5 GATT, can only be brought in NVNI complaints:[196]

> The concept of 'reasonable expectations', which the Panel refers to as 'legitimate expectations', is a concept that was developed in the context of NVNI complaints. As we stated in *India–Patents*, for the Panel to use this concept in the context of a violation complaint 'melds the legally-distinct bases for "violation" and "NVNI" complaints under Article XXIII of the GATT 94 into one uniform cause of action' and is not in accordance with established GATT practice (footnotes omitted).[197]

[192] *Ibid*, para 42.
[193] *Ibid*, para 14.
[194] *Ibid*, para 15.
[195] See *ibid*, para 14.
[196] See *India–Patents*, AB Report, para 36; *EC–LAN*, AB Report, paras 77, 80.
[197] *EC–LAN*, AB Report, para 80 with reference to *India–Patents*, AB Report, para 42.

NVNI complaints sanction members for *de jure* WTO-legal conduct, which offsets the trade liberalising effect of negotiated concessions. However, a WTO Member may also be required to make adjustments when its measures outrightly violate or 'conflict with the provisions of that Agreement' (Article 26 DSU).[198] Under GATT the 'nullification or impairment' can consist, pursuant to the text of Article XXIII:1(b) and confirmed by *EC–Asbestos* jurisprudence, either of a rule-violation or a measure which does not conflict with the GATT:

> It follows that a measure may, *at one and the same time*, be inconsistent with, or in breach of, a provision of the GATT 94 *and*, nonetheless, give rise to a cause of action under Article XXIII:1(b).[199]

Korea–Government Procurement *Panel Report (2000)* The *Korea–Government Procurement* Panel, despite expanding the PLE cause of action by introducing the concept of *pacta sunt servanda* as an additional basis for a PLE claim, refused to handle the case as a violation-type complaint. Had the *Korea–Government Procurement* Panel been consequent in its expansion of the scope of PLE, it would have had to agree that the logical consequence of violation of a positive rule of international law, which the principle of *pacta sunt servanda* embodies, is a violation-type complaint. Had the *Korea–Government Procurement* Panel completed its progressive approach, it should have allowed the claim of frustration of such legitimate expectations to be claimed under a rule-violation instead of a non-violation.

Possibly, extending the substantive scope of PLE to include the PLE as to the duty to negotiate in good faith under the general principle of law of *pacta sunt servanda*, was already a far-enough step for the Panel to take, so that in the end it seemed more acceptable to leave the claim unsubstantiated because the US could not prove the elements for successfully bringing PLE under a NVNI-type complaint. Instead the Panel preferred to maintain the NVNI-type complaint alleged by the US, with the result that it kept the US bound to the high threshold of showing the causal link between measure and benefit impaired and the non-foreseeability of Korea's change of legislation.

Had the Panel not stopped short at simply linking PLE with *pacta sunt servanda*, but had also changed the NVNI complaint into a violation of *pacta sunt servanda*, the likelihood that the US could have won the case on the ground of its legitimate expectations would have increased.[200]

EC–Asbestos *Appellate Body Report (2001)* In an important shift of its previous *India–Patents* and *EC–LAN* jurisprudence, the *EC–Asbestos* AB decisions argued that an Article II:5 or III GATT claim of violation can be brought together with a claim for compensation (NVNI) of frustrated expectations as to these provisions.

[198] Petersmann, 1991, pp 224, 226.
[199] *EC–Asbestos*, AB Report, para 187.
[200] See *Korea–Government Procurement*, Panel Report, para 7.100.

Nonetheless the acknowledgment in *EC–Asbestos* that Article II:5 and III GATT, or conceivably and Article I GATT XVII:3 GATS, constitute the basis for legitimate expectations differs from the *India–Patents* and *EC–LAN* jurisprudence of the Panels. The difference is that the AB in *EC–Asbestos* still held that any claim of a frustrated legitimate expectation would have to be brought under a NVNI-type complaint, even if the legitimate expectation related to conditions of competition guaranteed by Articles I, II:5, III GATT, and Article XVII:3 GATS. The Panels in contrast had found that in the specific cases of Articles I, II:5 and III GATT (conceivably also Article XVII:3 GATS), the ground of complaint of frustrated legitimate expectation could be contained in a claim of violation.[201]

Substantive Extensions: Articles I & II GATT 1994, Principle of WTO Law

EC–Citrus Products *(1985): Article I GATT*

The *EC–Citrus Products* case of 1985, which remained unadopted, expanded the PLE beyond tariffs, to so-called 'non-tariff benefits'. The US had alleged that the EC tariff treatment (preferences) accorded to citrus imports from Mediterranean countries nullified or impaired benefits accruing to the US under the MFN treatment (Article I: 1).[202]

The merit of *EC–Citrus Products* for the development of the principle of legitimate expectations is the expansion of the term 'benefit', which thereby opened NVNI complaints as to the impairment of legitimate expectations as to conditions of competition also to the competitive opportunities among the different importers into a foreign market.

The EC's preferential treatment did not offset bound tariff concessions; rather the preferences granted by the EC infringed upon 'only' unbound US tariffs. Although complaints brought previously under Article XXIII:l(b) had related to benefits arising from Article II, it believed that this did not signify that Article XXIII:1(b) was limited only to those benefits. The drafting history of Article XXIII confirmed that this Article, including paragraph l(b), protected any benefit under the General Agreement. This would include then the benefits accruing to the US under Article I:1, which applied to bound and unbound tariff items alike'.[203]

Nevertheless, the preferential tariff had operated in practice to affect adversely US–EC trade in these products and 'to upset the competitive relationship

[201] See *EC–LAN*, Panel Report, paras 8.23, 8.69–8.70; see *India–Patents*, Panel Report, para 7.20.

[202] See *EC–Citrus Products*, paras 1.5, 4.25. The countries favourably treated vis-à-vis other third country citrus importers were Algeria, Cyprus, Egypt, Israel, Jordan, Lebanon, Malta, Morocco, Spain, Tunisia and Turkey. See Cottier and Schefer, 1997, pp 159, 163; Petersmann, 1991, pp 210–13; von Bogdandy, 1992, pp 98–9, 104–6, for discussion of the case.

[203] *EC–Citrus Products*, para 4.36.

between the US and the EC's Mediterranean suppliers'.[204] The Panel found the grant of preferential tariffs to Mediterranean citrus exporters to be 'public knowledge' and thus 'foreseeable' to the US.[205]

The 'contracting parties had refrained from making a recommendation under Article XXIV: 7 on the EEC agreements with the Mediterranean countries on the understanding that the rights of third countries would thereby not be affected'.[206] Therefore, the Panel reached the conclusion that in this particular situation the balance of rights and obligations underlying Articles I and XXIV of the General Agreement had been upset to the disadvantage of the contracting parties, and that the US was therefore entitled to offsetting or compensatory adjustment to the extent that the grant of the preferences had caused substantial adverse effects to its actual trade or its trade opportunities.[207]

Because of objections by the Contracting Parties and the adoption of a bilateral agreement between the EC and the US, the Panel report of 7 February 1985 was not adopted.[208]

EC–LAN *Panel Report (1998): Article II:5 GATT*

The *EC–LAN* Panel extended the 'traditional' basis of a legitimate expectations complaint, namely Article III GATT, to Article II:5 GATT, which it found to implicitly contain in its first sentence, a measure of protection for legitimate expectations:

> [R]eceiving from another contracting party the treatment which the first contracting party believes to have been contemplated by a concession provided for in the appropriate Schedule annexed to this Agreement.

The EC had not modified the level of tariff concessions but had only switched the classification of certain computer equipment from one tariff heading to another. The US expectations therefore did not relate to competitive opportunities offset pursuant to Article III GATT, but rather to the EC violating Article II:5 GATT. In concreto, the US expectations related to the obligation to grant a product 'the treatment which the first contracting party believes to have been contemplated by a concession'. The Panel found the US legitimate expectations to consist in 'expectations regarding the continuation of the actual tariff treatment prevailing at the time of the tariff negotiations'.[209] '[T]he existence of this

[204] *Ibid*, para 5.1(j).
[205] See *ibid*, para 4.32.
[206] *Ibid*, para 5.1(g).
[207] *Ibid*.
[208] See Petersmann, 1991, pp 210–13; but see Jackson et al, 1995, p 363, who claim it was never adopted for 'lack of justification'.
[209] *EC–LAN*, Panel Report, para 8.55.

provision [Article II:5] confirms that legitimate expectations are a vital element in the interpretation of Article II and tariff schedules'.[210]

The Panel found that the US expectations deserved to be protected because 'the security and predictability . . . cannot be maintained without protection of such legitimate expectations'.[211]

In the result the Panel confirmed that the actual tariff treatment of LAN equipment by the EC differed from the negotiated tariff treatment during the Uruguay Round. In the Panel's view, this change entitled the US to legitimate expectations sufficient to establish a claim of violation of Article II GATT 94 by the EC:[212]

> We find that the United States was entitled to legitimate expectations that LAN equipment would continue to be accorded tariff treatment as automatic data-processing machines (ADP) machines in the European Communities, based on the actual tariff treatment during the Uruguay Round, . . . It is clear from evidence that these legitimate expectations were frustrated by the subsequent change in the classification practice in the European Communities. . . . We thus find that LAN equipment should have obtained the tariff treatment afforded to ADP machines in Schedule LXXX and that the European Communities has violated Article II:1 of GATT 94 by failing to accord imports of LAN equipment from the United States treatment no less favourable than that provided for under heading 84.71 or heading 84.73.[213]

However, since the Panel substantiated the claim of violation, it considered it unnecessary to examine whether or not the EC's reclassification had nullified or impaired 'the value of concessions accruing to the US'.[214] Moreover, the Panel refered to its practice of presuming a claim of nullification and impairment if a violation had been shown.[215]

Article II:5, last sentence provides for the remedy of 'compensatory adjustment' in cases where a reclassification may not have been contemplated by a concession. Where tariff treatment as claimed by the 'first contracting party . . . cannot be accorded' due to a court ruling of that other contracting party, a cause of action of PLE under a non-violation-type complaint may be given.

Providing for a compensatory adjustment remedy brings a potential violation Article II:5 GATT closer to a NVNI nullification and impairment, and thus also closer to the traditional remedy for the frustration of legitimate expectations.

[210] *Ibid*, para 8.24.
[211] *Ibid*, para 8.25.
[212] *Ibid*, paras 8.45, 8.60–8.62.
[213] *Ibid*, paras 8.60–8.62.
[214] *Ibid*, para 8.70.
[215] *Ibid*, paras 8.69–8.70.

Substantive Extension Towards a Principle of WTO Law

The third type of extension of PLE protects expectations related to the 'predictability needed to plan future trade'.[216] Instead of proposing a procedural tool for extending PLE, as for example a violation-type complaint, the expansion of PLE here occurs over a substantive principle of WTO law created by Panel practice. By attaching the concept of PLE to a creation of jurisprudence derived from the Preamble of the WTO Agreement and Article 3.2 first sentence of the DSU, the Panels have gone to great lengths to afford PLE protection. However, their concept of 'predictability needed to plan future trade', is in essence what the WTO is about, and could become, if followed by future Panel decisions, a WTO-Panel Principle.[217]

India–Patents *Panel Report (1997)* India's patent protection regime under construction neither guarantees the novelty of an invention nor safeguards, during the period of time of its transitional regime, the priority of patent applications. This situation had created uncertainty with respect to the future exploitation of patents in India, after the transitory regime cedes to a system of effective patent protection. This situation was at issue when the US asked the Panel to protect its legitimate expectations as to the US patent owners' 'right' under the TRIPS to obtain legally enforceable patent rights under Indian law, so that during the transitory regime—accorded to India under the TRIPS—the US patent owners could at least develop some type of business plans for selling their pharmaceuticals on the Indian market.

Under the transitional regime exception of Article 70.8 TRIPS, developing countries without operational patent protection for inventions at the time of the entry into force of the Uruguay Round results, are required to at least set in place the infrastructure for guaranteeing that the novelty of applications for pharmaceutical and agricultural chemical product patents is preserved until actual patent protection rights are granted. In India, this infrastructure had taken the form of a registry for filing patent applications according to their date of registry with the Indian authorities, in order to later calculate the time period of patent protection from the moment of registration.

In the *India–Patents* case, the US claimed that India's mailbox filing system infringed the minimal standard of legal security required for transitory regimes under Articles 70.8 and 70.9 and by this token also distorted the fair conditions of competition among different third-country inventors on the Indian market.[218]

In order to sanction India for frustrating the US's and the EC's patent applicants' legitimate expectations as to market exclusivity on the Indian market, the

[216] *India–Patents*, Panel Report, para 7.30.

[217] See Art 3.2 DSU first sentence, 'The dispute settlement system of the WTO is a central element in providing security and predictability to the multilateral trading system'.

[218] See *India–Patents*, Panel Report, paras 7.34, 7.41, 7.63, 8.1. Thomas Cottier served as Chairman of the *India–Patents* Panel.

Panel used the 'well-established GATT principle', which it derived from Article XXIII GATT. It thus sought to protect the US (specifically US patent applicants') expectations regarding their conditions of competition.[219]

> The protection of legitimate expectations of members regarding the conditions of competition is a well-established GATT principle, which derives in part from Article XXIII, the basic dispute settlement provisions of GATT (and the WTO).[220]

The Panel found that legitimate expectations under the TRIPS protected the foreseeable benefits of patent exploitation and the 'predictability to plan future trade', which an operational filing system for patent applicants would prospectively guarantee in lieu of the not yet available patent term protection.[221]

Curiously, even if India's limping patent registration system endangered the conditions of competitions for third-country applicants both vis-à-vis the domestic Indian operators, and vis-à-vis the other third-country applicants, the Panel did not relate—according to its previous practice—the 'well-established GATT-principle' either to Article III GATT (non-discrimination) or Article I GATT (MFN), notwithstanding the non-discrimination provision of TRIPS, under Article 3. Nonetheless, the Panel extensively, but convincingly, justified the transportation of a GATT principle to TRIPS:

> The protection of legitimate expectations is central to creating security and predictability in the multilateral trading system. In this connection, we note that disciplines formed under GATT 47 (so-called GATT *acquis*) were primarily directed at the treatment of the goods of other countries, while rules under the TRIPS Agreement mainly deal with the treatment of nationals of other WTO Members. While this calls for the concept of the PLE to apply in the TRIPS areas to the competitive relationship between a Member's own nationals and those of other Members (rather than between domestically produced goods and the goods of other Members, as in the goods area), it does not in our view make inapplicable the underlying principle. The Preamble to the TRIPS Agreement, which recognises the need for new rules and disciplines concerning 'the applicability of the basic principles of GATT 94 . . .', provides a useful context in this regard.[222]

In order to transpose 'a well-established GATT principle' to the TRIPS, the Panel advanced three arguments as to why PLE of members regarding the conditions of competition applies to and directs the interpretation of the TRIPS:[223]

> Since TRIPS is one of the Multilateral Trade Agreements, we must be guided by jurisprudence established under GATT 47 in interpreting . . . the TRIPS Agreement, unless there is a contrary provision', b) because the 'TRIPS Agreement was negotiated as a part of the overall balance of concessions in the Uruguay Round, it would be

[219] *Ibid*, para 7.20.
[220] *Ibid*.
[221] *Ibid*, para 7.30.
[222] *Ibid*, para 7.21.
[223] *Ibid*, para 7.20.

inappropriate not to apply the same principles in interpreting the TRIPS Agreements as those applicable to the interpretation of other parts of the WTO Agreement.[224]

Other adopted Panel reports had established the PLE as part of the GATT *acquis*. Thus because 'adopted Panel reports "create legitimate expectations among WTO Members, and, therefore, should be taken into account where they are relevant to any dispute"', PLE shall also be protected under TRIPS.[225]

Finally, PLE 'is central to creating security and predictability in the multilateral trading system'.[226]

The *India–Patents* Panel was criticised for its progressive jurisprudence, extending the principle of PLE to the TRIPS. The following section briefly summarises what the Panel could have done to escape the overturning of its decision by the AB.

'Predictability Needed to Plan Future Trade' Under the TRIPS, the concept of 'benefit' is more difficult to define than it is under the GATT, the GATS and the GPA, where there exist terms of value of tariff concessions or the price effect of tariff negotiations to measure an expectation by.

A 'benefit' is one constitutive element for claiming the frustration of legitimate expectations under an NVNI-type complaint. Article 64 TRIPS has exempted for a period of five years from the date of entry into force of the WTO Agreement, ie until 1 January 2000, the application of the NVNI-type complaints and situation complaints to the TRIPS. Since the negotiators have not been able to agree on whether or not to install the NVNI-type complaint for the TRIPS, the NVNI-type complaint is still suspended today.

Because the definition of 'benefit' as to the conditions of competition relating to tariff treatment or other negotiated market access concessions known to the GATT, the GATS or the GPA is not applicable to the TRIPS, defining PLE for the TRIPS is complicated. The TRIPS seeks to ensure 'worldwide recognition of extensive intellectual property rights'.[227] The TRIPS does not give the right-holders 'the assurance that they can actually sell' their inventions on another trading partners' market.[228] While the GATT, GATS and GPA aim at realising liberal market access concessions, the TRIPS is about setting up national legal systems of IP protection. The conditions of competition frustrated under a WTO-inconsistent behaviour cannot, under the TRIPS, be measured in terms of granting of concessions of market access for a certain good or service or a bidding offer for government procurement.

Roessler finds that the 'basic legal conceptions' of the TRIPS Agreement are so 'fundamentally different from the GATT and the GATS' that if a Panel or the AB were asked to find that a measure had nullified or impaired benefits under

[224] *India–Patents*, Panel Report, para 7.19.
[225] *Ibid*, paras 7.19–7.20.
[226] *Ibid*, para 7.21.
[227] Roessler, 1997, p 136.
[228] *Ibid*.

TRIPS, they 'would be facing a normative void which cannot be appropriately filled by judicial fiat'.[229] While concessions can be circumvented, traded off, and granted among the WTO members, a measure of compliance with the TRIPS obligations must be defined as the adherence with the TRIPS minimal standards. The benefit cannot be easily measured in terms of quantifiable trade volumes as it can be under the GATT, GATS and the GPA. Adherence or non-compliance with international legal standard setting is more difficult to measure in terms of economic benefits. Therefore under the TRIPS, the potential benefits impaired are more closely related to the ephemeral concepts of legal security and predictability. Some authors like Roessler, and the AB find that PLE, as a ground of non-violation complaints under the WTO DSU should not be expanded as to sanction benefits nullified or impaired because of a lack in legal security and predictability. Petersmann concedes however, that even if the NVNI ground of complaint has no legitimacy in TRIPS, general concepts such as the 'abuse of rights' or 'bad faith implementation of the TRIPS Agreement' may very well give rise to PLE, even in TRIPS.[230]

The *India–Patents* Panels share with Cottier and Schefer a broader definition of nullification and impairment of a benefit, one which is not restricted to benefits identified as a market concession.[231] The *India–Patents* Panel found that the concept of competitive opportunities underlies the multilateral trading system in its entirety, and thus applies also to TRIPS. Moreover, the *India–Patents* Panel argued that PLE relates to the concept of competitive opportunities as defined under Article III GATT as opposed to being inherent in NVNI complaints, as defined under Article XXIII:1(b) GATT.[232] Even if the competitive conditions in the TRIPS do not relate to market accession concessions as they do under the GATT and the GATS, the scenario of a disparate treatment impairing the conditions of competition of foreign versus domestic right holders or among foreign right holders on an internal market may very well arise under TRIPS as well. This is the *India–Patents* case scenario.

Thus, despite the lack of NVNI TRIPS complaints, adjudicators cannot escape their responsibility of protecting legitimate expectations, which in a somewhat broader format than under GATT and GATS may arise under TRIPS also.

Substantive Extensions under the Customary Rule of Pacta Sunt Servanda

The *Korea–Government Procurement* (2000) Panel expanded the scope of the PLE ground of complaint on the one hand, and the NVNI-type complaint on the other. The *Korea–Government Procurement* Panel introduced remedy for frustration of legitimate expectations not only for such actions, which would impair

229 *Ibid.*
230 See Petersmann, 1994, 1233.
231 See Cottier and Schefer, 2000, pp 60–1.
232 See *India–Patents*, Panel Report, paras 7.20–7.21.

upon the actual value of negotiated concessions, but, a fortiori, for measures which would impair upon the concessions under negotiation, as will be laid out in more detail below. The *Korea–Government Procurement* Panel found that legitimate expectations may also protect against the frustration of negotiations, where the disrespect for the negotiations has a 'material effect on competitive opportunities'.[233]

Korea–Government Procurement *Panel Report (2000)* The US had argued that 'inadequate bid-deadlines', and other GPA violations, had provoked a loss of US$6 billion vis-à-vis Korean suppliers in competitive bidding opportunities for the construction of an airport that it had agreed to build earlier for Korea.[234]

Contrary to the assurances Korea had offered the US during the negotiation of Korea's accession to the GPA, Korean government policies and measures were offsetting the 'competitive bidding opportunities' for US service providers on the Korean market.[235] The US alleged that the 'inadequate bid deadlines and insufficient challenge procedures', that Korea had introduced while negotiating an 'agreement regarding [its] accession to the GPA', violated the US' legitimate expectations as to its service providers' competitive bidding opportunities.[236]

Because the expectations related to the accord between the US and Korea pursuant to negotiating Korea's accession to the GPA and not the final list of concession itself, the US was barred from equating the discriminatory treatment to a violation of Article III GPA, and instead had to resort to a NVNI complaint, in order to demonstrate that the nullification and impairment of its competitive opportunity was the result of Korea's modifying the list of concessions.

The US filed a NVNI complaint alleging that Korea's measures unexpectedly and detrimentally modified US competitive opportunities, which in result led to a nullification and impairment of the benefits the negotiations on the concessions had come to count on.[237] Because Korea had not yet defined the scope of coverage of listed entities (ie, made any commitments in a binding schedule, but had only put out a list of government entities in charge of making them), the US loss relates to a 'broad[er]', less defined 'competitive opportunity' than to a negotiated concession.[238]

The issue was whether or not the entity conducting the procurement was at all listed in Korea's annexes or notes to its schedule. If the entity was not listed in Korea's schedule, the next question was whether it could still be considered 'covered' under the GPA if it related only to Korea's offer of commitments during negotiations. An affirmative finding would enlist Korea's responsibility for—what amounts to—GPA-inconsistent measures (inadequate bidding

[233] *Korea–Government Procurement*, Panel Report, para 7.95.
[234] See *ibid*, paras 7.87, 7.89.
[235] *Ibid*, para 7.103.
[236] *Ibid*, para 7.124.
[237] *Ibid*, para 7.103.
[238] Cho, 1998, p 333.

deadlines, insufficient challenge procedures), in the sense that they would nullify and impair for the US, Korea's level of concessions.[239]

'[U]nlike traditional NVNI claims', the Panel created a specific concept of NVNI,[240] designed to protect the US legitimate expectations as to Korea's 'duty to demonstrate good faith and transparency in GPA negotiations'.[241] The Panel found that in this case there were no 'actual Schedule commitments' upon which to base the US legitimate expectations under a traditional claim of frustration of legitimate expectations.[242] The Panel thus agreed to expand both the concepts of NVNI nullification and impairment and the scope of PLE to 'the *negotiations* which allegedly gave rise to the reasonable expectations rather than any *concessions*'.[243]

> A key difference [the Panel argues] between a traditional NVNI case and the present one would seem to be that, normally, the question of 'reasonable expectation' is whether or not it was reasonably to be expected that the benefit under an existing concession would be impaired by the measures. However here, if there is to be a NVNI case, the question is whether or not there was a reasonable expectation of an entitlement to a benefit that had accrued pursuant to the *negotiation* rather than pursuant to a *concession*.[244]

Unlike the traditional claim of PLE as to the competitive opportunities based upon the guarantees of the actual schedules of concessions, the *Korea–Government Procurement* Panel extended PLE to a customary rule of international law. Instead of the actual schedule of commitments, the basis for the PLE claim became *pacta sunt servanda*. The *Korea–Government Procurement* Panel created the concept of legitimate expectations as to 'Parties have[ing] an obligation to negotiate in good faith just as they must implement the treaty in good faith'.[245]

In the result, the Panel denied the US protection under the GPA with the following arguments: an NVNI complaint will not be successful in this case for a lack of non-forseeability:

— The Panel found that while the 'duty to demonstrate good faith and transparency in GPA negotiations' is particularly strong for the 'offering' party, this does not relieve the other negotiating partners from their duty of diligence to verify these offers as best as they can.[246] Thus, the Panel found the US to bear the responsibility for changes in Korean law and could not legitimately argue that these changes were unforeseeable.[247]

[239] See *Korea–Government Procurement*, Panel Report, para 7.29
[240] *Ibid*, para 7.118.
[241] *Ibid*, para 7.125.
[242] *Ibid*, para 7.118.
[243] *Ibid*, para 7.120, emphasis added.
[244] See *ibid*, para 7.87.
[245] *Ibid*, para 7.100.
[246] *Ibid*, para 7.125.
[247] See *ibid*, para 7.119.

— According to the Panel, the trade-distorting measures that the US blamed for the value of bidding opportunities, amount to an actual violation of the GPA rules. A fortiori, Korea's offer of concessions had concretised into an actual schedule of commitments. To that extent the Panel found that the US should have brought the case against Korea on grounds of a violation complaint instead of under a NVNI-type complaint:

> If there were a commitment, the case would properly be a violation case because the measures cited by the United States as the basis for the NVNI nullification case (eg, inadequate bid deadlines and insufficient challenge procedures) would, if they were substantiated, result in a violation. A traditional NVNI case could, therefore, not be sustained in this situation.[248]

'Good Faith Performance Has Been Agreed to Include Benefits Reasonably Expected' Scholars divide NVNI complaints into two categories, the *Korea–Government Procurement* case scenario exemplifying the 'wrong' NVNI complaints category.

The *Korea–Government Procurement* Panel ruling expanded the 'traditional NVNI complaint' into what it calls a complaint 'unlike traditional NVNI claims', thus avoiding digressing into the realm of vague and thus 'wrong' NVNI complaints.[249]

The Panel derived the legitimacy of expanding on 'traditional NVNI claims' from the 'general principle[s] of customary international law . . . [of] *pacta sunt servanda*':[250]

> In our view . . . observations by previous Panels are entirely in line with the concept of *pacta sunt servanda*. The vast majority of actions taken by members which are consistent with the letter of their treaty obligations will also be consistent with the spirit. However, upon occasion, it may be the case that some actions, while permissible under one set of rules (eg, the ASCM is a commonly referenced example of rules in this regard), are not consistent with the spirit of other commitments such as those in negotiated schedules. That is, such actions deny the competitive opportunities which are the reasonably expected effect of such commitments.[251]

Paradoxically, it is precisely the general principle of law of good faith, which has often been characterised as non-law, that is attributed the role of providing a legal basis for the GATT/ WTO-specific principle of PLE.[252]

The Panel also pointed out that by linking NVNI complaints to good faith it did not mean to introduce a new criteria ie, that for substantiating a NVNI claim, the complainant would have to actually prove bad faith:[253]

248 *Korea–Government Procurement*, Panel Report, para 7.118.
249 *Ibid*, paras 7.103, 7.118.
250 *Ibid*, para 7.93.
251 *Ibid*, para 7.99.
252 See, eg Zoller, 1977, pp 338–9, 'il ne semble pas qu'elle [la bonne foi] soit la source directe des solutions judiciaires' . . . "la bonne foi . . . n'est pas une règle juridique en tant que source de droit et d'obligation"'.
253 *Korea–Government Procurement*, Panel Report, para 7.99.

> However, we must also note that, while the overall burden of proof is on the complainant, we do not mean to introduce here a new requirement that a complainant affirmatively prove actual bad faith on the part of another Member. It is fairly clear from the history of disputes prior to the conclusion of the Uruguay Round that such a requirement was never established and there is no evidence in the current treaty text that such a requirement was newly imposed.[254]

The *Korea–Government Procurement* Panel deserves credit for unveiling that the origins of NVNI complaints are *pacta sunt servanda* and good faith: 'In our view, the NVNI remedy as it has developed in GATT/WTO jurisprudence should not be viewed in isolation from general principles of customary international law'.[255]

Externally, revealing the link between NVNI and good faith contributed to the WTO's greater integration into, and the WTO's pioneering role within, the international legal system. The Panel declared that NVNI complaints are but an extended expression of the good faith performance of WTO obligations agreed to by WTO Members:

> It seems clear that good faith performance has been agreed by the WTO Members to include subsequent actions which might nullify or impair the benefits reasonably expected to accrue to other parties to the negotiations in question.[256]

As if the Panel had prematurely heard its critics—that holding Korea responsible under the customary rule to negotiate in good faith is unlawfully aggrandising Korea's obligation under Article 3.2 DSU— the Panel stated that unless the WTO has expressly contracted out from general public international obligations, general public international law inherently forms part of members' WTO obligations.

Even when the Panel, as in this case, was asked to broaden the scope of the claim, a NVNI claim will still be WTO consistent for the following reasons:

— WTO Members have expressed their consensus to allow for such claims to complete the WTO legal system when they introduced the NVNI concept under GATT Article XXIII:1(b). As the *Korea–Government Procurement* Panels said, 'good faith performance has been agreed to by the WTO Members to include actions which might nullify or impair the benefits reasonably expected'.[257]
— As long as the complaining member is able to produce a detailed justification of its nullification and impairment, the claim is sufficiently grounded.
— Because 'the relationship of the WTO Agreements to customary international law is broader than this [one of customary rules of *interpretation* of public international law]', 'customary international law applies generally to the economic relations between the WTO Members'.[258]

[254] *Ibid.*
[255] *Ibid*, para 7.93.
[256] *Ibid*, para 7.94.
[257] *Ibid.*
[258] *Ibid*, para 7.96.

— The *Korea–Government Procurement* decision shows that the Panel clearly found that there is a prohibition of *non-liquet* for the WTO judiciary:

> If NVNI represents an extension of the good faith requirements in the implementation of a treaty and can also be applied to good faith and error in negotiations under the GPA, and we think it can, then the special remedies for NVNI contained in DSU Article 26 should also be applied rather than the traditional remedies of treaty law which are not apposite to the situation of the GPA.[259]

— The *Korea–Government Procurement* Panel refused to substantiate the NVNI complaint for lack of evidence that the US had 'reasonable expectation that a benefit had accrued'. Nevertheless, under the principle of good faith in negotiations, the Panel did find that Korea had violated customary international law,[260] because the government entity Korea had first declared in charge during negotiations was replaced by another one at the end of the accessions process.[261] However, the Panel's finding does not alter the fact that the US should have foreseen such a change.[262]

— The Panel clarified that, even if the US had confronted Korea with GPA violations (inadequate bid-deadlines and insufficient challenge procedures), a potential specific commitment would have been violated rather than impaired. '[A] traditional NVNI case could, therefore, not be sustained in this situation'.[263]

The *Korea–Government Procurement* case demonstrates that even if there is potential for true NVNI complaints based on the general principle of law of good faith, the procedural reality of the harsh burden of proof for 'non-foreseeability' with respect to 'reasonable expectations', will restrict NVNI cases from filling in intended gaps, and thereby limit the potential for WTO law to become increasingly judicially created.[264] PLE—while allowing a complainant to claim the protection of a reasonable benefit arising from a negotiated tariff or other concession (which another member has frustrated) as the basis of a non-violation cause of action, must be limited. It must be avoided that WTO law compensates for any loss of trading opportunities related to the WTO's objectives. The limits of the PLE are flexible; it expands as more areas of international trade fall under the WTO legal system's jurisdiction. The limits of PLE also depend on the viewpoint of specific adjudicators as to how much legitimate expectations it protects under its understanding of WTO law. The scope of PLE is a matter of interpretation of WTO law as will be seen in the following

259 *Korea–Government Procurement*, Panel Report, para 7.102.
260 See *ibid*, paras 7.109–7.110.
261 See, eg *ibid*, paras 2.38, 2.39, 7.5, 7.89, 7.124, 8.1.
262 *Ibid*, paras 7.111, 7.115.
263 *Ibid*, para 7.118.
264 *Cf ibid*, para 7.93, see *EC–Canned Fruit*, para 54 on non-foreseeability; see also *Japan–Film*, Panel Report, paras 10.152, 10.165–10.166.

discussion of the *India–Patents*, *EC–LAN* and *Korea–Government Procurement* Panel decisions. The limits of PLE depend upon how an adjudicator interprets the Vienna Convention rules on treaty interpretation. If the Panel's understanding of what may be a legitimate interpretation of WTO law is broader than what the AB believes, the rules of interpretation should be that protection for PLE will shift towards the AB's narrower interpretation of the Vienna rules on interpretation.

Limits on the Broad Principle of Legitimate Expectations in Appellate Practice

India–Patents *Appellate Body Report (1997)*

The AB in *India–Patents* was not prepared to protect the legitimate expectations as to *conditions of competition* under the TRIPS Agreement.[265] The AB only recognised violation complaints under the TRIPS Agreement, amongst which it did *not* consider conditions of competition to figure. As Cottier and Schefer observe:

> [T]oday it is unclear whether legal protection of legitimate expectations is a reserved domain of NVNI complaints or whether it can also be argued within the violation complaint framework.[266]

In *India–Patents*, the AB reprimanded the Panel for 'confusing' the distinction of previous GATT practice between:

— the protection of expectations as to competitive opportunities for third-country products on the internal market; and
— the protection of reasonable expectations relating to market access concessions, as developed in the context of NVNI complaints under GATT Article XXIII:1(b).[267]

Thus, the AB implied that a failure to install a certain legal instrument (eg, a mailbox application rule under Article 70.8 TRIPS) does not, in comparison to a violation of non-discrimination obligation, qualify as an impairment of a condition of competition, because PLE regarding conditions of competition protect only 'after a Panel has found a violation of, for example, Article III or Article XI'.[268] Nevertheless, the AB upheld the Panel's conclusions that India had violated Articles 70.8 and 70.9 of the TRIPS Agreement.[269]

[265] See *India–Patents*, AB Report, para 42.
[266] See Cottier and Schefer, 1997, p 181
[267] See *India–Patents*, AB Report, paras 36–41; see also *Japan–Alcohol*, AB Report, p 17, 'The broad and fundamental purpose of Art III is to avoid protectionism in the application of internal tax and regulatory measures. . . . Toward this end, Art III obliges Members of the WTO to provide equality of competitive conditions for imported products in relation to domestic products'.
[268] *India–Patents*, AB Report, para 40.
[269] See *India–Patents*, AB Report, paras 57, 71, 84, 97, (a) and (b).

Also the AB criticised the Panel for construing an 'overbroad' type of protection for legitimate expectations, by deriving the PLE in the case at hand from an incorrect, because 'overbroad', definition of the good faith rule of interpretation of Article 31 VCLT. By 'relying on the GATT *acquis*, the Panel relies also on the customary rules of interpretation of public international law'.[270]

The AB found that the Panel's failure is not so much grounded in the Panel's misunderstanding of substantive WTO law, but rather in the Panel's incorrect understanding of the VCLT rules.

The AB admonished the Panel for the missapplication of the Vienna rule of Article 31(1) on good faith interpretation, which shows that textual interpretation should be given preference over good faith interpretation. Under such a textual interpretation, a mere goal or objective (the 'predictability to plan future trade', which, according to the Panel justifies a protection of the US patent applicants' legitimate expectations in India's transitory registry) would not have granted a WTO Member State an enforceable right to protection of its legitimate expectations:

> The Panel misunderstands the concept of legitimate expectations in the context of the customary rules of interpretation of public international law. The legitimate expectations of the parties to a treaty are reflected in the language of the treaty itself.[271]

However, had the Panel not 'offer[ed] the interpretative principle' of 'good faith interpretation', the legitimate expectations of the US, as to the TRIPS transitory regime, which should be implemented for ensuring to the market participants a future, effective and enforceable patent protection in India, would not have been protected.[272]

EC–LAN *Appellate Body Report (1998)*

The US in its appeal of the Panel decision in *EC–LAN* had carefully distinguished as its bases of complaint three different types of PLE:

- — Articles III or XI
- — Article II GATT
- — the NVNI-type complaint

In a strategy identical with the one in *India–Patents*, the AB dismissed PLE on the basis of an incorrect use of the VCLT.[273]

[270] *Ibid*, para 43.
[271] *Ibid*, para 45.
[272] *Ibid*, paras 43 and para 44 referring *to India–Patents*, Panel Report, para 8.17.
[273] See Cottier and Schefer, 2000, pp 61–2; *India–Patents* AB Report, para 45; *EC–LAN* AB Report, para 83 referring explicitly to *India–Patents*, AB Report, para 45.

The AB referred to the argumentation it had used already in *India–Patents:* because NVNI complaints are PLE's only possible cause of action, a claim alleging the *violation* of PLE cannot be brought under current procedural WTO law.[274]

The AB in *EC–LAN* dismissed PLE on the basis that the Panel had incorrectly broadened the Vienna rules of treaty interpretation in order to protect PLE. In so doing, the AB adopted the EC's understanding of customary rules of treaty interpretation, which protects only those expectations reflecting the common intentions of the parties.[275] The AB overturned the Panel's interpretation of Article II:5 GATT 94. The AB identified the Panel's interpretation of Article II:5 GATT as protecting only the exporting member's expectations instead of the common intentions of the parties.[276]

Just as in *India–Patents,* the AB in *EC–LAN* found that the Panel had 'offered an interpretative principle', rather than applying the 'customary rules of interpretation of public international law'.[277] In the view of the AB this interpretive principle, namely 'good faith interpretation', had led the Panel to protect a wider scope of legitimate expectations, which was not warranted by the WTO Agreements.[278]

The *EC–LAN* appellate decision to find against protecting the US' legitimate expectations, has been criticised in scholarship. The views are that if the AB sought to deny the US protection of its expectations, it should have denied the US the protection of its expectations because EC Member practice was inconsistent, not because the Panel had introduced an overbroad application of the rule of good faith interpretation leading to an incorrect broadening of the scope of PLE. The scholaly counterproposal suggests that US expectations were not legitimate but 'anomalous'.[279]

In sum, the argument that US expectations in equal tariff treatment throughout the EC for LAN equipment was not legitimate because EC Member practice was inconsistent, would have been the better argumentation, because it would have been grounded in general public international law. Founding legitimate expectations upon 'subsequent practice' under Article 31(3)(b) VCLT would have invariably led to the same result as the *EC–LAN* Panel argument with PLE, because the EC's practice, as examined by the Panel, was revealed to be inconsistent, and the US legitimate expectations as to subsequent practice pursuant to Article 31(3)(b) VCLT would have had to be dismissed.

[274] See *EC–LAN*, AB Report, para 42.

[275] See Cottier and Schefer, 2000, pp 61–2.

[276] See *EC–LAN*, AB Report, para 82; see also Cameron and Gray, 2001, p 262.

[277] *India–Patents*, AB Report, para 43.

[278] Compare *EC–LAN*, AB Report, paras 79 and 83, with *India–Patents*, AB Report, para, referring *to India–Patents*, Panel Report, para 8.17.

[279] *EC–LAN*, Panel Report, para 8.46.

Japan–Film *Panel Report (1998)*

The US had proposed to extend NVNI complaints in order to correct anti-competitive behaviour which frustrated US legitimate expectations. The Panel responded that the US' legitimate expectations extended beyond the scope of protection of GATT law because GATT law does not protect competition between market participants in the sense of anti-trust law, but only conditions of competition as to market access and market conditions among WTO Member States. The Panel found the US case against the Japanese film industry to be a policy-driven 'wrong' case, which the security and predictability of the GATT/WTO system could not substantiate.

The US had claimed that its negotiated market access expressed by the tariff reductions exchanged with Japan was not at issue, but that rather its market conditions on the Japanese market were impaired.[280] Since the US claim went beyond WTO law covered by consensus, the Panel was unable to base PLE upon the customary rule of *pacta sunt servanda*, and thus did not substantiate such an extended claim of legitimate expectations.

The *Japan–Film* Panel clarified the difference between protecting legitimate expectations as to conditions of competition, derived from Article III GATT, and the concept of equal conditions of competition sanctioned under Article III GATT. *Japan–Film* (1998) is perhaps the only Panel decision to date where a Panel (and not the AB) has refused to expand the concept of legitimate expectations.

The Panel found that a broad interpretation of Article III GATT protects competitive opportunities absolutely—in the sense of prohibiting discriminatory treatment under Article III GATT. Basing a claim that one's legitimate expectations as to the competitive conditions provided for by the tariff concessions had been frustrated by a measure subsequently and unilaterally modifying the concessions, on Article III GATT, however, sets off only a 'relative' protection through a NVNI complaint. A relative protection for the Panel means that a GATT-legal measure without any other discriminatory effect than the one of modifying concessions, can nonetheless frustrate the legitimate expectation as to competitive opportunities, which must then be compensated for under Article 26:1(b) DSU.[281]

Divided Adjudicators

In contrast to the Panels, the AB has opposed substantiating any claim of PLE based on a NVNI-type complaint so far.[282] There are institutional reasons for the evasiveness with which the AB considers PLE. As a 'quasi-court of appeal

280 See Ohlhoff, 2003, p 739.

281 See *Japan–Film*, Panel Report, para 10.86.

282 See *India–Patents*, AB Report, paras 34, 36, 40–1; *EC–LAN*, Panel Report, paras 80–3.

and last resort' within a weak political decision-making process, the AB has more control than the Panels as to what becomes WTO case law.[283]

In order to safeguard the already unbalanced division of power between the quasi-judicial and political branches of the WTO, the AB, in NVNI cases, bears even more responsibility for not overstepping into the legislator's realm. Since the AB does not want to appear creative, and since it does not have to fear an over-broad legislative branch against which it must display its own power, the AB prefers not to base PLE cause of action on NVNI-type complaints.

If a WTO Member invokes NVNI, the AB could adopt an equity approach without endangering Member State sovereignty or the principle of consensus.[284] Equity would strengthen the WTO vis-à-vis civil society. Equity would require the AB to 'situate' under a post-modern function of equity, the case within the context of politics rather than trying to distance WTO law away from politics.[285]

Instead of issuing a one-dimensional sovereignty-friendly decision influenced by precepts of *in dubio mitius*, the AB will be asked to give greater consideration to international law.[286]

By relaxing the principle of consensus in favour of respecting the principle of equity, the AB will be more true to the WTO's multifaceted goals than if it were to stick strictly to the limits of consensus at the expense of equity. The AB can consider these goals through NVNI complaints, where PLE is impaired, and the general principle of law of good faith, when there is a violation of good faith.[287]

Scholarly Critique of Expanded Protection

Fragmentation and 'Non-discipline'

As PLE protects conditions of competition, making it a very GATT-specific concept, PLE is said to distance the WTO from other fields of international law,

[283] Ehlermann, 2003a, pp 606, 632.

[284] See Cottier and Schefer, 1997, pp 148, 166, 170, '[T]he WTO should recognise only those NVNI complaints, that are violations of the equity-based international law principle of good faith and its specific applications'; Cottier and Schefer, 2000, p 58; Petersmann, 1994, p 1171, 'There was also a widely felt need among the drafters of the GATT in 1947 for a sort of "equity law jurisdiction" (in Art XXIII:1, b and c) which would enable collective decisions to deal with unforeseen new situations such as a worldwide monetary crisis or a depression with widespread unemployment'; Petersmann, 1991, p 225, '[N]on-violation complaints are based on broader legal principles of effectiveness, . . . reciprocity, and *bona fide* protection of "reasonable expectations"'.

[285] See Koskenniemi, 2000, p 31.

[286] *Cf* Lennard, 2002, p 88, 'The reliance on the *in dubio mitius* principle, . . . demonstrates a deference to the notion of "sovereignty" which seems to unjustifiably and unprofitably differ from the approach taken by other modern international tribunals, and which will perhaps wane as the Appellate Body grows in confidence . . . and other more widely accepted principles (such as that of "effectiveness") become more obvious'; see also Hilf, 2001, p 118.

[287] See Cottier and Schefer, 1997, p 148.

instead of linking the WTO Agreements to related treaties.[288] A first group of scholars fear that NVNI-complaints, which are one way to vindicate the frustration of legitimate expectation, are a 'non-discipline'. These scholars fear that NVNI complaints will contribute to the fragmentation of international law and, worse, to *non-liquets*. There are valid arguments to demonstrate that NVNI might be a 'non-discipline'.[289] While it is true that NVNI appears to be a more abstract remedy compared to violation complaints, they do not randomly substitute for any type of legal vacuum. As shown above, they at least require the conditions for the 'well-established GATT principle' of legitimate expectations or the customary international rule of *pacta sunt servanda* to be fulfilled.[290]

Other scholars are critical of Article 3.2 DSU, which prohibits WTO obligations from being supplemented by additional obligations derived from public international law, as long as Article 3.2 is viewed to propagate *pacta sunt servanda*.[291] However, these authors ignore the fact that the Panel in *Korea–Government Procurement* invoked and incorporated *pacta sunt servanda* to protect the US legitimate expectations, and did not overreach the scope of Article 3.2 DSU. The Panel clarified that even if NVNI complaints are an 'exceptional concept within the WTO dispute settlement system', such complaints are not inconsistent with Article 3.2 DSU.

Yet a third group of scholars finds it too tempting for the judiciary not to resist the unlawful judicial law-making prohibited by Article 3.2 DSU.[292] They argue that PLE endangers the 'legitimacy' and 'stability' of the WTO system when 'misused', such as for integrating into WTO jurisdiction 'newly emerging areas' yet uncovered by the WTO legal texts.[293] On the other hand, there are those who believe that PLE is an 'important' concept precisely for its purpose of 'closing-up of a gap in substantive law'.[294]

Founded upon the 'well-established GATT principle' of protecting legitimate expectations, NVNI ensures the multilateral trading system's legal security and predictability.[295] The merit of the NVNI is to prevent the system from 'backsliding'.[296] NVNI-type complaints are an indispensable tool for consolidating

[288] Compare Council for TRIPS-Minutes of Meeting, 18–19 February 2003, 21 March 2003, WTO Document IP/C/M/39, para 170, which uses the term 'limit the use of flexibilities' along with Cottier and Schefer, 1997, p 182; Cottier and Schefer, 2000, p 68.

[289] Cho, 1998, p 323, for the term 'non-discipline'.

[290] Against von Bogdandy, 1992, p 103, who argues that the criteria of legitimate expectations is only required alongside the one of a nullification and impairment of a benefit, when there is no tariff binding in question.

[291] See McRae, 2003, p 713.

[292] See Roessler, 1997, p 133.

[293] Cho, 1998, pp 314, 319, 320; see also Cottier and Schefer, 1997, p 147; see Henderson, 2002, p 288 on 'new issues . . . swirl[ing] around the Organization for the last few years'; see generally, McRae, 2003, pp 7.10–7.13, for the AB jurisprudence's lack of predictability.

[294] von Bogdandy, 1992, p 110.

[295] *Cf India–Patents*, Panel Report, para 7.21.

[296] Cho, 1998, p 314.

the WTO legal system.[297] Economically, they guarantee that the WTO Agreements' underlying goal of realising fair competitive opportunities will not be offset.[298]

In the light of the 'weak' negotiations-based mechanisms for law-creation at the WTO, which are often blocked or paralysed by setbacks, such as those the 'major trade rounds' have suffered at Seattle or Cancún, NVNI complaints, in combination with general principles of law, provide the WTO judiciary with the legal basis to prevent the system from eroding.[299]

'Limit the Use of Flexibilities'

Certain scholars agree with those WTO Members who oppose NVNI complaints because NVNI 'limit the use of flexibilities'. However, flexibility is the key element to pursue non-trade goals with WTO trading rules, such as public health in the TRIPS and environmental protection in the GATT 94. Not only does the fear persist that NVNI complaints will isolate the WTO legal system (integration of non-trade values in related agreements), concern is further raised that NVNI will fragment the WTO system from within (create incoherence between the different agreements' different goals):[300]

> Critical observers ask whether the NVNI complaint scheme will still be viable with the increasing linkage to agreements that are wholly outside the WTO system-agreements relevant to, but not aimed solely at, trade-related matters (such as environment protection treaties, agreements harmonizing labour protection standards, and disciplines relating to export cartels).[301]

The argument goes that NVNI is biased towards free trade values, because NVNI protects the conditions of competition, against non-trade concerns expressed by such positive legal exceptions as Articles XX, XI GATT, Articles XIV and XIVbis GATS, Articles 13, 17, 24, 26:2, 30 TRIPS.

'Go Against . . . Rule-Orientation'

Jackson, a promoter of a rule-oriented WTO legal system, seems to be undecided about whether NVNI complaints go against the 'rule-orientation' of the WTO system. If dispute settlement focuses on 'specific treaty obligations', rather than on 'general and arguable notions of 'equity' or 'nullification and impairment', Jackson says only that it 'bring[s] the GATT into line with most other international dispute settlement procedures'.[302]

297 *Cf* Cottier and Schefer, 1997, p 147.
298 *Cf Japan–Film*, Panel Report, para 10.35.
299 Ehlermann, 2002, pp 632–6, see also Bourgeois, 2002, p 44.
300 Cottier and Schefer, 1997, p 182; Cottier and Schefer, 2000, p 68.
301 Cottier and Schefer, 1997, p 147.
302 Jackson, 2000, p 132.

Like the *Japan–Film* AB Report, Jackson seems to say that because members negotiate the rules they want to be bound by, they 'only exceptionally would expect to be challenged for actions not in contravention of those rules'.[303]

If Jackson is critical of the merits of NVNI complaints in WTO law, this does not yet mean that he is opposed to PLE guiding the adjudicators. If Jackson is ambivalent about the function of NVNI-type complaints at the WTO, his view would reflect a sovereignty-oriented and textual approach, which emphasizes the willpower of nations over an objectivated common interest. As such it would be in sync with the textualist tendencies of the AB.[304]

Pescatore more bluntly opposes NVNI claims, because they 'create[s] an easy escape from obligations imposed by the general agreement'.[305] Petersmann simply confirms, without advocating for an explicit recognition of the good faith principle in WTO law, that 'NVNI complaints are based on broader legal principles of effectiveness ("effect utile") of concessions, . . . and *bona fide* protection of "reasonable expectations"'.[306] Petersmann does not seem in favour of NVNI complaints, because he sees them as 'vaguely defined' and running counter the aims of 'progressive "legalization" and codification of GATT dispute settlement procedures'.[307]

Jackson, Pescatore, Petersmann and Roessler, clearly value the goals of trade liberalization more highly than the WTO's non-trade goals, and perceive a danger in expanding too vastly, the NVNI-type complaint, as it could backfire by devaluing trade related goals.

An Imbalance between Rights and Obligations

Developing countries criticise that '[t]he relevance of good faith duties has thus far been emphasized primarily by developed countries who seek recognition of NVNI nullification or impairment'.[308] Specifically in the TRIPS area, where developing countries are privileged by transitory regimes (Articles 65 and 66 TRIPS), developing countries anticipate expansive NVNI complaints, which would require developing countries' compliance with TRIPS beyond its text.

In particular, they fear that as industrialised WTO Member States will be able to (ab)use NVNI complaints to retrieve commercial benefits or preserve conditions of competition with regard to any WTO exempted non-trade value as was seen with Article XX(a–j) GATT 94, the non-trade concerns will be negatively affected:

303 *Japan–Film*, AB Report, para 10.36.
304 See Ehlermann, 2003a, p 616, on the AB's textualism; against Bagchi, 2003, p 1540.
305 See Pescatore, 1993, p 19.
306 Petersmann, 1991, p 225.
307 *Ibid*, 1994, 1187–8.
308 Bagchi, 2003, p 1534.

> [T]he application of NVNI . . . complaints was *unnecessary, undesirable and impossible*. First of all, NVNI . . . complaints were unnecessary to protect the delicate balance of rights and obligations inherent in the TRIPS Agreement . . . *Article 1 of the TRIPS Agreement* clearly stated that WTO Members shall not be obliged to provide *more extensive protection than that conferred*.[309] (emphasis added).

Developing countries find that drawing from the principle of good faith performance of treaties is the only way to prevent an expansive interpretation of the NVNI-type complaint. They introduce good faith application of the treaty provisions, in accordance with established principles of international law, as the way to prevent expansive interpretation of NVNI-type complaints and thus avoid an overbroad, and incorrect notion of PLE. This would result in tilting the negotiated balance of rights and obligations under the TRIPS Agreement, just as in any other WTO Agreement. For example:

> [The representative of Peru] believed that [t]hese principles [good faith, NVNI nullification or impairment] would allow home countries of patent-holding firms to sue for breach of the spirit and expectations behind the text of TRIPS, beyond its more limited literal meaning.[310]

Recently, certain developing-country WTO members led by Peru have argued that allowing NVNI complaints for TRIPS will endanger the preservation of biodiversity. Their claim is that TRIPS-related non-trade values (public health and access to medicines contained in the Doha Declaration[311] and biodiversity related issues in Article 27:3(b) TRIPS) will de facto be exposed to requirements of intellectual protection even if *de jure* exempted from Intellectual Property Rights (IPR) protection.

Parties who are ecologically oriented, consumer protection-directed, or more generally, WTO Members interested in invoking Article XX GATT or a TRIPS exception, fear that non-trade concerns will be drawn into trade liberalization through NVNI complaints, even if *de jure* exempted from trade liberalization.[312] In effect, these members fear that all the exceptions provided for in the TRIPS Agreement will become meaningless once a NVNI complaint is installed:

> They also considered that this remedy could limit use of the flexibilities contained in the TRIPS Agreement to secure objectives relating to public health, nutrition, protection of the environment and biodiversity, technology transfer, and other issues of

[309] Council for TRIPS-Minutes of Meeting, 18–19 February 2003, 21 March 2003, WTO Document IP/C/M/39, para 167.

[310] Bagchi, 2003, p 1534.

[311] See Declaration on the TRIPS Agreement and Public Health, 14 November 2001, WTO Document WT/MIN(01)/DEC/W/2.

[312] See Council for TRIPS-Minutes of Meeting, 18–19 February 2003, 21 March 2003, WTO Document IP/C/M/39, Peru's above cited statement was supported by Brazil, the ASEAN, China, and the EC.

public interest in sectors of vital importance to socio-economic, cultural and technological development'.[313]

Economically less robust or politically less influential WTO Members are in favour of keeping the NVNI remedy, as a 'mutually satisfactory adjustment' is more in their interest than the removal of the unlawful measure and the compensation or suspension of concessions that Article 22 DSU prescribes for violation cases.

Litigation also demonstrates that WTO Members approach NVNI complaints skeptically, as the NVNI ground of complaint 'has played only an auxiliary role as a precaution against the failure to win the first violation argument'.[314]

Balancing Legitimate Expectations with Good Faith Treaty Performance

A 'Catalyst for Integration'

The principle of protecting legitimate expectations may work as a catalyst for integration because it substitutes power-based treaty relations with the principle of co-ordination, according to Schwarzenberger.[315] Cameron and Gray similarly argue for the PLE to have a secured place in WTO jurisdiction, because its 'foundations rest in international law', together with other international legal principles related to the legitimate expectations doctrine, such as *pacta sunt servanda*, estoppel and *abus de droit*.[316]

Ehlermann a fortiori criticises the AB's reluctant embrace of PLE. As Ehlermann says, 'this cautious attitude [can be] regretted from a point of view of the security and predictability of the multilateral trading system'.[317]

Interpreting Article 3.2 DSU to encompass *substantive* general public international law was a step undertaken by the Panel in *Korea–Government Procurement*,[318] which recognised that PLE and NVNI are derivatives of the general principle of law of good faith. This is a measured acknowledgment by the Panel that WTO law stretches to include the general principle of law of good faith.

Legitimate expectations 'maintain the integrity of WTO law in the overall system of international law' generally and 'increase the linkages' to non-WTO treaties specifically.[319] Within the WTO, they enhance (through 'broad inter-

[313] Council for TRIPS-Minutes of Meeting, 18–19 February 2003, 21 March 2003, WTO Document IP/C/M/39, para 170.

[314] Cho, 1998, p 322.

[315] See Schwarzenberger, pp 295, 325.

[316] Cameron and Gray, 2001, p 260.

[317] Ehlermann, 2002, p 638.

[318] See *Korea–Government Procurement*, Panel Report, paras 7.102, 7.96; see Hilf, 2001, p 122 for gap-filling in the WTO discussed with reference to the *Korea–Government Procurement* case.

[319] Cottier and Schefer, 1997, pp 147–8, p 145.

pretations of treaty clauses that would extend the obligations beyond the language of the Agreement's text') the integrity between the different Agreements.[320] However, in order not to expand by adjudication the scope of the WTO Members rights and obligations, Cottier and Schefer propose to limit the concept of PLE (to violation complaints only) and to distinguish it from what they call 'true NVNI' or 'real non-violation complaints'.[321] To prevent a member's frustration of legitimate expectations, the duty to perform WTO obligations in good faith would be included in the DSU and replace the derelict notion of NVNI.[322]

According to Cottier and Schefer (1997), the other function of PLE, namely, gap-filling, should be assigned to the Trade Policy Review Mechanism (TPRM), much like restatements in the US assess legal developments.[323]

Authoritative Interpretation

In order to respect the WTO's institutional balance (empowering the WTO legislator to fill in gaps), while simultaneously rendering the general principle of good faith/legitimate expectations invocable WTO law, authoritative interpretations pursuant to Article IX.2 Marrakech Agreement must be made.[324]

The advantage of authoritative interpretations over TPRM is that the authoritative interpretation will be binding on all WTO Members and become part of the WTO *acquis*, whereas the TPRM only 'contributes to improved adherence by all members to rules, disciplines and commitments'.[325] Annex 3 to the Marrakech Agreement, which codifies the TPRM, expressly forbids the TPRM being used to 'impose new policy commitments on members'.[326]

It is important to maintain the institutional balance at the WTO (Articles 3.2 and 3.3 DSU) and to separate the gap closing and legislative from the regulative and judicial function of legitimate expectations. However instead of using the TPRM, it is proposed that the General Council adopts an authoritative interpretation of Article 3.2 DSU, which would once and for all specify and codify that general principles of law are part of the WTO *acquis* and can be used by the judiciary to fill in gaps.[327]

[320] *Ibid.*

[321] *Ibid*, pp 181–2.

[322] See *ibid*, p 181.

[323] See *ibid*, pp 148, 180–2; *cf* Kerse, 2000, p 210, on the value of restatements 'for shaping the disciplines of the law' in the US, and comparing it to the working groups in EC law, which have the task to provide for a comprehensive analysis of current law, which can be used as a 'guide by national courts in applying Community law', as well by legislators as a 'checklist'; see also 'Restatement', Black's Law Dictionary, 7 edn (1999), pp 1314–15.

[324] See Jackson, 1999, p 123–4, generally, on authoritative interpretations.

[325] TPRM, Annex 3 of the Marrakesh Agreement Establishing the WTO of 15 April 1994, in 'The Results of the Uruguay Round of Multilateral Trade Negotiations', The Legal Texts, GATT Secretariat, June 1994, WTO, Geneva, A. Objectives (i).

[326] See also Art III:3 WTO Agreement.

[327] See Ehlermann, 2002, p 636, 'Today, I consider it to be perfectly legitimate that the legislative branch clarifies a provision of a covered agreement, provided this is done in those forms that the

Every time a claim of NVNI is brought on grounds of a frustration of legitimate expectations, the judiciary could then point to the authoritative understanding of Article 3.2 DSU and safely use *pacta sunt servanda* to avert the circumvention of tariff or other concessions. The judiciary would be able to interpret the provision more effectively, pursuant to 'good faith interpretation', without being criticised for aggrandising the scope of WTO obligations under Article 3.2 DSU.[328]

Authoritative interpretations also address the positivist concern about security and predictability because the gap-filling will be accomplished via principles known to international law and derived from members' domestic laws.

REDEFINING THE RATIONALE OF PROTECTING LEGITIMATE EXPECTATIONS

This section discusses how the PLE and 'true' NVNI-complaints are both premised upon the assumption that the WTO law they protect and enforce is part of a 'complete' WTO legal system.

A 'Complete' WTO Legal System

Formative Principle of Good Faith

The precondition for a general principle of law to adopt a 'formative' function and to fill in the gaps of an international treaty is, according to general public international theory, that a legal system is 'complete' as to its rule of law.[329]

> The completeness of the rule of law—as distinguished from the individual branches of statutory or customary law—is an a priori assumption of every system of law, not a prescription of positive law . . . There may be gaps in a statute or in the statutory law as a whole; there may be gaps in the manifestations of customary law. There are no gaps in the legal system taken as a whole.[330]

Lauterpracht maintains that gaps in international law and the duty to fill these arise only in complete legal systems. Degan agrees with Lauterpracht and

respective "constitutive" charter prescribes. I would even go one step further and congratulate the WTO if its political organs were able to use Arts IX and X of the Marrakech Agreement to react to an interpretation of a covered agreement, given by a Panel or the Appellate Body, with which these political organs disagree'.

[328] *Cf India–Patents*, AB Report, paras 43–8.

[329] See Lauterpracht, 1933, pp 60–9; Scobbie, 1997, p 269, summarising Lauterpracht's emphasis on the importance of general principles of law to 'avoid delivering a non-liquet' and 'play[ing] a central role in Lauterpracht's conception of the Rule of Law'; see Schwarzenberger, 1955, p 325 ('good faith as a formative influence').

[330] Lauterpracht, 1933, p 64.

finds that the general public international system fulfills the conditions of completeness, not least for the simple reason that since the function of international law is to maintain peace, *non-liquet* rulings should be avoided. If the international system were considered incomplete as to the rule of law and open for *non-liquets,* it would dangerously liberate the international judiciary of its responsibility to oppose violence.[331]

Some post-1945 scholars maintain that GATT of 1947 was more of a power-oriented 'realist' legal structure assisting diplomats' negotiating rounds. However, others agree that the GATT 47 was one among the many post-war treaties established to promote the international rule of law.[332] The fact that GATT 47 Panels used the legally abstract concept of legitimate expectations demonstrates that GATT 47 drafters were at least exposed to, if were not out rightly espousing the idealistic approach defining post-war international legal thinking (modern objectivism):[333]

> It is a striking observation that much of what modern legal doctrines fought to achieve had been realised in the GATT system of carefully balancing trading rights and interests of the contracting parties.[334]

Koskenniemi and Leino, by contrast, have a sceptical view of post-1945 international law:

> The Cold War pragmatic consensus was that if international law had not become the 'complete system' as it had been imagined by the profession's great names—Kelsen, Scelle and Lauterpracht in particular—this was due to a hostile political environment.[335]

Foundations for Gap-filling

In WTO practice, the Panel statement in the *India–Patents* case was the first indication that the WTO legal system can be considered a complete system of law. Consequently, any gaps are unintended.

Panel Reports on India–Patents *and* Korea–Government Procurement
According to the *India–Patents* Panel, a NVNI-based complaint is the instrument of choice for filling in gaps. The condition for the NVNI cause of action to effectively substantiate is, for the 'well-established GATT principle' of PLE, to

[331] *Ibid*, pp 64–5, 'Under the normal rule of law it is inconceivable that a court should pronounce a *non-liquet* because of the absence of law. This is certainly not so because the positive law has provided a solution for all possible emergencies. The reason for it is that law conceived as a means of ordering human life—cannot without abdicating its function concede that there are situations admitting of no answer'; see Degan 1997, pp 45–7, 100, 112, 435–6.

[332] See Cottier and Schefer, 1997, p 166; but see Jackson, 2000, pp 121–2, who has argued that the GATT since its beginnings was more rule-oriented than power-oriented.

[333] Cottier and Schefer, 1997, p 170; Korhonen, 1996, p 17, for modern objectivism.

[334] Cottier and Schefer, 1997, p 170.

[335] Koskenniemi and Leino, 2002, p 559; see also, p 561.

step into the gap, which in turn requires that the *lacunae* negatively impacts upon the negotiated balance of tariff or other concessions.

> In the absence of substantive legal rules in many areas relating to international trade, [the *India–Patents* Appellate Report maintains] the 'NVNI' provision of Article XXIII:1(b) was aimed at preventing contracting parties from using non-tariff barriers or other policy measures to negate the benefits of negotiated tariff concessions.[336]

The *India–Patents* Panel Report recognised that substantive areas of law are not yet covered by the WTO and that the function falling upon the 'well-established GATT principle' is to substitute temporarily for the lack of adequate rules.[337] The *India–Patents* Panel Report did not explicitly use the term of gap or *lacuna* to describe the areas yet uncovered by WTO jurisdiction, but it did introduce the notion of a complete WTO legal system.

Not until three years later did the Panel in *Korea–Government Procurement* expressly admit to unintended gaps. The *Korea–Government Procurement* report implied by its express reference to gaps in WTO law that there exists a consensus among WTO Members as to the completeness of the multilateral trading system.[338] The Panel thereupon reaffirmed the necessity for the judiciary to fix such gaps. In a further development from earlier *India–Patents* jurisprudence, the Panel found itself not limited to the 'well-established *GATT* principles' for filling in the gaps, declaring that the 'general principles of customary *international law*' may step in as well (emphasis added).[339]

A Re-emerging Comittment to International (Trade) Law Among WTO commentators, Marceau, Lowenfeld, Pauwelyn and Bacchus amongst others, have demonstrated that the WTO judiciary is obliged to adjudicate, 'must secure a positive solution to the dispute', and may not, pursuant to Article 11 DSU, resort to a *non-liquet*. Consequently, the DSU is 'the most complete system of international dispute resolution'.[340] Others go even further and declare the WTO *mutatis mutandis* to the ICJ, a court of general jurisdiction.[341]

These proponents of a progressive WTO doctrine on PLE are generally scholars who were educated in the time between the GATT's creation in 1947 and the WTO's inception in 1994, when international legal thinking had already undergone changes that by the mid-nineties had cumulated in a renewed effort to 'defend the fortress' of international law. Instead of continuing nihilistically to dismantle the foundations of the international legal system, defenders of the fortress recognised their responsibility as well as that of international adjudica-

[336] *India–Patents*, AB Report, para 41.

[337] *Ibid*, Panel Report, para 7.20.

[338] See *ibid* ('absence of substantive legal rules'); see *Korea–Government Procurement*, Panel Report, para 7.101 ('gap').

[339] Compare *India–Patents*, Panel Report, para 7.20 with *Korea–Government Procurement*, Panel Report, para 7.93.

[340] *Cf* Marceau, 1999, p 108; Lowenfeld, 2002, p 150; see also Bacchus, 2003c, p 5, confirming Lowenfeld.

[341] See Palmeter and Mavroidis, 1998, p 399; against Marceau, 1999, p 108.

tion for maintaining a living international legal system. This entailed a restored commitment towards gap-filling.[342]

When the WTO was established almost fifty years later, in 1994, international legal thinking was caught in the post-modern dilemma between 'apology and utopia', realism and deconstructivism. Both doctrinal currents intended to negate the 'modern determinacy' that had shaped the post-war international legal order.[343] Both realists and deconstructivists defined the international legal system as being the mere tool of power politics, and consequently an incomplete answer to cross-border trade issues.

Some of the above-mentioned scholars understand the mandate of PLE to be a more limited one, and WTO law not to be a generally applicable legal system of last resort. Petersmann in 1991 describes NVNI under the heading of 'restor[ing] an agreed balance of reciprocal concessions'.[344] Similarly, Marceau finds that Articles 7 and 11 DSU 'suggest a limited mandate' for the WTO DSU.[345] Seen from this perspective, the WTO will hardly apply all international law pursuant to Article 38 ICJ. However, the WTO must respect the 'rule of law'.[346] Its judiciary is obliged to adjudicate disputes, 'even when involving the interpretation of the most obscure provisions of the WTO Agreement'.[347]

Later still, the 'fortress defenders' critically rejected such skeptical approaches, which tended to define international law by 'referring to the factual-political, economic, cultural or ecological-interdependence between States',[348] resulting in 'anti-foundationalism' and 'silence'. The fortress defenders thus sought to re-establish the responsibility of the judiciary for gap-filling and with it equity and concretivism, as 'relatively satisfactory tools for lawyers' because 'silence and suicide are no answers'.[349]

This study maintains that the fact that the WTO DSU has 'created an ever-expanding treasure of international jurisprudence' demonstrates its determination to leave no gaps and be complete.[350] The WTO system is complete, insofar as Articles 7 and 11 DSU do not allow *non-liquet*, because the judiciary should 'secure a positive solution to a dispute' (Article 3.7 DSU). Furthermore, Article 3.2 DSU refers to general public international law. Finally, the WTO Preamble propagates the further integration of yet unregulated subjects into the WTO.[351]

[342] See Korhonen, 1996, pp 3, 16.

[343] See generally Korhonen, 1996, pp 1–18 who traces back the development of international law scholarship in the post-war period, from modern objectivism over realism to post-modern deconstructivism and finally what he terms 'fortress defenders'; see Koskenniemi, 1989, pp 422–57.

[344] Petersmann, 1991, p 222.

[345] Marceau, 1999, p 108.

[346] See *ibid*, 2000; see generally, Bacchus, 2003b, pp 533–50.

[347] Marceau, 1999, p 108.

[348] Koskenniemi, 1989, p 425.

[349] Korhonen, 1996, p 19.

[350] Bacchus, 2003b, p 539; see also Pauwelyn, 2001, p 535, against Trachtman, 1999, p 342.

[351] *Cf* Marceau, 1999, p 108; *cf* Bacchus, 2003b, p 541; see Preambles of GATT 94 and the WTO (WTO Agreement), as well as Arts II:1 and III:2 WTO (WTO Agreement), the WTO considering itself competent on all multilateral trade-related issues,

Pauwelyn backs the 'completeness' of the WTO legal system, insofar as 'WTO rules cut across almost all other rules of international law', with the result that WTO rules are 'all-affecting'.[352]

For example, the relationship that the Panels build between PLE and *pacta sunt servanda* in *Korea–Government Procurement* and between PLE and good faith interpretation in *India–Patents* and *EC–LAN* demonstrates that general public international law, or the principle of good faith specifically, will strengthen (instead of weaken) the regime-specific principles of a more specialised regime (the WTO's balance of negotiated concessions, broadly, the WTO's liberalism).

At the same time as integrating the WTO more into general public international law, using the general principle of good faith will also contribute strongly to the persuasiveness of general principles of law.[353] As the *Korea–Government Procurement* Panel stated:

> Thus, on the basis of the ample evidence provided by both parties to the dispute, we will review the claim of nullification or impairment raised by the United States within the framework of principles of international law which are generally applicable not only to performance of treaties but also to treaty negotiation. *To do otherwise potentially would leave a gap in the applicability of the law generally to WTO disputes* and we see no evidence in the language of the WTO Agreements that such a gap was intended. If the *NVNI* remedy were deemed *not to provide* a relief for such problems as have arisen in the present case regarding good faith and error in the negotiation of GPA commitments (and one might add, in tariff and services commitments under other WTO Agreements), *then nothing could be done about them within the framework of the* WTO dispute settlement mechanism if general rules of customary international law on good faith and error in treaty negotiations were ruled not to be applicable. As was argued above, *that would not be in conformity* with the normal relationship between *international law* and treaty law *or* with the *WTO Agreements* (emphasis added).[354]

The *Korea–Government Procurement* Panel maintained that NVNI claims exist to avoid backsliding as to the status of trade liberalization (achieved through negotiated tariff/services/procurement concessions). However, compared to earlier NVNI cases, the emphasis of the *Korea–Government Procurement* decision lies more in the gap threatening to impair the WTO legal system rather than in the economics (and power) of the negotiated level of tariff concessions.

Today, NVNI, coupled with PLE, is a measure of recognition that the broader purpose of NVNI—in an era of integrated legal systems—is to fill in the gaps of the WTO texts when a WTO Member is found to infringe general public international law.

352 Pauwelyn, 2001, pp 539–40.

353 *Cf* Degan, 1997, pp 74–82.

354 *Korea–Government Procurement*, Panel Report, para 7.101.

'Equity Law Jurisdiction' of Non-violation Complaints

> Good faith may be understood as an objective value independent of the will of the Parties, and it may then conspicuously approach the idea of equity.[355]

> The substantive and procedural functions of equity as an instrument to achieve fairness and do justice in complex cases have a function similar to that of NVNI complaints in trade regulation. More specifically, this is true for the protection of good faith and legitimate expectations as emanations of equity.[356]

As a judge-based concept, equity has been said to infuse a rule with the flexibility required to address the particularities of specific cases.[357] 'Equity as an instrument to achieve fairness and do justice in complex cases has a function similar to that of NVNI complaints in trade regulation'.[358]

WTO-specific Equity of Non-violation Complaints

NVNI complaints and the PLE, as a procedural device[359] in the hands of the WTO judiciary[360], have been brought into connection with concepts of equity:[361]

> The substantive and procedural functions of equity as an instrument to achieve fairness and do justice in complex cases have a function similar to that of NVNI complaints in trade regulation. More specifically, this is true for the protection of good faith and legitimate expectations as emanations of equity.[362]

Although Cottier and Schefer maintain that equity 'is today clearly part of the law', they nevertheless warn against the danger of generalizing NVNI complaints to the point of according a full-fledged 'equity law jurisdiction' to the WTO judiciary.[363]

Only if WTO Members truly commit to the integration of general principles of law into the law of the WTO Agreements (especially the one of good faith) could the NVNI-type complaint become associated with equity.[364] As long as

355 Zoller, 1977, p 21.

356 Cottier and Schefer, 1997, p 170.

357 *Cf ibid*, 2000, stating that the concept of nullification and impairment, similarly to the principle of good faith, 'inserts an element of flexibility to take into account elements other than strict adherence to or violation of treaty provisions'; *cf* Cottier and Schefer, 1997, pp 163–4, comparing the civil law concepts of Billigkeit and équité, which 'recognise justice as a value . . . within the rule of law', with the 'Anglo–American conception of equity', where 'justice can more readily be pursued contrary to the narrow dictates of law'.

358 Cottier and Schefer, 1997, p 170.

359 *Cf ibid*, p 149, who state that 'NVNI complaint mechanism' is a 'procedural tool'.

360 See *ibid*, p 169, who state that 'the use of equity is in practice still open to a judge's subjective discretion as to what is "fair"'.

361 *Ibid*, pp 148, 170.

362 *Ibid*, p 170.

363 Cottier and Schefer, 1997, p 169.

364 See *ibid*, 2000, p 59.

this is not the case, the judiciary will be tempted either to over-broadly, and thus unlawfully under Article 3.2 DSU, use its adjudicative power to adjudicate 'wrong' cases, or to suddenly evade its responsibility by issuing a *non-liquet*.[365] For the systemic reason that Article 3.2 DSU prohibits judge-made law, the WTO legal system would seem precluded from using 'equity law jurisdiction'. Lennard therefore declares that it would be inconsistent with Article 3.2 DSU to integrate equity law jurisdiction at the WTO:

> If the Vienna Convention is not closely borne in mind, such general concepts may develop a life of their own and could lead the interpreters away from the text . . . to a 'quasi-equitable jurisdiction' which would be regarded by most as improperly enlargening the role of the AB.[366]

In general public international theory, Lauterpracht finds that equity law jurisdiction cannot replace gap-filling with general principles of law, but must be complementary to these.

> If, as the result of a deficient system of international legislation, there is a possibility and a necessity for developing by international organs jurisdiction of this kind, . . . then there is every reason why this should be done by a permanent body, of high authority, learning and, impartiality, which can be relied upon to shape international equity, not in a haphazard way, but in accordance with principles capable of general application.[367]

Equity as understood by Newman is 'the common principle that justice be done', rather than deciding *ex aequo ac bono*. It is an objectivating factor that judiciaries can use to fill in *lacunae*.[368] When equity is understood as the corollary to justice, then its function is identical to the one of the general principle of law of good faith and will equally be fact-oriented in order to be legitimate.[369] With Newman, however, using the general principle of good faith particularly to fill in a gap, which means finding a solution more broadly applicable than to the individual case at hand, is identical to ruling on basis of equity, which is nothing else than the Anglo-American way of objectivating an individual, subjective solution for the benefit of society at large.

> If the end of law is social justice, there is no longer need for a body of principles to relieve against injustice in special types of cases. . . . Our dual system of law and equity has come about because of accidents of history which should no longer be allowed to control the shape of our law. There area in which the principles of equity are to be

[365] *Cf* Lauterpracht, 1933, pp 63–9, in analogy.

[366] Lennard, 2002, p 89.

[367] Lauterpracht, 1933, p 327.

[368] Newman, 1961, p 266.

[369] See *ibid*, p 69 referring to Stone's saying that 'the effective basis of decision should be a full consideration of the facts and of the practical effect of the judgment', against Kelsen, 1960, p 196, 'Daraus, dass etwas *ist*, kann nicht folgen, dass etwas sein *soll;* sowie daraus, dass etwas sein *soll*, nicht folgen kann, dass etwas *ist* . . . Der Geltungsgrund einer Norm kann nur die Geltung einer anderen Norm sein'.

applied must be *enlarged so as to embrace the whole range of interests which may required judicial resolution*' (emphasis added).[370]

The Principle of Pacta Sunt Servanda *Takes Precedence Over Equity*

At the WTO, both the AB and the Panels emphasize the interaction between NVNIs and legitimate expectations, which is a substantive law-based concept, materializing as a 'well-established GATT-principle' or 'extended *pacta sunt servanda*'.[371] The WTO adjudicators demonstrate a certain preference for general principles of law over equity for the purpose of filling gaps.[372] As Cottier and Schefer say:

> In the context of the WTO, the goals of freer trade are therefore intricately bound to the question of whether the Members (and the Members' citizens) see the WTO processes to be sufficiently fair and transparent. Consequently . . . the legitimacy and fairness of the WTO system must necessarily be important guides for the future development of WTO law. The principle of good faith and its doctrinal branches of the doctrine of abuse of rights and the protection of legitimate expectations are key aspects to achieving this acceptance.[373]

Sometimes equity refers to its balancing function identified by Schwarzenberger,[374] based upon the Aristotelian and Grotian concepts of 'corrective justice',[375] other times equity to *abus de droit* and estoppel, which are considered 'equitable principles' without giving a definition to what the *überbegriff* of equitable principles should express, or why it is necessary.[376] The safest option is to state with McWhinney that equity serves to invalidate treaty law infringing upon *ius cogens*.[377] Underlying equity is a very basic gap-filling function, the gap between 'social needs and opinions . . . always more or less in advance of Law'.[378] However, this function is what renders equity difficult to concretise in the international legal system, precisely because as Nader and Starr say,

> [E]quity is not universal, but is dependent on time, place and the restraints set against 'naked power' which the dominant members of society might use.[379]

370 Newman, 1961, p 265.

371 *India–Patents*, Panel Report, para 7.20; *Korea–Government Procurement*, Panel Report, paras 7.102ff.

372 See *EEC–Oilseeds I*, Panel Report, para 144; *Japan–Film*, Panel Report, paras 10.50, 10.61; *cf India–Patents*, Panel Report, para 7.20, which less derives legitimate expectations from Art XXIII GATT generally, without clearly specifying that in the past it has been more used in the context of NVNI complaints; see also *EC–LAN*, Panel Report, paras 8.23–8.24, where legitimate expectations have also been associated with violation complaints in the context of conditions of competition pursuant to Art II GATT.

373 Cottier and Schefer, 2000, p 57.

374 See Schwarzenberger, 1955, p 324.

375 See Blum, 1997, p 232.

376 *Cf* Mc Whinney, 1973, p 587.

377 *Ibid*, pp 585–6.

378 Nader and Starr, 1973, p 125.

379 *Ibid*, p 136.

Korhonen and Koskenniemi found that equity today is more a situational than an idealistic concept equal to the principle of good faith[380] that Lauterpracht proposed for general public international law.[381] In this context, Lauterpracht and Rosenne have warned that equity loosely applied could itself result in inequitable solutions, endangering the predictability of law as well as the 'right of the parties to realise their legitimate expectations'.[382]

> 'Equity', by whatever name we call it, has been developed in legal systems in which the courts, are part and parcel of the society in which and for which the courts have been set up. . . . No universal international tribunal has yet attained such a degree of integration of its judges into the international society. . . .[383]

Equity in international law (and here Rosenne and Blum would agree with Koskenniemi and Korhonen) has found neither a foundation nor an identity.[384]

Because the WTO expressly prohibits judge-created law in Article 3.2 DSU and is known for its lack of a democratic basis, or at least for its credibility problem with the citizen-consumer, it is more legitimate to replace (with the legislative concept of TPRM than with elastic equity law) overbroad NVNI complaints which cannot be founded upon the WTO Members' legitimate expectations.

Currently, with no consensus as yet among the WTO members as to a 'justice concept' for the WTO, the WTO judiciary is, for lack of a democratic basis, unable to formulate a WTO-specific notion of equity. Before any concept of equity could become actionable at the WTO, the democratic foundation at the basis of the multilateral trading system must be strengthened and unified.

It is not the duty of equity to balance the WTO's multifaceted and often contradictory goals of liberalizing trade and preserving environment, culture, labour, etc; a fortiori it would even be dangerous if equity were conferred this task, because the WTO has no constituency, such as individuals, who rely and reflect upon the law-adducing function of justice.

As long as the WTO's legal development is in the hands of Members States' negotiating rounds, where decisions are often the result of exclusive and excluding green room debates, the WTO judiciary is not ready to have equity placed in its hands.

Inversely, however, one could argue that equity via NVNI complaints might replace exactly the societal values left unconsidered in trade round negotiations, and thus create the 'equitable' counterpart to WTO law's interest-group ori-

380 See Koskenniemi, 1989, pp 417–18, debating whether equity should be a moral or psychological concept; see also Korhonen, 1996, p 8.

381 See Blum, 1997, p 233 referring to Lauterpracht; see also Cottier and Schefer, 1997, who also derive good faith and the PLE from the principle of equity.

382 *Ibid*, pp 237–8, referring to Rosenne and Lauterpracht.

383 Rosenne, 1993, pp 204–5.

384 See Korhonen, 1996 p 8, in particular, fn 15 and 16, referring to others.

ented, State sovereignty-based positive rights and obligations. As such equity would (as it has ever since Roman *aequitas*) embody the function of 'correcting or overruling strict law'.[385]

CONCLUSIONS

Starting out when good faith was internationally unknown, the GATT Panels began to use the 'imaginative' concept of legitimate expectations to protect negotiated concessions from being circumvented by members taking advantage of *lacunae* in the GATT.[386] Under the WTO, the Panels sought to interpret, pursuant to the VCLT, the TRIPS and Member tariff schedules in good faith, in order to expand the PLE in to a broader concept of conditions of competition. In the Panels' view the goal was to include such considerations as 'the predictability to plan future trade' or even more broadly, 'security and predictability in the multilateral trading system'. The good faith principle was to be the tool to accomodate under the protection of legitimate expectations such broad notions of 'benefits', which, if impaired, could be claimed under a non-violation-type complaint.[387]

[385] Ziegler, 1997, pp 54–5.

[386] See Cottier and Schefer, 1997, pp 170, 180–1; see also Cottier and Schefer, 2000, pp 56, 58–9; see generally O'Connor, 1991, p 121, on the increasing importance of good faith for international law, especially when compared to municipal law.

[387] *India–Patents*, Panel Report, paras 7.21, 7.30.

7

Good Faith Interpretation of the WTO Agreements

As the ascertainment of this mutual understanding, ie the real and common intention of the parties, is a matter of interpretation, it is also said that treaty interpretation is governed by the principle of good faith.[1]

En réalité, ce principe [de la bonne foi] domine l'ensemble de la démarche interprétative, dans les recours en situations de violations comme dans les recours en situation de non violation.[2]

RULE INTERPRETATION FORMS part of the process of applying a norm to a factual situation.[3] Rule interpretation stands for legal reasoning. It consitutes one of the three pillars in the process of law-determination and is a task most often attributed to the judicial branch. The other three components of law-determination are the adjudicatory, the advisory and the law-making-processes.[4] If law is considered a manifestation of practical reasoning, its interpretation must also be guided by reasonableness.[5] However, doctrine has linked legal reasoning or rule interpretaton to practical reasoning only for common law. The question is therefore whether or not the interpretation of treaties must also be reasonable.[6]

It follows that if the law in question is a treaty provision, like any other law, it must be interpreted with reason. As agreements between Member States, the WTO Agreements are treaties, and they must be, like any other law, interpreted with reason.

Thus, in the process of determining the law applicable to a situation of international trade in goods and services, of international intellectual property protection or of government procurement, WTO treaty interpretation is a process that, just like law-creation, adjudication and advising on WTO law, must be guided by reason. This is how the interpretive principle of 'good faith interpretation' has become a necessary tool of WTO treaty interpretation.

[1] See Cheng, 1987, p 115.
[2] Canal-Forgues, 2001, p 8.
[3] *Cf* Atria and MacCormick, 2003.
[4] Detmold, 1989, pp 438–41.
[5] *Ibid*, pp 436–71.
[6] *Ibid*, pp 437–8.

The principle of 'good faith interpretation' mandates attributing a reasonable meaning to a norm of international law. Put more simply, 'good faith interpretation' as it is presently codified in the Vienna Convention on the Law of Treaties (VCLT) in Article 31(1), stands for 'legal reasoning', which in the author's view is no different from interpreting a treaty in good faith.

However the underlying question in treaty interpretation, as with all interpretive process in the law, is whether reason suffices as, or may be, a legitimate source of interpretation. Dworkin finds that the issue splits scholars insofar as there are some who believe that interpretation ought to be grounded in objectivity and must thus be reasonable and those who want to give free judgment to the interpreter in analysing the law. If reason is recognised as one element of the objectivity which an interpreter must find represented in applying a norm to a case, reason is a valid source of interpretive authority.[7]

'Good faith interpretation', as the *US–Gasoline* AB Report has termed the concept, is one element, source or tool of interpretation within the process of treaty interpretation. Whether or not it is an inalienable part of every treaty interpretation depends on the doctrinal opinion one has espoused about the 'general rule of interpretation'. Thus chapters seven and eight will examine whether the WTO judiciary considers 'good faith interpretation' an inherent part of the 'general rule of interpretation'.[8] These chapters will describe whether or not good faith interpretation is a mandatory step in all interpretive activities relating to each WTO-covered agreement.

Specifically, this study aims to analyse whether good faith interpretation and its corrolaries, codified in Article 31(1) of the VCLT, apply as 'customary rules of interpretation of public international law', which Article 3.2 DSU prescribes for clarifying the 'existing provisions of those [WTO] agreements'.[9]

The first aim of this section is therefore to determine whether Article 31(1) VCLT includes good faith as a source of interpretation. Only once this question has been answered can we ask whether Article 3.2 DSU includes a good faith element of interpretation. The question then becomes whether good faith interpretation falls under the notion of 'customary rules of interpretaton of public international law'[10] and is part (under Article 3.2 DSU) of the legitimate sources of clarification of the rights and obligations of the WTO Agreements. If not, good faith interpretation may still be a legitimate tool for the interpretation of the WTO Agreements, albeit one specifically applicable to WTO law, as opposed to one used in public international law. The question to be asked in considering the WTO as an institution is whether and how good faith inter-

[7] See Fish, 1989, p 387; see also MacCormick, 1999, pp 1575ff.

[8] *India–Patents*, Panel Report, para 7.18; *EC–LAN*, Panel Report, para 8.25; see also *US–Section 301*, *Panel Report*, para 7.67, which uses the term 'general rule of interpretation' when referring to Art 31(1) VCLT.

[9] Art 3.2 DSU.

[10] *Ibid.*

pretation has shaped the balance of power between the judicial and the legislative branches, and whether or not good faith interpretation divides the WTO Panels from the AB.

This chapter offers a brief introduction to the key issues of good faith treaty interpretation in general public international law, both under and outside the rules of interpretation of the VCLT. This discussion centres on the following questions:

— Is good faith a recognised element of interpretation under the VCLT when taken together with the text, the context and the object and purpose of a provision?
— What status does good faith interpretation have in relation to text, context, object and purpose; and does it come before or after the plain meaning of a rule?
— What are the sources of good faith under Article 31 VCLT, the 'general rule of interpretation'?
— Does good faith interpretation relate to the customary rule of *pacta sunt servanda*; does it embody a measure of equity; and does it lend effectiveness to a treaty?
— Are there conflicts between good faith and its corollaries of *pacta sunt servanda*, effectiveness and equity?
— How can good faith possibly enhance the effectiveness and contemporaneity of a treaty, while standing simultaneously for *pacta sunt servanda*?
— How can it develop a contemporaneous meaning for a treaty while embodying the consensus of the signatories?
— How can good faith provide an objective solution based upon the common intentions of the signatories, while the principle of equity simultaneously offers a case-by-case solution, ie individualised fairness to a party of the treaty?

In this chapter the first section will outline some of the key references made to the VCLT rules of interpretation by the working parties and Panels of the GATT 47 and the Panels and the AB of the WTO. The next section will describe how the WTO Panels have referred to 'good faith interpretation', which the Panels use more frequently and differently than the AB. The last section of this chapter will analyse the function of the element of good faith in WTO treaty interpretation, both within the general rule of interpretation of Article 31 VCLT and outside it.

THE 'GENERAL RULE OF INTERPRETATION' IN THE VIENNA CONVENTION ON THE LAW OF TREATIES

WTO jurisprudence, starting with the decisions in *US–Gasoline, Japan–Alcohol, India–Patents* and *EC–LAN*, usually declares in an obiter dictum that the 'customary rules of interpretation of public international law' pursuant to Article 3.2 DSU are applicable to WTO treaty interpretation.[11] WTO jurisprudence further states that this refers to the rules of interpretation under the VCLT as opposed to the entire set of provisions of the VCLT.[12]

The first section in this chapter seeks to understand the relationship between the general principle of law of good faith and the general rule of interpretation under Article 31 VCLT. Chapters two to five have addressed the general rule of interpretation, as well as the element of good faith interpretation, as it applies to WTO law,[13] ie the 'clarification by reference to the fundamental rule of treaty interpretation set out in Article 31(1) of the *Vienna Convention*'.[14]

Since *US–Shrimp,* the AB has sought 'interpretative guidance' from 'the general principle of law and general principle of international law'. Good faith has increasingly assisted the WTO judiciary's law-finding, but, for the AB, good faith has been associated with a general principle of law rather than with the customary rules of interpretation under the VCLT. Thus, this chapter is intended to shed light on why the AB has chosen to interpret the provisions of the WTO Agreements with the general principle of good faith, while simultaneously refusing to recognise that good faith is an element of the Vienna rules on interpretation referred to in Article 3.2 DSU.

The Panels, unlike the AB, have preferred to take into account good faith considerations pursuant to the VCLT's good faith interpretation under Article 31 (as in *India–Patents, EC–LAN* and *Korea–Government Procurement*).

Increasingly, adjudicative practice has found the general principle of law of good faith and its more specific emanations such as *abus de droit* doctrine to 'inform' the provisions of the WTO Agreements.[15]

Among the cardinal concepts contained in the VCLT is what the *India–Patents, EC–LAN* and *US–Section 301* Panel Reports called the 'general rule of interpretation' codified under Article 31 VCLT.[16] According to international court practice and doctrine, as well as AB jurisprudence, Article 31 VCLT has 'attained the status of a customary rule of international law'.[17]

Article 31 General Rule of Interpretation

1. A treaty shall be interpreted in good faith in accordance with the ordinary meaning to be given to the terms of the treaty in their context and in the light of its object and purpose.

[11] *US–Gasoline*, AB Report, p 17; *Japan–Alcohol*, AB Report, p 10; *India–Patents*, AB Report, para 43.

[12] *India–Patents*, Panel Report, para 7.18; *EC–LAN*, Panel Report, para 8.25; *US–Section 301*, *Panel Report*, para 7.67.

[13] *US–Gasoline*, AB Report, p 17.

[14] See *Japan–Alcohol*, AB Report, p 10.

[15] *US–Shrimp*, AB Report, para 158; *US–Japan Hot-rolled Steel*, AB Report, para 101.

[16] *India–Patents*, Panel Report, para 7.18; *EC–LAN*, Panel Report, para 8.25; see also *US–Section 301*, Panel Report, para 7.67.

[17] See *US–Gasoline*, AB Report, p 17 and fn 34; see *Chile–Agricultural Products*, AB Report, para 213, for a recent reference.

2. The context for the purpose of the interpretation of a treaty shall comprise, in addition to the text, including its preamble and annexes:

   (a) any agreement relating to the treaty which was made between all the parties in connection with the conclusion of the treaty;
   (b) any instrument which was made by one or more parties in connection with the conclusion of the treaty and accepted by the other parties as an instrument related to the treaty.

3. There shall be taken into account, together with the context:

   (a) any subsequent agreement between the parties regarding the interpretation of the treaty or the application of its provisions;
   (b) any subsequent practice in the application of the treaty which establishes the agreement of the parties regarding its interpretation;
   (c) any relevant rules of international law applicable in the relations between the parties.

4. A special meaning shall be given to a term if it is established that the parties so intended.

By contrast, the ILC and others maintain that good faith in international treaty law is based upon '*bonae fidei negotia*',[18] which refers to the 'substantive obligation' of *pacta sunt servanda* (separately codified in Article 26 VCLT):[19] 'The . . . interpretation in good faith flows directly from the rule of *pacta sunt servanda*, the interpretation of treaties in good faith and according to law is essential if the *pacta sunt servanda* rule is to have any real meaning'.[20] The ILC finds only the principles of effectiveness,[21] that of PLE ('to refrain from acts calculated to disappoint the legitimate expectations of its partner'),[22] and of integration (interpretation *in concreto*) to be implied in Article 31 VCLT.[23]

Other scholars suggest that what the *US–Gasoline* AB Report called 'good faith interpretation',[24] namely the references to good faith within the

[18] The principle of interpreting treaties in good faith can be traced back to the principle of *bonae fidei negotia*. Kolb, 2000, pp 87–93, finds that it was a Canonist lawyer, who, since the early stages of English treaty practice, had included separate clauses to the treaties concluded by the Kings of England with foreign princes to the effect that these were meant to be *bonae fidei negotia*, ie to be kept in good faith. Additionally to *pacta sunt servanda*, *bonae fidei negotia* determines the extent of the obligation, and provides for constitutive functions, Kolb, 2000, p 97–8. Similarly to *pacta sunt servanda*, *bonae fidei negotia* spells out that treaties must be both carried out and interpreted in accordance with standards of conduct which stand the test of good faith. Schwarzenberger, 1955, p 300; Kolb, 2000, p 98, '*pacta sunt servanda et bonne foi peuvent se renforcer mutuellement au regard d'une même finalité* . . .'; see also Kolb, p 91 referring to Sir Robert Philimore's statement that 'all international treaties are covenants *bonae fidei*'.

[19] Lennard, 2002, p 55.

[20] YBILC, 1966, vol II, p 221, p 219; see also Lennard, 2002, p 55; Marceau, 1999, p 127.

[21] *Ibid*, 1964, vol I, p 288, 'ut res magis valeat quam pereat . . . appeared in the jurisprudence of the ICJ and was inherent in the notion of good faith'; see similar citations on pp 288–9; Lennard, 2002, pp 58–61; Cameron and Gray, 2001, p 256.

[22] *Cf* Charme, 1992, pp 71ff.

[23] YBILC, 1966, vol II, p 221; YBILC, 1964, vol II, p 56.

[24] *US–Gasoline*, AB Report, p 17.

interpretive process under the 'general rule of interpretation' of Article 31(1) VCLT,[25] refers to interpretive maxims and canons not expressed in Article 31 VCLT.[26]

Cottier and Schefer, as well as Lennard, consider good faith interpetation to originate in Article 31 VCLT but find that the WTO judicial bodies refer to additional maxims of good faith outside this Article.[27]

Substance

The term 'interpretation *made in* good faith'[28] refers either to good faith as a single element of rule 31(1) VCLT (as opposed to ordinary meaning) or to the whole of rule 31(1) VCLT. The drafters use the term 'interpretation *in* good faith' to refer exclusively to good faith as the first principle in paragraph 1 of Article 31 VCLT.[29] Rosenne uses the term 'good faith in interpretation'.[30] The present study uses the equivalent term of 'good faith interpretation' introduced by the Panel in *India–Patents*[31] and subsequently adopted by the *EC–LAN* Panel Report.[32] The closest the AB has come to referring to good faith in Article 31(1) VCLT was when it stated in the *US–Offset ('Byrd Amendment')* case, 'Article 31(1) of the Vienna Convention directs a treaty interpreter to interpret a treaty in good faith'.[33]

25 *India–Patents*, Panel Report, para 7.18; *EC–LAN*, Panel Report, para 8.25; see also *US–Section 301*, *Panel Report*, para 7.67.

26 YBILC, 1964, vol II, p 53; YBILC, 1966 vol, II, p 219; Cottier and Schefer, 2000, p 64; Lennard, 2002, p 55.

27 YBILC, 1964, vol II, p 56, Sir G Fitzmaurice, a Special Rapporteur to the ILC Commission has derived this and five further principles, which he considered major principles of interpretation, from the PCIJ and ICJ jurisprudence. For the WTO, Petersmann found that, in addition to the general principle of effectiveness, in *US–Gasoline*, AB Report, p 12, the AB used the principle of fundamental fairness, Petersmann, 1998, pp 91–2; see Lennard, 2002, pp 55–76, identifies as canons of interpretation derived from the requirement to interpret in good faith and used by the WTO, presumption of consistency, legitimate expectations, *abus de droit*, effectiveness, in *dubio mitius*, *lex specialis*, evolutionary meanings, unilateral statements and *expressio unius est exclusio alterius*, against Marceau, 1999, pp 116–17, who opines that the principle of 'effective interpretation, the presumption against conflicts and the interpretative principle of in *dubio mitius*' are 'general principles of interpretation, to which the Panels and the AB have referred in addition to the provisions contained in the Vienna Convention . . .'.

28 YBILC, 1964, vol II p 60, para 27.

29 YBILC, 1966, vol II, p 221, para 12.

30 Rosenne, 1989, p 174.

31 *India–Patents*, Panel Report, para 7.18.

32 *EC–LAN*, Panel Report, para 8.25, referring to Art 31(1) VCLT.

33 Lester and Leitner, 2003a, p 15, '[The AB] takes a narrower view of the principle of good faith than the Panel', which had held that the Offset Act was evidence that the US had not acted in good faith, and thus based its finding on the *substantive* principle of good faith. The AB found that the Panel should have provided evidence that the US had violated more than a treaty provision, in order for the US to have not acted in good faith. In its finding, the AB did not provide further information on what *interpreting* in good faith under Art 31(1) VCLT entails.

Good faith can manifest either as the objective standard of a communication between the parties to a treaty or it can stand for the individual subjective intentions of each of the parties. This section will examine international scholarship on whether good faith interpretation expresses subjective or objective manifestations of the will of the parties to an international agreement, and how the WTO Panels and the AB are divided over the issue.

'Objective Good Faith'

'Objective good faith', the standard of reasonable expectation by which the binding rules of a treaty are interpreted,[34] emanates from '*Treu und Glauben*'.[35] Conversely, an interpretation according to subjective good faith seeks to determine the intentions of the parties[36] and is related to the concept of '*guter Glaube*'.[37] As opposed to subjective good faith, objective good faith can be said to function in the following way: when two or more parties enter into contact with each other and establish a dialogue, their relationship, before even being governed by law, is determined by their mutually shared expectations.[38] The general principle of law of good faith protects the expectations that are legitimate,[39] without the need for any positive rule in the form of treaty law. Nonetheless, states might choose to concretise the principle of good faith in positive legal rules, whether or not good faith will act as a standard or establish a right or obligation.[40]

In WTO practice, objective good faith primes subjective intent of the parties to a treaty. Despite the AB's findings to the contrary, ie that subjective intent is at the root of the PLE, the WTO's institutional structure preconditions a primacy of objective expectations over subjective intent;[41] in other words, the most-favoured nation and non-discrimination obligations, both of which are based on multilateralism, have primacy over reciprocity. In contrast to reciprocity, where a subjective intent may be the foundation of treaty relations, the

[34] Zoller, 1977, pp 224–46.

[35] Kolb, 2000, p 143–53, who also uses the term 'objective good faith'.

[36] Zoller, 1977, pp 343–5.

[37] Kolb, 2000, pp 115–34, who uses the term 'subjective good faith'.

[38] See Schwarzenberger, 1955, pp 291–326; in particular, p 290, '[L]aw of every type relies on the fulfilment of expectations'; see also Bernhardt, 1963 pp 23–5; Müller, 1971, pp 154–64, 176–81; see specifically Bacchus, 2003d, pp 23–4, for the WTO, '[t]hose of us who believe we need "law" and who believe especially, and increasingly, that we need "international law" must understand above all what it is that *precedes* "law". Law is preceded by a perception of a duty. Thus, an awareness of a duty precedes a willingness to abide by a law. Law will exist only to the extent that we see a need for law in fulfilling our "range of duty". Law will exist only to the extent that we see the need to be *bound* by law'.

[39] But see YBILC 1964, vol I, p 29, 'the expression "in good faith" should also certainly be retained, for those words were the very essence of the rule stated. The obligation was not only moral, but also a legal one'.

[40] See Müller, 1971, p 256, who finds that good faith protection often concretises in positive rules; similarly, Cheng, 1987, p 132; McDougal et al, 1994, p 42.

[41] *Cf* Howse, 2003, p 11; see also Koskenniemi, 1990, p 1.

multilateralism of the WTO, which becomes an operational principle through the most-favoured nation obligations, works only if trade relations are based upon 'standards [of reasonable] behaviour', that is objective good faith, or as GATT 1947 practice would say, legitimate expectations.[42]

'Subjective Intent'?

The subjective approach was rejected by the VCLT drafters,[43] who found that 'the starting point of interpretation is the elucidation of the meaning of the text, not an investigation *ab initio* into the intentions of the parties'.[44]

However, subjective intent was upgraded to an element of interpretation consistent with international law in Judge Schwebel's Separate Opinion to the Case concerning Fisheries Jurisdiction (*Spain v Canada*),[45] where he opined that when interpreting reservations of a state, those reservations that are inconsistent with international law or legally questionable—that is, where states comply objectively with the international rule but subjectively deviate from it by invoking a reservation—must also be taken into account.[46]

In his pledge to engage the ICJ's jurisdiction in cases where a state has built a reservation on subjective intentions, which may not be consistent with the objective international law at hand, Judge Schwebel took a Hobbesian view of international legal relations through the lense of political realism. Schwebel appears to agree with Hobbes' 'criticism of relying upon natural principles to justify political authority'. Koskenniemi finds that subjective intent primes objective good faith, because:

> [a]ppealing to principles which would pre-exist man and be discoverable only through faith or *recta ratio* was to appeal to abstract and unverifiable maxims which only camouflaged the subjective preferences of the speaker.[47]

To Koskenniemi an honest interpretation of a rule would lead to subjective intent becoming more important than objective interpretation in good faith. This is so because Koskenniemi finds objective interpretation or good faith interpretation to 'camouflage' and thus to hide the real reasons for adopting a

[42] *Cf* O'Connor, 1991, p 109, who describes the principle of good faith in the interpretation of treaties as 'a standard of behaviour'.

[43] The promoter of the subjective good faith approach, Sir Hersch Lauterpracht envisaged that the treaty interpreter seek out the intentions of the parties with the support of both '*effet utile*' and '*travaux préparatoires*'.

[44] YBILC, 1966, vol II, p 220.

[45] ICJ, Separate Opinion of President Schwebel in the the *Case Concerning Fisheries Jurisdiction (Spain v Canada)* of 4 December 1998.

[46] See *ibid*, para 4, where he says that '[I]f Spain means to maintain that a reservation is ineffective in so far as it excludes measures or actions by the declarant State that are illegal under international law, I cannot agree. As the Court's Judgment acknowledges, the very purpose, or one of the purposes, of States making reservations may be to debar the Court from passing upon actions of the declarant State that may be or are legally questionable'.

[47] Koskenniemi, 1990, p 1.

certain rule, ie the political power play underlying the value expressed by an international rule.

McDougal, Lasswell and Miller as well as Lennard confirm that the VCLT prefers to extrapolate the 'objectively ascertained intention of the parties, as opposed to the subjective intent of the parties'.[48]

Bernardez makes the criticism that since 1995, there has been a trend of 'subjectivity *redivivus*' within the ICJ, where the interpreter investigates alleged subjective intentions, as 'distinguished . . . from the common intention expressed in the treaty itself either in plain words or by necessary implication as established through the application of VCLT rules'.[49] He attributes this development to the strong role some interpreters attribute to *travaux préparatoires*.[50]

Cottier and Schefer diagnose a trend in the WTO AB towards a subjective approach to good faith interpretation, similar to the subjectivity *redivivus* of the ICJ. They consider that the reason why the AB 'bars the protection of legitimate expectations from the scope of Article 31 VCLT', 'stem[s] from fundamentally diverging views on treaty interpretation'.[51]

Up to now, only three AB reports have established the primacy of ordinary meaning over supplementary meaning. However, the AB did not explicitly acknowledge a priori or a fortiori text autonomy over good faith means of treaty interpretation. As the *EC–LAN* appellate report states: 'The application of these rules in Article 31 of the Vienna Convention will usually allow a treaty interpreter to establish the meaning of a term'.[52]

Although the AB has usually been 'less international law oriented' than the Panels—the latter have more often used good faith aspects of treaty interpretation, and have had to be 'disciplined' regarding their approach to interpretation[53]—there have also been cases where the AB has reprimanded the Panel for being 'overly literal and narrow'.[54]

Sequencing

This section on sequencing looks at the status and significance of the good faith method in comparison to the text-based approach of treaty interpetation. It

[48] Lennard, 2002, p 21.

[49] Bernardez, 1998, p 747.

[50] *Ibid*, pp 738–9, 746, for Bernardez, the VCLT-consistent application of subjective intentions as supplementary means, should never 'contradict the meaning arrived at by application of Art 31'. Their role is limited to 'confirm the meaning arrived at by the application of the general rule of Art 31' or to determine the meaning when the result of the interpretive process under Art 31(1) is 'ambiguous, obscure, manifestly absurd or unreasonable'.

[51] Cottier and Schefer, 2000, p 62.

[52] *EC–LAN*, AB Report, para 86; *Canada–Milk/Dairy*, AB Report, paras 132–6 (footnote omitted).

[53] Lennard, 2002, p 87.

[54] *Canada–Milk/Dairy*, AB Report, para 136.

considers the relative weight good faith has in the light of the 'plain or ordinary meaning' approach to treaty interpretation. If good faith has a function in treaty interpretation, what is its place and status in comparison to the sources of text, context, object and purpose?

Status

The VCLT represents itself as maintaining a 'balanced' approach between a valuation of the text (consensus) and other 'extrinsic' means of interpretation. Extrinsic instruments can include the search for the subjective intentions, the ascertainment of the parties' reasonable expectations as well as a teleological approach.[55] Clearly, the extrinsic approach was considered secondary to the meaning of text.[56]

However, there are scholars who consider that good faith has no place at all in the VCLT. Zoller believes that,[57] 'in consecrating the textual method, the Vienna Convention has limited the role of good faith'.[58]

In Müller's view, the ordinary meaning rule of the VCLT is already a compromise of the plain meaning rule (Vattel's maxim: '*qu'il n'est pas permis d'interpréter ce qui n'a pas besoin d'interprétation*'), which if the text of a term seems clear, any recourse to other interpretive elements, even if these would elucidate the true will of the parties[59], and which also precludes *Vertrauensprinzip* or Paley's rule, which is guided by the 'standard of reasonable expectation'.[60]

Müller's view that ordinary meaning is already a compromise between the autonomy of text and good faith, and thus an expression of good faith, is shared by O'Connor. Like Müller, O'Connor distinguishes the narrow function of good faith, expressed with ordinary meaning, from the 'the wider functions of the principle of good faith', which require regard for the spirit of a treaty emanating from the substantive rule of *pacta sunt servanda* and, in all cases, expressing honesty, fairness and reasonableness.[61]

The VCLT itself is apparently a combination of the textual approach and the standard of reasonable expectations[62] or common intentions.[63] The primacy of the text gives a basis for the interpretation of a treaty, while at the same time

[55] YBILC, 1966, vol II, p 218; Korhonen, 1996, p 7; Lennard, 2002, pp 20–2, who notes that using text as well as the 'expressed intent' (rejecting 'subjective intent') was seen as 'the best balance', p 22.

[56] See Art 32 VCLT.

[57] Zoller, 1977, p 214; McDougal, 1967, reprinted in McDougal et al, 1994, p 423, 'the rigor of the Commission's insistency upon the "primacy of the text" . . .'.

[58] Zoller, 1977, 'la jurisprudence international applique beaucoup plus les méthodes de l'interprétation stricte que celles de l'interprétation de bonne foi'.

[59] Müller, 1971, pp 138–40.

[60] *Ibid*, pp 145–6.

[61] *Cf* O'Connor, 1991, p 109.

[62] Müller, 1971, p 145; O'Connor, 1991, p 109.

[63] Bernardez, 1998, pp 727–32.

a role in the interpretive process is given to extrinsic evidence of the intentions of the parties and the objects and purposes of the treaty.[64]

McDougal and others make the criticism that good faith interpretation only vests when the ordinary meaning of the text is ambiguous or unclear.[65] The good faith aspects of interpretation should be taken into account together with the ordinary meaning from the beginning. In summary, the VCLT

— confers priority but not exclusivity upon the 'plain' or 'clear' meaning rule,[66] also called Vattel's maxim (represented by Bernhardt);[67]
— considers the Vertrauenstheorie/New Haven school (represented by McDougal Lasswell and Miller,[68] Dahm,[69] Bernardez,[70] Rosenne[71] and Müller[72]), acknowledging the additional interpretive element of reason or objectivity that the term 'good faith' represents in Article 31(1) VCTL.

The VCLT decisively bars use of the subjective/empirical approach (represented by Anzilotti,[73] Bernhardt[74] and Degan[75]) as the 'initial' approach to treaty interpretation. However, the VCLT drafters did not dismiss the subjective approach to treaty interpretation entirely. Representatives of such a dialectic approach, namely Sinclair and Zoller,[76] influenced the ILC, which declared: '[T]he *starting point* of interpretation is the elucidation of the meaning of the text, not an investigation *ab initio* into the intentions of the parties' (emphasis added).[77]

The answer as to whether or not good faith gives primacy to ordinary meaning, depends on the particular school of thought about the 'sequencing' of the sources of interpretation.[78]

Some authors, such as Müller (for general international law) and Lennard (for WTO law) say that the VCLT drafters' intent was to leave it up to the interpreter in each case to decide which element shall be guiding.[79] Under the VCLT, the treaty interpreter is free to choose depending on the nature and the substantive content of a treaty, as well as the circumstances of its conclusion, the rele-

64 YBILC, 1966 vol II, p 218.
65 McDougal et al, 1994, p 90, 'comes perilously close to . . .'.
66 Bernardez, 1998, p 732.
67 Bernhardt, 1963, pp 58–66.
68 McDougal et al, pp 29–39.
69 Dahm et al, 2002, pp 637–9.
70 Bernardez, 1998 pp 747–8.
71 Rosenne, 1989, p 179.
72 Müller, 1971, pp 145–6.
73 Zoller, 1977, p 207, 'Parmi les juristes modernes, il convient de relever tout particulièrement Anzilotti, défenseur intransigeant de l'interprétation subjective . . .'.
74 Bernhardt, 1963, p 24.
75 Degan, 1997, pp 28–48, for a summary on the different followers of the subjective method of treaty interpretation; see Zoller, 1977, pp 205–23.
76 Sinclair, 1984, 115; Zoller, 1977, pp 204–23.
77 YBILC, 1966, vol II, p 220.
78 See *ibid*, pp 219–21; see, eg, Müller, 1971, pp 127–53; O'Connor, 1991, p 109; Korhonen, 1996, p 7–8.
79 See Müller, 1971, p 123, Lennard, 2002, pp 21–3.

vance it wants to accord to the individual interpretive element.[80] This flexibility in the choice of elements of treaty interpretation reflects the fact that there is no hierarchical distinction between the sources of international law.[81]

Significance

A recurring question of treaty interpretation is whether or not good faith is an implicit, but nevertheless indispensable, element of the 'general rule of interpretation' of Article 31 VCLT, just as the explicit elements of text, context, object and purpose are. Good faith is said by some to refer to the subjective intentions of the parties,[82] and by others to express an 'objectivated' standard of reasonable expectation,[83] also termed a standard of behaviour[84] or test of reasonableness[85] (*Vertrauensschutz*).[86]

As the *US–Lead Bismuth Carbon* GATT 47 case, discussed in the following chapter, demonstrates, the conflicts between the textualists and the *Vertrauensschutz* school over the correct application of the VCLT interpretation rules were already being fought out at the time of the earliest GATT cases. The US argued that reasonableness is the VCLT-consistent standard of interpretation, and that good faith is to be disregarded because it expresses 'motives and intent' instead of the common intentions as the 'general rule of interpretation' requires.[87]

The *India–Patents* and *EC–LAN* Panel Reports, both issued in 1998, took the conflict up to another level, where, under what had become the WTO, the AB was forced to take a stand. The AB did, reversing the Panels' open consideration of reason and objectivity, ie good faith as a source of interpretation, in favour of textualism.[88]

[80] Müller, 1971, p 122.

[81] Villiger, 1997, p 283; Rosenne, 1989, p 179, emphasizing that good faith in treaty relations essentially functions to ensure the flexibility of the treaty language.

[82] See Kolb, 2000, p 273; Zoller, 1977, pp 205–23; against Müller, 1971, pp 129–30.

[83] See Müller, 1971, p 145, who equates the standard of reasonable expectation to Paley's rule, which express the contemporary approach to treaty interpretation generally, '*Eine Erklärung gelte so, wie berechtigterweise angenommen werden dürfte, dass sie verstanden worden sei*'.

[84] See O'Connor, 1991, p 109, who describes the principle of good faith in the interpretation of treaties as 'a standard of behaviour'; see also Cottier and Schefer, 2000, p 59.

[85] See Marceau, 1999, p 96, describes the AB's balancing test in *US–Shrimp* of the Chapeau of Art XX (balancing. the market access commitments against the right of countries to invoke an Art XX specific exception), as a 'test of reasonableness'.

[86] See Müller, 1971, p 104–8, 143–53.

[87] *US–Lead and Bismuth Carbon Steel*, para 104.

[88] See *India–Patents*, AB Report, para 45; *EC–LAN*, AB Report, paras 83ff.

Functions

Good faith interpretation embodies an array of non-literal interpretive elements,[89] such as the requirement to interpret *in concreto* (the norm in its context and in the light of the object and purpose), to enhance the effectiveness and to respect the integrity of the agreement. In addition, good faith has two interpretive functions in a wider sense: the gap-filling (constitutive) and balancing (regulative) functions. In the context of the latter, the question is; what is: the correlation between good faith interpretation as employed in a balancing function, and equity?

Resolving Gaps in Interpretation

What scholars define as the constitutive good faith function more intrusive upon a treaty text. It authorises judges to fill *lacunae* by way of creative jurisprudence.[90] The line between this constitutive, gap-filling function and interpretation is not fixed, and the judicial body will have to take a decision in one of two directions; it may either apply the general principle of law of good faith (or any other general principle of law or customary rule) *practer legem*, or it may decide that an existing norm leaves enough room for a good faith interpretation to expand the meaning of that norm so as to encompass the conflict to be adjudicated.

Since good faith interpretation derives from *pacta sunt servanda*, one of its principal functions is to limit the powers of the treaty interpreter. A fortiori it cannot be used to fill in gaps.[91]

However, good faith in treaty interpretation can also express the search for the reasonable intentions of the parties.[92] In this sense, the use of good faith avoids excessive formalism (a too strict adherence to *pacta sunt servanda*). Thus if a gap is unintended, it becomes eligible for gap-filling (constitutive good faith or good faith *praeter legem*), albeit within the limits of reason.[93]

> [L]orsque les Traités ne contiennent pas de disposition formelle et sont muets sur certains points, *la bonne foi va autoriser le juge* à subvenir par le biais d'une interprétation généreuse conforme à l'esprit de l'acte, *à suppléer au vide juridique* créé par les parties.[94]

McDougal, Lasswell and Miller agree that a treaty cannot afford to fail to apply an agreement because of some 'alleged verbal gap or infelicity in the text',

[89] *US–Gasoline*, AB Report, p 17.
[90] Zoller, 1977, p 223; Schwarzenberger, 1955, p 324.
[91] Zoller, 1977, pp 214–15.
[92] Zoller, 1977, pp 216–23.
[93] Zoller, 1977, pp 221–3.
[94] Zoller, 1977, p 223 (emphasis added).

simply because the plain meaning rules would consider an interpretation *contra legem* to be a revision of the 'genuine shared expectations of the parties'.[95]

For De Visscher it is equity rather than good faith which permits filling a gap. De Visscher argues in favour of gap-filling with equity, because equity, as opposed to 'good faith interpretation', is not attached to the positive law of a treaty's provisions:

> Tandis que le droit positif y compris le principale général de bonne foi, adossé à des principes et à des règles, opère par déduction, c'est par une démarche directe de l'esprit que l'équité en découvre les carences et en corrige les injustes rigueurs.[96]

Since the AB has adhered to the literal method of interpretation, which is 'relatively safe and its results . . . easily accepted . . .', it has been difficult to fill in gaps. According to Ehlermann, the AB's gap-filling has received mixed reactions.[97] Hilf believes that the *Korea–Government Procurement* Panel decision opened the way to 'fill unintended gaps in the WTO Agreements' with 'principles of customary international law'.[98]

It should be noted that the Panel did not refer to 'good faith interpretation', rather it applied what was identified as the customary principle of good faith in treaty negotiations. Thus, the Panel conveyed the view that gap-filling is not a function of treaty interpretation (in good faith), but rather of a substantive principle of good faith. Even if the AB in *US–Japan Hot-rolled Steel* and the Panel in *Egypt–Steel Rebar* did not qualify their interpretation of certain provisions in the anti-dumping agreement as 'filling in gaps', they actually used the principle of good faith to creatively clarify 'often imprecise anti-dumping rules' or 'alleged *lacunae*'.[99]

Correcting Restrictive Interpretation

Good faith may remedy textual interpretation. This means that the principle of good faith may be applied to correct interpretations of treaties that do not seem to be objectively reasonable, ie which do not seem to make good sense. In this function, 'good faith interpretation' is said to be a corrective to positive law.[100] In 1963, Bernhardt authoritatively defined the corrective function:

> Das Gebot der bona fides Rechnung zu tragen, hat schliesslich bei der Vertragsauslegung-wie in allen anderen Bereichen des Völkerrechts-noch eine weitere

[94] Zoller, 1977, p 223 (emphasis added).

[95] McDougal et al, 1994, p 90.

[96] de Visscher, 1972, p 4; see also Kolb, 2000, on the relationship between good faith and equity, pp 99–111.

[97] Ehlermann, 2002, p 617, who argues that while the AB's technique of 'completing the analysis' has been well received the 'controversial issue of the admissibility of the unsolicited amicus curiae briefs' has been 'severely criticized and hotly debated'.

[98] Hilf, 2001, p 122.

[99] Petersmann, 1997b, p 99; see also *US–Japan Hot-rolled Steel*, AB Report, paras 101, 193; *Egypt–Steel Rebar*, Panel Report, para 7.161.

[100] *US–Gasoline*, AB Report, p 17.

> Funktion: Es begrenzt den Bereich zulässiger Rechtsausübung, indem es den Rechtsmissbrauch untersagt und damit eine dem vertraglichen Treueverhältnis und seinem Sinn widersprechende Auslegung verbietet, auch wenn sie dem Wortlaut nach möglich erscheinen könnte.[101]

Sinclair and Zoller concur that 'good faith underlies the concept that interpretation should not lead to a result which is manifestly absurd or unreasonable'[102]: '*La bonne foi intervient pour rémedier aux excès que pourrait presenter le critère du sens ordinaire, la primauté du texte*'.[103]

However, Zoller warns against confusing the corrective function of good faith, which is to guard against an unreasonable result of an excessively strict literal interpretation, with the principle of equity:[104] '*La bonne foi écarte la solution déraisonnable, elle n'écarte pas la solution injuste*'.[105]

In 2000, Kolb, on the basis of Müller's work, stated that the corrective function of good faith is its only legitimate function in the interpretive process:[106]

> En conclusion on peut dire que le rôle de la bonne foi est ici de tempérer la textualité afin d'éviter ses excès.[107] Son objet est de protéger la confiance dans l'emploi raisonnable de la langue et du langage.[108]

'Balancing Conflicting Rights'

In 1955, Schwarzenberger introduced what he termed 'a regulative function' for good faith:

> [I]n the fields, in which good faith exercises a regulative function, be it the law of treaties or international customary law as applied by judicial institutions, good faith is a potent and persuasive factor in the process of *balancing conflicting rights* (emphasis added).[109]

'Balancing conflicting rights', the regulative function for good faith, may be a corollary of the corrective function. Although when used correctively good faith may avert an abuse of rights ('*Rechtsmissbrauchsverbot*'), the balancing function of good faith limits the exercise of one right in the light of another, rather than banning the use of a right altogether. Compared with corrective good faith, balancing good faith is less intrusive.

In WTO jurisprudence the regulative function of good faith has been used only occasionally by the AB, most importantly perhaps in the *US–Shrimp*

101 Bernhardt, 1963, p 25.
102 Sinclair, 1984, p 120; Zoller, 1977, pp 109–15, 257–63.
103 Zoller, 1977, p 214.
104 *Ibid*, pp 21, 240, who argues that arbitral decisions have confused equity with good faith.
105 *Ibid*, p 240; see p 21, for the English translation, 'in a general manner, the judge uses good faith to exclude the unreasonable solution, but he cannot use it to rectify the law in the sense that he considers to be the most equitable'.
106 Müller, 1971, pp 127–8; Müller, 1995, p 95.
107 Kolb, 2000, p 274.
108 *Ibid*, p 272.
109 Schwarzenberger, 1955, p 324.

decision, where the AB balanced with good faith, according to what it termed the 'line of equilibrium', the market access commitments of the US with the right of the US as a member to protect its market with a specific exception under Article XX(a–j) of GATT 94.[110]

EARLY WTO CASE LAW REFERENCES TO 'GENERAL RULES OF INTERPRETATION'

A precondition for the adoption of the rule of good faith interpretation under Article 31 VCLT by the GATT/WTO legal system was to establish the application of the VCLT rules of interpretation for the WTO Agreements overall. The following section will cite the most important milestones in case law marking the commitment of the WTO judiciary, under Article 3.2 DSU, to take into account 'customary rules of interpretation of public international law' when applying the VCLT rules of treaty interpretation.

GATT 47, GATT 94, and the WTO Agreements

The GATT 47 Panels declared that the VCLT rules of treaty interpretation were applicable to GATT law only relatively recently, in two cases, both in 1994. GATT 47 jurisprudence declared in the *US–Tuna II* and *US–Lead and Bismuth Carbon Steel* cases, that the VCLT was a codification of customary rules of interpretation of public international law, binding even those GATT members that had not ratified the VCLT, most notably the US.[111]

Early WTO Panel and appellate jurisprudence descriptively referred to rules of interpretation under VCLT Articles 31 and 32. WTO jurisprudence in the *US–Gasoline* case of 1996 declared that the term 'customary rules of interpretation' in Article 3.2 DSU was meant to be a reference to the VCLT. For the facts of the *US–Gasoline* (1996) and *Japan–Alcohol* (1996) cases we refer to the decisions themselves, available from various sources.

The WTO AB, since its very first case (*US–Gasoline* in 1996) has proclaimed that it will abide by the VCLT rules regarding the interpretation of the WTO Agreements.[112] By comparison, it had taken the ICJ 11 years, following the

[110] *US–Shrimp AB Report*, paras 156, 159; see also above Part I, ch III, 'Prohibition of *Abus de droit* as an 'application of good faith''.

[111] See Restatement (Third) of the Foreign Relations Law of the United States 112(2) (1987), 325 cnt., which suggests that the US subscribes to the interpretive provisions of the VCLT as these, 'represent [. . .] generally accepted principles and the United States has also appeared willing to accept them despite differences of nuance and emphasis', cited in van Alstine, 1998, fn 71 to p 706.

[112] Ehlermann, 2002, p 615.

entry into force of the VCLT in 1980, to recognise in 1991 (*Arbitral Award of 31 July 1989*) Articles 31 and 32 VCLT.[113]

Only two years before the AB declared that VCLT Article 31 is applicable as customary international law to non-parties to that treaty, the ICJ in the 1994 *Territorial Dispute (Libyan Arab Jamahiriya/Chad)* case had proclaimed the same.[114] The ICJ's 'lateness and hesitation' in adhering to the VCLT stemmed from the 'doctrinal division among the various schools of interpretation of treaties'.[115]

The WTO AB's quick and open recognition and definition of customary rules of interpretation was hailed as pioneering in the history of international adjudicative organs.[116] Apparently, the WTO AB was not much concerned about scholarly debates on treaty interpretation, but simply considered the VCLT system a solid enough basis for its work.

GATT 47 and WTO Case Law

US–Tuna II, *GATT 47 Panel Report (1994): 'Good Faith Expresses the Basic Rules of Treaty Interpretation'*

The issue of *US – Tuna* II was, 'whether, in the pursuit of its environmental objectives, the United States could impose trade embargoes to secure changes in the policies which other opposing parties pursued within their own jurisdiction'.[117]

The EEC and the Netherlands brought a complaint against the US trade restrictions on imports of yellowfin tuna from the Eastern Pacific. The US Marine Mammal Protection Act ('the Act') had set out restrictions affecting direct import of tuna to the US in the form of a 'primary nation embargo' and an 'intermediary nation embargo'. The latter required that imports of tuna products be certified and reasonably proven not be imports subject to a direct prohibition by the US.[118]

113 Arbitral Award of 31 July 1989 (*Guinea-Bissau v Senegal*), ICJ Judgment of 12 November 1991, pp 69–70, 'These principles [natural and ordinary meaning etc] are reflected in Arts 31 and 32 of the Vienna Convention on the Law of Treaties, which may in many respects, be considered as a codification of existing customary international law on the point'.

114 See Territorial Dispute (*Libyan Arab Jamahiriya/Chad*), Judgment, ICJ Reports 1994, p 21, para 41; the ICJ reiterated that Art 31 VCLT reflects customary international law in, Maritime Delimitation and Territorial Questions between Qatar and Bahrain (*Qatar v Bahrain*), Jurisdiction and Admissibility, Judgment, ICJ Reports 1995, p 18, para 33; Oil Platforms (*Islamic Republic of Iran v United States of America*), Preliminary Objections, Judgment, ICJ Reports 1996 (II), p 812, para 23; Kasikili/Sedudu Island (*Botswana/Namibia*), Judgment, ICJ Reports 1999 (II), p 1059, para 18.; and most recently in the *Case Concerning Sovereignty over Pulau Ligitan and Pulau Sipadan, (Indonesia/Malaysia)*, ICJ Judgment 17 December 2002, para 37.

115 Bernardez, 1998 pp 732–3.

116 See Ehlermann, 2002, pp 616, 618.

117 *US–Tuna II*, para 5.42.

118 *US–Tuna II*, para 2.14.

Under both embargoes, the Act required:

> reasonable proof of the effects on ocean mammals of the commercial fishing regulatory program in effect for such fish or fish products exported to the US. In the case of yellowfin tuna harvested with purse seine nets in the eastern tropical Pacific, the government of the harvesting nation must meet a number of specific conditions.

One of the conditions required the tuna fishing to be monitored by the Inter-American Tropical Tuna Commission or an equivalent body.[119]

The question before the Panel was whether bilateral or plurilateral environment and trade treaties had established an international subsequent practice pursuant to Article 31(3)(b) VCLT, whereby national jurisdiction protecting living natural resources (US–Marine Mammal Protection Act of 1972) was 'practice with respect to international environmental agreements'.[120] The international environmental agreements had often 'require[d] . . . "straightforward import prohibition" '.[121] Therefore, national legislation implementing such international agreements could apply outside the national scope of that jurisdiction, that is extraterritorially. If evidence of such a practice could be found, Article XX(g) GATT 47 could be interpreted to allow national environmental law to apply extraterritorially, as long as the exhaustible natural resources protected by the national law required a cross-border international protection regime.

The EC and the Netherlands argued that if there were no jurisdictional limitation to the objects of measures justified by these paragraphs, then each party could unilaterally determine policies on international conservation and protection of life and health, from which other contracting parties could not deviate without jeopardising their rights under the General Agreement.[122]

The EC opposed the argument of the US that subsequent practice, in the form of the international environmental agreements concluded by the US, requires that national legislation on the protection of living resources apply beyond the jurisdiction of a nation state. In fact, the EC found the contrary to be true, that the signatories of the agreements analysed by the US had 'merely promised to take conservation measures within their own jurisdiction, . . .'.[123] 'The Panel observed that, under general international law, states are not in principle barred from regulating the conduct of their nationals with respect to persons, animals, plants and natural resources outside their territory'.[124]

The Panel went on to say that the parties had based their arguments on international environmental treaties other than the General Agreement (GATT 47). Therefore, it was 'necessary' for the Panel to 'determine the extent to which

[119] *US–Tuna II*, para 2.11.
[120] *Ibid*, para 3.21.
[121] *Ibid*, para 3.22.
[122] *Ibid*, para 3.36.
[123] *Ibid*, para 3.40.
[124] *Ibid*, para 5.17.

these treaties were relevant to the interpretation of the text of the General Agreement'.[125]

The Panel recalled that it is generally accepted that the VCLT expresses the basic rules of treaty interpretation and that the parties to the dispute shared this view. It therefore proceeded to examine the treaties in this light.[126]

The Panel then found that the international agreements cited by the US could not be considered under 'subsequent practice' pursuant to Article 31(3) as a primary means of interpretation for GATT 47 Article XX, since many of these agreements had been concluded before the General Agreement.[127] The other reason why the cited agreements were not relevant to the interpretation of Article XX GATT 47 was that they were often bilateral and plurilateral treaties, and would therefore not qualify as 'applicable between the parties to the agreement' as Article 31(3)(c) VCLT required, because some GATT 47 members were not party to them. Practice under the bilateral and plurilateral agreements, said the Panel, 'could not be taken as practice under the General Agreement, and therefore could not affect the interpretation of it'.[128]

The Panel found as a result that bilateral and plurilateral treaties do not constitute subsequent practice but only supplementary means (Article 32 VCLT) of interpretation of the General Agreement.[129] In this case, the Panel found that as supplementary means, the bilateral and plurilateral treaties 'were of little assistance in interpreting the text of Article XX(g)'[130] and that the treaties had no standing as primary means of interpretation because no 'direct reference were made to these treaties', either in the 'text of the General Agreement, the Havana Charter, or in the preparatory work to these instruments'.[131]

As a result, the Panel found 'that the contracting parties, by agreeing to give each other, in Article XX, the right to take trade measures necessary to protect the health and life of plants, animals and persons or aimed at the conservation of exhaustible natural resources', had not agreed to accord each other the right to impose trade embargoes for such purposes.[132]

The Panel therefore concluded that the US import prohibitions on tuna and tuna products under the US Marine Mammal Protection Act of 1972 were not covered by the exceptions of GATT 47 Article XX(g). The Panel therefore recommended that the US 'bring its measure into conformity with its obligations under the General Agreement'.[133]

[125] *Ibid*, para 5.18.
[126] *Ibid*.
[127] *Ibid*, para 5.19.
[128] *Ibid*.
[129] *Ibid*, para 5.19.
[130] *Ibid*, para 5.20.
[131] *Ibid*.
[132] *Ibid*, para 5.42.
[133] *Ibid*, para 6.2; see also para 6.1.

US–Lead and Bismuth Carbon Steel, *GATT 47 Panel Report (1994): Reasonableness v Good Faith Interpretation*

In this case the US made the distinction between reasonableness and good faith in treaty interpretation; the US associated the first with rationality and logic and identified the second as motives and intent. The Panel came to the conclusion that reasonableness did not relate to treaty interpretation but rather informed about the standard of review for factual considerations. However, the Panel argued that good faith was a source of interpretation pursuant to the Vienna Convention and applicable to the interpretation of the GATT 47.

In *US–Lead and Bismuth Carbon Steel*, the Panel referred to the VCLT in answering the question posed by the EC as to whether Article 4.2 Tokyo Round Subsidy Code required that before a countervailing duty is imposed, it is first necessary to identify that a subsidy exists, despite the lack of the definition of a subsidy in the above-mentioned code. The EC argued that the US had misapplied Articles 31 and 32 VCLT, because it had sidestepped the interpretation of the ordinary meaning of the term with the argument that since there was no definition of a subsidy in the Code, there could be no ordinary meaning for the word 'subsidy'. Subsequently, the US directly derived its right to impose countervailing duties from the context, object and purpose of the Code overall.[134]

The EC, in contrast, argued that the lack of a definition did not mean that the word 'subsidy' has no ordinary meaning, and that subsequent practice in the form of a preceding adopted Panel report in *US–Canadian Pork* was to be drawn on to illustrate the meaning of the word.[135] The Panel in *US–Canadian Pork* had said that even if there was no definition of 'subsidy', the rules of interpretation nevertheless prohibited an interpretation contrary to a provision's clear wording. Even if policy considerations, such as defenceless farmers asking for a broader definition of 'subsidy' in order to be protected from cheaper imports, were to be advanced, the definition of subsidy should reflect the existing level of concessions, and if that seemed outdate, the issue was to be resolved through negotiations and not *contra legem* interpretation:

> The Panel moreover found that such an argument did not justify an interpretation of Article VI:3 contrary to its clear wording. As previous Panels have emphasized (BISD 35S/227; L/6568, page 20 and L/6513, page 33), the purpose of the dispute settlement procedures is to ensure the implementation of existing commitments; if it is considered that the existing mechanisms are not sufficient, any changes must be sought through negotiation.[136]

Since primary means of interpretation, ie subsequent practice, were available to the Panel in the *US–Lead and Bismuth Carbon Steel* case, it was not necessary to resort to supplementary means of interpretation under Article 32 VCLT, such

[134] *US–Lead and Bismuth Carbon Steel*, para 51.
[135] *Ibid*, para 55; see also *US–Canadian Pork*, para 4.7
[136] *US–Canadian Pork*, para 4.7

as preparatory material. (The US had found that the preparatory material had shown that a conflict existed as to the definition of a subsidy, between the concepts of 'cost to government' versus 'benefit to the recipient'.[137])

In *US–Lead and Bismuth Carbon Steel* a dispute emerged between the US and the EC over whether the VCLT rules required the imposition of a countervailing duty to be interpreted under the standard of reasonableness, or under that of good faith. The US argued that reasonableness expresses 'logic and rationality',[138] while good faith stands for 'motives and intentions', and that under the VCLT rules, interpretation had to be based on the standard of reasonableness rather than that of good faith.[139]

The Panel held that the GATT and the Codes, as an international agreement falling under the definition of Article 2 VCLT, had to be interpreted in conformity with the VCLT:

> As an international agreement within the meaning of Article 2 of the VCLT, the Agreement had to be strictly interpreted in conformity with the customary rules on treaty interpretation as laid down in Articles 31 and 32 of that Convention.[140]

The Panel, however, deviated from its above-mentioned statement on legal interpretation, by taking into account the standard of reasonableness the US had used to show that the imposition of the subsidy by the EC was arbitrary. The Panel found that the rules of interpretation of Article 31 and 32 VCLT did not necessarily suffice to guide it in a *legal* appreciation of the evidentiary issues. Consequently, the impact of such rules of interpretation on the Panel's standard of review relating to national law was limited to questions of interpretation.

In *US–Lead and Bismuth Carbon Steel* the Panel distinguished 'reasonableness as an element for the legal appreciation of facts'—which is a problem for the standard of review—from 'good faith', which pertains to the legal interpretation of an agreement. The Panel decided that the issue of reasonableness pertained to the 'legal appreciation of facts' and was thus a standard of review, while good faith pertained to the issue of interpretation, which relates to the provision of the Code:

> The Panel noted, however, that the rules of treaty interpretation in the Vienna Convention did not necessarily provide sufficient guidance to a Panel on issues involving the legal appreciation of facts in light of evidentiary requirements of the Agreement. For example, while these rules were relevant to an interpretation of the meaning of the concept of 'positive evidence' in Article 6 of the Agreement, these rules alone did not necessarily enable a Panel to determine whether or not in a given case certain facts qualified as 'positive evidence'. The Panel noted that it was mainly in this limited context of a review of factual assessments in light of evidentiary standards that several previous Panel reports had used terms like 'reasonable'.[141]

137 *US–Lead and Bismuth Carbon Steel*, para 56.
138 *Ibid*, para 104.
139 *Ibid*.
140 *Ibid*, para 368.
141 *US–Lead and Bismuth Carbon Steel*, para 56.

In the two other GATT 47 Panel decisions with findings referring to the VCLT, the *US–Salmon (AD)* and the *US–Stainless Steel Plate* cases, the Panel merely 'note[d]' that interpretive rules of the VCLT exist. The Panels did not, however, further clarify what the relationship between the VCLT and the GATT 47 should be.[142]

US–Gasoline, *Appellate Body Report (1996): 'Directed to Apply the "General Rule of Interpretation"'*

In *US–Gasoline* (1996), the AB held that the US gasoline baseline establishment rules, legitimately designed to promote clean air under Article XX(g) GATT 94, discriminated between US and foreign gasoline refiners and resulted in a disguised restriction on trade prohibited by the Chapeau of Article XX GATT 94. In overturning the Panel's finding of non-discrimination when applying Article XX GATT 94 to the US baseline establishment rules, the AB reprimanded the Panel because it had 'overlooked a fundamental rule of treaty interpretation, which has received its most authoritative and succinct expression in the Vienna Convention on the Law of Treaties'.[143]

In its first report, the AB laid down why the 'general rule of interpretation' (Article 31 VCLT) specifically, and the 'customary rules of interpretation of public international law' more generally (but not the entire VCLT) become 'related treaty' law applicable to the WTO.[144] The AB based the application of the VCLT's interpretive rules to the GATT and the other covered Agreements of the following three arguments:

— The AB refered implicitly, but without mentioning the decision, to the argument put forward by the Panel in *US–Tuna II*, that Article 31 VCLT applies because 'all of the participants and third participants', 'rely upon' the 'general rule of interpretation'.[145]

— The AB elevated the 'general rule of treaty interpretation' to 'a rule of customary or general international law'[146] by expressly referring in a footnote to the jurisprudence of the ICJ, the European Court of Human Rights and the courts of the Inter-American Court, as well to the writings of international publicists.[147]

— The AB considered Article 31 VCLT a rule of customary interpretation of public international law, which WTO law, specifically Article 3.2 DSU, obliges the WTO adjudicators to apply when 'seeking to clarify' the WTO Agreements; the 'general rule of interpretation' set out above has been relied

[142] *US–Salmon (AD)*, para 369; *US–Stainless Steel Plate*, para 235.

[143] *US–Gasoline*, AB Report, p 16; see also Petersmann, 1998, pp 90–1 for a discussion of the case in relation to development of the WTO DSU.

[144] Bartels, 2001, on the notion of 'applicable law in WTO Dispute Settlement Proceedings'.

[145] *Ibid*, first sentence of p 17 excluding the quotation of Art 31(1) VCLT.

[146] *Ibid*, second sentence of p 17 excluding the quotation of Art 31(1) VCLT and fn 34.

[147] See *US–Gasoline*, AB Report, p 17 and fn 34.

> upon by all of the participants and third participants, although not always in relation to the same issue. This general rule of interpretation has attained the status of a rule of customary or general international law. As such, it forms part of the 'customary rules of interpretation of public international law' which the AB is directed, by Article 3(2) of the DSU, to apply in seeking to clarify the provisions of the General Agreement and the other 'covered agreements' of the *Marrakesh Agreement Establishing the World Trade Organization*.[148]

Ultimately, the AB in *US–Gasoline* concluded that the US baseline for pollution must not be read so broadly as to restrict the scope of Article III:4 GATT, nor so narrowly as to fall outside Article XX(g) GATT.[149]

Although in its first report the AB did not specifically use the term 'good faith interpretation' to describe Article 31(1) VCLT,[150] the report is nevertheless important because it established the application of the general rule of treaty interpretation for the WTO.[151] Moreover, the report established the principle of effectiveness for WTO treaty interpretation, which the AB borrowed from ICJ case law and which scholars consider a 'corollary' to the general rule of treaty interpretation in Article 31 VCLT:

> One of the corollaries of the 'general rule of interpretation' in the *Vienna Convention* is that interpretation must give meaning and effect to all the terms of a treaty. An interpreter is not free to adopt a reading that would result in reducing whole clauses or paragraphs of a treaty to redundancy or inutility.[152]

According to Marceau, the *US–Gasoline* case also established an interpretation of the Chapeau of Article XX pursuant to the 'test of reasonableness', which would lead the AB in *US–Shrimp* to be guided by the principle of good faith/*abus de droit* when making the interpretation:[153]

> It is . . . important to underscore that the purpose and object of the introductory clauses of Article XX is generally the prevention of 'abuse of the exceptions of [what was later to become] Article [XX]'. . . . The Chapeau is animated by the principle that while the exceptions of Article XX may be invoked as a matter of legal right, they should not be so applied as to frustrate or defeat the legal obligations of the holder of the right under the substantive rules of the *General Agreement* . . . in other words, the measures falling within the particular exceptions must be applied reasonably, with due regard both to the legal duties of the party claiming the exception and the legal rights of the other parties concerned.[154]

[148] *Ibid*, third sentence of p 17 excluding the quotation of Art 31(1) VCLT.
[149] See *ibid*, p 18.
[150] *India–Patents*, Panel Report, para 7.18; *EC–LAN*, Panel Report, para 8.25; *US–Section 301*, *Panel Report*, para 7.67.
[151] See Marceau, 1999, p 95.
[152] *US–Gasoline*, AB Report, p 23, fn 45.
[153] Marceau, 1999, p 96.
[154] *US–Gasoline*, AB Report, p 22.

Therefore, in the *US–Gasoline* decision, the AB—while declaring that it followed the textual, or contextual means of interpretation—based the decision on a functional (object and purpose, effectiveness) approach towards the words in Article XX.[155]

Japan–Alcohol, *Appellate Body Report (1996): 'Words of the Treaty Form the Foundation for the Interpretive Process'*

In *Japan–Alcohol*, the AB reiterated the finding of *US–Gasoline*, which is that the WTO Agreements shall be interpreted according to the customary rules of interpretation of public international law, which includes Article 31(1) VCLT.[156] The AB expanded the reference in Article 3.2 DSU to encompass supplementary means of interpretation under Article 32 VCLT.[157] In addition, the AB declared its preference for the text-first approach. Finally, the AB established the sequence in which it believes all the interpretive processes at the WTO should be conducted.[158]

In this early example of the AB's preference for a text-first approach to treaty interpretation the AB stressed that the first step of every 'interpretative process' is the language of the provision itself. Only if the text-based approach leaves uncertainty, can the range of interpretive methods be broadened to include the wider applications of the general rule of interpretation, such as the principle of effectiveness.

Article 31 of the Vienna Convention provides that the words of a treaty form the foundation for the interpretive process: 'interpretation must be based above all upon the text of the treaty'. The provisions of the treaty are to be given their ordinary meaning in their context. The object and purpose of the treaty are also to be taken into account in determining the meaning of its provisions. A fundamental tenet of treaty interpretation flowing from the general rule of interpretation set out in Article 31 is the principle of effectiveness (*at rest mages valet qualm per eat*). In *United States–Standards for Reformulated and Conventional Gasoline*, it was noted:

> One of the corollaries of the 'general rule of interpretation' in the *Vienna Convention* is that interpretation must give meaning and effect to all the terms of the treaty. An interpreter is not free to adopt a reading that would result in reducing whole clauses or paragraphs of a treaty to redundancy or inutility.[159]

Up to and including the *Japan–Alcohol* decision, no Panel had mentioned good faith aspects of treaty interpretation. The only elements recognised as constitutive for treaty interpretation up to that point were text, context, object

[155] Petersmann, 1997a, pp 112–15.
[156] *Japan–Alcohol*, AB Report, p 10.
[157] *Ibid*, pp 10–11, fn 17.
[158] *Ibid*, p 11.
[159] See *ibid*, p 11.

and purpose and effectiveness. Only with the Panel decisions in *India–Patents*, *EC–LAN* and *US–Shrimp* and their subsequent appeals does the element of good faith, either in the 'general rule of interpretation' of Article 31(1) or as a general principle of law applicable in the relations between the parties under Article 31(3)(c), become an issue of WTO adjudication, if not an element of WTO law.

Usually, however, the AB follows the textual approach. It has applied good faith aspects of treaty interpretation only once to date, namely in the *US–Offset Act ('Byrd Amendment')* case (see chapter eight below), where it found that the ADA must be interpreted pursuant to the principle of *pacta sunt servanda*, the emanation of good faith, which it found the US was bound to respect. However, in *Japan–Alcohol*, the AB created the precedential value of adopted reports and based it upon PLE. The Panel in *Japan–Alcohol* chose a different legal basis for a judiciary's duty to follow previous reports. In this case the Panel accorded adopted Panel and AB reports a more significant function than had the AB, because it elevated the value of previous adopted reports to the rank of primary sources of treaty interpretation, which the adjudicator is obliged to take into account as 'subsequent practice' in every interpretive process in which he or she engages, pursuant to Article 31(3)(b) VCLT.[160]

'GOOD FAITH INTERPRETATION' IN THE LIGHT OF LEGITIMATE EXPECTATIONS BY THE PANELS

The WTO must continue to renew attention to the interpretive tool of good faith in the context of Article 31 of the Convention, as much as it already pays attention to the general principle of good faith in a number of different forms.[161]

This section examines in detail how the WTO Panels approach the element of good faith in their interpretation of the WTO Agreements. This section will show that the WTO Panels are using the good faith aspect inherent in the 'general rule of interpretation' under Article 31(1) VCLT.[162] The interpretation of the WTO-covered agreements by the Panels is thus referred to as 'good faith interpretation', using the term the AB used in *US–Gasoline* to describe a clarification of rights and obligations based upon good faith.[163]

Using case descriptions, this section will outline first how the Panels introduced a WTO-specific element of 'good faith interpretation',[164] which they

[160] *Ibid*, pp 12–13, and Panel Report, para 6.10.

[161] Cottier and Schefer, 1997, p 67.

[162] The first section set out the mainstay 'general rule of interpretation' under Art 31 VCLT and the function of the element of good faith therein. The following section illustrated that the WTO Panels and AB from their earliest cases in 1996 onwards had referred to the VCLT rules of interpretation, without considering, beyond the text of the provision itself, other sources of interpretation, namely good faith.

[163] *US–Gasoline*, AB Report, p 17.

[164] *Ibid*.

linked to the 'general rule of interpretation' of VCLT 31.[165] Secondly, we will observe how WTO Panel practice has subsumed the PLE, a GATT-specific emanation of good faith (see above), within the scope of Article 31(1) VCLT. Thirdly, we will examine how such a WTO Panel-specific approach to 'good faith interpretation' has successfully realised an effective protection of the legitimate expectations of WTO members. Fourthly, we consider how WTO appellate practice has overturned most of the Panel decisions on the specific issue of good faith interpretation, which the AB deems a misapplication of the VCLT rule of interpretation.

Protection of Legitimate Expectations Endemic to 'Good Faith Interpretation'

India–Patents *(1997): 'Lack of Legal Security . . . System Cannot Adequately Protect Legitimate Expectations'*

India failed to install a TRIPS-consistent measure. In effect, this left patent applicants without protection at the beginning of the mandatory protection period in 2005, which in turn deprived foreign patent applicants of the future benefits that should have been guaranteed under Articles 70.8 and 70.9.

The 'conditions of competition', which in the preceding cases related exclusively to the balance of negotiated *tariff* concessions, were interpreted broadly by the Panel, in order for PLE as to conditions of competition to encompass *market access for patentable products* of private, non-Indian right-holders. The Panel arrived at this broad interpretation by declaring 'conditions of competition' a 'well-established GATT principle', but found that beyond the GATT, 'the protection of legitimate expectations is central to creating security and predictability in the "multilateral trading system" '.[166]

In *India–Patents*, the absence of security and predictability could be measured by the lack of future effective patent protection.[167] Thus, when the Panel interpreted Articles 70.8 and 70.9 in the light of WTO Member States' reasonable expectations as to their ability to 'plan future trade', it was doing no more than enforcing the goal of security and predictability in the TRIPS Agreement:[168]

> [W]e find that the lack of legal security in the operation of the mailbox system in India is such that the system cannot adequately achieve the object and purpose of Article 70.8 and protect legitimate expectations contained therein for inventors of pharmaceutical and agricultural chemical products. . . . Thus, security and predictability in

[165] *India–Patents*, Panel Report, para 7.18; *EC–LAN*, Panel Report, para 8.25; see also *US–Section 301*, *Panel Report*, para 7.67.
[166] See *ibid*, para 7.21.
[167] *Ibid*, para 7.28.
[168] *Ibid*, paras 7.30, 7.41 referring to the *US–Taxes on Petroleum (Superfund)* case.

the multilateral trading system, which is one of the central goals of the dispute settlement mechanism, cannot be achieved.[169]

To reinforce its argument in favour of protecting the legitimate expectations of the US, the Panel argued with the 'standards of interpretation developed in past Panel reports, . . . in particular those laying down the principle of the protection of conditions of competition flowing from multilateral trade agreements',[170] and in particular emphasized that 'good faith interpretation' 'requires the protection of legitimate expectations derived from the protection of intellectual property rights provided for in the Agreement'.[171]

It was by invoking security and predictability as one of the DSU's goals and as the foundation for PLE, that the Panel provided the AB with counter-arguments (Articles 3.2 and 19.2 DSU). The AB was quick to point out that transposing the principle of legitimate expectations as to conditions of competition from the GATT to the TRIPS agreement would add to member obligations,[172] at least when the transposition was made by the adjudicator.[173]

EC–LAN *(1998): 'Security and Predictability . . . Cannot be Maintained without Protection of such Legitimate Expectations'*

The US claimed that LAN computer equipment (which does not have a tariff category of its own in the EC tariff schedule LXXX) should be classified as ADP machines. The EC in contrast considered that LAN equipment was being used for telecommunications and should thus be classified as such.[174] Since the ordinary meaning of the tariff category of neither computer nor telecommunications is illustrative, the US submitted evidence that LAN equipment in the EU and in the US had been treated as computer equipment and qualified as such under the tariff heading of ADP machines. According to the US, the UK, Ireland, Denmark, France, and the Netherlands had long classified LAN equipment as ADP machines. Based on this practice in these EU Member States, the US had a legitimate expectation that such tariff treatment would continue in the future.[175]

In contrast, the EC claimed that the actual tariff treatment of LAN equipment in the EC Member States was not uniform during the Uruguay Round, and therefore that the US was not entitled to such expectations.[176] The Panel accepted the evidence presented by the EC that Germany's practice was to treat LAN as telecommunications equipment and that the practice in France was

[169] *Ibid*, 7.41.
[170] *Ibid*, 7.22.
[171] *Ibid*, 7.18.
[172] See *ibid*, paras 46–7.
[173] *Ibid*.
[174] See *EC–LAN*, Panel Report, paras 8.30–8.32.
[175] See *EC–LAN*, Panel Report, paras 8.32–8.38.
[176] *Ibid*, para 8.32.

inconsistent. It did not accept as relevant the fact that in the UK and Ireland, one week before the conclusion of the Uruguay Round, one type of machine had been treated as telecommunications equipment, as opposed to the hitherto common practice of placing such machines under the category of computer equipment.[177]

The Panel thus had to determine, on the basis of the evidence submitted by both parties regarding the actual tariff treatment of LAN equipment in the EC, whether this treatment entitled the US to legitimate expectations in that regard.[178] The Panel found that the evidence produced by the EC did not rebut the presumption raised by the US concerning the accuracy of its claim regarding the actual tariff treatment of LAN equipment during the Uruguay Round.[179]

The question was when the expectations of the US regarding the tariff treatment of its LAN equipment vis-à-vis the EC's actual treatment of this equipment became legally protected. The Panel stated:

> [A]n exporting Member's legitimate expectations regarding tariff commitments are normally based on the assumption that the actual tariff treatment accorded to a particular product at the time of the negotiation will be continued unless such treatment is manifestly anomalous or there is information readily available to the exporting Member that clearly indicates the contrary.[180]

The Panel established that since the textual interpretation of a tariff schedule will not clarify the meaning of the terms of the schedule, it is the context, ie Article II and the PLE associated with it, that is relevant:

> In our view, it may, as a matter of fact, be the case that in nearly all instances, the ordinary meaning of the terms of the actual description in a tariff schedule accurately reflects and exhausts the content of legitimate expectations. . . . It must remain possible, at least in principle, that parties have legitimately formed expectations . . ..[181]

To ascertain whether the EC engaged in less favourable treatment, the Panel was asked to interpret the meaning of a particular expression in the schedule.[182] The rule that the value of a member's tariff concession is protected by the legitimate expectations of other members had already been established in a NVNI complaint (*EEC–Oilseeds I*).[183] Consequently, the Panel in *EC–LAN* found:

> [I]n cases where an actual violation of tariff commitments [under Article II GATT 94] is alleged[,] such a direct violation would involve a situation where expectations concerning tariff concessions were even more firmly grounded.

This was because:

[177] See *EC–LAN*, Panel Report, para 8.43.
[178] *Ibid*, para 8.33.
[179] *Ibid*, paras 8.36–8.44; see also Cameron and Gray, 2001, p 262.
[180] *EC–LAN*, Panel Report para 8.45.
[181] *Ibid*, para 8.26.
[182] See *ibid*, para 8.22.
[183] *Ibid*, para 8.23.

> [T]he importance of legitimate expectations in interpretation of tariff commitments can be confirmed by the text of Article II itself.[184]

The Panel found that interpretive practice as regards PLE is supported by the object and purpose of the WTO Agreement and the GATT 94 Preambles, as well as contained in the principle of good faith interpretation under Article 31 VCLT, which was established for the WTO by the *US–Underwear* Panel and subsequently confirmed by the *India–Patents* Panel.[185]

In conclusion, the Panel found that the US was entitled to legitimate expectations that LAN equipment 'would continue to be accorded tariff treatment as ADP machines in the EC, based on the actual tariff treatment during the Uruguay Round'.[186] Even if the tariff treatment was not uniform throughout the EC, the US was entitled to ADP tariff treatment of its LAN equipments, as long as 'major export markets for US products', particularly Ireland and the UK, would accord ADP tariffs to LAN equipment.[187] In addition, it was obvious that the US's 'legitimate expectations were frustrated by the subsequent change in the classification practice in the EC'.[188]

In the result, the Panel found that because the actual tariff treatment of LAN equipment by the EC differed from the tariff treatment negotiated during the Uruguay Round, this change entitled the US to legitimate expectations sufficient to establish a claim of violation of Article II GATT 94 by the EC:[189]

> This conclusion [that legitimate expectations are a vital element in the interpretation of Article II and tariff schedules] is also supported by the object and purpose of the WTO Agreement. . . . The security and predictability . . . cannot be maintained without protection of such legitimate expectations. This is consistent with the principle of 'good faith interpretation' under Article 31 of the Vienna Convention.[190]

The criticism of the *EC–LAN* Panel decision was that the factual conditions for PLE were not met, as only two WTO Member States and trading partners of the US, namely the UK and Ireland, were practising classification in the sense claimed by the US.

Had *EC–LAN* been decided on the basis of subsequent practice under Article 31 VCLT instead of with good faith interpretation, the legitimate expectations of the US—that the LAN equipment would be subjected to the lower tariffs of computer equipment rather than the higher ones of telecommunications apparatus—could not have been protected. This is because practices in the EC regarding the tariff treatment of LAN differed so widely between Member States that the Panel would have had to dismiss the legitimate expectations of the US regarding lower tariff treatment of LAN equipment.

184 *Ibid*, paras 8.23–8.24.
185 See *ibid*, para 825 and fn. 258; see also Cameron and Gray, 2001, p 262.
186 *EC–LAN*, Panel Report para 8.60.
187 *Ibid.*
188 *Ibid*, para 8.61.
189 See *ibid*, paras 8.45, 8.60–8.62.
190 *Ibid*, para 8. 25.

EC–LAN *(1998): 'Legitimate Expectations are a Vital Element in Interpretation'*

The *EC–LAN* case illustrates how good faith appears in WTO jurisprudence in its two functions, namely as a source of law *and* of interpretation.

The *EC–LAN* case involved a dispute about the tariff rate applicable for specific computer equipment. LANs comprise specific computer devices such as routers, patches and switches used for building computer networks and linking work stations. The EC's schedule of tariff concessions (schedule LXXX), under GATT 94 provides for a bound tariff class under the heading of 84.71 or 84.73 (0 per cent tariff rate to maximum 2.5 per cent) including computers and ADP. Distinct from the above-mentioned headings is heading 8.517, which includes telecommunications apparatus (3.0 per cent tariff rate to 3.6 per cent tariff rate).[191] LAN equipment is a relatively new item that gained importance with the emergence of the internet in the nineteen-nineties. This form of equipment did not yet exist when the list of tariffs was drafted. The US and many other members charged LAN equipment at the rate for ADP, considering it to be closely related to the items in that list. But at the beginning of May 1995 the EC issued a binding regulation ordering the customs authorities of Member States to charge LAN equipment under the tariff heading of telecommunications apparatus, namely 8.517. Subsequently, the EC customs authorities, particularly those in Ireland and the UK that had hitherto charged LAN equipment under the tariff rate for ADP, began charging LAN equipment from the US at the rates that applied for telecommunications apparatus, arguing that LAN equipment was not ADP, but rather telecommunications equipment.[192]

As telecommunications apparatus, the LAN equipment was taxed at a higher rate than it had been when regarded as ADP, and the US brought action against the EC. The basis of the US claim was that the tariff reclassification of the LAN equipment went against good faith because it ran counter to legitimate expectations that the tariffs negotiated for computer equipment would apply to all related items and that there would be no changes to the applicable rates that would significantly increase costs for exporters. The US claimed that it was entitled to the legitimate expectation that LAN equipment would continue to be accorded the tariff treatment of ADP that had applied until then in the EC.

The EC appealed the Panel's finding, 'considering that Article II.5 of the GATT 94 confirms the interpretive value of "legitimate expectations" ', because in the EC's view, it incorrectly rendered the concept of PLE.[193]

The WTO Panels have strengthened the GATT/WTO-specific function of good faith, namely, the PLE, by attaching the following GATT/WTO-specific and substantive good faith principle to the Vienna rule of treaty interpretation:

[191] See *EC–LAN*, Panel Report para 8.29.
[192] *Ibid*, para 8.2.
[193] *Ibid*, AB Report, para 74.

'[T]he existence of this provision [Article II:5] confirms that legitimate expectations are a vital element in the interpretation of Article II and tariff schedules'.[194]

The ingenious trick used by the Panels to restrain an overbroad use of NVNI complaints was to link a good faith principle indigenous to the GATT/WTO with a non-WTO treaty rule. Only through attaching the GATT-specific principle of PLE to the VCLT good faith rule of interpretation, could the destabilising effect of another GATT-specific instrument, the NVNI, be prevented from weakening the legal security and predictability of the multilateral trading system.[195]

The WTO Panels considered any alleged frustration of legitimate expectations an emanation of the good faith element of the general rule of interpretation of Article 31(1) VCLT. By subsuming PLE under the good faith element inherent in the general rule of interpretation under Article 31(1) VCLT, the Panels contained the GATT/WTO-specific constellation of NVNI complaints. Because the Panels attached PLE to treaty interpretation rules of the VCLT, they simultaneously succeeded in preventing a PLE cause of action from being brought under a NVNI complaint only. By considering PLE a corollary of good faith interpretation under VCLT 31(1), current Panel practice conditions any substantiation of a PLE cause of action upon the general rule of interpretation of Article 31(1) VCLT, using an interpretive rule of international treaty law instead of testing the claim solely on a GATT/WTO-specific basis.[196] Not only did WTO Panel practice enhance the legitimacy of PLE, by considering it as a GATT/WTO-specific emanation of good faith, and more generally a necessary interpretive element applicable to all parties of the VCLT under the general rule of interpretation of the Vienna Convention, it also preemptively reduced the impact of NVNI complaints.

However, the AB has overturned all Panel reports protecting legitimate expectations. The AB has argued that subsuming PLE under the Vienna rule of interpretation amounts to a misapplication of the general rule of interpretation under Article 31(1) VCLT:[197] '[T]he AB bars the protection of legitimate expectations from the scope of Article 31 Vienna Convention, limiting that provision to calling for a reliance upon the words and context of a treaty'.[198]

'Maxims' of Good Faith Interpretation in Panel Practice

This section will briefly show that the WTO adjudicators have, despite Article 3.2 DSU, referred to 'maxims', that is to non-VCLT rules of treaty interpretation, for analysing the WTO Agreements. This section will not try to reconcile

194 *Ibid*, Panel Report, para 8.24.

195 See Cottier and Schefer, 2000, p 62; similarly, Ohlhoff, 2003, p 740 and fn 441.

196 *India–Patents*, Panel Report, para 7.18; *EC–LAN*, Panel Report, para 8.25; see also *US–Section* 301, *Panel Report*, para 7.67.

197 See, eg, *India–Patents*, AB Report, para 45.

198 Cottier and Schefer, 2000, p 62.

the interpretive approach to maxims with the restrictive application of the general rule of good faith interpretation of Article 31(1) VCLT by the AB because this is beyond the scope of the present study. We will therefore only diagnose the conflict between propagating a 'cropped' good faith interpretation with the Vienna rules on the one hand, and extensively tapping non-WTO sources of law for interpretation of WTO law on the other.

The WTO Panels' Substitution of Article 31(1) Vienna Convention

While engaging in 'good faith interpretation' to protect legitimate expectations under the WTO Agreements, certain WTO Panels have not inferred the meaning of the term under the general rule of interpretation under Article 31(1) VCLT, but have been guided instead by so-called 'maxims' or 'canons' of interpretation.[199] Both these terms have been used to describe rules of treaty interpretation outside Article 31(1) VCLT. 'Maxims' and 'canons' of interpretation thus encompass all non-VCLT rules of interpretation.[200]

WTO judicial practice has, in addition to conceiving a limited use for 'object and purpose', distinguished itself by its wide use of 'maxims',[201] ie 'general principles for the interpretation of treaties',[202] which are either, according to Hilf, general principles of law under Article 38 ICJ statute, such as good faith, due process and estoppel, or principles under customary law, such as *pacta sunt servanda*.[203] McCall Smith has proposed that the AB refers to such 'legal doctrines', which may include interpretive principles outside the general rule of interpretation under Article 31(1), to increase its discretion for adjudicating on a case-by-case basis,[204] as opposed to establishing a line of precedent.[205] Such maxims are the WTO-specific interpretive principles of balancing test, multilateralism and progressive liberalization,[206] but also of judicial economy (also called the doctrine of self-restraint or of independence) and *non-liquet*.[207]

[199] Lennard, 2002, p 55; YBILC, 1966, vol II, p 219, uses the term 'canons' to describe 'basic principles of interpretation'.

[200] *Ibid*, p 76.

[201] *Ibid*, p 55; YBILC, 1966, vol II, p 219, using the term 'canons' to describe 'basic principles of interpretation'.

[202] Hilf, 2001, p 123.

[203] *Ibid*.

[204] McCall Smith, 2003, p 93, 'reducing the value accorded to Panel reports as precedents by the original Panel'.

[205] *Ibid*, pp 79, 93, 'limited legal status of adopted GATT Panel rulings'.

[206] See Hilf, 2001, pp 117–21.

[207] McCall Smith, 2003, p 93.

'Maxims' and the 'Good Faith Rule of Interpretation'

The legal status of these maxims is unclear. For Lennard all maxims not expressly mentioned in the VCLT are inherent in the good faith rule of Article 31(1):[208]

> The maxims appear to be relied on as convenient expressions of principles, a 'star chart' for Panels unfamiliar with public international law to assist in the development of a legally coherent text-based WTO jurisprudence and to bind together relevant international economic law and public international law.[209]

Marceau finds such 'general principles of interpretation' situated 'outside' the VCLT, to exist 'in addition to the provisions contained in the Vienna Convention'.[210]

It is proposed to separate the six maxims Fitzmaurice identified as the 'major principles of interpretation' of the World Court[211] (also called 'basic principles of interpretation'[212]) from the other 'general principles of interpretation', which I consider as 'outside' Article 31(1).

Principles of interpretation 'outside' 31(1) VCLT originate from the *general principle of law* of good faith as opposed to the 31(1) VCLT *rule* of good faith interpretation.[213] Outside of Article 31(1), such interpretive principles either are 'relevant rules . . . applicable between the parties' through Article 31(3)(c), or have a 'special meaning' under Article 31(4) or form supplementary means under Article 32 VCLT.[214] Interpretative principles or principles of interpretation are recognised 'general principles of law' according to Article 38(1)(c) ICJ statute, but can also be the 'result of practical application'.[215]

A subcategory of general principles of interpretation is what Hilf calls the 'principles expressed in the WTO Agreements when these are not applied but used to interpret WTO provisions'.[216] Lennard finds that 'WTO Panels and the Appellate Body have relied on several interpretative "maxims". . . . These are not explicitly referred to in the Vienna Convention, but they have been treated in WTO fora as emerging naturally from the expressed principles in the Vienna Convention. In particular, they are often seen as deriving from the requirement to *interpret* treaties in "good faith" . . .'[217] Lennard thus considers all principles as being derived from the obligation to interpret in good faith in Article 31(1) VCLT whether they were actually linked by the VCLT drafters to the good faith

208 Lennard, 2002, p 55.
209 *Ibid*, 76.
210 Marceau, 1999, pp 116–17.
211 YBILC, 1964, vol II, p 53.
212 *Ibid*, 1966, vol I, p 218.
213 *Cf* Lennard, 2002, p 55.
214 Hilf, 2001, pp 122–3.
215 *Ibid*, p 123.
216 *Ibid*, p 117.
217 *Ibid*, p 111 (emphasis in original).

rule (effectiveness, interpretation *in concreto*) or not (*in dubio mitius*, *lex specialis*).[218]

Hilf distinguishes general principles under Article 38 ICJ statute from customary principles and from WTO-specific principles, but does not indicate under what paragraph of Article 31 VCLT they would be relevant for interpretation. Moreover, Hilf does not trace back the origins of such principles used interpretively either to good faith interpretation of Art. 31(1) VCLT or to general principle of law.

The Consistency of Interpretive Maxims with Vienna Rules

WTO treaty interpretation with maxims,[219] ie general principles of interpretation of treaties,[220] is, with two possible exceptions, VCLT-consistent.

The two exceptions to this assumption are as follows:

— WTO Member States can contractually agree to an exemption from the VCLT.[221]
— There may be interpretive principles not (yet) recognised as sources of public international law, eg the precautionary principle.[222]

Not all interpretative principles are inherent in the good faith rule of Article 31(1). They often derive from another paragraph of Article 31 VCLT. When the AB in *Japan–Alcoholic Beverages* used the principle of effectiveness, it originated from the requirement of good faith in Article 31(1);[223] but when the AB uses *lex specialis*[224] it could be derived from Article 31(3)(c);[225] and when the AB interprets with *in dubio mitius* it is derived from Article 32 VCLT. Finally, when the AB refers to the principle of multilateralism[226] or reciprocity[227]—if it is not

218 Hilf, 2001, p 55.

219 Marceau, 1999, p 116.

220 Hilf, 2001, p 123.

221 *US–Japan Hot-rolled Steel*, AB Report, para 101, and fn 40.

222 *EC–Hormones*, AB Report, para 124, or conversely there can be a maxim that has fallen into disuse.

223 *Japan–Alcohol*, AB Report, p 12.

224 *EC–Bananas*, AB Report, para 96, 'Therefore, the ordinary meaning in the context of the relevant provisions of the Lomé Convention, confirmed by the application of the *lex specialis* principles of interpretation, shows that the Lomé Convention's only "trade instruments" on bananas are those set forth in Protocol 5'.

225 The AB does not indicate on what source of the VCLT it bases its interpretation with *lex specialis*. The only time the AB has referred to Art 31(3)(c) VCLT, was when it used *abus de droit* for interpreting the Chapeau of Art XX in *US–Shrimp* para 158; however, since *abus de droit* can be derived from good faith in interpretation under Art 31(1) VCLT, recourse to Art 31(3)(c) VCLT would not have been necessary.

226 *US–Shrimp* AB Report, paras 121–2, the AB actually refers to 'unilateral measures' that are prohibited; Hilf, 2001, p 119, situates the AB's statement in the context of multilateralism.

227 *EC–LAN*, AB Report, para 82, 'we agree with the Panel that the security and predictability of "the reciprocal and mutually advantageous arrangements directed to the substantial reduction of tariffs . . ." is an object and purpose of the *WTO Agreement*, generally, as well as of the GATT 94'. The AB considers reciprocity and object and purpose of the WTO, ie under para 1 rather than as a

considering these as the 'object and purpose' of a provision under Article 31(1)—then it uses a 'special meaning' in accordance with Article 31(4) VCLT.

However, had the AB interpreted the SPS Agreement according to the precautionary principle, it would have acted contrarily to the VCLT, because the principle is neither applicable law between the parties—because it is not yet considered customary international law—nor a general principle of law.[228] Neither is it a special meaning agreed upon by WTO Member States, because in the *EC–Hormones* case, the US, unlike the EC, did not recognise its existence.[229] There are limits to the interpretation of the WTO Agreements with 'maxims'. Lennard identifies such risks, as quoted below, as legal security and predictability of the multilateral trading system:

> They [maxims] have in many cases effectively fulfilled this role, and enhanced the predictability and certainty of WTO jurisprudence while aligning it closely to international treaty law more generally. The danger would be if the reliance on these maxims went beyond that role to lead Panels and the AB away from the Vienna Convention's primarily text-based approach to create greater uncertainty as to the applicable rules and to risk altering the balance of WTO institutions, with the Panels and AB having a greater 'law-making' role than designed.[230]

special meaning under para 4, because no party to the dispute invoked reciprocity as an interpretive principle of the WTO; see also Hilf, 2001, p 119.

[228] *EC–Hormones*, AB Report, paras 123–4; Hilf, 2001, pp 127–8.

[229] *EC–Hormones*, AB Report, paras 121–2.

[230] Lennard, 2002, 76.

8

Good Faith Non-interpretation by the WTO Appellate Body

'[The] Panel misapplies Article 31 of the Vienna Convention'[1]

THE FOLLOWING FEW chapters analyse WTO AB jurisprudence on the possible interpretive function of the GATT/WTO-specific principles of PLE and good faith interpretation in WTO appellate practice. As an opening statement let us quote Cottier and Oesch in saying that the AB 'has not hesitated to actively shape the methods and elements of interpretation'.[2] Overall, the AB has 'devise[d] formal doctrines that give it legal room for manoeuvre where the political circumstances require flexibility'.[3]

In analysing a Panel decision based on good faith or addressing PLE, the AB usually proceeds as follows. First, it treats PLE and NVNI complaints as two sides of the same coin, by examining whether or not the conditions for a NVNI complaint have been met. These conditions are:

— the non-foreseeability of the action;
— the existence of a benefit accruing under WTO law; and
— the nullification and impairment of the benefit.

The latter usually amounts to a competitive relationship being offset, whether or not the WTO agreement under dispute provides for such a remedy.[4]

In the next step of analysis, if the AB finds that there is no basis for a NVNI complaint, because a WTO Agreement such as the TRIPS does not (yet) recognise such a remedy or because of lack of evidence of nullification or impairment, the AB then discusses whether or not PLE is an interpretive principle.[5]

[1] *India–Patents*, AB Report, para 45.
[2] Cottier and Oesch, 2001, p 39.
[3] McCall Smith, 2003, p 79.
[4] See Cottier and Schefer, 1997, pp 160–3; *Australia–Subsidy*, para 12.
[5] See *India–Patents*, AB Report, paras 39–42; *EC–LAN*, AB Report, paras 80 and 98.

LEGITIMATE EXPECTATIONS, GOOD FAITH INTERPRETATION AND 'SUBJECTIVE' INTENTIONS

'Subjective and Unilaterally Determined Expectations'

When the Panels refer to Article 31(1) VCLT they are usually referrring to good faith interpretation.[6] In contrast, the AB has not agreed that good faith interpretation is a valid method under Article 31(1) VCLT. Moreover, the AB finds that the 'general rule of interpretation' of Article 31(1) does not contain a reference to the obligation of protecting the legitimate expectations of the parties:

> The Panel misapplies Article 31 of the *Vienna Convention*. The Panel misunderstands the concept of legitimate expectations in the context of the customary rules of interpretation of public international law. The legitimate expectations of the parties to a treaty are reflected in the language of the treaty itself.[7]

As Cottier and Schefer have stated, the AB has 'barred the protection of legitimate expectations from the scope of VCLT 31(1)'.[8] The AB dismisses a self-standing, objective good faith function for Article 31(1) VCLT.

The *US–Offset Act ('Byrd Amendment')* AB Report of 2003 may either be an exception or may mark the beginning of a new era in WTO appellate jurisprudence relating to good faith. In this case, the AB seemed to recognise for the first time that 'Article 31(1) VCLT directs a treaty interpreter to interpret a treaty in good faith'.[9]

As a general rule, however, the AB has expressed the concern that in interpreting the text of a treaty provision in the light of the subjective and unilaterally determined expectations of the exporting member, PLE would seriously undermine the security and predictability of tariff concessions.[10]

However, Bacchus, the longest-serving AB Member, clearly sees the WTO's 'overarching goal' as 'serv[ing] the "mutual self-interest of all WTO Member States"'.[11]

The AB dismisses the value of the concept of legitimate expectations in WTO and international law because it allegedly protects the subjective intent, which is incompatible with the common intentions required by Article 31 VCLT. However, as the *EC–LAN* Panel maintained, WTO law may be interpreted in view of PLE for the following reasons:

— The principle of consensus prevailing in public international law limits the significance and scope of subjective will in the different legal instruments.[12]

[6] *India–Patents*, Panel Report, para 7.18.
[7] *Ibid*, AB Report, para 45.
[8] Cottier and Schefer, 1997, pp 160–3.
[9] *US–Offset Act ('Byrd Amendment')*, AB Report, para 296.
[10] See *EC–LAN* AB Report, paras 82 and 84.
[11] Bacchus, 2003, p 434.
[12] See Zoller, 1977, p 205.

— WTO law specifically restrains the search for and relevance of subjective intent because its multilateral approach to trade liberalization is built around the 'single package' approach of the Uruguay Round.[13] The subjective intentions approach to 'good faith interpretation' may have been stronger under the 'old' GATT 47, where, according to Kuyper (1995), each code was a separate treaty with its own dispute settlement mechanism. Under the WTO, to a greater extent than under GATT 94, the potential impact for subjective intentions is limited because the WTO is an 'integrated system in the sense that disputes which touch upon different instruments annexed to the WTO Agreement can be treated by the same Panel', with the result that with an increase of subjective views and interests it might be better to follow a strictly objectivate approach to interpretation.[14]
— PLE is an emanation from the *Vertrauensschutz* approach to treaty interpretation.[15]

'Common Intentions are the Purpose of Treaty Interpretation'

The PLE, understood by the *EC–LAN* Panel as a subjective approach, cannot contribute to ascertaining the *common* intentions, which are 'the purpose of treaty interpretation under the Article 31 VCLT'.[16]

Interpreting tariff concessions in the light of PLE amounts to protecting the subjective views of the exporting member only. The AB has found that this is contrary to the maintenance of the security and predictability of the tariff concessions as promulgated both by the WTO Agreement and the GATT.[17]

The AB has not indicated the source for its argument about why VCLT interpretation should mirror the common intentions of the parties. According to Pauwelyn, the source is the 1995 ICJ *Case Concerning Maritime Delimitation and Territorial Questions between Qatar and Bahrain*, where the ICJ said:

> whatever may have been the motives of each of the Parties, the Court can only confine itself to the actual terms of the Minutes as the expression of their *common intention* and to the interpretation of them which it has already given (emphasis added).[18]

The AB has found four possible outcomes of interpretation:

— [i]nterpreting the meaning of a concession in a Member's Schedule in the light of the legitimate expectations of exporting Members is not consistent

[13] *Cf* Jackson et al, 2002, pp 226–31, and Jackson, 2000c, 3–45 on the single package approach and on multilateral trade liberalization; see also Lowenfeld, 2002, pp 45–109; see Kuyper, 1995, p 91 on the 'integrated system' of the new dispute settlement system under the WTO.

[14] Kuyper, 1995, p 91.

[15] See Zoller, 1977, p 346.

[16] *EC–LAN*, AB Report, para 84; see also Cameron and Gray, 2001, pp 262–3.

[17] See *EC–LAN*, AB Report, para 82; see also Cameron and Gray, 2001, p 262.

[18] *Case Concerning Maritime Delimitation and Territorial Questions between Qatar and Bahrain (Qatar v Bahrain)*, Jurisdiction and Admissibility, ICJ Reports, 1995, para 41, also cited in Pauwelyn, 2001, p 18.

with the principle of "good faith interpretation" under Article 31 of the VCLT'.[19]

— The Panel was 'misapplying Article 31 VCLT'.[20]
— '[T]he duty of an interpreter is to examine the words of the treaty to determine the intentions of the parties', and Article 31 VCLT 'neither requires nor condones the imputations into a treaty of words that are not there or the importation into a treaty of concepts that were not intended'.[21]
— '[T]he Panel, in this case has created its own interpretative principle, which is consistent with neither the customary rules of interpretation of public international law, nor with established GATT/ WTO practice'.[22]

REJECTION OF THE PANELS' OBJECTIVE GOOD FAITH INTERPRETATION

The AB's reversal of the Panel ruling on the principle of good faith has significant ramifications on the future of the WTO system.[23]

Two 1998 AB Reports— namely *India–Patents* and *EC–LAN*—illustrate how the AB objected to the Panels' repeated use of the 'good faith interpretation' rule, which the AB found to:

— run counter to a text-first approach, as propagated by the VCLT;
— indequately take into account the subjective intentions of the parties in dispute; and
— fail to protect legitimate expectations unless the treaty provision under consideration contains a measure of, or reference to, legitimate expectations.

However, we think that both in *India–Patents* and *EC–LAN*, the AB erroneously applied a subjective theory of good faith, and if the AB had embraced objective good faith, it would not have needed to reject the Panels' good faith interpretation.

India–Patents Appellate Body Report (1998)

'The Panel Misunderstands the Concept of Legitimate Expectations'

In the *India–Patents* case, the AB criticised the Panel for associating the concept of legitimate expectations with the customary rules of interpretation of public

[19] *EC–LAN*, AB Report, para 82.
[20] *India–Patents*, AB Report, para 45; *EC–LAN*, AB Report, para 83.
[21] *India–Patents*, AB Report, para 45.
[22] *India–Patents*, AB Report, para 46.
[23] Jung and Lee, 2003, p 922.

international law.[24] Consequently, the AB overturned the Panel's decision, first, on the basis that the Panel had erroneously created its own interpretive principle, with disregard for not only for the VCLT's customary rules of interpretation of public international law, but also the prohibition in Articles 3.2 and 19.2 DSU against 'adding to or diminishing' members' rights and obligations.[25]

Secondly, the AB disagreed with the Panel that PLE 'is a well-established GATT principle'[26] that guides jurisprudence[27] and applies in the TRIPS areas.[28] Legitimate expectations are not part of the interpretive rule of Article 31 VCLT, the AB said, unless they are part of the treaty text itself.[29]

Scholarly Discussion

In Ehlermann's view, the only elements of the 'good faith rule of treaty interpretation' are text, context, and object and purpose.[30] Ehlermann does not consider good faith to be an element of Article 31(1).[31] Thus, it comes as no surprise that the AB in this decision (even though Ehlermann did not sit on it), denied PLE any interpretive function or value.

By introducing 'real NVNI complaints', Cottier and Schefer distinguish the above-mentioned situation from 'politically important expectations impaired by the action of others'.[32] Simultaneously they warn that these real NVNI complaints can have a destructive potential. Perhaps the AB was concerned that the Panel's result would open, via legitimate expectations, the TRIPS to private parties.[33] But in early 1997 Cottier and Schefer had already stated that 'it is clear that, absent official statements to the contrary, there can be no objectively reasonable expectation that a member will arrange its existing and therefore known internal trade laws to protect another member's private actors in its markets'.[34]

Cameron and Gray seem to agree with Cottier and Schefer's critique of the AB's limiting the applicability of PLE to NVNI complaints in *India–Patents*,

24 See *India–Patents*, AB Report, para 45; for the facts of the *India–Patents* decision of (1997) we refer to the decision itself, available from various sources, and our brief description of the case above.

25 *Ibid*, paras 46–8.

26 *Ibid*, para 7.20.

27 *Ibid*, para 7.19.

28 See *ibid*, para 7.21.

29 *Ibid*, para 45.

30 Ehlermann, 2002, pp 615–16; see also *India–Patents*, Panel Report, para 7.18; *EC–LAN*, Panel Report, para 8.25; *US–Section 301*, *Panel Report*, para 7.67.

31 See O'Connor, 1991, p 109 considers that 'good faith' under Art 31(1) as the requirement for the tribunal to 'have regard to honesty, fairness and reasonableness', 'takes precedence' over the incomplete or ambiguous words which have failed to yield a 'plain meaning'; see also Kolb, 2000, p 273; see also Lennard, 2002, p 55.

32 Cottier and Schefer, 1997, p 182.

33 *India–Patents*, AB Report, para 48.

34 Cottier and Schefer, 1997, p 182.

which was reaffirmed in *EC–LAN*.[35] For them, it is the *US–Underwear* and *US–Taxes on Petroleum (Superfund)* cases that are constitutive for the GATT-specific expression of PLE.[36] The foundation of PLE is not NVNI complaints, but the goal that conditions of competition are to be protected 'in order to inject security and predictability into the multilateral trading system'. NVNI complaints, by contrast, only 'bolster the need for the protection of legitimate expectations'.[37]

Roessler agrees with the AB's argument that there is no basis in the TRIPS (or generally in any WTO agreement other than GATT) to justify the introduction of NVNI complaints for 'non-renegotiable obligations'.[38] The transfer of Article XXIII: 1(b) to such obligations would amount to a breach of the prohibition in Article 3.2 DSU against adding to or diminishing obligations.

Lennard opines that the AB adopted 'the correct approach both in the interpretation of WTO Agreements generally, and in the consideration of "legitimate expectations" more specifically'.[39] Lennard in endorsing the decision seems to be succumbing to the mistaken view of the AB. He comments that 'as only violation complaints were available under the TRIPS Agreement, it was improper for the Panel to apply principles from NVNI complaint jurisprudence'.[40]

Canal-Forgues concurs with the AB and Lennard, firstly that PLE is not a well-established principle of GATT law, and secondly, that the Panel confused the concept of PLE in violation complaints (competitive relationship between products of one member vis-à-vis those of another) with the one in NVNI complaints (concerning market access concessions).[41]

Critique

In our view, the Panel did not confuse concepts, but only referred to PLE under Article III, ie in relation to the competitive relationship between two members' products. It should be noted that the Panel had not derived PLE in *India–Patents* from NVNI jurisprudence, but consciously chose the concept of PLE as to conditions of competition under Article III GATT, as elaborated by the *US–Taxes on Petroleum (Superfund)* and *US–Section 301* cases, for its claim that since the Preamble of TRIPS refers explicitly to the applicability of GATT 94, PLE concepts under GATT apply equally to TRIPS.[42] It was the AB in its decision that confused the concept of PLE as the basis of NVNI complaints; this was not

[35] See Cameron and Gray, 2001, pp 262–3.
[36] *Ibid*, p 261.
[37] *Ibid*.
[38] Roessler, 1997, pp 137–8.
[39] Lennard, 2002, p 67.
[40] *Ibid*, p 66.
[41] See Canal-Forgues, 2001, p 10.
[42] *India–Patents*, Panel Report, paras 7.20–7.21.

alleged by the Panel who had derived PLE from Article III GATT.[43] Possibly, it was more comfortable for the AB to assume that the Panel had meant to refer to PLE as the basis of NVNI complaints, so that it could easily rebut this assertion with the argument that since TRIPS does not yet apply to NVNI complaints, the Panel had misapplied PLE. The AB did not consider that when the Panel referred to legitimate expectations, the Panel could have meant the objective approach to treaty interpretation, and not an additional element of interpretation. Moreover, the AB also failed to consider that PLE could be a self-standing principle of interpretation, which, deriving from the requirement to interpret treaties in good faith, needs to be taken into account in addition to text, context, object and purpose when interpreting a treaty.[44]

EC–LAN, Appellate Body Report (1998)

According to the AB,'The Panel was not justified to find that the United States was entitled to "legitimate expectations"' because the Panel had based PLE on 'erroneous legal reasoning'.[45] The AB in *EC–LAN* reasoned that interpreting with legitimate expectations was inconsistent with the VCLT because it reflected only the subjective perspective of a single party to a treaty, instead of the common intentions of the parties.[46]

'The Panel was Not Justified [in Finding] that the United States was Entitled to "Legitimate Expectations"'

The purpose of treaty interpretation under Article 31 of the Vienna Convention is to ascertain the common intentions of the parties. These common intentions cannot be ascertained on the basis of the subjective and unilaterally determined 'expectations' of *one* of the parties to a treaty.[47]

Because the text of the EC's tariff schedule was unclear, both the AB and the Panel were forced to look at the object and purpose and even at other instruments of treaty interpretation. Thus, to ascertain what the change of tariffication of LAN equipment in certain EC countries after the Uruguay Round meant for the US, the AB had no material in the text of the EC's tariff schedules to criticise an erroneous expansion of a textual interpretation of tariff schedules, but reprimanded the Panel for misinterpreting the concept of common intentions, to incorrectly include PLE.[48]

[43] See *ibid* 39–42.
[44] *Ibid*, paras 43–5.
[45] See *EC–LAN*, AB Report, para 92 with reference to *EC–LAN*, Panel Report, para 8.60.
[46] *Ibid*, paras 82–4.
[47] *Ibid* para 84.
[48] See *ibid*, para 86, where the AB says that all rules under Art 31 leave the meaning of the tariff categories in the EC's schedule unclear and that the AB therefore had to take recourse to the supplementary means of Art 32 VCLT.

Also, the AB criticised the Panel for not having used all of the tools of interpretation according to Articles 31 and 32 VCLT. The AB considered that the Panel should have used the Harmonized System (HS) and Notes as supplementary means of treaty interpretation. The Panel should have attempted to elucidate the meaning of the EC's tariff schedule in relation to its treatment of LAN equipment to determine whether the US was in fact entitled to treatment of its LAN equipment as ADP rather than telecommunications equipment.[49] According to the AB, the Panel had erroneously replaced the supplementary means of interpretation that the HS and Notes would have offered with PLE, which is a tool of interpretation inconsistent with the rules of the VCLT.

The AB argued that the HS and the Notes were the sources of law necessary to elucidate the textually ambiguous meaning of the EC's tariff schedule, rather than the US's legitimate expectations, even if these were evaluated under the concept of common intentions. However, the AB was not very clear as to whether the HS and the Notes constitute supplementary means (Article 32 VCLT) or perhaps primary means of interpretation under Article 31(3)(c) VCLT.[50]

In the result the AB found that because the Panel had neglected to examine the HS and the Notes, as well as the subsequent practice in the EC, there was insufficient evidence for the AB to conclude that the US was entitled to legitimate expectations regarding the EC's tariff treatment of LAN equipment as ADP.[51]

Moreover, the AB held that classification practices in individual Member States are relevant only as supplementary means of treaty interpretation, ie as circumstances of the conclusion of the WTO Agreement and not as primary means of treaty interpretation under Article 31 VCLT as the Panel had believed.[52]

When drawing from the classification practice of members as supplementary means, the AB found that the Panel was incorrect not to consider the classification practice of the US, as the exporting member, and, furthermore, to use as a basis, information regarding only five of the 12 EC Member States (which in addition had inconsistent classification practice), and to ascribe special importance to the classification practice by customs authorities in only two of these Member States, since the export market comprises the EC as a whole and not any individual Member State.[53]

The AB held that for the reasons set out above, the Panel erred in finding that the 'legitimate expectations' of an exporting member are relevant for the purpose of interpreting the terms of schedule LXXX and determining whether the EC violated Article II:1 of the GATT 94:[54]

[49] *EC–LAN*, AB Report, para 83.
[50] Marceau, 1999, p 118.
[51] *EC–LAN*, AB Report, para 99.
[52] *Ibid*, para 92.
[53] *Ibid*, paras 93–6.
[54] *Ibid*, para 97.

> On the basis of the erroneous legal reasoning developed and the selective evidence considered, the Panel was not justified in coming to the conclusion that the US was entitled to 'legitimate expectations' that LAN equipment would be accorded tariff treatment as ADP machines in the EC.[55]

In sum the AB found no single rule under Article 31 VCLT to accommodate PLE, but found instead that the Panel should have used other evidence for evaluating the classification practice in the EC, such as the HS of the World Customs Organization (WCO).

The AB maintained, identically to its finding in *India–Patents*, where it had found the Panel to have 'misapplied the principle of good faith interpretation under Article 31 of the Vienna Convention',[56] that in *EC–LAN*, the Panel had erred in believing that the VCLT rules of interpretation protect the legitimate expectations of the parties:

> On the basis of the erroneous legal reasoning developed and the selective evidence considered, the Panel was not justified in coming to the conclusion that the United States was entitled to 'legitimate expectations'.[57]

The AB reprimanded the Panel for its incomplete application of the VCLT rules.[58] While it conceded that the Panel correctly sought to clarify the meaning of schedule LXXX in the context and in the light of its object and purpose,[59] it held that the Panel had failed to take into account the other rules such as Articles 31(3)(c), 31(4) and 32 VCLT.[60] To the AB, the Panel had specifically neglected to check which interpretive role, if any, would accrue to the HS of the WCO and the Notes of the WCO, both of which were the basis for the Uruguay Round tariff negotiations.[61]

Scholarly Discussion

Canal-Forgues agrees with the AB, who in *EC–LAN*, denied PLE any role in the interpretive process. Both Canal-Forgues and the AB (incorrectly) view PLE as the expression of protection for the subjective intentions of the parties. Canal-Forgues explains why it would be detrimental to the stability of the WTO legal system to allow subjective, unilateral views to colour the interpretation of its norms:

> [L]e but de l'interprétation des traités conformément à l'article 31 de la Convention de Vienne est d'établir les intentions communes des parties, intentions *qui ne sauraient être établies sur la base des 'attentes' subjectives et déterminées de manière unilatérale d'une des parties à un traité*. Se manifeste ainsi le souci de ne pas permettre un amendement

[55] *Ibid*, para 98.
[56] *Ibid*, para 83.
[57] *Ibid*, para 98.
[58] *Ibid*, para 87.
[59] *Ibid*, para 88.
[60] *Ibid*, paras 85–6.
[61] *Ibid*, paras 89–92.

> ou une révision unilatérale des engagements mutuellement agrées entre les Membres de l'OMC, car il ne s'agirait plus alors d'une question d'interprétation, mais de révision. L'exigence de prévisibilité du droit l'emporte ici clairement (emphasis added).[62]

If not the subjective intentions of the parties to the agreement, then, the common intentions are the key to interpreting a treaty provision, where the text remains unclear.

Pauwelyn seems to agree with the AB that treaty interpretation should reflect the common intentions of the parties, and to share the AB's view that legitimate expectations express only the subjective intentions of the parties:

> The criterion of legitimate expectations of some WTO Member States only as a tool to interpret WTO rules in violation cases was twice rejected by the AB (in *India–Patents*, paragraph 36 ff and *EC–Computer Equipment*, paragraph 84). As noted, what counts is the 'common intentions' of all WTO Member States.[63]

Pauwelyn notes the difference between the *EC–LAN* decision where the AB looked for the 'common intentions' of all WTO Member States, and the later *US–Shrimp* decision, where the AB checked only whether the 'two WTO Member States in dispute (Malaysia and the United States)' were bound by the non-WTO law taken into account under Article 31(3)(c).[64] However, one could disagree with Pauwelyn that the *EC–LAN* AB Report focused on all the WTO Member States. The AB explicitly stated that 'during the Uruguay Round negotiations, both the EC and the US were parties to the HS'.[65] The AB did not seem to require that all WTO Member States be parties to the HS for it to be relevant in the interpretation of a member's tariff schedule in *EC–LAN*.

Critique

The AB overturned the Panel's examination of the meaning of a tariff concession in a member's Schedule in the light of the 'legitimate expectations' of an exporting member, by stating that while it agreed with the Panel that security and predictability is an object and purpose of the WTO Agreement and the GATT 94,

> [W]e disagree with the Panel that the maintenance of the security and predictability of tariff concessions allows the interpretation of a concession in the light of the legitimate expectations of exporting members, ie their *subjective* views as to what the agreement reached during tariff negotiations was (emphasis in the original).[66]

In addition to viewing PLE as a subjective interpretive approach diametrically opposed to the multilateralism of the WTO system, the AB found that the sub-

[62] Canal-Forgues, 2001, p 10.
[63] Pauwelyn, 2001, p 18; see also Canal-Forgues, 2001, p 10.
[64] *Ibid*.
[65] *EC–LAN*, AB Report, para 89.
[66] *Ibid*, para 82.

jective and unilaterally determined 'expectations' of one of the parties to a treaty, which it associates with PLE, are also contrary to the goals of the VCLT.[67] This is a continuation of the AB's argument in *India–Patents* (which the AB cited here), where the AB had reprimanded the Panel for not sticking to a textual interpretation and instead interpreting in the light of legitimate expectations.[68] The AB said:

> The purpose of treaty interpretation under Article 31 of the Vienna Convention is to ascertain the common intentions of the parties. These common intentions cannot be ascertained on the basis of the subjective and unilaterally determined 'expectations' of one of the parties to a treaty.[69]

Similarly to its rejection of the Panel decision in *India–Patents*, the AB in *EC–LAN* incorrectly associated the PLE with subjective views. However, in contrast to *India–Patents*, where the AB had concluded that protecting subjective expectations of the exporting member was opposed to the textual approach of the VCLT, in *EC–LAN* the AB found that subjective views are contrary to the VCLT's aim of determining the common intentions behind the terms of a treaty, namely, *in concreto*, the common intentions behind the negotiated concessions of a Uruguay Round tariff schedule.

Interpreting the *EC–LAN* decision pursuant to subjective expectations would have meant that tariff treatment of LAN equipment in the US's largest export market for LAN equipment (ie the UK and Ireland), but also in the Netherlands and Denmark, was as ADP machines, so that only Germany, where it was classified as telecommunications equipment, imposed a higher tax on LAN equipment.[70] Since the AB considered EC practice *as a whole* (and not only that of the US's largest export markets *within* the EC), it would have found EC practice to be inconsistent.

However, the AB was forced by its limited standard of review for facts to base its findings on those of the Panel, who had considered only five out of 12 EC members.[71] Consequently it was not the AB's dismissal of the PLE as a principle of interpretation that resulted in denying the US protection of its legitimate expectations in the EC's continued higher tariff treatment of LAN equipment, but rather its limited standard of review, which prevented it from examining the basis for a claim of legitimate expectations.

Even if there was no way around dismissing the US claim that its legitimate expectations had been frustrated by changes in EC practice, an alternative argument may have been for the AB to say that because the practice of EC Member States is inconsistent, the US could not have formed legitimate expectations that its LAN equipment would continue to be treated as computer

[67] See *ibid*, para 83,
[68] *Ibid*.
[69] *Ibid*, para 84.
[70] See *ibid*, paras 8.40–8.42.
[71] See *ibid*, para 95.

equipment, rather than to dismiss the concept of PLE altogether by alleging that it protects unilateral subjective intentions instead of the common ones. Moreover, it is very difficult to determine why the AB in *EC–LAN* linked PLE to subjective, unilateral views of members. It would be interesting to know the source from which the AB derived its assumption.

CLASSICAL WTO APPELLATE PRACTICE

Japan–Alcohol (1996)

The WTO AB decision in *Japan–Alcohol* illustrates the AB's reluctance to interpret the GATT 'in the light of its object and purpose'.[72] In this case, the AB stated that 'the treaty's "object and purpose" is to be referred to in determining the meaning of the "terms of the treaty" and not as an independent basis of interpretation'.[73]

In the statement 'first finding your dictionary meaning and then sequentially examining the context and object and purpose',[74] the WTO adjudicator's focus on dictionaries is perhaps closer to Vattel's plain meaning rule[75] than to the VCLT's 'ordinary meaning rule'. The latter 'take[s] into account all the consequences normally and reasonably flowing from the text'.[76]

US–Shrimp (1998)

In the *US–Shrimp* Appellate Report, the AB established the primacy of text over the VCLT rule of good faith interpretation:

> A treaty interpreter must begin with, and focus upon, the text of the particular provision to be interpreted. It is in the words constituting that provision, read in their context, that the object and purpose of the states parties to the treaty must first be sought. Where the meaning imparted by the text itself is equivocal or inconclusive, or where confirmation of the correctness of the reading of the text itself is desired, light from the object and purpose of the treaty as a whole may usefully be sought (footnote omitted).[77]

In *US–Shrimp*, the AB demonstrated its limited understanding of the object and purpose of a treaty and:

[72] Lennard, 2002, 27.
[73] See *ibid*, citing *Japan–Alcohol*, AB Report, p 20.
[74] Lennard, 2002, p 23.
[75] See Müller, 1971, pp 136–8.
[76] Sinclair, 1984, p 121.
[77] *US–Shrimp* AB Report, para 114, with references to similar citations in preceding cases.

criticised the Panel for too quickly jumping to the general object and purpose of the GATT 94 and for too broadly construing the object and purpose of the GATT in any case. The AB again emphasized the need to focus on the text at hand.[78]

Applied to the situation in the specific case at hand, the AB said:

> the Panel did not look into the object and purpose of the Chapeau of Article XX. Rather, the Panel looked into the object and purpose of the whole of the GATT 94 and the WTO Agreement, which object and purpose it described in an overly broad manner.[79]

US–Offset Act ('Byrd Amendment') (2003)

More recently, the AB has confirmed its 'text-first' approach in the *Byrd Amendment* decision:[80]

> Thus, the task of interpreting a treaty provision must begin with the specific words of that provision. Accordingly, we turn first to the texts of Article 5.4 of the Anti-Dumping Agreement and Article 11.4 of the ASCM Agreement.[81]

DOCTRINAL ANALYSIS: KEY ELEMENTS OF CLASSIC APPELLATE BODY INTERPRETATIVE PRACTICE

Ehlermann describes the AB's interpretive practice as a 'cautious attitude'.[82] To better evaluate the AB's approach to the good faith rule of interpretation under Article 31 VCLT, this section will first consider how the AB perceives the Vienna rules of interpretation in general, that is, whether the AB has referred to the VCLT either as constituting an additional WTO covered agreement[83] or merely as an issue of facts.

'Symbolic' Reference to the Vienna Convention

According to McRae, 'it is an illusion to think that the meaning can be devined from a text through a direct application of the Vienna Convention'.[84] McRae's view of the role of the VCLT in clarifying the rights and obligations of the WTO covered agreements matches de Visscher's understanding that rules of interpretation of the VCLT more closely resemble a 'working hypothesis' than 'rules

78 Lennard, 2002, p 27.
79 *US–Shrimp* AB Report, para 116.
80 See Jung and Lee, 2003, pp 923, 925–7, referring to the 'the AB's ostensibly diehard textualism'.
81 *US–Offset Act ('Byrd Amendment')*, AB Report, para 281.
82 Ehlermann, 2002, p 638.
83 *cf ibid*, p 616.
84 McRae, 1998, p 108.

of international law'.[85] Furthermore, the references to the VCLT in ICJ jurisprudence have often been 'symbolic rather than functional',[86] as well as being 'non-obligatory in character'.[87]

In contrast, the AB actions in overturning Panel decisions for 'incorrectly' applying the VCLT, demonstrate that the AB adheres to the VCLT as part of the WTO's jurisdiction. Rules of interpretation of public international law are, according to Ehlermann, not merely referred to by the AB as facts. Ehlermann elaborates further that the AB has determined the 'precise relevance of rules and principles of public international law for the covered agreements'[88] and has thus actively applied and deliberately chosen to apply the VCLT. Ehlermann predicts that, in the future, international law will be increasingly applied at the WTO, and that the 'true importance of the interrelationship between the WTO Agreements and public international law will become apparent only when more . . . problems of substance have to be addressed'.[89] Thus, it can be said that references to the VCLT in WTO case law are more than symbolic.

'Sequencing' versus a 'Holistic Approach'

Not only does the AB 'privilege "literal" interpretation, it also adheres to a "strictly sequential process" of interpretation'.[90] The AB's text-first approach relates more closely to Vattel's maxim than to the VCLT's 'single combined operation.[91] The latter reflects the statement that there is 'not any legal hierarchy',[92] because interpretation is 'to some extent an art, not an exact science'.[93] The WTO Panels, in contrast, have espoused a 'holistic' approach, which more closely resembles Vatttel's 'single combined operation'.[94] Hierarchical considerations are more important to the AB than equitable interpretive results, which is what, according to Sinclair, the VCLT drafters had in mind. As Sinclair says,

> [t]he principle of good faith applies to the entire process of interpretation, including the examination of the text, the context and subsequent practice. In addition, the result obtained must be appreciated in good faith.[95]

Of the seven WTO Appellate judges, only Ehlermann and Bacchus have provided information on the way the AB interprets the WTO covered agreements. Ehlermann states:

85 de Visscher as cited in YBILC, 1964, vol I, p 275.
86 *Ibid.*
87 YBILC, vol II 1966, p 219.
88 Ehlermann, 2002, p 618.
89 *Ibid.*
90 Lennard, 2002, p 618.
91 YBILC, 1966, vol II, p 219.
92 *Ibid*, p 220.
93 *Ibid*, p 218.
94 *US–Section 301*, Panel Report, para 7.22.
95 Sinclair, 1984, p 120.

> Among the three criteria [of Article 31.1 VCLT, ordinary meaning, context and object and purpose], the Appellate Body has certainly attached the greatest weight to the first, ie 'the ordinary meaning of the terms of the treaty'. This is easily illustrated by the frequent references in Appellate Body reports to dictionaries, in particular to the Shorter Oxford Dictionary, which, in the words of certain critical observers, has become 'one of the covered agreements'.[96]

Bacchus refrains from prioritising any of the sources used by the AB. More in line with Sinclair's understanding of the VCLT than with Ehlermann's perception of the international interpretive process, Bacchus combines text and the other remaining sources:

> The meaning of the words of the treaty is thus our constant focus in reaching and rendering our judgments. (. . .) this focus is in keeping with the rules of treaty interpretation that have been codified in the VCLT.[97]

The 'Text-First' and 'Text-Only' Methods

The text-first approach must not be confused with a text-only approach. In *US–Shrimp* the AB demonstrated that while it adhered to the text-first approach,[98] this did not mean that it was unable to consider other sources of interpretation outside the WTO Agreement, such as under rule 31(3)(c), the principle of *abus de droit*.[99] The text-first approach means only that there will be less opportunity for good faith/legitimate expectations to exert influence over interpretive results that are arrived at through analysing ordinary meaning.

The Report of the International Law Commission of 1966

The ILC in its report to the General Assembly in 1966 affirmed that a language-based approach shall be the primordial rule of treaty interpretation.[100] The reason for the text-first approach to treaty interpretation in international law has been said to originate in the customary rule of treaty law of *pacta sunt servanda*, which says that parties must observe what they have actually agreed to observe (Article 26 VCLT).[101] Besides its 1966 report to the General Assembly, however, the ILC is reported to have 'rejected the use of language suggesting a focus on the legitimate expectations of the other signatories', when confronted

[96] Ehlermann, 2002, p 616.
[97] Bacchus, 2002, p 1033.
[98] *US–Shrimp* AB Report, para 114.
[99] *Ibid*, para 158.
[100] See YBILC, 1966, vol II, p 221, para 9; see also O'Connor, 1991, pp 109, for the discussion of the relationship between the plain meaning of a provision and the obligation to interpret in good faith.
[101] O'Connor, 1991, p 109.

with the situation of 'acts calculated to disappoint the legitimate expectations of its partners'.[102]

Sinclair, a key drafter of the VCLT, confirms that independent of whether one subscribes to a text-first approach, equity and good faith will control the interpretive result. Good faith, according to Sinclair, 'applies to the entire process of interpretation, including the examination of text, the context and subsequent practice'.[103] In addition, the result obtained must be appreciated in good faith.

Critical WTO Doctrine

Bacchus implies that adhering to the VCLT requires interpreters to consider more than the language and grammar. In addition, Bacchus argues that the parties' 'responsibility in every appeal is to say everything about the meaning of the words of the treaty that must be said in order to . . . assist the WTO Member States in resolving that dispute with a "positive solution"'.[104] Bacchus thus implies that the WTO rule of Article 11 requires the treaty interpreter to take into account more than the text of a provision, because in the final analysis all treaty interpretation should arrive at 'a mutually satisfactory solution'.[105]

Canal-Forgues seems to endorse the view that the WTO interpretive process should arrive at a mutually satisfactory solution, independently of which interpretive element was used first, or whether the elements were combined.[106] Canal-Forgues pleads with the AB to recognise the constitutional nature of the WTO, and therefore to interpret with the aim of unifying instead of fragmenting its goals. Canal-Forgues argues in favour of a unifying interpretive method for the sake of creating acceptance and a fortiori recognition of the WTO. In addition, a more flexible rather than sequential, and a more comprehensive rather than exclusive interpretive approach will allow the WTO interpreter to apply WTO law consistently with goals propagated in other fields of general public international law.[107]

Good Faith as Subsidiary Means

When the text-based approach to interpretation fails, the treaty interpreter is empowered to use subsidiary means of interpretation, so-called 'maxims and principles' not mentioned in the VCLT, ie 'good faith' aspects of treaty inter-

[102] Charme, 1992, pp 71ff; see also *US–Offset Act ('Byrd Amendment')*, Panel Report, fn 314 to para 7.64, citing YBILC, 1966, vol II, p 211.

[103] Sinclair, 1984, p 120.

[104] Bacchus, 2002, p 1033.

[105] Art 11 DSU.

[106] See Canal-Forgues, 2001, p 22.

[107] *Ibid*, p 23; *cf* Oxman, 2001, p 279, who cites Tommy TB Koh, president of the Third United National Conference on the Law of the Seas, that 'UNCLOS is a constitution for the Oceans'.

pretation.[108] Among these figures the general principle of good faith, which either protects against an abuse of rights, or expresses the reasonable trust of one party regarding the dealings of another (legitimate expectations).[109]

To this day there is disagreement as to whether or not the VCLT *intended* to establish such a strict sequence of steps, ie a primacy of text, followed by the 'wider functions of the principle of good faith'.[110]

The AB's text-first approach is not unusual for general public international law. O'Connor identifies a sequencing of the sources of interpretation, with plain meaning giving primacy to good faith considerations: the 'wider function of the principle of good faith is called into service when the plain meaning approach fails'.[111]

The WTO judiciary's task can be compared with that of the ECJ. Both institutions are shaped by a multitude of goals that need to be reconciled.[112]

> [O]n peut se demander si les interprètes des Accord de l'OMC on en définitive le même souci de la finalité que les interprètes des textes communautaires.[113]

The Panel and the AB decisions of *India–Patents* and *EC–LAN* symbolise these two opposing approaches. The Panels believe that the VCLT does not prescribe such a strict hierarchy of sources. Thus, even before all the textual means, ie the context of schedule LXXX—which is the WTO Agreement and GATT 94—are exhausted, the Panels reverted to the general principle of legitimate expectations. The AB in contrast adheres to a strict 'text-first' approach and thus overturned the Panels' recourse to legitimate expectations with the argument that referring to PLE was premature because the non-good faith interpretive means had not yet been exhausted.[114]

In *US–Section 301* the Panel again proclaimed its view that the VCLT leaves the treaty interpreter free to choose the interpretive method it deems appropriate for a specific set of problems:

> However, the elements referred to in Article 31 text, context and object-and-purpose as well as good faith—are to be viewed as *one holistic rule* of interpretation *rather than a sequence of separate tests to be applied in a hierarchical order.* Context and object-and-purpose may often appear simply to confirm an interpretation seemingly derived from the 'raw' text.[115]

In the final analysis, it seems that the Panels embraced treaty interpretation as an art, with no fixed hierarchy of sources, and especially not a text-first

[108] See Lennard, 2002, p 55, who, branding the term of good faith aspects of treaty interpretation, does not necessarily share the view of O'Connor, 1991 that text comes first and the expressions of the good faith principle follow.

[109] See Zoller, 1977, pp 214.

[110] See O'Connor, 1991, p 109.

[111] *Ibid.*

[112] See Canal-Forgues, 2001, pp 22–3.

[113] *Ibid*, p 22.

[114] *India–Patents*, AB Report, para 45; *EC–LAN*, AB Report, para 83.

[115] *US–Section 301*, Panel Report, para 7.22.

obligation. WTO Panels are more inclined to adopt the broader reading of Article 31 VCLT. As the Panel in *US–German Steel Countervailing Duty (CVD)'s* confirmed, 'Article 31 of the Vienna Convention does not, in our view, limit us to a literal reading of the provision in question'.[116]

By contrast, the AB seems to adhere very strictly to the text-first approach. The consequence of this stance is that the opportunity for equity law jurisprudence is restricted, as a clear textual meaning will not be screened for flaws of equity and good faith.

The choice between prioritising text over objective intent in WTO treaty interpretation also reflects policy goals. The AB prefers a textual interpretive method to any other means and considers 'good faith interpretation' to be a subsidiary method, available to the WTO interpreter only if the text fails. Lennard summarises the advantages of adhering to the VCLT rules and specifically their textual approach with the following arguments:

— A key point is that new parties to the treaty (particularly developing countries with their generally more limited WTO-specific resources) can analyse and form judgments on the treaty against the well-understood and documented touchstone of customary international law rules of interpretation, rather than being disadvantaged greatly through not having participated in the original negotiations. The relative certainty of the primarily textual approach is best adapted to preventing disputes arising, as well as to solving those that have arisen.[117]
— The WTO must maintain its democratic legitimacy and ensure equal participation of all of its members, specifically the developing countries and the new members.

With the inception of the WTO in 1994, Cameron and Gray observed that 'Panels are now liberated from the need to satisfy all parties',[118] and since 1994 Panels have been empowered to interpret the WTO Agreements more boldly. Panels do not need to adhere to the limits of Article 3.2 DSU as stringently as does the AB. Good faith interpretation by Panels can be redimensioned where necessary by appellate reports which will reduce potentially audacious interpretations of Panels to textual ones.

On the one hand, good faith interpretation at the WTO will be necessary to prevent unclear text from being abused by the most imaginative and litigious among the WTO Member States: '[T]extual insufficiency of certain WTO rules must not serve Members as a justification for protectionism, which might then lead to further tribulation and disputes'.[119] On the other hand, the WTO judiciary will have to subscribe to the rule of good faith interpretation in order to arrive at meaningful solutions that are able to maintain the peace and stabil-

[116] *US–German Steel CVDs*, Panel Report, para 8.28.
[117] Lennard, 2002, p 22.
[118] Cameron and Gray, 2001, p 249.
[119] Horowitz, 2002, p 172.

ity in trade relations. The AB in *US–Shrimp* (detailed further below) qualified this specific, regulatory function of good faith interpretation[120] as 'marking out a line of equilibrium' between the rights of WTO Member States to call upon an exception, such as Article XX GATT, and the obligations of WTO Member States to adhere to trade liberalization obligations.[121]

Interpreting more expansively through good faith allows for gap-filling with public international law, which renders the WTO legal system less exposed to erratic legislative changes and additions to its rules during Ministerials. The long-standing traditions shaping customary and general principles of law would supplement the rapidly-changing WTO legislation and thus contribute, as the Preamble to the Marrakesh Agreement prescribes, to enabling the multilateral trading system to become both more durable and better integrated.

COMPARATIVE ANALYSIS: THE INTERPRETIVE METHODS OF OTHER INTERNATIONAL TRIBUNALS

Appellate practice has been found to compare closely to international scholarship on good faith. As described in detail above, the AB, in contrast to the WTO Panels, has refused to protect the legitimate expectations of an importing member as to the benefits it is entitled to enjoy in the future.[122] AB practice closely resembles international doctrine on good faith treaty interpretation, which cautions against letting good faith considerations influence textual interpretation. As Zoller describes,

> Il y aura toujours, compte tenu du milieu de la société internationale elle-même, une certaine rigueur, un certain formalisme dans l'interprétation du droit qui ne sera pas toujours forcément compatible avec les exigences de la bonne foi.[123]

Rosenne, who is open to the idea of good faith interpretation having a creative function,[124] warns that at times,

> it may be going too far to regard good faith as supplying a 'dynamic element' to this branch of law, for this would easily lead to trespass on revision, which is not permissible by way of judicial interpretation.[125]

Thus, in Rosenne's view, PLE employed to realise, by way of TRIPS, the wider goals of the GATT 94 (predictability to plan future trade, establish and maintain competitive relationships between different WTO Member States) would probably constitute a prohibited 'dynamic element' to interpretation.

[120] *Cf* Zoller, 1977, p 229.
[121] *US–Shrimp*, AB Report, para 159.
[122] See *India–Patents*, Panel Report, para 7.66.
[123] Zoller, 1977, p 215.
[124] See Rosenne, 1989, p 179, treaties are *bonae fidei negotia*.
[125] *Ibid* and fn 67, referring to Schwarzenberger, 1955.

Zoller attributes to the sovereignty of states the responsibilty for diminishing the role of good faith (interpretation) in international treaty relations. The adversarial attitude of States towards good faith interpretation, which Zoller describes, may also be behind the AB's restrictive practice and its cautious approach towards good faith interpretation under Article 31(1) and Article 31(3)(c) of the Vienna rules as well as towards a general principle of good faith:

> Or, c'est précisément lorsque la souveraineté surgit dans le processus interprétative que la bonne foi perd toute son originalité. Comprise comme l'expression de la volonté de l'Etat souverain, elle s'impose au juge avec une force toute particulière et l'oblige à interpréter strictement toute clause attentatoire à la souveraineté.[126]

When the AB ruled on the *India–Patents* case, it was guided by the purpose of protecting India's sovereign rights of exercising a transitory application of TRIPS, pursuant to the special transitory TRIPS regime for developing-country members under Articles 70ff TRIPS. As a result, the AB retained a textual interpretation of Articles 70.8 and 70.9 TRIPS, although the practice of India's administrative organs was not only unrestricted by any rule of law but also unchecked by courts, and thus the administrative organs were free to follow their filing practice without ensuring non-Indian nationals any court-enforceable patent protection.

Because the AB in *India–Patents* did not want to interfere when India was not yet committed to the full TRIPS *acquis,* it did not broaden the scope of interpretation of Articles 70.8 and 70.9 by introducing the element of good faith, which would have put an end to the unforeseen administrative practice, with its lack of legal protection for non-Indian patent applicants, as previous GATT 47 practice, in the light of legitimate expectations, would also have demanded.

While Steinberg finds that the 'AB [. . .] favours completeness and dynamism over doctrine that favours deference to sovereign states',[127] WTO appellate practice in *India–Patents* showed that, in contrast to Steinberg's finding, deference to and respect for national sovereignty guided the AB's decision at the expense of ensuring non-discrimination, multilateralism and the rule of law. By deferring to national sovereignty, the AB failed to guarantee the substantive standards of intellectual property protection, which a good faith interpretation of the TRIPS transitory regime would have required.

THE PROGRESSIVE INTERPRETATIVE PRACTICE OF THE WTO APPELLATE BODY

It has been suggested that future Panels and the AB subsume PLE as an element of good faith interpretation under Article 31(1) VCLT, as the *India–Patents,*

[126] Zoller, 1977, p 216.

[127] Steinberg, p 44.

[128] *India–Patents*, Panel Report, para 7.18; *EC–LAN*, Panel Report, para 8.25; see also *US–Section 301*, Panel Report, para 7.67.

EC–LAN and *US–Section 301* Panels have demonstrated.[128] In cases in which the WTO adjudicators acknowledge the GATT/WTO-specific function of PLE, they may prefer to subsume PLE as a principle of interpretation binding only the WTO Member States pursuant to Article 31(3)(c) VCLT. The advantage of Article 31(3)(c) VCLT is that the concept of PLE remains applicable to the WTO Member States regardless of whether or not it is binding upon the VCLT parties. In cases where PLE is an element of interpretation, which is foreign to general principles of law or customary law, it may still bind the WTO Member States, but not all VCLT parties, as long as there is consensus among WTO Member States that PLE is applicable between them as a well-established principle of GATT law. Article 31(4) VCLT is less advantageous for embracing PLE, because it is the party that invokes the special meaning in the dispute that will have to prove that such a special meaning exists.

Three Panels have considered PLE an inherent part of good faith interpretation under Article 31(1) VCLT.[129] Future WTO adjudicators are advised by those three Panel Reports to follow the obiter dicta of the *EC–LAN* AB Report, in which the AB suggested a more limited subsumption of PLE, under VCLT 31(3)(c), and not under Article 31(1) generally. Under VCLT 31(3)(c), PLE would be considered 'applicable law' between the WTO Member States, and would be binding upon WTO Member States only. On the one hand, PLE under VCLT 31(3)(c) would escape the continuing scholarly debate to which it would be exposed under 31(1), namely as to whether or not good faith interpretation is a mandatory element of the general rule of interpretation under Article 31(1). On the other hand, by proxy of VCLT 31(3)(c), PLE could retain its GATT/WTO-specific definition, scope, function and legal enforcement, whether through NVNI or violation complaints.

As the more recent Panel and AB Reports show, good faith interpretation has acquired a new significance in WTO jurisprudence since the year 2000. The next chapters will trace the process of development from the Panels' attempts to introduce a measure of good faith interpretation into WTO adjudicative practice in *India–Patents* and *EC–LAN*; through the *Korea–Government Procurement* Panel's application of the customary rule of international law of *pacta sunt servanda* in order to protect legitimate expectations as to pre-accession negotiations; to the AB's acknowledgement of the significance of the different expressions of good faith for *pacta sunt servanda* in the 2003 *US–Offset Act ('Byrd Amendment')* AB Report.

This chapter also notes that the WTO judiciary, starting with the *Korea–Government procurement* Panel in 2000, has embraced a more prominent role for good faith.[130] With the *US–Offset Act (Byrd Amendment)* decision

[128] *Ibid.*

[129] See Cho, 1998, p 313.

[130] See *US–Offset Act ('Byrd Amendment')*, AB Report, paras 296–8; see also McNelis, 2003, 658, 'Thereby, the AB confirmed that good faith is an obligation and that it can be examined in the context of dispute settlement, even though it did not end up finding a good faith violation in the case at hand'.

of 2003, even the AB was prepared to recognise good faith as positive WTO law.[131] However, as in the earlier *US–Shrimp* case (1998), its statements about good faith were not unambiguous. In its earlier decision in *US–Shrimp* the AB had let the 'general principle of law' of good faith 'guide' its interpretation of GATT Article XX, without yet fully recognising that good faith is a substantive rule of WTO law.[132] In *US–Offset Act ('Byrd Amendment'),* the AB found the EC's allegation insufficiently substantiated; at the same time, however, it failed to clarify the constitutive elements which a party would have to prove for a good faith violation complaint to succeed.[133]

US–Shrimp, Appellate Body Report (1998)

'Relevant Rule of International Law Applicable . . . Between the Parties'

In *US–Shrimp,* the AB firstly clarified the scope of the specific exception of Article XX(g) GATT 94. Secondly, it identified the *ratio* of the Chapeau of Article XX. In evaluating whether US Section 609 had been applied extraterritorially, contravening the Chapeau of Article XX GATT 94, the AB referred to the 'general principle of law of good faith' and protected the good faith of the US' trading partners under the 'relevant rule of international law applicable in the relations between the parties' pursuant to Article 31(3)(c) VCLT.[134]

In *US–Shrimp,* the AB further developed the concept it had established under *US–Gasoline*, which found that the object and purpose of the Chapeau 'is generally the prevention of "abuse of the exceptions of [Article XX]"'.[135] Consequently, the AB in *US–Shrimp* declared: '[T]he Chapeau of Article XX is, in fact, but one expression of the principle of good faith'.[136]

The AB subsumed the principle of prohibition of *abus de droit* under the Chapeau of Article XX GATT 94. In this way, the AB is free to use the doctrine of *abus de droit* as 'interpretative guidance' according to rule 31(3)(c) VCLT.[137]

Thus, the AB has evaded the difficult question of whether good faith interpretation is a mandatory element that each interpretive process is required to respect under the general rule of interpretation of 31(1) VCLT. By attaching the prohibition of *abus de droit* in the Chapeau of Article XX GATT 94 to Article 31(3)(c), the AB declared *abus de droit* doctrine a GATT-specific principle, which WTO Member States and *only* Member States must respect.

Because Article 31(3)(c) VCLT provides that substantive law applicable in the relation between the parties may become an interpretive principle, the AB was entitled to use interpretively the prohibition of *abus de droit*: 'Having said this,

[132] *US–Shrimp*, AB Report, para 158; see also Cottier and Schefer, 2000, pp 64–5.

[133] See *US–Offset Act ('Byrd Amendment'),* AB Report, paras 298–9.

[134] *India–Patents*, Panel Report, para 7.18; *EC–LAN*, Panel Report, para 8.25; *US–Section 301, Panel Report*, para 7.67.

[135] *US–Shrimp*, para 151, referring to *US–Gasoline*, p 22.

[136] *Ibid*, AB Report, para 158.

[137] *Ibid.*

our task here is to interpret the language of the Chapeau, seeking additional interpretive guidance, as appropriate, from the general principles of international law'.[138]

However, *US–Shrimp* remains the only case in which the AB has referred to rule 31(3)(c) VLCT in order to use the general principle of law of good faith/*abus de droit* as 'relevant rule of international law applicable in the relations between the parties', which according to Article 31(3)(c) VCLT, 'shall be taken into account, together with the context, "when interpreting a treaty in good faith in accordance with the ordinary meaning to be given to the terms of the treaty in their context"'.[139]

The general principles of law remain, by the proxy of the rule of interpretation of Article 31(3)(c), applicable to the WTO only as interpretive, and not as substantive rules. Nevertheless, the AB has moved into the realm of general public international law, declaring not only that the VCLT rules of interpretation are applicable to the WTO Agreements, but also that the general principles of law are applicable, as long as these bind the WTO Member States in dispute because they are 'applicable law in the relation between the parties' under Article 31(3)(c) VCLT. Therefore, *US–Shrimp* marks an important step in appellate practice, because it was the first time the AB broadened the scope of WTO interpretation to include non-WTO sources of international law, whether these are related treaties, customary law or, as in *US–Shrimp*, general principles of law. The threshold for the AB was Article 31(3)(c), which determines whether a non-WTO legal source applies for interpreting a WTO rule. As Marceau confirms,

> [I]t can be argued that Article 31(3)(c) requires the interpreter to consider and use, when relevant, a broad range of non-WTO legal instruments to interpret the WTO Agreements. However, it should be emphasized that the weight and value to be given to those non-WTO provisions would be left to each interpreter on a case-by-case basis. Nonetheless, Article 31(3)(c) imposes an obligation to take into account those other rules of international law with a view to avoiding conflicts between them and ensuring a greater coherence of international rules.[140]

Canal-Forgues, quoting Sands, finds that Article 31(3)(c) VCLT has a further impact. It establishes the *presumption* that the WTO legal system must be interpreted in conformity with public international law, and that the customary rule shall prime WTO law, unless it is demonstrated that such an application would evade the object and purpose of the WTO system.[141] Howse expands this finding by arguing that 31(3)(c) VCLT is the key provisions for promoting the legitimacy of the WTO treaties' interpretation of 'competing values':

> This [Article 31(3)(c)] mandates the consideration of non-WTO international legal rules in the interpretation of WTO treaties—rules that may reflect or prioritise other

[138] *Ibid*, para 157.
[139] *Ibid*, fn 157 to para 158.
[140] Marceau, 1999, p 128.
[141] Canal-Forgues, 2001, p 15, quoting Sands, 2000, p 232.

> values and interests than those of trade liberalization, thus countering the undue privileging of the latter in WTO interpretation.[142]

The issue in the future will be how the WTO adjudicators define the scope of Article 31(3)(c), specifically whether the WTO adjudicators will adopt a broad interpretation of 31(3)(c) VCLT, which binds WTO Member States who are parties to the particular dispute, or whether the AB adopts the narrower definition that all WTO Member States must be parties to such a non-WTO treaty or at least consent to being bound by the source of law in question for Article 31(3)(c) VCLT to vest.

'Marking Out a Line of Equilibrium'

A domestic regulation that is extraterritorially applied is no longer GATT-consistent (even if it is consistent with a specific exception under Article XX) unless it is applied in a manner that is fair and equitable to the parties, which in WTO-terms means that it must be non-discriminatory and non-arbitrary.[143] Applying and interpreting the Chapeau entails ensuring that a measure does not 'distort and nullify or impair the balance of rights and obligations constructed by the members themselves in that Agreement':[144]

> A fair and equitable (good faith) interpretation of the Chapeau of Article XX, aims to locate and mark out a line of equilibrium between the right of a Member to invoke an exception under Article XX and the rights of the other Members under varying substantive provisions (eg Article XI) of the GATT 94.[145]

Interpretation in good faith ensures that when using an exception, a member remains bound by its obligations under the WTO Agreements (MFN, NTO etc). In such a balancing function, good faith ensures that a legitimate and controlled escape from certain obligations is combined with a principled adherence to the WTO's main instruments of non-discrimination under NT and MFN obligations.

Influenced by the ICJ *Barcelona Traction* case,[146] general public international law attributes to good faith a self-standing judicial function that goes beyond interpretation and spills over into regulatory rule-creation:[147]

> La bonne foi tend à jouer le rôle d'un élément régulateur du rapport againstctuel établi entre les parties. Elle concilie les intérêts et les équilibres. Le juge l'utilise le plus souvent comme un balancier aux fins de fixer le contenu et la portée des obligations respectives des parties.[148]

[142] Howse, 2000, p 55.
[143] See *US–Shrimp*, AB Report, paras 119–20.
[144] *Ibid*, para 159.
[145] *Ibid*, similar citation in para 155.
[146] Zoller, 1977, p 229.
[147] Schwarzenberger, 1955, p 324.
[148] Zoller, 1977, p 229.

It is to the 'regulative' function of good faith that the AB referred when it considered applying the Chapeau of Article XX with respect to to 'marking out the line of equilibrium':

> The task of interpreting and applying the Chapeau is, hence, essentially the delicate one of locating and marking out a line of equilibrium between the right of a member to invoke an exception under Article XX and the rights of the other members under varying substantive provisions.[149]

When the AB cited Cheng in a footnote, it was to legitimise its reference to the balancing function of good faith:

> A reasonable and bona fide exercise of a right in such a case is one which is appropriate and necessary for the purpose of the right . . . It should at the same time be *fair and equitable as between the parties* and note one which is calculated to procure for one of them an unfair advantage in the light of the obligation assumed (emphasis added).[150]

The AB introduced equity law jurisdiction by means of the bias of interpreting Article XX GATT in good faith (in addition to analysing the traditional text, context, object and purpose):[151]

> [T]he application of a measure may be characterised as amounting to an abuse or misuse of an exception of Article XX . . . also where a measure, otherwise *fair and just* on its face, is actually applied in an arbitrary or unjustifiable manner. The standards of the Chapeau, in our view, project both substantive and procedural requirements (emphasis added).[152]

It is no coincidence that the AB introduced a measure of equity in a case requiring the analysis of an *exception* to trade liberalization. Because the judiciary risks overstepping its precisely defined judiciary role, Lennard warns against the AB's attempts to develop an equity law jurisdiction:

> The passage from Cheng relied on by the AB . . . could . . . lead to a greatly expanded role for the Panels and AB (perhaps in effect developing a general 'equitable' jurisdiction which it appears to lack under its constituent documents) . . . than is warranted under customary international law and the WTO Agreements.[153]

Because the AB introduced an element of equity law jurisdiction into the analysis of Article XX GATT, there are far-reaching consequences for the WTO legal system, and specifically, for the WTO Agreements' exceptions to trade liberalization.

For Marceau the line of equilibrium or 'balancing test' described by the AB in *US–Shrimp* is simply 'a requirement of reasonable balance (between Members' market access rights and the right of Members to take measures pursuant to other policies that may clash with market access)'.[154] Thus, Marceau proposes

149 *US–Shrimp* AB Report, para 159.

150 *Ibid*, fn 156 to para 158, where the AB cites this para on p 25 of ch 4 of Cheng, 1987.

151 Cottier and Schefer, 2000, p 64, cited the *US–Shrimp* case as the first express admission by the AB of the application of the 'equitable doctrines of estoppel, acquiescence, and abuse of rights'.

152 *US–Shrimp*, AB Report, para 160.

153 Lennard, 2002, p 68.

154 Marceau, 1999, p 105.

that the Chapeau is an expression of good faith, which necessitates a good faith interpretation of domestic regulatory measures. Marceau associates the Chapeau with a 'test of reasonableness' that ensures flexibility and coherence among systems of laws.[155]

Lennard, who most adamantly warned against introducing an equity law jurisdiction, limits the impact of good faith as used in *US–Shrimp*, stating, 'good faith gives flexibility' and 'slightly moderates the textual approach'.[156]

US–Offset Act ('Byrd Amendment'), Appellate Body Report (2003)

'Good Faith May be Said to Inform a Treaty Interpreter's Task'

Good faith according to the AB 'informs a treaty interpreter's task'.[157] The AB thus reinstated the legitimacy of good faith as an interpretive element after it had been dismissed as irrelevant to treaty interpretation in the context of legitimate expectation claims in the *EC–LAN*[158] and *India–Patents*[159] cases.

In *US–Offset Act ('Byrd Amendment')*, the EC alleged, and the Panel confirmed, that the US CDSOA textually conforms to Articles 5.4 ADA and 11.4 ASCM, but in effect 'defeats [their] object and purpose' and thus renders the above-mentioned provisions 'completely meaningless', amounting to a violation of substantive good faith.[160] The US, however, claimed before the AB that there existed no 'basis' or 'justification' in the WTO Agreements for the Panel 'to conclude that a Member has not acted in good faith, or to enforce a principle of good faith as a substantive obligation agreed to by WTO Member States'.[161] The Panel had found that the US CDSOA instigated dumping investigations because of financial incentives rather than because they were really necessary. Industry is incited to vote in favour of support dumping investigations, and, in the final analysis, imposing AD-duties on foreign competitors, through the financial incentive of prospective payments to the industry out of the sum of AD duties collected from foreign competitors. This was found to have 'undermined the value of Article 5.4 ADA and Article 11.4 ASCM to the countries with whom the US trades. The US may be regarded as not having acted in good faith in promoting this outcome'.[162]

Lester and Leitner criticise the Panel for disregarding the textual meaning of Article 5.4 ADA and Article 11.4 ASCM.[163] These authors also find that the

[155] Marceau, 1999, pp 96, 103, 105.
[156] Lennard, 2002, p 88.
[157] *US–Offset Act ('Byrd Amendment')*, AB Report, para 296.
[158] *EC–LAN*, AB Report, para 83.
[159] *India–Patents*, AB Report, paras 45 and 48.
[160] *US–Offset Act ('Byrd Amendment')*, AB Report, para 279.
[161] *Ibid*, para 296.
[162] *Ibid*, para 7.63.
[163] *Ibid*, para 7.64 and fn 314; see Lester and Leitner, 2003a, p 15.

Panel created an overlap between violation and NVNI complaints by emphasising that Article 5.4 ADA and Article 11.4 ASCM had been *violated* because the CDSOA *was contrary to good faith* in the sense that it diminished the value of Article 5.4 ADA and Article 11.4 ASCM.[164]

The EC invoked a violation of good faith in *US–Offset Act (Byrd Amendment)* to sanction the US for undermining the value of treaty provisions vis-à-vis their respective trading partners by conditioning the receipt of offset payments on support for anti-dumping measures.

The EC, India, Indonesia and Thailand claimed before the AB that:

> Members must observe the general principle of good faith, recognised by the AB as a pervasive principle that informs the covered agreements, in the application and interpretation of the Anti-Dumping and the ASCM Agreement.[165]

The EC, India, Indonesia and Thailand thus claimed that the duty to perform treaties in good faith has both a substantive dimension ('obligations "must not be evaded by a merely literal interpretation"') and an interpretive dimension ('parties "must abstain from acts that are calculated to frustrate the object and purpose of a treaty"').[166]

The VCLT rule of good faith interpretation had no impact on the outcome of this case. The AB found a textual interpretation of Articles 5.4 ADA and 11.4 ASCM to reveal that only the number of petitions conditions the initiation of an investigation and that the motive behind the number of petitions supporting the initiation of a dumping investigation is irrelevant.[167] Based upon such a textual interpretation of the ADA and ASCM, the AB found no violation of substantive good faith, and that there was no reason for good faith interpretation to apply.[168]

'Performance of Treaties is also Governed by Good Faith'

However, the AB did recognise that good faith may have both an interpretive value ('inform a treaty interpreter's task')[169] and significance as substantive law ('Moreover, performance of treaties is also governed by good faith').[170] To concede that good faith can be a self-standing principle was new for the usually strictly textualist AB, predated only by the AB's use of *abus de droit* as

[164] *Ibid.*

[165] *US–Offset Act*, AB Report, para 88.

[166] *Ibid.*

[167] *Ibid*, paras 286, 291, 294; see Bhagwati and Mavroidis, 2003, p 8, who advocate that the CDSOA is WTO-inconsistent, 'So, if the *US–Offset Act (Byrd Amendment)* were rejected by the Appellate Body, as it should be, the changes that should be recommended to the United States are obvious. The selective use of the tariff revenue to subsidise only the petitioners must go. And we should allow the anti-dumping tariff to be reduced and revenues to be used as a subsidy but only so that the joint support so provided does not exceed the dumping margin'; against Charnovitz, 2003, p 9.

[168] *US–Offset Act ('Byrd Amendment')*, AB Report, para 295.

[169] *Ibid*, para 296.

[170] *Ibid.*

interpretive guidance (albeit under the more specialised provision of Article 31(3)(c) VCLT) in *US–Shrimp*.[171]

For finding a good faith violation, the AB maintained, one would have had to prove 'more than a mere violation'. Possibly, the AB was alluding to a subjective element, ie that the EC would have had to show that the US *intentionally* circumvented Articles 5.4 ADA and 11.4 ASCM Agreement by using financial incentives to increase the number of applications in support of anti-dumping duties by or on behalf of the domestic industry.[172]

Critically, Lester and Leitner find that 'the basis for the AB's reversal of the Panel's finding on good faith is unclear'.[173] According to Lester and Leitner, the AB assumed that the Panel's finding that the US had not acted in good faith was based on its finding a violation, while for the Panel, 'good faith formed part of the basis for its finding of violation'.[174]

In order for the Panel's argument on good faith to stand before appeal, the Panel would have had to show a subjective element on the part of the US in addition to its objective violation of Articles 5.4 ADA and 11.4 ASCM. The Panel may have had such a subjective element in mind when it asked whether the US 'CDSOA defeats the object and purpose of 5.4 ADA and 11.4 ASCM', and whether, pursuant the 'principle of good faith as a general rule of conduct in international relations', 'a party to a treaty [is] to refrain from acting in a manner which would defeat the object and purpose of the treaty as a whole or the treaty provision in question'.[175]

To emphasize its finding the Panel referred in a footnote to the scholar D'Amato's reference in the *Encyclopedia of International Law*, to the ILC Commission's debate in 1966 on the meaning of good faith in international treaty law. D'Amato attributes to the ILC Commission the finding that a subjective element of good faith must be considered implicit in the obligation to perform a treaty in good faith.

In contrast there are those who would like to see the subjective good faith element (an intention, a calculated act) to constitute a self-standing precondition for a finding of a breach of good faith:

> some members felt that there would be an advantage in also stating that a party must abstain from acts calculated to frustrate the object and purpose of the treaty. The Commission however considered that this was clearly implicit in the obligation to perform the treaty in good faith and preferred to state the *pacta sunt servanda* rule in as simple a form as possible.[176]

[171] Lester and Leitner, 2003a, p 15, who find that in contrast to the AB the Panel, 'went [even] further than previous invocations of good faith in WTO dispute settlement decisions', because the principle of good faith is not tied to the language, ie the interpretation of a provision but to the US acting contrary to good faith.

[172] *US–Offset Act ('Byrd Amendment')*, AB Report, para 298.

[173] Lester and Leitner, 2003a, p 15.

[174] *Ibid.*

[175] *US–Offset Act ('Byrd Amendment')*, Panel Report, para 7.64.

[176] *Ibid*, fn 314 to para 7.64.

9

Towards a WTO-specific Good Faith Interpretation?

> It might be possible for the parties to a treaty expressly to agree that the rules of treaty interpretation in Articles 31 and 32 of the Vienna Convention do not apply, either in whole or in part, to the interpretation of a particular treaty. Likewise, the parties to a particular treaty might agree upon rules of interpretation for that treaty, which differ from the rules of interpretation in Articles 31 and 32 of the Vienna Convention.[1]

THIS CHAPTER BUILDS upon the findings of the previous one and investigates whether, in the final analysis, the WTO Panels and the AB, or both, have developed an idiosyncratic WTO-specific rule for interpretation in good faith. The goal of this chapter is to discuss the possible deviations from the VCLT rule that the WTO adjudicators might have purposefully or unintentionally developed. This chapter will thus consider the possible emergence of a WTO-specific principle of good faith interpretation. It will draw from the previous chapter, which established that the AB had refused to base WTO treaty interpretation on the good faith rule. In contrast, the approach of the Panels was to match the general rule of interpretation under the VCLT to the PLE in WTO law. Based upon these findings, this section attempts to determine whether the WTO adjudicators' application of the Vienna rules, coupled with their distinct interpretive patterns, have lead to a WTO-specific good faith rule of interpretation.

THE MEANING OF ARTICLE 3.2 OF THE DISPUTE SETTLEMENT UNDERSTANDING FOR WTO INTERPRETATION

Article 3.2 of the DSU implicitly attributes the task of adding to the rights and obligations under the WTO Agreement to the WTO legislators. The General Council, or exceptionally, the Ministerial Conference, decide upon the consensus, or occasionally on a qualified majority of the WTO Member States. The question is: how much room for manoeuvre does the judiciary have under

[1] *US–Japan Hot-rolled Steel*, AB Report, para 101, and fn 40.

Article 3.2 DSU to creatively adjudicate or to fill in the gaps in the WTO Agreements?

The Limitation of Judicial Power

Article 3.2 DSU explicitly delimits the scope of action of the WTO DSB, implying that the judicial bodies, the Panels and the AB of the WTO are not allowed to overstep their mandate as adjudicators. Article 3.2 DSU prohibits the judicial bodies from substituting their task with that of the legislator. As Sutherland says, 'Dispute Panels should resist the temptation to substitute their insight for lack of precision in the text'.[2] Similarly, Roessler has maintained that the AB ruling in *India–Patents* 'shifted decision-making authority from the political to the judicial organs of the WTO, and consequently changed the negotiated balance in the WTO',[3] which was prohibited by Article 3.2 DSU.

After *EC–Sardines*, the representative of Malyasia was quoted as voicing a similar concern about overly broad WTO treaty interpretation:

> International treaties shall be interpreted in a limited manner taking into account the sovereign rights of countries. Thus, the Appellate Body, although only an organ that adjudicated trade disputes between WTO Member States should, at least, respect the sovereign rights of all WTO Member States.[4]

WTO Member States and scholars alike are concerned that the element of good faith interpretation, even if an inherent part of the general rule of interpretation under Article 31(1) VCLT, is too broad for Article 3.2 DSU. Those who seek to preserve the negotiated institutional balance between the legislative and judicial bodies at the WTO argue that good faith interpretation, even if allowed under Article 31 VCLT, has to be sacrificed in order to maintain the WTO's institutional balance. The purportors of this view refer to what thay argue is the clear meaning of the last sentence of Article 3.2 DSU, which reads: 'Recommendations and rulings of the DSB cannot add to or diminish the rights and obligations provided in the covered agreements'.

The AB's 'clear option in favour of a predominantly literal approach' at the expense of good faith interpretation was seen as 'deny[ing] that the method of literal interpretation has its limits'.[5] Among others, the AB itself countered that Articles 3.2 and 19.2 DSU impose their limits on interpretation:[6]

> The heavy reliance on the 'ordinary meaning' to be given to the terms of the treaty has protected the AB from criticism that its reports have added to or diminished the rights

[2] Sutherland, 2000.

[3] Wilson and Starchuk, 2003, p 2.

[4] *Ibid*, referring to DSB, Minutes of Meeting, WT/DSB/M/134, held 23 October 2002, circulated 29 January 2003.

[5] Ehlermann, 2002, p 617.

[6] Bartels, 2001, p 518.

and obligations provided in the covered agreements (Article 3.2, third sentence, DSU).[7]

On the one hand, if good faith interpretation is based upon the PLE, an expansive approach is required to build coherence among treaty provisions through effective interpretation[8] or even to take into account non-WTO rules.[9] On the other hand, if good faith emanates from *pacta sunt servanda,* its interpretation requires refraining from binding WTO Member States to treaties to which they have not agreed.[10] Such conflicting views on how far good faith interpretation ought to go have been openly debated between the Panels and the AB of the WTO, as well as among scholars.

One group of critics argues that the WTO adjudicators have failed to make use of the full potential that the VCLT rules on treaty interpretation give to international judicial bodies. Such critics hold Article 3.2 DSU responsible for the restraint shown by the WTO judiciary when interpretating treaty provisions, because Article 3.2 DSU prohibits interpretations that would add to or diminish the rights and obligations of the members.[11]

Another group of critics counters that Articles 3.2 and 19.2 DSU impose their limits on interpretation by the WTO judiciary:[12]

> The heavy reliance on the 'ordinary meaning' to be given to the terms of the treaty has protected the AB from criticism that its reports have added to or diminished the rights and obligations provided in the covered agreements (Article 3.2, third sentence, DSU).[13]

The proponents of this opinion find that the process of GATT/WTO dispute settlement guided by the DSU has unfortunately 'taken a form characterised by expansive judicial law-making'.[14] However, there are others who say that the 'judicial law-making has not fundamentally upset the asymmetric package of rules, [. . .] because the WTO is developing along paths that are gathering ongoing support from the two members that matter most to its political survival: the EC and the United States'.[15]

[7] Ehlermann, 2002, p 617.

[8] YBILC, 1964, vol I, p 288, 'ut res magis valeat quam pereat . . . appeared in the jurisprudence of the ICJ and was inherent in the notion of good faith'; see similar citations on pp 288–9; see also *US–Gasoline*, AB Report, p 12; *US–Underwear*, AB Report, p 16; see Marceau, 1999, p 117.

[9] Marceau, 1999, pp 123–8 '. . . the purpose of this obligation to "take into account" non-WTO rules is not to impose, apply or enforce these non-WTO rights and obligations . . . the purpose is to take them into account, where relevant, in interpreting the WTO rights and obligations in order to ensure that the WTO sub-system of international law develops coherently with other systems of law in the light of the international principle of interpretation against conflicts and for effective interpretation'.

[10] *Ibid*, p 127.

[11] Bacchus, 2002, p 1034, former Chairman and current member of the WTO AB says that, 'In all our recommendations and rulings, we have been true to these [3.2 and 19.2 DSU] responsibilities'.

[12] Bartels, 2001, p 518.

[13] Ehlermann, 2002, p 617.

[14] Steinberg, 2003, p 2; see also Wilson and Starchuk, 2003, on 'judicial activism'.

[15] *Ibid*, p 56.

Holders of the first opinion consider the VCLT rules to have primacy over Article 3.2 DSU, while those who hold the second find that Article 3.2 DSU takes precedence, perhaps as a *lex specialis,* over the general rule of interpretation of Article 31(1) VCLT, by proscribing 'good faith interpretation' in favour of the more limited and exclusively textual approach purported by Article 3.2 DSU.

WTO Expression of *Pacta Sunt Servanda*

If Article 3.2 DSU, last sentence expresses *pacta sunt servanda* (as codified in Article 26 VCLT), one cannot say that Article 3.2 DSU imposes on the WTO adjudicator's a more restrictive interpretive regime than the VCLT rules on *performance* (Article 26) impose on the VCLT rules for the interpretation of treaties (Articles 31 and 32). Instead of unterstanding Article 3.2 DSU as a rule imposing a WTO-specific limitation on the Vienna rule of interpretation, one could also consider Article 3.2 DSU as a mirror image rule to the principle of *pacta sunt servanda* expressed in Article 26 VCLT, which general public international law considers a 'natural' limit to good faith interpretation.

While we have demonstrated that the AB's preference for literal interpretation is independent of the prohibition on adding to or diminishing members' rights and obligations under Article 3.2 DSU, the AB's literal approach 'has contributed to "providing security and predictability to the multilateral trading system" (Article 3.2, first sentence, DSU)'.[16]

Lennard finds that 'enhancing predictability and certainty of WTO jurisprudence' should be attributed to the 'AB's reliance on various interpretive maxims, bind[ing] together international economic law and public international law'. Under 3.2 DSU last sentence or *pacta sunt servanda*, according to Lennard,

> [t]he danger would be if the reliance on those maxims [were] to lead Panels and the Appellate Body away from the Vienna Convention's, primarily text-based approach to create greater uncertainty as to the applicable rules and to risk altering the balance of WTO institutions, with the Panels and the AB having a greater 'law-making' role than was designed.[17]

Because the AB cannot refuse to rule on sensitive cases, the AB has created a high level of discretion for itself and the means to handle cases flexibly. Such case-by-case adjudication, unencumbered by any *stare decisis* obligation of establishing a set of precedents, leads the AB to 'utilise legal doctrines' that are flexible enough to adjust to the factual setting and political constellation of the case at hand.[18]

The AB's use of legal doctrines to enhance its own discretion is also evident in the field of treaty interpretation, where it has more often than not deviated

[16] Ehlermann, 2002, p 616.
[17] Lennard, 2002, p 76.
[18] McCall Smith, 2003, p 79.

from the general rule of interpretation under Article 31(1) VCLT by introducing other elements into the interpretive process—so-called 'maxims' and 'canons' of interpretation (see below)—but mainly the principle of effectiveness as discussed below.

As early as its *Japan–Alcohol* decision of 1996, the AB introduced the 'principle of effectiveness' (*at res magis valeat quam pereat*), which it found to be 'one of the corollaries of the "general rule of interpretation" of the general rule of treaty interpretation'.

According to Lauterpracht, good faith interpretation means to privilege all interpretation which preserves the validity of the treaty (*favorem validitatis*).[19]

> The third possibility, which appears to me . . . in accordance with good faith and common sense, is to interpret the instrument as continuing in validity and as fully applicable . . . to maintain the effectiveness, though not more than that, of the . . . instrument.[20]

Therefore, it could be argued that should PLE enhance the effectiveness of a treaty, it could form part of Article 31(1) VCLT.[21]

Following this approach, the Panel in *India–Patents* could have argued that because TRIPS recognises in its Preamble 'the applicability of the basic principles of GATT',[22] it is also committed to the principle of equal conditions of competition. Thus, giving effectiveness to TRIPS would have entailed its being interpreted as protecting the legitimate expectations as to the installation of a patent registration system, in order to safeguard the conditions of competition between non-Indian nationals and Indian nationals relating to market access.

THE PRINCIPLE OF EFFECTIVENESS IN WTO TREATY INTERPRETATION

The second constitutive function of (objective) good faith interpretation is to enhance the validity of a treaty by applying the principle of effectiveness.

Foundations

Effectiveness aims to find the means by which to maximise the results in order to fulfil the objectives of a treaty.[23]

[19] See Kolb, 2000, p 277.

[20] See *Admissibility of Hearings of Petitioners by the Committee on South-West Africa*, ICJ, Advisory Opinion of June 1, 1956, Separate Opinion of Judge Sir Hersch Lauterpracht, in H Lauterpracht (ed), *International Law Reports, 1956*, London, 1960, p 60.

[21] See Müller, 1971, p 128.

[22] See *India–Patents*, Panel Report, para 7.21.

[23] Wälde, 1999, pp 181–2.

> L'interprétation in *favorem validitatis* serait, selon certains auteurs, une concrétisation de la bonne foi dans l'interprétation. Ces développements reposent sur la règle de privilégier toute interprétation qui préserve la validité du traité. Elle se rapproche de la règle de l'effet utile.[24]

Bernhardt finds that, in principle, to favour the interpretive method that contributes most effectively to the realisation of the treaty's goal, is a concretisation of the VCLT's rule of good faith treaty interpretation. However, modern treaty practice, he argues, has replaced the element of good faith with that of effectiveness:

> Die Zurückhaltung der Praxis bedeutet unzweifelhaft keine Ablehnung der bona fides im Rahmen der Vertragsauslegung, sie ist vielmehr anders zu erklären. . . . im Laufe der Entwicklung und in der modernen Praxis haben sich konkrete Auslegungsregeln kristallisiert, die—ohne Verleugnung der Herkunft-eine eigene rechtliche Bedeutung erlangt und den Interpreten vom Zwang enthoben haben, in jedem Einzelfall auf das allgemeine Gebot der Beachtung von Treu und Glauben zurückzugreifen.[25]

'[I]nherent in the Notion of Good Faith'

The drafts of the ILC Commissions confirm that the principle of effectiveness closely relates to that of good faith interpretation. Deemed 'inherent in the notion of good faith',[26] earlier drafts of the VCLT had codified effectiveness as a principle of interpretation in its own right. However, on 14 July 1964 the Commission decided to consider 'the principle of effective interpretation . . . to be implicit in the requirement of good faith'.[27] For the VCLT drafters the function of good faith interpretation is mainly to realise the rule of effectiveness:

> [I]n so far as the maxim *ut res magis valeat quam pereat* reflects a true general rule of interpretation, it is embodied in article 27, paragraph 1, which requires that a treaty shall be interpreted *in good faith* (italics in original).[28]

> When a treaty is open to two interpretations one of which does and the other does not enable the treaty to have appropriate effects, good faith and the object and purposes of the treaty demand that the former interpretation should be adopted.[29]

Like the principles of integration, contemporaneity and actuality, the principle of effectiveness is one of the major principles Fitzmaurice distilled from

[24] Kolb, 2000, p 277.
[25] Bernhardt, 1963, p 24.
[26] YBILC, 1964, vol 1, pp 288, according to Special Rapporteur, Sir Humphrey Waldock.
[27] *Ibid*, pp 288–91, Mr Verdross, was instrumental in convincing the other members of the Commission to drop a separate provision for effective interpretation.
[28] *Ibid*, vol II, p 219.
[29] *Ibid*, p 219.

World Court interpretive practice;[30] the principle of effectiveness was subsequently associated with interpretation made in good faith.[31]

Several drafters had expressed the concern that the principle of effectiveness entails teleological interpretation.[32] The drafters agreed that giving 'fullest weight and effect' as Fitzmaurice has described it, to the 'major principle of effectiveness', would lead to extensive treaty interpretations that did not correspond to the envisaged aim of the VCLT, namely, of being limited by the object and purpose of a treaty, and good faith.[33] The Special Rapporteur clarified that 'correctly understood, "effective interpretation" may be said to be implied in interpretation made in good faith'.[34]

ICJ jurisprudence did not relate the concept of effectiveness to the rule of good faith treaty interpretation, but relied instead on a 'self-standing' principle of effectiveness in the *Case Concerning the Territorial Dispute (Libya/Chad)* in 1994[35] and *Maritime Delimitation and Territorial Questions between Qatar and Bahrain* (Jurisdiction and Admissibility) in 1995.[36]

Similarly, the WTO AB in *Japan–Alcohol* also considered the principle of effectiveness as a self-standing fundamental of treaty interpretation, distinct from VCLT rules.[37]

In contemporary international law, effectiveness simultaneously 'denotes the politically and economically hegemonic powers' ability to impose their regulation on actors of the global economy'[38] as well as to 'attempt to recover the possibly lost or at least diminished grip of national law over business activities'.[39] The third and most legitimate function of effectiveness has contributed to the emergence of the 'youthful subjects of international environmental law, coupled with its sibling international human rights law'.[40]

The WTO-specific Principle of Effectiveness versus *Pacta Sunt Servanda*

For the WTO AB, effectiveness stands as an interpretive principle on its own and has nothing to do with good faith interpretation.

30 *Ibid*, vol II, pp 55, 60–1.

31 *Ibid*, vol I, pp 288, according to Special Rapporteur, Sir Humphrey Waldock; Lennard, 2002, p 58; Cameron and Gray, 2001, p 256.

32 YBILC, 1964, vol II, p 60.

33 *Ibid*, vol I, pp 288–91.

34 *Ibid*, vol II, p 60.

35 See *Case Concerning the Territorial Dispute (Libya/Chad)*, 3 February 1994, p 25, para 51, 'Any other construction would be contrary to one of the fundamental principles of interpretation of treaties consistently upheld by international jurisprudence, namely that of effectiveness'; see also Bernardez, 1998 pp 739–41.

36 See *Maritime Delimitation and Territorial Questions between Qatar and Bahrain*, Jurisdiction and Admissibility, ICJ Judgment 15 February 1995, para 41; see also Bernardez, 1998 pp 740–1.

37 *Japan–Alcohol*, p 18, 'fundamental principle of effectiveness in treaty interpretation'.

38 Wälde, 1999, p 179

39 *Ibid*, p 172.

40 *Ibid*, p 170.

The AB in *US–Shrimp* concluded that 'effectiveness' called for the term 'exhaustible natural resources' to be interpreted under Article XX(g) GATT 94 in the light of contemporary concerns and that such an interpretation entailed including living natural resources (sea turtles) under the term of 'exhaustible natural resources':

> Given the recent acknowledgement by the international community . . . to protect living natural resources, . . . we believe it is too late in the day to suppose that Article XX(g) of the GATT 94 may be read as referring only to the conservation of exhaustible . . . natural resources. We hold that, in line with the principle of effectiveness in treaty interpretation, measures to conserve exhaustible natural resources, whether *living* or *non-living*, may fall within Article XX(g) (emphasis in the text).[41]

The Relation between Effectiveness and Good Faith Interpretation

Where effectiveness expresses the assumption of regulatory responsibility by multilateral treaties in the face of the diminishing effectiveness of national regulatory power, turning back the clock and interpreting in favour of national sovereignty would be contrary to the legitimate expectations of global civil society, and thus, good faith.

When effectiveness expresses the values of global civil society and the cross-border concerns of citizens, giving a non-transnational interpretation to treaties, or at least turning a blind eye to global positions would be an interpretation against good faith, as good faith interpretation is *in concreto*, and, in accordance with the principle of integration, needs to take into account all available information.

In addition, good faith demands that the 'common intentions' of the parties be ascertained. Neglecting the concerns of civil society would be to arbitrarily disregard one segment of constituents and would result, contrary to good faith interpretation, in an incomplete apprehension of the 'common intentions'. Intentionally disregarding information, ie civil society concerns, would amount to an interpretation in bad faith.

H Lauterpracht notes:

> The principle *ut res magis valeat quam pereat* does not mean that the maximum of effectiveness must be given to an instrument . . .; it means that the maximum of effectiveness should be given to it consistently with the intention—the common intention—of the parties.[42]

Wälde says:

> If 'effectiveness' is about giving more strength and impact to 'legitimate' public policies aimed at correcting market failure, eg internalising the external costs of environmental

[41] *US–Shrimp* AB Report, para 131.
[42] YBILC, 1964, vol II, p 60, para 27.

pollution, . . . or where the issue is to create a 'global civil society' under the rule of law, then international law aiming at such global policy objectives should be effective.[43]

The only limit to the principles of 'effectiveness' and good faith, is an interpretation that leads to overturning the clear meaning. This would constitute treaty revision by the adjudicator.[44]

'GOOD FAITH INTERPRETATION' OF FUTURE DISPUTE SETTLEMENT REPORTS

This section follows upon the previous discussion of the possibly increased relevance of 'good faith interpretation' in the WTO, and attempts to foresee the future direction, function and scope of good faith interpretation at the WTO.

A Prospective Member's Perspective

A textual interpretation is preferred for 'multi-member' treaties—such as the WTO—over subjective intention and reasonable expectations. A textural as opposed to teleological interpretation or an interpretation in good faith is preferred because it does not 'greatly disadvantage newly entering and specifically developing countries for not having participated in the original negotiations'.[45] Prospective members might not have the same intentions as those that defined the original members' negotiations. Moreover, critics of good faith interpretation argue that the original Member States' reasonable expectations might have changed over time such that it is impossible to define the point in time that is decisive for the legitimate expectations to be binding simultaneously on all the members of the multilateral treaty.

However, evolutionary interpretation is crucial in an era of increased linkages between treaties and interconnections between civil society and law.[46] Another argument in favour of superimposing good faith interpretation over textual limitation is that the evolutionary approach is derived from good faith interpretation, as long as it respects *pacta sunt servanda* and is a corollary to predictability.[47]

WTO members, such as the EC in *EC–LAN*, have confounded the PLE, even with the sum of all individual expectations of all WTO Member States and/or with the subjective intentions of the exporting members only (EC in *EC–LAN*). Some members have even mismatched legitimate expectations with subsequent practice and/or negotiators' intent (US in).[48]

[43] Wälde, 1999 p 178.
[44] YBILC, 1966, vol II, p 219.
[45] Lennard, 2002, p 22.
[46] See Marceau, 1999, pp 120–3.
[47] *Ibid*, p 121 with reference to Sinclair, 1984, p 139; see also Canal-Forgues, 2001, p 16.
[48] See *EC–LAN*, AB Report, paras 18 (EC), 37–38 (US), 84 (AB).

Developing Country Members

Member States that are developing countries may find that the principle of good faith protection is in their interests. The principle of good faith is contained in the Chapeau of Article XX, where it expresses a measure of control against discriminatory, trade-restrictive application of the exceptions listed in Article XX(a–j). As case law has shown, the exceptions listed in Article XX(a–j) GATT are usually used by industrialised WTO Member States that have lost their comparative advantage to developing country WTO Member States because industrialised countries have to comply with stricter domestic environmental, labour and cultural standards. The principle of good faith in the Chapeau of Article XX GATT protects the comparative advantage of developing country against an industrialised WTO Member State applying a GATT Article XX exception with a protectionist intent. Thus, the rule of good faith interpretation is used to protect the values of trade liberalization, non-discrimination and multilateralism against the various exceptions to free trade, for which the WTO Agreements also provide.[49]

Unfortunately, the AB in *US–Shrimp* did not follow the good faith interpretation of the Chapeau of Article XX, which should have restrained the overbroad interpretation of the natural resources exemption. The interpretation in *US–Shrimp*, was similar to the one in *India–Patents*, where the AB, in deference to national sovereignty, broadly interpreted the right to environmental protection under the list of specific exemptions in Article XX(a–j).[50]

For developing countries, an overbroad interpretation of the WTO exceptions attributing primacy to health, labour, culture and environment over the free trade values and trade liberalization obligations—as under the general exceptions under Article XX GATT or Article XIV GATS—would run counter to a good faith interpretation of such exceptions. This is because, under good faith, such exceptions may not divert or gain primacy over the WTO's core *ratio* as an international trade organization.[51]

Senti finds that interpreting WTO exceptions too broadly would go against the developing countries' legitimate expectations that in entering into the WTO they would be joining a trade-based organisation committed to liberalising international economic relations without consideration being accorded to non-trade concerns. However, Trachtman retorts that AB practice is characterised by 'blanket subordination of the trade values incorporated in WTO law to other values'.[52]

[49] *Cf* Senti, 2005, p 29.

[50] Against Steinberg, p 44, who says that the 'members of the AB share an ideological predisposition that favours market opening, which may be effectuated through judicial law-making'.

[51] See Senti, 2005, p 29, 'Ein Abrücken von der WTO als reiner Handelsorganisation sei auch ein Verstoss gegen Treu und Glauben. Die Entwicklungsländer wären in seinem Urteil weder dem GATT noch der WTO beigetreten, hätten sie nicht die Gewissheit gehabt, dass es sich bei diesen um reine Handelsorganisationen handelt. Es sei staatspolitisch unredlich, nachträglich die Spielregeln zulasten der armen Länder zu ändern'.

[52] Trachtmann, 2004, p 861.

Full Acceptance of Vienna Rules on the Law of Treaties

A conservative, textual approach to the VCLT favours the interests of both new entrants to the WTO and developing-country members. However, a conservative, textual approach to WTO treaty interpretation does not satisfy the concerns of civil society or non-governmental organisations regarding consumer protection, sustainable development, fair labour conditions, etc. Nor does the focus on the text of the Agreements with a good faith interpretation that is too narrowly concentrated on trade liberalization values find acceptance in industrialised WTO Member States, whose citizens wish their food to be safer, their air cleaner and their environment better protected.[53]

One reason why the AB 'neglects' these issues is that it still has 'comparatively weak authority'. Thus, by 'religiously repeating' the VCLT standards of interpretation, the AB hopes to increase its legitimacy vis-à-vis its members.[54] However, it fails to take into account that a conservative approach to the VCLT bars interpretation with evolutionary meaning and restricts the potential impact of treaties related to the WTO Agreements under Article 31(3)(c). In other words, a strict text-centred interpretation of WTO rules results in the WTO neglecting to dialogue with civil society and losing its legitimacy in this respect.

Thus, the WTO AB is faced with a trade-off between choosing a pioneering role in the international arena by increasing its legitimacy with civil society through broad and often teleological interpretation of the exceptions in the WTO Agreements, or increasing its legitimacy and its legal certainty vis-à-vis potential new members (multilateralism) and developing-country members through adherence to textualist interpretation or through embracing good faith interpretation. The latter (textualist or good faith interpretation) protects the legitimate expectations of the WTO Member States as to trade liberalization obligations. Like the ECJ, the AB is faced with a two-speed development. Either it can consolidate its current *acquis* among its contemporary members, or it can opt for policy that will be attractive to new entrants.

WTO Institutional Limits

Institutional approaches to treaty interpretation find that the balance between formalism (strict textualism) and good faith interpretation depends upon a judiciary's authority, its degree of specialisation, and whether or not it operates under tight time—and information—constraints.[55] Scholars find that the

[53] Umbricht, 2001, pp 773–4, 791–2, while the WTO is (still) considered an intergovernmental organisation, concerns of civil society may enter its jurisdiction through *amicus curiae* briefs; Howse, 2000, pp 47–51 and Howse, 2003, pp 22–8, generally on *amici* before the WTO.

[54] Cottier and Oesch, 2003, p 297.

[55] See Sunstein and Vermeule, 2002, pp 29, 46–7.

emphasis on text is characteristic of international adjudication; deference to national sovereignty often prevents international courts from pursuing good faith interpretation.[56]

From an institutional perspective on interpretation, WTO adjudicators are prevented by the tight time constraints under which they operate from attaching value to objective good faith. The WTO Panels and the AB cannot research the preparatory material on objective intentions of the parties in dispute.[57] Given that WTO jurisprudence does not consider preparatory material too closely, this jurisprudence resembles that of the ECJ[58] but contrasts with later (1993–97) ICJ jurisprudence, in which *travaux* have played an increasingly important role.[59]

[56] See Zoller, 1977, p 214, 'La jurisprudence internationale . . . consacre une interprétation, sinon formaliste du moins stricte, des textes'.

[57] Art 17.5 DSU, the AB has 60 days and can request no more than 90 days from the date of filing notice of appeal, Arts 12.8 and 12.9, the Panels have 6 months, exceptionally 9 months, from the date of its composition and agreeing on the terms of reference; see Cottier, 1998 pp 341, 343–4, on the question of tight time-frames, describing the DSU's tight time-schedules a 'unique legal feature' of the WTO; see Sunstein and Vermeule, 2002, p 29, on institutions and interpretation.

[58] See Ehlermann, 2002, p 616.

[59] See Bernardez, 1998, pp 735–48.

10

Good Faith Rules and Procedures of WTO Dispute Settlement

> [T]he DSU also calls for a good faith interpretation of the . . . procedural provisions of WTO law, in light of general international law that binds WTO Member States. This would include notably the right and obligation of Panels to adopt specific rules of procedure on due process etc, as emphasized by the AB on a few occasions.[1]

THIS CHAPTER BEGINS by considering good faith as it applies to the settlement of disputes before the WTO dispute settlement body (DSB). The 'legalization'[2] of the WTO dispute settlement proceedings reflects the increasing relevance of procedural issues in the parties' submissions before the Panels and the AB. Good faith plays an important role in this process as will be shown below.

This chapter then looks at role of the general principle of law of good faith for clarifying the procedural rights and obligations of the parties to a dispute. In this context, it will be considered whether the general principle of law of good faith in WTO dispute settlement functions as a self-standing general principle of law, or whether its role is to provide a standard for the interpretation of the rules and procedures of WTO dispute settlement.

Throughout this chapter I will distinguish good faith *standards* that the Panels and the AB have introduced to the rules and procedures of dispute settlement from the good faith *obligations* in the Dispute Settlement Understanding (DSU), particularly in Articles 3.10 and 4.3 DSU.

I will consider whether good faith expression is applicable in the 'special or additional rules and procedures on dispute settlement contained in the covered agreements'[3] listed in Appendix 2 to the DSU.[4] These other rules and procedures referred to in Article 1:2 DSU, in combination with Appendix 2 to the DSU, are

[1] Marceau, 2002, p 20.

[2] Pauwelyn, 2003b, p 125, 'Legalization takes the form, for example, of a dramatic increase in procedural claims and objections raised by disputing parties, as well as in the number of pages spent by panels and the AB on procedural issues (eg burden of proof, mandate of the panel, submission of evidence, and participation in the proceedings)'.

[3] Art 1:2 DSU.

[4] Appendix 2 to the DSU.

located outside the DSU and spread out among the different covered agreements; they are found in the ADA, the CVD, the TRIPS, and sometimes express standards of 'due process'. In case of conflict, the *leges speciales* of the respective covered agreement have primacy over the *leges generales* of the DSU, pursuant to Article 1:2 DSU.[5] Issues of good faith protection have been cited in WTO cases not only in relation to the *leges generales* of dispute settlement, ie the rules and procedures under the DSU, but also with respect to the *leges speciales* on dispute settlement within the different covered agreements pursuant to Article 1:2 DSU in combination with Appendix 2.[6]

We will then move to the 'pervasive'[7] or 'organic'[8] general principle of law of good faith applied to the substantive rules of the covered agreements and good faith as the 'fundamental rule of treaty interpretation' (Article 31(1) VCLT),[9] and also deal with the duty to resolve disputes in good faith, the appellate standard of review of facts of good faith, as well as the legitimate expectation of a precedential value for adopted reports.

RULES AND PROCEDURES OF DISPUTE SETTLEMENT

The Dispute Settlement Body (DSB), the WTO's quasi-judicial body, includes all WTO Member States under the umbrella of the General Council (Article IV:3 WTO (Marrakesh) Agreement), pursuant to the rules and procedures of the DSU.[10]

The DSB issues rulings and recommendations (Articles 2, 3.2, 3.4 DSU) in cases based upon the findings of Panels (Articles 11, 19). The Panels are the first-level judiciary comprising trade law experts, who are selected by the DSB on an ad hoc basis (Article 6 DSU). At the appellate level, a standing AB hears Panel cases on appeal (Article 17:1 DSU).

The Panel or AB report, consisting of the findings, rulings and recommendations of the Panel or the AB respectively (Articles 11, 16, 19 DSU), is adopted by the DSB unless there is consensus among the WTO Member States not to do so (Articles 16:4 Panel reports, Article 17:14 AB reports, DSU).[11] With the adoption of the findings, rulings and recommendations of the Panel or the AB by the DSB, the respective report becomes a decision (Article 20 DSU). At this point,

[5] See Neumann, 2002, pp 80–1, who describes the conflict rule in case of a difference between the DSU and the special rules and procedures of dispute settlement contained in different covered agreements.

[6] *Ibid*.

[7] *US–FSC*, AB Report, para 166; *US–Cotton Yarn*, AB Report, para 81.

[8] *US–Japan Hot-rolled Steel*, AB Report, para 101.

[9] *US–Gasoline*, AB Report, p 16 and *US–Line Pipe Safeguards*, AB Report, para 244.

[10] See, eg Waincymer, 2002; Petersmann and Pollock (eds), 2003; Oesch, 2003b; Zimmermann, 2004, on more recent studies on the WTO DSU's structure and function.

[11] See Marceau, 1999, p 94.

the rulings and recommendations of the Panel or the AB become rulings and recommendations of the DSB (Articles 2, 3.2, 3.4 DSU).[12]

The WTO dispute settlement process operates under a two-tier system, meaning that appeals regarding Panel cases may be heard by the AB. Its possibility for appeal makes the WTO dispute resolution system unique among the judicial processes of dispute settlement in general public international law.[13]

THE TERM 'PROCEDURAL' GOOD FAITH

Good faith protection is termed 'procedural' when it relates to the settlement of disputes under the WTO, whether the rules and procedures of dispute resolution are codified under the WTO DSU, or are set out in the other covered agreements, where they express *leges speciales* of WTO dispute settlement.

The term procedural good faith protection is used here to distinguish it from both substantive and interpretive uses of the general principle of law of good faith and its corrolaries of *pacta sunt servanda*, PLE and prohibition of *abus de droit*. This term addresses good faith protection relating to the *leges generales* of WTO procedural law as it relates to the DSU, as well as with respect to the *leges specialis* of WTO dispute settlement rules contained in the covered agreements. Procedural good faith protection as it is used here is closely related, but not equivalent to, WTO due process, as demonstrated in the following sections of this chapter.

'The procedural rights of parties to a dispute settlement proceeding' were first described for WTO law by Bourgeois.[14] Ehlermann further elaborates the notion by introducing the phrase 'procedural rights and obligations of WTO Member States related to the dispute settlement procedure'.[15]

Another characteristic of good faith protection in WTO dispute settlement, hereafter termed WTO procedural good faith, is that it amounts to the only comprehensive good faith expression of WTOlaw. It not only engages the WTO Member States (the way substantive and interpretive good faith would do), but also binds the Panels as to their standard of review for facts and both the Panels and the AB as to the precedential value of adopted reports.

As it applies to the dispute settlement process, so-called procedural good faith is the only expression of good faith codified in a WTO covered agreement, specifically, the Understanding on Rules and Procedures Governing the

[12] See generally, *Ibid*.

[13] See Bacchus, 2003b, p 9, 'WTO dispute settlement system is as busy as it is because the WTO dispute settlement system is unique. We have much to do around our table in Geneva because, among all the international tribunals in the world, and, indeed, among all the international tribunals in the history of the world, ours is unique in two important ways. We have compulsory jurisdiction, and we make judgments that are enforced'.

[14] See Bourgeois, 1998, p 260.

[15] Ehlermann, 2003, p 701.

Settlement of Disputes, better known by its short title, the Dispute Settlement Understanding (DSU) in Annex II of the WTO (Marrakesh) Agreement.

As the only expression of good faith expressly mentioned in the treaty law of the WTO, the challenge is not so much one of knowing whether good faith enters WTO jurisdiction as a general principle of law or as a rule of interpretation under the VCLT.[16] Rather the question is one of knowing whether or not the procedural good faith rules of the WTO are part of the wider *corpus* of public international law.[17]

The interest in analysing the role of good faith in the DSU lies in knowing whether good faith forms part of the applicable law in WTO dispute settlement procedure. If so, the next question is whether good faith, as part of the rules governing the settlement of disputes, takes on the legal status of an obligation or rather consists of establishing a standard that guides the conduct of the dispute settlement procedure.

If procedural good faith expressions are obligations binding under the DSU, the next question is whether or not such a good faith obligation is binding only upon the WTO Member States who are parties to a dispute, or upon WTO Member States generally, or even upon the WTO judiciary as represented by the Panels and the AB. A further question is whether or not the 'unique characteristics' of the WTO DSU are exacerbated by the role of procedural good faith.[18] The 'unique characteristics' include:

— the binding nature of recommendations and rulings on both parties;
— the compulsory dispute settlement mechanism;
— the technical character of the WTO as an organisation; and
— the possibility for cross-retaliatory sanctions.

THE PROCEDURAL GOOD FAITH STANDARD OF 'FAIR, PROMPT AND EFFECTIVE' DISPUTE RESOLUTION

> The WTO procedure enshrines the rule of law and makes the trading system more certain and more predictable.[19]

Standards and obligations of good faith are necessary if WTO dispute settlement procedures are to be used fairly, promptly and effectively. As the AB in the *US–FSC* case found, 'The procedural rules of WTO dispute settlement are designed to promote, not the development of litigation techniques, but simply the fair, prompt and effective resolution of trade disputes'.[20] What this study

[16] See Hu, 2004, p 144.
[17] See Pauwelyn, 2001, p 543; ibid, 2003a, p 460.
[18] See Hu, 2004, pp 143, 153–4, 160, 165.
[19] Marceau, 2000, 'The General Legal Principles of the GATT and the WTO', Speech, Libreville 2000, Metting of African Trade Ministers, Libreville, Gabon, 13–15 November 2000.
[20] *US–FSC*, AB Report, para 166.

calls the procedural good faith standard of 'fair, prompt and effective' dispute resolution, gives content to the procedural rules of dispute resolution and codifies the rule of law for the WTO.

The AB first introduced the above-quoted formula in the *US–FSC* case, and it has become the standard illustration of what Article 3.10 refers to as settling disputes 'in good faith'. The *US–FSC* formula also expresses what is meant by references to 'due process', 'fairness', 'procedural justice', 'rule of law', and other references to good faith principles in the DSU, such as Articles 4.3 and 3.7.

First, the *US–FSC* formula illustrates the necessity for a fair dispute settlement procedure, or for achieving a 'satisfactory settlement of the matter in accordance with the rights and obligations under [the Dispute Settlement] Understanding and under the covered agreements'.[21] While the rules and procedures of the DSU cannot ensure 'a solution mutually acceptable to the parties to a dispute and consistent with the covered agreements' (Article 3.7 DSU), they shall nevertheless ensure that the process of dispute resolution remains a fair one, independent of the substantive fairness of the decisison's result.

Among the DSU rules and procedures are some that contain due process obligations, specifically those which see that DSU rules are applied in a manner consistent with the standard of good faith. Those rules, which prescribe that the WTO Member States and the Panels apply the rules and procedures of dispute resolution fairly, promptly and effectively, because the 'prompt settlement of disputes [. . .] is essential to the effective functioning of the WTO' (Article 3.3 DSU), express the concern that the dispute settlement system as a whole 'is a central element in providing security and predictability to the multilateral trading system' (Article 3.2, first sentence, DSU).[22]

Following the frequent references in later cases to the *US–FSC's* characterisation of the duty to 'engage in [dispute settlement] procedures in good faith in an effort to resolve the dispute', this has become a formula. The three adjectives 'fair, prompt and effective' express the three functions for good faith that the AB has identified for WTO dispute settlement and conciliation proceedings. The three elements of the *US–FSC* formula, to which the Panels and the AB have been referring since *US–FSC* in order to illustrate the function of good faith in dispute settlement rules and procedures, are discussed below, illustrating the different meanings that good faith in DSU proceedings has taken in jurisprudence about the settlement of disputes in the WTO.

Fairness, the first element, refers to the relationship between the complaining and responding party, but also involves a member's good faith obligations vis-à-vis a Panel, the AB and the DSB. Fairness guarantees that the procedural rights in the DSU are not abused, and thus assumes a corrective function.

Promptness expresses the element of time in dispute resolution, which must be read together with *US–FSC's* reference to 'trade disputes'. The AB explicitly

[21] Art 3.4 DSU; see Art 3.3 DSU: 'maintenance of a proper balance between the rights and the obligations of Members'. See also Art 3.7 DSU.

[22] See Petersmann, 2003, p 10.

refers to trade, highlighting the urgency of settling disputes quickly in the fast-changing world of global economics.

Last, but not least, the AB refers to effectiveness, meaning considerations of legal order, encompassing the stability, predictability and foreseeability of treaty relations. Possibly this function also refers to the relationship between the members party to the dispute, who are responsible for the successful dispute resolution on the one hand, and, on the other the Panel and/or AB, who are ultimately responsible for the successful and orderly settlement of disputes. In the context of effectiveness it should be noted that good faith in dispute resolution has been complemented by a reference to 'due process' and/or 'orderly procedure'.[23]

Fairness

In relation to the substantive rules in the WTO covered agreements, the principles of fundamental fairness and due process guard against 'unfair trade' practices. Examples include the protectionist (ab)use of substantive WTO rights—specifically dumping prices, subsidies, and other WTO-inconsistent import surges—as well as quantitative barriers to trade, such as discriminatory practices. As inherent elements of the good faith principle, fundamental fairness and due process ensure that the right 'commercial defence' is exercised fairly, that is, that the WTO Member States do not abuse the right to exercise a trade remedy, such as imposing anti-dumping duties, countervailing measures or safeguards.[24]

Fundamental fairness and due process not only exist in relation to substantive rules of the WTO covered agreements but also apply to WTO procedural law, namely to the rules and procedures of dispute settlement, whether such provisions are contained in the DSU (*leges generales*) or in the other covered agreements (*leges speciales*).[25]

The object and purpose of procedural fairness are expressed in Article 3.10 DSU, first sentence, which states that 'requests for conciliation and the use of dispute settlement procedures should not be intended or considered as contentious acts, [. . .]'[26] and 'that if a dispute arises, all Members will engage in these procedures in good faith in an effort to resolve the dispute'.

The prohibition against abusing the dispute settlement procedures as 'contentious acts',[27] is contained in a teleological interpretation of the duty to

[23] *Mexico–HFCS (Art 21.5)*, AB Report, para 47.

[24] O'Cunningham and Cribb, 2003, p 155; see also Durling and Nicely, 2002, p 2, for the term 'unfair trade'; Vermulst and Graafsma, 2002, pp 19–20, specifically, for the term 'commercial defence'.

[25] Art 1:2 and Appendix 2 of the DSU refer to the rules and procedures of dispute resolution outside the DSU.

[26] Art 3.10 DSU.

[27] *Ibid.*

resolve disputes in good faith under Article 3.10 DSU.[28] Article 3.10 DSU also clarifies that fairness, as an element of good faith in dispute resolution, relates to the process of dispute resolution as opposed to the substantive result of the decision.

The *EC–Sardines* Panel elaborated on fundamental fairness in proceedings before the DSU as being the capacity to defend and complain. The *EC–Sardines* Panel decision moreover demonstrated that there are two ways of ensuring that the complaining party respects procedural fairness in dispute resolution when filing or withdrawing a notice of appeal, as the following quote from the *EC–Sardines* Panel decision shows:

> [T]here may be situations where the withdrawal of an appeal on condition of refiling a new notice, and the filing thereafter of a new notice, could be abusive and disruptive. However, in such cases, we would have the right to reject the condition, and also to reject any filing of a new notice of appeal, on the grounds either that the Member seeking to file such a new notice would not be engaging in dispute settlement proceedings in good faith, or that Rule 30(1) of the *Working Procedures* must not be used to undermine the fair, prompt, and effective resolution of trade disputes. [T]he rules must be interpreted so as to 'ensure that appellate review proceedings do not become an arena for unfortunate litigation techniques that frustrate the objectives of the DSU, and that developing countries do not have the resources to deal with'.[29]

In order to render procedural fairness a binding obligation upon parties to a dispute, the *EC–Sardines* Panel introduced two ways of engaging a member party's responsibility as to the fair use of the dispute settlement procedures. The first option is to refer to Article 3.10 DSU, whereas the second comes closer to creative jurisprudence by the *EC–Sardines* Panel. It consists in interpreting Rule 30(1) of the Panel Working Procedures (Appendix 3 of the DSU) pursuant to the procedural good faith standard of 'fair, prompt, and effective resolution of trade disputes', which the AB introduced under the *US–FSC* decision.

Promptness

Article 3.3 of the DSU calls for the 'prompt settlement of situations in which a member considers that any benefits accruing to it directly or indirectly under the covered agreements are being impaired by measures taken by another member'.[30] Article 12:2 DSU illustrates the meaning of the postulate by reference to Article 3.3 DSU.

The *Mexico–HFCS (Article 21.5)* AB Report found that the element of time (promptness) is an obligation of the WTO Member States party to a dispute, the obligation being implied in the duty to 'engage in [dispute settlement]

[28] See Petersmann, 2003, p 10.
[29] *EC–Sardines*, AB Report, para 146.
[30] Art 3.3 DSU.

procedures in good faith in an effort to resolve the dispute' under Article 3.10 DSU.[31]

The *Mexico–HFCS (Article 21.5)* AB explained that the duty to resolve disputes in good faith functions in combination with the principle of due process to oblige the responding Member to bring claimed procedural deficiencies to the attention of the complaining member in a 'prompt' manner.[32] To the AB, the procedural obligation of a WTO Member State to be prompt in the duty to resolve disputes in good faith, is one element of Article 3.10 DSU and is also implied in Articles 3.2 and 3.3 DSU, thereby 'reflect[ing] the importance to the multilateral trading system of security, predictability and the prompt settlement of disputes'.[33] Article 3.3 DSU is situated under the so-called General Provisions of the DSU and thus expresses guiding principles, as opposed to a duty or a binding obligation.

In addition to the duty of timeliness under Articles 3.10 and 3.3 DSU—and/or the *US–FSC* formula on procedural good faith and due process—Article 12.2 DSU says that Panel procedures shall not 'unduly delay [. . .] the panel process'.[34] Consequently, Article 12.2 DSU cannot be used to sanction a responding party for abusing its due process rights under the DSU as a litigation technique to draw out the resolution of the dispute, because it relates to the adoption of the Panel Working Procedures in Appendix 3.

The AB has defined an untimely manner for raising objections as the failure of a member to raise objections under Article 16 DSU when it had one or more opportunities to do so. The AB has also introduced the legal consequence for failing to respect the consideration of promptness in the settlement of disputes, by stating that a Member failing to raise objections even though it had had several opportunities to do so 'may be deemed to have waived its right to have a Panel consider such objections'.[35]

In our view, assuming that Mexico had explicitly raised these issues before the Panel, the Panel could reasonably have concluded that Mexico's 'objections' were not raised in a timely manner, because as the AB later in the case said, 'when a Member wishes to raise an objection in dispute settlement proceedings, it is always incumbent on that Member to do so *promptly*' (emphasis added).[36]

The AB in *Mexico–HFCS (Article 21.5)* subsumed the duty of timeliness or promptness under Article 3.10 DSU, thereby filling in with content the duty to resolve disputes in good faith in the WTO DSU.

We have already said that the principles of good faith and due process require:

[31] Art 3.10 DSU.
[32] *Mexico–HFCS (Art 21.5)*, AB Report, para 79 and fn 45 to para 50.
[33] *Ibid.*
[34] Art 12:2 DSU.
[35] *Mexico–HFCS (Art 21.5)*, AB Report, para 50.
[36] *Ibid.*

> . . . that responding Members *seasonably and promptly* bring claimed procedural deficiencies to the attention of the complaining Member, . . . The procedural rules of WTO dispute settlement are designed to promote, not the development of litigation techniques, but simply the fair, prompt and effective resolution of trade disputes (emphasis added).[37]

In its *US–Offset Act ('Byrd Amendment')* decision, the AB construed a violation based upon the duty of timeliness, upholding the Panel's finding that the US had not made its request in a timely manner, because it had let seven months pass since the composition of the Panel and two months since the issuance of the descriptive part of the Panel report.[38] In so-doing, the AB did not cite Article 3.10 DSU, but instead referred to the standard of fair, prompt and effective dispute resolution, which had been introduced earlier in the *US–FSC* formula. In *US–Offset Act ('Byrd Amendment')* the AB referred to case law in order to construe the duty of timeliness in dispute settlement. In particular, the timely manner for filing a procedural request was measured according to whether or not a member party has used the 'opportunities' for doing so, in reference to *Mexico – HFCS (Article 21.5)*.[39]

Effectiveness

In addition to expressing a duty of promptness in bringing and resolving disputes before the WTO Panels and the AB, WTO appellate practice in *US–Lamb*, *EC–Sardines*, *Thailand–Steel* and *Chile–Agricultural Products*, attributes to Article 3.3 DSU the function of guaranteeing the effectiveness of the WTO legal system overall.

Article 3.3 DSU maintains that

> prompt settlement of situations in which a Member considers that any benefit accruing to it . . . are being impaired by measures taken by another Member is essential to the *effective* functioning of the WTO and the maintenance of a proper balance between the rights and the obligations of Members (emphasis added).[40]

Effectiveness in dispute settlement procedures has been defined in more detail in the *US–Lamb Safeguards* AB Report, where it stands for a prohibition against improperly withholding arguments with a view to raising them later. The AB in *US–Lamb Safeguards* said:[41]

> We wish to emphasize that the discretion that WTO Member States enjoy to argue dispute settlement claims in the manner they deem appropriate does not, of course, detract from their obligation, under Article 3.10 of the DSU, 'to engage in dispute

[37] *Ibid*, fn 45 to para 50 with references to *US–FSC* AB Report and others.
[38] See *US–Offset Act ('Byrd Amendment')*, AB Report, para 314.
[39] *US–Offset Act ('Byrd Amendment')*, AB Report, para 313.
[40] Art 3.3 DSU.
[41] See *US–Lamb Safeguards*, AB Report of 1 May 2001.

> settlement procedures "in good faith in an effort to resolve the dispute" '. It follows that WTO Member States cannot improperly withhold arguments from competent authorities with a view to raising those arguments later before a Panel. In any event, as a practical matter, we think it unlikely that a Member would do so.[42]

Like in the *US–Lamb Safeguards* decision, the AB in *EC–Sardines* emphasized the elements of effectiveness, legal security aand predictability in order to fill the gap which the lack of conditional withdrawal creates in WTO procedural law. Neither the DSU nor Rule 30 of the Working Procedures contain a provision on conditional withdrawal.[43] In the *EC–Sardines* AB Report, the question was whether it is lawful under Article 3.10 DSU to withdraw a Panel request under the condition of filing a replacement notice of appeal.[44] The *EC–Sardines* AB found the principle of effectiveness as derived from good faith in Article 3.10 DSU to be the most appropriate interpretive method for filling in the gap.

In *Chile–Agricultural Products*, the AB related the element of effectiveness to the duty to resolve disputes in good faith by linking effectiveness and good faith with due process rights, which are 'inherent in the WTO dispute settlement system'.[45]

Based on this jurisprudence, it is proposed that the element of effectiveness contained in the good faith obligations of Articles 3.10 and 4.3 DSU prohibits an abuse of due process rights. As mentioned above, such due process rights apply in the context of settling disputes (Panel request must be sufficiently precise,[46] claims must be made explicitly and not implicitly,[47] and the filing of replacement notices of appeal must be timely and early[48]). In addition, due process rights exist for the *leges speciales* of dispute settlement rules under other WTO Agreements. See for example Article 6 ADA: investigating authorities must disclose evidence during investigation to interested parties;[49] Article 12 ADA: duty to inform during final determination;[50] and Article 6.7 ATC: requirement for consultations.[51]

Article 12.2 DSU expresses what Panel and Appellate Reports understand specifically by effectiveness in WTO dispute settlement proceedings. Although it relates to Panel reports only, Article 12:2 DSU formulates a mandate that could equally apply to AB Reports: '[P]rocedures should provide sufficient flexibility so as to ensure high-quality [Panel] reports, while not unduly delaying the

[42] *US–Lamb Safeguards*, AB Report, para 115.
[43] See *EC–Sardines*, AB Report, para 140.
[44] *Ibid*, para 139 and further references in paras 141, 142 and 146.
[45] *Chile–Agricultural Products*, AB Report, para 176.
[46] See *Thailand–Steel*, AB Report, paras 84–9.
[47] See, eg *Chile Agricultural Products*, AB Report, para 164; *EC–Hormones*, AB Report, paras 78–9; *Brazil-Coconut*, Panel Report, p 22.
[48] See *EC–Sardines*, AB Report, para 105.
[49] See *Thailand–Steel*, AB Report, paras 109, 117.
[50] *Ibid*, paras 110, 117.
[51] See *US–Underwear*, AB Report, p 15.

[Panel] process'.[52] The balance of flexibility with high quality and promptness is what effectiveness in dispute resolution before the WTO should stand for.

Bacchus, a former Chairman of the AB, may have had the principle of effectiveness in mind when he urged the AB to ensure that the DSU remains an efficient tool:

> Members of the WTO [shall] establish a useful, workable, practical, enduring institution that will contribute to the continuing success of the WTO and the WTO dispute settlement system, and that will, in time, serve all the people of the world.[53]

Similarly, Ehlermann, another former Chairman of the AB, is reported as saying that the goal of the DSU 'from the very start was the establishment of an independent, quasi-judicial institution that would serve all the Members of the WTO equally and effectively'.[54]

Van den Bossche associates the element of effectiveness in dispute settlement with the security and predictability that the WTO legal system and dispute settlement understanding, in particular, shall bring to international trade relations: 'While the WTO dispute settlement system is definitely still open to improvement, it currently already constitutes an effective and efficient system for the peaceful resolution of disputes. It brings a degree of security and predictability, in international trade, to all its Members and their citizens'.[55]

Conclusions

The *US–FSC* formula of 'fair, prompt and effective' dispute settlement and the standard of procedural good faith it propagates embody the procedural guarantee that the dispute settlement rules and procedures will be used in a fundamentally fair manner. The due process rights ensured by this *US–FSC* formula of 'fair, prompt and effective', stand for the impartiality of the adjudicative tribunal and 'its corollary, the juridical equality between the parties in their capacity as litigants'.[56] Procedural good faith thus expresses 'the principles of fundamental fairness and due process that underlie and inform the provisions of the DSU'.[57]

If procedural good faith standards in dispute settlement are to ensure *in concreto* the fair settlement of disputes, they must also guard against the abuse of these rights. Therefore the procedural good faith standard of 'fair, prompt and effective dispute settlement'[58] may function as a prohibition of (procedural) *abus de droit* by condemning ineffective or otherwise unduly prolonged dispute

[52] Art 12.2 DSU.
[53] Bacchus, 2003b, p 8.
[54] *Cf* Ehlermann, 2003b, as reported by Bacchus, 2003d, p 7.
[55] Van den Bossche, 2003, p 24.
[56] Gaffney, 1999, p 1179.
[57] *Mexico–HFCS (Art 21.5)*, AB Report, para 107.
[58] *US–FSC*, AB Report, para 166.

setttlement proceedings, which reduce the rules and procedures of the DSU to litigation techniques.

In addition, the good faith standards of fundamental fairness and due process apply to the *leges speciales* of WTO procedural law (see below), namely the rules of procedure contained outside the DSU in the different covered agreements. Applied to these *leges speciales* the prohibition against abuse of due process rights guards against 'unfair trade', that is the protectionist (ab)use of substantive WTO rights, specifically AD/CVD, ASG/ATC safeguards and GATT Article XX exceptions. As to *leges speciales*, the procedural good faith standards embodied in the *US–FSC* formula ensure that these due process rights, intended to maintain fair 'commercial defense', are themselves not abused.[59]

To sum up, without the duty to solve disputes in good faith, all other good faith issues in treaty relations (negotiation, interpretation and implementation) would stand no chance of being adjudicated.[60]

PROCEDURAL GOOD FAITH OBLIGATIONS OF DISPUTE SETTLEMENT'S *LEGES GENERALES*

The dispute settlement provisions of the WTO DSU contain two explicit and one implicit reference to good faith. The first of the codified procedural good faith expressions imposes on all WTO Member States the obligation to engage in dispute resolution in good faith:

Article 3.10 DSU applies once it has been found that bringing a dispute before the WTO will be (in the word of Article 4.3 DSU) 'fruitful'. Article 3.10 DSU may apply either to conciliation under Article 5 DSU or to adversarial dispute resolution with Panel (Articles 6–16) and appellate (review) proceedings (Article 17).

The second codified good faith obligation is found in Article 4.3 DSU and applies to only those Member States 'to which the request for consultations is made', binding them to 'enter into consultations in good faith'. Article 4.3 DSU relates only to Panel proceedings, and only to the consultations phase.[61] This is the most narrowly focused good faith obligation as it relates neither to conciliation nor to appellate review.

A third good faith obligation is, according to Panel and appellate jurisprudence, implicitly contained in Article 3.7 DSU. It binds the WTO Member

[59] O'Cunningham and Cribb, 2003, p 155; see also Durling and Nicely, 2002, p 2, for the term 'unfair trade'; Vermulst and Graafsma, 2002, pp 19–20, specifically, for the term 'commercial defence'.

[60] *Canada–Aircraft*, AB Report, para 182 (and paras 51–3); the statement was issued as the AB's preliminary reaction to the argument and counter-arguments raised by the parties in this dispute. Brazil's complaint against Canada was that Art 3.10 DSU (the rule of collaboration as Brazil termed it in reference to the Panel report in *Argentina–Textiles and Apparel*) required that once Brazil had laid down that its case was supported by prima facie evidence, Canada was under the obligation provide the Panel with the relevant documents in its possession. It was then that the AB responded that the issues raised questions of fundamental and far-reaching consequences for the WTO dispute settlement system.

[61] Art 4.3 DSU.

States before they even become parties to a dispute. A potential complainant must:

> exercise its judgment as to whether action under these procedures would be fruitful . . . [thereby reflecting] *a basic principle* that Members should have recourse to WTO dispute settlement in good faith . . . .[62]

Similar to Article 3.10, the duty to consult in good faith under Article 3.7 DSU applies to both conciliatory and adversarial dispute resolution. Procedural good faith obligations exist not only for dispute settlement in WTO law; Article 2 paragraph 2 UN Charter codifies the duty of states to settle disputes in good faith:

> All Members, in order to ensure to all of them the rights and benefits resulting from membership, shall fulfill in good faith the obligations assumed by them in accordance with the present Charter.[63]

Article 2 of the Charter does not specifically address good faith in judicial proceedings.64 ICJ jurisprudence has derived from this universal duty of both Members and UN organs, to fulfil the treaty obligations under the UN Charter in good faith, the specific obligation to settle disputes in good faith.65

As the *Case Concerning the Aerial Incident of 10 August 1999 (Pakistan v India)* shows, Article 2 paragraph 2 of the UN Charter might constitute more of a binding obligation for the UN Member States than does Article 3.10 DSU for WTO Member States:

> The Court's lack of jurisdiction does not relieve States of their obligation to settle their disputes by peaceful means. The choice of those means admittedly rests with the parties under Article 33 of the United Nations Charter. They are nonetheless *under an obligation to seek such a settlement, and to do so in good faith* in accordance with Article 2, paragraph 2, of the Charter (emphasis added).[66]

Secondly, the principle of good faith in the judicial settlement of disputes is said to be *implicitly* contained in the International Criminal Court statute (ICC statute) Article 86, which requires states to 'fully [reference to good faith] cooperate with the Court in the investigation and prosecution of crimes within the jurisdiction of the Court'.[67] In international criminal judgments, the duty to provide information as a specific emanation of the good faith obligation in disputes, was concretised in the 1997 *Blaskic* Subpoena Judgment, where the

[62] *Mexico–HFCS (Art 21.5)*, AB Report, para 73, referring to Art 3.7 DSU.

[63] Art 2.2 UN Charter

[64] See Art 2.2 UN Charter; see also Müller, 1995, pp 89–97 for a discussion of Art 2.2 UN Charter; see also Rosenne, 1989, p 159.

[65] See *Case Concerning the Aerial Incident of 10 August 1999 (Pakistan v India)*, Jurisdiction of the Court, para 53.

[66] *Ibid.*

[67] Art 86 ICC Statute, of 17 July 1998, ILM 37 (1998), pp 999ff, also available at http://www.un.org/law/icc/statute/romefra.htm; see also Peters, 2002, pp 131–3, for a cross-comparison of the principle of good faith as a source of States' duty to co-operate specifically in dispute settlement procedures in various treaties.

Appeals Chamber of the International Criminal Tribunal for the Former Yugoslavia (ICTY) held that 'the degree of bona fide cooperation and assistance' is an element the tribunal will take into account 'throughout the whole process of scrutinizing the documents'.[68]

In general, public international tribunals are very cautious about acknowledging the bad faith of a Member State.[69] As of 2000, there are nine judgments of the ICJ that express the prohibition against abuse of procedural rights.[70]

Moreover, Article 294 UNCLOS contains a prohibition against the abuse of procedural rights within the law of the sea.[71] The history of the provision stems from the concern about finding an equilibrium between the interests of coastal states and those of land-locked states, the land-locked states in particular wanting to see their rights safeguarded under the Convention.[72]

Article 3.10 DSU: 'Engage in these Procedures in Good Faith . . . to Resolve the Dispute'

This section focuses on the 'duty to engage in dispute settlement procedures in good faith in an effort to resolve the dispute'.[73] Particular emphasis is placed on analysing jurisprudential clarifications of Article 3.10, which the WTO adjudicators pursuant to their duty of analysing the 'existing provisions of those agreements in accordance with the customary rules of interpretation of public international law' (Article 3.2, second sentence, DSU), have only recently begun to address. The 1999 *Canada–Aircraft* AB Report[74] was the first to mention Article 3.10 DSU in the context of WTO jurisprudence; the *US–FSC* in 2000 and the *US–Lamb Safeguard* case in 2002 continued the trend.[75]

The use of Article 3.10 DSU in WTO jurisprudence has coincided with the surge in trade remedy cases, a trend which can be dated back to 2001, when party submissions had presumably discovered that Article 3.10 DSU, together with the other due process and good faith obligations of the DSU (Articles 4.3 and 3.7 DSU), provided a new tool for adversarial process.

[68] Case no IT-95-14-T, *Prosecutor v Tihomir Blaskic*, Judgment of 29 October 1997, para 68, cited in Peters, 2002, p 132.

[69] See Zoller, 1977, 141.

[70] See, eg *Case Concerning the Aerial Incident 10 August 1999 (Pakistan v India)*, where in para 30, Pakistan alleges that the reservation valid for Commonwealth is a disguised discrimination that amounts among other things to a breach of good faith, which is an argument the Court denied; Ambatielos (*Greece v United Kingdom*) (1951–1953), p 23; Military and Paramilitary Activities in and against Nicaragua (*Nicaragua v United States of America*) (1984–1991), para 21; Application of the Convention on the Prevention and Punishment of the Crime of Genocide (*Bosnia and Herzegovina v Serbia and Montenegro*) (1993–present), p 336 and 349; see Kolb, 2000, pp 640–6, for a summary and discussion of all cases relating to abuse of judicial process.

[71] See UNCLOS.

[72] See Kolb, 2000, p 639.

[73] Art 3.10 DSU.

[74] See *Canada–Aircraft*, AB Report, para 190.

[75] See *US–FSC*, AB Report, para 166.

The GATT 1947 Contracting Parties who negotiated the Uruguay Round Agreements did not have to create the wording for such a duty because it already existed. A wording identical to Article 3.10 DSU informed Paragraph 9 of the Tokyo Round DSU Code of 1979, but that Tokyo Round Code had never been used.[76] Thus, during the establishment of the DSU in the Uruguay Round, the Contracting Parties established Article 3.10 DSU by simply referring to the wording of paragraph 9 Tokyo Round DSU Code.

The Tokyo Round Understanding Regarding Notification, Consultation, Dispute Settlement and Surveillance of 1979 reads:

> 9. It is understood that requests for conciliation and the use of the dispute settlement procedures of Article XXIII:2 should not be intended or considered as contentious acts and that, if disputes arise, all contracting parties will engage in these procedures in good faith in an effort to resolve the disputes.

Article 3.10 DSU represents both treaty law and a general principle of law pursuant to the *US–FSC*, AB Report.[77] Hudec, in 2000, warned that the obligation in Article 3.10 DSU to engage in dipsute settlement procedures in good faith could be abused by larger WTO Member States who could insist that smaller Member States had not implemented a Panel's recommendations in good faith.[78] Article 3.10 DSU says:

> It is understood that requests for conciliation and the use of the dispute settlement procedures should not be intended or considered as contentious acts and that, if a dispute arises, all Members will engage in these procedures in good faith in an effort to resolve the dispute. It is also understood that complaints and counter-complaints in regard to distinct matters should not be linked.

The WTO judiciary has only relatively recently started to use Article 3.10 DSU. The AB in *Canada–Aircraft* (1999) took the lead when it said that Article 3.10 DSU would 'give teeth' to the rules and procedures for the settlement of disputes.[79] Since *Canada–Aircraft*, references to Article 3.10 DSU have been made in almost every case dealing with an issue of dispute settlement procedure. In the *Mexico–HFCS* (Article 21.5) AB Report of 2001, the AB is quoted as having 'continued its recent trend of citing to the principles of good faith, fundamental fairness and due process in its decisions'.[80]

The WTO judiciary's well-intentioned attempts to strengthen the dispute settlement procedures by invoking the good faith obligation under Article 3.10 DSU have also had some undesirable consequences. Certain WTO Member States began to realise that disputes could be prolonged and time gained by

[76] Understanding Regarding Notification, Consultation, Dispute Settlement and Surveillance, 28 November 1979, available at http://www.worldtradelaw.net, Tokyo Round Agreements, Understandings, Decisions and Declarations.

[77] See *US–FSC*, AB Report, para 166.

[78] *Cf* Hudec, 2000, p 15.

[79] *Canada–Aircraft*, AB Report, paras 48–53.

[80] *Cf* Lester and Leitner, 2003c, p 14.

manipulating the WTO rules and procedures for the settlement of disputes. This insight that procedural rights under the DSU may be used as litigation techniques went hand-in-hand with the development, by the WTO judiciary, of its Article 3.10 DSU jurisprudence.

Such an adversarial approach to dispute settlement rules proliferates in the jurisprudence on trade remedies, notably in cases dealing with anti-dumping and Agreement on Subsidies and Countervailing Measures (ASCM).[81] Not surprisingly, procedural good faith as in the duty to settle disputes fairly, promptly and effectively, has thus acted as the ultimate weapon against abuses of (due process) rights, mostly in 'trade remedy' cases.[82]

The following listed entries consider how good faith obligations under Article 3.10 DSU were used by the AB to counter possible abuses of the rules and procedures of WTO dispute settlement:

— *Canada–Aircraft* (1999): The AB introduced the principle that a member has no right (except if there is business confidential information (BCI) at issue) to refuse to supply the Panel with information (under Article 13 DSU in combination with Article 3.10 DSU), but conversely, the Panel is under an obligation limited only by its standard of review vis-à-vis domestic authorities, to objectively assess the facts under Article 11 DSU.

— *US–FSC* (2000 appeal): A scenario for using Article 3.10 DSU arose, specifically in a situation of *venire contra factum proprium*, where the defendant may not appeal on the basis that the 'statement of available evidence' is insufficient under Article 4.2 ASCM Agreement, when it has acted as if it had accepted the establishment of the Panel and the preceding consultations.

— *US–Lamb Safeguards* (2001): The AB construed a third constellation with respect to Article 3.10 DSU, namely the prohibition against withholding information from investigating authorities.

— *Thailand–Steel* (2001): A defending party is not entitled to appeal on the basis that the statement of available evidence is insufficient for the establishment of a Panel, when it has already been given the opportunity to request clarifications.

— *Mexico–HFCS (Article 21.5)* (2001): The AB found that Article 3.10 imposes the obligation to raise objections 'explicitly and timely', that is, not after a party has already had the opportunity to speak up, for example in written submissions to the Panel. The AB gives three examples of valid objections:

  (i) when no consultations were held;
  (ii) where no indication was given that they were held; and
  (iii) when the defendant neglected to evaluate whether an action would be 'fruitful'.

[81] *Cf* Jackson, 1999, p 347.

[82] Jackson and Benke, 2003, p 111.

— *EC–Sardines* (2002): The AB found with respect to Article 3.10 DSU that conditional withdrawals of notices of appeal are DSU-consistent as long as they do not violate the Article 3.10 DSU principles.

Canada–Aircraft *Appellate Body Report (1999)*

Canada failed to provide information on the Export Development Corporation's financing of the Atlantic Southeast Airlines (ASA) transaction. Canada justified its actions by claiming firstly that Brazil had not established a prima facie case to establish why Canada's export subsidy on the airlines transaction was prohibited under Part II of the ASCM. Canada considered that its own claim had already been fruitful *before* the Panel had requested the information because, according to Canada, the obligation to provide the Panel with information under Article 13(1) DSU vests only after the opposing party has established that the claim is valid.

Secondly, Canada claimed that the information Brazil was requesting was business confidential and thus protected under the last sentence of Article 13(1) DSU.[83]

The AB was not persuaded by Canada's first argument. Under Article 13(1) it is the Panel that requests information and decides when it needs which piece of information. The Panel may request information before the opposing party has established a prima facie case, since a fortiori information may become necessary to enable the opposing party to establish the prima facie case. Moreover, if a member were to make its duty to provide the Panel with information dependent on the opposing party's formulation of a claim, the decision as to whether or not a prima facie case is established would erroneously become the responsibility of the member and not the Panel.[84]

The AB also rejected Canada's second claim justifying its refusal to cooperate with the Panel with BCI, because the AB found it 'curious' that Canada asked the AB to adopt the same special procedures for the protection of BCI that it had previously characterised as sufficiently inadequate to allow it to refuse to provide the Panel with the information sought.[85]

Brazil considered Article 3.10 DSU a binding obligation upon a responding party to provide information. With its broad interpretation of Article 13(1), Brazil expanded the right of the Panels to seek information and transformed it into a duty of WTO Member States to collaborate with the dispute settlement bodies.[86] 'Brazil had, in its submission before the AB, introduced the "duty of collaboration" which it had derived from Article 3.10 DSU as an argument against Canada's refusal to provide the requested information'.[87]

[83] See *Canada–Aircraft*, AB Report, paras 188, 191–2.
[84] *Ibid*, paras 192–4.
[85] *Ibid*, paras 195–6.
[86] *Ibid*, para 52.
[87] *Ibid*, paras 48–53.

'Article 3.10 DSU "Gave Teeth" to the Member's Duty to Provide the Panel with the Information Sought' The AB, it seems 'took inspiration from the Brazilian' broad analysis of Article 3.10 DSU, linking Article 3.10 DSU with Article 13(1) DSU and thereby engaging in creative jurisprudence by which it derived the duty of WTO Members to provide the Panel with information.[88] The AB, with Article 3.10 DSU thereby gave teeth to the Member's duty (implied in Article 13.1 DSU) 'to provide the Panel with the information sought'.[89]

The AB upheld the Panel's finding that the Canada EDC's debt financing was not proven to confer a 'benefit' and therefore fulfilled the necessary criteria of a subsidy.[90] The AB thus rejected Brazil's appeal, which would have established from the information Canada had withheld that the Canadian financing scheme for aircraft constituted a subsidy prohibited under the CVD Agreement.

Evaluation of Canada–Aircraft: *Article 3.10 DSU Establishes the Duty of Collaboration with the Panel* The issue of the *Canada–Aircraft* case was the refusal of a party to a dispute (Canada) to comply with the Panel's request for certain information regarding payments made by the Canadian government to Canada's aircraft industry under Article 13(1) DSU.

Canada–Aircraft links the Panel's right to request information under Article13(1) DSU with the obligation of the WTO Member States to resolve disputes in good faith pursuant to Article 3.10 DSU. Insofar as the AB balances the '*right* of the Panel to seek information' (Article 13(1) DSU) with the WTO Member's *right* to a good faith dispute resolution (Article 3.10 DSU), it ensures respect for the content of Article 3.10 DSU, which prohibits WTO Member States from 'consider[ing] "the use of the dispute settlement procedures . . . as contentious acts"'.[91]

The AB in *Canada–Aircraft*, inspired by Brazil, succeeded in reinforcing the object and purpose of Article 3.10 with those of Article 13(1) DSU, thereby strengthening, or as the AB put it, 'giving teeth' to this procedural good faith obligation:

> We believe also that the duty of a Member party to a dispute to comply with a request from the Panel to provide information under Article 13.1 of the DSU is but one specific manifestation of the broader duties of Members under Article 3.10 of the DSU not to consider the 'use of the dispute settlement procedures . . . as contentious acts', and, when a dispute does arise, to 'engage in these procedures in good faith in an effort to resolve the dispute'.[92]

Even if a member party to a dispute is not legally bound to provide the Panel with information, the AB found that a member obstructing the Panel's right to seek information under Article 13(1) DSU acts against the right of the members to

[88] *Canada–Aircraft*, AB Report, paras 48–53.
[89] *Ibid*, para 203.
[90] See *ibid*, paras 205 and 182.
[91] *Ibid*, para 190.
[92] *Ibid*.

have disputes settled in good faith under Article 3.10 DSU, or the 'fundamental right of Members to have disputes arising between them resolved through the system and proceedings for which they bargained in concluding the DSU'.[93]

In adjudicating *Canada–Aircraft,* the AB may have been influenced by duties of cooperation with judicial bodies codified elsewhere in international law. The ICSID, referring to disputes between governments and foreign investors, specifically qualifies the duty to provide information for conciliation proceedings in Rule 23 ICSID.[94]

Sanctions By interpreting Article 13(1) DSU in the light and context of Article 3.10 DSU, the AB created a *positive* duty of members to collaborate; but it nevertheless found that members must not obstruct the Panels' obligation to conduct an objective assessment of facts (Article 11 DSU) or the Panel's right to seek information (Article 13(1) DSU).[95] To better enforce its *Canada–Aircraft* good faith in dispute-settlement jurisprudence, the AB bolstered its jurisprudence by introducing sanctions to be imposed for acting against the right of a member to have disputes resolved in good faith, in particular if the infringement of Article 3.10 DSU consists in a WTO Member refusing to provide a Panel with the information sought.

From the refusal to co-operate with a Panel under Article 13(1) DSU in combination with Article 3.10 DSU, the AB created the Panel's right to draw 'adverse inferences' against the non-co-operating member party. The AB in *Canada–Aircraft* did this by extending a Panel's right to draw adverse inferences from a member's refusal to cooperate, which exists for actionable subsidies under Annex V ASCM Agreement, to the category of prohibited subsidies.[96]

The following discussion of the *US–Wheat Gluten* case will show that depending upon whether the Panel was able to conduct an objective assessment of facts (Article 11 DSU), a Panel *must or may* draw such adverse inference (obligatory or discretionary).[97] The AB in *Canada–Aircraft* merely stated that drawing adverse inferences was neither a 'punishment' nor a 'penalty' for Canada's withholding of information:[98]

> We note, preliminarily, that the 'adverse inference' . . . is not appropriately regarded as a punitive inference in the sense of a 'punishment' or 'penalty' for Canada's

[93] *Ibid*, para 189.

[94] Rule 23 ICSID, Rules of Procedure for Conciliation Proceedings (Conciliation Rules) of January 1985, available at http://www.worldbank.org/icsid/basicdoc/basicdoc.htm, 'Cooperation of the Parties (1) The parties shall cooperate in good faith with the Commission and, in particular, at its request furnish all relevant documents, information and explanations as well as use the means at their disposal to enable the Commission to hear witnesses and experts whom it desires to call. The parties shall also facilitate visits to and inquiries at any place connected with the dispute that the Commission desires to undertake'.

[95] See *Canada–Aircraft*, AB Report, paras 188–90.

[96] *Ibid*, para 201.

[97] See Steger, 2001, pp 819–20.

[98] *Canada–Aircraft*, AB Report, para 200.

withholding of information. It is merely an inference, which in certain circumstances could be logically or reasonably derived by a Panel from the facts before it.[99]

What the *Canada–Aircraft* AB did not clarify is whether the refusal to comply with the Panel's request for information under Article 13(1) only becomes actionable with the consequence of 'adverse inference' if it is combined with Article 3.10 DSU, or whether that article simply adds to the seriousness of a member's non-compliance under Article 13(1) DSU.[100]

If Canada had refused to give the information only *once*, the facts in *Canada–Aircraft* show Article 13(1) DSU would not have been triggered and Article 3.10 DSU would therefore not have been automatically breached. In contrast, when Canada refused 16 times to provide the information, such repetitive infringement triggered the Panel's right to draw 'adverse inference'.[101]

Steger derives a member's 'duty and an obligation to "respond properly and fully" to requests made by Panels for information directly from Article 13.1 of the DSU' without implicating Article 3.10 DSU.[102] Steger describes a 'Panel's discretionary authority under Article 13(1) DSU', in contrast to the AB in *Canada–Aircraft*, which spoke of the Panel's *right* to seek information.[103]

By refusing to categorise Article 13(1) DSU as a right, Steger implies that it cannot be violated and thus cannot be invoked by a member, nor may a non-complying member be sanctioned. Steger thus adopts the view that to draw adverse inferences from a member's non-compliance with Article 13(1) DSU is not a punishment or penalty.[104]

In contrast to Steger, the AB in *Canada–Aircraft* suggested that the Panels' 'right to seek information' under Article 13(1) DSU was actionable in and of itself. In combination with a members' good faith obligation under Article 3.10 DSU it is only rendered *more* effective. Non-compliance under Article 13(1) DSU had already become sanctionable when the Panel was unable to establish the facts under Article 11 DSU. Thus, it is non-compliance with Article 13(1) DSU and not Article 3.10 DSU alone that triggerd the Panel's sanction, which was to draw adverse inferences.[105]

Even more radically, Kuyper views Article 3.10 DSU in and of itself, without a *nexus* to Article 13(1) DSU, to be a sufficient basis for sanctioning a member's failure to provide information:

> A refusal to provide . . . information is simply a demonstration of bad faith; this in itself would be basis enough to justify the drawing of negative inferences; a duty to

[99] *Ibid.*

[100] *Cf* Kuyper, 2000, p 320.

[101] See Steger, 2001, p 819; see also *Canada–Aircraft*, AB Report, para 48, relating to Canada's repeated refusal to provide information.

[102] Steger, 2001, referring to *Canada–Aircraft*, AB Report, para 187.

[103] Compare Steger, 2001, p 819 with *Canada–Aircraft*, AB Report, para 188.

[104] See *Canada–Aircraft*, AB Report, para 200.

[105] *Ibid*, paras 188, 190.

provide information an unnecessary . . . step and construed on the basis of that flimsy contextual analysis.[106]

In the final analysis, the merit of *Canada–Aircraft* was that it introduced a new obligation under good faith in disputes, which is to prohibit members from behaving in a way that renders the Panels' rights ineffective or meaningless.[107] Another merit of the case is that it introduced a sanction, namely, that a Panel under Article 11 DSU in combination with Annex V ASCM can draw adverse inferences from a member's refusal to provide information under Article 13(1) DSU,[108] if the breach of the Panel's right amounts to a violation of Article 3.10 DSU.[109]

Following Canada's refusal to provide the Panel with the information the Panel had requested, the Panel was entitled under Article 11 DSU to draw the inference that Canada's allegation that its EDC programmes payments were not prohibited subsidies, was 'not proven'. However, the AB also said that the right to draw adverse inferences has no punitive character.[110]

US–FSC *Appellate Body Report (2000)*

In *US–FSC,* the EC had claimed that the US had applied prohibited subsidies under Article 3 ASCM Agreement to certain types of tax revenue. The EC pointed the AB to Sections 921–27 of the United States Internal Revenue Code (IRC) relating to tax breaks. However, the EC failed to lay out for the AB why it found the tax breaks to constitute prohibited subsidies under Article 4.2 ASCM.

Thus the issue on appeal in *US–FSC* was whether or not, according to Article 3.10 DSU in combination with the *lex specialis* of Article 4.2 ASCM, it sufficed that the EC simply identified and mentioned the IRC's relevant provisions. The question was whether or not the EC should have (and failed to) provide a 'statement of available evidence' explaining why the US tax law acts as a system for subsidising US industries (which have supported the US government's imposition of anti-dumping tariffs on imports to the US market) and why such a law falls under the definition of a prohibited subsidy under Article 4.2 ASCM.[111]

The AB found that since the US had been given the opportunity to raise its objections but had kept silent on the issue for an entire year,[112] it was not

[106] Kuyper, 2000, pp 320–1.
[107] See *Canada–Aircraft*, AB Report, paras 188, 190.
[108] *Ibid*, para 201.
[109] *Ibid*, paras 197–205.
[110] *Canada–Aircraft*, AB Report, paras 197–205.
[111] See *US–FSC*, AB Report, paras 155–7, 161, referring to the Panel report which had rejected the US's preliminary objection that the claim by the EC under Art 3 ASCM Agreement should be dismissed because the request for consultations by the EC did not include a 'statement of available evidence', as required by Art 4.2 of the ASCM Agreement.
[112] See *US–FSC*, AB Report, para 165.

necessary to rule on the issue of the consistency of the EC's request for consultations under Article 4.2 ASCM Agreement.[113]

Following the EC's request for consultations (the US and the EC held three separate sets of consultations over a period of nearly five months, during which the US did not raise any objections) as to the content of the EC's request for consultations under Article 4.2 ASCM Agreement, the US twice had the opportunity to raise the objection of an insufficient statement of evidence.[114] The US did not object to what it held to be an insufficient request for consultations during the DSB meetings when the EC's request for the establishment of a Panel was discussed.[115] The first time the US did object to the request for consultations was in the request to the Panel for preliminary findings.[116]

'Good Faith Compliance' as 'Opportunity to Defend' and to 'Bring Claims of Procedural Deficiencies' While the AB did not sanction the US for conduct that was in violation of the obligation in Article 3.10 DSU, it nevertheless reminded the parties to the dispute that:

> By good faith compliance, complaining Members accord to the responding Members the full measure of protection and opportunity to defend, contemplated by the letter and spirit of the procedural rules. The same principle of good faith requires that responding Members seasonably and promptly bring claimed procedural deficiencies to the attention of the complaining Member, and to the DSB or the Panel, so that corrections, if needed, can be made to resolve disputes. The procedural rules of WTO dispute settlement are designed to promote, not the development of litigation techniques, but simply the fair, prompt and effective resolution of trade disputes.[117]

The behaviour of the US was associated here with the 'development of litigation techniques', which the AB found to be disallowed by the 'design' of the WTO dispute settlement rules.[118]

Challenged by the claim of the US that the EC's request for consulations was insufficiently precise, the AB found it unnecessary to rule on the question of whether the EC's request for consultations included a 'statement of available evidence' that satisfied the requirements of Article 4.2 ASCM,[119] because, according to the AB, the US had 'acted as if it had accepted both the establishment of the Panel, and the consultations preceding such establishment'.[120] The

[113] *Ibid*, paras 155 and 165. The Panel, as opposed to to the AB, had based its refusal to dismiss the EC's claim under Art 3 ASCM Agreement on the fact that neither the ASCM Agreement nor the DSU contains a provision that would sanction a failure to comply with Art 4.2 with dismissal of a claim under Art 3 ASCM Agreement.

[114] *Ibid*, para 162.

[115] *Ibid.*

[116] *Ibid*, para 163.

[117] *Ibid*, para 166.

[118] *Ibid*, para 165.

[119] See *ibid*, para 165.

[120] *Ibid.*

AB even implied that the invocation by the US of its right to a statement of available evidence was contrary to good faith.[121]

Because the *US–FSC* case dealt with a procedural rule outside the DSU, a *lex specialis*, namely Article 4.2 ASCM, the *US–FSC* case is an example of a *lex specialis* rule of procedure in the WTO. Nonetheless, this procedural *lex specialis* relates to Article 3.10 DSU, as the AB showed in its analysis. Therefore, the *US–FSC* case may also be discussed under the *leges generales*.

Good Faith in Disputes Fills Gap in Appellate Standard of Review In *US–FSC*, the AB introduced the concept whereby it outweighs or compensates for the lack of a standard of review with respect to facts by the good faith obligations of members. AB Reports subsequent to *US–FSC* further developed the concept of substituting with good faith the factual standard of review, which, not least for its judicial economy, seems to be a successful way of filling in gaps in the appellate standard of review.[122]

Evaluation of US–FSC, *AB Report*: Venire Contra Factum Proprium Starting with *India–Patents* (1998) the AB has repeatedly declared that due process and fundamental fairness underlie the DSU. Thus since 1998, it has given all parties free reign to use and abuse these procedural guarantees, which they had probably started using by 2000 with the *US–FSC* case.[123] To reinforce the legitimacy of permissible limitations to the 'free flow of trade', WTO Member States party to a dispute used due process rights *against* the complaining Member.[124] In *US–FSC*, the AB applied Article 3.10 DSU for the first time, to curb such defendants' abuse of due process (litigation techniques).

The *US–FSC* decision emphasizes that the origins of the duty to settle disputes in good faith lie in the general principle of law of good faith. In order to emphasize the similarity between WTO substantive and procedural law, as well as the continuity of its jurisprudence, the AB in 2000 reiterated the 'formula' for good faith that it had used since *US–Shrimp* in 1998:

> Article 3.10 of the DSU commits Members of the WTO, if a dispute arises, to engage in dispute settlement procedures "in good faith in an effort to resolve the dispute". This is *another specific manifestation of the principle of good faith which, we have pointed out, is at once a general principle of law and a principle of general international law* (emphasis added).[125]

The set-up of the next case, the *Thailand–Steel* AB Report, is very similar to that of *US–FSC*. It depicts a claim by the responding party that the defending

[121] See *ibid*, para 166.
[122] See *US–Cotton Yarn*, AB Report, para 81.
[123] See *India–Patents*, AB Report, para 94; *Mexico–HFCS (Art 21.5)* AB Report, para 105; *Chile–Agricultural Products*, AB Report, para 176.
[124] See O'Cunningham and Cribb, 2003, pp 155, 160–70.
[125] *US–FSC*, AB Report, para 166.

party had issued an insufficient Panel request.[126] However, thereupon, the responding party conducted itself in a manner that would either negate the alleged necessity for the AB to enter into the matter or lead to the outright dismissal of the claim. Next, the AB reminded both the responding and complaining party, in an obiter dictum, of the need to apply the rules of the DSU in good faith. The final statement of the obiter dictum suggested that the responding party may have abused the WTO procedural rules for litigation techniques and thus violated the good faith obligation under Article 3.10 DSU.

Thailand–Steel *Appellate Body Report (2001)*

In *Thailand–Steel*, the AB was asked by the defendant—Thailand—to consider whether Poland's request for a Panel fulfilled the requirements of Article 6.2 DSU. The complaining party had 'merely repeated the language of an article'. However, the defending party had made no attempt to obtain more information from the complainant on why it was being accused of violating WTO law. Because the defendant (Thailand) had failed to seize the opportunity to request further clarification,[127] the AB refused to find that it had been prejudiced by the lack of clarity of the Panel request. Although the Panel request was not clear, the AB balanced the lack of clarity against Thailand's conduct in not requesting further clarification, and implied that Thailand might not have acted in good faith.[128] The AB concluded that 'Thailand did not feel at that time that it required additional clarity with respect to these claims'. To the AB this was 'a strong indication that Thailand did not suffer any prejudice on account of any lack of clarity in the Panel request'.[129] This is the point at which the AB introduced Article 3.10 DSU, the duty to 'engage in dispute settlement procedures "in good faith in an effort to resolve the dispute" '.

'Article 3.10 of the DSU Enjoins Members of the WTO to Engage in Dispute Settlement Procedures in "Good Faith"' In *Thailand–Steel*, the AB set Thailand's due process right relating to a sufficiently clear Panel request by

[126] Recall that in *US–FSC* the AB had to consider the sufficiency of a statement of available evidence.

[127] The *Thailand–Steel* decision is almost identical to that in the earlier *US–FSC* case, where it was asked whether the EC's reference to relevant statutory provisions (Sections 921 through 927 of the United States Internal Revenue Code) fulfilled the requirement for a 'statement of available evidence' included in the request for consultations under Art 4.2 ASCM Agreement, *US-FSC*, AB Report, paras 155–7. In its reasoning, the AB drew in an obiter dictum from the commitment of WTO Member States under Art 3.10 DSU to 'engage in [dispute settlement] procedures in good faith in an effort to resolve the dispute'. Thus, the finding on Art 3.10 DSU replaced an investigation under Art 4.2 ASCM. The question is whether in *Thailand–Steel* the AB used a similar argument to dismiss the claim of Thailand that Poland's request for establishment of a Panel was insufficient under Art 6.2 DSU. The AB in *US–FSC* had found it unnecessary to rule on this question because the 'US had acted as if it had accepted the establishment of the Panel in this dispute, as well as the consultations preceding such establishment'.

[128] *Thailand–Steel*, AB Report, para 95.

[129] *Ibid.*

Poland (6.2 DSU) against Thailand's good faith obligation (Article 3.10 DSU) to request more material before claiming a prejudice under Article 6.2 DSU:

> In view of the importance of the request for the establishment of a Panel, we encourage complaining parties to be precise in identifying the legal basis of the complaint. We also note that nothing in the DSU prevents a defending party from requesting further clarification on the claims raised in a Panel request from the complaining party, even before the filing of the first written submission. In this regard, we point to Article 3.10 of the DSU, which enjoins Members of the WTO, if a dispute arises, to engage in dispute settlement procedures 'in good faith in an effort to resolve the dispute'. As we have previously stated, the procedural rules of WTO dispute settlement are designed to promote, not the development of litigation techniques, but simply the fair, prompt and effective resolution of trade disputes.[130]

Although the AB found that the Panel had erred in assessing the sufficiency of the Panel request under Article 6.2 DSU relating to Articles 2 and 5 ADA, it found that Thailand was not prejudiced by the lack of clarity in Poland's Panel request. It found Poland to have met the minimum requirements of Article 6.2 DSU[131] and therefore refused to substantiate Thailand's claim because when Thailand had asked the Panel for a preliminary ruling on the sufficiency of Poland's Panel request with respect to Articles 5 and 6 of the AD Agreement at the time of filing its first written submission, 'it did not do so at that time with respect to Articles 2 and 6 ADA'.

Article 6.2 DSU in combination with Article 3.10 DSU expresses the minimal standards for Panel requests. Good faith thus prevents a dispute from lingering in the initial, procedural stages. Both the AB and the Panel believe that the good faith obligation imposes a limitation on the ability to submit claims of a procedural nature when either the complainant or respondant have had the opportunity to clarify substantive legal issues.[132]

Evaluation of Thailand–Steel: *the Right to Due Process versus the Obligation of Good Faith in Dispute Resolution* The AB in *Thailand–Steel* reiterated the exact wording of the *US–FSC* case relating to Article 3.10 DSU. This can be explained by the similar set of facts: the complaining party raising procedural objections relating to its due process rights[133] while not acting in good faith when applying the rules of the DSU. Also, the AB is guided by a concern for continuity and predictability in the development of the WTO legal system.[134]

Both the *US–FSC* and the *Thailand–Steel* cases juxtapose the right to due process with the obligation to invoke DSU rules in good faith.[135] The AB in *Thailand–Steel* identified due process as the right of

[130] *Ibid*, para 97.
[131] *Thailand–Steel*, AB Report, paras 95–6.
[132] See *ibid*, para 97; *Thailand–Steel*, Panel Report, para 7.40.
[133] *Thailand–Steel*, AB Report, para 88; *US–FSC*, AB Report, para 155.
[134] *Thailand–Steel*, AB Report, para 97 and fn 46 referring directly to para 166 of the *US–FSC* AB Report.
[135] See *US–FSC*, AB Report, paras 155 and 166.

> [the] defending party to know what case it has to answer, and what violations have been alleged so that it can prepare its defence, as well as the obligation of the complaining party to inform those Members of the WTO who intend to participate as third parties to be informed of the legal basis of the complaint.[136]

It is possible that good faith functions to ensure that due process rights, which lend themselves to litigation, are not abused. Once again, good faith takes on a balancing function or, a fortiori, expresses the prohibition against an *abus de droit*, relating to due process rights under the DSU.

US–Lamb Safeguards *Appellate Body Report (2001)*

US–Lamb Safeguards introduced a situation of *venire contra factum proprium* similar to that in *US–FSC*. In *US–Lamb Safeguards*, Australia and New Zealand violated the obligation to engage in dispute settlement in good faith. On the one hand they claimed an erroneous application of facts before the AB, while on the other hand they withheld certain evidence from the complainant, the US and its government trade agency, the United States International Trade Commission (USITC).[137] Australia and New Zealand replied that the Panel had erred in applying a standard of review to the USITC that was limited to the facts made available by the interested parties.

The issue before the AB was whether Australia and New Zealand had the right to claim that the Panel had misapplied its standard of review. The Panel had found a threat of serious injury to the US domestic lamb meat industry, but both New Zealand and Australia had purposefully avoided bringing the full scope of evidence before the competent authorities, who were in this case, the USITC. Thus, the question of procedural good faith in *US–Lamb Safeguards* became one of knowing whether Australia and New Zealand had violated the obligation to engage in dispute settlement in good faith, when they first withheld evidence from the USITC only to claim later that the Panel had failed to conduct a full investigation into the USITC's evaluation of a threat of injury to US producers.[138]

'WTO Member States Cannot Improperly Withhold Arguments from Competent Authorities with a View to Raising those Arguments Later before a Panel' While the AB found the *US–Lamb Safeguards* Panel guilty of narrowing down the Panel's standard of review, it nevertheless abstained from sanctioning the Panel, because Australia and New Zealand were to blame for refusing to submit to the USITC the evidence to which it was entitled, at least until the Panel had completed its review:[139]

[136] *Thailand–Steel*, AB Report, para 88.
[137] See *US–Lamb Safeguards*, para 115.
[138] *Ibid*, AB Report, paras 99, 106.
[139] *Ibid*, paras 149, 111–13, 115, 116.

> As *competent authorities* themselves are obliged, in some circumstances, to go beyond the arguments of the interested parties in reaching their own determinations, so too, we believe, Panels are not limited to the arguments submitted by the interested parties to the competent authorities in reviewing those determinations in WTO dispute settlement (emphasis in the original).[140]

Stopping short of labelling the behaviour of Australia and New Zealand as *abus de droit* (the AB implied that Australia and New Zealand lacked the intention), the AB, by implicating Article 3.10 DSU, nevertheless found that Australia and New Zealand had purposefully withheld evidence from the USITC in order to be able to claim later that the Panel had violated their 'due process right' in a full *de novo* review:

> We wish to emphasize that the discretion that WTO Member States enjoy to argue dispute settlement claims in the manner they deem appropriate does not, of course, detract from their obligation, under Article 3.10 of the DSU, 'to engage in dispute settlement procedures in good faith in an effort to resolve the dispute'. It follows that WTO Member States cannot improperly withhold arguments from competent authorities with a view to raising those arguments later before a Panel. In any event, as a practical matter, we think it unlikely that a Member would do so.[141]

Australia and New Zealand withheld evidence from the competent authorities, in order to later base a claim on the 'application of the standard of review', with a view to gaining time and avoiding a ruling on the substance.[142]

Evaluation of US–Lamb Safeguards*: Clean Hands Doctrine* In *US–Lamb Safeguards* the obligation of WTO Member States to engage in dispute settlement proceedings in good faith under Article 3.10 DSU was described not only as the corollary duty of Panels to conduct an objective examination of facts (similar to the scenario of a Panel's right to collect evidence by seeking information under Article 13(1) DSU in *Canada–Aircraft*), but also as the right of WTO Member States to demand that the Panels' standard of review go beyond the evidence that WTO Member States have brought before the competent authorities, under Article 4(2)(a) ASG.

The AB said that the *US–Lamb Safeguards* Panel, should, on its own initiative, have looked more carefully at the material that the competent authorities had submitted. A duty similar to that of the Panels, the AB found, lay upon the competent (national) authorities, who should take on the task of looking beyond the factual and legal arguments submitted by the interested parties. However, the AB also added that the Members' due process rights vis-à-vis the Panels' standard of review could not go so far as to require a Panel to look into evidence that this Member had newly introduced, and which it had not filed before the competent authority.[143]

140 *Ibid*, para 114.
141 *US–Lamb Safeguards*, para 115.
142 *Ibid*, para 110.
143 Compare *US–Lamb Safeguards*, AB Report, para 197(d) with para 115.

Because it lacked the standard of review to effectively change the outcome of this case, the AB introduced the obiter dictum argument of good faith. Because investigations as to whether or not a certain mode of conduct violates the duty to engage in good faith dispute settlement is a legal, as opposed to factual issue, it is only through reference to good faith that the AB became empowered at least to judge the behaviour of the governments of Australia and New Zealand, without being able to change the outcome of the case.

The *US–Lamb Safeguards* has provided guidance for subsequent Panels as to their scope for review under Article 4(2)(a) ASG, which had first been circumscribed in *US–Wheat Gluten*. The *US–Lamb Safeguards* case both specifies the limits of the Panel's review and describes the extent of the power of factual review of national investigating authorities under Article 4(2)(a) ASG in combination with Article 3.10 DSU.

Article 3.10 DSU as a Standard or an Actionable Right There are two views represented in jurisprudence on the issue of whether Article 3.10 DSU is an actionable right, ie whether violating the good faith duty can be sanctioned under WTO law or whether this Article merely constitutes a standard, which neither imposes an obligation nor confers a right to claim a violation of good faith, and thus can only be brought as a claim together with a right or obligation under the WTO Agreements.[144]

A first view, expressed in the *Canada–Aircraft* AB Report, apparently considered Article 3.10 DSU as a right that may be the basis of an appeal only when combined with Article 13.1 DSU. Under *Canada–Aircraft*, Article 3.10 DSU only becomes a right if it is linked with the Panel's explicit right to seek information, which implicitly contains the duty of the WTO Member party to provide the Panel, if so requested, with information. This is what the AB calls the 'specific manifestation of the broader duties of Members under Article 3.10 of the DSU when a dispute arises, to "engage in these procedures in good faith in an effort to resolve the dispute"'.[145] Non-compliance with Article 13(1) DSU empowers the Panel to draw adverse inferences from the member's refusal to cooperate.

Following the reasoning of *Canada–Aircraft* one could argue that Article 3.10 DSU becomes invocable as an enforceable obligation for WTO Member States if combined with a WTO provision codifying a more concrete duty for member parties than that of the obligation to settle disputes in good faith.

US–Lamb Safeguards[146] and most recently, *EC–Sardines*,[147] also spoke of an 'obligation' to engage in these procedures in good faith in an effort to resolve the dispute.

[144] See Parlin, 2002.
[145] *Canada–Aircraft*, AB Report, para 190.
[146] See *US–Lamb Safeguards*, AB Report, para 115.
[147] *EC–Sardines*, AB Report, para 140.

But there are also indications as to why Article 3.10 DSU is more of a principle than a legal right. One of these is that in all cases involving good faith in disputes, Article 3.10 DSU consists of an obiter dictum and is not referred to as the principle argument in a dispute over a procedural issue under the WTO DSU. Nevertheless, at least in the *Canada–Aircraft* case, the AB admitted that these questions have 'fundamental and far-reaching implications for the entire WTO dispute settlement system'.[148]

Zoller gives a good explanation as to why claims based on good faith are rarely, if ever, substantiated in general public international law. Good faith is regarded as a concern of secondary nature to judges when compared to the precepts of legal security and predictability. Convincing a state that it will be able to fight for its rights (for example when it is confronted with a claim that it has infringed good faith) is more important than protecting the opposing, and usually defending, party against a failure to respect good faith.[149] This argument may be equally valid for the WTO, where to date there has been no sign in jurisprudence that Article 3.10 DSU is actionable on its own without being accompanied by another right or obligation.

Mexico–HFCS (Article 21.5) *Appellate Body Report (2001)*

Mexico–HFCS (Article 21.5) is the follow-up case to the original dispute between NAFTA partners Mexico and the US. During the original dispute Mexico had alleged before the Panel that the US was selling domestic High Fructose Corn Syrup (HFCS) at dumping prices in order to protect itself from cheaper imports of HFCS from Mexico. Mexico had thus claimed that its imposition of anti-dumping duties on US HFCS was justified under the ADA. However Mexico's imposition of the definitive anti-dumping measure on imports of HFCS from the US was inconsistent with the requirements of the AD Agreement, because Mexico had inadequately considered the impact of dumped imports on its domestic industry. Among others, the US held against Mexico that Mexico had examined only a part of the domestic industry's production, rather than the the industry as a whole, and that this was not consistent with the threat of material injury investigation under Articles 3.1, 3.2, 3.4, 3.7 and 3.7(i) of the ADA.[150] The Panel decision was not appealed. Instead Mexico brought a case under Article 21.5 DSU.

In this follow-up case, known as *Mexico–HFCS (Article 21.5)*, Mexico alleged that by 'remaining silent' on the issue of missing consultations as to Mexico's redetermination, the Panel had acted inconsistently with Articles 12.7, 3.4, 7.2 and 19 of the DSU.[151] Mexico claimed that the Panel's redetermination—which had revised the original resolution imposing the

[148] *Canada–Aircraft*, AB Report, para 182.
[149] See Zoller, 1977, p 146.
[150] See *Mexico–HFCS*, Panel Report, para 8.2.
[151] *Ibid*, AB Report, para 35.

anti-dumping duties on the US imports—had found it 'appropriate' to keep in place the 'final' offsetting duties imposed.[152] Mexico in *Mexico–HFCS* (Article 21.5) reaffirmed the Panel's finding in *Mexico–HFCS* that during the period of investigation, the threat of injury as a consequence of discriminatory pricing of US HFCS imports into Mexico still persisted.

Firstly, the AB had to determine whether Mexico had the right to raise objections against the US when, at the DSU meeting, it had not objected to the US having missed consultations on Mexico's redetermination. Secondly, the AB had to review whether the Panel had the authority to address the redetermination when no prior consultations had been held.

It may be that Mexico's right to raise objections was limited by its procedural good faith obligation, which, under Article 3.10 DSU, would have meant that if the issue of missing consultations had not been explicitly or at least promptly raised, the Panel had no obligation to consider this on its own motion.[153]

The AB did not find that a lack of consultations beforehand deprives a Panel of its authority to adjudicate a dispute.[154] Thus, the AB held that the fact that Mexico had filed its objection *after* the Panel had been established had no consequence for the authority of the Panel, but that by filing the objection (that the Panel had no authority to adjudicate a dispute when there had not been consultations beforehand), Mexico had invalidated its own right to claim that the Panel had violated Mexico's rights of due process:[155]

> In sum, the 'observations' raised by Mexico were not expressed in a fashion that indicated that Mexico was raising an objection to the authority of the Panel. The requirements of good faith, due process and orderly procedure dictate that objections, especially those of such potential significance, should be explicitly raised. Only in this way will the Panel, the other party to the dispute, and the third parties, understand that a specific objection has been raised, and have an adequate opportunity to address and respond to it. In our view, Mexico's objection was not explicitly raised. Thus, in making its 'observations', Mexico did not meet this standard.[156]

'Good Faith, Due Process and Orderly Procedure Dictate that Objections Should be Explicitly Raised' Mexico had not complied with the requirement emanating from good faith and due process to raise an objection promptly, and thus its conduct amounted to 'waiving its right to have a Panel consider such objections'.[157] The AB said:

> When a Member wishes to raise an objection in dispute settlement proceedings, it is always incumbent on that Member to do so promptly. A Member that fails to raise its objections in a timely manner, notwithstanding one or more opportunities to do so,

[152] *Ibid*, para 3.
[153] *Ibid*, para 21.
[154] *Ibid*, paras 63 and 64.
[155] *Ibid*, paras 47, 49, 50, 63, 64, 65, 75.
[156] *Ibid*, para 47.
[157] *Ibid*, para 50.

may be deemed to have waived its right to have a Panel consider such objections (emphasis added).[158]

The AB on the one hand considered good faith and due process similar objectives, as both express the element of promptness; specifically they both require that a member file an objection in a timely manner. On the other hand, it was the same due process in combination with good faith that limited Mexico's due process right (to claim that the Panel failed to consider an objection) by imposing a requirement of time (and to a lesser extent, specificity).

The second issue of good faith in the *Mexico–HFCS (Article 21.5)* case was linked with the obligation in Article 3.7 DSU not to frivolously set in motion the procedures contemplated in the DSU. This aspect of the duty—to have recourse to WTO dispute settlement in good faith—will be dealt with later in the section on Article 3.7 DSU.

Evaluation of Mexico–HFCS (Article 21.5): the *Good Faith Standard of Due Process* Mexico's failure to comply with the standard of raising objections to the Panel, which good faith, due process and orderly procedure require, did not entail any adverse consequence for Mexico, notwithstanding that the AB considered the objection as not explicitly raised and thus did not consider the issues brought by Mexico on appeal. This means that in *Mexico–HFCS (Article 21.5)*, the duty to engage in dispute settlement procedures in good faith is, as the AB itself pointed out, a 'standard' as opposed to a right that can potentially be violated and for which sanctions exist. For the *Mexico–HFCS (Article 21.5)* AB, this meant that the duty to resolve disputes in good faith was not an actionable one in the sense that a party cannot allege that another party has violated this provision, nor can it expect the violator to be sanctioned for its breach: 'The requirements of good faith, due process and orderly procedure dictate that objections, . . . should be explicitly raised. Thus, in making its 'observations', Mexico did not meet *this standard*' (emphasis added), said the AB in *Mexico–HFCS (Article 21.5)*.[159]

EC–Sardines *Appellate Body Report (2002)*

In order to prevent frivolous appeals, the AB in *EC–Sardines* applied the obligation to engage in dispute settlement proceedings in good faith (Article 3.10 DSU) to the EC. Peru had questioned the EC's withdrawal of the EC's original Notice of Appeal, which the EC had conditioned upon the filing of a new notice.[160]

Peru submitted that the EC's withdrawal of its original notice of appeal upon the condition of filing a new notice of appeal was 'impermissible' and that

[158] *Ibid.*
[159] *Mexico–HFCS*, Panel Report, para 47.
[160] See *EC–Sardines*, AB Report, para 135.

consequently, the new Notice of Appeal should be 'inadmissible because there is no right to appeal twice'.[161]

The EC defended its decision not to appeal twice by stating that its reason for withdrawing the original notice of appeal was simply to respond to Peru's request for additional information. Therefore, the EC claimed, its new notice of appeal—filed in a timely manner—was based on the same legal grounds as the original notice, so that in the EC's view, Peru did not suffer any prejudice.[162]

It is a fact that Rule 30(1) of the Working Procedures for Appellate Review (Working Procedures) accords the appellant a broad right to withdraw an appeal at any time. This broad right appears to be 'unfettered on its face' insofar as there is nothing in the rule to prohibit the attachment of conditions to a withdrawal.[163] Even if the AB in *EC–Sardines* did not prohibit conditional withdrawals outright, it used the threshold of good faith of Article 3.10 DSU to ensure that it would neither prevent a conditional withdrawal in a particular case from diminishing the right of the appellee or of any other participant in any way, nor otherwise obstruct the 'fair, prompt and effective settlement of disputes'. Another reason why the AB in *EC–Sardines* interpreted Rule 30 narrowly was to limit the right to attach conditions to a withdrawal, which may pose the danger of nullifying any effort to resolve the dispute in good faith.[164]

'Appellate Review Proceedings do not Become an Arena for Unfortunate Litigation Techniques' The AB in *EC–Sardines* examined whether the EC, in retracting its original notice of appeal only to replace it later with a new one, had violated the obligation to 'engage[d] in [dispute settlement] procedures in good faith in an effort to resolve the dispute'.[165]

The AB concluded that because the EC's withdrawal was intended to remedy the allegation of insufficiency raised by Peru rather than disguising a further delay of the DSU proceedings, under these circumstances, the conditions underlying the withdrawal were 'not unreasonable'.[166]

Although any condition attached to the right to file a new notice of appeal is unilaterally declared,[167] and although the EC did in fact file a new notice of appeal, the AB in *EC–Sardines* nonetheless shared Peru's concern that withdrawals conditioned upon the refiling of a new notice, and that filing thereafter

[161] *Ibid.*

[162] *Ibid.*

[163] *Ibid*, para 138, even if in two previous cases, notices of appeal were withdrawn subject to the condition that new notices would be filed, these cannot be compared with the case here, because the divisions hearing those appeals and the appellees had previous knowledge of, and agreed with, the process, see para 138 and fn 31 to para 138 referring to *US–FSC*, AB Report, para 4 and *US–Line Pipe Safeguards*, AB Report, para 13.

[164] See *EC–Sardines*, AB Report, p 141.

[165] *Ibid*, para 142.

[166] *Ibid*, para 144.

[167] See *ibid*, para 146.

of a new notice could be 'abusive and disruptive' and create 'immense potential for abuse and disorder in appellate review proceedings'.[168]

In such cases, the AB would have the right to reject the condition as well as the filing of the new notice of appeal based upon either the duty to resolve disputes in good faith as expressly stated in Article 3.10 DSU, or the abuse of Rule 30(1) of the Working Procedures, which implies a violation of good faith:

> [I]n such cases, we would have the right to reject the condition, and also to reject any filing of a new notice of appeal, on the grounds either that the Member seeking to file such a new notice would not be engaging in dispute settlement proceedings in good faith, or that Rule 30(1) of the *Working Procedures* must not be used to undermine the fair, prompt, and effective resolution of trade disputes. We agree with Peru that the rules must be interpreted so as to 'ensure that appellate review proceedings do not become an arena for unfortunate litigation techniques that frustrate the objectives of the DSU, and that developing countries do not have the resources to deal with'. The case before us, however, presents none of these circumstances.[169]

The AB added that there may be actions that while not 'abusive practices', would be in violation of the DSU, 'compelling the AB to disallow the conditional withdrawal as well as the filing of a replacement notice'.[170] In this case, because the replacement notice of appeal was provided before the submissions were filed, this replacement notice had the effect of conditionally withdrawing the original notice.[171]

A second charge laid by Peru, was that the AB declared the new Notice of Appeal inadmissible because it would accord the EC the right to appeal twice.[172] But the AB responded that because the conditional withdrawal of the original notice of appeal was 'appropriate and effective', the replacement notice did not constitute a second appeal.[173] In addition, the replacement notice did not contain new or modified grounds of appeal but merely constituted a timely and appropriate response to Peru's objections regarding the initial notice.[174]

In response to Peru's third allegation that the AB would create a new procedural right not contained in the DSU if it were not to sanction the EC's withdrawal, the AB argued in congruence with its jurisprudence in *US–Shrimp*, that it was giving full meaning to the right of appeal. Moreover, the AB found that it had given Peru a full measure of due process to the appellee, because the EC had filed in a timely manner and early in the process and Peru had been given adequate opportunity to respond and had not demonstrated that it had suffered prejudice.[175]

168 *Ibid*, para 146 with reference in footnote 41 to Peru's appellee's submission, para 45.

169 *EC–Sardines*, AB Report, para 146 (footnote omitted).

170 *Ibid*, para 147, ie where the conditional withdrawal were to take place after the 60-day deadline under Art 16.4 of the DSU.

171 See *ibid*, para 145.

172 *Ibid*, para 148.

173 *Ibid*, para 149.

174 See *ibid*, paras 149, 150, 151.

175 *Ibid*, para 150.

Evaluation of EC–Sardines: *Prohibition of the Abuse of DSU Rules and Procedures* The AB in *EC–Sardines* declared that the right to withdraw a notice of appeal is limited by the duty to engage in dispute settlement proceedings in good faith, pursuant to Article 3.10 DSU. In addition, the AB used the *US–FSC* formula, its judge-made law, to limit the use of the right to withdraw notices of appeal by subjecting the right to conditions of 'fair, prompt and effective' dispute settlement, and the prohibition of litigation techniques.[176]

The AB agreed with Peru, and listed the acceptable reasons for curbing a too expansive exercise of the DSU's procedural rights:

— the risk of undermining the effectiveness of the DSU;
— the aim of securing a positive solution to a dispute;
— the possibility that the development of litigation techniques will be detrimental to the rights of developing countries at the WTO.[177]

The AB in *EC–Sardines* warned that aggressive use of the DSU's procedural rights as opportunities for delaying dispute resolution, poses a threat for developing countries, who would be unable to defend themselves effectively because they do not have the means to sustain disputes of long duration.

Like Peru in the *EC–Sardines* case, developing countries now have the option of using the cost-adapted services of the Advisory Centre and can in addition solicit the support of consumer groups, which Peru in *EC–Sardines* also did.[178] However, as Mengozzi has said, for developing countries 'still more than for developed countries, time is money'; and 'for them an expeditious settlement can in many instances be vital'.[179]

In the *EC–Sardines* case the AB argued in favour of the EC and against Peru, even after hearing Peru's concerns and having voiced its own concern over the EC's conduct in dispute settlement. The AB's final argument in support of the EC was reminiscent of that of the ICJ in the *Barcelona Traction* case.[180] In its

[176] *EC–Sardines*, AB Report, paras 139, 146.

[177] *Ibid*, para 146.

[178] See Schaffer et al, 2002, pp 15–16.

[179] Mengozzi, 1995, p 122.

[180] In the *Case Concerning the Barcelona Traction, Light and Power Company Limited (New Application: 1962) (Belgium v Spain)*, Judgment of 24 July 1964 (Preliminary Objections) Spain had invoked estoppel and good faith in the Barcelona Traction case against Belgium who had given notice of discontinuance, in order to replace dispute procedures with direct negotiations. Spain said that, '[O]blige de déclarer formellement qu'est againstire au principe de la bonne foi . . . toute tentative de réintroduire l'affaire devant la Cour internationale de Justice, puisque cette affaire-en tant que prétendu litige international-est définitivement et irrévocablement close'. The Court however, found that since notices of discontinuance are a procedural and 'neutral' act, the Parties' ignorance must be established in 'attendant circumstances'. In this case, there was no real renunciation nor was the discontinuance made in circumstances that 'must preclude further proceedings'. Moreover, the Court did not find that Belgium's action had in any way injured Spain and that Belgium had not created any legitimate expectations vis-à-vis Spain, so that in consequence, the claim of good faith and estoppel related closely to an abuse of procedure by Belgium was unfounded and Belgium was free to submit all the preliminary objections it had invoked before the original (and now retracted) request. *Case Concerning the Barcelona Traction, Light and Power Company Limited (New Application: 1962) (Belgium v Spain)*, Judgment of 24 July 1964 (Preliminary

findings, the AB in *EC–Sardines* apparently even cited the *Barcelona Traction* case, arguing that a missing prejudice to the defendant, in the end justifies a conditional withdrawal of the notice of appeal:

> The replacement Notice was filed in a timely manner and early on in the process, and the replacement Notice contained no new or modified grounds of appeal. Also, Peru has not demonstrated that it suffered prejudice as a result. Moreover, Peru was given an adequate opportunity to address its concerns about the European Communities' actions during the course of the appeal.[181]

However, the AB neither directly quoted nor referd to *Barcelona Traction* as the source of its finding that when the EC withdrew its original notice of appeal subject to the condition of filing a new one, its unilateral action did not amount to an (illegal) litigation technique.

US–Offset Act ('Byrd Amendment') *Appellate Body Report (2003): Good Faith as a Standard of Procedural Justice*

The AB in the *US–Offset Act ('Byrd Amendment')* referred to the *US–FSC* formula of fair, prompt and effective resolution of trade disputes (but not to Article 3.10 DSU) in support of Article 9.2 DSU, the latter of which codifies the right of a member party to obtain separate Panel reports.[182]

The AB in the *US–Offset Act ('Byrd Amendment')* case referred to Article 9.2 DSU in order to reject the US grounds of appeal that the Panel had acted beyond its margin of discretion under Article 9.2 DSU by not issuing a separate Panel report on behalf of the US in the dispute brought by Mexico.[183]

The Panel found that while it is true that Article 9.2 does not specify a timeframe during which a party to the dispute may apply for a separate Panel report, the right to request such a separate Panel report is not, according to the Panel in the *US–Offset Act ('Byrd Amendment')* case, an unqualified right, in the sense that a separate report can be requested at any time only if there is a good reason.[184]

In this context, the Panel had found that making the request two months after the issuance of the descriptive part of the Panel report and more than seven months after the composition of the Panel was not timely.[185]

The AB reference to the *US–FSC* formula is auxiliary only; its first choice was Article 3.3 DSU.[186] At no point did the AB refer to Article 3.10 DSU or cite case

Objections), Summary, cited in International Law Reports, vol 46, E Lauterpracht (ed), London, 1973, p 4; see Zoller, 1977, p 145, citing Spanish Note of 5 March 1962 addressed to the Belgium Foreign Ministry at the Belgian Embassy in Madrid; see also Kolb, 2000, p 641, for a discussion of the case.

[181] *EC–Sardines*, AB Report, para 150.

[182] See *US–Offset Act ('Byrd Amendment')*, AB Report, para 313.

[183] *Ibid*, paras 316–17.

[184] *Ibid*, para 311.

[185] *Ibid*, para 314.

[186] *Ibid*, para 311.

law referring to the DSU's central procedural good faith obligation. However, the AB stated:

> Having made these observations, we note that Article 9.2 must not be read in isolation from other provisions of the DSU, and without taking into account the overall object and purpose of that Agreement. The overall object and purpose of the DSU is expressed in Article 3.3 of that Agreement which provides, relevantly, that the 'prompt settlement' of disputes is 'essential to the effective functioning of the WTO'.[187]

The AB added:

> Our view is supported by our decision in US–FSC, where we observed that: The procedural rules of WTO dispute settlement are designed to promote . . . the fair, *prompt and effective* resolution of trade disputes (emphasis added).[188]

The AB not only found that the Panel's decision that the US had requested the separate report too late was correct, but also denied the US the chance to prevail because, as the appellant requesting the AB to reverse a Panel's ruling on matters of procedure, the US failed to demonstrate that it suffered a prejudice generated by such legal ruling.[189]

Conclusions

Article 3.10 DSU has many facets, which the AB jurisprudence summarised above sought to capture:

— Article 3.10 DSU requires a fair exercise of members' procedural rights in dispute settlement proceedings, that is *due process rights* (right to object, right to consultations, right to withdraw notice of appeal, right to request information). The AB has argued that Article 3.10 DSU, the obligation to engage in dispute settlement in good faith, is to express and protect the '*fundamental right* . . . to have disputes arising between them resolved through the system and proceedings for which they bargained for in concluding the DSU' of the other WTO member party to a dispute.[190]
— The AB in the *EC–Sardines* case attributed to this duty to engage in dispute settlement in good faith, a specific significance for developing countries, which have neither the expertise nor the means to sustain disputes prolonged by controversies over procedural issues.
— The *Canada–Aircraft* AB Report added a measure of protection against *abus de droit* to Article 3.10 DSU, by finding that the good faith obligation under Article 3.10 DSU obliges Members not to render a Panel's right or

[187] *Ibid*.
[188] *Ibid*, para 313.
[189] See *ibid*, paras 315–16 with further reference to *EC–Hormones*, AB Report, fn 138 to para 152.
[190] See *Canada–Aircraft*, AB Report, para 189.

obligation meaningless.[191] By 'facilitating the effective conduct of the adjudication', good faith 'provides sufficient fact-gathering opportunities concerning a dispute and thereby enables a tribunal to provide a well-reasoned and just adjudication of the controversial claims'.[192] As such, good faith 'assists' the adjudicative body in reaching a decision.[193]

— When combined with Article 13(1) DSU, good faith in the settlement of disputes, as codified under Article 3.10 DSU, gives Panels the right to seek information and to accept only fair withdrawals, while Members have an obligation to collaborate with Panels, eg by providing requested information.

— Good faith under Article 3.10 DSU not only concerns the individual parties to a dispute and/or the Panels, but is moreover a general objective of the DSU, 'to secure a positive solution to a dispute' (Article 3.7).[194] As Gaffney says, 'Failure to observe procedural justice, . . . will adversely affect the perception of the legitimacy and fairness of WTO dispute settlement, which could undermine the commitment of its Members'.[195]

Good faith under Article 3.10 DSU functions to ensure that such 'procedural justice' is observed. It entails ensuring that procedural rights are protected against abuse, and specifically that all WTO Member States, especially developing countries, have an equal chance of winning a case before the AB. However, there are also those who call upon WTO Member States themselves to limit the extent to which they make use of procedural rights as strategies to gain time and money on dispute settlement procedures before the WTO. As O'Cunningham and Cribb say, there is a call for WTO Member States to 'auto limit' the use of due process rights in the profession, because '[t]o the extent that the United States is busy defending charges of procedural unfairness, efforts to defend more substantive decisions will suffer'.[196]

Article 4.3 DSU: 'Entering into Consultations in Good Faith'

Having discussed the general duty of WTO Member States to resolve their disputes in the DSU under good faith, this section will examine how good faith controls the mandatory consulation mechanism at the beginning of any litigation before the WTO.

Article 4.3 DSU may be considered a sub-function of the more general obligation of Article 3.10 DSU to engage in 'dispute settlement procedures' in good faith. The obligation under Article 4.3 DSU sets out a more specific duty than its

191 *Ibid*, para 188.
192 Gaffney, 1999, p 1185.
193 *Ibid*.
194 See *EC–Sardines*, AB Report, para 139.
195 Gaffney, 1999, p 1184.
196 See O'Cunningham and Cribb, 2003, p 170.

counterparts in Articles 3.7 and 3.10 DSU. Article 4.3 DSU, which pertains to the consultation phase of a dispute, says:

> If a request for consultations is made pursuant to a covered agreement, the Member to which the request is made shall, unless otherwise mutually agreed, reply to the request within 10 days after the date of its receipt and shall enter into consultations in good faith within a period of no more than 30 days after the date of receipt of the request, with a view to reaching a mutually satisfactory solution. If the Member does not respond within 10 days after the date of receipt of the request, or does not enter into consultations within a period of no more than 30 days, or a period otherwise mutually agreed, after the date of receipt of the request, then the Member that requested the holding of consultations may proceed directly to request the establishment of a Panel.

Article 4.3 has a more limited scope and addresses only the 'Member to which the request [for consultations] is made', unlike Article 3.10, which engages both Members involved in conciliation and/or dispute settlement procedures.

Four Panel reports, not all of which are linked to the *Mexico–HFCS* case complex, contain references to Article 4.3 DSU: *EC–Bananas*, *US–FSC*, *Turkey–Textiles* and *Brazil–Coconut*.[197] Only one, the *Mexico–HFCS (Article 21.5)* Panel Report, offered any additional commentary on Article 4.3 DSU.

Davey has argued that the duty of good faith in the procedures before the WTO DSU starts with an existing duty of the parties to engage in consultations in good faith. Despite this, the author notes that in some cases, such as *EC–Bananas*, it is 'undoubtedly true that consultations were treated as an annoying procedural step to be overcome as soon as possible'. However, Davey notes that *EC–Bananas* does 'not demonstrate that the consultation requirement is undesirable'.[198]

Bourgeois, in the light of GATT 47 practice under *US–Salmon (AD)*, *EC–Audio Cassettes* and *US–Cement*, which held that consultation and conciliation requirements are still 'mandatory preliminary steps', agrees that entering consultations in good faith under Article 4.3 DSU should imply that 'all claims be aired at the consultation phase in order to be properly before a Panel'.[199] Thus, good faith under Article 4.3 DSU may either allow a Panel to refuse to consider the subject and/or authorise the complainant or respondent to claim a Panel's incompetence.

US–Cement *GATT 47 Panel Report (1992)*

Bourgeois argued pre-WTO that the 1992 cement case (*US–Cement*) referred implictly to the duty to conduct consultations in good faith as a procedural obligation of the complainant. In *US–Cement*, the US claimed that Article 15 of

[197] See Research on http://www.worldtradelaw.net with 'Art 4.3 of the DSU' on 15 May 2004.
[198] Davey, 2000, p 291.
[199] Bourgeois, 1998, p 266.

the then-Tokyo Round anti-dumping Code mandated that there was a 'hierarchy' in dispute settlement procedures, whereby consultations were the first step. In this context, the US also argued, but without expressly claiming good faith, that Article 15 mandated that all claims be brought at the consultations phase. Article 15 of the Tokyo Round anti-dumping Code said under paragraph 4 that 'Parties shall make their best efforts to reach a mutually satisfactory solution throughout the period of conciliation'. The US hoped to convince the Panel that Mexico could not bring in issues relating to the initiation of the anti-dumping investigation and the cumulation of Japanese and Mexican claims before the Panel, because it had failed to raise these issues in bilateral consultations.[200]

In *US–Cement*, the Panel had to answer the question of whether it should consider an issue not brought in at the consultations phase, *ex officio* or only upon complaint.[201] The Panel, however, found evidence (in the form of a letter from the Mexican authorities to the US) that the US had been informed by Mexico bilaterally on these issues, before Mexico started multilateral conciliation. Thus, Mexico had not violated Article 15 of the anti-dumping Code, and the Panel was entitled to look into the issues of initiation and cumulation of anti-dumping claims.[202] Since the Panel in *US–Cement* had found evidence in the form of a letter showing that consultations had in fact been held, it considered itself disengaged from the responsibility of ruling on the contentious issue.

Bourgeois argues that the *US–Cement* Panel decision lay the foundation for the following procedural rule: whoever 'does not put a claim on the table at the consultation stage' may not 'subsequently raise it before the Panel'.[203] To Bourgeois, not only does good faith under Article 4.3 DSU bind both the complainant and the respondent to refrain from claiming a gap in the case when they did not use the consultations phase, it moreover creates a positive obligation for all parties to 'put the whole matter, ie all their claims on the table'.[204] Bourgeois, who situates the duty to engage in consultations in good faith into the context of the WTO Member States' procedural rights', says ' "Good faith" has to work both ways'.[205] This, according to Bourgeois, is especially true for disputes brought under the ADA, because Article 17.3 ADA not only reiterates that the first procedural step in a dispute is consultations but also specifies that these consultations shall lead to 'mutually satisfactory resolution of the matter'.[206]

Like *US–Cement*—which dealt with 'best efforts' in consultations under Article 15 ADA Code—*Mexico–HFCS (Article 21.5)* dealt with 'good faith' in consultations under Article 4.3 DSU. In both cases, the Panels had to deal with delimiting their scope of consideration, as well as the parties' rights as to the issues brought by the opposing party before a Panel. While Article 15 paragraph

[200] See *US–Cement*, Panel Report, para 5.6.
[201] *Ibid*, paras 5.12–5.13.
[202] *Ibid*, para 5.12.
[203] Bourgeois, 1998, p 267
[204] *Ibid.*
[205] *Ibid.*
[206] See *ibid.*

4 of the Tokyo Round anti-dumping Code of 1979 uses the term 'best effort' to qualify the parties' rights and obligations in the consultations phase, the Uruguay Round WTO DSU extends the scope of the consultations requirement to all subjects under the WTO umbrella (not just AD) and replaces the relic of diplomatic-speak ('best effort') with the legally enforceable instrument of good faith.[207]

Whether or not jurisprudence on the legal requirements for the consultations phase has made any progress since *US–Cement*, the fact that the negotiators at Marrakesh introduced 'good faith' to substitute for 'best efforts', demonstrates the increasing confidence in a WTO trading system governed by law as opposed to diplomacy. Moreover, the substitution of best efforts with good faith may even demonstrate the intention to lay the foundations for procedural rights at the WTO. The Tokyo Round negotiators had used good faith only in relation to the entire process of dispute settlement without including a specific good faith obligation relating to the consultations phase.[208]

Mexico–HFCS (Article 21.5) *Appellate Body Report (2001)*

In the *Mexico–HFCS (Article 21.5)* case, the AB elaborated on the issue of whether consultations are a 'prerequisite'[209] or an 'indispensable element'[210] for initiating a Panel procedure. The language of Article 4.3 DSU denies the necessity for consultations before bringing a dispute before the DSB, so the AB in *Mexico–HFCS (Article 21.5)* clarified that because the consultations phase was created for the benefit of the respondent, who is confronted with an alleged infringement of the WTO Agreements, it is only the respondent who bears the responsibility for no consultations having been held.[211]

Article 4.3 of the DSU links the responding party's conduct towards consultations with the complaining party's right to request the establishment of a Panel. When the responding party does not respond to a request for consultations, or declines to enter into consultations, the complaining party may dispense with consultations and proceed to request the establishment of a Panel. In such a case, the responding party, by its own conduct, relinquishes the potential benefits that could be derived from those consultations.[212]

[207] See Agreement on Implementation of Art VI of the General Agreement on Tariffs and Trade ('Tokyo Round Anti-dumping Code') Art 15, para 4, available at http://www.worldtradelaw.net 'Parties shall make their best efforts to reach a mutually satisfactory solution throughout the period of conciliation'.

[208] See Understanding Regarding Notification, Consultation, Dispute Settlement and Surveillance, 28 November 1979, available at http://www.worldtradelaw.net, Tokyo Round Agreements, Understandings, Decisions and Declarations, para 9.

[209] *Mexico–HFCS (Art 21.5)*, AB Report, para 58.

[210] *Ibid*, para 52.

[211] See *ibid*, paras 58–9.

[212] *Ibid*, para 59.

As with GATT 47 *US–Cement*, where consultations had in fact been held, albeit not on all issues, the first issue in this case was whether the Panel should have acted on its own motion, ie considered certain issues without consultations. The second issue was whether or not the Panel had committed a 'fatal error' by not addressing the lack of consultations prior to the redetermination proceedings between the US and Mexico. The third issue relating to Article 4.3 DSU was whether the US should be held responsible under 6.2 DSU because it had failed to indicate whether consultations had been held before seeking a re-determination.[213]

The AB held that Mexico had consented to the consultations phase being left out, had simply reduced the issue of consultations to 'observations of a general nature', had not asked the Panel whether it had the authority to rule on such issues and/or had not asked the Panel to rule on the legal consequences of procedural deficiencies, and finally had expressly declared that it was not complaining as to the lack of consultations. Therefore the Panel considered that Mexico was not entitled under good faith to raise the issue of lack of consultations before appeal.[214]

The AB held that even if either the AB or the Panel had found that Mexico had raised these procedural objections, good faith under Article 4.3 DSU would still permit a refusal to rule on the issue, given that Mexico had not submitted its objections in a timely manner.[215] Thereby, the AB evaded ruling on the substance of whether or not the DSU foresees that in cases when no consultations have been held, a Panel is required to look into the issues raised before it *quasi ex officio*.[216] However, the AB hypothetically held Mexico responsible for not submitting its objections relating to the lack of timely consultations under Article 3.10 DSU. Interestingly, the AB neither mentioned Article 3.10 DSU expressly nor accused Mexico directly of failing by good faith standards; rather it simply referred in a footnote to previous case-rulings on good faith under Article 3.10 DSU, for instance, *US–FSC*, paragraph 166.[217]

Good Faith in Article 4.3 DSU: Balancing the Respondant's Right to Consultations with the Complainant's Right to the Establishment of a Panel

Article 4.3 DSU imposes a good faith obligation onto the right of the complaining party to request the establishment of a Panel. Good faith under Article 4.3 DSU also balances the right of the responding member to request consultations with the right of the complaining member to move the dispute resolution along and to request the establishment of a Panel.

213 See *Mexico–HFCS (Art 21.5)*, AB Report, paras 35, 36.
214 *Ibid*, paras 38–47.
215 *Ibid*, paras 49–50, 58–9.
216 *Ibid*, para 35.
217 *Ibid*, para 50.

Good faith also imposes a limitation on the right of the responding member to enter into consultations, prohibiting the abuse of this right as a litigation technique either to gain time or to detract from the substantive issues, as Mexico was implicitly accused of doing in *Mexico–HFCS (Article 21.5)*. Article 4.3 DSU thus functions in a manner identical to that of Article 3.10 DSU. Even if compared to Article 3.10 DSU, entering into consultations in good faith less directly delimits members' rights vis-à-vis Panels (consultations involve Panels less than dispute settlement procedures), members' rights may be indirectly affected by a Panels' right to refuse to enter into the subject matter when the member has neither raised the issue of lack of consultations explicitly nor done so in a timely manner.[218]

Nonetheless, Article 4.3 DSU, in combination with Article 6.2 DSU, establishes that Panels are not obliged to delay the adjudication of a dispute because no consultations have been held.[219] Good faith limits a party's right to claim that a Panel has exceeded its authority if the Panel adjudicates a dispute established without prior consultations. Conversely, however, good faith limits the Panel's obligations vis-à-vis members' conduct of consultations.[220] In addition, Article 4.3 DSU does not have to be claimed together with another provision such as Article 4.7 or 6.2 DSU to be actionable, as was sometimes the case in the context of Article 3.10 DSU.[221] Articles 4.7 DSU and 6.2 DSU in *Mexico–HFCS (Article 21.5)* illustrate only that consultations are not a necessary prerequisite for a Panel's becoming operational,[222] even if they are 'as a general matter . . . a prerequisite to Panel proceedings'.[223]

Bourgeois adds that the good faith obligation of Article 4.3 DSU prohibits the complainant from refusing consultations and later claiming before the Panel an issue not brought in at the consultations phase; in addition a respondent who 'does not *comment* on an issue raised at the consultation stage, [may not] subsequently claim that the issue is not properly before the Panel' (emphasis added).[224]

Article 3.7 DSU: 'Whether Action . . . Would Be Fruitful'

Related to the duty to resolve disputes (Article 3.10) and conduct consultations in good faith (Article 4.3 DSU) is the duty to assess whether bringing an action

[218] *Ibid*, paras 36, 49.

[219] *Ibid*, paras 62–70.

[220] *Ibid*, paras 62–5.

[221] See, eg *EC–Sardines*, AB Report, para 147 (Art 16.4 DSU); *Thailand–Steel*, AB Report, para 96 (Art 6.2 DSU).

[222] See *Mexico–HFCS (Art 21.5)*, AB Report, paras 61–3.

[223] *Ibid*, para 58, confirms that, on the basis of previous practice, consulations are important as a precursor or even a prerequisite to Panel proceedings.

[224] Bourgeois, 1998, p 267, '"[G]ood faith" has to work both ways. If the complainant does not put a claim on the table at the consulation stage, it should not be permitted to subsequently raise it before the panel. Likewise if the respondent does not comment on an issue raised at the consultation stage, it cannot subsequently claim that issue is not properly before the panel'.

before the DSU proves 'fruitful' (Article 3.7 DSU). Article 3.7 DSU does not mention good faith. Nevertheless, practice has often implied that the act of ascertaining whether bringing a dispute is useful or not involves a measure of good faith.[225] However, it has also been said that ascertaining the fruitfulness of lodging a dispute is to be understood as a duty of WTO Member States who must exercise political judgment and seek to negotiate a mutually acceptable solution before engaging in the formal dispute settlement procedures.[226] Article 3.7 DSU says:

> Before bringing a case, a Member shall exercise its judgment as to whether action under these procedures would be fruitful. The aim of the dispute settlement mechanism is to secure a positive solution to a dispute. A solution mutually acceptable to the parties to a dispute and consistent with the covered agreements is clearly to be preferred.

EC–Bananas *Appellate Body Report (1997)*

In *EC–Bananas*, the matter of procedural good faith in dispute settlement arose as one of the preliminary issues before the AB. The question was whether the US had a right or a 'standing',[227] or in the terminology of the ICJ, a 'legal interest', in bringing a claim under GATT 94.[228] The AB agreed with the Panel that neither Articles 3.3 DSU nor 3.7 DSU, nor any other provisions of the DSU explicitly require a member to have a 'legal interest' as a precondition for requesting a Panel.[229]

The Panel had argued that even in the absence of a specific legal interest requirement in the DSU, there was no reason for concern that the system might become overburdened with cases 'by all against all', because Article 3.7 'obliges Members to exercise restraint in bringing cases and the cost of cases is such, . . . that this admonition is likely to be followed'.[230]

The AB found both Article XXIII:1 of the GATT 94 and Article 3.7 of the DSU relevant to the issue of standing. From the first provision it extracted the words '[i]f any Member should consider . . .' and, from the second, which it deemed consistent with Article XXIII, it derived the requirement that the action should prove 'fruitful':[231]

> Of special importance for determining the issue of standing, in our view, are the words '[i]f any Member should consider . . .'. This provision in Article XXIII is consistent

[225] *Mexico–HFCS (Art 21.5)*, AB Report, para 73; see also Parlin, 2002; but see Martha, 2001, pp 1035–59.

[226] See Zimmermann, 2004, p 57.

[227] *EC–Bananas*, AB Report, para 132 with further references in footnote 65 to the dictionary meaning of 'standing'.

[228] See *ibid*, paras 132 and 133 with further references in footnote 66 to ICJ and PCIJ Judgments on 'legal interest'.

[229] See *EC–Bananas*, AB Report, para 132.

[230] *Ibid*, para 7.51.

[231] *Ibid*, paras 134–5.

> with Article 3.7 of the DSU, which states: Before bringing a case, a Member shall exercise its judgment as to whether action under these procedures would be fruitful. . . . Accordingly, we believe that a Member has broad discretion in deciding whether to bring a case against another Member under the DSU. The language of Article XXIII:1 of the GATT 94 and of Article 3.7 of the DSU suggests, furthermore, that a Member is expected to be largely self-regulating in deciding whether any such action would be 'fruitful'.[232]

Thus, the standing of a Member wishing to become a party to the dispute is determined by Articles XXIII:1 GATT 94 and 3.7 DSU, and specifically hinges upon the term 'fruitful' in the latter provision. Since no other specification offering a more precise definition of 'fruitful' is given in the treaty text, the AB found that 'a Member is expected to be largely self-regulating in deciding whether any action would be "fruitful"'.[233]

Thus, in this case the AB declared itself 'satisfied that the US was justified in bringing its claims under the GATT 94 in this case'.[234] To the AB the argument by the US that it is a producer of bananas and has a potential export interest cannot be ignored. Moreover, even from an internal market perspective, the US market would be affected by the EC banana regime (ie the term for the EC's regulations on bananas) on world supplies and the world prices of bananas. Ironically in the *EC–Bananas* case, the AB said that effects of the EC's banana regimes were global, so that any WTO Member State would be justified in finding its request for dispute settlement 'fruitful' and would have the standing to bring a claim even if that Member were only an importer of bananas.[235]

Mexico–HFCS (Article 21.5) *Appellate Body Report (2001)*

Mexico wanted to know from the AB whether the Panel, who had remained silent and had ignored the failure of the US to assess the fruitfulness of bringing its dispute with Mexico, had failed to comply with the first sentence of Article 3.7 DSU. In *Mexico–HFCS (Article 21.5)* AB Report (2001), the question was whether Article 3.7 DSU binds the Panel. More specifically, if both parties have conducted a defective evaluation or no evaluation at all regarding the fruitfulness of the dispute settlement proceedings, does Article 3.7 DSU still oblige the Panel to examine the fruitfulness of bringing a case? Would the Panel's silence upon the member's lack of action deprive the Panel of its authority to deal with and settle a matter?

Fruitfulness as Prohibition of Frivolous Disputes In *Mexico–HFCS (Article 21.5)*, the AB addressed the contentious issue of Article 3.7 DSU with two considerations:

232 *Ibid*, paras 134–5.
233 *Ibid*, para 135.
234 See *EC–Bananas*, AB Report, para 136.
235 See Martha, 2001, p 1039, for a discussion of the case relating to Art 3.7 DSU.

— The AB in *Mexico–HFCS (Article 21.5)* cited its *EC–Bananas* report, in which it stated:

(a) 'A Member has a broad discretion in deciding whether to bring a case against another Member under the DSU'; and

(b) The 'language of Articles XXIII:1 GATT 94 and 3.7 DSU suggests; that a Member is largely self-regulating in deciding whether any such action would be fruitful'.[236]

— The only new and supplementary comment the AB offered in *Mexico–HFCS (Article 21.5)* was an elaboration on what is meant by fruitfulness, which is described in opposition to frivolous dispute settlement procedures:

> In our view, this sentence reflects a basic principle that Members should have recourse to WTO dispute settlement in good faith, and not frivolously set in motion the procedures contemplated in the DSU.[237]

However, the AB in *Mexico–HFCS (Article 21.5)* left unanswered the issue of whether Article 3.7 DSU, in the absence of a party's claim of violation, obliges either the Panel or the AB to examine *ex officio* a defect in the sense of absence of frivolousness, fruitfulness, or good faith in bringing a case before the DSU.

Presumed Fruitfulness In addition to firstly establishing the duty of fruitfulness relating to a dispute and, secondly, deriving the prohibition to bring frivolous disputes before the DSB from the duty to settle disputes in good faith (Article 3.10 DSU), the AB in its *Mexico–HFCS (Article 21.5)* Report introduced a presumption of fruitfulness under Article 3.7 DSU. The AB translated the obligation of WTO Member States to first assess the fruitfulness of a dispute under Article 3.7 DSU, into a presumption. As a presumption, Article 3.7 DSU considers that whenever a Member submits a request for establishment of a Panel, 'such a Member does so in good faith, having duly exercised its judgment as to whether recourse to that Panel would be fruitful'.[238]

It is by qualifying Article 3.7 DSU as a presumption that the AB introduced the principle of good faith in dispute settlement into the obligation of Article 3.7 DSU first sentence. By considering Article 3.7 DSU a presumption of good faith, the AB shifts the burden of proof from the Panel or AB to the responding Member, regarding whether the complaining Member submitting a request for establishment of a Panel has assessed the fruitfulness of engaging in DSU procedures.[239] If a Member claims that the Panels' presumption was in error, the AB will review the presumption for possible violations of WTO law, which, in turn, affect a Panel's authority when the Member has established that an action

[236] *Mexico–HFCS (Art 21.5)*, AB Report, para 73.
[237] *Ibid.*
[238] See *ibid*, para 74.
[239] *Ibid.*

would be fruitful.[240] However a Member cannot claim that the Panel breached Article 3.7 DSU by not evaluating a Member's exercise of discretion as to the fruitfulness of bringing a dispute before the DSB.

The Standard of Good Faith for Judgment on Bringing a Dispute Since Members are 'self-regulating' in assessing whether it is fruitful to start an action before the WTO, the AB has not only found that the Panels and the AB must presume that Members submit requests for establishment of Panels in good faith, but also deduced that Article 3.7 DSU does not even *authorise* a Panel to consider a Member's exercise of judgment.[241]

One author suggests that in certain situations, the judiciary should not even presume that the Member has exercised its judgment in good faith as to whether the action is fruitful:

> Any action entailing that a Panel is asked to examine the consistency of a measure with an obligation that is not included in one of the covered agreements would not be fruitful under the DSU procedures, and should be dismissed at the outset. The latter situation arises in cases involving other international instruments, such as environmental treaties, labor conventions and regional trade arrangements.[242]

The AB is not authorised to scrutinise a Member's behaviour as to that Member's obligation to exercise judgment relating to the fruitfulness of an action. A fortiori a Panel has even less right to do so on its own motion.[243] Thus, the Panel's authority is not impaired when the defending Member fails to claim the defective judgment of the complaining Member relating to the fruitfulness of an action.[244]

The Self-regulating Presumption of Good Faith Exempts Panels from Investigating on Their own Motion The AB in *Mexico–HFCS* (Article 21.5) stated that if the defendant WTO Member State fails to object to the complaining Member State's lack of judgment on the fruitfulness of a dispute, the Panel still has no authority to examine fruitfulness of an action.[245] The AB stated:

> Given the 'largely self-regulating' nature of the requirement in the first sentence of Article 3.7, Panels and the AB must presume, whenever a Member submits a request for establishment of a Panel, that such Member does so in good faith, having duly exercised its judgment as to whether recourse to that Panel would be 'fruitful'. Article 3.7 neither requires nor authorises a Panel to look behind that Member's decision and to question its exercise of judgment. Therefore, the Panel was not obliged to consider this issue on its own motion.[246]

[240] See *ibid*, para 75.
[241] *Ibid*, para 74.
[242] Martha, 2001, p 1058.
[243] See *Mexico–HFCS (Art 21.5)*, AB Report, para 74.
[244] Analogous to *ibid*, para 67.
[245] See *ibid*, para 75 and compare with paras 63 and 64.
[246] *Ibid*, para 74.

In this decision two points remained undecided:

— Does the presumption of exercising judgment in good faith pertain only to the exercise of judgment or to both the exercise of judgment and the outcome of that judgment? In other words, does the Panel's presumption involve asking only whether judgment has been exercised?
— Does the presumption encompass the question of 'fruitfulness'?

The question of fruitfulness is addressed before the WTO judiciary at the appellate level to the extent that if a Panel presumes the fruitfulness of an action the AB could find that the Panel had erred in presuming a Members' evaluation of the fruitfulness of a dispute.[247]

Common Features of Procedural Good Faith Obligations

The following section discusses firstly the addressees of the procedural good faith obligations under Articles 3.10, 4.3 and 3.7 DSU. Secondly, it examines the justiciability of procedural good faith obligations for dispute settlement as codified in the above-mentioned provisions. A third question is whether each of the three codified procedural good faith provisions is binding upon all WTO Member States or only upon those WTO Member States that are parties to a dispute.

Binding on the Complaining Member Only? Article 3.7 DSU pertains to the complaining Member only, while Article 3.10 DSU binds all WTO Member States obliged under good faith. Article 4.3 DSU as opposed to Article 3.7 DSU, is binding upon the responding member only: the 'Member to which the request is made'.[248]

An Actionable 'Basic Principle'? Is it possible to claim the violation of the 'basic principle' of good faith in the settlement of disputes? Might a WTO Member base a claim upon the principle of good faith, when it feels that another Member has violated the requirement to proceed in good faith before the WTO DSU? Is the implicit reference to good faith under Article 3.7 DSU an actionable obligation, imposing the duty upon a Member to evaluate whether or not an action would be at all 'fruitful'?[249] The AB has stated:

> [I]n our view, [Article 3.7 DSU] *reflects a basic* principle that Members should have recourse to WTO dispute settlement in good faith, and not frivolously set in motion the procedures contemplated in the DSU.[250]

[247] See *ibid* para 75.
[248] Art 4.3 DSU.
[249] See Parlin, 2002.
[250] *Mexico–HFCS (Art 21.5)*, AB Report, para 73 (emphasis added).

Therefore, Article 3.7 is apparently more of a 'basic principle' than a right or obligation for Members.[251] As to the the issue of whether or not the good faith obligation in Article 3.10 DSU confers a 'right' on Member parties to a dispute, the *Mexico–HFCS (Article 21.5)* case took the position that Article 3.10 DSU did not express a right, but rather a 'requirement' or a 'standard'.[252]

Mexico–HFCS (Article 21.5) AB Report and *EC–Bananas* AB Report are the only cases to date that address the legal nature of Article 3.7 DSU. The single most important conclusion we can draw is that Members bringing a case have an obligation to exercise judgment as to whether their case will be fruitful. This exercise of judgment is controlled by the principle of good faith under Article 3.10, which applies to Article 3.7 DSU. While on the one hand a Member can be sanctioned for exercising its judgment in bad faith, as the *India-Autos* Panel suggested, it is the defending party that has the burden of showing bad faith.[253] For Panels on the other hand, there are no sanctions when they remain silent regarding the failure of a Member to exercise judgment. This is so because the rights of Members to exercise judgment as to the fruitfulness of a dispute under Article 3.7 DSU do not touch upon the authority of Panels to dispose of a matter. As the AB in *Mexico–HFCS (Article 21.5)* stated, the Members are 'self-regulating' as to whether or not to bring an action.[254]

Conclusions

Procedural good faith obligations as in Articles 3.10, 4.3, as well as those implied in Article 3.7 DSU, function to prohibit the abuse of the due process rights contained in the DSU and scattered about in the procedural *leges specialies* of the different WTO Agreements, namely the ASCM and ADA. The obligation to resolve disputes in good faith may combine different addressees, such as WTO Member States in Article 3.10, the responding member in Article 4.3, and, to some extent, the Panels in Article 3.7 DSU; but it has a single function as summed up by the *US–FSC* case: the principle of good faith in dispute settlement procedures guarantees that due process rights 'underlying the DSU' are not used unfairly.

The cases brought before the DSU in the late 1990s saw an increase in abuses of due process rights, the purpose of which was usually to detract from the substantive problems at issue. As a result, the AB has linked Article 3.10 DSU not only with the rights of Members to an effective resolution of the dispute in a timely fashion, but also to the Members' obligations vis-à-vis the Panels. Article 4.3 DSU, the duty to engage in consultations in good faith, aspires to the same

[251] *Cf US–Japan Hot-rolled Steel*, AB Report, where the AB referred to both good faith and due process as 'basic principles'.

[252] *Mexico–HFCS (Art 21.5)*, AB Report, para 47.

[253] See *India–Autos*, Panel Report, para 7.141.

[254] *Mexico–HFCS (Art 21.5)*, AB Report, para 74.

goal, ie the responding Member's due process rights protects it against the establishment of a Panel for the wrong reasons.[255]

Good faith in Articles 3.10 and 4.3 DSU prohibits the abuse of procedural rights relating to the settlement of disputes in six ways:

- A complaint against an insufficient Panel request (Article 6.2 DSU, here in combination with Articles 2, 5 ADA) must be preceded by a request for more information.[256]
- The Panels have the authority to settle disputes despite lack of consultations, unless the objection is brought explicitly and in a timely manner (4.2 ASCM and 4.4. DSU).[257]
- A conditional withdrawal of a notice of appeal under Rule 30 of the Working Procedures is legitimate only if it is fair to the responding party.[258]
- A lack of consultations cannot be invoked to claim that the Panel is deprived of authority to settle the dispute.[259]
- A Panel's right remains effective only if Article 3.10 DSU is respected and the commitment to achieving a positive solution to a dispute is secured, pursuant to Article 3.7 DSU, if a Panels' standard of review relating to competent investigation authorities is not rendered meaningless.[260]

Together, the formula created by the AB in *US–FSC* of a fair, prompt and effective dispute settlement and the principle in Article 3.10 DSU encapsulate the role and function of the procedural good faith standard and obligations so that ultimately 'the use of the dispute settlement procedures should not be intended or considered as contentious acts'.

Thus, it can be said that for the role of good faith in the DSU, the century-old traditions and 'synthesizing' force of good faith[261] guided the usually 'circumspect' AB to create a well-balanced WTO procedural law.[262]

PROCEDURAL GOOD FAITH OBLIGATIONS OF DISPUTE SETTLEMENT'S *LEGES SPECIALES*

The WTO's procedural good faith obligations under Articles 3.10, 4.3 and 3.7 DSU apply not only to the rules of settling disputes in the DSU. According to Article 1:2 of the DSU in combination with Appendix 2 of the DSU, there exist additional rules of procedure in certain WTO covered agreements. These

[255] See *Mexico–HFCS (Art 21.5)*, AB Report, para 59.
[256] See *Thailand–Steel*, AB Report, paras 95–7.
[257] See *US–FSC*, AB Report, paras 161–6.
[258] See *EC–Sardines*, AB Report, para 140.
[259] See *Mexico–HFCS (Art 21.5)*, AB Report, para 64.
[260] See *US–Lamb Safeguards*, AB Report, para 115.
[261] Virally, 1990, p 204, who likens general principles of law to 'synthesizing traditions rather than to innovative instruments of the law'.
[262] Ehlermann, 2002, p 606.

so-called 'Special and Additional Rules and Procedures', which are outside the DSU but part of certain WTO Agreements, such as the TRIPS, the GATS and the GATT covered agreements, are summarised in Appendix 2 of the DSU.[263] The good faith obligations of the DSU also apply to these *leges speciales* of WTO procedural law.

This section distinguishes the application of procedural good faith obligations to special rules of dispute settlement, situated outside the DSU, the *leges speciales*, from the good faith obligations applicable to the procedural rules of the DSU, the *leges generales*.

The codified, express, procedural good faith obligations under the DSU control the exercise of 'procedural' (also called 'due process') rights. Other, non-DSU procedural rights in the WTO Agreements are in Articles 17 ADA, 30 ASCM, 11 SPS, 14 TBT.[264] Furthermore, there are other such 'procedural rights' in the WTO Agreements that do not relate to dispute resolution, namely Article 6.2 ADA (opportunity to be heard in anti-dumping investigations), Article 6.5 ADA (right to protect BCI), Article 12 ASCM (the right to reply in CVD investigation), and Article 23 ASCM (the right to a judicial review of administrative decisions at the domestic level).

A question worth asking is whether Articles 3.10 and 4.10 DSU apply to these extra-DSU procedural guarantees, which are often due process rights. One answer would be that the single package approach of the WTO leads to the effect that DSU rules govern all agreements. This argumentation would justify an expansive interpretation of Articles 3.10 and 4.3 DSU to include non-DSU procedural rights and obligations. A counter-argument would be that the clear meaning of Articles 3.10 and 4.3 shows that they apply to the procedural rules of the DSU only (*leges generales*).

The AB finds that good faith under Article 3.10 DSU 'raise[s] a number of questions with fundamental and far-reaching implications for the entire WTO dispute settlement'.[265] Indeed by using good faith to limit the exercise of due process rights, the AB has developed WTO procedural law. However, it may have contributed to more than that, since the rules it has derived from DSU provisions may also promote the development of international procedural law, for which 'no accepted doctrine of procedural principles' exists as of today.[266]

The other substantive functions of good faith, such as *pacta sunt servanda* and the prohibition of *abus de droit,* are, with the exception of the WTO-specific principle of PLE, generally and directly applicable sources of international law and apply to the entire WTO jurisdiction. In contrast, the litigation-specific substantive good faith obligations of the DSU control only

[263] Art 1:2 DSU and Appendix 2 to the DSU.

[264] *Cf* Ehlermann, 2003, p 700–1, who uses the distinction between substantive and procedural rights and obligations; see also Marceau, 2002, p 20.

[265] *Canada–Aircraft*, AB Report, para 182.

[266] Gaffney, 1999, p 1179; see Ehlermann, 2003, pp 698, 701, for the development of WTO procedural law.

the law and practice of settling disputes. Depending on the interpretation given, the good faith obligations of the DSU may even extend to the procedural rights and obligations outside the DSU, the so-called procedural *leges speciales*.

In *US–Hot-rolled Steel*, the procedural obligation of the interested party to provide evidence to the anti-dumping investigating authorities was qualified under the 'organic' principle of good faith as the duty to balance the interest in obtaining information in the best possible format with the 'practical abilities' of the interested party to comply with such a request.

The AB held that the 'organic' general principle of law of good faith expressed in Articles 2 and 5 Annex II, ADA 'informs' the ADA, as well as the other covered agreements. In the context of this case, the AB found good faith to give content to the 'best of their abilities' standard of paragraphs 2 and 5 Annex II, ADA. Relating to the collection of evidence, the good faith standard transforms the duty to provide information from an 'absolute' to a relative one. In the words of the AB, good faith 'informs' paragraphs 2 and 5 Annex II, ADA, insofar as good faith 'restrains investigating authorities from imposing on exporters burdens which, in the circumstances, are not reasonable'.[267] In *US–Hot-rolled Steel* the AB confirmed that the procedural good faith standard of the *US–FSC* formula of fair, prompt and effective dispute settlement, as well as the procedural good faith obligations of Articles 3.10, 4.3 and 3.7 DSU all apply to the *leges speciales* of WTO procedural law as well.

[267] *US–Japan Hot rolled Steel*, AB Report, para 101.

11

The Good Faith Standard of Factual Review

THE MEMBERS OF the WTO are bound by procedural good faith not only when engaging in dispute settlement procedures. As this chapter shows, a Panel's assessment of facts is determined by good faith as standard.

A Panel's good faith obligations as to the factual review of a case, as well as the good faith threshold for review by the AB of facts both emanate from the jurisprudence of the AB. In contrast, the AB has come to reject that procedural good faith obligations of the WTO Member States are codified in DSU Articles 3.10, 4.3 and 3.7. Nevertheless, the procedural good faith obligations of the Panels compare to those of the WTO Member States. As this chapter will show, procedural good faith limits the Panels' discretion vis-à-vis the members, while as seen in chapter 10 above, good faith ensures that members, on the other hand, do not abuse due process rights.[1]

As discussed below with regard to the following cases, the AB did not use any source of general public international law when it introduced the Panel's procedural good faith standard with respect to the facts of a case. As with the PLE described in chapter 6 above, a Panel's duty to refrain from surpassing the limits of a good faith factual evaluation may be considered a WTO-specific good faith principle.

'AN EGREGIOUS ERROR . . . CALLS INTO QUESTION THE GOOD FAITH OF A PANEL'

The WTO Panels are under the obligation to respect the confines of good faith when reviewing the facts presented to them by WTO Members. Such a limit to a Panel's discretion was introduced by the AB in *EC–Hormones* in 1998 but has since been abandoned. The *EC–Hormones* appeal introduced the Panels' good faith standard for factual review with the quote that the Panels, when assessing

[1] See, eg *EC–Hormones*, AB Report, para 154; *US–1916 Act*, AB Report, paras 149–50; *US–FSC*, AB Report, para 243, on how due process limits a Panel's discretion.

the facts of a case, must avoid 'an egregious error . . . that calls into question the good faith of a Panel'.[2]

The *EC–Hormones* appeal has had a certain amount of influence, but is no longer of any significance. Current appellate practice allows the Panels to delegate the duty to respect good faith in the assessment of the facts to the members for whom the good faith duty with respect to the establishment of the facts of a case forms part of their procedural good faith obligations pursuant to Articles 3.10, 4.3 and 3.7 DSU.

EC–Hormones Appellate Body Report (1998)

The EC alleged in this appeal that the Panel had 'disregarded or distorted or misrepresented' the evidence as well the opinions and statements expressed by the Panel's own scientific expert advisors.[3] The AB in *EC–Hormones* was called upon to define when an error made by the Panel in the appreciation of evidence may be characterised as a failure to objectively assess the matter before it.[4]

The *EC–Hormones* case was the first case in which the AB had to deal with allegations that the Panel had 'disregarded', 'distorted' or 'misrepresented' the evidence before it. The AB linked these allegations 'to charges that the Panel had violated its duty under Article 11 of the DSU', allegations which in the final analysis it found to be 'unsubstantiated'.[5]

The AB found that it is only if the Panel commits an 'egregious error that calls into question the good faith of a Panel', is it entitled to review the factual considerations of the Panel.[6]

Even if the EC's allegations related to findings of fact, which, pursuant to Article 17.6 DSU, do not fall within the AB scope of review, the AB took responsibility for assessing whether the Panel made an objective assessment of the facts before it. In order to conduct an assessment of the Panel's factual analysis while simultaneously maintaining the balance of power defined by the DSU and acting in accordance with the two-tier judicial structure of the WTO Agreements, the AB introduced the standard of good faith to limit the Panel's appreciation of facts. This application of good faith meant the AB was engaging in a review of the law. With this construct of good faith limiting the Panel's factual review, the AB effectively substituted its prohibition on reviewing facts with an obligation to determine whether the Panel overstepped the limit of good faith. This means that the AB, by law, reviews the Panel's good faith, while in effect examining the Panel's assessement of the facts of a case.[7]

[2] *EC–Hormones*, AB Report, para 133.
[3] *Ibid*, para 131.
[4] See *ibid*, para 133.
[5] *Korea–Alcohol*, AB Report, para 162.
[6] *EC–Hormones*, AB Report, para 133.
[7] See *ibid*, para 133.

The AB defined and delimited what constitutes a violation of the Panel's duty to objectively assess the facts before it:

— 'Not every error in the appreciation of the evidence (although it may give rise to a question of law) will be considered incompatible with a Panel's duty under Article 11 of the DSU'.[8] This implies that although the assessment might constitute a question of law, it is not reviewable by the AB.
— 'simply an error of judgment in the appreciation of evidence' is not sufficiently incompatible with a Panel's duty under Art. II DSU, 'rather an egregious error that calls into question the good faith of a Panel' is to be considered inconsistent with an objective assessment of facts.[9]
— A Panel that disregards or distorts the evidence is one that 'to a greater or lesser degree, denies the party submitting the evidence fundamental fairness, or what in many jurisdictions is known as due process of law or natural justice'.[10]

The AB summarised as follows:

> When may a Panel be regarded as having failed to discharge its duty under Article 11 of the DSU to make an objective assessment of the facts before it? . . . 'Disregard' and 'distortion' and 'misrepresentation' of the evidence, . . . imply not simply an error of judgment in the appreciation of evidence but rather an egregious error that calls into question the good faith of a Panel. A claim that a Panel disregarded or distorted the evidence submitted to it is, in effect, a claim that the Panel, to a greater or lesser degree, denied the party submitting the evidence fundamental fairness, or what in many jurisdictions is known as due process of law or natural justice.[11]

Although, in the result the AB found that the Panel had misinterpreted the evidence submitted by the EC as well as its own, it nevertheless refuted the claim that the Panel had failed to conduct an objective assessment of the matter before it.[12]

Although in *EC–Hormones*, the Panel may have made a 'mistake' in interpreting evidence, or appeared to consider certain evidence irrelevant by remaining 'silent' on the issue, this failure did not amount to a breach of a WTO treaty provision. A Panel would have violated its duty to establish the facts of the case only if it had 'ignored' the evidence or breached mandatory rules establishing an expert review group. In the cases in which it determined the evidence relevant, the Panel had at least examined the evidence.[13] Thus, in *EC–Hormones*, the AB implied that when examined in the light of the members' fundamental due process rights, the Panel's failure was not serious enough to be considered a

[8] *Ibid* paras 131 and 133.
[9] *Ibid*, para 133.
[10] *Ibid*.
[11] See *ibid*.
[12] See *ibid*, paras 137, 142, 144, 145, and 149; see also para 131 for the EC's claim against the Panel.
[13] See *EC–Hormones*, AB Report, paras 135–49.

breach of such rights, as would necessarily have been the case if the Panel were to be sanctioned under its duty of Article 11 DSU.

Why is the limit to a Panel's discretion set so high? The AB's standard of review is defined by two opposing rationales: on the one hand the obligation to ensure 'the party submitting evidence fundamental fairness, . . . due process or natural justice', calls for an intrusive review of a Panel's factual assessment; on the other hand, the seriousness of an Article 11 DSU allegation limits the AB's power to sanction a Panel and extends a Panel's margin of discretion.[14]

Limited Factual Discretion of the Panels and the Duty of Members to Provide Information

The standard of 'egregious error calling into question the good faith of a Panel limits the Panels' discretion to seek out the facts of the case. However, that limit is relaxed by the Panels' right to seek information under Article 13(1) DSU. As a result, while the Panels' discretion for factual review is limited pursuant to the judge-made (*EC–Hormones*) good faith standard inferred from Article 11 DSU, it is compensated by the Panel's right to seek information under Article 13(1) DSU.

Under the *EC–Hormones* standard of factual review, a Panel's scope for factual review ends where the discretion of the domestic investigating authorities begins. The information on which a Panel misses out, comes back to the Panel in the form of members' good faith duty to supply that Panel with the requested information, pursuant to the Article 13(1) DSU *Canada–Aircraft* jurisprudence.

As *US–Lamb Safeguards* illustrates, a member may not abuse the Panels' limited standard of review of facts established by domestic authorities (Article 11) in order to mask the fact that it does not cooperate with the Panel.[15] Members are prohibited under good faith from abusing the limiting function of good faith on the discretion of Panels under Article 11 DSU. In *US–Lamb*, the US had purposefully withheld evidence from its own investigating authorities, so that it would not fall under the Panels' review. The US had the intention of producing the evidence on appeal, thus rendering the Panel, under Article 11 DSU, culpable of failing to conduct its factual review, which in turn would prevent the AB from adjudicating on the substance, ie holding the US' safeguard unjustified.[16]

[14] *EC–Hormones*, AB Report, para 133.
[15] See *US–Lamb Safeguards*, AB Report, para 115.
[16] *Ibid*, para 110.

The Judge-made Good Faith Standard of Factual Review

The next section describes the impact for Article 11 DSU of the AB's reading into the limit of the Panel's standard of review for facts, its own opportunity for a limited factual review. Specifically, the issue is whether the AB's creative jurisprudence is consistent with the other provisions of the DSU.

The first question is whether the limit of good faith to the Panel's power of factual review introduced by the AB under Article 11 DSU, is an importation of the general principle of law of good faith into the DSU, or whether it amounts to a judge-made principle of WTO law.[17] A second question is whether the AB's creative gap-filling, controlling the 'objectivity' of a Panel's factual assessment (Article 11 DSU), is incompatible with the prohibition against adding to or diminishing Members' obligations.

The language of Article 3.2 DSU prohibits only judicial activism that adds to or diminishes the legal obligations of WTO Member States, whereas Article 11 DSU is directed at the Panels. Also, neither Article 11 DSU nor jurisprudence describe the legal consequence of a Panel's committing an egregious error calling into question the good faith of a Panel, meaning that it is not permitted under Article 11 DSU for the AB to adjudicate on a factual issue.

THE GOOD FAITH STANDARD FOR APPELLATE REVIEW OF FACTUAL CONCLUSIONS

As described above, the AB in *EC–Hormones* introduced the good faith standard as it relates to the duty of the Panels to assess the facts of a case; conversely, the AB wanted its good faith jurisprudence to be understood as providing the AB itself with the possibility of reviewing a Panel's assessment of facts too.

Not only does the good faith standard inferred from Article 11 DSU define the limit of a Panel's power to assess objectively the establishment of facts with the degree of discretion available to national governments, but in addition the good faith limit to factual review empowers the AB, pursuant to Article 17.6 DSU, to review a Panel's factual consideration if the Panel's assessment 'calls into question' the Panel's good faith.[18]

Only when a Panel's good faith is called into question, is the AB called upon to assess whether a Panel 'abuse[d] [its] discretion' and thereby infringed members' rights.[19] It is through a good faith standard that the AB measures a Panel's abuse of discretion, which is defined by the the amount of deference a Panel owes to the national investigating authorities under Article 11 DSU. In other

[17] See *US–Cotton Yarn*, AB Report, para 81.
[18] *EC–Hormones*, AB Report, para 133.
[19] *EC–Poultry*, AB Report, para 133.

words, good faith stands for the prohibition against allowing the Panels to 'substitute their own judgment for that of a competent authority'.[20] Good faith implied in Article 11 DSU functions as the prohibition of *abus de droit* and acts correctively.[21]

In addition, the appellate good faith standard of factual review also fills in a gap in the rules on standards of review. As the threshold for the AB's assessement of facts of a case, good faith supplements the AB's lack of power to review facts. When the AB reviews the limits of a Panel's assessment of facts, it is, in fact, reviewing law, that is, the standard good faith.

By being attached to a Panel's objective assessment of facts, good faith can be used by the AB to control a Panel's factual assessment.[22]

The good faith obligation of the Panels vis-à-vis the AB and the members is created judicially. However, it nevertheless constitutes Article 3.2 DSU-consistent judge-made law, because it only adds to the obligations of WTO *organs* and does not add to or diminish the obligations of *members*.

The question of the AB's factual standard of review has been well described elsewhere. Oesch (2003) comprehensively addresses both the Panels' standard of review relating to facts and law vis-à-vis national authorities and the AB's standard of review relating to the Panels.[23] Jackson (2000), and Jackson and Croley (1996), focus on the specific issues of the Panels' standard of review and the deference paid to national governments (national sovereignty), dismissing the analogy to a Chevron-like approach, because Panels do not have the 'fact-gathering resources' of an administrative agency.[24] Cottier and Oesch (2001), as well as Cottier and Hertig (2003), link the impact of the standard of review to the WTO's constitutionalisation and point to the 'paradox' that the structurally weak international order defines more 'rigorous' standards of review for members' national legislations, giving no 'leeway to Members', than regional judiciaries (EC) accord the national laws of their members.[25] Finally, Bronckers and McNelis (1999) and Kuyper (2000) debate the differences between the AB's review of facts and law and whether the standard for the AB's factual standard of review is set too high.[26]

[20] *US–Lamb Safeguards*, AB Report, para 106; *US–Cotton Yarn*, AB Report, para 74.

[21] *Cf* Cheng, 1987, p 132; Schwarzenberger, 1955, p 324.

[22] *Cf* Schwarzenberger, 1955, who equates gap-filling with the formative function of good faith.

[23] See Oesch, 2003b, pp 133–48 (for the Panels' standard of review relating to facts), pp 157–69 (for the AB's standard of review relating to facts).

[24] See Jackson, 2000, pp 133–61, based on Jackson and Croley, 1996, pp 193–213.

[25] See Cottier and Oesch, 2003, pp 299–300; Cottier and Hertig, 2004, pp 262–328.

[26] See Bronckers and McNelis, 1999, pp 241–53; Kuyper, 2000, pp 310–23.

Factual Review Based upon a Panel's Good Faith Standard

Pursuant to the *EC–Hormones* jurisprudence, the AB's factual review is triggered when a Panel is accused of having conducted a factual review in bad faith. Only under the circumstance of a Panel having acted in bad faith, may the AB, which under Article 11 DSU does not usually have a standard of review relating to the facts of the case, engage in a review of the Panel's factual assessment.

Pursuant to the text of Article 11 DSU, the AB, in contrast to the Panels, is not empowered to review the facts of the case brought before it. Factual review is a duty reserved for the Panels under Article 11 DSU. However, the AB in *EC–Hormones* engaged in expansive jurisprudence to expand its own review to include factual issues, and not only the law of the case, if and when a Panel's factual review has resulted in an 'egregious error calling into question the good faith of a Panel'.[27]

As in the section on good faith in resolving disputes, where subsequent Panels and AB Reports reiterated the *US–FSC* formula on the duty to resolve disputes in good faith, the AB in the *EC–Hormones* case introduced the 'egregious error' formula, which has been used repeatedly to trigger the AB's review of a Panel's factual conclusions.

The formula used by the *EC–Hormones* AB calls upon the AB to evaluate the Panel's factual assessments. The *EC–Hormones* formula for the AB's standard of review has remained valid for cases subsequent to *EC–Hormones* until the *US–Wheat Gluten and US–Lamb Safeguards* cases introduced a new appellate standard of review.[28]

Systemic Context

In the earlier *Canada–Periodicals* case, adopted 30 July 1997, the standards that allowed the AB to reverse the fact-finding by the Panel were: a Panel's failure either to carry out the necessary analysis or to base its findings on the facts and exhibits before it; and incorrect reasoning by a Panel, for example, inapposite comparisons, logical jumps or drawing conclusions which cannot reasonably be drawn.[29]

Bronckers and McNelis (1999) criticise that 'basically requir[ing] that the appellant allege bad faith on the part of the Panel, [is] too high a standard'. A finding of bad faith is, in these authors' view, 'an extreme allegation that . . . would almost never be appropriate'. In addition, they argue that it is particularly important that factual errors should be reviewable by the AB, without alleging bad faith. Given the 'extremely tight' time limits that characterise the

27 *EC–Hormones*, AB Report, para 166.
28 See Oesch, 2003b, pp 163–4.
29 See Lugard, 1998, pp 323–5.

dispute settlement procedures for Panels, the risk that Panels will 'certainly make errors without having the will to do so', is real.[30]

Functional Rationale

The likely reason why the AB introduced the good faith test in 1998, with regard to to Article 11 DSU, was to emphasize the legal nature of reviewing the Panel's assessment of facts (Article 17.6 DSU). As a legal standard, good faith serves to stress that despite the term 'facts' in Article 11 DSU, the AB remains within the boundaries of its mandate of reviewing questions of law and legal interpretations, as specified in Article 17.6 DSU, when reviewing the Panel's assessment of facts. 'Whether or not a Panel has made an objective assessment of the facts before it, as required by Article 11 of the DSU, is also a legal question which, if properly raised on appeal, would fall within the scope of the appellate review'.[31]

Once it had abandoned the good faith test in later cases, the AB demonstrated that there could be other legal questions linked to an objective assessment of facts, of a lesser degree than a violation of good faith, which could necessitate an AB review. The AB thus substituted the more stringent good faith test with other legal questions that were less alarming, such as a Panel substituting a member's judgment in *US–Cotton Yarn*, examining claims that had not been made in *Chile–Agricultural Products*, and a double standard of proof discriminating the defendant in favour of the complainants in *Korea–Alcohol*.

The AB in *EC–Hormones* basically stated that it reviews only such assessments by Panels that have the gravity to constitute a violation of a member's right (the right to due process) rather than those relating to 'a question of law' (which does not infringe upon a member's right) or merely a question of fact.

Under the good faith test in *EC–Hormones*, the AB intervenes only when the assessment of the Panel gives rise to a *new violation* of a member's right (and not to the violation, which a member may claim another member has committed). Thus, good faith seems to translate into the duty of Panels to respect, and the duty of the AB to safeguard and enforce, the right of members to fundamental fairness and due process of law or natural justice.

In subsequent cases, the AB has relaxed this standard and determined that because an objective assessment of facts is a question of law, its violation, in the absence of any additional conduct contrary to good faith or that infringes the rights of members to fundamental fairness, is sufficient to render its review consistent with its obligation under Article 17.6 DSU.

What function does good faith embody in Article 11 DSU? In my opinion it serves to delimit the extent of the Panel's rights and obligations in relation to the AB's power of review and more importantly, enforces the members' procedural rights against the Panels.

[30] Bronckers and McNelis, 2000, p 243.
[31] *EC–Hormones*, AB Report, para 132.

The Good Faith Standards of WTO Factual Review and ICJ Factual Review

The ICJ usually functions as court of first and final instance. It is only where it functions as a tribunal of review that questions of standard of review arise.[32] The ICJ's standard of review relating to facts will be briefly compared with the AB's development of its own standard of review for factual considerations of the Panels, which shifted from 'an egregious error calling into question the good faith' to 'empower[ing] itself to review the process of fact-finding by a Panel',[33] which amounts to 'neither engage in a *de novo* review nor to apply "total deference"'.[34]

The ICJ reviews judicial decisions of the following inferior courts:

— administrative tribunals, such as the Governing Body of the ILO and Administrative Board of the Pensions Fund (ILOAT), UN Secretary General, members of his or her staff (UNAT) and the WB;
— ad hoc international tribunals, such as the Arbitral Award of the King of Spain[35] and Arbitral Award of 31 July 198936; and
— decision-making bodies in the exercise of judicial or quasi-judicial functions, such as the UN Compensation Commission and the UN Iraq-Kuwait Boundary Demarcation Commission.[37]

In all other instances the ICJ acts as a tribunal of review to non-judicial organs, such as: when firstly 'the constitutive convention and other instruments of an international organization provide Member States with a general right of "appeal" against the acts of one or more of its internal organs' (Appeal Relating to the Jurisdiction of the ICAO Council, where the ICJ held that the Council's action was within its powers contrary to what India had argued);[38] secondly, when it is explicitly requested to review the validity of an act of an organ or specialised agency (IMCO Maritime Safety Committee Advisory Opinion);[39] thirdly, when asked by the General Assembly or the Security Council to review the validity of decisions of international organisations other than those in Article 96, paragraph 2 of the UN Charter.[40]

It can be concluded that the AB's use of a standard of review vis-à-vis the Panel demonstrates that the WTO is a relatively advanced legal system within the international legal order because:

32 Kaikobad, 2000, pp 43, 77–90.

33 Oesch, 2003b, p 160, who states that the AB 'should not accept as lawful such a large amount of error in the assessment of the facts'.

34 *Ibid*, p 161.

35 ICJ Reports, 1960, p 192.

36 *Ibid*, 1991, p 53.

37 Kaikobad, 2000, p 33.

38 ICJ Reports 1972, p 69.

39 *Constitution of the Maritime Safety Committee of the Inter-Governmental Maritime Consultative Organization* (1959–1960), ICJ Advisory Opinion of 8 June 1960.

40 Kaikobad, 2000, pp 77–9.

— UN Members have only to a limited extent accepted judicial review of (administrative) tribunal decisions by the ICJ.
— The tribunals involved all are administrative tribunals (in contrast to the Panels, which have jurisdiction over Member States but not over administrative matters at the WTO).
— The entities entitled to demand review by the ICJ are not States (UNAT, ILOAT).[41]
— The fact that it was agreed on 11 December 1995 to delete the option of judicial review of UNAT decisions by the ICJ from the statute of the UN Administrative Tribunal, demonstrates the lack of interest shown by the UN system in judiciaries.[42]

The new Article 11 of the UNAT statute simply provides that the Secretary General or the applicant may apply to the UNAT for a revision of a judgment 'on the basis of the discovery of some fact of such a nature as to be a decisive factor'.[43] Even if this revision procedure applies to facts, it is of no interest for a comparison with the appellate standard of review relating to facts at the WTO, because since 1995 it is the UNAT itself that 'reviews' its own opinion and not a superior court that assesses the factual considerations of a lower court.[44]

Under the now deleted Article 11 UNAT statute were the grounds for legal action which the UNAT had:

— exceeded its jurisdiction or competence;
— erred on a question of law relating to the provisions of the UN Charter;
— failed to exercise jurisdiction vested in it; or
— committed a fundamental error in procedure that had occasioned a failure of justice.

As a court of appeal, the AB, in contrast to the ICJ, is entitled within certain limits—which have fluctuated from strict to more relaxed over time—to conduct a review of the Panels' factual considerations. The issue of good faith as a threshold to trigger a review on factual considerations is—in terms of international law—unique to the WTO, and even within WTO law, has its critics.

[41] Even if Art 34, para 1 of the ICJ statute, says that only States may be parties in cases before the Court, Arts XII ILOAT and the pre-1995 Art 11 UNAT statute are considered 'to avoid this difficulty while nevertheless securing an examination by and a decision of the Court by means of a Request, emanating from the Executive Board, for an Advisory Opinion'. *Judgments of the Administrative Tribunal of the International Labour Organization upon Complaints Made Against the United Nations Educational, Scientific and Cultural Organization*, ICJ Advisory Opinion 3 October 1956, p 522.

[42] Kaikobad, 2000, p 278, referring to Resolution 50/54.

[43] Art 11 of the statute of the Administrative Tribunal of the UN.

[44] Compare Art 11 of the statute of the Administrative Tribunal of the UN, with Art 11 of the statute of the Administrative Tribunal of the UN adopted by a 1955 General Assembly Amendment: vide Resolution 957(X) 8 November 1955 and amended on 11 December 1995 by resolution 50/54.

Case Law of Appellate Decisions

This section will describe how the *EC–Hormones* and other AB reports have introduced a standard of good faith under Article 11 DSU to allow the AB to assess the objectivity of a Panel's appreciation of facts. After laying out the jurisprudence which introduced the AB's standard of review, the next part of this chapter will describe the development of a new AB standard of factual review which replaces the *EC–Hormones* standard of appellate review.

EC–Hormones *Appellate Body Report (1998)*

The good faith standard of Article 11 DSU in *EC–Hormones* introduced procedural rights for the WTO Member States against the Panel. Good faith implied in Article 11 DSU thus functioned to balance the members' good faith duties vis-à-vis a Panel derived from Article 3.10 DSU. While the first creates members' due process rights, the other protects one member from the consequences of the other member's abuse of its due process rights. However, both obligations are narrow, as the first relates only to the factual considerations of the Panels and does not expand to legal assessments, and the second applies only to due process rights which relate to the settlement of disputes.

EC–Poultry *Appellate Body Report (1998)*

Brazil brought an appeal based on the Panel's alleged failure to make an 'objective assessment of the matter before it' as required by Article 11 DSU.[45] The AB found the allegation that the Panel failed to conduct 'an objective assessment of the matter before it'[46] unsubstantiated because it had neither engaged in an abuse of discretion (*Argentina–Footwear Safeguards*),[47] nor committed 'an egregious error calling into question the good faith of the Panel' (*EC–Hormones*).[48] According to the AB, the Panel had merely exercised 'judicial economy' in deciding not to hear all arguments in support of the various claims that Brazil had submitted to the Panel, but had not engaged in 'an abuse of discretion amounting to a failure to render an objective assessment of facts before it'.[49] The AB said:

> We note, furthermore, that Brazil's appeal under Article 11 of the DSU relates, in effect, to the judicial economy exercised by the Panel in its consideration of a number of arguments in support of the various claims that Brazil submitted to the Panel. Brazil argues that the Panel, in effect, abused its discretion in not addressing in the Panel

[45] *EC–Poultry*, AB Report, para 132.
[46] See *ibid*, para 134.
[47] *Ibid*, para 133.
[48] *Ibid*.
[49] *Ibid*, para 135.

Report a series of arguments Brazil made in relation to GATT/WTO law and practice.[50]

The AB added that since an allegation under Article 11 DSU 'is a very serious allegation' that 'goes to the very core of the integrity of the WTO dispute settlement process',[51] the failures imputed to the Panel by Brazil 'do not approach the level of gravity required for a claim under Article 11 DSU to prevail'.[52]

For its argument in the *EC–Poultry* case, the AB derived from the *US–Shirts and Blouses* decision, that nothing in Article 11 DSU requires a Panel to assess all the legal claims. Pursuant to the *US–Shirts and Blouses* jurisprudence, a Panel may choose to address only those legal claims that contribute to dispose of the matter being disputed. A fortiori, according to the AB, the Panel enjoys 'the discretion to address only those arguments it deems necessary to resolve a particular claim'.[53] For these reasons the AB found that if the Panel had failed to consider member practice relating to tariff rate quotas under Article XXVIII or other evidence (namely the MFN exceptions) and had instead based its finding that the *EC–Brazil Oilseeds* Agreement contained MFN inconsistent, specific tariff rate quotas for frozen poultry meat, solely on Article XXVIII, per se, the level of gravity of the Panel's failure did not approach that required for finding a breach of Article 11 DSU.[54]

EC–Poultry follows in the footsteps of *EC–Hormones* because it bases its standard of review of facts on the stringent criteria established in *EC–Hormones*.[55] As in *EC–Hormones* the AB found the Panel's failure to consider member practice under an MFN exception not serious enough to substantiate the claim of an Article 11 violation.[56]

The importance of *EC–Poultry* lies in its two additional rationales for understanding why the AB 'developed a fairly rigorous system for determining when a Panel failed to make an objective assessment of the facts'.[57] First, a finding that a Panel breached Article 11 of the DSU 'goes to the very core of the integrity of the WTO dispute settlement process itself'.[58] Secondly, Panels are guided by the principle of judicial economy (eg they need not examine member practice relating to the implementation of GATT Article XXVIII, but can simply rely on the fact that Article XXVIII exists).[59]

A comparison between *EC–Hormones* and *EC–Poultry* shows that the AB offered different *ratio legis* for identical claims alleging a violation of Article 11

[50] *EC–Poultry*, AB Report, para 135.
[51] *Ibid*, para 133.
[52] *Ibid*, para 134.
[53] *Ibid*, para 135.
[54] See *ibid*, paras 133–6; see also paras 24–5 for Brazil's allegations under Art 11 DSU.
[55] See Kuyper, 2000, p 317.
[56] Compare *EC–Poultry*, AB Report, paras 134–6 with *EC–Hormones*, AB Report, paras 132–49, 253(e); see also Oesch, 2003b, p 159.
[57] Oesch, 2003b, p 159.
[58] See *EC–Poultry*, AB Report, para 133.
[59] *Ibid*, para 135.

DSU. The AB in *EC–Hormones* emphasized that a claim under Article 11 DSU 'is, in effect, . . . denies the party submitting the evidence fundamental fairness, or what in many jurisdictions is known as due process of law or natural justice'.[60] In contrast, in *EC–Poultry* it said that an allegation of a failure of the Panel to conduct the 'objective assessment of the matter before it' required by Article 11 of the DSU 'is a very serious allegation'. 'Such an allegation goes to the very core of the integrity of the WTO dispute settlement process itself'.

Moreover, in *EC–Poultry* the AB implied that judicial economy (limitation of the AB's scope of factual review) overrides members' rights to fairness and due process (initially advanced by the AB in *EC–Hormones* as the reason for introducing its review of the Panel's factual considerations under Article 17.6 DSU).

Thus, while the *EC–Hormones* decision emphasized arguments of fairness and due process, with which we are already familiar from the obligation of parties to resolve a dispute in good faith under Articles 3.7, 3.10 and 4.3 DSU, the later *EC–Poultry* decision stressed the systemic consequences of an allegation of violation of Article 11 DSU. Both concerns are of equivalent weight and consequence, but have opposing goals. Whereas the members' due process rights 'inform', 'underlie' and 'are inherent' to the DSU, accusing a Panel of violating the members' due process rights is an equally fundamental allegation against one of the two pillars of an effectively functioning dispute settlement system.[61] While the first goal would favour aggrandization of the AB's scope of factual review, by applying less stringent criteria than for good faith, the second would favour a restriction of the AB's standard of review for Panel's factual decisions.

Why was a different *ratio legis* put forward by the AB in these two different cases? Is it because in the *EC–Hormones* case it was more the fairness of the evidence-gathering that was at issue, whereas in *EC–Poultry* the claim was more against the judicial economy exercised by the Panel in evaluating the arguments of the parties relating to the claims submitted to the Panel, and thus touching more upon the general nature of WTO dispute settlement rather than being an issue of fairness between the parties to a dispute?

The AB in *EC–Poultry* argued that a negative effect on the rights of a member, or a more serious question of law, must be involved rather than mere considerations of judicial economy by the Panel, in order for the AB to review a Panel's factual conclusions.

It seems like the *EC–Poultry* AB Report had already lowered its standard from the very high standard of egregious error, finding a violation of law sufficiently serious to trigger the AB's review, because the AB only delimits the lower threshold for its factual review, ie it must not become active for a simple exercise in judicial economy by the Panel.[62]

[60] *EC–Hormones*, AB Report para 133.

[61] Compare *India–Patents*, AB Report, para 94; *Mexico–HFCS (Art 21.5)*, AB Report, para 105; *Chile–Agricultural Products*, AB Report, para 176 with *EC–Poultry*, AB Report, para 133.

[62] See *EC–Poultry*, AB Report, para 135.

Australia–Salmon *Appellate Body Report (1998)*

The *Australia–Salmon* Panel had found that Australia's SPS measures, which prohibited the entry of fresh, chilled and frozen salmon, were overly broad for the risk assessed.[63] Australia alleged on appeal that the Panel had considered scientific studies ('Vose Report') that were either irrelevant or 'too general' (eg the Panel looked only at smoked salmon) for assessing the risk to Australia's salmon population. Based upon Article 11 DSU, Australia added that the Panel had 'seriously mischaracterised' the process relating to, as well as the character and purpose of the Australian government draft reports, the government's recommendations and legislation.[64] Australia also contended that the Panel had 'partially or wholly ignored relevant evidence placed before it, or misrepresented evidence in a way that went beyond a mere question of the weight attributed to it, but constituted an egregious error amounting to an error of law'.[65]

The AB concluded that even if Australia alleged that the way in which the Panel misrepresented evidence constituted an 'egregious error amounting to an error of law',[66] the two allegations described were in no way serious enough to constitute an 'allegation that goes to the very core of the integrity of the WTO dispute settlement process'. The AB said:

> In our view, the Panel did not 'deliberately disregard', 'refuse to consider', 'wilfully distort' or 'misrepresent' the evidence in this case; nor has Australia demonstrated in any way that the Panel committed an 'egregious error that calls into question the good faith' of the Panel. We, therefore, conclude that the Panel did not abuse its discretion in a manner, which even comes close to attaining the level of gravity required for a claim under Article 11 of the DSU to prevail.[67]

As regards the allegation by Australia that the Panel had failed 'to accord "due deference" to matters of fact it put forward',[68] this failure also did not amount to an infringement of the fairness the Panel has to guarantee the parties to a dispute, because 'Panels, however, are not required to accord to factual evidence of the parties the same meaning and weight as do the parties'.[69] Thus, a Panel is not under an obligation to consider every factual issue submitted by the parties to a dispute; a Panel's duty is only not to 'ignore' such facts. This in turn means that Article 11 DSU requires a Panel to give a reasoned statement as to why it considers certain facts irrelevant.

Even if members have a due process right that their evidence be considered, Kuyper made the criticism that conditioning the realisation of their right (the AB's review) on showing that the Panel had considered the 'Vose report' (in

[63] See *Australia–Salmon*, Panel Report, paras 9.2–9.3.
[64] *Ibid*, AB Report, para 263; see also paras 7–8 for Australia's arguments.
[65] *Australia–Salmon*, AB Report, para 262.
[66] *Ibid.*
[67] *Ibid*, para 266.
[68] *Ibid*, para 267.
[69] *Ibid.*

Australia–Salmon) was 'charging Australia with [an] impossible task'.[70] Thus, members have a due process right under the DSU that their findings of evidence be considered; however, members can enforce this right only if they can prove that a Panel dismissing evidence submitted by the members has failed to provide a reason for the non-consideration.

Because *Australia–Salmon* concerned the erroneous consideration of a deliberate disregard of scientific evidence as grounds for Article 11 DSU, it is more closely related to *EC–Hormones* than to *Korea–Alcohol*, which concerned the allocation of a double standard of proof, and where the AB would have examined the claim if Korea could have proven discriminatory treatment, without the need for it to prove the Panel's breach of good faith.

Thus, it seems that the good faith test has to date been limited to issues of objective assessment of scientific evidence and member practice relating to MFN exceptions (*EC–Hormones*, *Australia–Salmon*, *EC–Poultry*), but has not been used to review the 'simple' procedural issue of discriminatory allocation of the burden of proof (*Korea–Alcohol*).

The AB created the *good faith test* and subsequently applied it, exclusively in cases of *exceptions* to the multilateral trading system (Article XX, SPS Agreement and regionalism, Article XXIV GATT), where it had an interest in having a standard so high as to be able to avoid reviewing the Panel decisions, which had carried out their duty by concentrating exclusively on free trade to the exclusion of the other values inherent in the WTO system (human, plant and animal health, consumer protection and regionalism).[71]

Korea–Alcohol *Appellate Body Report (1999)*

In *Korea–Alcohol*, Korea asked the AB to 'lower the present standard'[72] of factual review by the Panel as the AB would be 'introducing new criteria' for the term 'objective assessment'.[73] The US suggested that the AB reject these proposals, as they would require the US to undertake a *de novo* factual review, thereby contradicting Article 17.6 of the DSU.[74] Korea did not assert that the Panel had acted in bad faith, but 'believes that the matters it has raised under Article 11 of the DSU are, nonetheless, serious enough to merit reversal of the Panel's conclusions'.[75]

Korea alleged that the Panel also failed to accord due deference to Korea's description of its own market. Korea believed that, when faced with conflicting descriptions of a foreign market, a Panel should be very careful in making

[70] Kuyper, 2000, p 319.

[71] *Cf* Howse, 2000, p 54, who argues that the AB should adhere to general public international law in order to avoid 'privileging a single value, that of free trade'.

[72] See *Korea–Alcohol*, AB Report, para 85, Korea alleges this because showing an error so egregious that it calls into question the good faith of the Panel is a high standard.

[73] *Ibid*, paras 40 and 86.

[74] See *ibid* para 86.

[75] *Ibid*, para 40.

assertions about what this market is like and should certainly not engage in speculation about its possible future development. Where there was disagreement between the parties about the Korean market, the Panel should have accepted Korea's description, unless the complainants brought compelling evidence to the contrary.[76]

However, the EC (the appellee), like the US, said that 'the "deferential" standard of review advocated by Korea finds no support in either the DSU or the GATT 94'.[77] Although Korea did not allege or succeed in showing that the Panel committed an egregious error, the AB, nevertheless considered whether the Panel had failed to conduct an objective assessment.

The AB found the allegation that the Panel had applied a double standard of proof (more exacting on the defendant (Korea) than on the complainants) was a sufficiently legal issue to cause it to enter into consideration of the matter under Article 11.[78] The AB no longer requires a member to bring a claim under Article 11 and to challenge the Panel's good faith. It has thus relaxed, to a certain extent, its *EC–Hormones* jurisprudence, where the egregious error test had to be proven before an appellate review of a Panel's factual misinterpretation could start:

> In our view, notwithstanding Korea's express disclaimer that it is not challenging the good faith of the Panel, an allegation of a 'double standard' of proof in relation to the facts is equivalent to an allegation of failure to render an 'objective assessment of the matter' under Article 11 of the DSU.[79]

Although there is no codification of allocation of burden of proof in the Agreements, the AB, on the basis of its jurisprudence in *US–Underwear*, nevertheless considered Korea's allegation an issue of law, because it refered to the burden of proof.

Consequently, the AB held that, an allocation of the burden of proof discriminating in favour of the defendant over the complainant is such a 'serious allegation that it goes to the very core of the integrity of the WTO dispute settlement system process itself'. The AB was careful to emphasize, through the use of its language ('rules') and preceding decisions (*US–Underwear*), not only that burden of proof, specifically its allocation, is a '*rule*', and thus a legal question (in the sense of paragraph 132 *EC–Hormones*), but in addition, that equal allocation of the burden of proof equally between the complainant and defendant is a due process *right* of the dispute. However, in result, the AB denied Korea a finding that the Panel's factual assessment was in breach of Article 11 DSU. It held that Korea could not prove a discriminatory allocation of burden of proof by the Panel, ie that the Panel had imposed a different burden of proof on the parties to the same dispute.[80]

[76] *Korea–Alcohol*, AB Report, para 39.
[77] *Ibid*, para 68.
[78] See *ibid*, para 163.
[79] *Ibid*.
[80] See *ibid*, paras 164–5.

The *Korea–Alcohol* appellate decision shows that the AB is prepared to apply a looser standard than good faith/bad faith for reviewing a Panel's assessment of facts. It merely needs to be a question of law (which it automatically is when a party alleges a violation of Article 11 DSU) and, according to the *EC–Poultry* formula, go 'to the very core of the integrity of the WTO dispute settlement process itself', as the AB cited in *Korea–Alcohol*.[81]

However, similarly to *EC–Hormones*, where the AB had found the EC's claim as to distortion of evidence unsubstantiated,[82] the AB in *Korea–Alcohol* also found Korea's claims to be unsubstantiated, because 'it is not an error, let alone an egregious error for the Panel to fail to accord the weight to the evidence that one of the parties believes it should be accorded to'.[83]

While, in theory, in *Korea–Alcohol*, maintaining a double standard of proof qualified, as with a distortion of evidence in the *EC–Hormones*, as failure to objectively assess the matter before it, in practice the AB found the arguments brought by the parties when 'read together with the Panel Report and the record of the Panel proceedings' 'not to disclose' the failure alleged by the parties.[84]

Doctrinal Division on the Good Faith Standard of Factual Review

In conclusion, we will discuss how different authors in literature have interpreted the *EC–Hormone's* good faith standard of Panel and appellate review for factual issues.

Oesch proposes the most stringent standard, saying that it must be established by the appellant that a Panel deliberately disregarded or distorted the evidence *and* that the egregious error calls into question the good faith of a Panel.[85] Oesch's view that a deliberate disregard coupled with an egregious error calling into question the good faith of a Panel is the standard threshold level of evidence, seems to disregard the fact that the AB itself has suggested that there can be instances where a Panel does not deliberately disregard or distort evidence, but where there is gross negligence amounting to bad faith. Thus, Oesch seems to reduce the formula with the effect that the AB can effectively pursue only intentional, but not grossly negligent conduct by Panels.

Lugard supports a considerably lower threshold level of evidence. Parties alleging an infringement of Article 11 DSU would have to show *either* that a Panel deliberately disregarded or distorted evidence *or* that the Panel engaged in gross negligence amounting to bad faith.[86] Unlike Oesch, Lugard asserts that the element of good faith need not be proven for every allegation of an Article 11

[81] *Ibid* para 163.
[82] See *ibid*, para 165; *EC–Hormones*, AB Report, para 145.
[83] *Korea–Alcohol*, AB Report, para 164.
[84] *Ibid*; *EC–Hormones*, AB Report, paras 135–9, 143–5.
[85] See Oesch, 2003b, pp 160–1.
[86] See Lugard, p 325.

DSU infringement.[87] According to Lugard, the AB should find proof of deliberate disregard or distortion of evidence sufficient for reversing a Panel's factual findings.

The criteria of an action contrary to good faith (or bad faith) need not be proven each and every time a member alleges a violation of Article 11 DSU by the Panel, because the 'disregard, distortion and misrepresentation of the evidence' '*implies*' 'an egregious error that *calls into question* the good faith of a Panel' (italics added), said the AB in *EC–Hormones*. This statement somewhat contradicts Lugard's assertion that parties alleging a Panel's failure to comply with the duty to assess the facts, must show that a Panel has acted in bad faith, or has demonstrated behaviour contrary to good faith.[88] While paragraph 133 of the *EC–Hormones* decision and a subsequent paragraph do say, 'However, this mistake on the part of the Panel in interpreting Dr Lucier's statement does not constitute a *deliberate* disregard of evidence or *gross* negligence amounting to bad faith'(italics in original),[89] it can nevertheless be interpreted to mean that once deliberate disregard or gross negligence has been shown, the AB *implies* a good faith violation.

The later *Australia–Salmon* case, which based itself on a narrow interpretation of the standard of review introduced in *EC–Hormones*, clearly required that the member alleging an infringement of Article 11 DSU by the Panel prove an egregious error calling into question the good faith of the Panel, in addition to the deliberate disregard of evidence.[90]

Wirth criticises the AB's standard of review as 'highly deferential to the Panels'.[91] Similarly, Lugard has predicted that the AB's decisions not to 'immediately reverse the findings of a Panel, even where it made mistakes' will lead to systemic consequences for future Panels, which will 'perform a less accurate assessment of the facts'.[92]

Lugard warned in 1998 that the deliberate distortion or bad faith standard would be much more difficult to prove than earlier criteria developed in the *Canada-Periodicals case* (which did not include a subjective element).[93]

Organs of an international organization must exercise their power in good faith. The inverse also applies, ie the organs are prohibited from exercising their power arbitrarily, whether the arbitrariness constitutes unreasonable conduct or is associated with the manifest intention to commit wrong. In the general public international legal context, Zoller does not distinguish good faith and bad faith from subjective elements such as arbitrariness or intention. According

[87] *Ibid.*

[88] See *EC–Hormones*, AB Report, para 133.

[89] *Ibid*, para 138.

[90] See *Australia–Salmon*, AB Report, para 266; see also Kuyper, 2000, p 317, who agrees that the *Australia–Salmon* case 'maintained' the good faith standard of *EC–Hormones*.

[91] Wirth, 1998, p 758.

[92] Lugard, p 325.

[93] See *ibid*.

to Zoller, acting contrary to good faith already constitutes subjective conduct.[94]

Deliberate Disregard (Intention) or Gross Negligence ('Unreasonable Conduct')

A pertinent question is whether for the WTO, good faith or bad faith express a reasoned and objective conduct, distinct from subjective expressions of conduct such as negligence and intention.[95] For Lugard, who does not compare the AB's standard of review with that of other international appellate courts, the WTO standards of showing either deliberate disregard or gross negligence amounting to bad faith, 'seem to request that the parties prove that a Panel had the *aim* or the *intention* to act contrary to due process requirements' (italics in original).[96] Oesch, who does compare WTO adjudication with general public international court practice, says that the AB does not adopt the 'clearly or manifestly erroneous' or 'substantial evidence' standard of traditional (international) appellate courts.[97]

If the WTO AB's standard of review, or the limits of a Panel's assessment of facts, are compared with the limits imposed on the actions of organs in general public international law, the AB's definition seems either less stringent (Oesch) or more stringent (Lugard) than standards of public international law.[98] It's standard is equal to that of international law if it is a matter of either deliberate disregard (intention) or gross negligence ('unreasonable conduct').

The WTO's good faith standard for controlling the actions of its organs is more stringent than in general public international law, if the condition under which the AB will intervene is that the appealing party must show that the Panel deliberately disregarded the evidence (intention) *and* committed an egregious error, which called into question its good faith (arbitrariness).[99]

Oesch apparently distinguishes the demonstration of a subjective element (deliberate disregard) from the standard of good faith. Oesch does not consider deliberate disregard to be the same thing as acting contrary to good faith, as Zoller does. Oesch's view dissociates good faith and bad faith from the subjective element, because good faith expresses a reasonable measure for the conduct of Panels and not a purely subjective expression that varies from case to case.

In the last few years fewer members have brought appeals based on disputes over issues of fact, perhaps because of the practical impossibility of proving deliberate disregard or bad faith. The AB, only two years after its introduction

[94] See Zoller, 1977, pp 190–1.
[95] See Lugard, p 325.
[96] *Ibid.*
[97] See *EC–Hormones*, AB Report, paras 133 and 138 and *Australia–Salmon*, AB Report, para 266.
[98] See Oesch, 2003b, pp 159–69, pp 239ff.
[99] *Ibid*, p 160.

of the good faith/bad faith standard for appellate review of facts, relaxed the standard by dismissing the bad faith standard.

Science and the Facts: Narrow or Broad Appellate Standard of Review

The way the AB upheld the Panel's findings relating to science in *EC–Hormones* and *Australia–Salmon* has been found to 'concentrate[s] substantial, virtually unreviewable discretion on questions of science in the dispute settlement Panels'.[100] It was precisely because science was involved, this study maintains, that the AB during *Australia–Salmon* tightened its standard of review regarding factual considerations of the Panels.

The AB's very high standard was purposefully chosen to avoid a stream of members appealing against the Panels' considerations of scientific expert opinion, which in contrast to other factual considerations such as dumping margins or determination of injury in relation to safeguards or countervailing duty action, usually brought by interest groups, do not pass a first review by national investigating authorities before being brought to the Panel. These opinons are thus more subject to the influence of interest groups and are consequently more vulnerable to allegations that the Panel did not objectively assess them.

Jackson finds that because a Panel's fact-gathering resources 'compare negatively to national agencies', the 'expertise argument' speaks for a rather 'deferential standard of review of factual conclusions' by the Panels.[101] An identical argument reduces the scope of the AB's standard of review for facts in the light of the Panels' assessment of facts. The AB lacks the resources and the knowledge (because the WTO is composed of economists and lawyers) to properly investigate the Panel's factual findings on scientific matters.

REPLACING THE GOOD FAITH STANDARD OF FACTUAL REVIEW WITH THE GOOD FAITH OBLIGATIONS OF MEMBERS

In connection with the scope of the Panel's and, under certain circumstances, the AB's review of facts, the issue arises as to what extent the good faith obligations of a member engaging in a dispute (such as the obligation to provide the Panel with information on the facts of the case) may be used to substitute for a Panel's examination of facts. If such a construct proves both consistent with the DSU and effective in practice, the substitution of the factual review by the Panels with the good faith obligation of the members under Articles 13.1 and 3.10 DSU could then also serve to dispense with the AB having to review the facts.

100 Wirth, 1998, p 758.
101 Jackson, 2000, p 154.

As WTO practice shows, such a development has taken place in WTO jurisprudence, where the AB's standard of factual review has evolved, eventually leading to it 'abandoning the *EC–Hormones* criteria':[102]

— The AB has conceded that all allegations criticising a Panel's consideration of facts are legal issues because the objective assessment of facts by the Panels is regulated by *positive law* (Article 11 DSU).[103] Moreover, the AB has followed through on its reasoning in *EC–Hormones* that factual issues touch upon *general principles of law* such as fundamental fairness and due process.[104] Thus, it considers the strict 'bad faith' standard for factual reviewed no longer necessary for complying with the terms of Article 17.6 DSU, since questions of fact would all become legal questions given that either Article 11 or the general principle of law of due process would be at stake.
— The good faith standard may be a one-time, intentional creation by the AB for the resolution of conflicts involving scientific and other non-trade values. In order to promote the values of free trade over the conflicting values of consumer protection, regionalism, and in particular, health, the *EC–Hormones*, *Australia–Salmon*, and *EC–Poultry* AB Reports developed the depth of factual review for the AB. As there have since been no such cases, the AB has not had to resort to its *EC–Hormones, Australia–Salmon* and *EC–Poultry* good faith standard. Thus, it is only by chance, rather than a fundamental shift in AB jurisprudence, that the factual standard of review has been relaxed.
— In most cases adjudicated with the principle of good faith, scientific evidence has had to be reviewed. As the WTO has limited 'fact-gathering resources', the AB has preferred to set the standard of review high.[105]
— The predictability and impartiality,[106] as well as the credibility[107] of the WTO legal system may be impaired because the AB is unable to overturn correct decisions based upon wrong facts.[108] Thus, there need not be a violation of a member's right, but a violation of rule (such as Article 11 DSU) for the AB to address factual review.
— None of the claims based on the *EC–Hormones* standard of review were successful.[109]

[102] See Oesch, 2003b, pp 163–6.
[103] *Ibid*, p 161; *EC–Hormones*, AB Report, para 132.
[104] See *EC–Hormones*, AB Report, para 133; see also Bronckers and McNelis, 1999, p 242, pleading that the AB consider reviewable a Panel's failure to respect the 'general principles of law, such as due process'.
[105] Jackson, 2000, p 154.
[106] See Oesch, 2003b, p 160.
[107] Bronckers and McNelis, p 243.
[108] Based on an interview with Lothar Ehring, WTO Legal Division, 5 June 2003; see also Bronckers and McNelis, pp 243, 252.
[109] See Oesch, 2003b, pp 161ff.

— It is possible that the AB sought to move closer to the less stringent standards of other appellate courts under public international law.[110]
— As suggested by Tarullo, the AB might have 'chosen to disregard' the good faith test in AD/CVD cases in order to be able to review (and overturn) national authorities' restrictions on free trade.[111] The AB dismissed the egregious error/good faith standard and opened the way for reaching decisions that were both correct in terms of the law and, especially, accurate on the facts. With the possible exception of the *US–Cotton Yarn* case, the AB lowered its standard of review for factual issues. The resulting increase in legal security, stability and credibility enhances the constitutional dimension of WTO law.[112] Thus, it is not the presence of the good faith standard of review, but its abolition, that establishes the WTO legal order as a constitutional order.

In later cases relating to the standard of review for factual considerations by the Panels, the AB has dismissed the good faith criteria and allowed for 'simple' questions of law linked to facts to be reviewed by the AB. Oesch has proposed two factors as being mainly responsible for this shift in jurisprudence.

The first factor involves the three sub-standard that actually make up the standard. A Panel must have a) *deliberately* disregarded or distorted the evidence, which must b) comstitute an *egregious error*, which must c) call into question the *good faith* of the Panel. These sub-standards make up an 'extremely stringent' criterion, which 'appears to be almost impossible to establish in practice'.[113] The second factor is that neither *EC–Hormones* nor the subsequent cases that supposedly followed its standard, contributed to further clarification of the standard of review of facts.[114]

Since 1999, there have been calls for the AB to change its standards for dealing with Panel errors of fact that infringe upon members' due process rights.[115] Even if 'letting clear errors' stand would be the price of the 'remarkable speed' 'for which the WTO dispute settlement system is known', Bronckers and McNelis in 1999 pleaded for the AB to relax its 'bad faith' standard, because they rated the detrimental impact of correct Panel decisions based on wrong facts on the credibility of the DSU higher than the benefits of the relative speedy dispute resolution of the DSU following the AB's limited review of facts.[116]

[110] *Ibid*, pp 159–60, who defines these standards as 'clearly or manifestly erroneous' or 'substantial evidence'.

[111] See Tarullo, 2002, p 153.

[112] See Cameron and Campbell, 1998, p 21, 'the AB displays the attributes of a constitutional legal chamber, which contributes rules, to guide the conduct of members. Recent cases have included observations on the correct way to interpret obligations; general principles of international law applicable to the conduct of the dispute, such as legitimate expectation, due process or procedural fairness'.

[113] Oesch, 2003b, p 160 with references to Kuyper, 2000, p 317 and Lugard, 1998, p 325.

[114] See *ibid*, pp 157–66.

[115] Bronckers and McNelis, 1999, p 243; see also Kuyper, 2000, p 317.

[116] See *ibid*, pp 243, 252; see also L Ehring, interview.

General public international law applies a less stringent standard for containing the powers of organs than good faith.[117] As Zoller says, in this case the principle of legality suffices for delimiting the powers of organs, which includes considerations based upon the object and purpose of an organisation. The major difference between the good faith delimitation of powers and the non-good faith means to control the conduct of an organ is that the latter do not contain any subjective element. It is pure recourse to the adequacy, proportionality (between the objective and the final result) and the object and purpose of the treaty that determine whether an organ has overstepped its discretion.[118]

However, it should be noted that in none of the cases adjudicated under the new standard of review, was science involved. Under the previous standard, two of the five cases adjudicated had involved science.[119] The last case before the shift of jurisprudence in *US–Wheat Gluten* on 22 December 2000, was *Australia–Salmon* on 6 November 1998, which related to the evaluation by the Panel of scientific facts. At issue was whether the Panel had considered—contrary to its own determination—the 'Vose Report',[120] and this stringent standard (of *EC–Hormones*) was applied precisely.[121] Thus, the question is whether the stricter *EC–Hormones* standard remains valid for appellate review of scientific facts. A future case will show.

Another reason for the AB to relax its standard of review regarding facts, is that it has no remand authority;[122] thus, factual assessments cannot be given back to the Panel for further deliberations. Therefore, the responsibility to ensure that the WTO 'DSU remains the central element in providing security and predictability to the multilateral trading system' vests within the AB.[123]

US–Cotton Yarn Appellate Body Report (2001)

In *US–Cotton Yarn*, the Panel had to review the US authority's determination of serious damage or actual threat thereof. The US had imposed a transitional

[117] See Zoller, 1977, p 196, '[L]e manquement à la bonne foi n'est parfois pas nécessaire pour vicier la compétence exercée'.

[118] *Ibid*, p 197, '[C']est à dire que dans la determination de cette illicéité, aucun élément subjectif n'entre en considération. Il s'agit de rechercher l'adéquation, la compatibilité enter le but de la compétence exercée (résultat final) et le but et l'objet du trait constitutif'.

[119] See Oesch, 2003b, pp 122ff, the two cases were *EC–Hormones* (16 January 1998) and *Australia–Salmon* (6 November 1998), the others where *Japan–Agricultural Products*; *EC–Poultry* and *Korea–Alcohol*.

[120] *Australia–Salmon*, AB Report, paras 268–78.

[121] See *ibid*, para 266.

[122] See Bacchus, 2002, p 1028.

[123] Art 3.2 DSU; in analogy to Davey, 1992, pp 309–10, who explains that because of the remand authority of the CIT, appeals to the Federal Circuit are greatly delayed and often never reviewed. For this reason, the CIT has adopted an 'intensive review'.

textile safeguard against Pakistani cotton imports under Article 6 ATC.[124] The *US–Cotton Yarn* AB Report of 2001 is the only case to date which links a member's obligation of procedural good faith to cooperate in investigations with the Panel's standard of review relating to the facts.

The US asked the AB whether the Panel was entitled to take into account evidence relating to facts which predated the US authority's determination of damage.[125]

The US had objected against the use by the Panel of the Official US Census data for 1998. Pakistan had submitted to censure the US safeguard measure for being based on 'unverified, incorrect and incomplete data'.[126] The Panel ruled in favour of Pakistan and in line with its earlier decision in *Argentina-Footwear*.[127] The Panel concluded that it was entitled to use such data—even if they had neither been available nor had been considered at the time of the investigation.[128]

On appeal, the US argued that the Panel had exceeded its mandate under Article 11 DSU.[129] The new data was not found by the Panel to 'vitiate' the result of the US determination and did not lead the Panel to ask the US to lift its safeguard.[130] The US nevertheless appealed to the AB that its due process right—that Panels abstain from substituting their own judgment for that of the members—had been violated, because the Panel had considered evidence that was not in existence at the time the US made its determination of serious injury.[131]

The AB summarised its jurisprudence on the Panel's standard of review, citing jurisprudence specifically relating to safeguards in the ATC and ASG (*US–Shirts and Blouses, US–Underwear, Argentina–Footwear, US–Lamb, US–Wheat Gluten*).[132] The *US–Cotton Yarn* decision consolidated the key elements of the Panel's standard of review relating to facts.[133] *US–Cotton Yarn* concluded that Panels must not conduct a *de novo* review of the evidence nor

[124] See *US–Cotton Yarn*, AB Report, para 74.

[125] *Ibid*, para 67; see also Oesch, 2003b, p 120.

[126] *US–Cotton Yarn*, AB Report, paras 62–3.

[127] See *ibid*, para 63; see also Oesch, 2003b, pp 118, 135, 174, for an overview of the *Argentina–Footwear* Panel decision and AB Report relating to the standard of review. The author describes how the Panel considered evidence which was not presented to the national authority at the time of the investigation regardless of whether it was possible to submit it at that time or not. (The evidence related to transactions which took place after the consultations had begun, but furnished further evidence of the transactions that had taken place earlier).

[128] See *US–Cotton Yarn*, AB Report, paras 62–3, with references to paras 7.33, 7.35 and 7.94 of the *US–Cotton Yarn* Panel Report where the Panel narrowly delimited the use of this evidence and stated that it would not be used to reinvestigate the market situation, but for examining whether the US investigating authority had thoroughly and sufficiently investigated and whether it had been justified to rely exclusively on the American Yarn Spinners Association data.

[129] *Ibid*, para 65.

[130] *Ibid*, para 64.

[131] *Ibid*, para 66, 78–80.

[132] *Ibid*, paras 70–3.

[133] See Oesch, 2003b, pp 107–8, 118; Oesch, 2003a, pp 648–50.

substitute their judgment for that of the competent authority.[134] Specifically, it pointed out that the Panel took into account census data the US had not known about at the time of its determination, in the context of assessing the due diligence of an importing member in making the determination under Article 6.2 ATC.[135]

The AB reprimanded the Panel for considering the census data, which amounted to using pre-determination evidence for establishing post-determination facts. The AB based its argument on the grounds that the Panel had exceeded its standard of review, because it had ventured beyond the examination of a member's due diligence and had substituted its judgment for the members' judgment which amounts to a *de novo* review.[136]

However, in its obiter dictum, the AB suggested, on the basis of the general principle of law of good faith, that the US lift the safeguard on its own motion, if the census data were to show that the determination had been incorrect. This obiter dictum demonstrates that even if a member has respected due diligence, it is not released from the duty to act in good faith.[137] Thus, the general principle of law of good faith adopts the corrective function.

The AB refrained from examining whether the US should be held in violation of good faith for not withdrawing the safeguard, possibly because the Panel's (unlawful) review of predetermination evidence brought to light that the safeguard was legitimate in the first place.

But not only was the good faith obligation unsubstantiated in *US–Cotton Yarn,* it could not become operational in practice. The question remained: who would be the entity charged with finding that a member has based its determination on incorrect facts when Panels are prohibited from investigating post-determination evidence relating to predetermination facts? This shows that good faith does not fill a *lacuna* in WTO law, but serves to diffuse a politically sensitive situation. The standard of good faith excludes the Panel from reviewing certain facts but still ensures the same result the WTO desired in the first place: the only exception being that the duty shifts from the Panel to become an obligation of a member. The AB says:

> There is no need for the purpose of this appeal to express a view on the question whether an importing member would be under an *obligation*, flowing from the 'pervasive' general principle of *good faith* that underlies all treaties, to *withdraw* a safeguard measure if post-determination evidence relating to pre-determination facts were to emerge revealing that a determination was based on such a critical factual error that one of the conditions required by Article 6 turns out never to have been met.[138]

[134] *US–Cotton Yarn*, AB Report, para 74; *cf* Cottier and Oesch, 2005, p 168 on *de novo* review.
[135] *Ibid*, para 67; see also Oesch, 2003b, pp 120, 127–8.
[136] See *US–Cotton Yarn*, AB Report, para 80.
[137] *Ibid*, para 81.
[138] *US–Cotton Yarn*, AB Report, para 81 (italics in original, footnote omitted).

Thus, the AB found that a Panel had exceeded its mandate without there being any necessity for showing that a Panel had committed an egregious error that calls into question its good faith, or may otherwise have acted in bad faith. A finding that the Panel 'substituted its own judgment for that of the competent authority or that it conducted a *de novo* review'[139] is sufficient for finding that the Panel acted 'inconsistently with the standard of Panel's review under Article 11 of the DSU'.[140]

In the final analysis, the AB Report left the findings of the Panel, ie that the US safeguard measure was justified, unaltered, conceding to Pakistan only that the Panel had overstepped its standard of review. The AB said that it would not force members to have Panels investigate matters that will, in any case, be influenced by interest groups and thus not be objective (the determination of injury), but that in exchange it held the member should take the overall responsibility for imposing a fair safeguard.

Evaluation of *US–Cotton Yarn* Appellate Body Report (2001)

This decision of the AB has been described as inconsistent with Panel practice (which had considered post-determination evidence relevant to predetermination facts in *Argentina–Footwear*)[141] and 'as a limitation at odds with the active role which Panels have generally played in reviewing the "raw" evidence', but also as consistent with 'the established principle that Panels must not conduct a *de novo* review of the matter'.[142]

The gist of the AB's proposition was that it was not interested in encroaching upon the members' national sovereignty by expanding the Panel's standard of review in exchange for more WTO-consistent safeguard measures. Safeguards run counter to the WTO's aims of free trade anyway, and when they are allowed, they exist only on a temporary basis. Thus, there is no merit—or so the AB argued—for Panels to invest resources in order to achieve accuracy in reviewing safeguard determination.

Good faith to the AB substitutes for a more intrusive standard of review. The AB does not want the Panels to apply such an intrusive standard, because it does not want the Panels to waste time and resources in investigating national authorities' determinations, which will in any case be influenced by those interests that called for the safeguard in the first place.

In order to eliminate the too-high threshold to the Panel's standard of factual review (egregious error calling into question the good faith), the AB substantiated the claim that the Panel had exceeded its authority.[143] However, to balance

[139] *Ibid*, para 74.
[140] *Ibid*, para 78.
[141] See Oesch, 2003b, pp 117–24.
[142] *Ibid*, p 124.
[143] See *US–Cotton Yarn*, AB Report, para 80.

out the unfair result for the exporting party, the AB introduced the good faith duty of the importing member to withdraw a safeguard 'if post-determination evidence relating to pre-determination facts reveal that a determination was based on such a critical factual error that one of the conditions required by Article 6 turns out never to have been met'.[144]

As noted above, the pertinent question is who should investigate a claim that, under a good faith obligation, a member should have withdrawn a safeguard? Would a Panel still be prohibited from taking into account post-determination evidence relating to predetermination facts? We think not, because:

- the member, under *US–Cotton Yarn*, is now held responsible not under due diligence but under good faith for post-determination evidence relating to predetermination facts; and
- the duty of members does not stem from either the ATC or the Safeguard Agreement but from the pervasive general principle of good faith.

With this change in AB jurisprudence, the Panels are no longer substituting their authority with that of a member's investigating authority. Now, under the principle of good faith, the obligation for a correct determination of facts lies in the responsibility of the defendant WTO Member State.

The AB has noted two points about this general principle of good faith:

- The obligation to withdraw a safeguard measure when 'post-determination evidence relating to pre-determination facts' reveal that the determination was based on 'such a critical factual error that one of the conditions required by Article 6 turns out never to have been met', flows from the 'pervasive general principle of good faith that underlies all treaties'. Thus, the good faith obligation is not a creation by jurisprudence in the manner of the 'egregious error that calls into question the good faith of a Panel' standard for objective assessment of facts under Article 11 DSU.
- It is an obligation for WTO Member States and does not function only as a standard. This conclusion flows directly from the fact that it represents the corollary to the right of members under Article 6 ATC to apply transitional safeguards.

EC–Bed Linen (Article 21.5) Appellate Body Report (2003)

In *EC–Bed Linen (Article 21.5)* India claimed that the Panel had violated Article 11 DSU twice. India first said that the Panel had failed to apply the rules on the burden of proof developed in the *US–Wool Shirts and Blouses* jurisprudence, which would have shifted the burden of rebutting the prima facie case to the EC.[145] Secondly, India accused the Panel of distorting evidence under Article 11

[144] *Ibid*, para 81.

[145] See *EC–Bed Linen, (Art 21.5)*, AB Report, para 155.

by accepting for a 'fact' the 'mere' assertion by the EC that it had collected data on all relevant economic factors including stocks and capacity utilisation.[146] India expressly conceded that the Panel had not committed an egregious error calling into question the good faith of the Panel,[147] but nevertheless claimed that the above-mentioned acceptance by the Panel of the EC's assertion constituted a failure by the Panel to make an objective assessment of the matter as required by Article 11 DSU.[148]

The EC in reply denied that EC Regulation 1644/2001 contains mere assertations.[149] Moreover, since India did not allege that the Panel had committed an egregious error calling into question the good faith of the Panel, India's claim of an incorrect determination of facts by the Panel in violation of Article 11 DSU was unfounded.[150]

The AB confirmed the downscaled threshold for measuring a Panel's determination of facts (factual standard of review) of *US–Cotton Yarn*, and cited three situations in which a violation of Article 11 DSU without finding an egregious error could be conceivable:

> it has not always been the situation that the Panel had made an egregious error calling into question its good faith. Indeed, we have found a violation of Article 11 of the DSU when Panels have failed to ensure that a competent authority evaluated all relevant economic factors and that the authority's explanation of its determination is reasoned and adequate.[151] In those instances, the error related to the evaluation conducted by the *competent authorities*. We also found that a Panel exceeded its mandate under Article 11 by considering evidence that was not in existence at the time of a member's determination imposing a safeguard measure on imports of textiles.[152] In another case, we determined that the Panel had not made an objective assessment of the *matter before it* because it examined a *claim* that had not been raised by the complainant.[153]

The AB in this case found that none of the cited examples supported India in its appeal. India had not appealed against the evaluation by the EC's investigating authorities of the relevant factors in Article 3.4, as had been the issue in *US–Wheat Gluten*. Rather, India appealed only against the Panel's assessment of the *facts of the case*, and not of the *matter* before it. According to India, the Panel had distorted the evidence by placing greater weight on the statements made by the EC than on those made by India. Since jurisprudence holds that the weighing of evidence is at the discretion of the Panel as a trier of facts, and India

[146] *Ibid*, para 156.
[147] See *ibid*, para 158 and India's appellant submission, para 87.
[148] *Ibid*, para 156.
[149] *EC–Bed Linen, (Art 21.5)*, AB Report, para 158.
[150] See *ibid*, para 180.
[151] *Ibid* referring to *US–Wheat Gluten*, AB Report, paras 161–2; *US–Lamb Safeguards*, AB Report, para 149.
[152] *Ibid*, para 180 referring to *US–Cotton Yarn*, AB Report, para 80.
[153] *Ibid*, para 180 referring to *Chile–Agricultural Products*, AB Report, para 177 (footnotes in original).

did not succeed in convincing the AB that the Panel had exceeded the bounds of this discretion, the AB rejected India's argument that the Panel had distorted evidence.[154]

Thus, the AB found that the Panel had properly complied with its duty under Article 11 of the DSU and therefore upheld the Panel's finding that the EC had information before it on the relevant economic factors listed in Article 3.4 of the AD Agreement when making the determination of injury.[155]

Evaluation of *EC–Bed Linen (Article 21.5)* Appellate Body Report (2003)

The *EC–Bed Linen (Article 21.5)* case demonstrates that it is no longer necessary to demonstrate that there has been an egregious error calling into question the good faith of the Panel. The cases preceding *EC–Bed Linen (Article 21.5)*, which had also abandoned the use of good faith in Article 11 DSU, were *Korea–Alcohol* (mainly because the party claiming a violation of Article 11 dismissed good faith of its own), *US–Wheat Gluten* and *US–Lamb Safeguards*.

The good faith element in Article 11 DSU is discretionary. It is possibly applied by the AB against a Panel only in cases based on scientific evidence or in all cases covering an exception to free trade.

The AB is more intrusive now than formerly vis-à-vis Panels, because a mere legal issue connected to a fact suffices to trigger a review. No longer will bad faith be the sole factor prompting the AB to actively review a Panel's factual conclusions. Invariably, with the more intrusive review, the AB has also acquired a heavier workload. This might be the real reason why the AB in the cases immediately following *EC–Bed Linen* has re-introduced the good faith test. In contrast to the good faith egregious error test used in the past, this new good faith obligation puts a heavier burden on the defendant WTO Member State to correctly determine the contested facts.

CONCLUSIONS

In the first set of cases (*Australia–Salmon*,[156] *Japan–Agricultural Products*,[157] *EC–Poultry*[158] and *Korea–Alcohol*)[159] in which the AB applied the good faith standard of review relating to the Panel's appreciation of facts, the AB followed the high standard for the threshold of good faith that it had established in *EC–Hormones*.

154 See *ibid*, para 181.

155 See *ibid*, para 182.

156 See *Australia–Salmon*, AB Report, para 266.

157 See *Japan–Agricultural Products*, AB Report, para 141.

158 See *EC–Poultry*, AB Report, para 133 (although the reference to good faith/egregious error is contained in a quote from *EC–Hormones* and was not reformulated specifically by that AB).

159 See *Korea–Alcohol*, AB Report, para 162 and 164.

With *US–Wheat Gluten* and *US–Lamb Safeguards*, the AB loosened its 'stringent', 'rigorous'[160] and 'too strict'[161] criteria for assessing a Panel's factual conclusions and, in the process, dismissed the good faith threshold. Once it had dismissed the good faith threshold, the AB only reviewed factual conclusions when such conclusions were connected to some legal problem. Thus, the AB burdened itself with more work and was quite intrusive upon the Panels and, indirectly, upon domestic investigation authorities.

With *Chile–Agricultural Products* in 2003, the AB re-introduced good faith, with a view to firmly grounding the Panels' duty to respect members' due process rights. This had the effect of increasing the defending WTO Members' responsibilities vis-à-vis factual issues and formalized the complaining party's due process rights while relieving the AB of some of its workload.

Appreciation

The AB introduced the measure of good faith to prevent Panels from abusing their power of factual appreciation by intruding into areas of sovereignty reserved for the domestic authorities' factual considerations.

There were three main reasons for the reintroduction of good faith to limit the Panel's discretion in assessing facts:

— to protect the 'integrity of the WTO dispute settlement';[162]
— to maintain the much appreciated speedy resolution of complex issues as required by Article 12.2 DSU, which would no longer be possible if the Panels had to conduct more fact-intensive searches; and[163]
— to avoid the WTO judiciary, with its limited resources for expert-intensive disputes, being pulled into scientific debates.[164]

Moreover, it seems like the AB purposely introduced this standard with the intention of later dropping it.

This study argues that the AB created the high standard of 'bad faith' because it was at that time faced with trade and linkage cases on which it wanted to reserve its opinion (possibly to preserve some consensus at the WTO), so it conveniently let the Panels—which were more pro-free trade—assess the facts, and would intervene only in cases in which an error called into question the good faith of a Panel. Perhaps the fact that good faith is a 'fact-intensive' principle for determining whether or not a Panel has abused its limits of factual assessment added to the AB's reluctance to use it, leading the AB to dismiss the standard

[160] Oesch, 2003b, p 159.
[161] *Ibid*, p 160.
[162] *EC–Poultry*, AB Report, para 133.
[163] See Bronckers and McNelis, 1999, p 252.
[164] *Cf* Jackson, 2000, pp 152–4.

later on.[165] However, at the same time the AB threw in references scattered here and there in the text of its decisions indicating that the standard of review existed to ensure the members' due process rights and fundamental fairness vis-à-vis the Panel.[166]

It was not until the 2001 *Chile–Agricultural Products* case that the AB finally recognised that a Panel need not have acted against good faith in the appreciation of evidence, before the AB could enter into the picture; it sufficed that the Panel had disregarded the 'fundamental tenet of due process' for the AB to actively review the Panel's conduct.[167]

While in its early years of jurisprudence the AB had searched for ways to balance its different substantive goals, which led to the linkages debate of the late 1990s, the reality of the trade remedy cases and their harsh litigation techniques has forced the AB to organise its procedural checks and balances.[168]

Critics may say that the AB's 'heightened scrutiny' is directed at 'controlling the hegemon's protectionist impulses' (ie, the US).[169] The AB has done its job in continuing to use the general principle of law of good faith and its corollary, due process, as the guarantee of fair dispute procedures and ultimately, fair trade. It has protected the WTO dispute settlement system from becoming a single litigation machine fed by those members who can 'afford' to have a trade concern because they possess the financial resources and weight to rally litigious lawyers who can succeed in deterring the Panels and the AB from investigating the underlying substantive issues.

As has been described elsewhere, the evolution of the AB's standard of review for facts is a measure of the WTO's constitutionalisation and of the role therein of the WTO judicial bodies.[170] It can be argued that the WTO's constitutionalisation has partially hinged upon the eventual abandonment of the good faith standard in the AB's review of factual considerations. While the good faith standard brought the WTO close to public international administrative law, where the ICJ's standard of review of lower tribunals is similarly based on breaches of good faith, the elimination of this standard has firmly established the WTO as a more constitutionalised international order.[171]

[165] Kolb, 2000, p 69.

[166] See *EC–Hormones*, AB Report, para 133; *India–Patents*, AB Report, para 94; *Australia–Salmon*, AB Report, para 272.

[167] *Chile–Agricultural Products*, AB Report, para 175 referring to *Australia–Salmon*, AB Report, para 278.

[168] Compare *US–Shrimp* AB Report, para 156 and *EC–Hormones*, AB Report, para 177 with *US–Japan Hot-rolled Steel* AB Report, para 172, see also Ehlermann, 2003, p 704, also pp 698, 701.

[169] Tarullo, 2002, p 169.

[170] See Cottier and Oesch, 2003, pp 287–306; Oesch, 2003b, p 234, 'juridification' of the DSU, instead of constitutionalisation of the WTO; Cottier and Hertig, 2004, pp 261–328; Jackson and Croley, 1996, p 195; on the correlation between the standard of review, its incursion on national sovereignty and consequent strengthening of the WTO's 'constitution'.

[171] See *Canada–Aircraft*, AB Report, para 190.

12

Legitimate Expectations as to the Precedential Value of Dispute Settlement Reports

ADOPTED PANEL AND AB Reports create legitimate expectations for members that 'following Panels dealing with the same or similar issue' will take into account the relevant previous WTO rulings.[1] Legitimate expectations confer upon WTO Member States the principle that, in general, the finding of a previous report to a similar set-up of facts in a case will be 'taken into account' by the subsequent Panel or appellate ruling.

Despite creating legitimate expectations, such prior reports are not precedents, because they are not binding on all WTO Member States but rather only between the parties to a particular dispute.[2] The AB overturned the *US–Japan Alcohol* Panel, which had attributed to prior reports the status of subsequent practice.

Nonetheless, it is a notable achievement for the diplomacy-oriented GATT 47 system to have abolished the rule that the adoption of reports could be blocked in order to establish dispute settlement reports as 'legally binding decisions', even if not binding on all the WTO Member States.[3]

THE WTO-SPECIFIC BASIS OF THE PRINCIPLE OF PROTECTION OF LEGITIMATE EXPECTATION

The AB in *Japan–Alcohol* created the precedential value of adopted WTO Panel reports and based such value on PLE. The Panel in *Japan–Alcohol* had chosen a different legal basis for the adjudicator's duty of following previous reports from that chosen by the AB, and had accorded adopted Panel reports the rank of a primary source of treaty interpretation as 'subsequent practice' pursuant to Article 31(3)(b) VCLT.[4]

[1] Cottier and Oesch, 2001, p 29.
[2] See Cameron and Gray, 2001, p 263.
[3] Cottier and Oesch, 2001, p 28.
[4] *Japan–Alcohol*, AB Report, pp 12–13, and Panel Report, para 6.10.

Under GATT 47, the *Dessert Apples* Panel had already refused to concede that adopted reports are subsequent practice, which the GATT 47 interpreter is bound to respect under Article 31(3)(b) VCLT. Nevertheless, the *Dessert Apples* Panel held that a party may harbour the legitimate expectation that the adopted Panel report will be followed in the future.[5] In 2002, the WTO Secretariat sent out a note to confirm the role of legitimate expectations of adopted Panel and AB Reports.[6]

Article XVI(1) of the WTO Agreement is the only exception to the rule that adopted reports shall create legitimate expectations for the future rulings. Article XVI(1) WTO Agreement confers adopted GATT 47 Panel reports a precedential value.[7] However, the provision is of limited practical use, because under GATT 47 few reports were actually adopted.

It is generally agreed that adopted reports create the legitimate expectation that similarly situated ones will follow the argumentation of the preceding ones. So far, no scholar has argued in favour of attributing adopted reports a more fundamental role as the primary source of interpretation of subsequent practice under Article 31(3)(b) VCLT.[8]

The substantive and WTO-specific principle of legitimate expectation as to the precedential value of adopted reports, trumps the interpretive and general international legal rule of subsequent practice. Apparently, the WTO legal system before 2002, as the Note of the WTO Secretariat showed, was not yet prepared to attribute to its reports the status of subsequent practice.[9] This study argues that in 2002, the AB decision in *US–Line Pipe from Korea* dismissed the principle of legitimate expectations in favour of the binding interpretive rule of subsequent practice. WTO reports adopted since 2002 have the precedential value of subsequent practice, which obliges adjudicators to take similarly situated, preceding reports into consideration as a primary means of WTO interpretation.

'Subsequent Practice' of Article 31(3)(b) VCLT and Rule of Precedents in International Law

The *US–Line Pipe from Korea* AB Report of 2002 indicated that the situation may be changing. In this case, the AB made the following statement in paragraph 174:

[5] See Cameron and Gray, 2001, p 263 and fn 74.

[6] See GATT/WTO Dispute Settlement Practice Relating to GATT Art XX, paras (b), (d) and (g), Note by the Secretariat, 8 March 2002, WTO Document, WT/CTE/W/2038.

[7] See Cottier and Oesch, 2001, p 29.

[8] See Palmeter and Mavroidis, 1998, p 401f; Cameron and Gray, 2001, p.263.

[9] See Cottier and Oesch, 2001, pp 29–30.

> Following the *Vienna Convention* approach, we have also looked to the GATT *acquis* and to the relevant negotiating history of the pertinent treaty provisions. We have concluded that our view is reinforced by the jurisprudence under the GATT 47 (emphasis in the original).[10]

If this statement is to be taken in the way its textual interpretation suggests, it would mean that since 2002, the AB has been prepared to recognise that previous GATT/WTO practice has the status of subsequent practice today. Since 2002, the AB has substituted the status of prior reports, as a GATT-principle of legitimate expectations, with the binding obligation to take into consideration prior reports as a primary source of treaty interpretation pursuant to the VCLT. Insofar as the AB intended to shift its jurisprudence towards a binding obligation to take into consideration prior reports, the role of precedents in WTO law today is equal to the role that precedents have in general public international law. Moreover, having been attributed the primary interpretive value of subsequent practice under Article 31(3)(b) VCLT, prior reports at the WTO have a more decisive influence on adjudication than judicial decisions have in general public international law under Article 38(1)(d) of the ICJ statute, where judicial decisions are categorised as subsidiary means for the determination of law.[11]

The Obligatory or Voluntary Nature of Legitimate Expectations as to Precedential Value of WTO Reports

The question then arises of whether the Panels or the AB may voluntarily, or must mandatorily, take into consideration similarly situated previous reports. The issue is whether or not the principle of legitimate expectations as to the precedential value of adopted reports is an obligation for the judiciary, or only a principle, that sets a general rule, from which it remains possible to deviate.

Cottier and Oesch argue that the case law of the Panels—short of constituting 'judicial decisions', as the *Japan–Alcohol* Panel report proposed—is to be considered 'an important part of the GATT *acquis*'. Insofar as adopted prior reports constitute GATT *acquis,* Cottier and Oesch argue that the Panels and the AB 'may be obliged to articulate particularly good and convincing reasons when departing from a previously developed line of argumentation and reasoning'.[12] For Cottier and Oesch the obligation for the Panels and the AB to follow the legal reasoning of previous reports, exists 'in order to give due respect to the principle of legal certainty'.[13]

Appellate practice in *US–Shrimp (Article 21.5)* in contrast, found that the principle of legitimate expectations as to adopted reports imposed no obligation

[10] *US–Line Pipe from Korea*, AB Report, para 174.
[11] Cottier and Oesch, 2001, p 29.
[12] *Ibid*, p 30.
[13] *Ibid.*

upon a Panel to follow the line of reasoning of previous reports, or, in the negative, to offer a thorough justification for why it has chosen to deviate from the arguments of similarly situated preceding reports.

The *US–Shrimp (Article 21.5)* AB Report clarifies that the legitimate expectation of 'WTO Member States of taking into account the reasoning in an adopted report', 'where relevant to any dispute' means that 'a Panel can us[e] . . . findings as a tool for its own reasoning'.[14] In contrast to the earlier *Japan–Alcoholic Beverages* Report, this wording suggests a more voluntary than mandatory nature for the obligation to adhere pursuant to PLE to preceding reports. The earlier report stated: 'Adopted Panel reports are an important part of the GATT *acquis*. [. . .] They create legitimate expectations among WTO Member States, and, therefore, should be taken into account where they are relevant to any dispute'.[15]

The *Argentina–Textiles* Panel mentioned the 'experience' acquired by the contracting Parties as well as the 'importance' of adopted Panel reports to the GATT *acquis*.[16] The *Argentina–Textiles* Panel did not define more clearly whether PLE as to the precedential value of adopted reports creates a binding obligation to respect preceding decisions, or whether it leaves the WTO adjudicator the choice between adhering to the ruling or ignoring it.

The *US–Shrimp (Article 21.5)* AB decision expanded the concept of legitimate expectations of preceding Panel reports to AB Reports.[17] Nowhere is it more obvious that a subsequent AB decision will follow in the footsteps of a preceding one as in Article 21.5 DSU complaints.

So it was only logical that the preceding *US–Shrimp* AB Report provided the basis for the subsequent *US–Shrimp (Article 21.5)* AB Report. The question is whether the concept of legitimate expectations as to adopted Panel and AB reports will lead eventually to recognition of *stare decisis*, or whether it resembles more the 'the law of the case' common law doctrine.[18]

In any case, it may be that the era of legitimate expectations as to the status of prior adopted reports came to an end when the *US–Line Pipe from Korea* AB decided in 2002 to attribute similarly situated prior reports the status of subsequent practice. However, since no AB Report has since expressed its opinion on the precedential value of adopted prior reports, the substantive but less incisive role for adopted prior reports under the concept of legitimate expectations may still be applicable concurrently or exclusively to the interpretive yet more stringent obligation to follow the rulings of prior reports under subsequent practice.

[14] *US–Shrimp (Art 21.5)* AB Report, para 109 with reference to *US–Shrimp (Art 21.5)* Panel Report, para 5.138.

[15] See *Japan–Alcohol*, AB Report, p 14, for the legitimate expectations adopted Panel reports create.

[16] See *Argentina–Footwear, Safeguards*, Panel Report, fn 175 to para 6.24.

[17] See *US–Shrimp (Art 21.5)*, AB Report, para 109.

[18] See Kearns and Charnovitz, 2002, p 350 and fn 66.

The Binding Precedent or Discretionary Precedential Nature of WTO Reports

The evolution of the value of prior adopted reports, from the principle of legitimate expectations under GATT 47, to subsequent practice for WTO practice today, demonstrates once more how the principle of good faith and its emanation of the PLE may further anchor the interpretation of the WTO Agreements in the rules of the Vienna Convention. By the proxy of the GATT-specific principle of legitimate expectations, the WTO judiciary has once again integrated the WTO legal system more firmly into the rules (of interpretation) of the international legal order.

THE TRIANGLE OF PROCEDURAL GOOD FAITH

Procedural good faith functions for the following reasons as a triangle that binds the three actors making up the WTO legal system, namely the WTO Member States, the Panels and the AB.

On the one hand, procedural good faith protection in WTO dispute settlement prohibits WTO Member States from abusing the WTO dispute procedures and due process rights, as a tool for vexatious litigation practices. Such an obligation of good faith is codified in the duty to resolve disputes in good faith (Article 3.10 DSU) and to enter into consultations in good faith (Article 4.3 DSU).

On the other hand, procedural good faith functions as a standard in Article 3.7 DSU and not as an obligation. The *EC–Bananas* and the *Mexico–HFCS (Article 21.5)* AB Reports implied a standard of good faith when requiring WTO Member States to only engage in dispute settlement proceedings when the result would prove 'fruitful'.[19]

Case law in *EC–Hormones*, *EC–Poultry*, *Australia–Salmon* and *Korea–Alcohol* inferred from Articles 11 and 13 DSU that factual standard of review of a Panel and of the AB was based on good faith. As a standard of review, the 'procedural' function of good faith is to limit the Panels' and the AB's standard of review relating to facts.

The later cases of *US–Cotton Yarn* in 2001 and *EC–Bed Linen (Article 21.5 DSU)* in 2003, reversed the standard of good faith review and substituted the good faith threshold for the Panels and the AB with a Panel's right to seek information, which reinforces good faith as inferred from Article 13(1) DSU with the good faith duty of the WTO Member States.

Article 13.1 DSU, the right of a Panel to seek information from Members, has been interpreted with the good faith obligation in Article 3.10 DSU as obliging Members to cooperate with the Panels.

[19] See *Mexico–HFCS (Art 21.5)*, AB Report, para 73; *EC–Bananas*, AB Report, paras 134–5.

More concretely, the *Canada–Aircraft* AB report found that while the language of Article 13.1 establishes the right of a Panel to seek information, a contextual interpretation of Article 13.1 DSU in the light of Article 3.10 DSU establishes the obligation of Members to provide the Panel with information.[20] *Canada–Aircraft* equipped its newly created obligation upon the WTO Member States with a legal consequence, ie, the adjudicator may draw adverse inferences pursuant to the ASCM based upon a member's non-compliance with its duty to inform the Panel.[21]

It has been shown that the obligation to engage in dispute settlement procedures in good faith under Article 3.10 DSU has far-reaching implications insofar as it has been drawn upon to create additional obligations for the members in terms of WTO procedural law. In construing the main procedural rights and obligations for dispute settlement rules and procedures, such as the duty of members to provide the Panel with information and the standard of factual review of the Panels and the AB, the principle of good faith has 'judicialised' the WTO.[22] For this reason, the AB found that Article 3.10 DSU has 'far-reaching implications for the WTO dispute settlement system'.[23]

As early as 1955 Schwarzenberger was already predicting that good faith would become a cornerstone in the development of international institutional law, organizing not only the relations horizontally between the members, but also vertically between the members and the organs ('superstructures'):

> If the ever-growing importance of treaty law, as compared with international customary law, and the multitude of international institutions, which impose on their members positive duties of actions and cooperation are duly taken into account, the actual and still more the potential, significance of this principle for the superstructures of international law strengthens still further the arguments in favour of such a positive assessment of the place of good faith in international law.[24]

In fact, at the WTO, and particularly for the WTO's procedural law of dispute settlement, good faith is the 'impetus for legal development', be it by effective interpretation or by gap-filling.[25] Such an ability to link a specialised legal order to more general international rules—as good faith for the WTO has demonstrated with respect to the rights and procedures of its dispute settlement—is what characterises good faith as an 'essential principle of international law'[26] or 'general principle of international law'.[27]

[20] See *Canada–Aircraft*, AB Report, para 190.
[21] *Ibid*, paras 200–1; Steger, 2001, p 819.
[22] Goldsmith and Posner, 2005, p 161.
[23] *Canada–Aircraft*, AB Report, para 182.
[24] Schwarzenberger, 1955, p 325.
[25] Degan, 1997, p 139.
[26] Cheng, 1987, p 105.
[27] *US–Shrimp*, AB Report, para 158; Brownlie, 1998a, p 18.

Despite criticisms[28] that the WTO has moved towards a 'trade constitution',[29] the WTO's judiciary is to be credited for carefully constructing a web of rights and obligations relating to the rules and procedures governing the settlement of WTO trade disputes. By unveiling links between 'due process rights', the abuse of such rights, standards of procedural fairness, the PLE and good faith,[30] and, in particular, by drawing from good faith to limit the Panels' factual standard of review under Article 11 DSU,[31] the AB has created a system of procedural checks and balances, which are the *ratio* and foundation of any constitutional order.

[28] See Koskenniemi and Leino, 2002, pp 571–2; see also Howse and Nicolaidis, 2003, pp 308–43.

[29] See Jackson, 1999, pp 339–51; see also Petersmann, 2000, pp 111–34; Cottier and Hertig, 2004, pp 261–328; Cottier and Oesch, 2003, pp 299–301; Cottier and Mavroidis, 2003, 353–7; Cottier and Oesch, 2005, pp 532–42.

[30] Cameron and Campbell, 1998, p 21, on the AB having 'to deal with some of the procedural concerns in a direct way' and the AB as a 'constitutional legal chamber', setting rules on 'general principles of international law applicable to the conduct of the dispute, such as legitimate expectations, due process or procedural fairness; the question of where the burden of proof lies in making and defending complaints; the distinction between legal argument and claims; judicial economy; deference and the standard of review'; and pp 22–3 on constitutional principles in the daily business of the WTO, including dispute settlement.

[31] By interpreting 'teleologically' the obligations of Articles 13(1) DSU and 11 DSU in combination with the good faith obligation of Article 3.10 DSU, to bind the WTO Member States parties to a dispute to the obligation to provide the Panel with information, even if such information is not being sought by the Panel.

13

Conclusions

THE PRINCIPLE OF good faith has been part of the GATT *acquis* in the form of the basic tenet of PLE ever since the beginnings of GATT 1947 adjudication.[1] This 'well-established GATT principle'[2] has formed the grounds of non-violation nullification and impairment complaints. Since the establishment of the WTO, it applies more broadly, both in violation and non-violation complaints *(Korea–Government Procurement)*.[3] By 1998, the WTO Panels and the AB were drawing from the general principle of law of good faith and its corrolaries of *pacta sunt servanda* and prohibition of *abus de droit*. It remains debatable firstly whether the Panels and the AB meant to expand the jurisdiction of the WTO to include a source of law other than the covered agreements. Secondly, the question is whether they just meant to apply, in the sense of Pauwelyn, the general principle of law without considering that principle or the customary rule of *pacta sunt servanda* as sources of WTO jurisdiction. Thirdly, the question is whether or not good faith enters WTO jurisprudence pursuant to the 'rule of good faith interpretation' of Article 31(1) VCLT to interpret the WTO Agreements.

THE RULE OF WTO GOOD FAITH

Substantive Good Faith

Substantive good faith protection manifests in WTO substantive law firstly as the principle of the PLE. GATT Articles II and III have been interpreted to

[1] *India–Patents*, AB Report, para 34:

> [T]he Panel noted that whereas the 'disciplines formed under GATT 1947 (so-called GATT *acquis*) were primarily directed at the treatment of the goods of other countries', [. . .] the concept of the protection of legitimate expectations in relation to the *TRIPS Agreement* applies to 'the competitive relationship between a Member's own nationals and those of other Members (rather than between domestically produced goods and the goods of other Members, as in the goods area)' (footnote omitted, emphasis in the original).

The AB was quoting from *India–Patents*, Panel Report, para 7.21.

[2] *India–Patents*, Panel Report, para 7.21; *India–Patents*, AB Report, para 36.

[3] Against Zeitler, 2005 p 752, who diagnoses a negative impact of using the principle of good faith broadly, because such a broad use would 'destroy' the distinction between violation and non-violation type complaints, a result, which according to Zeitler, is noxious to the WTO legal system.

protect legitimate expectations as to the conditions of competition, ie to offer protection against the frustration of benefits by measures not inconsistent with the rules but which nevertheless reduce the value of the negotiated concessions. This rule is expressly codified in the GATS Articles VI:5(a)(ii) and XVII:3 (see chapter six). The PLE constitutes the cause of action of non-violation nullification and impairment complaints. This type of complaint is codified in Articles II and III GATT, GATS Articles VI:5(a)(ii), XVII:3 as well as in Articles 3.10 and 4.3 DSU. NVNI is still suspended for the TRIPS, even if negotiations on the issue started in 1999 pursuant to Article 64 TRIPS. Under a NVNI action, the complainant has the duty of demonstrating the benefit of a specific negotiated level of tariff concessions. Under the definition of the benefit, the categories of PLE may be split into several sub-categories:

— If PLE relates to conditions of competition, a traditional NVNI complaint brought under the cause of action of either GATT or GATS is the rule.
— If PLE relates to a concept of 'conditions of competition' extended beyond negotiated trade concessions, the benefit is the 'predictability to plan future trade'; but the cause of action of a NVNI may be overbroad and thus 'wrong', and is thus replaced by a violation complaint.
— If PLE relates to the concept of conditions of competition as to trade concessions under negotiations, the benefit is the customary rule of *pacta sunt servanda*, and the preferred cause of action a 'broad' but nevertheless 'true' NVNI, because *pacta sunt servanda* is a legitimate and recognised legal basis.

Not recognised as the basis for a claim is PLE relating to conditions of competition nullified or impaired by non-WTO law. In such cases, neither Panels nor the AB would substantiate PLE, because the the NVNI claim is overbroad and 'wrong' and a violation complaint not available.

Interpretative Good Faith

The second category of good faith in WTO law is interpretive good faith. Chapters seven to nine of this study examined the interpretive uses the WTO adjudicators could make of good faith. The study argued that while the Panels have found that the general rule of interpretation under Article 31(1) VCLT prescribes what they have called a 'good faith interpretation' for every interpretive process, given that good faith is one of the mandatory sources of interpretation under Article 31(1)VCLT. However, the AB has not in addition to text, context, object and purpose, recognised good faith as an interpretative tool, specifically not if it is intended to protect the legitimate expectations that a member may claim.

Procedural Good Faith

In WTO procedural law, good faith protection firstly stands for good faith in efforts to resolve trade disputes and, secondly, for engaging in fruitful disputes, as opposed to submitting frivolous complaints. Thirdly, good faith in WTO procedural law determines that every dispute settlement procedure should start with good faith consultations (see chapters ten to twelve). These procedural good faith obligations are expressly codified in DSU Article 3.10. This study found that procedural good faith obligations in dispute resolution primarily function to limit the exercise of due process rights by the litigants. Procedural good faith obligations thus promote fair, prompt and effective procedure. As the analysis of the case law since 2000 has shown, the AB uses the procedural good faith obligations in the following ways:

— Good faith dispute resolution defines the extent to which a litigant may exercise its due process rights against the other party to the dispute.
— Procedural good faith reinforces the Panels' right to seek information under Article 13(1) DSU. Following a submission by Brazil, which had interpreted the duty to settle disputes in good faith as the litigants' duty to cooperate with the Panel, the AB created the duty of the members party to a dispute to provide the Panel with information.
— The well-established GATT-principle of protecting legitimate expectations has a procedural function in WTO law because it attributes precedential value to the adopted reports of the Panel and AB. As such, the procedural law function of PLE is to empower the members party to a dispute to demand that the WTO adjudicators follow the pattern established for similar cases in previous disputes. The procedural PLE as to the precedential value of adopted reports paves the way for installing a principle of *stare decisis* for WTO adjudication.

In procedural law, good faith may close the gaps in the DSU and *leges speciales* on dispute settlement in the other WTO Agreements which could otherwise lead litigants to abuse the WTO dispute settlement system. In the face of a missing rule on *stare decisis*, the PLE may fill in the gap by attributing precedential value to adopted dispute settlement reports. Furthermore, good faith may shape the rules of negotiations to ensure that they are 'forthright', 'open' and 'transparent'.[4]

[4] *Korea–Government Procurement*, Panel Report, para 7.110.

GOOD FAITH'S ROLE FOR THE WTO JURISDICTION'S REACH

The Jurisdictional Role of Good Faith

The initial question was whether the general principle of law of good faith protection has enlarged the scope of WTO jurisdiction, which was previously been limited to the law of the WTO covered agreements The principle of good faith defines the scope of the positive treaty law of the WTO Agreements and the limits of jurisprudence about these agreements.

— It has been shown that the GATT and later WTO rules have been shaped by the general principle of law of good faith. The answer to the question of whether or not the Panels of the WTO have acted inconsistently with their obligations under the DSU by using the general principle of good faith to clarify the rights and obligations of the WTO Member States party to a dispute (Article 3.2 DSU), has been shown to hinge on whether the general principle of law of good faith is used only to interpret the WTO law of the covered agreements, or whether it is directly applied as a general principle of law to the trade relations between the WTO Member States.

- On the one hand, a first doctrinal path would lead to the argument that interpretation and application are but the two sides of the same coin, so that there is no distinct difference between the two concepts.
- On the other hand the general principle of law of good faith may be used only when interpreting the existing WTO law of the WTO covered agreements, and not for extending the scope of rights and obligations of the WTO Member States, which the WTO Member States had contracted into when they established the WTO.

— Within the multilateral treaty system of the WTO, the general principle of law of good faith and the rule of interpretation in good faith under Article 31(1) VCLT, each express a different function:

- The principle of protecting legitimate expectations, the obligation to perform and implement the WTO Agreements in good faith, as well as the prohibition of *abus de droit* and apply as substantive legal principles, somewhat expand the law and jurisdiction of the WTO.
- The rule of interpretation in good faith under Article 31(1) VCLT clarifies the rights and obligations of the WTO Agreements and, as such, is consistent with Article 3.2 DSU.
- The obligation to consult and settle disputes in good faith, codified in Articles 3.10 and 4.3 of the DSU, is a procedural expression of good faith that prevents members from abusing their right to a dispute settlement procedure. In combination with Article 3.7 DSU, which contains the obligation to engage in dispute settlement proceedings only if such proceedings are seen as leading to a fruitful solution for a dispute, Article 3.10 prohibits

vexatious disputes. The good faith standard created by the AB in *US–FSC*, namely that the rules and procedures for settling disputes in the WTO be used 'fairly, promptly and effectively', also prohibits abuse of the DSU rights and obligations. Procedural good faith obligations have contributed to the 'judicialization' of the WTO, which is the term used to describe the process of adjudicating disputes according to 'formal rules of evidence and procedure administered by independent judges who employ conventional tools of legal reasoning, rather than left to negotiations among the affected parties'.[5]

Whether substantive, interpretive or procedural, the general principle of law of good faith is an example of how the WTO has successfully absorbed the three sources of public international law into its applicable law. Together with its corolary in custom, *pacta sunt servanda*, as well as the non-WTO treaty rule of 'good faith interpretation' of Article 31(1) VCLT, WTO judicial practice, namely, Panel reports, has pioneered the search for a mutual interconnection between WTO treaty law and general sources of international law. Vice versa, the GATT-specific priniciple of PLE may have found its way into non-WTO treaty law, namely NAFTA and bilateral investment treaties.[6]

The gains from good faith in WTO are law identified as follows:

— In future WTO negotiations, good faith may be of strategic value to the relationship between the WTO and other international agreements.
— More specifically, in a strategic function, good faith may be used to lay out the rules by which the norms and standards created by these other international treaties may be integrated into WTO law and practice.
— Expressions of good faith, and the way the WTO judiciary uses them, may provide insights into the broader relationship between general public international legal sources, such as treaty law (VCLT), customary international law *(pacta sunt servanda)* and general principles of law (good faith) and the WTO Agreements.

Pacta Sunt Servanda Limits to Normative Content

Certain treaty norms of the different WTO covered agreements imply a good faith obligation or inherently express a good faith standard. Primarily, good faith is found in exceptions to the trade liberalization obligations of the WTO Agreeements, namely in the Chapeau of Article XX GATT 94. It is also inherent in other obligations crucial to the object and purpose of the various WTO Agreements.

Functioning as the gate keeper of the negotatiated level of WTO trade liberalization, the general principle of law of good faith and the prohibition against

[5] Goldsmith and Posner, 2005, p 161; see also Petersmann, 1998, p 83.
[6] Weiler, 2005, pp 727–8.

abus de droit prohibition were first introduced in Article XX GATT jurisprudence under *US–Shrimp*. In this case of 1998, the prohibition of *abus de droit* ensured that the extraterritorial effects of the US legal regime for sea turtle protection remained proportionate to the policy goals of environmental protection and that the US factual import quota for shrimp originating in Thailand, Mexico and other WTO Member States remained free from protectionist intention and design.

The general principle of international law of good faith was furthermore implied in Article 7 TRIPS according to the *US–Section 211 ('Havanna Club')* Panel Report, as well as in the Enabling Clause according to *EC–Tariff Preferences*, AB Report. Implied in Article 5 ASPS, the general principle of law of good faith ensures a level of fairness, promptness and effectiveness in risk assessment procedures according to *US–Hormones*. When conducting anti-dumping investigations, a similarly inherent good faith standard of procedural fairness is impliedly required by Annex 2 ADA *(Japan–Hot-rolled Steel,* AB Report and *EC–Bed Linen (Article 21.5)* and AB Report*)*. Panels of GATT 1947 and the WTO have implied a measure of good faith in the legitimate expectations of GATT/WTO Member States as to the conditions of competition created by the negotiated level of tariff concessions.

For scholarship, such implied expressions of good faith in WTO provisions are evidence that the concept of good faith in the WTO is an 'abstract' obligation, which needs to be filled with content,[7] as opposed to a free-standing obligation existing in its own right as a principle of WTO law.[8] According to this approach, WTO good faith is normatively tied to WTO treaty provisions and functions *infra legem*. As an integral part of the Chapeau of Article XX GATT, the principle ensures that the domestic regulation for environmental protection, on labour standards, cultural diversity, human-, plant- and animal-health are designed and applied in a WTO-consistent manner.

It was demonstrated that the AB will not afford good faith protection beyond the limits of consensus. The proof is that the Panels and the AB recognise *pacta sunt servanda*, which Panel practice expanded to an 'extended *pacta sunt servanda*', covering gap-filling with non-violation complaints and the duty to negotiate in good faith, as lawful judicial applications of this customary international rule. [9]

'Pro-trade' Limits to Substantive Content

Another result of this study on the implications and applications of the good faith principle in WTO law, is that the WTO Panels and, a fortiori, the AB will

[7] Zeitler, 2005, p 721.

[8] *Cf ibid*, p 754, denying good faith in the WTO what the author calls a 'substantive and independent good faith obligation'.

[9] See *US–Offset Act ('Byrd Amendment')*, AB Report, paras 295–8; *Korea–Government Procurement*, Panel Report, paras 7.102ff, see also McRae, 2003, p 713.

only substantiate good faith if it serves the multilateral system's principle goal of trade liberalisation. Proof for such jurisprudential practice is the Panels' broad protection of competitive opportunities ranging from the negotiated tariff concessions (*Australia–Subsidy*, *EEC–Oilseeds*) over concessions under negotiations (*Korea–Government Procurement*) to the predictability of future trade opportunities (*India–Patents*).

THE ENFORCEABILITY OF WTO GOOD FAITH

Not all good faith obligations are enforced to the same extent. Four levels of enforceability can be distinguished in the jurisprudence of the AB and the Panels:

- The most stringent protection for good faith are the procedural good faith obligations codified in the DSU.
- The protection of legitimate expectations, *pacta sunt servanda*, and the prohibition of *abus de droit* are enforceable as rights; however these principles offer less protection than a codified right, in the sense that it is difficult to predict whether the AB will effectively enforce these rights.
- The expressions of good faith implied in WTO treaty rules have the status of general principles of law and are read into specific WTO rules where they give these rules a meaning or reinforce their object and purpose of the norm.
- The final category is good faith interpretation, which may give meaning to any rule of the WTO Agreements whether or not that rule implies a standard of good faith.

These four categories of enforceability are summarised below starting with the good faith principle that offers the most stringent degree of protection.

None of the three rules on procedural good faith has to date ever been the principal subject of a claim. Rather, good faith in the DSU has featured as an obiter dictum in the arguments of the Panels or the ABs, where it usually functions to set a 'good faith' limitation to a Member's exercise of due process rights. Appellate practice attributes to procedural good faith the function of enabling disputes to be brought and resolved in a prompt fair and effective manner. The most recent Panel and AB reports have repeated the formula that good faith in dispute settlement limits the exercise of due process rights in favour of a prompt, fair and effective dispute resolution with a view to maintaining the legal security and predictability of the WTO legal system by averting abusive litigation techniques. Therefore, the AB's clarification of good faith acquired the status of a quasi-precedent. To this extent WTO Member States may have a protected legitimate expectation that future Panels and the AB will put reasonably into context an opponent's due process rights under a legally secure, predictable and stable dispute settlement system.

Next in the descending hierarchy of legal enforceability of good faith in WTO law comes the self-standing good faith obligations *praeter legem* other than the protection of legitimate expectations. The WTO Panels and the AB have attributed binding force to the obligation of *pacta sunt servanda* and to the prohibition of *abus de droit*: *US–Offset Act ('Byrd Amendment')* and *Korea–Government Procurement* for *pacta sunt servanda, US–Shrimp* and *US–Cotton Yarn* for the prohibition of *abus de droit*.

Among the corollaries of *pacta sunt servanda*, both the Panels and the AB have recognised the duty to negotiate in good faith, and the obligation to implement the WTO Agreements in good faith: *Korea–Government Procurement*, *US–Havana Club* and *US–Shrimp (Art. 21.5)*. Good faith negotiation and implementation shall be subsumed under *pacta sunt servanda* because both address and demand respect for the consensually agreed treaty terms as opposed to adapting the stringency of a rule to an individualised solution. Yet, neither of the two WTO judiciaries has so far attributed an obligatory force to good faith either correcting and balancing the rigor of a rule or gap-filling a missing norm.

Except for *pacta sunt servanda* and the prohibition of *abus de droit*—which are closely linked or even part of positive treaty law—the general principle of law of good faith in its gap-filling function has yet not been recognised as a substantive, self-standing obligation of substantive WTO law. For this reason, at the WTO, equity as yet has neither the authority nor the legitimacy to impose a fair solution upon a positive ruling, or to replace rule-abiding stringency with distributive equity.

In the penultimate category of enforceability, just before good faith interpretation, comes what the AB calls 'expression[s] of the general principle of law of good faith'. By ascribing certain good faith functions to specific WTO treaty provisions, the AB is testing the grounds for acceptance of a new WTO good faith principle. It has done so with the Chapeau of Article XX GATT 94, Articles 3(1), 5.4 ADA, 11.4 ASCM, 6(2) ATC, 5.2 SPS, and Article 7 TRIPS. In each of these instances good faith has had a balancing, regulative function such as in the Chapeau of Art XX GATT 94 in the *US–Shrimp* case, and in *US–Japan Hot-rolled Steel* for paragraphs 2 and 5 of Annex II ADA. Good faith *infra legem* moreover had a corrective function in *US–Offset Act ('Byrd Amendment')* for Articles 5.4 ADA and 11.4 ASCM as well as in *US–Cotton Yarn*, for Article 6.2 ATC, and a constitutive function in *EC–Hormones* for Article 5.2 SPS Agreement.

Finally, in the last category comes the weakest form of good faith protection, which is the interpretation of the WTO Agreements with the element of good faith under the general rule of interpretation of Article 31(1) VCLT. Similarly to the protection of legitmate expectations, the Panels and the AB have opposing views on the matter. While the Panels have subscribed to what they call a 'good faith interpretation' under Article 31(1) VCLT, the AB has restricted itself and overturned the Panels in order to promote a text-first interpretive practice, which may be reinforced by the elements of context, object and purpose, but in which good faith has no place. In order to promote an acceptance of 'good faith interpretation', it has been suggested that the Panels use good faith when focusing on subsequent practice under either Article 31(3)(b) or, more likely, Article 31(3)(c), and perhaps even consider good faith interpretation under 'special meaning' in Article 31(4) VCLT. In choosing the latter, the Panels would run the risk of isolating good faith interpretation from the more general rule of interpretation in Articles 31(1)—(3) whereas our suggestion is to convince the AB of a primordial role of good faith in the interpretive process at the WTO.

Bibliography

ABBOTT, F (2002) 'The Doha Declaration on the TRIPS Agreement and Public Health: Lighting a Dark Corner at the WTO' 5 *Journal of International Economic Law* (JIEL), pp 469–505.

ABBOTT, F, Cottier, T and Gurry, F (1999) *The International Intellectual Property System, Commentary and Materials* (The Hague, Kluwer Law International).

ALLOT, P (1996) 'The International Court and the Voice of Justice in The International Court of Justice and Sources of International Law', in V Lowe and M Fitzmaurice (eds) *Fifty Years of the International Court of Justice, Essays in Honor of Sir Robert Jennings* (Cambridge, Grotius Publications), pp 17–39.

ATRIA, F and MACCORMICK, DN (2003) *Law and Legal Interpretation* (Dartmouth, Ashgate).

BACCHUS, J (2002) 'Table Talk: Around the Table of the Appellate Body of the World Trade Organization' 35 *Vanderbilt Journal of Transnational Law*, pp 1021–39.

—— (2003a) 'The Bicycle Club: Affirming the American Interest in the Future of the WTO' 37 *Journal of World Trade*, pp 42–441.

—— (2003b) 'Groping Towards Grotius: The WTO and the International Rule of Law' 44 *Harvard International Law Journal*, pp 533–50.

—— (2003c) '"Woulda, Coulda, Shoulda": The Consolations of WTO Dispute Settlement', Address by James Bacchus, Chairman, Appellate Body, WTO, to the International Bar Association, Geneva, March 20, 2003, http://www.worldtradelaw.net/articles.htm#bacchus (21 December 2005).

—— (2003d) "Lecky" Circle: Thoughts from the Frontier of International Law', Address by James Bacchus, Chairman, AB WTO, at the Institute of Advanced Legal Studies, University of London, April 10, 2003, http://www.worldtradelaw.net/articles.htm#bacchus (21 December 2005).

BAGCHI, A (2003) 'Compulsory Licensing and the Duty of Good Faith in TRIPS' 55 *Stanford Law Review*, pp 1529–55.

BARFIELD, CE (2001) *Free Trade, Sovereignty, Democracy: The Future of the World Trade Organization* (Washington, DC, American Enterprise Institute (AEI) Press).

BARTELS, L (2001) 'Applicable Law in WTO Dispute Settlement Proceedings' 35 *Journal of World Trade*, pp 449–519.

BENEDEK, W (1990) *Die Rechtsordnung des GATT aus völkerrechtlicher Sicht, Beiträge zum ausländischen öffentlichen Recht,* Band 100 (Berlin, Springer Verlag).

BERNHARDT, R (1963) *Die Auslegung völkerrechtlicher Verträge, insbesondere in der neueren Rechtsprechung internationaler Gerichte, Max-Planck-Institute für Ausländisches Öffentliches Recht und Völkerrecht, Beiträge zum ausländischen öffentlichen Recht und Völkerrecht,* Band 40 (Köln, Karl Heymanns Verlag).

BERNARDEZ, ST (1998) 'Interpretation of Treaties by the International Court of Justice Following the Adoption of the 1969 Vienna Convention on the Law of Treaties' in G Hafner, G Loibl, A Rest, L Sucharipa-Behrmann and K Zemanek (eds) *Liber Amicorum Professor Seidl-Hohenveldern* (The Hague, Kluwer Law International), pp 720–48.

BHAGWATI, J and Mavroidis, P (2003) 'Why the Byrd Amendment Must Be Buried' 7 *Bridges*, 7, January/February 2003, http://www.ictsd.org/monthly/bridges/BRIDGES7-1.pdf pp 8–9 (21 December 2005).

Black's Law Dictionary (1999) BA Garner (ed) 7th edn (St Paul, Minn, West Group).

BLOCHE, MG (2002) 'WTO Deference to National Health Policy: Towards an Interpretive Principle' 5 JIEL, pp 825–48.

BLUM, YZ (1997) 'The Role of Equity in International Law' in Alfredo Mordechai Rabello (ed) *Aequitas and Equity: Equity in Civil Law and Mixed Jurisdictions* (Greene Fund for Equity Studies, Jerusalem Hamaccabi Press (Jack)), pp 229–38.

BOURGEOIS, JHJ (1998) 'WTO Dispute Settlement in the Field of Anti-Dumping Law' 1 *JIEL*, pp 259–75.

BRONCKERS, M (2001) 'More Power to the WTO?' 4 *JIEL*, pp 41–56.

BRONCKERS, M and MCNELIS, N (2000) 'Fact and Law in Pleadings before the WTO Appellate Body' in MCEJ Bronckers (ed) *A Cross-Section of WTO Law* (London, Cameron May), pp 241–74, first published, 1999, in 5 *International Trade Law and Regulation.*

BROWN WEISS, E (2000) 'The Rise or Fall of International Law? The Robert L Levine Distinguished Lecture Series' 69 *Fordham Law Review*, pp 345–72.

BROWNLIE, I (1998a) *Principles of Public International Law*, 5th edn (Oxford, Oxford University Press).

—— (1998b) *The Rule of Law in International Affairs, International Law at the Fiftieth Anniversary of the United Nations* (The Hague, Martinus Nijhoff Publishers).

CAMERON, JK and CAMPBELL K (1998) 'Introduction' in J Cameron and K Campbell (eds) *Dispute Resolution in the World Trade Organization* (London, Cameron May), pp 18–27.

CAMERON, JK and GRAY, KR (2001) 'Principles of International Law in the WTO Dispute Settlement Body' 50 *International and Comparative Law Quarterly*, pp 248–98.

CANAL-FORGUES, E (2001) 'Sur l'interprétation dans le Droit de l'OMC' 105 *Revue Générale de Droit International Public*, pp 5–24.

—— (2003) *Le règlement des différends à l'OMC* (Bruxelles, Etablissement Emile Bruylant, SA).

CHARLESWORTH, H and CHINKIN, C (2000) *The Boundaries of International Law: A Feminist Analysis* (Manchester, Manchester University Press).

CHARME, JS (1992) 'The Interim Obligation of Article 18 of the Vienna Convention on the Law of Treaties: Making Sense of An Enigma' 25 *George Washington Journal of International Law and Economics*, pp 71ff.

CHARNOVITZ, S (2003) 'The Byrd Amendment Ruling Needs Careful Review' 7 *Bridges* January/February 2003, http://www.ictsd.org/monthly/bridges/BRIDGES7-1.pdf, pp 9–10 (21 December 2005).

CHENG, B (1987) *General Principles of Law as Applied by International Courts and Tribunals* (Cambridge, Grotius Publications Limited).

CHUA, ATL (1998) 'Precedents and Principles of WTO Panel Jurisprudence' 16 *Berkeley Journal of International Law*, pp 171–96.

CHO, S-J (1998) 'GATT NVNI Issues in the WTO Framework: Are They the Achilles' Heel of the Dispute Settlement Process?' 39 *Harv Int'l LJ*, pp 311–55.

COTTIER, T (1993) 'Constitutional Trade Regulation in National and International Law: Structure-Substance Pairings in the EFTA Experience' in M Hilf and E-U Petersmann (eds) *National Constitutions and International Economic Law, Studies in Transnational Economic Law* (Deventer, Kluwer Law and Taxation Publishers), pp 409–43.

—— (1998) 'Dispute Settlement in the World Trade Organization: Characteristics and Structural Implications for the European Union' 35 *Common Market Law Review*, pp 325–78.

—— (2000) 'Limits to International Trade: The Constitutional Challenge' in *Proceedings of the 94th Annual Meeting of the American Society of International Law*, Washington DC, pp 220–2.

—— (2001) 'A Theory of Direct Effect in Global Law' in A von Bogdandy, PC Mavroidis and Y Mény (eds) *European Integration and International Co-ordination, Studies in Transnational Economic Law in Honor of Claus-Dieter Ehlermann* (The Hague, Kluwer Law International), pp 99–124.

COTTIER, T and HERTIG, M (2004) 'The Prospects of 21 Century Constitutionalism' in A von Bogdandy and R Wolfrum (eds) *Max Planck Yearbook of United Nations Law* 7 (2003) (Leiden, Boston), pp 261–328.

COTTIER, T and MAVROIDIS, PC (2003) 'Concluding Remarks' in T Cottier and PC Mavroidis (eds) *The Role of the Judge in International Trade Regulation: Experience and Lessons for the WTO, The World Trade Forum, vol 4* (Ann Arbor, University of Michigan Press), pp 349–57.

COTTIER, T and NADAKAVUKAREN SCHEFER, K (1997) 'NVNI Complaints in WTO/GATT Dispute Settlement: Past, Present and Future' in Ernst-Ulrich Petersmann (ed) *International Trade Law and the GATT/WTO Dispute Settlement System, Studies in Transnational Economic Law, Volume 11* (The Hague, Kluwer Law International), pp 145–83.

—— (1998) 'The Relationship between World Trade Organization Law, National and Regional Law' 1 JIEL, pp 83–122.

—— (2000) 'Good Faith and the Protection of Legitimate Expectations in the WTO' in M Bronckers and R Quick (eds) *New Directions in International Economic Law: Essays in Honor of John H Jackson* (The Hague, Kluwer Law International), pp 47–68.

COTTIER, T and OESCH, M (2001) 'WTO Law: Precedents and Legal Change' 3 *Turku Law Journal*, pp 29–30.

—— (2003) 'The Paradox of Judicial Review in International Trade Regulation: Towards a Comprehensive Framework' in T Cottier and PC Mavroidis (eds) *The Role of the Judge in International Trade Regulation: Experience and Lessons for the WTO, The World Trade Forum, vol 4* (Ann Arbor, University of Michigan Press), pp 287–306.

COTTIER, T, OESCH, M and FISCHER, TM (2005) *International Trade Regulation Law and Policy in the WTO: The European Union and Switzerland. Cases, Materials and Comments* (London and Berne, Cameron May and Stämpfli Publishers).

COTTIER, T and PANIZZON, M (2004) 'Legal Perspectives on Traditional Knowledge: The Case for Intellectual Property Protection' 7 *JIEL*, pp 371–99.

—— (2006) 'International Trade Regulation for Plant Genetic Resources and Related Products' in S Biber–Klemm and T Cottier (eds) *Rights to Traditional Knowledge and Plant Genetic Resources for Food and Agriculture* (Wallingford, CABI Publishing).

DAHM, G, DELBRÜCK, J and WOLFRUM, R (2002) *Völkerrecht,* 5th edn, Band I/3 'Die Formen des völkerrechtlichen Handelns; Die inhaltliche Ordnung der internationalen Gemeinschaft' (Berlin, De Gruyter Recht).

D'AMATO, A (1992) 'Good Faith' in R Bernhardt (ed) *Encyclopedia of Public International Law*, Volume I (Amsterdam, Elsevier North-Holland), pp 559–601.

DAVEY, WJ (1992) 'The United States Court of International Trade and the Court of Appeals for the Federal Circuit' in E-U Petersmann and G Jaenicke (eds) *Adjudication of International Trade Disputes in International and National Economic Law* (Fribourg, University Press Fribourg Switzerland), pp 297–322.

DAVEY, WJ (2000) 'WTO Dispute Settlement: Segregating the Useful Political Aspects and Avoiding "Over-Legalization"' in M Bronckers and R Quick (eds) *New Directions in International Economic Law, Essays in Honor of John H Jackson* (The Hague, Kluwer Law International), pp 291–307.

—— (2001) 'Has the WTO Dispute Settlement System Exceeded its Authority?' 4 *JIEL*, pp 79–110.

DEARDORFF, AV (2001) 'Market Access for Developing Countries' in R Porter, P Sauvé, A Subramanian and AB Zampetti (eds) *Efficiency, Equity, and Legitimacy, The Multilateral Trading System at the Millenium* (Washington, DC, Brookings Institution Press), pp 159–73.

DEGAN, VD (1997) *Sources of International Law* (The Hague, Martinus Nijhoff Publishers).

DEKKER, IF and WERNER WG (1999) 'The Completeness of International Law and Hamlet's Dilemma, Non-Liquet, The Nuclear Weapons Case and Legal Theory' 68 *Nordic Journal of International Law*, pp 225–47.

DETMOLD, MJ (1989) 'Law as Practical Reason' 48 *Cambridge Law Journal*, pp 436–71.

DE VISSCHER, C (1972) *De l'Equité dans le Règlement Arbitral ou Judiciaires des Litiges de Droit International Public* (Paris, Editions A Pedone).

DE WITTE, B (2000) 'Institutional Principles: A Special Category of General Principles of EC Law' in U Bernitz and J Nergelius (eds) *General Principles of European Community Law, European Monographs* (The Hague, Kluwer Law International), pp 143–59.

DOLLAR, D (2001) 'Fostering Equity through International Institutions' in R Porter, P Sauvé, A Subramanian and AB Zampetti (eds) *Efficiency, Equity, and Legitimacy, The Multilateral Trading System at the Millenium* (Washington, DC, Brookings Institution Press), pp 212–21.

DWORKIN, R (1987) *Taking Rights Seriously: New Impression with a Reply to Critics* (London, Duckworth).

DURLING, JP and NICELY, MR (2002) *Understanding the WTO Anti-Dumping Agreement, Negotiating History and Subsequent Interpretation* (London, Cameron May).

EHLERMANN, C-D (2002) 'Six Years on the Bench of the "World Trade Court": Some Personal Experiences as Member of the Appellate Body of the World Trade Organization' 36 *Journal of World Trade*, pp 605–39.

—— (2003a) 'Reflections on the Appellate Body of the WTO' 6 *JIEL*, pp 695–709.

—— (2003b) 'Reflections on the Appellate Body of the WTO', Address to the American Society of International Law, Washington, DC (April 3, 2003).

EHLERMANN, C-D and EHRING, L (2005) 'The Authoritative Interpretation under Article IX:2 of the Agreement Establishing the WTO' 8 *JIEL*, pp 803–24.

EHRING, L (2002) 'De Facto Discrimination in World Trade Law, National and Most-Favoured Nation Treatment—or Equal Treatment?' 36 *Journal of World Trade*, pp 921–77.

ESTY, DC (2002) 'The World Trade Organization's Legitimacy Crisis' 1 *World Trade Review*, pp 7–22.

FISH, S (1989) 'Working on the Chain Gang: Interpretation in Law and Literature' in S Fish (ed) *Doing What Comes Naturally: Change, Rhetoric and the Practice of Theory in Literary and Legal Studies* (Oxford, Clarendon Press), pp 87–102.

FOOTER, M and ZIA-ZARIFI, S (2002) 'Case Notes, European Communities—Measures Affecting Asbestos and Asbestos-Containing Products, The World Trade Organization on Trial for its Handling of Occupational Health and Safety Issues' 3 *Melbourne Journal of International Law*, pp 120–42.

FRANCK, TM (1995) *Fairness in International Law and Institutions* (Oxford, Clarendon Press).

GAFFNEY, JP (1999) 'Due Process in the World Trade Organization: the Need for Procedural Justice in the Dispute Settlement System' 14 *American University International Law Review*, pp 1173–221.

GARCIA-RUBIO, M (2001) 'On the Application of Customary Rules of State Responsibility by the WTO Dispute Settlement Organs: A General International Law Perspective', Working Paper, Graduate Institute of International Studies (Geneva, the Graduate Institute of International Studies Geneva).

GOLDSMITH, JL and POSNER, EA (2005) *The Limits of International Law, Part 2, Treaties, Section 5, International Trade* (Oxford, Oxford University Press).

GROTIUS, H, 'The Rights of War and Peace (De Jure Belli ac Pacis, In quibus ius naturae & Gentium)', Book II, chapter XVI, *The Interpretation of Treaties,* Paris: 1625, English translation by Campbell AC, London, 1814, http://www.constitution.org/gro/djbp.htm (21 December 2005), original Latin version at http://visualiseur.bnf.fr/Visualiseur?Destination=Gallica&O=NUMM-58022 (21 December 2005).

GROUSSET, X (2000) 'General Principles of Community Law in the Creation and Development of Due Process Principles in Competition Law Proceedings: From Transcoean Marine Plant (1974) to Montecatini (1999)' in U Bernitz and J Nergelius (eds) *General Principles of European Community Law, European Monographs* (The Hague, Kluwer Law International), pp 185–204.

GATT SECRETARIAT (1994) *The Results of the Uruguay Round of Multilateral Trade Negotiations, The Legal Texts* (Geneva, World Trade Organization).

HARTLEY, TC (2003) *The Foundations of European Community Law: An Introduction to the Constitutional and Administrative Law of the European Community* (Oxford, Oxford University Press).

HENDERSON, D (2002) 'WTO 2002: Imaginary Crisis, Real Problems' 1 *World Trade Review*, pp 277–96.

HERDEGEN, M (2000) 'The Origins and Development of the General Principles of Community Law' in U Bernitz and J Nergelius (eds) *General Principles of European Community Law: European Monographs* (The Hague, Kluwer Law International), pp 3–21.

HILF, M (2001) 'Power, Rules and Principles—Which Orientation for WTO/GATT Law?' 4 *JIEL*, pp 111–30.

HILF, M and PUTH, S (2002) 'The Principle of Proportionality on its Way into WTO/GATT Law' in A von Bogdandy, PC Mavroidis and Y Mény (eds) *European Integration and International Co-ordination: Studies in Transnational Economic Law in Honour of Claus-Dieter Ehlermann* (The Hague, Kluwer Law International), pp 199–218.

HOROWITZ, D (2002) 'On Good Governance and WTO Disputes' 6 *International Trade Law and Regulation*, pp 169–72.

HOWSE, R (2000) 'Adjudicative Legitimacy and Treaty Interpretation in International Trade Law: The Early Years of WTO Jurisprudence' in JHH Weiler (ed) *The EU, the WTO, and the NAFTA: Towards a Common Law of International Trade*? (Academy of European Law, European University Institute; Oxford, Oxford University Press), pp 35–69.

Howse, R (2003) 'The Most Dangerous Branch? WTO Appellate Body Jurisprudence on the Nature and Limits of the Judicial Power' in T Cottier and PC Mavroidis (eds) *The Role of the Judge in International Trade Regulation: Experience and Lessons for the WTO, The World Trade Forum, vol 4* (Ann Arbor, University of Michigan Press), pp 11–41.

—— (2003a) 'The Jurisprudential Achievement of the WTO Appellate Body: A Preliminary Appreciation', Preliminary First Draft, copy with author.

Howse, R and Nicolaidis, K (2003) 'Legitimacy through "Higher Law"? Why Constitutionalizing the WTO Is a Step Too Far' in T Cottier PC Mavroidis (eds) *The Role of the Judge in International Trade Regulation: Experience and Lessons for the WTO, World Trade Forum vol 4* (Ann Arbor, University of Michigan Press), pp 307–48.

Hu, J (2004) 'The Role of International Law in the Development of WTO Law' 7(1) *JIEL*, pp 143–67.

Hudec, RE (2000) 'Broadening the Scope of Remedies in WTO Dispute Settlement' in F Weiss and J Wiers (eds) *Improving the WTO Dispute Settlement Procedures* (London, Cameron May Publishers), pp 345–76, http://www.worldtradelaw.net/articles.htm#hudec (21 December 2005).

Iwasawa, Y (2002) 'WTO Dispute Settlement as Judicial Supervision' 5 *JIEL*, pp 287–305.

Jackson, JH (1992) 'Status of Treaties in Domestic Legal Systems: A Policy Analysis' 86 *American Journal of International Law*, pp 310–40.

—— (1998) 'The WTO Dispute Settlement Understanding—Misunderstandings on the Nature of Legal Obligation' in J Cameron and K Campbell (eds) *Dispute Resolution in the World Trade Organization* (London, Cameron May), pp 69–74.

—— (1999) *The World Trading System: Law and Policy of International Economic Relations,* 2nd edn (Cambridge, MA, The Massachusetts Institute of Technology Press).

—— (2000) *The Jurisprudence of GATT and the WTO* (Cambridge, Cambridge University Press).

—— (2002a) 'Afterword: The Linkage Problem, Comments on Five Texts' 96 *AJIL*, pp 118–25.

—— (2002b) 'Perceptions about the WTO Trade Institutions' 1 *World Trade Review*, pp 101–14.

Jackson, JH and Croley, SP (1996) 'WTO Dispute Procedures, Standard of Review, and Deference to National Governments' 90 *AJIL*, pp 193–213, also published in Jackson JH (2000) *The Jurisprudence of GATT and the WTO* (Cambridge, Cambridge University Press), pp 133–67.

Jackson, JH, Davey, WJ and Sykes, AO (1995) *Legal Problems of International Economic Relations: Cases, Materials and Text,* 3rd edn, *American Casebook Series* (St Paul, Minn, West Publishing Co).

—— (2002) *Legal Problems of International Economic Relations: Cases, Materials and Text,* 4th edn, *American Casebook Series* (St Paul, Minn, West Publishing Co).

Jackson, JH and Benke, RTJ (2003) 'The WTO Cases on US "Trade Remedies": Opening a Discussion' 6 *JIEL*, p 111.

Joyner, CC (2005) *International Law in the 21st Century: Rules for Global Governance,* New Millenium Books in International Studies (Oxford, Rowman and Littlefield Publishers).

KAIKOBAD, KH (2000) *The International Court of Justice and Judicial Review: A Study of the Court's Powers with Respect to Judgments of the ILO and UN Administrative Tribunals, Studies and Materials on the Settlement of International Disputes, vol 6* (The Hague, Kluwer Law International).

KEARNS, JE and CHARNOVITZ, S (2002) 'Adjudicating Compliance in the WTO: A Review of DSU Article 21.5' 5 *JIEL*, pp 331–52.

KELSEN, H (1960) *Reine Rechtslehre* (Wien, Verlag Österreich).

KENNEDY, D (1992) 'The Sources of International Law' in M Koskenniemi (ed) *International Law, The International Library of Essays in Law and Legal Theory, Areas 5* (Aldershot, Dartmouth Publishing Company Limited), pp 293–388, reprinted from: (1987) 2 *American University Journal of International Law and Policy*, pp 1–96.

KERSE, CS (2000) 'General Principles of Community Law: Procedural Guarantees—A Note' in U Bernitz, J Nergelius (eds) *General Principles of European Community Law, European Monographs* (The Hague, Kluwer Law International), pp 205–11.

KIM, DW (2004) *NVNI Complaints in WTO Law: Theory and Practice*, Doctoral Dissertation (World Trade Institute, University of Berne, Switzerland).

KISS, A (1992) 'Abuse of Rights' in R Bernhardt (ed) *Encyclopedia of Public International Law*, Volume I (Amsterdam, North Holland), pp 4–8.

KOLB, R (1998) 'La Bonne Foi en Droit International Public' 2 *Revue Belge de Droit International*, pp 661–732.

—— (2000) *La Bonne Foi en Droit International Public, Contribution à l'étude des principes généraux de droit, Publications de l'Institut Universitaire de Hautes Etudes Internationales* (Paris, Presses Universitaires de France).

KORHONEN, O (1996) 'New International Law: Silence, Defence or Deliverance?' 7 *European Journal of International Law*, pp 1–28.

KOSKENNIEMI, M (1985) 'Reflexions on Constructivist Thinking in International Law' 18 *Oikeustiede-Jurisprudentia (Yearbook of the Finnish Law Society) 1985*, pp 117–63.

—— (1989) *From Apology to Utopia, The Structure of International Legal Argument* (Helsinki, Finnish Lawyers' Publishing Company).

—— (1990) 'The Politics of International Law' 1 *EJIL*, pp 4–32.

—— (1997) 'Lauterpracht: The Victorian Tradition in International Law' 8 *EJIL*, pp 215–63.

—— (2002) *The Gentle Civilizer of Nations: The Rise and Fall of International Law 1870–1960* (Cambridge, Cambridge University Press).

KOSKENNIEMI, M and LEINO, P (2002) 'Fragmentation of International Law, Postmodern Anxieties' 15 *Leiden Journal of International Law*, pp 553–79.

KUYPER, PJ (1995) 'The New WTO Dispute Settlement System: The Impact on the Community' in JHJ Bourgeois et al (eds) *The Uruguay Round Results: A European Lawyers' Perspective* (Brussels, European Interuniversity Press and College of Europe), pp 87–114.

—— (2000) 'The Appellate Body and the Facts' in M Bronckers, R Quick (eds) *New Directions in International Economic Law, Essays in Honor of John H Jackson* (The Hague, Kluwer Law International), pp 309–23.

LANG, JT (2000) 'Legal Certainty and Legitimate Expectations as General Principles of Law' in U Bernitz, J Nergelius (eds) *General Principles of European Community Law, European Monographs* (The Hague, Kluwer Law International), pp 163–81.

LAUTERPRACHT, H (1933) *The Function of Law in the International Community* (Oxford, Oxford University Press); reprinted 1966, with the permission of Oxford University Press in Hamden, CT by Archon Books.

LEE, SH and JUNG, Y (2003) 'The Legacy of the Byrd Amendment Controversies: Rethinking the Principle of Good Faith' 37(5) *Journal of World Trade*, pp 921–58.

LENNARD, M (2002) 'Navigating by the Stars: Interpreting the WTO Agreements' 5 *JIEL*, pp 17–89.

LESTER, S and LEITNER, K (2003a) 'Dispute Settlement Commentary (DSC): *US–Offset Act ('Byrd Amendment')*' AB Report, http://www.worldtradelaw.net, update of 28 April 2003.

—— (2003b) 'Dispute Settlement Commentary (DSC): *US–Cotton Yarn*', AB Report, http://www.worldtradelaw.net, update of 4 April 2005.

—— (2003c) 'Dispute Settlement Commentary (DSC): *Mexico–HFCS (Article 21.5)*', AB Report, http://www.worldtradelaw.net, update of 22 March 2005.

LEVI-FAUR, D (2005) 'The Political Economy of Globalization: Juridification, Adversarial Legalism, and Responsive Regulation. A Comment' 59 *International Organization*, pp 451–62.

LOWE, V (1992) 'The Role of Equity in International Law' 12 *Australian Yearbook of International Law 1992*, pp 54–81.

—— relates to Lowe, Vaughan (2000) 'The Politics of Law-Making: Are the Method and Character of Norm Creation Changing?' in M Byers (ed) *The Role of Law in International Politics: Essays in International Relations and International Law* (Oxford, Oxford University Press), pp 207–26.

LOWENFELD, AF (2002) *International Economic Law* (Oxford, Oxford University Press).

MACCORMICK, N (1999) 'Reasonableness and Objectivity' 74 *Notre Dame Law Review*, pp 1575–603.

MARCEAU, G (1999) 'A Call for Coherence in International Law: Praises for the Prohibition Against "Clinical Isolation" in WTO Dispute Settlement' 33 *Journal of World Trade*, pp 87–152.

—— (2000) 'The General Legal Principles of the GATT and the WTO', Speech, Libreville 2000 (Meeting of African Trade Ministers, Libreville, Gabon, 13–15 November 2000).

—— (2001) 'Conflicts of Norms and Conflicts of Jurisdiction: The Relationship between the WTO Agreement, MEAs and other Treaties' 35 *Journal of World Trade*, pp 1081–131.

—— (2002) 'WTO Dispute Settlement and Human Rights' 13(4) *JIEL*, pp 753–814.

MARTHA, RSJ (2001) 'The Duty to Exercise Judgment on the Fruitfulness of Actions in World Trade Law' 35 *Journal of World Trade*, pp 1035–59.

MATSUSHITA, M, SCHOENBAUM, T and MAVROIDIS, PC (2003) *The World Trade Organization: Law, Practice, and Policy* (Oxford, Oxford University Press).

MCCALL SMITH, J (2003) 'WTO Dispute Settlement: The Politics of Procedure in Appellate Body Rulings' 2(1) *World Trade Review*, pp 65–100.

MCDOUGAL, MS (1967) 'The International Law Commission's Draft Articles Upon Interpretation: Textuality Redivivus' 61 AJIL, pp 992 ff, reprinted in MS McDougal, HD Lasswell and JC Miller (eds) *The Interpretation of International Agreements and World Public Order, Principles of Content and Procedure* 1994 (New Haven, New Haven Press) Appendix 2, pp 419–42.

MCDOUGAL, MS, LASSWELL, HD and MILLER, JC (1994) *The Interpretation of*

International Agreements and World Public Order, Principles of Content and Procedure (New Haven, New Haven Press).

McLinden, G (2005) 'Trade Facilitation: Progress and Prospects for the Doha Negotiations' in R Newfarmer (ed) *Trade, Doha, and Development: A Window into the Issues* (Washington, DC, World Bank Publications), pp 179–89.

McNelis, N (2003) 'What Obligations are Created by World Trade Organization Dispute Settlement Reports?' 37 *Journal of World Trade*, pp 647–72.

McRae, DM (1998) 'The Emerging Appellate Jurisdiction in International Trade Law' in J Cameron and K Campbell (eds) *Dispute Resolution in the World Trade Organization* (London, Cameron May), pp 98–110.

—— (2003) 'Claus-Dieter Ehlermann's Presentation on "The Role and Record of Dispute Settlement Panels and the Appellate Body of the WTO"' 6 JIEL, pp 709–17.

McWhinney, E (1973) 'Equity in International Law' in RA Newman (ed) *Equity in the World's Legal Systems: A Comparative Study* (Brussels, Etablissements Emile Bruylant), pp 581–8.

Mendelson, M (1996) 'The International Court of Justice and Sources of International Law' in V Lowe and M Fitzmaurice (eds) *Fifty Years of the International Court of Justice, Essays in Honor of Sir Robert Jennings* (Cambridge, Grotius Publications), pp 63–89.

Mengozzi, P (1995) 'The Marrakesh DSU and its Implications on the International and European Level' in JHJ Bourgeois et al (eds) *The Uruguay Round Results, A European Lawyer's Perspective* (Brussels, European Interuniversity Press and College of Europe), pp 115–40.

Müller, JP (1971) *Vertrauensschutz im Völkerrecht, Max-Planck—Institut für Ausländisches Öffentliches Recht und Völkerrecht, Beiträge zum ausländischen öffentlichen Recht und Völkerrecht*, Band 56 (Köln, Carl Heymanns Verlag).

—— (1995) 'Article 2(2)' in B Simma (ed) *The Charter of the United Nations: A Commentary* (Oxford, Oxford University Press), pp 89–97.

Müller, JP and Cottier, T (1992) 'Acquiescence' in R Bernhardt (ed) *Encyclopedia of Public International Law*, Volume I (Amsterdam, Elsevier North Holland), pp 14–16.

—— (1995) 'Estoppel' in R Bernhardt (ed) *Encyclopedia of Public International Law*, Volume II (Amsterdam, Elsevier North Holland), pp 116–18.

Nader, L and Starr, J (1973) 'Is Equity Universal?' in RA Newman (ed) *Equity in the World's Legal Systems: A Comparative Study* (Brussels, Etablissements Emile Bruylant), pp 126–37.

Neuhaus, RK (1984) *Das Rechtsmissbrauchsverbot im heutigen Völkerrecht, Eine Untersuchung zur Entwicklung und Anwendbarkeit eines Begriffes, Schriften zum Völkerrecht*, Band 80 (Berlin, Duncker und Humblot).

Neumann, J (2002) *Die Koordination des WTO—Rechts mit anderen völkerrechtlichen Ordnungen, Konflikte des materiellen Rechts und Konkurrenzen der Streitbeilegung, Rechtsfragen der Globalisierung*, Band 4 (Berlin, Duncker und Humblot).

Newman, RA (1961) *Equity and Law: A Comparative Study* (New York, Oceana Publications Inc).

O'Connor, JF (1991) *Good Faith in International Law* (Aldershot, Dartmouth Publishing Company).

O'Cunningham, R and Cribb, TH (2003) 'Dispute Settlement thought the Lens of "Free Flow of Trade": A Review of WTO Dispute Settlement of US Anti-Dumping and Countervailing Duty Measures' 6 *JIEL*, pp 155–70.

OESCH, M (2003a) 'Standards of Review in WTO Dispute Resolution' 6 *JIEL*, pp 635–59.
—— (2003b) *Standards of Review in WTO Dispute Resolution* (Oxford, Oxford University Press).

OHLHOFF, S (2003) 'Streitbeilegung in der WTO' in H-J Priess and GM Berrisch (eds) *WTO Handbuch* (München, Verlag CH. Beck), pp 677–750.

OHLHOFF, S and SCHLOEMANN, H (1998) 'Rational Allocation of Disputes and "Constitutionalisation": Forum Choice as an Issue of Competence' in J Cameron and K Campbell (eds) *Dispute Resolution in the World Trade Organization* (London, Cameron May), pp 302–29.

OXMAN, BH (2001) 'Complementary Agreements and Compulsory Jurisdiction' 95 *AJIL*, pp 277–312.

PALMETER, D and MAVROIDIS, PC (1998) 'The WTO Legal System: Sources of Law' 92 *AJIL*, pp 398–413.

PANIZZON, M and COTTIER, T (2005) 'Developing Country Interests and Negotiating Positions on Protection of Geographical Indications and Traditional Knowledge', in E-U Petersmann (ed) *Developing Countries in the Doha Round: WTO Decision-Making Procedures and WTO Negotiations on Trade in Agricultural Goods and Services* (Florence, Robert Schuman Centre for Advanced Studies, European University Institute Publishing), pp 227–68.

PARLIN, CC (2002) *The Formation of the WTO Dispute Settlement Mechanism—Its Features and Principles; Disputes Involving Developing Countries, Law and Policy of International Economic Relations: The WTO Dispute Settlement System*, Fall 2002 Seminar, Georgetown University Law Center.

PAUWELYN, J (2001) 'The Role of Public International Law in the WTO: How Far Can We Go?' 95 *AJIL*, pp 535–87.
—— (2003a) *Conflict of Norms in Public International Law: How WTO Law Relates to other Rules of International Law* (Cambridge, Cambridge University Press).
—— (2003b) 'The Limits of Litigation: "Americanization" and Negotiation in the Settlement of WTO Disputes' 19(3) *Ohio State Journal on Dispute Resolution*, pp 121–40.
—— (2003c) 'Does the WTO Stand for "Deference to" or "Interference with" National Health Authorities When Applying the Agreement on Sanitary and Phytosanitary Measures (SPS Agreement)?' in T Cottier and PC Mavroidis (eds) *The Role of the Judge in International Trade Regulation: Experience and Lessons for the WTO, World Trade Forum vol 4* (Ann Arbor, Michigan University Press), pp 175–92.
—— (2004) 'The Jurisdiction of the World Trade Organization' in *Proceedings of the 98th Annual Meeting of the American Society of International Law*, Washington, DC, pp 135–8.

PESCATORE, P (1993) 'The GATT Dispute Settlement Mechanism: Its Present Situation and its Prospects' 27 *Journal of World Trade*, pp 5–20.

PETERS, A (2002) 'Cooperation in International Dispute Settlement' in J Delbrück (ed) *International Law of Cooperation and State Sovereignty: Proceedings of an International Symposium of the Kiel Wlather-Schücking—Institute of International Law, May 23–26, 2001* (Berlin, Duncker und Humblot), pp 107–62.

PETERSMANN, E-U (1991) 'Violation Complaints and NVNI Complaints in Public International Trade Law' 34 *German Yearbook of International Law*, pp 175–229.
—— (1994) 'The Dispute Settlement System of the World Trade Organization and the Evolution of the GATT Dispute Settlement System since 1948' 31 *CML Rev*, pp 1157–244.

—— (1997a) *The GATT/WTO Dispute Settlement System, International Law, International Organizations and Dispute Settlement* (The Hague, Kluwer Law International).

—— (1997b) 'International Trade Law and the GATT/WTO Dispute Settlement System 1948–1996: An Introduction' in E-U Petersmann (ed) *International Trade Law and the GATT/WTO Dispute Settlement System* (The Hague, Kluwer Law International).

—— (1998a) 'How to Promote the International Rule of Law? Contributions by the WTO Appellate Review System' in J Cameron and K Campbell (eds) *Dispute Resolution in the* WTO (London, Cameron May), pp 75–97.

—— (1998b) 'From Hobbesian International Law of Coexistance to Modern Integration Law: The WTO Dispute Settlement System' 1(2) *JIEL* 1998, pp 175–98.

—— (1999) 'Dispute Settlement in International Economic Law—Lessons for Strengthening International Dispute Settlement in Non-Economic Areas' 2(2) *JIEL*, pp 189–248.

—— (2000) 'The WTO Constitution and the Millenium Round' in M Bronckers and R Quick (eds) *New Directions in International Economic Law, Essays in Honor of John H Jackson* (The Hague, Kluwer Law International), pp 111–33.

—— (2003) 'Transatlantic Economic Disputes: The EU, the US, and the WTO' in E-U Petersmann and MA Pollock (eds) *Oxford International Economic Law Series*, John H Jackson (ed) (Oxford, Oxford University Press), pp 3–64.

Raghavan, C (2001) 'Developing Nations Reject Labour Issues in WTO' in South North Development Monitor No. 4564 of 2 December 2001, available at Third World Network, http://www.twnside.org.sg/title/deb9-cn.htm (29 December 2005).

Roessler, F (1997) 'The Concept of Nullification and Impairment in the Legal System of the World Trade Organization' in E-U Petersmann (ed) *International Trade Law and the GATT/WTO Dispute Settlement System, Studies in Transnational Economic Law, Volume 11* (The Hague, Kluwer Law International), pp 125–42.

Rosenne, S (1993) *An International Law Miscellany* (Dordrecht, Martinus Nijhoff Publishers).

—— (1989) *Developments in the Law of Treaties 1945–1986* (Cambridge, Cambridge University Press).

Rub, A (1995) *Hans Kelsens Völkerrechtslehre Versuch einer Würdigung* (Zürich, Schulthess Polygraphischer Verlag AG).

Sapir, A (2001) 'Who's Afraid of Globalization? Domestic Adjustment in Europe and America' in R Porter, P Sauvé, A Subramanian and AB Zampetti (eds) *Efficiency, Equity, and Legitimacy: The Multilateral Trading System at the Millenium* (Washington, DC, Brookings Institution Press), pp 179–201.

Schachter, O (1991) *International Law in Theory and Practice* (Dordrecht, Martinus Nijhoff Publishers).

Schaffer, G, Mosoti, V and Qureschi, A (2003) 'Towards a Development-Supportive Dispute Settlement System in the WTO' (ICTSD Series: Sustainable Development and Trade Issues), ICTSD Resource Paper No. 5, http://www.ictsd.org/pubs/ictsd_series/resource_papers/DSU_2003.pdf (21 December 2005).

Sands, P (2000) 'Vers une transformation du droit international', *Cours de l'HEI, Droit International 4* (Paris, Pedone).

Schermers, HG (1980) *International Institutional Law*, 1 edn (Alphen aan den Rijn, Sijthoff & Noordhoff).

Schermers, HG and Walbroeck, DF (2001) *Judicial Protection in the European Union*, 6 edn (The Hague, Kluwer Law International).

SCHWARZENBERGER, G (1955) 'The Fundamental Principles of International Law' in *Academie de Droit International, Recueil des Cours,* vol II 1955, 88, (Leiden, AW Sijthoff), pp 270–326.

SCOBBIE, IGM (1997) 'The Theorist as Judge: Hersch Lauterpracht's Concept of the International Judicial Function' 8 *EJIL*, pp 264–98.

SENTI, R (2005) 'Überlegungen zu Reformmöglichkeiten für die WTO, Im Spannungsfeld zwischen Handel, Gesundheit, Arbeit und Umwelt' in *Neue Zürcher Zeitung*, Nr. 60 of 12–13 March 2005, http://nzz.gbi.de/webcgi?WID=27572-5570435-03066_2 (21 December 2005).

SINCLAIR, SIR I (1984) *The Vienna Convention on the Law of Treaties,* 2nd edn (Manchester, Manchester University Press).

—— (1996) 'Estoppel and Acquiescence' in V Lowe and M Fitzmaurice (eds) *Fifty Years of the International Court of Justice, Essays in Honor of Sir Robert Jennings* (Cambridge, Grotius Publications), pp 104–20.

SOETEMAN, A (1991) 'Hercules aan het werk. Over de rol van rechtsbeginselen in het recht' *Rechtsbeginselen* (Nijmegen, Ars Aequi), pp 41–56.

STEGER, DP (2001) 'Appellate Body Jurisprudence Relating to Trade Remedies' 35 *Journal of World Trade*, pp 799–823.

STEINBERG, RH (2003) 'Judicial Law-Making, Internal Transparency, and External Transparency: Recent Institutional Developments at the WTO' 37(1) *The International Lawyer*, p 56, available at: http://www.law.berkeley.edu/cenpro/ils/papers/steinbergwtO17.pdf (21 December 2005).

STERN, B (2000) 'How to Regulate Globalization?' in Michael Byers (ed) *The Role of Law in International Politics, Essays in International Relations and International Law* (Oxford, Oxford University Press), pp 247–68.

SUNSTEIN, CR and VERMEULE, A (2002) 'Interpretation and Institutions' (Chicago John M Olin Public Law and Legal Theory Working Paper No. 28), http://www.law.uchicago.edu/academics/publiclaw/resources/28.crs-av.interpretation.pdf; The Social Science Research Network Electronic Paper Collection, http://ssrn.com/abstract_id=320245 (22 December 2005).

SUTHERLAND, P (2000) 'Is Free Trade Fair? Has it Gone Too Far?' (Fellow's Papers, Harvard University Weatherhead Center for International Affairs), http://www.wcfia.harvard.edu/fellows/papers/1999-00/sutherland.pdf (22 December 2005).

TARULLO, DK (2002) 'The Hidden Costs of International Dispute Settlement: WTO Review of Domestic Anti-Dumping Decisions' 34 *Law and Policy of International Business*, pp 109–81.

THIRLWAY, HWA (1996) 'Procedural Law and the International Court of Justice' in V Lowe and M Fitzmaurice (eds) *Fifty Years of the International Court of Justice, Essays in Honor of Sir Robert Jennings* (Cambridge, Grotius Publications), pp 389–405.

TRACHTMAN, J (2005) 'Book Review, *Conflict of Norms in Public International Law: How WTO Law Relates to Other Rules of International Law*, by Joost Pauwelyn, Cambridge: Cambridge University Press, 2003' 98(4) *AJIL*, pp 855–61.

—— (1999) 'The Domain of WTO Dispute Resolution' 40 *Harv Int'l LJ*, pp 333–77.

TREBILCOCK, M and HOWSE, R (1999) *The Regulation of International Trade*, 2nd edn (London, Routledge).

UMBRICHT, GC (2001) 'An "Amicus Curiae Brief" on Amicus Curiae Briefs at the WTO' 4 *JIEL*, pp 773–94.

VAGTS, DF (1993) 'Treaty Interpretation and the New American Ways of Law Reading' 4 *EJIL*, pp 472–505.

—— (2004) 'International Relations Look at Customary International Law: A Traditionalists Defence' 15(5) *EJIL*, pp 1031–40.

VAN ALSTINE, MP (1998) 'Dynamic Treaty Interpretation' 146 *University of Pennsylvania Law Review*, pp 687–793.

VAN DEN BOSSCHE, P (2003) 'The Doha Development Round Negotiations on the Dispute Settlement Understanding, DSU Negotiations' (WTO Conference Paper, New Agendas in the 21st Century, Taipei, 28–29 November 2003), http://www.worldtradelaw.net/articles/vandenbosschedohadsu.pdf, (22 December 2005).

—— (2005) *The Law and Policy of the World Trade Organization: Text, Cases and Materials* (Cambridge, Cambridge University Press).

VERHEIJ, B, HAGE, JC and VAN DEN HERIK, HJ (1998) 'An Integrated View on Rules and Principles' 6 *Artificial Intelligence and Law*, pp 3–26.

VERMULST, E and GRAAFSMA, F (2002) *WTO Disputes, Anti-Dumping, Subsidies and Safeguards* (London, Cameron May).

VIERDAG, EW (1996) 'The International Court of Justice and the Law of Treaties' in V Lowe and M Fitzmaurice (eds) *Fifty Years of the International Court of Justice, Essays in Honor of Sir Robert Jennings* (Cambridge, Grotius Publications), pp 145–65.

VILLIGER, ME (1997) *Customary International Law and Treaties: A Manual on the Theory and Practice of the Interrelation of Sources*, fully revised 2nd edn (The Hague, Kluwer Law International).

VIRALLY, M (1990) *Le droit international en devenir, Essais écrits au fil des ans, Publications de l'Institut Universitaire de Hautes Etudes Internationales Genève* (Paris, Presses Universitaires de France).

VON BOGDANDY, A (1992) 'The NVNI Procedure of Article XXIII: 2 GATT, its Operational Rationale' 26 *Journal of World Trade*, pp 95–111.

WAINCYMER, J (2002) *WTO Litigation, Procedural Aspects of Formal Dispute Settlement* (London, Cameron May).

WÄLDE, T (1999) 'Non-Conventional Views on "Effectiveness": The Holy Grail of Modern International Lawyers: The New Paradigm? A Chimera? Or a Brave New World in the Global Economy?' 4 *Austrian Review of International and European Law*, pp 164–203.

WEIL, P (1996) 'L'équité dans la jurisprudence de la Cour Internationale de Justice, Un mystère en voie de dissipation?' in V Lowe and M Fitzmaurice (eds) *Fifty Years of the International Court of Justice, Essays in Honor of Sir Robert Jennings* (Cambridge, Grotius Publications), pp 121–44.

WEILER, T (2005) 'Good Faith and Regulatory Transparency: The Story of *Metalclad v Mexico*' in T Weiler (ed) *International Investment Law and Arbitration: Leading Cases From the ICSID, NAFTA, Bilateral Treaties and Customary International Law* (London, Cameron May) chapter 19.

WHITE, G (1996) 'The Principle of Good Faith' in V Lowe and C Warbrick (eds) *The United Nations and the Principles of International Law, Essays in Memory of Michael Akehurst* (London, Routledge), pp 230–55.

WILSON, D and STARCHUK, L (2003) 'Judicial Activism in the WTO—Implications for the Doha Negotiations' in Johnston & Buchan LLP, Publications: International Trade, http://www.johnstonbuchan.com/pubs/trade/Judicial%20Activism%20in%20the%20WTO.pdf (22 December 2005).

WIRTH, DA (1998) 'European Communities—Measures Concerning Meat and Meat Products' 92 *AJIL*, pp 755–9.

WOOD, DP (2003) 'A US Perspective on Ducks' in T Cottier and PC Mavroidis (eds) *The Role of the Judge in International Trade Regulation: Experience and Lessons for the WTO, The World Trade Forum, vol 4* (Ann Arbor, University of Michigan Press), pp 119–31.

WTO Secretariat, *WTO Analytical Index: Guide to WTO Law and Practice,* 1st edn (2003) (Geneva and Lanham, MD, WTO Publications and Bernan).

ZEITLER, HE (2005) '"Good Faith" in the WTO Jurisprudence Necessary Balancing Element or an Open Door to Judicial Activism?' 8(3) *JIEL,* pp 721–58.

ZIEGLER, K-H (1997) 'Aequitas in Roman International Law' in AM Rabello (ed) *Aequitas and Equity: Equity in Civil Law and Mixed Jurisdictions,* Greene Fund for Equity Studies (Jerusalem, Hamaccabi Press (Jack)), pp 48–62.

ZIMMERMANN, TA (2004) *What Direction Should the DSU Take? Negotiations and Proposals to Review and Reform the WTO Dispute Settlement Understanding* (Bamberg, Difo-Druck).

ZOLLER, E (1977) *La Bonne Foi en Droit International Public* (Paris, Editions A Pedone).

Index